The Stiftung Wissenschaft und Politik (SWP) is a foundation established in 1962 for the purpose of furthering analytic research into problems of international politics and security. Publicly funded, but politically independent, the SWP today maintains the largest research institute of its kind in the Federal Republic of Germany. The SWP receives almost all of the operating funds for the institute through annual non-project appropriations from the Federal budget. These are supplemented by grants for specific projects, obtained from private foundations in the Federal Republic and abroad. The SWP's professional staff, some 45 out of a total permanent staff of 120, is drawn from a variety of disciplines and professional backgrounds.
The research activities of the SWP seek to combine the requirements of general research in international affairs with the specific needs of policymakers. To that end, the institute develops its own research agenda, giving due regard to specific questions raised by *Bundestag* members or governments departments.
Results are usually disseminated in the form of non-classified studies and position papers. Many of these are intended primarily for the attention and specific needs of policymakers. Chief recipients are the *Bundestag* and its committees, the Chancellery, and various Federal Ministries.

Aktuelle Materialien
zur Internationalen Politik

herausgegeben von der
Stiftung Wissenschaft und Politik, Ebenhausen
Redaktion: Dr. Albrecht Zunker

Band 40/2

Klaus Segbers/Stephan De Spiegeleire (Eds.)

Post-Soviet Puzzles

Mapping the Political Economy of the Former Soviet Union

Volume II
Emerging Geopolitical and Territorial Units.
Theories, Methods and Case Studies

Nomos Verlagsgesellschaft
Baden-Baden

Die Deutsche Bibliothek – CIP-Einheitsaufnahme

Post-Soviet Puzzles : Mapping the Political Economy of the Former Soviet Union / Klaus Segbers/Stephan De Spiegeleire (eds.). – Baden-Baden : Nomos Verl.-Ges.
(Aktuelle Materialien zur Internationalen Politik ; Bd. 40)
NE: Segbers, Klaus [Hrsg.]; GT
Volume 2. Emerging Geopolitical and Territorial Units: Theories, Methods and Case Studies. – 1. Aufl. – 1995
ISBN 3-7890-4043-6

1. Auflage 1995

Table of Contents

1

Post-Soviet Developments: A Regional Interpretation (A Methodological Review)

Sergei Medvedev

1 Introduction

Three years after the dissolution of the Soviet Union has been announced (September 1991), decomposition of the state is still far from over. Break-up, it turned out, is not a fixed point in history, but a long process which will probably spread over decades.

Since 1991, the situation in the area has continued to intensify. The break-up [*raspad*] has become a multi-functional and multi-dimensional process taking place in all spheres of politics, economics, and society. Indeed, break-up – or regionalisation – seem to be more adequate terms than the much-used word 'crisis' which implies a single system, a subject of crisis. For instance, when a plane in the air runs out of fuel, or loses control, or its engine sets on fire – this is a crisis. But when the plane hits the ground, it ceases to exist as a subject of crisis, and one needs to apply different terms to describe the fate of the debris.

In the case of the Soviet Union, the plane is ruined, but its parts are more or less preserved, and passengers (more or less) alive. A new reality has been born which requires a different logic. This may well be the logic of regionalisation or regional interpretation of post-Soviet developments.

It should be stressed that regionalisation is not simply just one of a number of processes taking place in the former Soviet Union, along with economic, social, political, ideological and other transformations. It is the principal shaping factor, the paradigm defining all other trends, and the future arrangements in the wide Eurasian space.

In this paper, the term 'region' is treated in a broad sense which implies local units and communities, territorial enclaves, ex-territorial functions and programmes, zones of special economic regime, ideological and cultural regions.

'Regionalisation' is also treated broadly: as de-unification, de-centralisation, de-regulation (and not necessarily disintegration or decomposition).

This paper reviews a number of theories that have been developed in Russia over the last decade, first of all the ideas of Vladimir Kaganskii ('the revolution of regions', 'the society of regions' and others), and to some extent the concept of the 'administrative market' (Vitalii Naishul', Simon Kordonskii). Citing and interpreting their theories and combining them with his own findings, the author looks for the grounds for creating an alternative methodological framework for the analysis of post-Soviet developments.

2 Regionalisation: A Soviet Heritage

2.1 Administrative/Territorial Division: The Region as a Functional Unit

Paradoxical as it may sound, one of the principal reasons behind regionalisation was the extreme centralisation of the Soviet system as it emerged at the heyday of Stalin's era (1930s to the early 1940s). State and society were not divided, they existed as a single whole. No individuality was accepted – be it personal, ethnic or regional. The authorities sought to create a homogeneous and governable space, penetrated by vertical relationships of command, control and communication. This was a space in which, according to Kaganskii, „nothing existed but the universal state/society and its territorial structures".[1] Any personal, social, ethnic or territorial (regional) differentiation was entirely defined by the administrative status of a person, ethnic or social group, or region in this state/society.

The effective functioning of this system in the enormous Soviet landmass required a certain territorial arrangement. This was sought in the unique Soviet system of the 'administrative/territorial division' (ATD), a universal structure, embracing the entire territory of the former USSR. ATD was „a system of multi-functional institutional districts, a framework, in which all state functions were performed." (Kaganskii[2]) ATD was created to control the Soviet space with all its 'contents', to organise the operation of state institutions as well as the people's everyday existence. The whole spectrum of state activities (law enforcement, military draft, ideology, education, health care, housing, day-to-day management of

---

1 Kaganskii, V.L. „Sovetskoe prostranstvo. Konstruktsiya i destruktsiya (teoreticheskaya geografiya sovetskogo prostranstva [Soviet Space. Construction and Destruction (Theoretical Geography of Soviet Space)]." *Inoe*, Vol. 1. Moscow, 1995 (forthcoming).

2 Ibidem: 4.

local industry and agriculture, etc.) was carried out entirely on the regional level and almost never went beyond it. All state functions were concentrated in the regions, which became focal points, vital centres, „the cells of guaranteed survival of the local population."[3] Regions did indeed emerge as principal institutions of the state.[4]

ATD was an artificial network imposed on a vast territory with its inherent natural divisions (ethnic, social, geographical, etc.). For instance, ATD had full priority over ethnicity; according to Kaganskii, „ethnicity could be legalised exclusively in the form of special ethno-administrative regions."[5] ATD turned ethnicity (as well as economy, local cultures) into a state institution, ethnic relations – into relations of ethno-administrative regions of different status (a republic, an autonomous *oblast'*, a district) which gave birth to the strict hierarchy of ethnic groups. Administrative division had an enormous ethno-genetic effect; the infrastructure of ethnicity (the use of language, etc.) existed only within ethnic regions.[6]

In other words, the logic of administrative subordination contradicted the natural logic of territorial relations; the former suppressed the latter. Vertical (artificial, hierarchical) chains of command prevailed over horizontal (natural, territorial) connections. But ATD could not completely abolish horizontal relations, which nevertheless existed in a latent form, and where an enormous potential of problems (economic, territorial, demographic, ethnic, social) was accumulating.

Therefore, this is to say that hyper-centralisation of the Soviet state/society was prone to conflict. Instead of an organic, regional system which would respect all geographical, historical, ethnic, demographic differences and in which local communities could interact in a natural manner, it set up an artificial system of ATD in which any territorial or ethnic differences and natural interaction of localities were disregarded and regions simply became functional units, agents of the universal state/society. Instead of promoting unity by nature (which would have been much more flexible and adaptable to change), it imposed unity by order which turned out to be superficial and non-resistant to future transformations of the Soviet system. Under the cover of formal, 'vertical', hierarchical unity, regions started to emerge as self-sufficient cells, and a number of unresolved 'horizontal' (territorial) problems started to accumulate. In this sense, the centralisation imposed on the Soviet territory

3 Ibidem: 4.
4 Ibidem: 4.
5 Ibidem: 5.
6 Ibidem: 5.

contained seeds of disunity, and today's regionalisation is the „revenge of the territory“ (Kaganskii).[7]

2.2 The Region as a Territorial Unit

As basic functional units in which most state activities were concentrated, regions also emerged as basic territorial units. Every region has an administrative centre – the largest city or town (at least 3 to 5 times bigger than the second largest) which dominates in the territory of the region as does a metropolis over a colony. The space of the region is hierarchically and functionally centralised. All essential objects are one of a kind and situated in the region's centre. (For instance, the monument symbolising the geometrical centre of Asia was moved to Kyzyl, the capital of Tuva, from its original (i.e. logical) location.) The region's capital is the economic, transport and communications centre; the region's roads and traffic are essentially centripetal. (Probably, up to 80 per cent of all roads in the regions serve hierarchical relations). The centre draws masses of the population; most migrations (especially the pendulum ones) proceed along centripetal routes.[8]

Main forces of industry and agriculture are concentrated around the region's centre; the level of development, the density of the population and other parameters decline drastically as one moves from the centre to the periphery. „The administrative rank of the centre and the distance from the centre are main criteria that define the status of the peripheral territory and its living standards.“[9] The administrative borders of the region become quite real: this is where many roads and communications are interrupted, the specialisation of agriculture is changed, etc. The borders of the regions are clearly readable on photographs taken from space.[10]

The region's population is thus a kind of closed community, a collective, vitally linked to the centre and confined by the borders of the region. Some experts point out that up to 90 per cent of all migrations on the Soviet territory took place within regions of the *oblast'* level. The greater part of the Soviet population identifies itself with regions which are, in turn, often identified with regional centres (in modern Russian, when a resident of a regional periphery „goes to the *oblast'*“, this means he

---

7 Ibidem: 23.
8 Ibidem: 5-6.
9 Ibidem: 6.
10 Ibidem.

goes to the centre of the *oblast'*: a telling metonymy). Life in the region is a closed cycle; the region is the stage for the everyday activities of the population.[11]

Centralisation and concentration of people, functions and activities in regional centres, combined with an almost complete lack of direct inter-regional (horizontal) connections, leads to 'centralist polarisation'.[12] This makes a region a compact and controllable unit, an object (and a subject) of possible claims. On the political level, regions became principal actors of Soviet political dynamics, the basic units in negotiating, trading and defining the balance of power on the Soviet political scene.

2.3 The Region as a Key Element in the Administrative Market

Apart from being primary functional units in the Soviet state/society and basic territorial units in the Soviet space, regions had a third vocation: they were key agents and 'trading places' in the so-called system of the 'administrative market'.[13]

According to the theory of the administrative market (Simon Kordonskii, Vladimir Naishul), the hard-core administrative-and-command system (a heavily centralised, hierarchical system of decision-making, planning and distribution) existed in the USSR in the 1930s and early 1940s. In the late 1940s it started to evolve towards a 'softer' variant, the 'economy of agreements'. Relationships between different interest groups (including regions) began to lose their hierarchical character and to turn into a system of 'heterarchical trade-offs' (or agreements): each interest group, being in possession of specific resources (human, natural, industrial, organisational, bureaucratic, political, etc.), applies pressure on other groups in the pursuance of its bureaucratic goals.

In other words, the administrative market emerged in the process of privatising the administrative-and-command system. In this case, privatisation means the transfer of the separate fragments of the planning and management system, of

---

11 Ibidem.

12 Ibidem.

13 Kordonskii, S.G. „Nekotorye sotsiologicheskie aspekty izucheniya khozyastvennykh otnoshenii [Some Sociological Aspects of the Study of Economic Relations]." In *Teoreticheskie problemy sovershenstvovaniya ekonomicheskogo mekhanizma* [Theoretical Problems of the Further Refining of the Economic Mechanism]. Moscow: VNIISI, 1986; Naishul' V.A. „Vysshaya i poslednyaya stadiya sotsializma [The Highest and Final Stage of Socialism]." In *Pogruzhenie v tryasinu* [Sliding in a Slump]. Moscow: Progress, 1991. Naishul', V.A. „Liberalizm i ekonomicheskie reformy [Liberalism and Economic Reforms]." *Mirovaya ekonomika i mezhdunarodnye otnosheniya* [World Economy and International Relations], no. 8 (1992).

information and decision-making channels into the full private or collective property of bureaucracy within the regions and the branches of the economy.[14]

The basic currency of the administrative market is an 'administrative service' which can be exchanged for another service between bureaucrats involved in the management process. Distribution, re-distribution or exchange of resources, supplies, planning or non-planning – virtually any bureaucratic activity can become an administrative service. Shipping of goods to their destination, inclusion into state plans and programs 'by a separate line', easing of social tension, housing programmes, granting a minimal wage in exchange for a minimal output: all these services are traded on the administrative market.

The administrative market is characteristic not only of Soviet or post-Soviet society; it exists everywhere. However, in the Soviet example it shapes all other markets: the market for commodities, services, information, means of production, and likewise, the labour market. Even in the post-Soviet economic environment all these markets function within and conform to the rules of the administrative market.

Normal economic logic i.e. the criteria of cost-and-benefit do not apply to the administrative market. In this market, the bureaucratic corporations struggle exclusively for their own stability, and economic considerations often fall victim to their corporative goals. For instance, a factory director tries to get the highest possible number of workers (as this will upgrade his status on the market and allow him to claim more resources), regardless of whether these people can be engaged in productive labour. The same bid for resources explains why it is preferable, in terms of the administrative market, that employees work in a hard climate, or live in bad housing conditions.

The administrative market has nothing to do with competition: this is an oligopolistic market. Its principal function is distribution and re-distribution of resources among four main functional/territorial groups of the Soviet economy:

- the fuel and resource complex;
- the military-industrial complex;
- the agro-industrial complex;
- the 'power ministries' (the army, KGB, the Ministry of the Interior) with their economic activities.

---

14 Kordonskii. „*Nekotorye sotsiologicheskie aspekty*".

All these groups, including the army, were organised along regional lines and so the administrative market ultimately provided for the flow of resources between donor-regions and subsidised regions.

Consequently, the administrative market functions almost exclusively in the regional framework. Historically, until early 1990s, it was organised in accordance with the regional Communist party structures and the regional structure of the soviets. Regions have emerged as key agents of the administrative market, and at the same time – its 'marketplaces'.[15] 'Trading' on the administrative market takes place either between regions or branches of the economy (the 'agreement' of various interest groups on the functioning of the Soviet economy as a whole), or within regions (the 'agreement' on the functioning of the local economy). This implies both official forms of agreements (e.g. those codified in the state plans), and unofficial ones (the shadow economy, tenevaya ekonomika). The black market of production, too, was organised along regional lines, in almost complete accordance with the administrative/territorial division (ATD). The administrative market has thus reinforced the positions of regions as basic units of Soviet politics and economics with their specific interests, pressure groups, procedures and bureaucracy.

2.4 Local Elites: The Region as a Cell in Cadres Structure

Playing a key role in Soviet politics, economics and society, regions started generating specific models of behaviour in the Soviet political class. In fact, their function in the Soviet space made them basic formative cells of the political elite.

The emergence of local elites was inherent in the structure of ATD, and so the institutional foundation was laid over many decades. However, this process was visibly accelerated in the early 1960s when the Soviet political system started to evolve from Stalinist centralisation to the more flexible model of the Khrushchev and Brezhnev years ('feudal socialism'). This model, underpinned by the cadre-based infrastructure of the Communist Party, put forward local structures, notably the *oblast'* Committees of the CPSU, as key actors of Soviet politics. „You are masters of the country!“, overtly claimed Konstantin Chernenko, addressing the first secretaries of the *oblast'* Party Committees at the conference he held after his election as General Secretary in 1983.

---

15 Ibidem. See also Naishul'. „Vysshaya i poslednyaya stadiya sotsializma.“

Over the years, local elites have emerged (and continue to develop) in virtually all regions of the former USSR and, as a rule, are composed of the following six elements[16]:

- The *traditional clan and tribal system* most representative of the region's history and culture. Despite the 'internationalist' indoctrination, clan relations were well preserved over the Soviet period (especially in the Caucasus and Central Asia) in the communist power structures.
- The *former party functionaries* who have retained extensive connections throughout the entire territory of the former USSR and still comprise a kind of a network of common cadres. The authorities in certain regions (including those that are considered 'democratic') are almost completely staffed by former *nomenklatura* cadres. For example, the staff of Nizhnii Novgorod *oblast'* Administration under Boris Yeltsin's former protégé Boris Nemtsov remains virtually unchanged when compared with the communist period.
- *Heads of major industrial and agricultural enterprises* of the region.
- *Influential representatives of the private sector*, many of whom are connected with the old *nomenklatura*. This link goes back to the mid 1980s, when members of the *nomenklatura* covertly started investing state and party capital in joint ventures and private businesses. This part of the local elite is sometimes strongly influenced by the criminal world.
- *Local heads of law enforcement* authorities, state security, and the army.
- The *representatives of the central republican authority* (in Russia these are representatives of the President, and heads of the local administration also appointed by his hand). As a rule the majority of them are incorporated into local elites and, in a manner of speaking, become captive to the local establishment. These figures play an important role in legitimising local elites and are sometimes used for applying pressure on the centre.

One can point out at least four major formative models of local elites[17]:

- A *local elite in the region with traditional (archaic) structures*, and/or with deeply rooted ethnic and confessional traditions. These can be either ethnic regions (the Chechen Republic, Dagestan, the Turkic and Finno-Ugric lands of the Volga region, Yakutia-Sakha, etc. in the Russian Federation) or areas with local differences in language, mentality, habits and ways (Galicia in Ukraine,

---

16 Sultanov, Sh.Z. *Razvitie regional'nykh politicheskikh elit i dinamika konfliktov*. Manuscript, 1992.

17 Ibidem.

Mengrelia in Georgia, the Fergana valley in Uzbekistan etc.). In most such cases, the local elites have emerged on the basis of archaic social structures (family clans, regional tribal unions, etc.), and 'modern' elements were incorporated later. In this model, the formation of the local elite takes place most rapidly.

- A *local elite on a wider traditional territory*: the Lvov area and adjacent lands that form the traditional community of West Ukraine, opposed to Central (Podolia), East and South Ukraine; Mengrelia, Guria and part of Abkhazia constitute West Georgia in contrast to East Georgia (Kartli); the Fergana, Namangan and Andizhan *oblasts* form the wider Fergan region as opposed to three other major areas of Uzbekistan: Tashkent, Samarkand-Bukhara, and Khiva.
- A *local elite in industrial areas* containing a high percentage of the urban population. (This is especially the case in Russia and Ukraine.) The main formative feature of the local elite is the control over natural resources (as seen in the regions producing raw materials such as the Komi and Yakutia-Sakha Republics, Kuznetsk and Vorkuta coal basins, etc.). The elite is then based on the heads of major enterprises, joined by other elements, listed above.

  In a number of cases, this model applies for agrarian regions: then the formative feature of the local elite is the control over land.
- A special kind of *regional elite* develops *in large cities and administrative and industrial centres* (Moscow, St.Petersburg, Kiev, Sverdlovsk, Tomsk, Dnepropetrovsk, etc.). A stable local elite has emerged in Moscow under the previous (Gavriil Popov) and the present (Yurii Luzhkov) mayors.

To put it more simply, these four models can be boiled down to two:

- elites, formed on the traditional (family, tribal, clannish, or wider historical) basis (a+b);
- elites, formed on the industrial (agro-industrial) basis in large cities (b+c).

It is important to stress that neither tradition, including ethnicity, nor the industrial base themselves constitute the necessary foundation for the emergence of a local elite. Elites have emerged everywhere as a function of the administrative-territorial division and as a necessary model of political behaviour. Ethnic, traditional, industrial or urban structures simply accelerate the formation of the elite.

To sum up the contents of this section, the creation of a unitary Soviet structure (state/society) in a wide and heterogeneous Eurasian space was prone to contradictions. It sought unity and uniformity, but instead it non-intentionally put forward regions and their elites as key actors of Soviet (and post-Soviet) political dynamics. This system made regions into autonomous units from four different perspectives:

- the functional (including social and political) perspective;
- the territorial perspective;
- the economic perspective (key units of the administrative market);
- the cadre perspective (local elites).

This Soviet heritage – such a concentration of functions, resources, procedures, bureaucracy and even geographical concentration on specific fragments of territory – laid the ground for the process of regionalisation which started in the post-Soviet period.

3 The Logic of Post-Soviet Regionalisation

3.1 Destruction of the Regional Pyramid

Post-Soviet regionalisation was inherent in the structure and composition of the regionalised space of the USSR and does not need additional explanations. This was a logical continuation of the functional and territorial fragmentation of the Soviet space in which every element had a specific place and status and sought to retain or upgrade this status. Those elements were regions and/or regional elites that simply extended their functions in the economic, political, ethnic and other fields.

The structure of the Soviet Union already allowed the regions to 'behave themselves', but within certain administrative limits and norms.[18] As those limits and norms were becoming more flexible, the regions started to behave in a more daring manner, but the model remained essentially the same. The only difference between the Soviet-era latent regionalisation (with regions being proto-subjects of politics) and the post-Soviet actual regionalisation (with regions becoming active subjects) is simply the extent of independent behaviour. In this sense, the USSR was a 'self-dismembering space' (Kaganskii).[19]

However, the Soviet political class did not come to realise this fact. By seeking to upgrade their status, the majority of the regional elites did not understand that they were dismantling the upper levels of the regional hierarchical pyramid and thus

---

18 Kaganskii. „Sovetskoe prostranstvo“: 12.
19 Ibidem: 11.

actually destroying the very pyramid which sanctioned and guaranteed their own existence. Paradoxically, „the USSR was destroyed by forces which were not interested in its dissolution“[20]; the 'tragic' decisions of Soviet and Russian leaders simply legitimised the actual state of things.

According to Kaganskii, the logic of regionalisation was rather simple: „upgrading their status, the regions acquired the competencies of the upper level of the hierarchy, and this led to dismantling the functionally unnecessary level. In other words, the regions were 'taking over' the Centre, the structures of which were regionalised themselves.“[21] As a matter of fact, the politics of the Centre further promoted regionalisation: opposing the regions, pursuing a special policy towards them (ranging from support to the use of force, e.g. in Lithuania) the Centre treated them as equal partners thus supporting their self-determination.

The regional system was only stable if the vertical hierarchy (the 'pyramid' of regions) dominated over horizontal links. Bringing the regions onto an equal footing with the Centre (or rather degrading the Centre's role to the regional level) ruined the vertical subordination and brought about a horizontal (i.e. 'political') kind of relationship. „The regional system was not conceived for political activity; any 'politics' further destabilised it and led to the autonomisation of its elements.“[22] For instance, regionalisation was visibly accelerated by the 1989 election campaign in which voting districts corresponded to the administrative/territorial division of the country and by the ensuing work of the First Congress of the USSR People's Deputies in regional delegations. From that time on, 'politics' became a game played on a regional field and all political forces had to fit into it – i.e. correspond to its constituent parts, the regions. Non-regional political forces were increasingly marginalised.[23]

Political dynamics were increasingly defined by the conflict-type interaction of various levels and elements of the unstable regional pyramid. In this game, the regional levels (and sometimes separate regions) employed various conflict strategies: the coalition of non-adjacent levels (the upper + the lower vs. the middle); the coalition of the regional level with the weak structure (the opposition) of the upper level; using the conflict of the upper levels to attain local goals („the monkey, watching the struggle between the lion and the tiger“, in Mao's metaphor), etc.

---

20 Ibidem: 10.
21 Ibidem: 11.
22 Ibidem.
23 Ibidem.

One can cite a number of such ad hoc coalitions[24]:

leaders of union republics	vs.	the USSR Centre
+		
the 'democratic opposition' to the USSR leadership		

the RSFSR leadership	vs.	the USSR Centre
+		
the centres of lower levels (the so-called 'democratic cities')		
+		
the leaders of union republics		

In a similar fashion, *oblasts* and autonomous republics of the RSFSR were using the conflict between the RSFSR and the USSR to claim additional rights and privileges

Later cases:

The Russian Federation	vs.	Moldova Georgia Ukraine
+		
The region of the lower level in the neighbouring state (Transdnestria in Moldova, Abkhazia in Georgia, Crimea in Ukraine)		

Russia's regions	vs.	The Centre of the Russian Federation
+		
The weakened part of the Moscow political establishment (the parliamentary opposition in 1993)		

Though regions did not directly participate in the events of August 1991, the failure of the 'coup' was their victory. Horizontal relations in the power pyramid clearly prevailed over the vertical ones. From that moment on, horizontal (including inter-regional) relations (and armed conflicts as well) became the dominant trend on the political scene.

---

24 Ibidem.

The events of September-October 1993 were even more telling: the regions virtually ignored the institutional and military confrontation in Moscow. Only one region was involved (Moscow), simply because the conflict was taking place on its territory. This lent weight to the fact that the Centre and the regions exist in different dimensions. „If the first putsch proved the independent existence of the regions, the second one questioned whether 'the Centre of the regions' exists at all" (Kaganskii).[25]

3.2 Modernisation of the Administrative Market

The economic logic of the process of regionalisation is closely connected with the modernisation of the administrative market. This modernisation, which started in the mid-1980s, was motivated by two basic factors. Firstly, by the external challenge of the world economy and secondly (and more importantly), by the internal necessity of capitalising on the achieved level of privatisation of the administrative-and-command system by basic elites in the administrative market.

Consequently, the elites started converting their rank, status and channels of influence in the administrative market into financial and material assets. This process has resulted in re-evaluation of many administrative ranks. For instance, a regional economic boss (e.g. a director of a major factory) and the chief of the *oblast'* traffic police (GAI) used to have a similar rank and influence in the *nomenklatura*. In the new era, the director privatises his position and economic leverage and enters into a new economic environment with a certain chance of success. However, this harder to do in the case of the GAI chief. The redrawing of the status pyramid, its 'marketisation' and adaptation to the new, quasi-liberal criteria was the principal form of modernisation of the administrative market in 1985-1990.

It is necessary to stress that this modernisation has nothing to do with social changes or the emergence of a new class of proprietors. It only concerns the models of behaviour among what are essentially the same bureaucratic elites, and does not change the structure of the Soviet society.

Already at this stage of modernisation, many regions (especially donor-regions) became actively involved. As key agents of the administrative market, they were vitally interested in converting their status on the market into material assets. From the very beginning, the principle of 'regional self-accountability' (regionalnyi

25 Ibidem: 13.

khozraschet) implied the regions' bid for the 'state property' of the Soviet Union.[26] Regionalisation during this period was the first phase of privatisation, carried out several years before the state programme of privatisation was announced (1991).

The conversion of military production which started during this period can also be interpreted as gradual withdrawal of part of the military-industrial complex from the jurisdiction of the central 'authorities' i.e. as regionalisation and privatisation of the military-industrial complex.[27] It has become evident that „the economy of the region is organised in such a way that any division or re-distribution of 'state property' can take place only within regions“: i.e. that privatisation can be legalised or implemented exclusively on the regional level.[28]

However, in 1985-1990 regionalisation and privatisation was still largely restricted by state monopolies and regulated prices. In the early 1990s, with the elimination of 'branch ministries', the ban on the regional structures of the Communist party (and then on the CPSU itself), the coup of August 1991 and finally with Egor Gaidar's attempt at liberal reform in early 1992, the modernisation and privatisation of the administrative market was dramatically accelerated.

Elimination of state control over prices in January 1992 triggered the comprehensive process of dividing up the former 'state property' of the USSR among the main groups and figures in the administrative market, primarily the regional elites. Implementation of the liberal doctrine gave those groups a free hand in taking over and re-distributing 'state resources', converting their administrative status into material assets, essentially in hard currency which could be taken out of Russia. The attempted reform finally emancipated the main agents of the administrative market from any political, administrative or economic restrictions.

As a result of Gaidar's quasi-monetarist reform the agents of the administrative market began to comprehend that, instead of the complicated distribution of hundreds of different resources, it suffices to control and distribute just two: finances and rights. In this sense, the modernisation of the administrative market is the transfer from the natural economic forms (including barter trade) to a more sophisticated manipulation of financial resources, rights and privileges.

This was the ultimate economic logic behind the process of regionalisation. The key difference between post-Soviet regionalisation and the similar global trend is that the former is the result of the transformation of the administrative market. In

---

26 Ibidem.
27 Ibidem.
28 Ibidem.

this transformation, the regional elites realise the possibility of converting their virtual property (administrative status) into actual property: the fragment of territory with all its natural resources, its potential taxation base, the possibility of claiming financial resources as well as special rights and privileges.

At present, unilateral actions on the part of the regions such as imposing special import and export regimes on their territory, collecting taxes and customs, introducing local currencies and bonds indicate that many regions have successfully privatised their administrative positions and acquired most of the economic competencies of the state. This is further confirmed by the fact that regions now have an almost complete command of resources (including natural resources) on their territory, and an actual right of veto in the implementation of the state programme of privatisation.[29]

3.3 The Mechanisms of Regionalisation

Post-Soviet regionalisation is a complex process which involves not only regions as territorial and functional units but also extra-regional functional components and structures of the former USSR. The regionalisation of the USSR (a super-region, the upper level of the regional pyramid) will be complete only when all its functional components are re-integrated and accommodated in its constituent parts (regions). In this sense the regionalisation of the USSR is not yet over, while the regionalisation of the former Union republics, above all Russia, still has a long way to go. At present, the processes of regionalisation at different levels interfere with each other.[30]

Regionalisation of the USSR level implies autonomisation of its following key components[31]:

- The *regions themselves* as territorial and functional units;
- *Regionalised sectors* of the USSR's functional components (part of the armed forces, of the military-industrial complex, of the energy and transport infrastructure, etc.);
- *Non-regionalised sectors* of the USSR's functional components (strategic nuclear forces, the atomic complex, the space complex, etc.).

---

29 Ibidem: 13.

30 Ibidem: 16.

31 Ibidem: 16-17.

- A special component: the *Centre* (Moscow with its as yet unclear functions and unclear borders).
- The special case of *separatist districts* (sometimes a sub-region, or a 'counter-region') which form part of one administrative region and are vitally linked with another: e.g. Nagorno-Karabakh, Transdnestria, Abkhazia, the Prigorodnyi district in North Ossetia, etc.

Regions that become the entities of the upper level in the hierarchy (i.e. independent states) construct their statehood from some of these five components. For instance, the Baltic states use components 1 and 2 while ridding themselves of component 3; Ukraine and to a lesser degree Kazakhstan (see the Baikonur issue) try to combine components 1,2 and 3; Armenia consolidates its statehood using components 1, 2 and 5.[32]

Sometimes the souvereignisation of a region can take place only at the cost of losing component 5 – a separatist district: this is the case of Azerbaidzhan and Moldova. In other cases, components 2 and 3, which are territorially defined, become the basis of souvereignisation of a separatist district (Transdnestria, Abkhazia).

However, full souvereignisation and assembly of statehood from these components does not render new independent states immune to further regionalisation. The level of the USSR has nearly been completely dismantled and the regions which have become the upper level of the hierarchical pyramid are themselves regionalised. Regionalisation continues on different territories at various speeds and in various forms. (On the types of regionalisation in Russia, see Appendix A.) The diversity of lifestyles in different regions increases; „the fragmentation of space is accompanied by the fragmentation of time" (Kaganskii[33]).

The political space, too, becomes subdivided into many levels and influenced by an increasing number of subjects. For instance, factors involved in decision-making on the issue of the South Kurile Chain, disputed with Japan, are: fragments of the dismembered USSR level (the armed forces, the navy), the Russian Federation, the Russian Far East (a coalition of regions), the Sakhalin *oblast'* (the disputed islands being on its territory) and finally, the islands themselves (as administrative and political units, based on a military infrastructure). In this sense, the 'old state'

32 Ibidem: 17.
33 Ibidem: 23.

(USSR) has not simply been replaced by the 'new states': the process is much more complex and takes place on a number of different, simultaneous levels.[34]

Regions form coalitions with each other and also with the states of the 'far abroad' (Moldova-Rumania, Azerbaidzhan-Turkey, etc.). It is hard to find a difference between regions and states, between inter-regional and inter-state relations, especially since the regions of the upper level acquire the attributes of independent statehood (army, including strategic forces, law enforcement agencies, etc.). The armed forces and the military-industrial complex are similarly being regionalised. In a number of new post-Soviet states the central authority becomes no more than a superstructure over the regions which possess the real power, or a 'cover' for certain regions' rule over others.[35]

At the present stage, the administrative/territorial division as a matrix of regionalisation is augmented by other models of souvereignisation. This primarily concerns ethnic groups which are settled outside of the regional framework. An important new development is the increased activity of ethnic groups that do not possess their own ethnic regions (e.g. the peoples of the North that are settled in various regions). Meanwhile, multi-ethnic regions are being fragmented (the North Caucasus).[36]

One final note concerning the logic of regionalisation. In this process, functional and territorial fragmentation is combined with functional and, to some extent, territorial re-integration. Regions and local elites consolidate their authority, re-assembling functional components of the former USSR and sometimes absorbing or annexing other territories. „Disintegration takes place on the level of the USSR; however, on the lower level (new independent states and greater regions) disintegration (their further regionalisation) is amalgamated with centralisation (consolidation of authority in the new centres)."[37] In this sense, it would be more correct to denominate this process as the reshaping of the territorial structure of the former Soviet Union, which implies both disintegration and integration.

---

34 Ibidem.

35 Ibidem: 24.

36 Ibidem.

37 Ibidem: 24.

4 Regionalism as a Universal Interpretation

4.1 'The Bourgeois Revolution of Regions'

The key role of regions in politics, economics and society in the Soviet period has been further enhanced following the break-up of the USSR. In actual fact, regions become the principal subjects of post-Soviet developments. Regionalisation becomes the prevailing trend, the main shaping factor. This can lead to re-evaluation of existing interpretations of post-Soviet developments (a systemic crisis, popular revolution, ethnic revolution, 'the conspiracy of the elite', etc.). Vladimir Kaganskii puts forward the hypothesis of the 'bourgeois revolution of regions' and the emerging 'society of regions' as a result of the transformation of the totally regionalised Soviet space.[38]

The increased and varied activities of regions can be interpreted in terms of the classic bourgeois revolution under the slogans of 'liberty, equality, property'. In this revolution, 'tiers état' is represented by the community of regions which find their identity in opposing the state (the Centre) and in claiming their 'inalienable' right of property.[39] The liberty of the region is its autonomy, sovereignty, independence. The equality of the regions implies the 'horizontalisation' of the administrative/territorial hierarchy; By this logic, Russia, Tatarstan or the Chechen Republic have essentially equal rights and privileges.[40] As for the property, the 'revolution of regions' means privatisation of all state resources and assets by subjects of the administrative market, namely by regions. The 'bourgeois revolution of regions' is a spontaneous institutional liberalisation.[41]

According to this concept, regions prove to be the analogue and the equivalent of the population. This is further confirmed by the fact that the populace itself in the Soviet system was engaged primarily in the regional framework; they were no more than a substance in the regional structure. It is no wonder that in the present situation

---

38 For the evolution of the argument, see: Kaganskii, V.L. „Sotsializm: dal'she – bol'she (zametki realista) [Socialism: Further – More (Notes of a Realist)]." *Vek XX i mir* [The 20th Century and the World], no. 12 (1990); Kaganskii, V.L. „Voyna i revolyutsiya rayonov (K 'anatomii' sovestkogo prostranstva) [War and Revolution of Districts (On the 'Anatomy' of the Soviet Space)]."; Kaganskii, V.L. „Real'nosti regionalizatsii: osnovnye aspekty protsessa [Realities of Regionalisation: Basic Aspects of the Process]." In *Kuda idet Rossiya?* [Where Is Russia Going?] Moscow: Interpress, 1994.

39 Kaganskii. „Sovetskoe prostranstvo": 18.

40 Kaganskii, V.L. „Pryzhok v neizvestnost' [A Leap into the Unknown]." *Vek XX i mir*, no. 6 (1992): 30.

41 Naishul'. „Liberalizm i ekonomicheskie reformy."

various Centres appeal to regions in the same instances where one would appeal to a population.[42]

In the regionalised Soviet space and especially so in the post-Soviet space, each region can be compared with an individual.[43] This explains many practical activities of the regions, in particular their declarations of sovereignty. Full sovereignty and inviolability of property are attributed only to individuals – i.e. to regions. In the modern secular culture only the individual can potentially be rendered sacral; therefore the regions and regional elites translate their specific interests into a symbolic, ideological form, and ethnic regions and elites – into a sacral form of individuality. Hence the extreme sensitivity of the regions over the questions of territorial integrity, rights and privileges and especially over ethnic issues (ethnicity is the most sacred form of regional individuality) as well as their relentless struggle for a place in the regionalised space.[44]

This analogy can be further extended in the political sense. The idea of the 'social contract' of individuals is translated into the idea of the 'direct contract of regions' (i.e. without the Centre) as the only possibility of a new agreement in the absence of the administrative hierarchy.[45] This ideology is gaining momentum and can result in the complete regional rearrangement of the Soviet territory without the participation of the Centre.

The 'socialisation' of regions, their transformation into 'individuals', is least of all their intentional strategy. The making of the 'society of regions' is a product of the evolution of the Soviet system which presupposed regional differentiation and autonomisation, vested the regions with main functions of the state, and made them focal points of everyday life of the Soviet population.

In their 'revolution' the regions rid themselves not only of administrative subordination but also of any legal and other norms and rules: the situation is bordering anarchy. The regions start setting their own norms which are sometimes even coarser for the local population than the old Soviet ones. Indeed, souvereignisation and individualisation often does not go below the regional level – to the real individual. By becoming 'individuals' in the public (political) sphere, regions occupy this functional niche and eventually force the people out of this field.

42 Kaganskii. „Real'nosti regionalizatsii."

43 Kaganskii. „Sovetskoe prostranstvo": 23.

44 Ibidem: 19.

45 Ibidem.

Kaganskii supposes that this identification of the region with an individual is the perverse form of the Russian *sobornost'* (conciliation, communalism).[46]

Thus the ideology of regionalism becomes universal to the extent that the ideology of human rights was universal in the French revolution. Regionalism is a meta-ideology.[47] Any other political or social ideologies are simply instrumental for the regions; time has shown that regional elites are utterly undiscriminating in ideological or political preferences. Regionalisation is the politics of bare interests. In fact, the question is whether in the 'society of regions' politics in the usual sense of the word exist at all.

4.2 Politics in the Regional Interpretation

Traditional political concepts and schemes are hardly applicable in the case of a totally regionalised, fragmented space; even if these schemes sometimes apply they turn out to be highly ambivalent. The usual political criteria of 'left' and 'right' can not explain the multi-level relationships on the regional scene.[48]

Most importantly, in the absence of a one-level, single political space, political parties cannot exist as real forces.[49] Artificial entities that call themselves 'parties' are largely symbolic; these are the products of a politicised mentality and their activity has no regional grass roots basis. The system of central power institutions and 'political parties' becomes more and more autonomous and self-sufficient. In this sense 'politics' becomes a special trade for several thousand individuals in the Centre (in Moscow, or in the Centres of the new independent states).

Not only the dichotomy of the 'left' and the 'right' but also the dichotomy of the 'government' and the 'opposition' is irrelevant (or at least ambivalent) in the multi-level regionalised space.[50] Since there is no single political process the notions of the 'government' and the 'opposition' are different for each level of the regional hierarchy. 'Government-opposition' relations are inverted as one goes down the regional levels: the *oblast'*-level authorities are the opposition for the central government in Moscow, but they are, in turn, the government for the regions below the *oblast'* level, which are 'their own' opposition.

---

46 Kaganskii. „Sovetskoe prostranstvo": 20.
47 Kaganskii. „Pryzhok v neizvestnost'": 29-30.
48 Kaganskii. „Sotsializm: dal'she – bol'she."
49 Kaganskii. „Sovetskoe prostranstvo": 20.
50 Ibidem.

Consequently, the 'centralism-separatism' antithesis is also ambiguous. It applies only in cases where there is a single state authority and one level of politically defined regions. The Post-Soviet scenario is very different. Every region seeks sovereignty from the structures of the upper level (separatism), and at the same time tries to preserve its own territorial integrity (centralism).[51] For instance, those who championed the separatist drive of the former Union republics (including the RSFSR leadership) turned out to be the centralists and even imperialists of their own republic after the USSR level had been dismantled. This testifies not to their inconsistency but to the fact that political conduct is totally defined by the regional status of a political subject.[52]

It is noteworthy that the subjects (regions) of the same level have essentially the same interests and programmes, which cannot be the case in any normal political process. The behaviour of regions hardly depends on political preferences and the origin of their authorities ('communists', 'democrats', 'nationalists', 'technocrats' etc.). Certainly, regions pursue varying strategies (see Appendix A) but this difference stems from such non-programmatic and non-ideological factors as the completeness of their structure (the availability of components mentioned above: II.3), the possibility to obtain the lacking components or to compensate for their absence (e.g. by entering into a coalition).

Pursuing a policy of interests (and not of programmes), the regions seek to support and legitimise their claims by any available means of justification. In particular, they proclaim the 'restoration of justice' through souvereignisation (which in fact simply means compensating for the deficit of administrative status). Such justification of regional demands is often very eclectic and contradictory.[53] Regions refer to the violation of their rights, to their unequal treatment during the Soviet period and, at the same time, to their former special rights and privileges in the Soviet administrative structure which have been taken away in recent years. References to any historical period are provided: Recalling Kievan Rus (X century), Ukraine claims that it has a longer tradition of statehood than Russia, yet in claiming Crimea, it refers to the Khrushchev period (1954). Regionalism is a non-discriminating meta-ideology, fraught with regional chauvinism and xenophobia. An important fact, however, is that through regionalisation the ideology and exercise of socialism and communism lose any substance and practical relevance. In a strange

51 Ibidem.

52 Ibidem.

53 Kaganskii. „Sotsializm: dal'she – bol'she."

way, Soviet communism is eliminated by regionalisation[54] – i.e. by local elites and leaders, a large proportion of whom still believe themselves to be communists.

Similar models of behaviour among communists, liberals, nationalists etc. in the regional framework render all these political identifications senseless. „Regions are quasi-political subjects in an essentially non-political situation"; „regionalisation is the mechanism of depolitisation and de-ideologisation in the post-Soviet space."[55])

Forced out to the margins of the universal regional structure, politics turns into a sphere of 'active marginal behaviour': a trade for several thousand individuals in the Centres, as stated earlier. 'Political life' becomes more and more alienated, isolated, and this renders any purely political interpretation of the post-Soviet developments largely irrelevant.

4.3 Ethnicity and Group Behaviour in the Regional Interpretation

Ethnicity is viewed by many as one of the main driving forces of post-Soviet developments. It is true that this issue has surfaced quite vividly, but it is far from sufficient to use it to explain regional and other trends. Ethnicity has emerged more in its instrumental function; this issue appears where and when local elites and interest groups formed in the administrative/territorial framework and in the Soviet-era administrative market can use it to justify their move towards souvereignisation and privatisation. As mentioned before, ethnicity or archaic structures (tribes, clans) can also be used for the consolidation of the local elite.[56] In this sense, ethnicity is simply one of the resources of regionalisation (ethnic consecration of the regional 'individuality'), but not its underlying reason. This resource is available only to a limited number of local elites.

In cases where it is available, local groups realise their specific interests by taking control over the existing ethno-administrative regions or by trying to create an ethnic proto-region and to integrate it into the existing regional system[57] (e.g., the Crimean Tartars). Most attempts to upgrade the administrative status of ethnic regions provoked conflicts (see III.4), particularly in cases when the actual settlement of the ethnic group did not coincide with the administrative borders of the region. A special case is the 'second wave of ethnic separatism'[58] – the formation of a proto-region by

---

54 Kaganskii. „Pryzhok v neizvestnost'": 30; Kaganskii. „Sovetskoe prostranstvo": 22.

55 Kaganskii. „Sovetskoe prostranstvo": 21.

56 Sultanov. *Razvitie regional'nykh politicheskikh elit.*

57 Kaganskii. „Sovetskoe prostranstvo": 15.

58 Ibidem.

a compact ethnic minority within a larger region (e.g., Transdnestria); such proto-regions are often used by the Centre as counter-regions and supported by the power structures of the Centre (the army).

Although this strategy can not be adopted by all ethnic groups (largely because of a complex poly-ethnic composition of most regions in the former USSR), it is quite natural in the post-Soviet situation with its inherited administrative/territorial division. Ethnic realisation is only possible in the regional framework; Kaganskii argues that „at present, there is no other way for ethnic realisation than the formation of an ethno-administrative region".[59] (For example, the failure to restore an autonomous German region on the Volga has led to the increased emigration of Russia's Germans.) Quasi-ethnic groups (especially the Cossacks) pursue virtually the same strategy.

The same is true of all large groups of the population and of large professional communities (the miners' movement of the Kuznetsk coal basin has an almost complete control of the Kemerovo *oblast'*). Each group can pursue its activities only in the regional framework.[60]

Smaller non-ethnic groups realise their interests by utilising functional components from the regional structure.[61] As mentioned earlier, regionalisation destroys the old mechanisms of agreement between regions (the administrative market), but the functions of agreement, distribution etc. remain intact.[62] Consequently, a large part of the 'new business' (banks, exchanges, etc.) assumes the distributing, negotiating, mediating and even symbolic functions of the former Centre.[63] This was vividly exemplified by the centralised barter trade concentrated in the hands of several major commodity exchanges in Moscow before 1992; price liberalisation has led to stagnation in their activities.[64] The current situation is more diversified; with the partial implementation of the monetarist reform, trading on the administrative market has been transferred from commodities to financial resources.

---

59 Ibidem.

60 Ibidem.

61 Ibidem.

62 Kaganskii, V.L. „Dezintegratsiya gosudarstva i strategiya negosudarstvennykh struktur: prostranstvennyi aspekt (rezyume monografii *Anatomiya sovetskogo prostranstvo*) [The State's Disintegration and the Strategy of Non-Governmental Structures: The Spatial Dimension (Resume of the Monograph *Anatomy of Soviet Space*)]." *Issledovaniya i razrabotki/IKI KB*. Vol. 2. Moscow, 1992: 2.

63 Kaganskii, V.L. „Rossiiskoe prostranstvo: chasti sil'nee tselogo [The Russian Space: The Parts Are Stronger than the Whole]." *Vek XX i mir*, No. 5, 1992.

64 Kaganskii. „Sovetskoe prostranstvo": 15.

Now it is primarily the banks that assume the functions of the Centre and pursue their activities along the old administrative/territorial lines (e.g., the regional system of money transfers of the *Tver'universalbank*).

In fact, all new forms of economic and public activity (politics, business, mass communication etc.) fill in the existing framework of the administrative regions.[65] The new structures even exaggerate certain features of the Soviet-era administrative/territorial division. They are more centralised (nine of ten biggest banks are based in Moscow, thus making the Centre even more influential than in the previous epoch) and they more clearly allocate their activities among the regional levels.[66] With the total break-up of the Soviet state/society its fragments became autonomous but their activities genetically reproduce the specific character and functions of the Soviet system. „There are virtually no groups or structures that would behave regardless of the regional matrix“[67]: every kind of activity is oriented towards obtaining control over the regions, regional levels, or functional positions in the regional structure.

The process of regionalisation involves all components of the Soviet state/society. The behaviour of various groups depends on their position, influence and adaptability to the regional structure. On the one hand, massive groups, settled in accordance with the regional structure and powerful enough to influence the regions, are regionalised in an almost natural way and adjust to the territorial fragmentation (e.g. the Ukrainians, miners, ground troops in military districts, etc.). On the other hand, smaller groups, vitally linked with the Centre, find it difficult to adjust to the post-Soviet fragmentation and become marginal elements in the regionalised space (e.g., Russia's Germans, air controllers, politically charged intelligentsia in large cities, the strategic nuclear forces etc.). They either find a place in the weakened structures of the Centre or are inclined to emigrate (emigration is another consequence of regionalisation).[68]

Religious communities and their institutions are also regionalised and have to accommodate themselves in the regional structures (e.g. the independent Ukrainian Orthodox Church under the Metropolitan Filaret or the Ukrainian Catholic Church based in the regional community of West Ukraine). In other words, regionalisation puts on trial all groups of the population which subsequently have to identify

---

65 Kaganskii. „Chasti sil'nee tselogo.“
66 Kaganskii. „Sovetskoe prostranstvo“: 16.
67 Ibidem.
68 Ibidem.

themselves either with a specific region (regional level) or the weakened structures of the Centre, or have to become marginal.

4.4 Conflicts in the Regional Interpretation

Emergence and escalation of various types of conflicts, including high-intensity armed conflicts, seem to be the most threatening trend in the former Soviet area. Once again, this process does not need external or subjective explanations (influence from abroad, specific ambitions of local leaders), nor can it be completely explained by ethnic, clannish, or confessional factors. Conflicts were inherent in the regional structure of the USSR[69] (administrative/territorial division), especially in the system of local elites.

As noted earlier, local elites with their specific and often contradictory interests have been present on the Soviet political scene for many decades. Their interaction was institutionalised in a number of mechanisms (most essentially in the CPSU structures and in the administrative market); there was a system of checks and balances (e.g. trade-offs in the administrative market) that moderated their contradictions, as well as a set of strict rules applying to political behaviour that excluded unilateral violent actions on the part of the subjects on the political market.

In the late 1980s-early 1990s, most of these institutions and checks were progressively removed: the system of 'branch ministries', the local CPSU committees, the system of soviets. The administrative market was being commercialised: a binding vertical structure was turning into a horizontal one. The old rules of the political game were no longer valid and the new ones were not yet established.

The smashing of the controlling unit in a giant corporation has rendered its basic elements – regions and local elites – completely autonomous. By trial and error they started to define a new balance of power on the political scene and to establish new rules for the political game. While in the old days regional groups could apply pressure along vertical lines, thus elevating any kind of tension (social, economic, ethnic, political) to a bureaucratic level, in the new circumstances they started to apply this pressure horizontally i.e. directly on other regions. A critical mass of

---

69 Kaganskii, V.L. „Sovetskaya territorial'naya tektonika (administrativno-territorial'noe delenie kak istochnik politicheskikh krizisov) [Soviet Territorial Tectonics (The Administrative-Territorial Division as a Source of Political Crises)." *Sostoyanie strany: Analiticheskie vestniki informatsionnogo agenstva Postfaktum* [The State of the Land: Analytical Bulletins of the Postfaktum Press Agency], no. 6 (1991).

horizontal tension started to accumulate in the post-Soviet environment. In other words, inter-regional conflicts have become a new (and probably temporary) rule of political conduct.

The political situation in the post-Soviet world is thus characterised by two basic types of conflict interaction between regional elites[70]:

- conflicts between neighbouring local political elites
- conflicts between local elites and the new republican centres (which have themselves been regionalised).

After the break-up of the Soviet Union the legitimacy, stability and efficiency of the republican centres are principally defined by their ability to maintain a balance of power between the inner republican local elites. However, it is far more difficult to maintain such balance in the context of the paramount social and economic crisis and the lack of effective mechanisms of power. This brings about the situation whereby the new republican centres (whose legitimacy has not yet been established since it had traditionally ensued from above, from Moscow, and not from the localities) are compelled to yield to the pressure of local elites. The failure to find a compromise between regional centres of power leads to the forced ousting of the republican regime and to permanent instability in the country, as plainly shown by the example of Rakhmon Nabiev's regime in Tadzhikistan in 1992.

In this sense, all post-Soviet conflicts can be regarded as a function in regional developments in the former USSR. On the one hand, conflicts emerge in the process of interaction between neighbouring regions, which, with no institutional channels in operation, can only settle their mutual claims by means of conflict. On the other hand, conflicts can be used as political instruments by local groups in the process of making (or consolidating or reshaping) the regional elite.

In the latter case, conflict can be employed as a means in the struggle for influence within the regional elite, often used by the opposition group. This is shown by the regulated interstate conflict between Armenia and Azerbaidzhan, which has actually brought to power leaders of both Transcaucasian states. Each Azeri leader in the last six years (Abdurakhman Vezirov, Ayaz Mutalibov, Yagub Mamedov, Abulfaz Elchibei, Geidar Aliev) has replaced his predecessor at the peak of public discontent over defeats in Karabakh. The Armenian president, Levon Ter-Petrosyan, for his part came to office with the 'Karabakh Committee' and represents a specific 'Karabakh dimension' in the Erevan political elite.

---

70 Sultanov. *Razvitie regional'nykh politicheskikh elit.*

Alternatively, conflict can be used as a means of retaining power by a leading group within the regional elite. This is clearly exemplified by the political continuity of the Tbilisi regime from Zviad Gamsakhurdia to Eduard Shevardnadze. Both leaders were vitally interested in the 'war of attrition' in South Ossetia as a means of consolidating the nation and strengthening the regime. Since that conflict was scaling down, Shevardnadze shifted the cross hairs of confrontation onto Sukhumi. The war in Abkhazia enabled Shevardnadze to legitimise his power and to assume the role as the 'defender of the nation' on the eve of the parliamentary elections in autumn 1992 which he subsequently won by a landslide.

In Moldova, President Mircia Sneghur has repeatedly encouraged confrontation in Transdnestria in order to appear more nationalist-minded than the opposition. For example, the opposition was planning a nation-wide meeting on March 29 1992 (being the anniversary of the unification of Bessarabia) at which it intended to demand the resignation of the president. Sneghur cast a preventive blow and on March 28, precisely on the eve of the meeting, declared a state of emergency in Transdnestria which eventually led to war between Moldova and this its own region.

Gen. Dzhokhar Dudaev in the Chechen Republic acted very much in the same manner, pursuing the politics of regulated conflict with Moscow with the purpose of consolidating the Chechen nation, the ruling elite and, above all, his hold on power.

The most striking example is the ruling Ukrainian elite for which the policy of controlled tension with Moscow is one of the main instruments for the consolidation of the elite itself.

Here an observation must be made pertaining, once again, to the question of ethnicity. The widespread term 'ethnic conflict' (or 'ethno-political conflict') seems to miss the point. This is not a conflict of nations or ethnic groups but a conflict of regional elites that use ethnic rhetoric and ethnic mobilisation to shape their specific interests.[71] In doing this, local elites often place an emphasis on the construction of an independent state by nations and groups, most of which lack any tradition of independence and statehood. Virtually all new states on the territory of the former USSR, including the Russian Federation, have a weak historical legitimacy, especially within their current frontiers and with the current ethnic composition of the population.

---

71 Medvedev, S.A. „Etnopoliticheskie konflikty na territorii byvshego SSSR [Ethno-Political Conflicts on the Territory of the Former USSR].“ *Rossiya i mir* [Russia and the World], no. 1 (1993).

The process of self-determination, imposed on the nation or ethnic group by the elite, generally outpaces the restructuring of the economic, political and social institutions of the society and is usually accompanied by a surge of national self-consciousness which deems 'the right of the nation' superior to the rights of the individual. Hence the violent and aggressive manner of self-determination and assertion of national identity in the new states. However, one should not be misled by nationalist phraseology – it is the interaction of regional interest groups in the absence of comprehensive vertical institutions and mechanisms of mediation that underlies most post-Soviet conflicts, including the 'ethnic' ones.

To summarise, recourse to conflict (including the use of military force) is, in a certain sense, an unavoidable political instrument in the regionalised post-Soviet environment, in the 'society of regions'. Now that the centralised power structure has collapsed and the old rules of the political game are no longer valid, conflict temporarily becomes a new ruling force of politics, the means to establish the subjects of political power (regional elites), to define their status and to set up a new balance of regional forces on the post-Soviet scene.[72] Unless new legitimate norms of political conduct are set, stable and legitimate regimes are established in the ex-USSR countries, and an appropriate international structure on the entire territory of the former Soviet Union takes shape (the CIS or whatever may replace it: a federation, confederation, a new commonwealth or a recognised system of nation states), the very political environment will produce conflicts as a transitory (and highly dangerous) form of post-Soviet regional developments.[73]

5 Conclusion: The Prospects of Regionalisation

Assessing the prospects of post-Soviet regional fragmentation, one should keep in mind that the conflict potential of the 'Soviet heritage' (the administrative/territorial division, specific interests of local elites etc.) is far from exhausted. Regionalisation will continue, spreading to the new levels of the regional hierarchy and to territories where it has not been manifest so far.[74]

---

72 Medvedev. „Etnopoliticheskie konflikty"; Medvedev, Sergei. „Security Risks in Russia and the CIS: A Case Study." *The International Spectator* 24, no. 1 (1994): 69.

73 Medvedev. „Security Risks in Russia and the CIS": 70.

74 Kaganskii. „Real'nosti regionalizatsii"; Kaganskii, V.L. „Spektr stsenariev dlya Rossiiskoi Federatsii [A Spectrum of Scenarios for the Russian Federation]." In *Kuda idet Rossiya* [Where Is Russia Going?] Moscow: Interpress, 1994.

In theory, regionalisation can continue to proceed until it finally determines all the economic subjects able to take possession of former state property or, in the case of economic collapse, the optimal size of the units that will prove most viable in a crisis environment.[75] In real terms, developments will be much more complex, ambiguous and asynchronous as processes at different regional levels interfere. An external factor will probably play a larger role: a number of foreign countries and communities can apparently choose autonomous regions as targets and as instruments for influencing the course of post-Soviet developments. This external influence can be both stabilising and destabilising (this issue is briefly treated in Appendix D). In other words, a number of uncertain factors will come into play and the final picture will be different from that provided in theory.

At present, one can only outline the phases of regionalisation. The first stage, at which the USSR was regionalised, is almost complete. By saying 'almost' we mean that the subjects of souvereignisation (the Union republics) have not yet consolidated their statehood and have still not assembled the different components left after the break-up of the Union. Furthermore, some functional components of the Centre have not yet been regionalised (the strategic nuclear forces).

The current (second) stage, which is still far from over, implies souvereignisation of regions of the republic, *oblast'*, or similar level i.e. of the level which is now the highest in the regional hierarchy. Further descent of regionalisation is a much less likely development, at least for the entire post-Soviet area: most regions below the *oblast'* level have substantially less resources for souvereignisation. However, disintegration of a number of larger *oblasts*, souvereignisation of some major industrial centres and other kinds of local restructuring are feasible at this level as well.[76]

At the following (third) stage, which has already started in some places, „the Soviet-era administrative/territorial division ceases to be the only, and then the main matrix of regionalisation".[77] For example, problems have already emerged concerning the regional borders, drawn in an arbitrary manner decades ago. Sooner or later, the inherent contradiction between the existing regional system (including borders) and the actual settlement of ethnic, cultural, historical etc. groups which are not legitimised and institutionalised in the existing system will come to the forefront. (In fact, this will be 'regionalism' in the proper sense of the word.) Questions of

---

75 Medvedev. „Security Risks in Russia and the CIS": 66.

76 Kaganskii. „Sovetskoe prostranstvo": 26.

77 Ibidem.

ethnic and cultural communities as well as pre-Soviet historical heritage will assume a primary importance.[78] At this stage, regionalisation will be far more ideologically charged and will be accompanied by ethnic mobilisation. The emergence of 'alternative' ethnic or quasi-ethnic communities (e.g. Siberians in Russia, the 'Poleshchuk' group (dwellers of Poles'e region) in Belarus, etc.) can bring into question today's concepts of nations and ethnic groups.

Another possible development at this stage is the formation of coalitions between a number of adjacent *oblasts* and autonomous republics in order to be able to lead a more effective struggle against the Centre (just as the national-democratic movements of the Soviet Union formed alliances to oppose Gorbachev's Centre). Regional coalitions of this kind are already being established, such as the Association of *oblasts* of Central Russia, the 'Greater Volga' Association, the Confederation of the Mountain Nations of the Caucasus, which has armed forces of its own, and so on. The emergence of such coalitions will accelerate regionalisation in the first and second phases.

It is probable that the third stage of regionalisation will be accompanied by the spread and escalation of armed conflicts and, generally speaking, by the spread of violence as a distinct lifestyle. Regional differentiation along the stability/instability axis will be even greater: more stable regions will endeavour to separate themselves from conflict zones, a proportion of the remainder will enter into the regime of permanent instability. The role of the Centre's armed components will be dramatically increased[79]: they too will be able to start forming proto-regions regardless of the existing administrative borders.

A special group of regional trends is connected with the privatisation (commercialisation) of regional institutes of authority. This has already started in a number of localities (Kislovodsk, which is being transformed into a joint-stock society, 'the free economic zone of Nakhodka' and so on). Kaganskii supposes that „if the mechanisms of power in the regions turn into something akin to corporations, this will probably weaken the state ambitions of local elites."[80] However, the restoration of the union cannot be achieved through this process.

Contrary to widespread opinion, the elements and promises of stability can only be provided by regions (see Appendix C: Scenarios of Regionalisation in Russia);

78 Ibidem.

79 Ibidem.

80 Ibidem.

the policies of the Centres will almost certainly prove destabilising. „Stability can not be reached by the means of counter-regionalism.“[81]

At present it is impossible to imagine a situation whereby the process of regionalisation will cease; such a 'common' situation could hardly ever arise: „regionalisation is regional“[82] and there is no common future (in the institutional sense) for the entire post-Soviet expanse. By means of regionalisation this enormous territory will undergo an irreversible transformation. It is of little value to argue whether this transformation could be prevented or avoided, whether it is benign or malign. As a logical product of the Soviet period, regionalisation was unavoidable. The universal Soviet state/society was a violation of the whole territory and its inherent diversity. Regionalisation is the self-determination of this territory[83], a return to the normal state of things, a return into history.

6 Appendices: Regionalisation in Russia

6.1 Appendix A: Regional Differentiation in Russia

The Russian Federation formed the territorial and functional nucleus of the USSR. Largely due to this fact, the regionalised structure (ATD) and the process of regionalisation are particularly vivid in Russia. The Russian Federation is now acquiring the 'Soviet heritage' and actually following in the footsteps of the USSR. The central authority of the RF (with which the functional and territorial fragments of the USSR not integrated into other new independent states are associated) is on the verge of losing control over its own regions. Russia's regions do in fact have the right to veto any of the Centre's activities on their territories (e.g., the Saratov and Volgograd *oblasts* have blocked the establishment of German autonomy on their respective territories).[84]

Special privileges granted to the subjects of the Russian Federation furnish them with a large degree of economic autonomy. The autonomous republics are entitled to establish their own national banks (agreements have been duly concluded with 20 republics of the Russian Federation); a special provision in the unpublished 'Annex

---

81 Ibidem: 27.

82 Ibidem.

83 Ibidem: 23.

84 Medvedev. „Security Risks in Russia and the CIS“: 60-65.

to the Federal Treaty' rendered republican courts the highest authority in legal procedure; land and natural resources are removed from the Centre's control; and certain regions such as Sakhalin are not obliged to comply to the all-Russian investment law.

Furthermore, over 40 regions have imposed their own quotas on the 'export' of commodities beyond their frontiers and have set up self-fashioned customs houses and procedures. Tatarstan, Yakutia-Sakha, Chelyabinsk *oblast'* and the Council of Siberian *oblasts* unilaterally introduced the so-called 'one-way' taxation system (i.e. they independently decide the amount of taxes they are to pay to the federal budget).

Regionalisation in Russia is aggravated by a visible usurpation of authority in the localities. The functions of state power are assumed by local political, social, ethnic, military and sometimes criminal groups. This is bluntly demonstrated by the evolution of the politically-charged Cossack movement which has become an issue of major-league politics; by the armament of Cossacks who assume the rights of law enforcement bodies; and by unwarranted participation of Cossacks in military conflicts beyond the borders of Russia (in Transdnestria, North Caucasus, Bosnia).

The current policies of Moscow vis-à-vis separatism in the peripheral regions as well as the autonomisation of the regional level in general are an almost complete repetition of the actions of the USSR Centre (although the Russian Centre has much less leverage and far fewer possibilities). The main difference from the regionalisation of the USSR is the absence of a region that could claim, acquire and control the 'indivisible common heritage' (Moscow as a region is too weakly defined to play this role). This improves the Russian Federation's chances of surviving in a more or less single, whole form, although its regionalisation is already irreversible.

The regionalisation of Russia has dramatically increased regional differentiation in political, economic, social, cultural and ideological terms. Over the last three years the following divisive lines and models of differentiation have emerged[85]:

1. Regional differentiation on the basis of specific models of *political behaviour*:
   - the *confederative model*: political conduct of the leadership of the Chechen Republic;
   - the *federative model*, based on separate bilateral treaties: the leadership of Tatarstan, Bashkortostan, Sakha. This model seems to be of particular

85 Sul'tanov, Sh.Z. *Politicheskoe vzaimodeistvie v perekhodnyi period: smena pravil igry v usloviyakh sistemnogo krizisa* [Political Interaction in the Transition Period: Changes in the Rules of the Game under Conditions of Systemic Crisis]. Manuscript, 1994.

importance since the signing of the bilateral treaty between the Russian Federation and the Republic of Tatarstan in March 1994 which sets a legal precedent;

- the model of initial regional self-determination by *self-compensation for the lack of administrative status*: the proclamation of republican status by a number of autonomous *oblasts* (Chukotka, etc.);
- the emergence of *specific geopolitical orientations*, especially among ethnic regions: the Republic of Karelia (the Scandinavian orientation), the Tuva and Buryat republics (the Mongolian orientation), Karachaevo-Cherkessia and Adygea (the Abkhazian orientation), etc.;
- the models of *new inter-regional coalitions* of various kinds: the 'Greater Volga' Association, association of the regions of the non-black-earth belt, association of the cities of the Moscow region, etc.

2. Regional differentiation on an economic basis. In this instance, two basic models can be discerned:
   - *Differentiation between donor-regions* (the Kaliningrad, Rostov, Perm, Yaroslavl, Leningrad, Moscow *oblasts*, Tatarstan, Bashkortostan etc., totalling 17 regions) and subsidised regions (Daghestan, Tuva, Kabardino-Balkaria, Marii-El, the Kamchatka, Pskov and Astrakhan *oblasts* etc., totalling 72 regions);
   - *Differentiation according to the types of resources*:
     - regions with a considerable *fuel export* potential (the Tyumen oblast', Tatarstan, Bashkortostan, the Chechen Republic);
     - regions with a considerable and diversified *mineral resources* potential (Sakha, the Sverdlovsk, Chelyabinsk Krasnoyarsk *oblasts* etc.);
     - regions with an export potential for main *agricultural products* (the Krasnodar and Stavropol territories, the Belgorod and Kursk *oblasts* etc.);
     - regions with a considerable *technological potential* (Moscow, St. Petersburg, Nizhnii Novgorod etc.);
     - *other regions*.
3. Regional differentiation on the basis of ideological models:
   - initial development of *concepts of 'uniqueness'* and a 'special way' for separate regions: the concept of Siberian independence, the idea of a 'Enisei Republic', a 'Urals Republic', a 'Far Eastern Republic', an 'Irkutsk Republic', a 'Republic of Sakhalin' etc.;

- promulgation of the *advanced ideologies of new geopolitical, ethnically based communities*: the 'Russian Republic', the Turkic confederation ('Greater Turan'), the federation of Finno-Ugric nations etc.;
- creation of *new types of regional political parties* and organisations (the Confederation of the Mountain Nations of the Caucasus, the Siberian Party of Independence, etc.).

6.2 Appendix B: Areas of Regional Instability in Russia

The process of regionalisation is taking place throughout the entire territory of the Russian Federation; it is universal to the same extent that Soviet state/society was universal. However, due to the increasing regional differentiation (see Appendix A) certain groups of regions have emerged where regionalisation is proceeding more rapidly and where local elites are more cohesive and more ambitious. At the RF regional level these areas pose greater risks (but not necessarily above and below this level), and as far as the RF still exists as a quasi-federative state with a certain kind of regional balance, developments in these areas are worth detailed consideration.

One can point out at least four main areas or 'belts' of regional instability in the Russian Federation:

- the North Caucasian area
- the 'Volga belt'
- the 'Transbaikal belt'
- the 'Northern belt'.

Possible developments in these areas are treated below in consecutive order.[86]

- In the case of the *North Caucasian area* it is hardly possible to speak of openly separatist or anti-Russian trends among the forces involved (the only exception being part of the Chechen leadership). The situation is rather to be described in terms of long-term instability and gradual distancing from Moscow. The main political forces on the scene are: 'the Chechen bloc', headed by the extremist leadership of Chechnya; 'the Adyg bloc' (Kabardins, Cherkessians, Adygs, Abazyns, Shapsugs); 'the Karachaevo-Balkarian bloc', and finally, Ossetia.

---

86 Sal'min, A.M. „Desintegratsiya Rossii? (Tezisy doklada Soveta po vneshnei i oboronnoi politike) [Disintegration of Russia? (Theses from the Report of the Council on Foreign and Defence Policy)]. *Nezavisimaya gazeta* 10 December 1992: 5.

Though the majority of these nations joined to form the 'Confederation of the Mountain Nations of the Caucasus', their cohesion should not be overestimated. It principally serves to promote or at least to demonstrate a number of communal interests to Russia, Georgia and possibly to Azerbaidzhan. The prospects of this confederation are obscured by century-old historical, ethnic, religious and economic contradictions in the region. The confederation can probably serve some of its members as a vehicle in the move away from Moscow but it is hardly capable of uniting them in a strategic opposition to Russia.

The common fear of a 'Lebanonisation' of the North Caucasus is largely exaggerated. 'Lebanonisation' does in fact signify a power struggle for constitutional influence and the representation of different ethnic and religious communities in a state, the very existence of which is not questioned by the opposing forces. Thus, in order to become a 'second Lebanon', the North Caucasus still has to be united in a kind of federation or confederation, which now seems highly improbable. There is not even a steady interaction of official authorities, ethnic movements and the Confederation of Mountain Nations: these three forces exist separately, in different dimensions. Thus the most probable scenario for the North Caucasus holds that there will not be any kind of protracted 'trench warfare' between several major opposing forces, but rather occasional outbreaks of conflicts throughout the area.

Provided that the North Caucasian 'conflict knot' is effectively localised, it will not pose an immediate threat to the very existence of the Russian Federation or to its state system. However, the risks involved are relatively high. Firstly, conflicts will most probably produce situations of mass migration (the 'exodus' of the Russian-speaking population from the North Caucasus has already been underway for a number of years) and terrorism (Chechens already account for a large part of organised crime in Russia). Secondly, the proliferation of arms in this region, already heavily charged with weapons, will continue. Thirdly, Russia will probably have to retain a large military contingent in or near the area. However, the possible separation or isolation of the North Caucasus is not likely to provoke popular resentment – for most Russians this is already a 'lost area'.

- In the case of the '*Volga belt*' (Tatarstan, Bashkortostan, Mordovia, Chuvashia, Marii-El), the majority of key risks of instability are connected with Tatarstan's policies. Its long-time independent stand on the Federal Treaty finally culminated in the signing of a separate bilateral treaty with Moscow in the spring of 1994 which grants Tatarstan a special status among Russia's regions and sets a legal precedent for other subjects of the federation.

Tatarstan's special status is further enhanced by the fact that the Tatars constitute the second largest (after Russians) ethnic group in the Russian Federation (4% of the population) which, in terms of traditions of statehood, is older than the Russian group. Furthermore, the separatism (or at least isolationism) of Tatarstan and Bashkortostan has sound material reasons: large resources of oil and a tangible industrial potential (military, chemical, electronic industries etc.). A low level of ethnic tension and the wide-spread conviction that economic ties with Moscow are unprofitable combine to form a relatively popular consensus around the separatist course of the leadership of Tatarstan and Bashkortostan with the result that even Russians in these two republics are mostly in favour of such policies.

Internal tensions in Tatarstan are still further reduced by the balanced ethnic (49% Tatars, 43% Russians), linguistic and religious composition of the population; by traditional links between both nations, a high percentage of mixed marriages (which is somewhat unusual in terms of the coexistence of Christian and Islamic cultures), and also by the fact that only 1/3 of all Tatars living in Russia reside in Tatarstan. For this reason, the prospects of the nationalist opposition ('kurultai', or the congress of Tatars, and its standing parliament 'milli-mejlis'), remain remote, despite its impressive performance. In Bashkortostan as well, the titular ethnic group is only the third largest after Russians and Tatars, which provides for relative internal stability.

As regards the other republics of the 'Volga belt', separatist zeal is weakened by the presence of an ethnic Russian majority in their populations (except in Chuvashia), as well as by a cultural affinity with Russia (they are all Orthodox except Marii-El which has strong pagan traditions) and a lack of substantial natural resources.

Though internal tensions in the 'Volga belt' are relatively low, the external effect of 'Volga separatism' is much higher. Indeed, this is potentially the most dangerous and ruinous form of separatism in Russia. In as much as it concerns an essential 'nucleus' in Russia, formed in the 16th century, and is surrounded by the Russian territories (to say nothing of the Volga being a symbol of the nation), it arouses considerable popular resentment and is actually a very sensitive issue for many Russians. This is especially the case among the nationalist opposition, which tends to regard it as a threat to the very existence of the Russian state. The secession of the Volga republics from Russia could virtually disrupt the major transport routes and power lines running from East to West and from North to South. Therefore Moscow's reaction (or overreaction) could indeed have serious repercussions.

- The '*Transbaikal belt*' is composed of Tuva, Buryatia, Khakassia, and the Agin Buryat and Ust-Ordyn Buryat National Districts. Ethnic tensions in this area and the general crisis of statehood and the economy could lead to regional separatism. However, the only candidate for real self-determination and probably secession from Russia is Tuva, where the titular ethnic group accounts for 2/3 of the population and Russians are largely forced to leave (in certain cases there was almost a genocide of Russians, though it did not provoke a major reaction in Moscow). Tuva is one of the few territories in the Russian Federation with a genuine tradition of independent statehood (having been incorporated in the USSR only in 1944).

  In the meantime, however, the possible separation of Tuva is hardly going to have major destabilising effect on the situation in Russia as a whole. Such destabilisation could take place only if the general balance of forces in this geopolitical area is ruined, which entails the highly hypothetical scenario of the disintegration of China. However, such a contingency is worth consideration. One cannot exclude that processes of self-determination in this part of the Russian Federation can be tempting for: (a) the regime in China, which is now entering the phase of economic and political expansion, comparable to Western expansionism of the early imperialist period; (b) national minorities in the bordering provinces of China seeking self-determination (primarily in Tibet).

  Therefore, developments in the 'Transbaikal belt' are fraught with risk in the context of Sino-Russian relations (which are in any case sure be uneasy in the years to come) and of general stability in the Far East.

- The '*Northern belt*' is a chain of former or current autonomous republics, stretching from the Komi Republic and the Yamalo-Nenetsk Autonomous District in the West to the Chukotka and the Koryak Autonomous Republics in the East. Destabilisation in this enormous area (which constitutes almost half of the territory of the Russian Federation) is provoked not so much by actual or latent ethnic conflicts (which have already occurred in Yakutia-Sakha and in other places) than by the 'natural resource' separatism or isolationism of wealthier regions: Yakutia-Sakha, Komi, the Yamalo-Nenetsk District.

Possession of natural resources is actually the key political issue on the agenda, defining the degree of the republics' autonomy. Territories rich in resources sometimes enter into an alliance with more radical separatist leaders of other republics in order to form a more effective coalition against Moscow. For example, such an alliance was formed in August 1991 between Tatarstan, Bashkortostan and Yakutia-Sakha

The greatest risk for the Russian Federation in this area is mainly in connection with the enormous republic of Yakutia-Sakha which remains one of the world's largest producers of gold and diamonds and has a relatively legitimate presidential regime in comparison to other republics in the Russian Federation. The Yakut President Mikhail Nikolaev pursues a relatively long-term strategy based on economic self-sufficiency and gradual distancing from Moscow in the political sphere. Though full separation of this republic is highly unlikely to ever take place, the greater economic insulation of Yakutia-Sakha will deal a heavy blow to Russia's economy and finances, and cause a serious setback in popular psychology in as much as Yakutia is considered an essential part of traditional Russian territory.

In general, the 'Northern belt' is more likely to add to general destabilisation in Russia than directly provoke it. It can contribute to the possible disintegration of Russia by further loosening the financial and taxation system, economic links within the country, or by promoting Siberian and Far Eastern regional separatism. This kind of separatism is still essentially hypothetical (slogans of the 'Enisei Republic', the 'Far Eastern Republic' etc. are mostly rhetorical), but Moscow's failure to introduce economic reforms and large-scale privatisation, as well as the continuing power struggle in the centre could greatly promote this trend.

If this occurs, regional risks will greatly intensify. Besides being a dramatic step towards the real disintegration of Russia (in as much as ethnic issues will no longer be concerned, simply boiling down to a blunt Russians vs. Russians confrontation), a territorial change of such scope will completely destroy the fragile geopolitical balance in the Far East. China and Japan will be greatly tempted (or even compelled) to come into play. Japan, for example, could regard this as a unique opportunity to get back its part of the Kurile chain (or the entire chain, or even half of Sakhalin, as Japanese radical nationalists insist).

In other words, given a certain set of circumstances the separation of Siberia and the Russian Far East could, with the possible involvement of China and Japan, pose real threats for Russia and the outside world.

6.3 Appendix C: Scenarios of Regionalisation in Russia

As mentioned earlier, it is hardly possible to envisage a 'common' situation for all Russia's regions, a 'common future' for the process of regionalisation. Current developments are extremely diversified and poly-variant, taking place on different regional levels, and the meaning of each new development may be different for each level. In this sense, any prognostication and scenario-based forecasts for regionalisation in Russia are highly dubious.

However, it is possible to outline some hypothetical models, or rather vectors, of regionalisation. These are ideal, alternative scenarios. None of them can serve as a forecast but their combination can give an indication in which direction the state structure of Russia may be evolving.

First of all, one has to mention two extreme (and most unlikely) scenarios: the full break-up of Russia and the full re-integration of the country. Complete disintegration can be of two kinds. On the one hand, it can take a violent course: the regionalisation of Russia can result in the dramatic increase of ethnic, inter-regional or inter-*oblast'* contradictions, in the 'Balkanisation' or 'Lebanonisation' of Russia and the entire territory of the former Soviet Union. On the other hand, full disintegration can proceed in a less conflicting manner, as the gradual establishment of a number of virtually independent region-states (and their coalitions), which are partly associated with adjacent countries. This will be a loose system of closed and self-sufficient local communities with primitive non-market economies. In this scenario, the Centre ceases to exist and Moscow turns into one of the regions, into a city-state. The army, strategic forces etc. become sovereign and are completely regionalised.[87]

Another unlikely scenario is the restoration of the single state (of Russia and/or of the greater part of the former USSR). This can take place either in the framework of the communist or the nationalist revanche, the latter being more probable. These developments are connected with re-militarisation, attempts to exert military control

87 Medvedev, S.A. „Raspad Rossii: tendentsii i perspektivy [The Break-Up of Russia: Trends and Prospects]." *Rossiya v mire*, no. 1 (1993).

over the greater part of the former Soviet territory, and with permanent armed conflicts.[88]

However, any final and radical arrangement (full disintegration, full re-integration) is highly unlikely to take place in Russia in the immediate future. In more likely contingencies, regionalisation will contribute to the development of a totally new political system in Russia. It is possible to envisage the following alternatives:

- '*Peace between the regions*' and the *Centre as a mediator*.[89] The Russian Federation is represented by Moscow, acting as a mediator between the regions, the countries of the CIS, the 'far abroad' and the armed forces as a sovereign component (probably with its own territories). The Centre assumes monetary, legal, judicial, mediatory and other functions.

  In this contingency, the Centre can use the increasing controversy between the 17 donor-regions (which are striving towards greater autonomy and may choose the 'Tatar way' in striking a separate deal with Moscow) and dozens of subsidised regions which are more dependent in their political attitudes. This may form a classical political triangle: two confronting groups and the Centre which acts as a mediator (and actually exerts control over both groups by pursuing a strategy of managed conflict). The armed forces and security forces thus obtain a higher profile by acquiring a balancing meaning in the regional interaction.
- A '*soft' federation*[90] in which the regions form a central authority which functions as an inter-regional economic committee, to which they cede a small proportion of their rights; most foreign and defence policies are conducted from Moscow, while foreign economic policies are pursued by the regions within one general framework.
- A '*two-speed' variant*[91], in which the Centre manages nation-wide affairs (security, foreign policy etc.) and the regions are in charge of the economy.
- A *flexible association with several levels of affiliation*[92], in which a proportion of the regions enter into a federation with the centre (*oblasts* of Central and North-Eastern Russia, the Urals etc.), some opt for a confederation (Yakutia-

88 Medvedev. „Raspad Rossii."
89 Kaganskii. „Spektr stsenariev"; Kaganskii. „Sovetskoe prostranstvo": 25.
90 Kaganskii. „Spektr stsenariev"; Kaganskii. „Sovetskoe prostranstvo": 25.
91 Medvedev. „Raspad Rossii."
92 Ibidem.

Sakha, Komi, Bashkortostan) and some, such as Tatarstan, become associate members. The Russian Federation becomes an amorphous superstructure over a mixed community of regions, some of which are states. The Centre, however, retains control over the strategic armed forces.

- 'The *minimal Russia*'.[93] The Russian Federation is preserved as a state only on part of its former territory, while the rest becomes completely sovereign. The boundaries of the 'new Russia' are defined by the dislocation of the strategic armed forces, the resource and industrial base, by conflicts with and between the regions and by a number of other factors (among which ethnicity does not play a major role).

Within this range of choices (probably with the exclusion of Scenario 5), a totally new political structure might take shape in Russia. It will be based on the principle of the division of three major state functions: provision of security; the provision of social stability (including the interests of local, ethnic, religious, political etc. groups); and provision for economic development. This can to a certain extent be regarded as a single structure, operating on three levels:

- the *security* level (a strong mono-centric vertical structure, unitary integration);
- the *economic* level (a horizontal framework structure with a limited number of administrative centres, federative integration);
- the level of *regional, social, political, administrative, ethnic and cultural relations* (a poly-centric structure, confederative integration).[94]

6.4 Appendix D: Russia's Regionalisation in International Perspective

Regionalisation in Russia will have a certain impact on international relations, especially in the security sphere. In the years to come, Russia will most probably remain a single, yet substantially weakened and unstable state with internal regional contradictions leaving a deep mark on its domestic perspectives, foreign and security policies and on economic performance. Instead of introducing structural reforms, the central authority will be increasingly preoccupied with settling regional disputes; the federal government and the Central Bank will be losing control over finances, the state budget and the system of taxation (which will invalidate most attempts to pursue a strict monetary policy); additionally, they will not fully dispose of Russia's

---

93 Kaganskii. „Spektr stsenariev"; Kaganskii. „Sovetskoe prostranstvo": 25.

94 Sul'tanov. *Politicheskoe vzaimodeistvie v perekhodnyi period.*

natural resources, the country's major source of hard currency. The nation can plunge into the 'state- of-war' psychological atmosphere, favourable for authoritarian and chauvinist trends and fascistic demagogy. The armed forces will be seen as the major guarantor of the RF's integrity and will acquire a higher profile in its political life. In foreign and security policies Russia will be more closed, inclined to isolationism and more suspicious of the outside world. Military build-up will be justified not only by regional separatism but also by hypothetical 'hostile interventions' from the outside into separatist regions.

The regionalisation of Russia is also a destabilising factor in itself, a dangerous temptation for many countries and ethnic groups outside Russia. Firstly, the ex-USSR states appear to be largely challenged by this seeming opportunity and will possibly try to profit from the decentralisation of Russia in terms of territorial acquisitions, direct access to natural resources (many have direct oil contracts with Tyumen *oblast'*), upgrading their political positions, and also in terms of weakening Moscow, regarded as the main rival and threat to their national security. Ukraine, for instance, has already attempted to play the regional card, officially establishing 'diplomatic relations' with a number of *oblasts* in Central Russia.

Secondly, the countries bordering Russia or the former USSR area can similarly regard the disintegration of Russia from the same perspective. In simple terms, Russia is just too big and many of its regions, especially along the borders, may be perceived by a number of states (though almost never openly) as belonging to their 'spheres of interest'. Such countries as Japan, China, Turkey, Romania, Poland and even Finland may endeavour to get 'their share' in the course of the regionalisation of Russia. For example, Turkey has already staked a claim in developing 'special relations' with Turkic republics in the Volga region. All of these countries may be willing to exert larger influence, but in the case of Japan territorial reasons may also be involved.

Thirdly, the temptation to 'profit' from the disintegration of Russia is valid for Western Europe and the United States. This is hardly a matter of territorial acquisition; this can more readily be described in terms of 'introducing democracy' and gaining a larger influence on the post-Soviet political scene through a type of 'direct diplomacy' over the head of Moscow. Such short-sighted policies have proved to be a complete failure in Yugoslavia, yet this has not discouraged some members of Western parliaments, who have given mixed signals to delegations of Tatars, Chechens and other groups in autonomous republics within the Russian Federation who are demanding independence. Some people in the West maintain the position that Russia remains a colonial empire and must therefore must be broken up.

In direct contrast to this, the West should rather display a commitment in assisting in the creation of a more decentralised, federal Russian state. It would be a serious mistake for the West to meddle with the regionalisation of Russia. The experience of Yugoslavia shows that the traditional Western answer to ethnic nationalism – self-determination – cannot be applied continually until it reaches its lowest denominator.

Fourthly, separatist movements in Russia can prove an inspiring example for national minorities all over the world (e.g. in Tibet) and notably in the countries of Eastern Europe undergoing similar transformation. All further regional separatist gains in Russia will contribute to the creation of an international environment in which ethnic separatism will gaining momentum.

2

Russian Regions and Territories

Vladimir Kaganskii

This brief study will begin with a standard interpretation of the processes taking place on the territory of the former Soviet Union, an interpretation that is widespread. Nevertheless, the author has great doubts about it, and will then introduce alternative notions and set forth the essence of the matter as he perceives it. Finally, there will be some brief methodological remarks. The concept developed by the author as well as field observations made upon the basics of this concept over the last two or three years are the source of this analysis.

An explanation of the Soviet space based on theoretical geography (which will be examined later on) presents an interpretation of the current situation and contemporary geopolitical developments. When talking about the events on the territory of the FSU, attention is focused on the territory of the RF as the nucleus of this space and the nucleus of what is considered typical.

The standard interpretation is a stereotypical cliché of the geopolitical processes on the territory of the former Soviet Union. According to this cliché, the break-up of the USSR is regarded as an absolute and practically completed process. Out of the ashes of the single state, 15 newly formed states emerged. The major problem on this territory is the formation of new states, including the establishment of international relations between them. Separatism, especially typical for the outlying districts, became a challenge for every single state. The main geopolitical processes in Russia are determined by the relations between the centre and the regions. The country is seeking its place along the federalism–unitarism axis. The role of politics, especially in the centre, is thought to be extremely important. It is considered that the peak of activity in reconstructing the Soviet space which was reached during the so-called break-up of the USSR has already passed and that the energy of destructive processes has been decreasing. It is also considered that either a pure disintegration is prevailing – a notion that causes extreme apprehension – or a new integration and even restoration is approaching. The processes in the neo-Soviet spaces, as the author calls them, or in the post-Soviet spaces, as they are commonly called, are thought to be similar to the processes of federalisation and decentralisation that are so typical for the modern western nations, especially for western Europe. The geopolitical and economic processes are regarded as being connected, yet autonomous and different. In other words, the spatial geopolitical framework and the phenomena taking place within this framework are regarded as being independent from each other. This is essentially the standard interpretation.

It is now necessary to introduce some basic notions. Under the term 'Soviet space' the author understands not the former USSR's territory but rather a certain type of spatial organisation that is typical for the USSR and a number of other socialist countries. It is characterised by the fact that there is a common hierarchy of administrative districts and their centres including all spheres of state rule and all activities in general. There is a hyper-centralised structure enveloping the whole territory, and the main units of this structure are the complex total districts which will further be called regions. These total districts simplify the whole spatial differentiation and serve as a universal spatial framework for the Soviet society and state. Hence in terms of this idealisation, the region appears to be the main 'natural' unit of analysis. The regions are enclosed one in another like a Russian doll. As an example for regions of different ranks one can cite the Soviet Union until 1991 (Estonia or Georgia); and nowadays and during the Soviet period any of the *oblasts* of the Russian Federation or Ukraine, any of the administrative districts, even towns. In this respect, the Soviet Union, Georgia and Moscow are regions of different ranks. For simplicity's sake, the term 'regions' will denote all the units that are smaller than the former Soviet Union. In this Soviet space, which represents a rigid system of co-ordinates, a process of regionalisation is taking place, characterised by a combination of four major components or four main particular processes. *Firstly*, the sovereignisation of the structural components, regions in particular. Other structural components will be discussed later. *Secondly*, the sovereignising structural components dismantle the higher administrative level in the same way as the ex-USSR republics dismantled the USSR's level. *Thirdly*, components start coalescing inside the sovereignised regions. Having formerly been under the authority of higher hierarchical links (e.g. the union's centre), territories and objects commence to integrate into a single republic or region. *Finally*, the fourth aspect of regionalisation is the reconstruction of spatial relations, the formation of the new inter-regional relations.

The Soviet space in which the regionalisation is in progress provides us with an example of an object that is characterised by a special type of reasoning – a structural determination. The essence of structural determination is that the object's condition and its transformation, including the spectrum of probable future conditions, are determined by its structure – not completely defined but largely determined. The author considers regionalisation to be the process of transformation of the Soviet space on the basis of structural determination. In this respect it is not necessary to seek other sources of explanation except the Soviet space's structure. The Soviet space is a self-dismembering one.

We can now turn to the actual realities of the neo-Soviet space, distinguishing not only those that seem to be the most significant but also those that normally receive less attention.

Current geopolitical developments, which frequently feature separatism and inter-regional conflicts, are internally structurally determined. In particular, one of the reasons for these conflicts is that being structurally identical, regions of the same rank and those of different ranks find themselves in tough competition for the same resources. In particular, those regions of similar rank – *oblasts* and republics – compete for the same resources within the framework of their authority, i.e., they compete for institutional resources. Since the process of sovereignisation within the Soviet space got under way, it is possible to observe a picture of unexpected spontaneous activity from structural components that to a significant extent used to be adjusted to one another.

We can single out at least two major types of structural components. The first type is obvious and tends to attract most attention – the *spatial components*. These are meant when talking about the break-up of the Soviet Union into 15 parts. These parts are republics, *oblasts*, etc. Apart from these, one can distinguish the *functional components* which provide the unity of every region, and which used to provide the unity of the Soviet Union. These are technical, military-industrial, military proper, cultural, ideological components and so on. We should not think that only republics, *oblasts* and other territorial units make up the sovereignisation components. The functional components also are become 'sovereignised': they display activity, act as subjects and conduct their own policy. Much of what we observe on the territory of the FSU can be explained by interference, i.e., super-positioning of actions of regional and functional components. Good examples of this are territories with indeterminate status (e.g. Transdnestria or Abkhazia), which, in a way, are military colonies and therefore are both territorial and functional units – essentially with the Armed Forces of the former Soviet Union.

Taking into account these super-positionings as well as the fact that the functional components have their own, although indeterminate, territories, the question about the number of existing political units on the territory of the former Soviet Union is indeed not a trivial one. It is quite natural that the Soviet Union did not break up into 15 part because it had never consisted of them. Into how many parts it broke up is an extremely difficult question, a question with no immediate answer. Within the space of the former Soviet Union new relations between the former constituent parts are now starting to take shape. More new combinations are developing all the time, and these permutations are far from exhausted: this is a kind of open space. Essentially, horizontal relations have been dominating in this space for at least two or three years, yet these horizontal relations are not of an administrative co-ordinate nature. They represent direct relations of conflict, interaction, trade. The most simple example of inter-regional relations are military conflicts or armed actions. It should also be noted that even within formally unified states such as Georgia or the Russian Federation, military action type relations exist between certain regions.

The space within which the constituent parts display this activity is a multi-level one, since regionalisation is occurring at several levels. It is also a poly-subjective space in so far as there are a great deal of complex subjects acting in it. It is very important that the multi-levelled and poly-subjective nature of the post-Soviet space is acknowledged by foreign political partners. It will suffice to give the excellent example of the South Kuril Isles claimed by Japan. The de facto 'partners' of Japan in the problem of obtaining the South Kurils are: *firstly*, the functional fragments of the former Soviet Union – its Armed Forces which have now become Russian. *Secondly*, the Russian Federation itself, its political centre. *Thirdly*, a coalition of Far Eastern regions which, in the question of the islands' transfer proceed in a relatively united fashion. *Fourth*, Sakhalin *oblast'*, to which the islands administratively belonged. *Fifth*, Primorskii *krai* which is clashing with Sakhalin *oblast'* over these islands. *Finally*, the islands themselves and their population. Japan has to deal with all these hierarchically correlated level partners. Practically any particular case, if we look at it properly, will express itself in a similar manner with different levels and politico-economic subjects. The uncertainty associated with this is bound to have implications for such a stable state formation as the Russian Federation. If we regard the state's territory as being the territorial sphere of the centre's competence, then in this case there is nothing that would allow us to definitively identify this competence. This is an open political issue. If we imagine a scale from nil to one, whereby nil characterises the territories which are by no means subordinate to the

Russian centre's authorities, and one characterises the territories that are fully subordinate to it, then the territory of the RF will look like a rather whimsical mosaic, covering the whole spectrum of meanings: from totally loyal to the Centre (according to venomous tongues this is Moscow within the 'Garden Ring') to those territories which are de jure independent. In other words, the territory of the RF is in a manner of speaking a testing ground for many possible proto-states, one of which the present central authority and Moscow are associated with and which could be identified as a possible city-state. When one considers that the regions of *oblast'* rank have efficiently devised strategies of survival in such an uncertain climate (one of these strategies was direct barter), that they have built up their own armed structures while the Russian armed forces are quickly becoming regionalized, and that their units are entering into vague or distinct coalitions with regional authorities, then we can talk about a process which is sweeping away differences between regions and states. The multiple unions between regions (even across national borders), entered into independently of the federal centre and often even in opposition to it, are a symptom of this process. In such an uncertain space certain other restoration tendencies are active, but they are especially typical for those regions which cannot conduct an efficient assembly of the components that happened to be on their territory. They have to form coalitions with larger and more powerful regions.

In this respect the question arises to what extent the customary notion of state sovereignty and state territory can be applied to the given situation? Moreover, if it cannot, what kind of conceptual tools *can* be used? In the conventional model, as presented earlier, the break-up of the USSR had been regarded as an event already completed. In reality, it is a long process that is far from over. Firstly, the conflicts over the partition of the Soviet heritage are still in progress. Under the Soviet heritage we understand not only material, financial and other resources, but also resources of authorities, property rights and historical continuity. The regional conflicts that were embedded in the structures of the Soviet space are thus taking their course.

One can say that the more the Soviet Union stops existing as a state, the more its territory integrates in a new way. In geography there is the notion of a 'problem region'. In this same vein, the Soviet Union, while disappearing as a state, continues to exist on the world map as a problematic macro-region and, moreover, as one that is attaching itself to the neighbouring territories. For example, Afghanistan is now a part of the problematic macro-region that emerged on the territory of the former

Soviet Union. And yet, in this complicated and precarious reality there nevertheless exists a quite normal life, quite normal economic processes and the cataclysms we were all afraid of a few years ago have not materialised.

In conclusion we should consider some intuitive ideas, some expert evaluations which cannot be supported by any empirical material or statistics. In the authors opinion, a change has taken place in the main framework of life and activity; and the so-called subjects of the Russian Federation turned out to constitute this framework. It is precisely within this framework that most of the problems are currently solved. We can call it either a framework or a sphere of action. To use a more simplified terminology, these are the spheres in which property issues are being resolved and privatisation is taking place. The regions and processes within them are now emerging.

To a considerable extent, a *regionalisation of property* has taken place. Strictly speaking, the idea of regional self-support was the first step towards and the predecessor of privatisation. A *regionalisation of the law* took place. The law, in most meanings of the word, differs greatly from region to region. The *regionalisation of the Armed Forces* took place. We are faced with a multi-level situation in which the centre of different kinds of processes, both constructive and destructive, has shifted to the regional level. However, it would be wrong to suppose that with the centre of gravity of real power shifting down to the *oblast' level*, everything is over. Regionalisation can be regarded as a sort of machine which eats away and dismantles level after level. The level of the Soviet Union has been dismantled, and the machine has reached the level of the RF and other republics. Now the same process is taking place at the level of *oblasts, krais*, etc. An extremely active inner process is taking place at this level, and although it is not common to use the term 'geopolitics' for this level, the fact that these processes are going on and can be described in the same way as those under way in Russia, other republics and the FSU, indicates that this is a kind of strange inner-regional geopolitics. The *de facto* subdivision of many *oblasts* and republics is taking place. The conflicts between the *oblast'* centres and their territories or their administrations can be observed almost everywhere. The fragmentation of many cities and regions is taking place, i.e., a peculiar form of internal urban separatism.

Let us take Arkhangel'sk *oblast'* as an example. What can we observe here? A conflict with the Nenets national *okrug* which used to be a part of the *oblast'*. Manifest separatist trends of the city Kotlas and its surroundings. (Kotlas is the second large city located in another part of the *oblast'*, economically far closer to

Moscow and the Centre). Demands for the restoration of some administrative districts that used to exist and were later abolished. Fears of the *oblast'* administration caused by the loss of control over potential diamond mining operations. Tension between Arkhangel'sk *oblast'* and Arkhangel'sk city. Finally, the conflict between Arkhangel'sk city and one of its administrative districts which used to be an independent city and is aspiring to this status again. In addition to this, there is a de facto special status for the Solovets islands, famous for their monastery. This is the situation in one *oblast'*. One can consider it quite an instructive and typical one.

One very significant and rapidly increasing though barely noticeable process, typical for the situation in the regions is the 'privatisation of regions'. By this is meant that the mechanisms for the administration of regions, which are hierarchically lower than the republics, are being subordinated to the power of corporations, which is leading to situation where the regions are ruled in that manner. The city of Kislovodsk, for example, is practically the property of a little known corporation. Another example is the free economic zone of Nakhodka. That the *oblasts* and similar regions behave as normal economic subjects on the market is confirmed by the fact that these regions establish bargaining relations with each other with regard to trading their own territory. Recently, the Sokolskii administrative district of Ivanovo *oblast'* was officially transferred to the authority of Nizhnii Novgorod *oblast'*. Although a referendum was held there, it is nevertheless more appropriate to describe this bilateral process as a normal deal. One *oblast'* sells its territory together with its people (who must of course approve of such a move) to another *oblast'*. There are several examples like this. Another example is Bratsk, a large industrial centre in Irkutsk *oblast'*, which entered into a *de facto* alliance with adjoining agricultural districts and formed a new administrative unit within Irkutsk *oblast'*. It is based on some political and economic interactions. Such phenomena can be observed all over. The privatisation of the whole institutional structure of the expanse is taking place. Moreover, as far as the situation in Bratsk is concerned, there are specific investors (at least, so it seemed to the author) interested in the existence of this new administrative-institutional unit.

To conclude, it should be stressed that the processes are multi-levelled. The common opinion is that regionalisation, and in particular of Russia, is primarily a disintegration of its space and a decentralisation. This understanding is not really incorrect, but rather incomplete. On the level of the regions themselves one can say that there processes of integration and consolidation are taking place. Considering that not only border regions are forging co-operative links with other countries, one can say that a new integration is taking place, but in another spatial framework. In other words, regionalisation remains a suitably complicated issue.

Finally, it is instructive to enumerate the most essential methodological problems that, in the authors opinion, require some comprehension in terms of the processes in which the neo-Soviet space is involved.

- The problem of the spatial approach, which is a kind of cross-section of the Soviet and neo/post-Soviet state. The spatial approach does not depend upon the subjective construction of economic sociology and political science. It provides this cross-section, a kind of X-ray, a general picture. Here, theoretical geography becomes geopolitics.
- The regional approach is an interpretation of geopolitical events making use of many interesting tools.
- The situation of the Soviet Union is not unique, but it stands out. Is very obvious and can be regarded as a prototype. In particular, it could be regarded as a prototype for China.

Obviously, there are many more problems, but let us close by emphasising that the processes under way on the territory of the former Soviet Union are also of paramount importance for other countries for the simple reason that they provide a wealth of material for consideration.

3

Administrative Regionalism: Stages, Actors, Legitimisation and Prospects

Sergei Pavlenko

Today, it seems as though Russia's movement towards a new federalism is inexorable. Administrative relations in the sphere of territorial governance are being reviewed, reflecting the reformulation of relations between the centre and the subjects of federation and between different levels of local authorities within those subjects. The consequences of that process may be even more dramatic than those that followed an analogous change of administrative relations in the sphere of sectoral management (a process sometimes called economic reform in the public sector). The speed of these changes is such that one can expect with an equal amount of probability both that Russia will miraculously transform itself into a different country in two or three years or that absolutely nothing will happen. The author of this paper enjoys prognosticating in his private life, but on this theme he prefers to leave that to more well versed experts. From a scientific point of view, it is more important to consider the issue of relations between regionalism and separatism, the nature of regional authority as well as the mechanism of its functioning and, most important, its legitimacy.

1 Territorial Structure

Today the Russian Federation includes several groups of territories that differ in their status. Some of them can be viewed as states or quasi-states. The situation in other territories provides sufficient grounds for classifying them as states in a stage of formation.

The fact that some territories of the Russian Federation are becoming increasingly sovereign is a natural result of the interaction between on the one hand territorial elites (conventionally called local authorities) and on the other hand sectoral elites (groups managing the enterprises situated in those regions) and entrepreneurial elites (large non-governmental economic structures operating in those regions). Before 1985 the latter led an underground existence, and relations between the first two were regulated by the Communist party structures and by the branch ministries. After the collapse of those structures, regional elites acquired more freedom of manoeuvre in their fight for the domination of their respective territories. The following factors contributed to the expansion of the zone of 'interest clashes':

- the existence of a power vacuum: the aftermath of the August coup was characterised by the destruction of the central bodies of sectoral regulation. The image of 'power lying in the street' was not just a mere metaphor – at the very least power remained without supervision.
- transition to new economic relations: the liberalisation of prices and the launch of economic reform has essentially changed both the relations between producers and the hierarchical structure of elite groups.
- privatisation of state property: the current accelerated privatisation of state property (conducted mainly for political reasons) initiated clashes of different groups fighting for control over privatisation and over the property that was already privatised. Taking into account that a real market has not yet been created and that a deep restructuring has not begun, it is very difficult to give even an approximate estimate of the future real value of the assets offered for privatisation now. The right strategy under present conditions is to buy everything as cheap as possible and to push aside every rival.

Up to the autumn of 1991 the dominant position in the territories of the Russian Federation had been held by sectoral elites. At the beginning of December 1991, however, local authorities, having received broader powers from the federal centre, began to take control of the situation. An apparent reason for that was the need to provide some certainty after economic reforms were declared but not yet clearly understood by the local authorities. In the middle of December it became clear the sectoral supply system failed to respond promptly to wild changes in demand both on the consumer market and on the market for equipment and raw materials. Local authorities set restrictions on export of agricultural products from their region (70% of all regions) and created special barter funds (50% of all regions). For the first time, local authorities used military troops to deliver bread, to repair hot-water systems in the cities, etc. In the winter of 1991-92 local authorities enjoyed absolute power on their limited territory, something never achieved either by the CPSU or by the State Planning Committee.

But after economic reform had gained impetus and not only the social structure but also the lifestyles of all social and territorial groups without exception had begun to change, regional elites faced the necessity to reformulate their strategies of relations both with the centre and with each other. Those strategies (be they tacit or overt) can be reduced to the following points:

- accelerating the tempo of economic reforms (especially in the institutional sense). It was presumed that overall social costs of reforms would be minimised thanks to a faster resolution of the crisis. It was also supposed that the more 'advanced' regions would soon gain an essential advantage over the 'backward' regions and would be able to exploit them;
- closing-off the administratively controlled space in order to control export resources of the regions. It was believed that this strategy would draw a maximum profit from exports from the regions while at the same time minimising social costs;
- closing-off the administratively controlled space in order to control the level of supply and demand on local consumer markets. It was supposed that would help curb sharp falls and rises of supply and demand and, accordingly, prices and real income of population, thus minimising the risks of a probable social outbreak.

The sole goal of those strategies was to prevent any social upheaval. Regional elites feared any large-scale disturbances while they were busy with the redivision of power. But it was not easy to avoid disturbances. Firstly, the federal pro-reform government continued to rock the boat in its attempt to make the reforms more radical. Secondly, a delayed response of the producers (state enterprises) to the changing economic rules ran the economy into a crisis of mass defaults on payment that was deeper than expected. By the end of May, 1992 it became quite evident that slowness of mind could also serve as a weapon. It was at that moment that the sectoral elites presented an ultimatum insisting on the clearing of non-payments (which in fact meant that all the costs of that settlement would fall upon the federal budget, which would have to pay for the inefficient work of the enterprises). Having suppressed the government's resistance (and having factually stopped the attempt at radicalisation of reforms), sectoral elites sharply raised their status at the regional level. Except for several regions that are major exporters, this threatened the interests of the territorial and entrepreneurial elites. These elites faced a hard choice: either to stick to the support of an only partially controllable pro-reform government or to try to supplement administrative regionalisation legislatively and to come to grips with the unleashed sectoral elites within the regional 'ring' that was shielded from external interference. Most of them chose the second alternative. From that moment, the process of regionalisation became irreversible.

2 Stages of Restructuring

Regionalisation is developing as follows:

2.1 The First Stage

- regulation of the flow of goods and resources (including those in transit) in a region through the introduction of an obligatory procedure of co-ordination, licensing and limitation of exports, and the creation of a territorial fund of resources and products;
- regulation of prices in a region through the setting of price ceilings, regulation of the level of marketing margin and profitability, and regulation of the VAT rate;
- regulation of money circulation, of the amount and order of payments both with and without cash.

These measures were used by local authorities from January through June 1992. Regulation of movement of goods and resources is still going on (the legislative basis for it is constituted by the decisions and acts of the federal ministries and government departments as well as by decisions of local administrations and soviets). Regulation of money circulation is periodically used by the local authorities in order to address specific issues (for example, to finance planting campaigns and harvesting, or to regulate cash payments in case of shortage of cash money).

2.2 The Second Stage

- the actions of the first stage are given a legislative basis through decisions and enactments of local representative bodies. As a result of conflicts between different branches of power, representative bodies very rarely take decisions approving the actions of local executive bodies.

2.3 The Third Stage

- creation of territorial security systems by reorganising the federal security systems to serve the regions, and by gaining of control over the military units deployed on the territory of the regions.

- arrangement of direct contacts with foreign partners (including independent determination of the terms of foreign investments).

Local administrations of the Ministry of Internal Affairs are practically under control of local authorities (including special militia forces like OMON). The only exceptions are the inter-regional structures of departments dealing with organised crime and internal security services of the Ministry of Internal Affairs. Along with the MIA structures, municipal militias (which include special departments) and 'private' security services (licensed by the local authorities) are being created in the regions. The structures of the Ministry of Security and the departments of the Ministry of Defence are not subordinated to local administrations.

Local administrations of many regions of Russia have opened trade offices in a number of foreign countries, representations of the corresponding countries are being opened in Russia. The legal status of these representations and that of their activities has not been defined yet. Practically every region has its own customs office (they were introduced by a decision of the Ministry of External Relations). Rules of tender submission for foreign investments are in fact set up by local administrations.

This stage was completed by the spring of 1993.

2.4 The Fourth Stage

- declaration (the wording might be different) of the necessity to achieve economic sovereignty;
- declaration (its wording different in every individual region) of the necessity to achieve management and execution sovereignty.

Administrations and soviets of all regions announced in the spring of 1993 their determination to achieve expansion of their economic rights and the right to determine their own future.

2.5 The Fifth Stage

- creation of regional blocks through agreements on maintaining economic ties; agreements on the creation of preferential regimes; agreements on co-ordination of claims against the federal government.

The above-mentioned agreements were adopted in the autumn of 1992 and declared by chairmen of soviets and administrations. Parallel talks on bilateral agreements between individual regions have been conducted since the beginning of 1993.

2.6 The Sixth Stage

- declaration of exclusive local control over the process of privatisation of federal property;
- declaration of exclusive local control over natural resources;
- implementation of a one-channel tax system.

Declarations about the exclusiveness of local control over privatisation were adopted by the soviets of three regions over the period of January-April 1993. Declarations of the exclusiveness of the local control over natural resources were adopted by the administrations of autonomous bodies during the same period, although these adoptions did little to change their status.

2.7 The Seventh Stage

- institutionalisation and legitimisation of sovereignty – establishment of a Constitution, a presidency, institution of plenipotentiary representatives, flag, anthem, etc.

All the territories are represented in the federal government. National autonomies have adopted constitutions, many regions are working out drafts of 'regional charters'.

After a territory has reached the 7th stage it can be considered as a quasi-state, and in some cases as a state de facto, the legal international status of which is just a question of time.

Nevertheless, regionalisation of territories of the Russian Federation has by no means been drawn by the rules of logic. The process of regionalisation often seems quite illogical, at least at first glance. Local elites undertake seemingly 'unreasonable' steps. Law often seems a misnomer. The irregular character of the process sharply decreases its predictability and, accordingly, any chances to exercise control over it.

The differentiation of regions in that process depends upon many factors, but foremost are the functioning of the regulation mechanism of interests and the behaviour of regional elites in their interaction both with each other at the local level and with the federal structures of power.

3 Regulation Mechanism

The behaviour of a Soviet citizen was regulated by a complex system of rules which included the written law, the whole body of legislation, as well as the operational system of rules comprising: a) norms of behaviour commonly socially approved; b) norms of behaviour not approved by other groups but binding upon the members of an individual group.

Behaviour was thus regulated by an integrated system of formal and informal social norms, while the rather high level of integration was determined both by the under-differentiation of society and by the existence of a vertical hierarchy of institutions co-ordinating activity of different groups (CPSU committees of all levels).

The collapse of co-ordinating structures and the weakening of the real power of central bodies of regulation was followed by a differentiation of operational systems of rules and by the legitimisation of formerly common laws. This allows us to talk about an evolving process of creation of differentiated local systems of behavioural regulation.

In the course of economic reform, the positions of different social groups constantly change because of factors external to the local system of interaction. This destabilises the system of hierarchy and, naturally, the structures of real power. As a result, regulation mechanisms break down, and turn from being systems of deals and agreements into a sum of confrontations and manipulations.

The instability of the regulation system essentially blunts its current effectiveness. When there is no operational system of sanctions punishing breaches of the fixed norms, when the very notion of norm is rather relative, the interacting social groups are forced to leave the field of 'fixed norms' and to move into the field of 'norms practised by convention', otherwise the very idea of regulation of social relations is jeopardised. In fact this means that 'the social contract' has to be constantly renegotiated, turning the search for inter-group consensus into a permanent process.

It is quite evident that a constant renegotiation of 'the social contract' is possible only at the local level and among a limited number of participants. Consequently, a certain degree of localisation of norm-making is a prerequisite for the development of that process. Moreover, some independence of the participants of that process from the influence of other groups, including federal regulation bodies, is equally necessary. So, we can say that regionalisation of the norm-making is a decisive element of a broader process of regionalisation of the territory of administration. Regionalisation of the territory of administration is in its turn a key factor of the regionalisation of the political and governmental space, that is of separatism.

Thus, regionalism is inseparable from separatism. The main motive of regionalism is the need for local elites to create more or less stable system of inter-group relations. This logically leads to the formulation and solidifying of the local legislative system, that is to the formation of local territorial entities which have one of the main attributes of the state. The fact that the supporters of regionalist movements do not declare their desire to form independent states means only one thing: the creation of an independent state is not an end in itself for them. The difference between a separatist and a regionalist in Russian conditions lies in the fact that for a separatist the declaration of the need to form an 'independent state X' is the declaration of the ultimate objective of his activity, whereas for a regionalist that is just a means of achieving other goals.

4 The Objectives of the Interested Groups

The objectives of the different groups that take part in the organisational shaping of regionalisation vary:

4.1 Radical regionalists

Radical regionalists pursue the following general objectives:

- to turn the region into a state entity- into a subject of international law;
- to sign a 'state agreement' with the Russian Federation which would give the region the status of an 'associated state';
- to fix by means of economic 'inter-government agreements' between the Russian Federation and the new state the volumes of compulsory supply of raw materials at reduced prices;
- an analogous agreement to fix a compulsory supply of consumer goods and industrial equipment, also at reduced prices;
- to turn transcontinental transport communications into the objects of joint possession and control.

It is clear that achievement of these objectives would mean preservation of the dual-standard pricing policy that includes administrative price-setting and control over the movement of goods. In the long run this will result in the preservation of a direct administrative control and regulation of economy by the state structures. Otherwise agreements concerning selling of resources to the manufacturers at reduced prices seem to be absolutely unreal. So, this assumes restoration of a 'real socialist state in its purest form'.

The radical wing of the regionalist movement is frequently made up mainly of the 'up-rooted intelligentsia' backed by new business structures that finance and support radical groups. The interest of the these business structures (for instance in Siberia) is quite obvious: to gain control over the functioning of the whole economic system. Representatives of this group are quite aware of the fact that control over export operations is not enough. To maintain stable functioning of the extraction complex different regional elites must come to an agreement (even if that includes elimination of intractable groups), otherwise the social tension inspired by them may not just increase investments risks but current costs too.

These business structures suppose that the task of gaining control over the extraction complex can be fulfilled by means of 'bribing' regional branch elites and by blocking administrative elites in co-operation with them. This strategy can be assessed as rather effective taking into account that a significant part of the new business is controlled by the people springing up from 'traditional' elites who have not lost because of their 'social origin' personal and business contacts with them. But the problem is that there people who are ready to pay even more for the same thing. Business structures from Moscow, St.-Petersburg and the Urals that have accumulated quite some capital are ready to invest money not only into production but also to pay transaction costs (or, put more simply, bribes). The business elites cannot compete with these 'aliens'. Regional branch elites are connected with central business elites through the central ministries and departments that have survived. Therefore, closing-up the regional financial and administrative markets is the only way for regionalist business elites to preserve their status and to develop. Hence the paradox of a 'new business′' desire to restore 'the old state' within the region. In the mind of these regionalists, administrative autonomy is a projectionist mechanism. Let us note that it is quite logical that none of them speaks for the restoration of state regulation of economy embracing the whole federation. In this case the advantages of regionalisation would be reduced to zero.

4.2 Moderate Regionalists

Moderate regionalists have the following general objectives:

- to turn regional structures of power into the subjects of a system of inter-group management relations at the federal level as well as to divide 'zones of influence' of the regional and federal structures of power;
- institutional and juridical legalisation of the special rights of the regional governing structures to draw and to use large appropriations from the federal budget in order to support enterprises that are uncompetitive on the world and Russian markets;

- to create a legal basis for the preservation of a part of the national resources rent and of the 'institutional rent' (payments for conducting export-import operations) under the control of the regional structures.

Achievement of these goals would mean the preservation of the 'command and permission' system of state regulation of the economy. As a result the administrative power of the subjects of regulation would be converted into capital in the form of the low-interest credits distributed for other than economic reasons. So, they talk about restoration of the 'state of the perestroika period'.

Moderate regionalists are in their majority representatives of regional branch elites. They include representatives of the scientific sector of the military industrial complex. Accordingly, their real objective is to create conditions for the continuation of financial support of their enterprises and organisations from the federal budget either in the form of direct appropriations or in the form of low-interest credits. To get that they need first of all to retain control over the status of their enterprises. Sectoral elites want to determine themselves the right time and order of privatisation of the assets that they actually possess and which is still traditionally called state property. They do not possess considerable financial means at the present moment, but they prefer those sources of financial means that are not designated 'creditor-receiver of credit', for relations of this kind include the potential complete loss of control over assets, which in turn means that they can lose their only advantage, i.e. their status as manager and de facto, of a proprietor.

That group is also interested in creation of more powerful centres of authority in the region because that will facilitate achievement of the above-mentioned objectives. However, unlike the radicals the moderate regionalists, instead of elimination of 'the power of the Centre,' think it necessary to 'reform the Centre', which does not exclude withdrawal from it as a means of pressure, in order to restore the system of relations which existed in 1987-91. Thus, regionalisation is a forced measure and self-determination is an unwelcome extreme.

4.3 The Activities of Radical and Moderate Regionalists

The activity of these two groups is directly dependent upon the tempo and character of economic development of the country and is determined by the following two chief factors- by the degree of rigidity of the financial and budgetary policy of the federal government and the Central Bank and by the tempo of the institutional liberalisation of the economy.

In a schematic way that can be described as follows:

1. *Liberal financial policy, low tempo of institutional liberalisation.*

   The situation is characterised by mass appropriation of low-interest credits to the manufacturer accompanied by slow privatisation. An eventual growth of inflation makes structures of the new business break through to the 'real values', national resources. This movement is however being obstructed by the sectoral elites. The regional economy short-circuits. Regionalism as an instrument falls into disuse. The federation's integrity is not threatened directly in this case, but economic development may become disastrous.

2. *Liberal financial policy and high tempo of privatisation.*

   Unreserved credit policy and high rate of inflation make sectoral elites use institutional changes to their advantage, that is invest in privatisation of the enterprises that they control. Structures of the new business prefer to avoid competition with sectoral elites, as they are unlikely to succeed under the conditions of an expanded supply of the property market. Nevertheless, regional branch elites start competing for the low-interest credits. As the 'credit consuming capacity' of the Siberian sectors of industry is relatively high, they resort to the threat of regionalisation as a means of pressing central authorities to allocate credits. However, ministries and departments do not care much about the preservation of the federation, so they are usually immune to such threats. Accordingly, the regionalist reason is not effective.

3. *Rigid financial policy and low tempo of privatisation.*

   Stopped credits, puts sectoral elites in a different situation. The low tempo of privatisation makes legitimisation of possession of property impossible. A possibility to resell is reduced to a minimum. In such a situation sectoral elites try, on the one hand, to expand their participation in the still profitable export operations and, on the other hand, to soften the rigidity of the financial policy of the federal authorities. They are then supported by structures of the new business.

   Such policy results in claims for the expansion of the regions' control over licensing and setting of export quotas as well as for more credits to the local enterprises. Regionalisation in this case is both a threat and a real claim.

4. *Rigid financial policy and high tempo of privatisation.*

   In this case a split-up of local elites takes place, as the threat of regionalisation is resorted to by that part of the sectoral elites which controls losing enterprises. In this case the investment attractiveness of such enterprises does not practically play any role. While others are busy dividing property by all possible means, this group of 'potential failures' becomes more and more radical and finally undertakes actions aimed at real regionalisation.

Let us note that this scheme does not include description of the actions of the third player, the local administration elites.

Local administration elites are the most difficult group to analyse and prognosticate. They are the most diverse of composition, including both people springing from the former power structures and representatives of sectoral and business elites, and at the same time they are the most integrated by the problems they face. Theoretically, an administration elite should express interests of other groups, but in fact it behaves as a rather independent force. There are several reasons for that:

- Administration elites are considered by other groups usually as their potential lobby, and, on the other hand, as a source of low-interest credits and free money. But the lobbying capacity of local administrations is not unlimited, nor are the budgets they control. A range of groups belonging to sectoral elites, having understood that, do not any longer take them into account and exclude them from their relations. Administration elites give a unanimous response- they raise their status by all possible means. As exclusion from the system of inter-group relations is lethal to any elite group, one of the ways to raise one's status is to threaten to undertake the steps which may completely change the system of relations between regional elites. In this way local administrations pushed aside as useless managed to turn into an 'active independent (uncontrolled-led) group'- in order to stop being perceived as useless.
- The mechanism of relations of local administration elites and other elite groups is essentially different. On of the reasons being that administration elites are not much interested in serving the interests of those 'sentenced to death', or the first enterprise to go bankrupt.
- Administration elites have found their own relatively independent and stable source of income. Privatisation of the property that they control turns them from managers of that property into its real proprietors. Being proprietors they not only prefer to serve their own 'business' but also show very little interest in serving anybody else's business.
- Finally, administration elites feel that they are responsible for safeguarding social stability in the territories they control. Protection of stability that was initially imposed upon them as a duty by the present moment turned into a

means of their survival because in case the people flare up in rage, they are going to be the first to fall victim to that rage. Moreover, administration elites seek to block any possible changes in the structure of local authority. Otherwise the tricks that they have previously done may come to the surface. So administration elites put distance between them and other groups and start playing 'their own game,' disguising that as 'being outside the fight'.

Relative autonomy of administration elites results in a reaction to the policy of the federal centre which is different from reactions of other regional elites:

- In the case of a *flexible financial policy accompanied by inflation* they try to conceal the incomes that come their way, tax money and incomes from introduction of quotas on export-import operations. The main problem is to save that money from devaluation. If there is a privatisation campaign underway, administration elites make deals with sectoral elites, which are eager to invest money from privileged credits into real property, and with business elites, which just look for profitable placement of their investments. On the regional level 'purpose blocs' of elites are created. They are formed by those wishing to take part in the division of state property. This division requires a certain intimacy as it goes on according to the law of convention. One of the basic conditions of that intimacy is the minimisation of external interference, particularly minimisation of the participation of organisations of the federal level which bring written law into the process. In this situation administration elites try to obtain real power over their territories, to become legislators rather than executors. Regionalisation of the juridical space is regarded by them as a means of strengthening their position in the inter-group relations on the regional level.
- If a *liberal financial policy privatisation is being checked* then a different situation emerges: administration elites try to form coalitions with other elites in order to get even more financial resources (as adjustment to inflation) which in fact turns their regionalist activity into serving interests of other elites. In this case administration elites guarantee for themselves a stable status but have to put up with the shortage of resources at their disposal.
- In the case of a *rigid financial policy*, which entails the risk of bankruptcy of a number of enterprises, mainly large enterprises, administration elites try to increase revenues of local budgets. That includes supporting sectoral elites' claims for 'selective support of the most important sectors of industry'. Of course, sectoral elites try to cadge subsidies from the budget on their own too,

but in the case of more or less austere financial policy nothing but a powerful lobby can help. But powerful lobbying, when demands exceed those 'to pay debts of individual enterprises', becomes a dangerous game. Individual enterprises always get something from government anyway, but when if all enterprises make demands government may just promise to give nothing as a punishment for 'being in the opposition'. Therefore, sectoral elites take pains to be very cautious. An open 'opposition' may cause negative results for them.

- If an *austere financial policy is attended by an expanded privatisation*, some sectoral elites tend to compromise with the federal centre, trading for more favourable conditions for their eventual activities as private entrepreneurs. In this situation administration elites begin to worry about the integral character of their group. The federal centre, once having succeeded in splitting the 'regional front', may start a campaign of the final destruction of its separate parts. Unlike business and sectoral elites, administration elites can be radically renewed over a relatively short period of time, either through a 'staff purge' or by means of extraordinary elections. Being fully aware of that danger, administration elites resort in such situations to radical actions, often becoming panic-stricken. Regionalisation in this case is a means of survival.

The problem of survival is a very serious one for administration elites. After they began to act as representatives of regional elites in general, the position of the central (federal) departments started also to change. The appearance of an intermediate link on the one hand facilitates co-ordination of decision-making, on the other hand, administration elites become a 'scapegoat' when the central authorities begin to get a feeling that their interests are being neglected. It should be noted that regionalisation of the administrative space does not make the federal authorities ecstatic. The Ministry of Finance furiously resists expansion of the share of tax revenues that remain at the disposal of regions. That narrows the tax base of the federal budget and, accordingly, undermines the position of the collector and distributor of tax revenues. The Ministry of external economic relations opposes the expansion of rights of local authorities concerning licensing export activity. The Ministry of economy does not want rights of the local administration for setting export quotas to be expanded. The Committee on the state property does not want to lose control over privatisation. The Ministry of fuel and energy does not think it expedient to give regions the right to take decisions concerning the exploitation of mineral resources. The positions of those official bodies are supported by the Chief Board on Legislation supervising observance of the written law. The Ministry of security considers any attempts at regionalisation as a direct blow to the national security of the Russian Federation.

It is paradoxical, but different federal structures, at loggerheads on all other issues, are unanimous in their rejection of regionalisation. It is even more paradoxical that their misgivings are based upon contrary assessments of the potential. for regional elites to turn into allies of a rival bloc. 'The radicals' think that regionalisation will secure position of local pro-Communist elites. Advocates of the state think that it creates a possibility of their opponents' alliance with the 'local corrupted new bourgeois groups'. At the same time both sides are trying to use local elites as a third force, which, of course, requires its acknowledgement as a 'force'. So, central authorities surreptitiously legitimise the status of local elites as equal participants of competition at the federal level and, doing so, they acknowledge them as their equals. In this situation a concept 'subject of federation' is understood as a subject of political competition at the federal level. Nurturing an ally, central authorities thus legitimise regionalism.

5 Legitimisation of Separatism

At first glance, separatist movements have two main aspects: one moral, the other legal. Actions of violence (terrorism, acts of civil disobedience) are evidently based upon the 'moral' aspect (they are inspired by moral reasons), while negotiations between the central government and the separatists are conducted within the framework of juridical legitimacy. In short, if the central government has enough forces (including armed forces), will and desire to confront separatist movements, then the confrontation dialogue will take a propaganda and ethical rhetorical tone. Nevertheless, the legal basis of separatism seems have a separate existence. The players see before them an open field for dialogue and try to reach it. The legal basis of separatism exists in the form of the 'right to self-determination' in three different forms: 'the natural law', the historical precedent norm, and international law.

5.1 Separatism as Natural Law

The idea of 'natural law' is based upon an extended interpretation of the 'natural rights of man', foremost among which are the right of individual freedom, the unlawfulness of any compulsion, independence from power which is seen as unlawful, and in the long run the right to resist that power until it is destroyed. So the problem of the territorial structure of a country (and, accordingly, the problem of relations between the elements of that structure and the managing centre) is reduced to the problem of relations between the person and the state.

It would be a mistake to say that this reduction always existed in its purest variant – the contrary is more likely to be true. In the majority of cases the central structure of power personified the 'state' and territorial 'immediate communities' represented the individual. Generally speaking, theoretical models concerning the communalisation of relations of an individual with the world around him say two things. On the one hand, they are supposed to encourage separatist initiatives (by means of declaring the supremacy of the natural rights of a community with regard to a state that is artificial by its nature), but, on the other hand, they create internal tensions in the theory itself (why should the alienation of the natural rights of a person be regarded as more legitimate in favour of the immediate community than in favour of the greater state?). Nevertheless, the federalist theory of social stratification founded by Johannes Althusius, based upon the principle of 'communal structure' of the state and society, assumed a territorial projection of the vertical hierarchical relations within the social structure and created a juridical prerequisite for the sovereignisation of territorial communities. That is why despite a 'ban on the separation of provinces' the right to separate was not excluded in the cases when the very existence of communities was under a threat. Let us note that in this case it is the existence of communities as such that was meant, not a physical survival of people constituting those communities (Hugo Grotius). Such application of the 'natural law' can be regarded as a mechanism of self-protection of social groups. When the social structure changes rapidly and these changes result in losses (of one's status, well-being, feeling of social and psychological security) for a considerable part of these groups, then the development of a 'group separatism' (which transforms social groups into territorial ones) is quite natural.

The legitimacy of separatism of that kind is very relative, though, as in the long run it means not only the supremacy of the rights of a group over the rights of a person, but also that 'large groups' (population of a territory, nation, social group) are more privileged in that respect than 'small groups' (families, households, national minorities).

Being a mixture of individual and group understandings of rights, 'communal separatism' cannot be considered by any of 'purely' theoretical schemes as undoubtedly legitimate, which, however, does not prevent its use as a means of propaganda. Relative legitimacy also means the necessity of violence towards separatists on the part of 'others', i.e. other groups or the state structures (which can be considered as 'groups' only in a somewhat strained interpretation).

5.2 Separatism as Historical Precedent

The norm 'historical precedent' is a rather relative one in Russia. The October Revolution and the seventy years of the power of soviets that followed made it practically impossible to appeal to the norms which existed before the revolution. Moreover, such appeals are in fact meaningless because the history of the Russian Empire has no precedents of separation of its parts from it (the case of Alaska is a specific one). Authorities of the Empire always emphasised the indivisibility of its territory and always suppressed by violence any separatist movements. Even special territories (Poland, Finland) up to the revolution were considered by the authorities under the special status of having self-government while being integral parts of the state. Thus, the precedent law or, more precisely, the possibility of legitimisation on the grounds of past precedents is operational only within the soviet period of Russia's history.

The right to separate during the soviet period (for the sake of simplicity we also include in this period opinions of the leaders of the communist movement before the Revolution) was regarded as a subordinate part of the right of nations to self-determination. Therefore, the right of a territorial group to separate was not unreserved even theoretically, the group aspiring to separate had to have properties of a nation forming a state system of its own.

In theory, the right of nations to self-determination was regarded as absolute and inalienable, however, in fact it had many limitations. Lenin gave a rational reason for the right of nations to self-determination. The costs of suppressing a nation's aspiration to separation are rather cumbersome, while the declaration of the right to separation creates a psychological restraint keeping the dominant state from 'being too hard' on the minor nations. Thus the right of nations to self-determination was distinctly discriminated from a real separation of territories, which was considered to be an ultimate consequence to be realised only in the situation of a deadlock (Lenin's work 'National question and internationalism of proletariat'). The dismemberment of capitalist multinational states was considered as a transitional stage, a possible (but not necessary) condition for the formation of a union of socialist republics.

The communist party's transformation into the ruling party, when Russia was exposed both to external threat and to the threat from within, was the reason for the reformulation of the doctrine of self-determination. The right of nations to self-determination was understood as contradictory to the task of preservation and expansion of the new regime (and, accordingly, proletarian internationalism was opposed to bourgeois nationalism). Stalin in the course of discussion on the national issue frequently underlined the right of nations to self-determination should not stand in the way of the dictatorship of the working class, on the contrary, it should serve that task. So, that right even on a theoretical level was applied only to the territories which were not yet 'free from capitalism'. Accordingly, the right of the republics of the Soviet Union to free separation from the Union declared by the Constitution of 1937 was not supported even by the slightest practical indication. Nevertheless, in the eyes of the people of the republics of the USSR the declaration of the right to leave the Union at the end of the 80s and early 90s was a rather forceful argument legitimising the breakdown of the Soviet Union. However, for the Russian Federation this precedent has only slight validity.

Even at the initial stage of elaboration of the constitution of 1937 Stalin listed the special conditions necessary for autonomous regions (republics) to raise their status to that of a constituent republic which has the right to leave the Union:

- actual status of autonomy;
- an external border (which excluded from the list of claimants regions situated inside the territory of the Federation);
- the titulary nation must constitute the majority of the region's population;
- 'new states' must be large enough so that they do not fall under the control of hostile states, thus becoming centres of anti-Soviet activities.

So, self-determination was regarded as potentially possible for a limited number of territories, but the criteria for classification of specific territories reduced that number to zero. Still, the very existence of such declarations was used as a precedent by Gorbachev's administration to raise the status of the autonomous territories of the Russian Soviet Socialist Republic to that of the subjects of the Union agreement, which later on logically transformed into a desire by the territories with lower status (autonomous regions) to raise their status to that of subjects of the federative agreement of 1992.

Summing up the above we note the absence of actual precedents of a legitimate separation of territory of the Russian Federation in a specifically juridical sense of this word, although there is a 'probable (declared)' legitimacy of such separation in the geopolitical space of the former USSR.

5.3 Separatism and International Law

The international law concerning separation of territories is based upon the idea that the right to self-determination is one of the fundamental rights of man. However, the practical application of this concept has always been accompanied by many conflicting interpretations. Thus, the Charter of the United Nations does not clarify such terms as 'state', 'people' and 'nation', leaving their interpretation to the member states. Accordingly, the Charter does not give a clear-cut definition of the relation between rights of an individual and rights of a group as well as the relation between groups and social institutions.

A discussion in the international organisations that began in the mid-50s mainly dealt with the question whether the right to self-determination is absolute or relative. The position of the USSR and other socialist countries was in support of an absolute character of the right of nations to form new (independent) states, which in its turn meant an absolute character of the right to separation. The majority of other states centred around the following two positions:

- the right to self-determination is rather a moral objective and cannot serve as a rigid restraint of the policy of the states, it should be realised through self-government rather than separation;
- the right to self-determination is a basic right of a person and it must be regarded as the right to self-determination in all dimensions of the world around him, which means the right of a nation to express its will with regard to self-determination and an obligation to respect and take into account that will.

Let us note that the problem of self-determination was initially discussed with respect to the colonies. However, it was in the early 60s that a range of countries, member states of the UN, had to face the problem of 'internal separatism' (Congo, Nigeria, Pakistan. Iraq). In those cases the position of the international organisations was modified. On the one hand, the right of minorities to self-determination continued to be considered as lawful, but in fact it was confronted by the right of state, a plenipotentiary member of the UN, to the internationally acknowledged existence, which under certain conditions meant preservation of territorial unity. In fact such cases were determined by the balance of forces and interests of the superpowers. Accordingly, with the collapse of the system of control of the superpowers over the world order processes of self-determination and separation broke free from under the control of the world community and their further development is steered in accordance with an internal logic (Yugoslavia).

Thus, international law can be viewed as an indisputable precedent for legitimisation of regionalism and separatism.

5.4 Propaganda as a Means of Legitimisation

Propaganda is one of the main methods of legitimising regionalism. Regional elites use propaganda in order to emphasise in the minds of people that they are the ruling elites as well as to secure a proper status in their relations with the federal authorities. In the course of propaganda campaigns regional elites achieve a whole range of goals:

- uphold in the population's eyes their legitimacy as the defenders of mass social groups' interests from the 'anti-social policy of the anti-social Centre';
- uphold in the eyes of other elites their legitimacy as the 'best organisers of pressure on the Centre';
- uphold their legitimacy in the eyes of politically engaged groups as the organisers of struggle against the 'anti-Communist' ('nomenclature-communist' as a variant) Centre.

The psychological influence of such propaganda is determined mainly by the absence of 'enemies' after the collapse of the communist regime. The traditional Soviet society confrontational ideology and, corresponding psychology can not serve any longer as a valve for reducing the existent social and psychological tension. The society naturally searches for an enemy. The one who points at this enemy will not only ward the blow off oneself, but also will gain some sort of appreciation.

Within the frames of this analysis we shall not dwell on the analysis of the mechanism of how the regional elites control mass media, but we would like to mention that this control covers 'central' mass media as well. Nor will we describe the psychological war methods used. We just want to point out that when conducting propagandist campaigns, the regional elite-controlled mass media use the following arguments:

- based on the statutes: appeals to the normative documents, first of all, to the Constitution and to legislation on local governments and the regional (district) Council. Regional elites use these normative acts for proving the legality of their position, interpreting any activity directed at changing their position as illegal and anti-constitutional;
- based on the common law: when speaking of mass social groups – appeals to the necessity to maintain income in the region and to maintain employment; when speaking of different groups of regional elites – appeals to maintain the

existent production structure and to legalise local control over natural resources.

In whole these arguments create the basis for legitimisation of regionalism as way of co-operation of regional elites with the federal centre.

6 Legitimisation of Suppression of Separatism

Unlike the right to self-determination based upon rather vague moral norms (humanitarian norms, individual values) anti-separatist activity is based upon quite workable postulates which combine both openly declared 'state interests' and hidden interests of 'group security'. Along with all that, the rights of one group are controlled by those of other groups.

6.1 External Security of 'Other States'

Separation of one of several regions of a country upsets international balance and undermines world stability. Thus, separation of several countries which possess nuclear weapons (Ukraine, Kazakhstan, Belarus) has radically changed the composition of the 'nuclear club' and has weakened the juridical foundations of the regime of nuclear non-proliferation. Moreover, an expanded interpretation of international agreements means that the states must preserve the status which they had at the moment when they signed those agreements. That is the contracting parties implicitly agree to preserve their unity because its preservation on one side prevents threat to the security of the other side.

6.2 Internal Security of 'Other States'

Separation of some regions of a country creates a precedent for groups of population of other countries which seek separation. So legitimisation of the separatist movements in one country creates a basis for legitimisation of other movements.

The 'right of nations to self-determination' once realised creates a precedent threatening internal security of 'other states'. There is no definite interpretation of the concept of 'nation' both in the international law and in the 'internal' state legislation, and the criteria as to what groups of population could justly claim realisation of that right are also unidentified. Therefore, that right if realised by one state with respect to a group of population which identifies itself as a 'nation' potentially stimulates similar self-identification of this or that group of population of other states. It is inevitable that the process of the expansion of self-identification 'suffered' by one country may cause much more serious changes in the national structures and, accordingly, in the balance of interests and forces of different social groups in other states.

The possible negative consequences of creation of new states can be categorised as follows:

- Formation of economically unviable states creating a dilemma for the world community – whether to keep afloat economies of large states or to put up with the existence of smaller states inevitably prone to social and economic crises.
- Formation of states incapable of self-defence, which may encourage an external aggressor and increase international tension.
- Formation of states without mature political and governing structures, which may result in internal chaos that will inevitably affect both neighbouring countries and the world community in general.
- Formation of states with undemocratic governing structures, which occurs when within a united democratic state the undemocratic character of local authorities failed to transform in the course of self-determination of the territory.
- Formation of states which will continue to disintegrate.

Another factor of instability is the troubled relation between the 'mother' country and the 'new-born' state. 'New minorities' will emerge, particularly those that before the separation belonged to the dominant national and ethnic groups. In the great majority of cases these groups suffer from real discrimination or feel that their status is falling.

On the other hand, separation of a region from a formerly united state can cause significant deterioration of the position of the former state. That region may have provided a significant part of the national product of a country, or that region may have provided through redistribution a considerable part of the income of the population of other regions. The economy of the rest of the state is also likely to suffer from an increased pressure because of the growth of costs of direct or indirect aid to the related ethnic groups of the population of the 'separated part'.

7 The Prospects of Regionalism

It is possible to say that both the population and the central authorities begin to consider regionalisation as the first (constituent) stage of separatism. Now, we can also speak of the fact that regional elites begin to show the first signs of dissatisfaction with such state of affairs.

Firstly, the method of pressure can sooner or later play against its initiators. Central administrations now begin to reduce the allotted resources on the ground of 'forthcoming separation' ('soon you'll be not ours, anyway'). Secondly, real regionalisation can weaken considerably the positions of those local elite groups, which are now connected functionally with the federal authorities. This will mean the beginning of repartition of power at the local level, which is not a piece of good news for some people. Thirdly, the perspective of changing the territorial status of the region becomes a strong impeding factor for foreign and Russian investors, which is considered to be an unfavourable phenomenon. Regional elites want to control these investments, and not to lose them. Fourthly, the fixation of regionalisation in the mentality of the population as the goal of elites' activities worsens their manoeuvrability- every new co-operation with federal authorities is regarded as apostasy and decreases the people's confidence in representatives of regional elites, which are constantly changing their positions. This is especially painful for those who are planning to make a political career in the regional organs of power. Fifthly, regionalisation which implies resubordination of local structures of ministries of security and internal affairs to local authorities, excites apprehension in many groups of regional elites- obviously, those who will take them under control will be 'an unjustly high authority'.

Thus, since the spring of 1993 regional elites are trying to return to the preferential use of traditional methods of co-operation with the federal centre, i.e. to direct lobbyism.

Lobbying of regional elites is carried out in two directions: through the apparatus of central ministries and bodies, including presidential structures, and through territorial representatives in representative organs of power, especially in the Federal Assembly. Traditional lobbying between leaders of deputies groups and representatives of executive power ('we give to the territory certain privileges and preferences, and you provide the votes in the elections'), was coming to nought. In the course of the 1992-93 congresses of people's deputies the representatives of executive power had become convinced that deputies corps were uncontrollable. Even more, became convinced the majority of people's deputies were not ready to make compromises in their eagerness to overthrow the existent regime by all means, including regionalist confrontation.

Lobbying aimed at receiving privileges 'from the hands' of executive power has also reached the highest degree. Under the tightening of financial policy, preferential resources are not enough for everybody. They are allotted on the basis of either providing 'the right' electoral behaviour of population (that is they are directed to densely populated regions), or of subsidising export.

It is obvious that the opportunities of regional elites to influence the federal authorities have decreased considerably since spring 1993. Now their expansion is connected mainly, if not exclusively, with the constitutional process which has emerged since the beginning of summer. The beginning of the constitutional conference has initiated a new rise in the status of administrative elites – they directly and unequivocally connected their participation in the conference and the results of voting with granting regions state status. The 'regional integrism' of administrative elites is used to raise their status in trade with the centre.

The traditional situation of trade is aggravated by the fact that the federal government asserts its permanent intention at least not to increase the expenditure part of the federal budget. This means that the 'aggregated demand on privileges' cannot be satisfied even in principle. Regional blocks appear to be useless as an instrument for knocking out privileges – the government will not give them the money they ask for, anyway. That is why the administrations of some regions, foreseeing the government won't let them have their share, since mid-summer 1993, have tried to use regional integrism and the threat of regionalisation 'till total separation' as an instrument of struggle with the government. The problem of overthrowing the existent regime has not yet become the major one in the regionalist movement, still it is steadily coming to the forefront.

Nevertheless, it would be oversimplifying to interpret the tolerance, which the federal government displays towards ambitious statements, and towards no less ambitious actions, of some regions exclusively or mainly as 'the weakness of the Centre'. The sanctions against 'the mutinous territories' are blocked not only by groups in federal structures, which use regional tendencies as an instrument of struggle, but also by the universal acknowledgement within the federal structures of the necessity of 'new federalism'.

8 New Federalism

In our opinion, 'new federalism' is becoming the main subject of purely political contradictions between the main political forces and the structures of power. In the nearest future it will become one of the main components of the economic policy of the federal authorities.

The strategic objective of the so-called liberal wing of the government is transferring the largest possible responsibility for the realisation of social programs aimed at supporting the population to the regional level during the stage of structural reforming of economy. The tax basis of local budgets must be expanded accordingly, including revenues presently going to the federal budget, and the regional authorities are given more freedom in conducting tax policy.

The strategic objective of the so-called 'modernisers' (the advocates of state intervention in the economy aimed at accelerated modernisation, not waiting until the financial system is stabilised) is transferring to the regional coalitions the responsibility for carrying out large investment projects. Accordingly, it is intended to create a mechanism for the purpose of pumping financial resources out of the federal budget and into the inter-regional (regional) investment funds ('funds of regional development'). However, the tax basis of local budgets is not expanded in this case, not markedly, at any rate, but the wide-range redistribution of tax incomes through the federal budget into the 'funds of regional development' is taking place.

The strategic objective of the so-called 'statesmen' (the advocates of expanding state intervention in the economy in order to preserve its 'controllability' – in other words, in order to preserve the centralised control system) is the formation of the joint management structures at the local level. These structures must unite, as intended, the corresponding structures of local administrations and federal ministries and bodies to restore the vertical co-ordination structures ruined by the collapse of the communist regime (in other words, to reproduce the managerial vertical line which at those times was provided by party committees).

Concretising the 'new federalism', filling it with real managerial sense, will be dependent on the balance of forces on the political arena. However, at any rate, the realisation of a new course of the central power in relation to regions will demand reconsidering the normative basis, the informal relations between regions and the federal centre and, what is quite obvious, the elaboration of an 'insurance' system.

The realisation of strategic objectives by liberals is hampered by their fear of giving too much freedom to a former party nomenclature which preserves control over local authorities. In an economic crisis the local authorities may use the widening of their plenary powers in the sphere of taxation to increase the rates of taxes on private entrepreneurs, which will lower the rates of growth of the regime's social base. Hence, in theory, the realisation of the concept of a 'new liberal federalism' requires a preliminary shift of power at the regional level, that is, ideally, new elections or voluntary change of structure and personnel of local soviets and administrations. New elections are constrained by the constitutional process, because logically they must become the result of the adoption of a new constitution. Forceful actions are constrained by fears of destabilising the achieved economic balance.

Nevertheless, it is clear that the course towards 'new federalism' will face significant difficulties, for it will demand reconsidering a great number of legislative acts:

- the constitution and part of the federal agreement dealing with differentiation of plenary powers and rights of federal and local authorities;
- the complex of laws which define the country's budget system, particularly the part dealing with the formation of multi-channel system of taxation and giving local authorities the right to introduce local taxes, as well as the part dealing with normative definition of the system of formation and spending of local budgets;
- the complex of laws and under-law acts which define the system of financing and functioning of the social welfare sphere.

Also it is clear that the realisation of such a course will not please the local authorities of the regions, which constitute a zone of structural crisis- the Urals, the Volga basin, Siberia (except Tyumen' and Kuzbass).

But most important in the course of the realisation of such a strategy, it is necessary to reconsider the status of different regions, that is to adjust the status of republics and 'Russian-speaking regions'. The situation resembles 'a catch-22 effect'. To adjust the status it is necessary to adopt a new constitution, which, as the course of the constitutional process shows, may be adopted only if the differences of status are preserved. The only way out of such an impasse may be the continued of development of an informal legal system, that is building a system of centre-periphery relations on the basis of non-law-based acts and orders, and the achievement of consensus in the process of administrative bargaining about their implementation, as well as the observance of agreements achieved in the course of implementation.

Realisation of the strategic objectives of 'modernisers' seems to be the most likely scenario. In principle, regional elites welcome the idea of concentrating considerable volumes of financial resources in their hands. Realisation of such a course does not require reconsideration of a large number of legislative acts. In practice, the normative execution may come to elaborate of some laws which will guide the formation and functioning of regional and inter-regional funds of development. But the problem of defining a system of controlling and managing the investment projects of these funds seems to be surmountable only with great difficulty. Vast differences in the economic situation and the need for investments, make it necessary to create a new (inter-regional) level of control system for these funds to function properly. The experience of the last two years shows that regional elites of different territories are deeply suspicious of neighbours aspiring to make a profit at their expense, and not without reason. This suspiciousness is even more sharp if within the regional block there are territories with budget deficits and others with budget over-expenditures (the situation in Siberia). The talks between regional elites of different territories may be more or less constructive only within a stable political atmosphere. In this case, stability and predictability is necessary not only at the local level, but at the federal one as well. Thus, realisation of the 'modernisers' federalism' depends upon the preservation of the existent configuration and personnel of structures of power of all levels, which is hardly a likely prospect for the near future.

The realisation of the strategic objectives of 'statesmen' is constrained only by the fears of regional elites to fall under 'very rigid' control of central authorities. In principle, the restoration of the managerial vertical line requires only the under-law registration of a new organisational structure of a central 'basic' administration (the Ministry of economy in this case) and reconsideration of functions of other central bodies (the Ministry of external economic relations and the State Committee on Property in this case), which can be implemented through issuing a presidential decree or an order of the head of the government, because the law on the government limits the President only relatively to reconsideration of structure of the government, and not in transferring functions from one department to another. However, for actual restoration of the vertical line it is necessary either to change the law on regional council, not to mention the constitutions of the republics within the federation, with possible but, not obligatory, reconsideration of some articles of the federal agreement, or to reach a consensus of the central power with local authorities relative to the range of plenary power of lower (joint) managerial structures. In the first case the main obstacle would be the purely technical impossibility to reconsider the constitutions of the autonomies in time. Reaching consensus with local authorities following the principle 'let's come to an agreement that we'll do this and this not wait until the law is adopted', which could be done in the form of agreements between local authorities and the corresponding central structure, is made difficult by the contradictions at the regional level.

Thus it is quite obvious that, on the one hand, it is necessary to reconsider federal relations, but, on the other hand, this is blocked by the very structure of power at both the regional and federal levels. It is noteworthy that the development of regionalism is to be expected in both cases: if existent relations inside the federation are preserved the regionalisation of 'poor' territories will continue; if relations are changed the 'rich' ones will regionalise. Assessing in whole, it is possible to say, that the second case would be preferable. The number of 'rich' regions in the Russian Federation is far less than the number of 'poor' ones, and with them it will be easier to come to an agreement. Moreover, the regionalisation of the 'rich' may create under certain circumstances prerequisites for concentration of the capital ready for investments into the less prosperous regions. One of the main dangers of political and economic reform in the Russian Federation – the restoration of 'big government' – can be eliminated by dividing the federal budget itself and the investment resources. Of course, such a decision cannot be regarded as theoretically optimal, but it is likely to be the only possible one.

4

Regional Alternative Approaches to Economic Reform

Oleg Grigor'ev, Mikhail Malyutin and Andrei Neshchadin

The first stage of reforms in Russia revealed an important and, in principle, expected peculiarity in their practical implementation, namely a difference in reactions to the nature and pace of the nation-wide reforms in various Russian regions. What is more important and seems to have been less expected is that the Russian provinces initiate an often poorly considered and designed policy of active adaptation of reforms to local conditions. Two main factors shape the situation to date:

- First, the USSR's former economic relations were established to ensure unity of the state. New economic relations will be set up in accordance with the purposes and priorities of Russia as a newly forming ethnic state and political system.
- Second, regions differ very much in their production and consumption rates, despite the official policy of levelling their social, economic and cultural development standards. According to the Rostov scale, Russian regions cover the whole range of development from the 'agrarian' to the 'industrial' stage, extending even to enclaves of post-industrialism (at least in the mid-1980s there were attempts to create technically-oriented regions). Surveys show that the regions of the 'agrarian' stage are less receptive to radical reforms than regions at the 'industrial' stage. In any case, it is absolutely clear that during the present stage of Russian development, the regions are decisive in determining the outcome of reforms.

1 Prospects of Development and Restructuring

Given the enormous territory of Russia, with its utterly diverse local situations, the prospects for regional economic and social development are quite different in various areas of the country.

While in the past the centre used to even out differences in regional development through the centralized redistribution of resources, its abilities to do so are now severely limited. Regions now have to use their own resources and opportunities more, and therefore regional differentiation in levels and paces of development have appreciably increased. The current crises of the Russian economy are likely to affect regions and enterprises, separating them into declining, stable or prosperous units.

It should be borne in mind that those regions which are stable today can run into crisis tomorrow and, conversely, those suffering the gravest depth of crisis at the present moment may be able to pass the stabilization phase more quickly and be able to start active reconstruction. In the Russia of today there are relatively stable zones, but none of them seriously merit being classified as totally prosperous. In the long run it is the orientation of restructuring and industrialization rates that will greatly determine the rate of reforms in Russia. It is no secret any more that the most significant reason for the crisis in the Russian economy was a very serious distortion of the reproduction system developing over centuries, not only over the recent years. In 1992-1994 the liberalization of prices, a sharp drop in the state's influence upon the economy, and the liberalization of foreign economic activities sparked large-scale restructuring of the economy, affecting all regions and sectors. It is worth mentioning that in world history this is a unique case of such large-scale and rapid changes in the structure of a highly-developed industrial economy (e.g., the share of services in the GDP increased by approximately 9% over the first nine months of 1994), which causes tangible difficulties in both appreciation and anticipation of the events in progress.

With respect to factors that have influenced the process of economic restructuring, it is possible to identify at least three periods. During the period up to the autumn of 1992, the main factor consisted of changes in relative prices in the domestic market. At that time the leading positions were taken by the fuel and energy sectors, although pricing for their products was controlled by the state administration. Periodical changes in fuel prices caused global changes in pricing for the whole economy; since the established system of distribution was unable to react quickly to changes in the market, an insolvency crisis developed, coming to its peak early in the autumn of 1992 and resulting in a sharp recession. Over time, changes in pricing proportions started to be less important. In July 1993 most price controls were removed and, starting in 1994, price controls for monopolists' products were eliminated.

However, the linkage of domestic prices to international ones became the main factor influencing restructuring in this period. Starting with the exporting sectors, the process affected the whole of the domestic market in the spring of 1993. By the autumn Russia encountered the problem of lack of competitiveness of domestic industries in the local market-place, which led to a mass replacement of domestic goods by imported products. This further aggravated the economic crisis.

Starting early in 1994, price changes in the domestic market-place, this time influenced by international prices, again began to influence the orientation of economic restructuring. If exporting enterprises previously had had an opportunity to save on expenses due to the relative cheapness of domestic products, they now had to deal with costs equivalent to those on the world market. The chief factor behind rising production costs was transportation expenditures, which are increasingly burdensome for exporting enterprises, many of which are located quite far from Russia's borders.

Each stage of economic restructuring affected the view of regional prospects in a different way. If, during the period before 1992, it was agrarian and locally oriented regions that were considered to have prospects, as of spring 1992 resource-based regions enjoyed the advantage. At present, however, the latter are encountering serious difficulties resulting from the sharp increase in transportation expenses. This circumstance had especially grave implications for the mining industry in the Kuzbass, since even in the European part of the domestic Russian market, priority today is given to Ukrainian coal. Forestry products from Krasnoyarsk are not competitive when moved over the Urals and are barely so when transported through the Far East. A more favourable situation is enjoyed by those industries geared towards the primary processing of materials, e.g., ferrous metallurgy and certain engineering sectors. However, this sector has its own problems. If, in 1990, the share of transportation expenses constituted only 2-4% of the cost of metal products, in 1994 it accounted for 18-22% or, counting raw material transportation expenses, up to 38%. Of the leaders of the previous stage, only those oil and gas extracting industries using pipeline connections have not been affected by the rise in transportation costs.

At any rate, the potential for restructuring has not yet been exhausted. Increases in transportation expenses will entail large-scale restructuring within the country as well as changes in relations with international markets. At present, the consequences of such changes may be anticipated only in a most general way. Only the possible end results and probabilities of various scenarios can be more or less clearly evaluated.

2 Three Directions of Restructuring

At the present moment there exist at least three different theoretical views as to which industries have the best prospects in the medium-term:

- *Extracting industries* (first and foremost oil and gas extraction). As far as Russia's place in the international market is concerned, these are the only efficient domestic industries capable of bringing substantial profits to the state at the present time.
- *Science-based manufacturing industries*, connected primarily with the military sector. In Russia there is a sufficiently large intellectual and industrial potential which may generate successful development of a number of sectors and regions, which will act as an 'engine' of restructuring. However, enormous investments are necessary in order for such technological industries to become self-reproducing, and in fact this cannot be achieved very soon.
- The third way lies in counting not so much on a breakthrough into external markets, as on *meeting demand on Russia's domestic market* by means of stimulating the demand of most local consumers. This variant is oriented toward production of a wide range of consumer goods and development of the agricultural sector and of related machine building and chemical industries. In this view, defence industries will be able to implement true conversion only if they manage to reorient themselves toward manufacturing activities that will serve the domestic market.

3 Regional Strategies

Depending on the availability of resources in the territories, we observe three types of regional strategies with regard to the pace of reform.

- Dislike and sometimes opposition to reforms.
- Slow adaptation to reforms, accompanied by partial price controls and the retention of some old distribution mechanisms.
- Accelerated reform, in some cases overtaking Russia-wide processes.

There are also three types of regional strategies of economic development and restructuring.

1. *Formation of an internal regional market.* The strategy suggests implementation of purposeful regional policy in order to strengthen, expand and diversify economic links in the region. Parallel to the formation of an internal market, expansion can be directed at external markets in order to attract additional

resources. Such a strategy may be recommended to regions that have their own resources and where extracting and heavy industries, consumer goods production and agriculture are relatively balanced; or, alternatively, where there is a possibility of making agriculture and housing construction the engine of economic development.

To implement a strategy of this kind the following measures are required:

- creation of a regional information system catering to local abilities and needs;
- creation of a system that stimulates efficient intra- regional relations;
- guaranteed consumer demand for goods produced in the region;
- creation of incentives for local savings and investment, which could be achieved by facilitating access of regional structures to resources and by providing them with a favorable business environment;
- creation of a system protecting the internal regional market against external expansion.

2. *Strategy of outward expansion.* This is feasible for regions with unique natural resources that have a high export potential, including export throughout Russia. During implementation of such a strategy, the region's viability and self-efficiency is to be ensured by activating relations with the outside world. This strategy may be pursued by all primary extractive regions as well as, to some extent, food-producing regions in the southern part of Russia. To follow this strategy, the appropriate regions need to remove all restrictions on foreign economic activity and to liberalize trade. In this strategy, legally binding commitments to supply local markets with a certain amount of products might be a reward for facilitating access to the international market.
3. *Strategy of passive enthrallment.* Such a strategy may be carried out by the regions which are unable to use their own resources and to expand outwards. Extreme structural disproportions, lack of machinery sufficient for utilization of resources, and/or immaturity of infrastructure are the reasons for choosing such a strategy. Under such conditions, a region would have no alternative other than to offer its resources as a possible object of expansion from other regions. This strategy seems likely to be chosen by resource-based regions located in an assimilation zone and by regions in the European part of Russia. To implement this strategy, regions must have an opportunity to create conditions that will attract external investments. Besides, these regions must have the opportunity to protect themselves against inefficient expansion, i.e., expansion that uses the

region's resources in a way that does not accord with the interests of the population. Such a situation is possible when the host region's understanding of certain resources' value differs from that of the expanding region. Another danger lies in selective expansion, whereby a region's resources are used unevenly. This situation can aggravate the disproportions in the region's economy.

4 Economic Interests of the Regions

With changes in the general economic situation, various approaches to industrial restructuring in Russia's regions bring the regions into conflict. The economic situation in Russia has evolved over recent years. The main sources of income for enterprises and firms have significantly changed and, therefore, so have the budgets of the members of the federation. It should be borne in mind that, for instance, over 40% of Vologda *oblast's* budget is formed from the taxation of the Cherepovets metallurgy enterprise and the joint-stock venture 'Amophos', while 30% of tax-based incomes of Krasnoyarsk *krai* come from the Krasnoyarsk affiliate of the Noril'sk metallurgy enterprise.

Changes in the economic situation are first and foremost connected with the following two factors:

- Firstly, liberalization of prices eliminated the divergence between state prioces and commodity exchange prices, which made it impossible to generate considerable profits from commodity exchange operations. The fact that domestic prices came closer to international ones made the export of certain raw materials and goods less profitable.
- Secondly, the pricing structure changed, which led to a more rapid growth of prices for machine building products as compared to that of prices for fuel and energy resources.

This led to a situation where the export of raw materials is losing its former attractiveness and can sometimes be not only unprofitable, but also loss-making. However, machine-building enterprises which managed to master their reconstruction and to enter the world market are gaining speed in their development.

In contrast to the previous reform stage, regional bodies started to set other objectives for themselves to achieve, primarily that of raising additional financial resources from various sources, such as:

- export and import operations which still generate considerable profits;
- operations in banking and finance;

- direct budget aid and preferential loans;
- taxation privileges, favourable tariffs for exporting and importing.

All this leads to conflicts between industries and also between regions.

5 Regional Interests and Regional Policy

As had become clear even in 1992-1993, incompleteness of the processes of decentralization and federalization makes the regions an even more substantial factor in restructuring at the present moment than they are going to be in the future. With the limited resources of the centre and its shapeless policy, it is the regions that must cope with acute problems. Their interests will largely be determined by the structures of their economies, which are often dominated by just a few industries or economic activities. In this respect, the following groups of regions can be identified:

- *extracting industries*: Tyumen', Komi, Magadan, Buryatya, Khanty-Mansy and Yamal-Nenets *okrugs*;
- *urbanized industrial regions* where traditional light and heavy industries and traditional or technology-based military industries exist in various proportions: Nizhnii Novgorod, Samara, Yekaterinburg, Perm', Chelyabinsk, Krasnoyarsk, Tomsk, territories of the central non-black-earth zone and Udmurtia. The Kuzbass is the most industrialized of the extracting regions and most extraction-oriented of the industrial regions, but at the same time it does not have any prospects of active export development and therefore is bound to the domestic market;
- *trading and industrial regions* specializing in external comprador-oriented trade, especially coastal regions with large ports: Murmansk, Arkhange'lsk, Astrakhan', Primorskii *krai*, Kaliningrad and also Moscow and St.Petersburg. The latter two have very complex structures with large shares of technology-based military industries and traditional sectors and are therefore characterized as seriously depressed, although the situation is somewhat ameliorated by a concentration of financial capital and intensive trade;
- *regions with a balanced combination of agriculture and industries*, oriented towards the domestic market: the central black-earth zone, the major part of Povolzhi'e; the south of Russia: the Don area, Kuban, Stavropol' *krai*; the south of Siberia: Kurgan, Orenburg, Omsk, Novosibirsk, Irkutsk;

- *regions with a clear ethnic profile*: Tatarstan and Bashkortostan, which are economically close to well-developed industrial and agricultural regions, and also Tuva and the republics of the North Caucasus, which are definitely depressed.

As early as 1993 it was clear that the creation of independent regional entities would be more likely to constitute the exception than the rule in the real conditions of Russia. In fact, spontaneous differentiation accompanied by various degrees of independence is the most likely outcome.

Evidently, extracting regions as well as trading and financial regions longed for the first variant of restructuring. However, they were too worried by their own growing problems to think of either their own future or the consequences of their actions for the country as a whole; thus, they left all responsibility to the central administration (with the possible exception of the Moscow administration under Luzhkov).

The referendum held in April and the elections of December 1993 proved that the reforms, understood as a policy of price liberalization and free economy, are supported in Russia not only by local administrations and businessmen, but also by a considerable part of the electorate.

However, at the same time it became clear that extracting regions were keen to turn the advantages of this federal policy to their own benefit and to become as independent from Moscow as possible. This is also true for coastal regions. However, they are too sparsely populated to seriously influence the results of nation-wide elections. Besides, the border zone turned out to be susceptible to speculatory changes of the national map by Zhirinovskii, which made Yeltsin substantially adjust and correct national policy in 1994.

However, as of 1994 it was not the case that the extracting, trading and industrial regions had chosen an outward expansion strategy. Instead of being applied for expansion purposes, all profits were used to counteract the drop in living standards. Considerable amounts of capital were being stashed abroad and neither the business sector nor the administration were able to initiate investment projects, even though financing was available. Evidently, the central administration failed to solve the key tasks, namely regulation of the activities of exporters and trading and financial capital and retention of a part of profits to redistribute them for the sake of implementing national structural policy.

We expected that for all the diversity of their economic structures, urbanized industrial regions – especially those with technology-based military industries –

would for the most part adhere to the second variant of the structural policy. Regions with traditional heavy and light industries were expected to choose to the third variant, oriented towards the markets of the region itself and of the CIS. Quite a few of them managed to break through to the external market, only to face limitations imposed by COCOM and the Jackson-Vanik amendment. On the whole, according to estimates, the first strategy is being implemented spontaneously, while the second and third variants require a definite, purposeful policy. Nevertheless, these regions still remain the most ardent supporters of a united Russia and are oriented towards active relations with the centre. This is so because only this kind of policy offers some possibilities to employ the revenues from the sale of raw materials and fuel abroad in such a way so as to secure the way for technology-based products onto the international market.

At the same time these regions are facing the prospect of severe economic and social hardship, since they have accumulated various distortions which must be eliminated. A huge exertion – on the part of the centre as well as the regions – is required to assist enterprises in adapting to market conditions and gaining access to international markets.

Since such efforts are not being made in a suitably active way, in some cases prospects of development have bee lost. Centres of outward expansion could appear in these regions, but it is more likely that they will ultimately orient themselves towards the domestic market of Russia. The small size of domestic markets is a serious constraint, however, since the industrial base was designed for a substantially larger market. Therefore, an interest in the preservation of a united Russia and of the common economic space of the CIS will remain.

These regions could also use the strategy of passive enthrallment, which entails opening the regional market to other regions and to foreign investors. Not only urbanized industrial regions, but also northern and eastern zones under development could use this strategy. To this end they would need to create extremely favourable conditions for foreign investments, yet in most cases the situation is still in the propaganda and declaration stage. In fact, potential foreign investors are still searching out the most favourable regions for their activities, and regional administrations should seriously think of ways to attract them through, e.g., supplying complete and trustworthy information about local conditions.

Agricultural and industrial regions, which are more or less self-sufficient in terms of food products, are primarily striving to form internal regional markets. They tend to shield themselves from other regions' problems, and accordingly, they show a tendency towards greater independence from Moscow. As internal regional markets emerge and are filled and as problems of sales and profits becomes more acute, the strategy of expansion, above all into other regions of Russia, will be pursued on a wider scale. However, taking into account that the 'first zone' lives on food imports and that the second cannot pay for them, the agricultural and industrial zone is today in favour not only of state subsidies but also of stringent protectionism. These contradictions were fully revealed in the conflicts around customs tariffs of mid-1994. Because of the constraints upon their outward expansion abilities, urbanized industrial and agro-industrial regions will more often defend the policy of protecting domestic manufacturers and encouraging local demand – which, in turn, could lead to a sky-rocketing of the inflation rate. However, it should be remembered that it is in these regions that most of Russia's population lives and, as the present central administration is likely to hold nation-wide elections in 1996, it will have to take their opinion into account.

The natural path of market development leads from regional to national markets, and eventually to international markets. Unfortunately, this path is not entirely suitable for Russian conditions because of the high degree of interdependence within the national economy. Nevertheless, all regions should assist in the development of regional markets. To this end, development of small-scale entrepreneurship and trade should be encouraged, local market infrastructure including transport, roads, communication system and storage facilities should be accessible to everyone, and a system for market information-sharing should be created.

A special problem is presented by the regions with clear ethnic domination, where separatist tendencies are determined by the national rather than the economic factor. However, the majority of these regions are economically depressed, with quite doubtful prospects for development (diamonds are found only in Yakutia, oil and timber – in Komi, where the native ethnos forms the minority). Diffusion of people from the Caucasus region all over Russia is to a great extent caused by their inability to find jobs and stable income sources in their own regions. The North Caucasus seems likely to remain a worrisome issue for the federal authorities over the coming years. Long before the Chechnya war it was evident that it would be fatal for this region to separate from Russia, although for Russia it represented a considerable burden, especially during the crisis period. A different situation exists in Tatarstan and Bashkortostan, where national and economic factors combine to push elites toward separatism.

One way or another, the economic positions of regions and their differing interests must sooner or later compel the federal administration to create and pursue a careful regional policy in order to balance their interests and at the same promote reforms. Restructuring and Regions

Although all regions have experienced a sharp drop in living standards since the 1980s, the degree of decline varies, and we can identify depressed regions and relatively well-off zones. This differentiation is due to an uneven recession rate in Russia's industries. For example, in April 1994 the level of industrial production in the fuel and energy sector was 70.1% as compared to that of January 1990, but in light industry it equalled only 20.5% and in machine-building – 29.1%. The distribution of industries across the territory of Russia was very uneven, and this strongly affects local situations. For instance, the traditional location of the textile industry in Ivanovo and Vladimir *oblasts* made their social and economic situation rather critical. Of course, it should be born in mind that territorially depressed regions do not necessarily coincide with administrative borders of *krai*s and *oblasts*; more often than not, they are more localized and are essentially concentrated in minor towns. When there are many such locally depressed areas in a region, the region may be classified as depressed. When factories close down, unemployment rises, and factories are unable to support social infrastructure, local and regional budgets are severely impacted. In such cases some form of aid or another from the centre to these regions is necessary. According to recession rates, officially reported incomes of the population, and unemployment rates, the most depressed regions are the following:

- republics of the North Caucasus: Kabardino-Balkaria, Karachaevo-Cherkessia, Kalmykia, Adygeya, Dagestan;
- Altai *krai*, Pskov and Chita regions, Chuvashia, Ivanovo, Novosibirsk and Kostroma regions, Mordovia, Tuva and the Republic of Altai.

The mostly resource-extracting regions of Tyumen' (oil and natural gas), Sakha-Yakutia (diamonds account for 95% of the budget as gold and coal became unprofitable in 1994), Belgorod *oblast'* (metals, ores) and others may be regarded as the most well-off regions. Similarly, a group of post-industrial regions with high rates of restructuring including Moscow, St.Petersburg, Nizhnii Novgorod and, to an extent, Ekaterinburg may be called well-off. However, even here the economic situation is determined not so much by the level of industrial development, which is undergoing the same stagnation as the rest of the country, as by development of services – and above all, financial services.

A forecast prepared by the Ministry of Economics in mid-1994 shows the expected ratio of industrial output in 1994 compared to that of 1991. Their conclusions were as follows:

Industrial output will constitute less than 40% of the 1991 output in the following regions:

- Pskov *oblast'* (1 out of 4 in the North-west district);
- Bryansk and Kaluga *oblasts* (2 of 13 in the Central zone);
- all national republics (7 of 10 in the North-Caucasian zone);
- Kurgan *oblast'* (1 of 7 in the Urals zone);
- Altai *krai* (1 of 7 in the West-Siberian zone);
- Chita *oblast'* (1 of 6 in the East-Siberian zone).

Output will be under 50% of the 1991 level in:

- St.Petersburg (1 of 4 in the North-west zone);
- Vladimir, Ivanovo, Kostroma, Moscow, Orel, Tula, Yaroslavl' regions and Moscow regions (8 of 13 in the Central district);
- Kirov *oblast'*, republics of Mari-El, Mordovia, and Chuvashia (4 of 5 in the Volga-Vyatka zone);
- Voronezh *oblast'* (1 of 5 of the Central-Chernozem zone);
- Volgograd, Penza, Saratov *oblasts*, Kalmykia and Tatarstan (5 of 8 in the Povolzh'e zone);
- Stavropol' *krai* and Rostov *oblast'* (2 of 10 in the North Caucasian zone);
- Sverdlovsk and Chelyabinsk *oblasts* and Udmurtia (3 of 7 in the Urals zone);
- Novosibirsk *oblast'* (1 of 7 in the West-Siberian zone);
- in Khabarovsk *krai* and Kamchatka (2 of 6 in the Far-East zone);
- Kaliningrad *oblast'*.

Although in the above list there is not one single region from the Northern zone of Russia, this area has the highest percentage of unprofitable enterprises in the European part of the country (28.5%), and also a relatively high level of indebtedness to suppliers.

Output will equal more than 65% of the 1991 level in:

- Vologda *oblast'* and Komi (2 of 5 of the Northern zone);
- Belgorod *oblast'* (1 of 5 of the Central Chernozem zone);
- Astrakhan' and Ulyanovsk *oblasts* (2 of 8 of the Povolzh'e zone);
- Tomsk and Tyumen' *oblasts* (2 of 7 of the West-Siberian zone);
- Irkutsk *oblast'* and Khakassia (2 of 6 of the East-Siberian zone);
- Yakutia (1 of 6 of the Far East).

This disastrous decline stimulates competition for investments. Real economic progress for such depressed regions can only come through reconstruction and reprofiling of the enterprises located on their territories, which requires large investments.

Two contradictory approaches to the development of production in Russia exist:

- investment in resource industries and further investment in technology-based industries at the expense of profit redistribution;
- investment in depressed industries in order to make them competitive in international or domestic markets even at the cost of insufficient financing for the fuel and energy and resource industries.

It seems that neither of these approaches will be implemented in its pure form, but compromises to address issues of restructuring are being sought. A compromise could lie in investment in the fuel and energy sector with the condition that enterprises in this sector order equipment from domestic manufacturers to accelerate the reconstruction process in engineering.

In the sphere of taxation, most clashes take place over the Tax Code. The position taken by the Ministry of Finance, which is opposed by resource-extracting regions, lies in making the least possible changes despite the obvious flaws in the current system of taxation. The position of the Committee of the State *duma* on economic policy and that of technology-based and industrial regions seeks to shift the burden of taxation onto resource-connected payments and taxes on real estate.

Although a new system of taxation will take effect no sooner than 1996, regional interests differ so greatly that the solution of this problem affects the very fundamentals of regional budgets. Disagreements arise around the fact that at the present moment, the major form of taxation lies in the tax on profits of an organization or an enterprise, regardless of its sectoral identification and real assets. In this case, industries – primarily technology-based ones – are identified as unprofitable and cannot become self-reproductive because of a lack of accumulation opportunities. On the other hand, profits are mostly accumulated in the resource-extracting industries, thus making resource-extracting regions the most successful. Transfer of the burden of taxation onto rent payments and real estate tax is in fact a way of re-distributing profits from resource-extracting industries to manufacturing sectors, which obviously will hurt the interests of the resource regions. It is not without reason that the regions and enterprises of the Urals are pushing for changes in taxation. Conversely, the Ministry of Finance advocates the transfer of the main tax burden from legal entities, levied as the tax on the profit of enterprises and organizations, to physical persons in the form of income tax, which is quite reasonable from the viewpoint of stability in taxation. Suffice it to say that over the first six months of 1994, incomes of the population increased by 13% despite a production recession of 25%. The amount of savings, including accessible cash, reached 20% in terms of incomes, although this figure is somewhat dubious for a number of reasons. Besides, in March 1994 more than 50% of savings were used for the purchase of hard currency, with a drop in pure savings. However, this will lead to a greater differentiation among regions, depending on income levels. Consequently, issues of fiscal federalism are becoming increasingly important.

As was previously mentioned, the structure of Russia's GDP underwent quite substantial changes connected with a sharp growth of services, a major part of which is formed by financial services. These changes become even more prominent when the regional factor is considered. Moscow banks account for 53 positions among the 100 largest banks of Russia, with only one regional bank, the *Zapsibkombank*, to be found in the top 20. At the same time it should be taken into account that the data are incomplete, particularly since one of the largest Russian banks, the *Sberbank*, is not mentioned in the list.

Overall, of 2132 banks working in Russia as of 1 April 1994, 690 were Moscow banks with investment funds totalling 583 billion roubles – only marginally less than half of the total of all commercial banks' collective investment funds (1,344 billion roubles). It should be mentioned here that the 'other capital', St.Petersburg, is far behind in this respect and, regarding the total of investment funds in its banks, ranks fourth in the country (33.5 billion roubles) after Saratov (40.5 billion roubles) and Nizhnii Novgorod (34 billion roubles) *oblasts*. The share of Moscow banks in interbank loans is close to two-thirds, i.e., 1936 billion roubles out of 3191 billion.

The decline in banking conditions which started in the spring of 1994 as a result of a drop in both inflation and interest rates affected regional banks the most, as they had had no easy access to the centralized loans of the Central Bank and therefore had offer a high interest rate in order to attract money. Six of the 100 largest banks suffered losses in the first six months of 1994, and such banks as Komibank (located in the Northern zone where we noted a high level of unprofitability of enterprises) and Altaikreditprombank completely lost their own capital and exist on clients' deposits.

Most regional banks are formerly branches of previously existing specialized banks transformed into commercial banks. Commercial banks which were created anew failed to operate. This conclusion is proved by the analysis of the hundred largest banks. The first group of 19 largest banks is formed by Moscow banks, the majority of which are transformed specialized state banks. The second group which extends to the 70th position consists mostly of regional banks (34 of 51) which were commercialized from specialized banks. The rest are also Moscow banks, mostly created anew with segments of reformed regional branches of former specialized state banks. Even such a well-known bank as Vostok of Bashkiria had not been listed among the 100 largest banks and has lately even found itself on the verge of bankruptcy.

It is possible to speak today of a serious regional imbalance in the development of banking. The over-accumulation of financial capital in Moscow and its obvious absence in the regions are evident. Of 37 trillion roubles in short-term deposits as of 1 April 1994, Moscow's share accounts for approximately 11%, i.e., just under four trillion roubles. Moscow's share in long-term loan deposits is about the same. Money accumulated in Moscow is sent to the market of interbank loans, to the currency-dealing stock exchange, and to speculatory financial operations, which leads to a further divergence between real and financial sectors of the economy.

As a matter of fact, another source of impulses for further restructuring was created in banking. The financial sphere has sufficient means to manipulate the dollar exchange rate, as happened on 11 October 1994. Such manipulations significantly affect the situation of importers (at present almost half of all consumer goods in Russia are imported) and exporters, thereby changing the incentives for economic development. This will continue to be the state of affairs until Moscow banks join the process of loan-based servicing of industry in the regions.

As of spring 1993, financial structures in Moscow, having encountered obvious over-accumulation of capital in the centre, began to actively consider projects of investment in the regions of Russia. However, the acute deficit of circulating assets in the regions resulted in the failure of many projects. Money was immediately transferred to enrich circulating assets in the region, and Moscow structures lost control over them. As a result, a number of banks suffered serious losses. At the present moment financial structures in Moscow are actively creating a subsidiary network which also features the inclusion of weak regional commercial banks. However, this is a long process and it is impossible to talk about possibilities of large-scale investment in the regions until it is complete.

With regard to the situation in customs policy, in spite of an existing Act on Customs Policy, presidential decrees and government resolutions have offered considerable tax favours to certain regions and enterprises. In fact, this is a most common means of budget support to regions and enterprises. Since it is quite uncontrolled and non-addressed, it is absolutely impossible to determine the real amount of preferential payments and to check ways of spending. Such relations are being established with Sakha-Yakutia and the Republic of Komi as well as with a number of other regions including Kaliningrad *oblast'*, Primorskii *krai*, etc. The customs policy pursued by the president also elicits different reactions from the regions since it directly influences the direction of structural changes in the economy.

This concerns, first of all, regions that produce agricultural products and regions that are net importers of agricultural goods. The creation of import duties for food products (meat, milk products, sugar, etc.) was negatively received by large regions importing such products in huge amounts from abroad, primarily Moscow, St.Petersburg, Ekaterinburg and other regions; on the other hand, this action was seen as a sign of concern for agrarian region, mainly the South and Central Black-earth zones of Russia.

However, in mid-1994 the import duty for certain food products was lowered to 10% as a result of pressure from consumer regions. Interests similarly run counter to each other with respect to the establishment of export duties, above all for raw materials and energy resources. Consumer regions are interested in establishing high export duties which would retard the growth of domestic prices and increase the profits of processing enterprises. Conversely, such a situation is unprofitable for exporting regions as it reduces profitability of exports as well as local budget revenues. Import duties play an especially important role for depressed regions, and regions with light and food industries and engineering. For instance, Ivanovo *oblast'* would prefer a considerable increase in import duties for textile goods, and reduction of import duties for cotton to support textile production. Quite often the interests of regions and industrial lobbies coincide, as in the case of introducing import duties for automobiles, since this affected the interests not only of the VAZ, KamAZ, ZIL and GAZ automobile-manufacturing enterprises, but also of administrations of the host cities and territories. In the event that these enterprises had had to stop production, regional budget revenues would not only have dropped, but it would have become more difficult to maintaining housing and social infrastructure and to employ laid-off workers.

6 Political Self-Determination of Regions: Dynamics of Changes in Mass Consciousness

In the chapter 'Political and Economic Geography' of the above-mentioned research work on *Regions of Russia in the Transition Period*, we presented a hypothesis that economic and social tendencies currently forming in the regions would in the near future influence the positioning of political forces, not only locally, but on a nation-wide scale as well.

The starting point for further assessment was based on the results of the referendum of 25 April 1993, a unique 'sociological poll on no-choice elections'. Conclusions were corrected based on an appraisal of the elections of 12 December 1993 and further local elections.

The primary question is how opinions formulated on the basis of the referendum take the rapidly changing political situation into account. By showing that there is a certain connection between the results of the referendum and interests of certain regions in reforms and restructuring, we could demonstrate a certain stability of electors' opinions. Of course, the results were not only influenced by the economic preferences of the regions; on the contrary, it is surprising that from the viewpoint of economic typology of territories the results turned out to be so instructive. As further research showed, a major factor influencing voting results and the economic preferences of the regions is the long-established system of population settlement: the alignment of the rural and urban population and sizes of towns and cities.

Our results showed this to be true.

It became clear from the very start that the voting results in typologically homogeneous zones (e.g., in Kaliningrad and Astrakhan, in Altai *krai* and Kuban, in Primorskii *krai* and Murmansk *oblast'*, in Krasnoyarsk *krai* and Vladimir *oblast'*) are unbelievably similar despite all the differences in the geographic location of regions. This pattern proved especially clear in the position of the Russian North (i.e., the territory between Chukotka and Sacha in the east and Karelia and Komi in the west) which is a resource-extracting region. Such regions try to achieve a high level of independence from Moscow, since they specialize in the extraction of raw materials. The Russian North generally approved of the president himself and of his liberal policies, which seemed to lead toward the first restructuring model. The picture that emerged from the parliamentary elections of 12 December 1993 was less clear, but in general, liberal blocs like *Russia's Choice* and *Yabloko* (Yavlinskii-Boldyrev-Lukin Bloc) did well in these regions. Still, the top place was won by Zhirinovskii who, with a slight majority, harnessed the votes of the discontented. Local elections held in the Russian North mostly failed to make it at the first attempt as electors did not attend. Bearing in mind that less than 4% of all registered voters of Russia live in the North, this zone plays an insignificant role in elections for the lower chamber of Parliament, especially in those held with party-lists, but it has quite a number of mandates in the Federation Council. As usual, the head of the local administration and the director of the largest enterprises were elected to the Federation Council.

The April 1993 referendum showed that under certain conditions, an unpredictable wave of changes in the mass mood could bring about results different from those predicted. It was known that the ardent electorate of the 'party of power' accounted for approximately 25%, the opposition –15-20%, scattered forces – 10%, and that 10-15% were still uncertain but occasionally attending elections. The geographic location of the electorate was quite obvious, too, with a domination of the pro-Yeltsin forces in capitals, major cities, sea ports, resource-extracting regions of the North and East, and in the Urals. The opposition supporters were generally to be found along the western and southern borders of Russia, from Pskov to the Amur, and especially in the densely populated agrarian zone, while the bulk of the population of the industrial 'central zone' was neutral or undecided.

6.1 The Referendum in the Far East

Despite all the talk of a Far Eastern Republic, Kamchatka and Magadan, Sakhalin and the Kurils, Khabarovsk and Vladivostok have failed to come to a positive agreement over the recent years. Taken individually, they are all sparsely populated and, except for Primor'e and, possibly, Khabarovsk, are not even remotely self-sufficient. The future of the Far Eastern region will be determined by its specific nature, since it is a resource-extracting and not a processing region. Utilization of potentially abundant resources is not, however, large-scale enough to ensure economic prosperity. Therefore the Far East is more likely to become a zone for neighbouring states to develop. Indeed, in the past this was the case every time when the influence of the central Russian administration was weakened (e.g., during the initial development phase in the early 19th century and immediately after 1917).

The population of the Far East was not active during the referendum. On the whole, the region voted in support of Yeltsin. Votes 'for' Yeltsin were higher than the average throughout the whole country, but because of the relatively small size of the electorate, the region is close to the middle group. During the elections of

December 1993 (with the exception of Khabarovsk where, with difficulty, *Russia's Choice* almost equalled the performance of the *Liberal Democratic Party of Russia* (*LDPR*), gaining 19% of the votes), Zhirinovskii's *LDPR* won by party-list throughout the Far East. At 36.9%, Sakhalin yielded almost the highest level of support for Zhirinovskii in the whole of Russia. In Magadan this number was 29%, in Kamchatka – 27%, and in Primor'e – 23%. However, the blocs in favour of the new constitution (*Russia's Choice* and *LDPR*) performed splendidly, receiving over 70% in Khabarovsk and Primorskii *krai*s and in Kamchatka, 68.6% in Magadan *oblast'* and 64% in Sakhalin *oblast'*.

Attendance during local elections was very low. The current big shots in charge of the administration and successful enterprises ensured the election of their people, although certain opposition representatives also won seats. In this area, communists and moderate radicals failed altogether during the general federal elections. Everyone was for Russia in word and against the centre in deed. The democrats may make some further gains if elections are held in Vladivostok, but they have become more marginal with respect to the new central and local administrations.

It is tempting to recall that Yeltsin won the presidential elections of 1991 and even the referendum of 1993 throughout the whole zone, and that as of 1990 the democratic movement and various reformist experiments (Sakhalin under Fedorov, Nakhodka under Ustinov, establishment of Vladivostok as a sea port, border trade with China), were the most radical in the Far East, and brought about noticeable changes in the living standards of the masses. Of course, only four million voters live in this huge – and rich! – territory.

There is no significant presence in the centre of the political spectrum. Only the *Women of Russia* gained over 10% in Khabarovsk and Primorskii *krai*s and in Sakhalin. The *LDPR*'s presence was well established (although after their unexpected victory through the party-list in the region, the candidates failed to distinguish themselves) and the party is now trying to gain more influence, pointing to the 'external threat' and the pauperization of some parts of the population. The *CPRF* marginally survived in Vladivostok (gaining around 9% of votes) and in Khabarovsk (12%) – it has over 50,000 votes in each case. The agrarians do not constitute an important factor since, with the exception of some minor farming areas in Primorskii *krai*, the Far East has no agriculture. In this area and in Khabarovsk *krai* some land is cultivated by the Chinese, who were urged to rent land there, Generally speaking, no true entrepreneurs have been elected anywhere in the Far

East; instead, the directors of privatized state firms enjoy the largest number of mandates.

Results of the local elections in Sakhalin proved the forecast absolutely true – previously, the administration and directors managed to be elected through the system of multi-mandate districts, even with the average attendance percentage of 25%. In Primor'e, honest democrats not belonging to the 'Party of power' declared a state of war against the head of the administration, Nazdratenko, who had removed the mayor of Vladivostok by force but had not run the risk of holding his own elections counter to the president's decree.

Khabarovsk *krai* is the easternmost of the large centres where local elections successfully took place. Of blocs represented on the federal level, only the *Communist Party of the Russian Federation* [*CPRF*] and the local *Demokraticheskii Vybor* [*Democratic Choice*] made a serious bid for election. The former nominated 11 candidates, the latter – 15, for a total of 25 seats (five for Khabarovsk, three for Komsomolsk and one for each of the other areas). Sector-based trade unions united to nominate their candidates in practically all districts. All in all, 20 associations, movements and blocs participated, and a total of 118 candidates were registered (ten were rejected). However, this politicization came to nought because of the utterly low attendance; the elections failed in 7 districts. Of course, in such a situation, *Russia's Choice* suffered a severe defeat; it had only one deputy elected from Komsomolsk (who previously worked on the district council of Deputies and at the moment is unemployed). The *Communist Party* performed a little better: a lawyer and a school teacher from Komsomolsk were elected as candidates from a party-list of the *CPRF*, although they lost to an unofficial democrat during the elections to the *duma*. Actually, the communists are themselves unofficial, having nothing in common with the former Soviet *nomenklatura*. Local democrats regard as pro-communists Bubenin, Hero of the Soviet Union, who participated in the battles of Damanskii Isle with China in 1969 and is now the head of Khabarovsk Academy of Border Guard Forces; the managing director of the joint-stock venture *Amurkabel*, delegated by the trade union bloc *For Social Justice*; and the head of Komsomolsk area administration. Others falling into this category are, as everywhere, from the administration and enterprise managers. In early 1995 the local Khabarovsk *duma* unanimously adopted the decision to withdraw from the Agreement on Public Accord. The same was done by the regional *duma*s of Sakhalin and Amur *oblast'*.

6.2 East Siberia (from the Jewish Autonomous *Okrug* to Altai and Krasnoyarsk *krais*)

Strictly speaking, if political preferences and their economic basis are taken into account, all local regions may be divided into three categories:

- *Stable 'traditional' anti-Yeltsinists* since the elections of 1991: Altai with the Republic of Gorny Altai, the Amur and Chita *oblasts*;
- *'Ditherers'*, all from ethnic districts: Buryatia with two Buryat autonomous districts in Irkutsk *oblast'*, the Jewish AO and Khakassia;
- Finally, the *two largest and most developed regions*: Krasnoyarsk and Irkutsk (together with Altai *krai* they each have 2 million voters), which, as of 1990, began to oppose Yeltsin. If Irkutsk ensured average Russian (i.e., moderate pro-president) votes on all issues, Krasnoyarsk provided a voting model for 'reforms' in Siberia.

The regions around Baikal (Zabaikalya) belong to those which have not chosen a strategy of development. This enormous region, relatively underdeveloped and remote from industrial and financial centers, faces serious economic problems. In the long-term, it may become a conflict zone for expansion tendencies from both East and West. The region is not homogeneous. For example, Chita *oblast'* is more drawn toward the southern belt of Siberia, while Amur *oblast'* is drawn toward the Far East. Buryatia, which is more economically dynamic, is oriented toward co-operation with Mongolia and China. Whatever the case, the Zabaikalya region is obviously depressed, yet has potentially promising prospects. Hence the anti-Yeltsin votes.

In both Amur and Chita *oblasts*, Yeltsin lost both the presidential elections and the referendum by a narrow margin. The results of the referendum showed that the Siberian region, barring a few exceptions, presents quite a homogeneous picture of voters' behaviour. The attendance rate is slightly less than the average; in Southern Siberia the question on personal confidence in Yeltsin was answered positively by 48% (Altai) to 57% of the electorate, which is less than the average in Russia as a whole. Moscow's economic policy was supported by approximately half of the voters, and in some regions the negative answer prevailed. Obvious exceptions were Tomsk *oblast'* and Krasnoyarsk *krai*, which yielded a positive 67% and 66% for the first question and around 60% for the second question) and, to some extent, Irkutsk *oblast'* with positive 58% for the first question, although the second question received a lesser number of positive votes than the average in Russia.

Voting results in Irkutsk *oblast'* are quite understandable. The region is into active international trade, primarily with China, and is a center of tourism. Attendance at elections here is the lowest in the region, excluding Kemerovo. At the same time, voting results are significantly lower than those in the northern and Far East regions because of the developed rural sector. On one hand, voting in Krasnoyarsk *krai* closely resembles voting in the Russian North (in fact, this region may be regarded as northern for a number of reasons), while on the other it displays voting tendencies similar to those in the centres of the defence and heavy industries of the Urals and Central Russia (and, like Tomsk region which produced similar voting, it may be regarded as belonging to these industrial centres). Southern Siberia borders with Orenburg *oblast'* which produced voting results very much similar to those of Kurgan *oblast'*.

What was new in the results of voting on 12 December and of local elections of 1994? Except for Krasnoyarsk (where V. Zubov, head of the moderate, democratic *krai* administration is supported by the *Democratic Party of Russia* (*DPR*), and was elected in April 1993 'for the referendum') and Irkutsk (where Yeltsin regularly threatened to dismiss Nozhikov, the head of the local administration, for being overly independent and deviating towards centrism), heads of local administrations did not stand for election for various reasons. In most cases directors were elected into the Upper House, including P. Romanov, linked with the irreconcilable opposition in Krasnoyarsk, and a more moderate head of a construction firm in Irkutsk who managed to beat the head of the *oblast'* council in the elections to the Federation Council. On 27 March 1994 Nozhikov was elected as head of administration in Irkutsk, with over 80% of the votes.

According to local experts, Irkutsk creates the same impression regarding the consolidation of its administration as Nizhnii Novgorod in the European part of Russia did in December 1994: 'strangers' and 'the questionable' were not let into the *duma* at all. In the city province district a *Grazhdanskii Soyuz* [*Civic Union*] candidate was elected, having beaten a *Russia's Choice* candidate and minor local administration officials; in '*uezd*' districts (i.e., local sub-districts) a director from Angarsk and a local head of the region council were elected, beating competitors from *Yabloko* and *Russia's Choice*, and in the rural district the head of local administration, a member of the *Agrarian Party of Russia* (*APR*), was elected, which was expected in view of his position. The *Party of Russian Unity and Accord* (*PRES*) performed well, gaining 13.2%, with the *CPRF* gaining a poor 9.5%. The democrats did not make headway anywhere. *Russia's Choice* received 16.9% and *Yabloko* – 6.7%. Zhirinovskii received only 21.4% of the votes.

Russia's Choice failed to have a single candidate elected during local elections in Irkutsk *oblast'*. Elected were Levchenko, First Secretary of the *oblast' CPRF* committee and a manager of Angarsk construction enterprise *Stalkonstruktsia*, and 15 more delegates who are considered 'pro-communists and national patriots' by local democrats. It was not only the local administration but also the local union of manufacturers and entrepreneurs – closely connected with Y. Nozhikov – that participated in the elections. Therefore, it is not surprising that 21 deputies (almost a half) represent economic management and 17 Deputies are administration officials including Govorin, formerly head of the Irkutsk administration, who was elected as mayor, receiving over 60% of the votes. These figures and more than 80% of votes given to Nozhikov prove the theory of high level of consolidation of local authorities.

In Krasnoyarsk, where pro-president voting was referred to our earlier article as an 'anomaly', voting this time tilted towards the opposition and resulted not only in the election of P. Romanov (currently a leader of nation-wide opposition) to the Federation Council and in the *LDPR*'s gaining first place in Eastern Siberia with 31.2%, but also in the election of three opposition activists in four districts of the *krai*. In fact, the range was complete; in Gubernsk, V. Tikhonov won, a left-wing figure now adhereing to the *Rossiiskii Put'* [Russian Way]; an *LDPR* member in Achinsk *uezd*; and an agriculturalist in a rural district. A chief of the Noril'sk MVD (Police Committee) just managed to overtake another *LDPR* candidate. *Russia's Choice* had 14%, and only *Women of Russia* and the *CPRF* were even close to reaching the level of 10%.

It is hard to say what the concrete results of these changes after the local elections will be, but many people would like to see a Enisei Republic and an alliance with Irkutsk (to a lesser extent with Altai and the Kuzbass). This enormous, wealthy zone is rather poorly consolidated; it has no leader of regional development. In this situation an ex-secretary of the regional committee, (who is also head of the regional council), assisted by Yu. Skokov (head of the local Federation of Manufacturers), led the movement of those discontented with the actions of V. Zubov, a moderate reformist. However, the results of the local elections did not allow the enterprise managers to radically change the situation – they were able only to shift the alignment of forces in their favour. One mandate is with the Union of Labour, which is connected with the *SDPR* and all trade unions, and another is with the democratic party-list in Krasnoyarsk.

The bloc of communists, agrarians, pro-Soviets and patriots came second after the administration, proving that the results of the elections of 12 December held in the *krai* had not been accidental. The republics of Altai, Buryatia and Tuva comprise a zone where the administration is ethnically quite consolidated, having a more traditional basis than the neighbouring regions which are larger and richer in natural resources. Regarding voting results, Altai *krai* produces quite an unusual picture; Yeltsin has consistently lost here since 1991. According to scientific analyses based on research in the Altai, the weak position of the *Communist Party* (which gained 1% less in the party-list than *Russia's Choice* with its 10%) and the complete absence of activists from various anti-government movements, be they red or white, led to a situation in cities and towns, especially in the provinces, whereby the anti-system and anti-establishment mood are amorphous and have no active supporters. At the same time it is well-known that the agrarian lobby in the country is oriented towards compromise with the regime.

It is not clear in what way the local situation will change, bearing in mind the fact that minor *LDPR*-oriented towns have overtaken *Agrarian Party*-oriented rural areas and that large cities voted for the administration officials. Such a situation is absolutely contrary to that prevailing in European Russia, where minor southern towns vote differently. Many people in Altai had long awaited an opportunity to tell the Moscow regime 'where to go' quite openly rather than in a furtive manner! In fact, there are sufficient numbers of those discontent with the agrarian, administrative and 'democratic' compromise of the present authorities and of the resource-holders, and thus the elections agitated the local situation. Sudden shifts in the distribution of forces in the agricultural region are quite unlikely to happen, but there will definitely be certain changes since the elections resulted in A. Surikov, head of the *krai* council, taking charge of the *krai duma*, while only a few candidates from the radical opposition were elected.

Finally, with the exception of the Amur region proper, where two communist representatives were elected to the Upper House, fierce clashes took place 'on the steep banks of the Amur' between democrats and opposition activists throughout the area covering Chita and the Jewish Autonomous *Okrug*. Yeltsin had managed to win the April 1993 referendum in the Jewish AO with the average Russian vote percentage, and now an agrarian defeated a *Russia's Choice* candidate on the single-mandate basis and the Upper House was joined by the chairman of the *SPT* council and by the head of the administration, who had no party affiliation. Thus, an obvious shift in balance to the opposition occurred and the *LDPR*, *CPRF* and *Russia's Choice* received votes similar to the Russian average.

However, something peculiar happened in Chita: elections pushed the head of administration 'down' to the Upper House; the editor of the local *Demrossia*-oriented newspaper and a moderate opposition member (formerly a deputy) and head of the local railroad network were elected. The head of the council slipped down to the Lower House, having gained 27% of votes and trailing (together with candidates from *Russia's Choice*, the *Party of Russian Unity and Accord* and the *Agrarian Party of Russia*) 2% behind the winner, the director of the *Zabaikalzoloto* association. In another district, the candidates of the *LDPR*, which won in Chita by the party-list, and *RDDR* candidates were beaten by head of the State Committee on Property. For some reason, the communists did not participate as a separate force, although their local organization was quite powerful, overtaking *Russia's Choice* by 3,000 votes in the party-list (the latter gaining 10% and the *LDPR* – 30.4%). One possibility is that Chita constituted a case where the long-established elite unsuccessfully tried to cover and 'close' the region, disguising itself under red banners and with aggressive anti-governmental propaganda. Following 4 October 1993, a disaster struck the local administration system, and the 'ideological fighter' turned out to be unprepared for such changes in the action. Our information may be unreliable, but it indicates that in the majority voting by party-list *Russia's Choice* barely overtook the *CPRF*, with the *Agrarian Party* achieving the Russian average of 8%. Local elections will clarify the situation.

On the whole, it is possible to conclude that the Krasnoyarsk disaster left no regions loyal to Yeltsin in Eastern Siberia, though it is difficult to forecast their behaviour during the new period. Moreover, the abundance of republics leads to a situation whereby voting on the Russian constitution is 'nailed' in true Bashkortostan style (as happened in Tuva) with 31% voting in favour, and irreconcilable clashes between the branches of power (according to the most recent information, another round has started in Buryatia) led to no-election local situations. Buryatia councils represented by the leaders of their administration won both local elections and those of 12 December. Altogether, just over eight million voters live in a region containing three urban centres of two-million inhabitants, forming a 'Moscow' in themselves, with a couple of satellite towns on the city ring-road.

Taking the results of the vote on the constitution as an indicator of integral loyalty in Eastern Siberia, it had a slight majority in Altai and Buryatia (55% and 57%) and a scarce 51% and 50% in Altai *krai* and the Amur *oblast'*, a positive 61% and 62% in Krasnoyarsk *krai* and the Kuzbass, 74% in Irkutsk, 57% and 64% in Chita and the Jewish AO. The opposition level of the zone in question should not be overestimated, as nothing in the south of Siberia has any similarity to the southern parts of Russia. Attendance is average, being just slightly over 50%.

6.3 Western Siberia

The seven regions of West Siberia have one million people more than the 'easterners', with a certain symmetry in its sub-division: the Kuzbass and Novosibirsk – two million each; Omsk and Orenburg *oblasts* – one and a half million each; and approximately one million in Kurgan, Tomsk and Southern Tyumen' respectively. The latter has almost completely lost the Khanty-Oil and Yamal-Gas districts, classified here as being part of the North.

In the party-list elections, *Russia's Choice* survived only in Tomsk, where its representatives were elected to both the Upper and Lower Houses. In other cases the *LDPR* won by party-list followed by different forces, depending on the particular region.

A more detailed examination is called for in the case of Novosibirsk. The local elite made numerous optimistic comments on the results, longing for the city to be regarded as the capital of the region. The *LDPR* had its 'classic 24%', with *Yabloko* and *Russia's Choice* each gaining half as many votes, followed by the *CPRF* with 10.7% and the *Agrarian Party* with 8.1%, *Women of Russia* with 7.3%, the locally influential Democratic Party of Russia's with 6.8%, and the *Party of Russian Unity and Accord* with 5.2%. The Constitution bloc enjoyed 50.3% pro and 47% contra.

The Upper House was joined by I. Indinok, temporary head of the administration, clearly ahead with 31%, and by democrat A. Manannikov, a former deputy of the Russian Federation, with 23.4% of votes and 0.5% margin victory over A. Sychev, chairman of the council, who obviously lacked the votes of the opposition. In Zavodskoy district a director with 19.5% of the vote enjoyed a 1% margin victory over a woman *DPR* candidate, and had a 2% advantage over a *Russia's Choice* candidate and a 4% advantage over the leader of the *oblast's DPR* branch. Being a *GS* candidate, the head of the city council tried to hinder the director in gaining the votes but ended up having only 8.8%.

In another municipal polling district, V. Lipitskii gained 13.7% with a 0.3% advantage over a *Partiya Ekonomicheskoi Svobody (PES)* [Party of Economic Freedom] candidate and a 3% advantage over a *Demrossia* representative. In an *uezd* constituency a *Russia's Choice* candidate triumphed, having collected 27% of the votes, or twice as much as the vote percentage won by the *LDPR* runner-up. Finally, in the agricultural Barabinskii district an *APR* nominee received over 50% of the votes, far ahead of *Yabloko* (17%) and the *CPRF* (8%). This data is very illustrative: as one would expect, the region's capital city reveals the type of political behaviour appropriate to other capitals (here, a man in the street would hardly confuse *Yabloko* and *Russia's Choice*, and Democratic Russia is also active). In smaller towns and the countryside the voters have different considerations when voting and the discrepancy between the poll results is large. We can conclude that the resignation of Mr. Mukha did not affect the oppositional mood of the region (the parties of this trend having polled more than 50% votes) and his revenge should have been expected during the municipal elections.

Against the general political background of Siberia, Novosibirsk is highly politicized. Nevertheless, out of 34 deputies elected from 49 single-mandate constituencies to the regional *duma*, only five were proposed by voters' associations, just one by *Russia's Choice*, one represented a certain 'Deputies' and Voters' Club', two more – regional organizations, and there was one communist. 11 were the former regional Soviet deputies, 12 – heads of administration and their deputies, 6 – directors of enterprises of various property forms, 4 – chief agrarians, and as many professors and scientists. None represented commercial structures. The ostracized V. Mukha, one of the leaders of the 'Siberian Accord' obstructing Decree No. 1400 was convincingly elected as head of administration, as was Yu. Nozhikov. The November by-elections added one mandate to each: a politically engaged democrat, a communist, and the centre in the person of a trade-union bound social-democrat.

Such tendencies, in terms of anti-Yeltsin revenge at local elections, can be said to be applicable to the Kuznetsk Basin. Regardless of the significant diversity of the regions belonging to this geo-political zone (they have little in common apart from the highest rate of population density and increased political activity), the regional electoral canvases are almost identical (although the candidates have little to do with parties – for some reasons party affiliation has never been popular here).

Here as well, the ardent opposition candidate, Tuleev, easily won the elections to the Upper Chamber, followed by a democrat and editor of a strike-committee newspaper, Mr. Aslanidi, just scraping in ahead of communist Avaliani (a still more zealous member of the opposition). In Gubernsk, after a hard struggle and only 1% ahead of the rival, one of Tuleev's closest collaborators, S. Burkov, collected a little over 20% of the votes and came in first. In two *uezd* constituencies the director of the regional social policy department and the high-school professor polled over 50% accordingly, in a third a business woman collected 30% – twice the number of votes of *NPG* leader A. Sergeev. All directors and party-bound candidates failed. Tuleev staked his all on winning the local elections and had been thoroughly preparing himself to this end. As far as the party-list is concerned, the number of votes received by the *LDPR* and *Women of Russia* exceeded the average level in Russia (29% and 10.7%), unlike *Russia's Choice* and the *CPRF* (13.7% and 9.6%), while the rest were of minor significance (*DPR* – 7%).

The moderate attendance rate of 34% in the local elections in the Kuzbass allowed the election of deputies in 30 districts out of 35 (in Kemerovo the attendance exceeded 25% in all cases but one, in Novokuznetsk there were three such districts). The list headed by A. Tuleev (the back-bone of it being formed by eight ex-regional Soviet deputies) attained 20 seats, i.e., two-thirds of those elected the majority of which are not vulnerable to any by-elections and therefore consolidate the actual tendency. Meanwhile, the communists from *Trudovoi Kuzbass*, along with the Patriotic Union of the Kuzbass declared their support for 37 candidates from 33 constituencies. Having entered this bloc, *Women of Russia* successfully fielded three candidates. We have already noted the successful performance of this party in this region, in particular during the elections to the regional *duma* from the districts (two seats out of four available), whereas their list was the third with a 10% poll, over 100,000 votes, following *Russia's Choice* by only 30,000 votes and having twice as many as those coming after them. A. Tuleev was unanimously elected chairman. As expected, the pro-Yeltsin administration of Mr. Kislyuk was defeated. Nevertheless, some of the district and municipal administrators made their way to the *duma* – but only five of them, from entirely different political camps. After the humiliating failure of *NPG* leader A.Sergeev in the December 1993 election the miners' committees did not dare to run in the local election with their list. The democrats, however, took their chances in several constituencies and were thwarted once again.

Surprisingly enough, the balloting patterns of Omsk and Orenburg *oblasts* bear a marked resemblance to each other: together with heads of administration, opposition hard-liners triumphed: left-wing intellectual O. Smolin, who had defended Parliament against the President in October of 1993, and the patriotic director P.

Gurkalov. In two districts out of four, ardent opposition members succeeded – S. Baburin (30%) beat 'the independent democrat' S. Nosovets by 10%, the director of the 'Russkoe' joint-stock association from an agrarian constituency in Omsk, as well as an agrarian and a communist in two *uezd* districts in Orenburg. The regional election, however, was dominated by others: a member of the *Russian Ecological Union* – the Orenburg regional Soviet deputy, enlisted in the *Yabloko* list; and the head of the department of regional internal affairs (the latter polled over 40%). The situation was almost the same in Tyumen', where together with the governor, N. Pavlov's brother was elected. The zealous patriot himself missed by a few percentage points the chance to arrange a political 'brotherly reunion in two chambers', and yielded to a popular journalist, receiving 28% of Tyumen' electorate. In the countryside agrarians were elected.

As for party lists, Omsk and Orenburg feature parallel tendencies as well: 21% and 22% for the *LDPR*, 13% for both branches of the *CPRF*, and 16% and 13% for *Russia's Choice*. The only considerable, rational difference between the two was a gap of 10% in the case of the *APR*: almost 18% in Orenburg compared to the national average 8% in Omsk. It would seem that Tyumen' also voted according to this 'profile' – 21% for the *LDPR*, 13% for *Russia's Choice*, 11% for the *CPRF* and 10.6% for the *APR*. The only important deviation was 14% for *Women of Russia* (which, incidentally, collected 10.7% of the Omsk vote). The poll for the constitution in Omsk and Orenburg produced approximately the same results – 57% and 58% respectively, compared to as much as 67% in Tyumen'. Nevertheless, it is generally understood that the constitution was passed in these regions not simply due to the votes collected by *LDPR* and *Russia's Choice*, evidently insufficient for such an all-out campaign, but also due to certain centrist figures. In Orenburg the issue ended up with the former regional Soviet chairman V. Grigoriev taking control over the regional *duma*, in Omsk – an administrator took hold of the reins.

Kurgan *oblast'* manifested its protest against the pro-Moscow course in a specific way: the Upper Chamber let in the regional Soviet chairman and the *GS*-associated agrarian, the Lower Chamber admitted the director of the military school, who had backed Rutskoi, and a *GS*-supported director. Zhirinovskii and the communists harvested their average of 23% and 12% correspondingly, an above average performance was given by the *APR* (11.4%), average by the *DPR* (7.35%) and *Women of Russia* (15.5%). All democrats' lists were far below their average (*Russia's Choice* 11.6%, *PRES* – 5.6%, *Yabloko* – 4%). We have already discussed the 'Tomsk fluctuation': it is possible that it is not the voters' view of Yeltsin-Gaidar that mattered, but rather the popularity of the local authorities personally. The results of the referendum on the constitution were Siberia's highest here – 57% and 68% respectively. It should be stressed once again that the constitution was adopted all through Siberia with the exception of Tuva.

The southern regions of eastern and western Siberia constitute a zone where the domestic market is gradually being formed. These regions (from Kurgan through South Tyumen', Tomsk, Novosibirsk, Omsk, Kemerovo, the south of Krasnoyarsk *krai* and the north of Altai *krai* to Lake Baikal) are not simply resource mining centres, but also industrially developed; their remoteness from industrial agglomerations of central European Russia contributed to their efforts to achieve self-sufficiency. The core of the regions' economy is made up by the mining industry and the production of machinery, processing of raw materials and a relatively sophisticated range of consumer goods. This region attracts the industrial potential of the central and southern Urals, the resources of which are of interest for the southern Siberian industrial complex.

In turn, the latter may be of essential interest as a sales market or industrial base for the agricultural regions in the south of Russia and the black-earth region. In many respects southern Siberia resembles Kazakhstan (out of all CIS republics, perhaps the only one capable of creating a relatively wholesome regional market) and in some aspects these two regions complement each other. Kazakhstan can supply provisions and oil products; South Siberia – timber, machinery and engineering products. Kazakhstan represents a passage to the markets of South and Central Asia, where Siberian products could be competitive. However, in 1994 the formation of the southern Sibirian integral economic complex slowed down, despite its rate of progress in the past. The reasons for this are to be found both in the consequences of the events of late 1993, along with the delusions of local leaders with regard to the government's policies. As a result, the region is gradually losing any prospects for economic development. In fact, 1994 could be called the year of lost opportunities for South Siberia. Here, just as in South European Russia at the beginning of the year, exaggerated expectations gave way to frustration. The search for development models terminated and was replaced almost everywhere by models of survival, with varying degrees of success.

6.4 The Urals

Historically, the Urals resemble the Ruhr, Lorraine, Liverpool and the Appalachians, and the region's industry today is at the state of development where it faces the prospect of experiencing the gloomy fate of its foreign counterparts. In the referendum the Urals voted in support of Mr. Yeltsin with a striking majority. Yeltsin's home-town of Ekaterinburg as well as Chelyabinsk collected over 71% 'fors' on the first question and over 65% on the second, and in Perm' – over 76% and almost 70% respectively. The situation is quite a paradox: the regions which suffered the most under the president's policies, having a concentration of industrial enterprises which had been declared inefficient and even harmful, yielded the best results for Yeltsin.

However, this is just an illusion. The situation in this region is, in fact, hopeless from any point of view. There was nothing to rely on other than a sheer miracle and that was the miracle that the people voted for, voting for the president's miraculous promises. As we had predicted, should the president fail to keep his promises to perform a miracle, both Ekaterinburg and Chelyabinsk could become the first to confront him. The election in the Urals was the least politically grounded or motivated. Evidently the population of the Urals cast their votes in defiance of the opinion of the regional elite, which was dissatisfied with Yeltsin as early as April 1993 (in Chelyabinsk region the opposition elected the head of administration, whom the president did not recognize until the October putsch itself). However, this does not mean that the elite enjoys little confidence among the people. Thus, we can identify voting behavior that is peculiar to the Urals – the 'vote of hope'.

Very geographically compact, this territory (including Udmurtia) outnumbers the whole of entire Western Siberia in terms of population. In 1993 the Moscow regime managed to retain control over the whole region in the course of the parliamentary elections (primarily thanks to the polls of Chelyabinsk-Magnitogorsk and Perm-Ekaterinburg). Nevertheless, the first unloyal tendencies and discontent could be discerned with the victory of the two local administrators in Chelyabinsk region who had been ostracized after the October putsch. In Sverdlovsk, a woman agrarian won, with a close second place being taken by V. Isakov; and in Perm, an agrarian and a professor connected with the *GS* were the winners.

Apart from this, the attendance rate, which along with levels of pro-Yeltsin support had been considerably higher than the national average at the referendum, crumbled (in Udmurtia it was below 50%). Small towns were taken here by the *LDPR*, but it was not sufficient to be considered a victory, due to the high proportion of bigger industrial cities in the region. The communists do not constitute any significant factor here, and agrarians are influential in only a few localities. It is worth noting, however, that the *LDPR* only managed to put forward one candidate prior to the campaign in both Udmurtia and Chelyabinsk. The constitution, as expected, was triumphantly welcomed by 79% of the voters in Sverdlovsk and Perm *oblasts*, by over 77% in Chelyabinsk, but by only 57.5% in Udmurtia.

In general, it appears that deviation from the position of firm support for the reformers in the centre and Yeltsin personally has lately been subject to the local authorities' greater preoccupation with purely domestic problems. It is characteristic of both Sverdlovsk and Perm' *oblasts* that there was only one 'pure' *Russia's Choice* candidate in each, while Chelyabinsk had three *Russia's Choice* candidates. Very few candidates were nominated in all the districts, and the elections failed to take place in one district.

The results of the local election to the legislative assembly of Perm' *oblast'* turned out to be quite unusual. The attendance rate was near the national average of 34%, and the elections were carried in 37 of 40 constituencies. The former administration was in a relative majority (ten seats), representatives of the local business circles took nine seats, and the current administration a mere seven. This is much like what happened in December 1993, when the chief administrator failed to get elected to the Upper Chamber. Since *Russia's Choice* won the party-list poll, he only could put forward one candidate, whereas the opposition put forth two. Formally, they were on the *GS* list; presently one is in the *APR*, the other in the *CPRF*. The fourth candidate was an economic administrator. Two *APR*-connected agrarians made it into the regional legislative assembly. As we have already remarked, the *Communist Party* does not play the first fiddle in the Urals. The entrepreneurs essentially comprise one vaguely formed grouping of 'reform backers' (totalling a dozen). There are six 'centrists', among whom are three enterprise managers, two doctors, and the regional agricultural department chairman.

Thus, we have a kind of legislative medley, where the ultimate political balance depends to a great extent upon 'the hesitating seven', comprised of a couple of managers and heads of district administrations, a businessman, a school principal, and a chief doctor.

Among those who ran on the behalf of parties, there was the unique social-democrat V. Zotin, formerly deputy chairman of the municipal Soviet, who nevertheless made his way through both municipal and regional structures as an independent.

Naturally, in the far more politicized Ekaterinburg and Sverdlovsk *oblast'* the struggle between blocs was conducted in a more purposeful way than in the neighbouring Perm'. In the end the results could hardly be termed 'a party-list' in the proper sense: seven constituencies were preserved as in the election to the *duma* in December, but this time they were the four-mandate ones. The parties were indignant over the fact that in almost every constituency, about fifty candidates ran for four seats, and they feared that ignoring the party-list principle might create an ideal opportunity to falsify the results. All that the political organizations achieved was the opportunity to nominate candidates in their name to 'majority' constituencies.

Russia's Choice finally split after 12th December, with a bloc named *Deistvie* [Action] separating from it. In fact, this bloc had been formed from the team of G. Karelova (presently a Federal Assembly Deputy, formerly the deputy chairman of the regional Soviet and a member of the *Russia's Choice* list, unregistered by Tsentrizbirkom[1]). The actual leader of the bloc was T. Alaiba, who had earlier been from the local *RPRF* [Workers' Party]. The parliamentary centre of Ekaterinburg and the public movement named *Harmony and Honour* as well as the regional women's association joined the bloc (G. Karelova is the chairman of the first and the last of these).

In almost every constituency *Deistvie* nominated four candidates for deputy status, in two districts – three candidates for each spot. The list also included several former regional Soviet deputies – supporters of moderate reforms (*RDDR*, *Kedr*), some of them balloting to the *duma*. The list lost completely, having pushed through one and only one deputy.

It was not *Deistvie* that became the favourite in the election race, but rather E. Rossel's team *Preobrazhenie Rossii*' [Transformation of Russia], which had been formed before the Federal Assembly elections. The adversaries were well aware of the slim chances of winning over a bloc of major state-owned enterprises, commercial structures exporting non-ferrous metals abroad and that part of the 'Party of power' which stood for the Urals Republic. Nevertheless, they met with hardly any serious competition at all. *Russia's Choice* was able to fully 'cover' one four-mandate polling district, while in three other constituencies two candidates were proposed for election; in two others – three and one candidates respectively. Four of them were on the *Russia's Choice* list on 12th December, but only one actually balloted in the district, and failed to pass again (a university professor, Popov). *Russia's Choice* suffered the same shattering defeat as *Deistvie*, having

---

1 The Central Election Committee (note of the editor).

placed one candidate – ex-chairman of the regional Soviet, Grebenkin – a university assistant professor, who was in fact supported by *Preobrazhenie*.

One way or another, 227 candidates submitted applications (109 on behalf of blocs and 118 on behalf of electors' groups), and 189 were registered. Six public associations out of 32 which took part (the second biggest number after St.Petersburg) withdrew from the struggle as early as the registration stage. Finally, every constituency listed on average 30 names of candidates, and even more, as was the case in municipal constituencies of Ekaterinburg. The discrepancy between the hyperactivity of the thin politicized stratum of society and the virtually inert general public did not lead to such confusion as it did in St.Petersburg. As had been supposed, *Preobrazhenie Rossii* outpolled the others at the attendance rate of 32%. Unlike its opponents, this party kept its nominees' list a secret and did not openly put forward as many candidates as the others: four 'zealots' including Rossel himself, and seven more allegedly proposed by voters' groups. Two regional administration workers won immediately in one district with the help of *PRES*, and two were put forward by the *APR* (one of whom was dubbed the 'stubborn reactioneer' by the democrats), one represented the *DPR* (unsuccessfully running for the *duma* on 12th December), and two more self-nominated losers were lucky this time as independents. Consequently, 12 out of 28 deputies who had declared the parties they belonged to in advance were elected to the regional *duma* on 10 April 1994, but in reality there were a little more than a half. 50% of the deputies work in administration, and one third are industrial directors.

Overall, the poll results in the various regions of the Urals closely correlate to one another. The best record of *Russia's Choice* was collected on 12th December in Perm' *oblast'*, and the administration representatives failed. It is thus not surprising that formally having six seats in the legislative assembly of the region out of a total of 40 (the same number as the opposition and the centre each have), the opposition democrats could ally themselves with a dozen or so businessmen and thereby enjoy a relative majority. Rossel was himself successful and his list *Preobrazhenie* won the election in Sverdlovsk *oblast'*, whereas *Russia's Choice*, having split from the moderate democrats personified by Karelina-Alaiba, was crushed and lost its mandates in the *duma* to the *PRES* (2), the *APR* (2), and even the *DPR* (1). At present we do not have at our disposal the data on Chelyabinsk *oblast'*, where the election to the Upper Chamber has not been carried out. However, the clear favorite is a member of the hard-line opposition who was elected on 25 April 1993 in the turmoil of the referendum and who has not been acknowledged by Yeltsin.

6.5 European Russia: A Bird's-Eye View

This is the most heterogeneous region, where the most advanced high-tech branches of industry are to be found side by side with backward agriculture. Leaders of the regions in the European part of Russia do not regard the areas they govern as integral territories, and in this respect they differ from the leaders of the Siberian regions. They can be aware of the problems of particular enterprises, specific branches, separate cities but not the problems of the territories on the whole. The problems they face are resolved in Moscow, or rather it would be nearer the truth to say that they are not really being solved; these territories live off a diet of promises. Thus they are always centre-oriented and are psychologically dependent upon the centre. Local authorities, especially in the regions to the north and east of Moscow, are normally powerless. The fate of the regions depends on a few large enterprises where the directors do not particularly include the local authorities in their calculations, letting the latter deal with routine problems of the area where the enterprise is situated and using them as 'go-getters' in Moscow.

The scientific and technical potential of this region (except *KamAZ* and a few similar enterprises) is of no interest to Western countries, although it may present some interest to the southern and southern Siberian regions, especially if they start to penetrate into the markets of developing countries more actively. In connection with this, the region can be expected to fall subject to Siberian economic expansion, especially in the event that an integrated local market is created in this territory. The 'last hope voting' in the referendum as a polling pattern might have become apparent in a less obvious form in many regions of European Russia, especially in the regions to the north and east of Moscow (because of the support by the remaining village population). These are the Vladimir, Vologda, Ivanovo, Leningrad, Moscow, Nizhnii Novgorod, Novgorod, Samara, Tula (geographically Tula lies to the south of Moscow but it adjoins this whole region and gives a similar picture of voting) and Yaroslavl' *oblasts* and Udmurtia.

The results of the voting in national autonomies in central Russia were worse for Yeltsin than in the neighbouring, purely Russian regions. Possibly, due to the lack of significant natural resources on their territories these regions cannot upgrade their status to something more important and thus the gap between their expectations and reality is particularly painful for them. The results of the voting displayed suprising similarity. Attendance ranged from 63% (Samara, Nizhnii Novgorod) to 70% (Vladimir, Ivanovo), a rate higher than in the Urals (except Sverdlovsk *oblast'*, which can be easily explained). This is apparently connected with the higher percentage of the rural population which, on the whole, participated more actively in the election throughout the country. Positive responses to the first question ranged from 59.5% (Novgorod) up to 69% (Yaroslavl'), with the difference being even more marginal for the second question at a mere 8%. The third question revealed considerable variations (from 28% as per list in the Moscow *oblast'* up to 36.5% in the Vologda *oblast'*), yet they are not too striking to prevent us from placing these regions in one group.

Four more *oblasts* belong geographically to this area, namely those of Tver', Kostroma, Pskov and Smolensk. Here the situation is quite different. If Tver' and Kostroma outlined a moderate pro-Yeltsin picture of the poll ('yes' to the first question on a lower level than the average throughout Russia and 50/50 – to the second one), Pskov gave half-and-half to the first question and 'no' to the second. Smolensk turned out to be in the group of strongly anti-Yeltsin oriented areas. All four *oblasts* belong to the least industrially developed areas in this part of the country, and additionally Tver' and Kostroma have a half-paralyzed agriculture and are incapable of even feeding themselves. It is possible that the pattern of the voting characteristic of the Baikal region was revealed here; one which could be referred to as 'absolutely hopeless', though the high rate of attendance makes such a hypothesis questionable but impossible to entirely rule out because Tver' and Kostroma are much closer to the political centres than Chita.

The central black-earth zone includes Belgorod, Bryansk, Voronezh, Kursk, Kaluga, Lipetsk, Orel, Ryazan and Tambov *oblasts*. These are the regions with a considerable percentage of the tradition-oriented rural population. They are quite able to feed themselves and have a developed traditional industry which can be re-oriented towards the needs of agriculture. The area (with the exception of the Kaluga region which voted very similarly to Tver' *oblast'*) displayed a surprising unanimity in voting.

First, the rate of attendance was much higher than the average for Russia, with Belgorod *oblast'* following by only 1% the all-national record turn-out of Ryazan *oblast'* at 78.5%. Secondly, the results revealed a vehement anti-Yeltsin stance. Nowhere did he poll more than half of the votes on the first question, and in almost half of the regions he collected less than 40% on the second question. Belgorod *oblast'* nearly yielded a constitutional majority for re-election of the president, having stopped at the point of 48.6%. The distinctive peculiarity of this type of voting is that in the majority of republics and regions more voters supported the re-election of the president than the re-election of the parliament. The Belgorod,

Bryansk, Kursk, Penza, Smolensk, Tambov and Ulyanovsk *oblasts* as well as Bashkiria, Mordovia and Chuvashia voted this way. The Voronezh and Orel *oblasts* supported both Parliament and President in equal measure.

Voronezh *oblast'*, the most industrially developed in this region, supported Yeltsin with almost 50% on the first question and the highest level of loyalty (more than 46%) on the second, resembling a typically southern Siberian voting pattern, except in one respect. Low attendance is typical of South Siberia (a little lower than the average), while more than 72% of voters attended the election in Voronezh. The central black earth zone pattern of voting is characteristic of such neighbours to the east as the Penza, Ulyanovsk and Saratov *oblasts* (the latter is the most pro-Yeltsin among all members of this type, but evidently it strongly resembles the Urals pattern of voting) as well as of the national republics of the Volga and Kama areas: Mari El, Mordovia, Bashkiria and Chuvashia (the latter producing the worst results for Yeltsin outside the North Caucasus, with only about 37% answering 'yes' to the first question). In this region, Udmurtia is the area of transition from the black earth zone to the Urals type of voting: attendance is lower (61%), but there are more Yeltsin supporters (56% on the first question, 50% on the second question).

The south of Russia – the Don, Kuban and Stavropol' regions (joined by the Vologda *oblast'*) – yielded a picture similar to that of southern Siberia. Attendance was approximately average (maybe a little lower, but definitely not higher); 'yes' votes on the first question – lower than the average Russian figure and 50% on the second question with a very high density of results (the difference does not exceed 3%).

As far as the extreme west of Russia is concerned (the Kaliningrad region), voting was moderately liberal, almost coinciding with the voting results in Astrakhan (with a slightly higher level of attendance). This region will be a zone of exploration for the neighbouring countries, but rather than natural resources, it will of course be the region's advantageous geographical position that will be probed (although oil and amber are to be found here). Moscow and St.Petersburg voted exactly as expected i.e., for the president and the reforms, with St.Petersburg voting in a more mercantile fashion (62% attendance as compared with 64% in Moscow).

Now it is necessary to look at this picture in the light of the elections on 12 December 1993, giving concrete data about the results of the election in some regions. To this end we may divide European Russia into five zones: the Baltic coast (including Karelia, which is a border area), the non-black-earth zone, the black-earth zone, and the South (in the area between the Don, Kuban and Volga rivers). Such special 'cases-in-themselves' as St.Petersburg, Nizhnii Novgorod, Samara and Saratov should be regarded separately, since their political behaviour is unlike that of the neighbouring regions. The dichotomy 'non-black-earth zone – black-earth zone' has already been considered, and so it will be enough to discuss only the exceptions from the average results. The opposition won two victories in the majority districts (not taking into account the steep banks of the Amur river) in seven European *oblasts*: Belgorod and Bryansk (after the OMON forces' expedition to dismiss Lodkin, nothing else could be expected in these two provinces, including the election to the Upper Chamber – they tried to use the latest experience of Bryansk in Belgorod *oblast'*); Vladimir (two people from the local administration were elected to the Upper Chamber, which we will discuss separately); a similar picture of distribution of votes could be seen in Kirov where the candidates from the *LDPR* and the *Agrarian Party* were elected to the Lower Chamber, and the local administration head and the rector of the Institute of socio-economic problems – to the Upper Chamber; Kursk, Smolensk, Tambov (in these three cases the results of the election to the Upper Chamber are the same – only the opposition); Tver', where the head of the local administration is accompanied by a communist in the Federal Assembly; in Pskov, the situation is similar to that in Tver' (both the head of the local administration and an agrarian deputy are elected to the Upper Chamber and an *LDPR* deputy to the Lower Chamber).

It is necessary to point out once again that with the exception of Vladimir *oblast'* (where a far worse fate awaited the administration in the elections), the results were as expected.

In the non-black-earth zone it was generally a local administrator who was voted in as leader of the local *duma* (Kirov, Novgorod, Yaroslavl'), although there were some exceptions (Vologda, Vladimir). In the black-earth zone, representatives of the Soviets were voted in (Belgorod, Voronezh, Lipetsk, Tambov), with two exceptions nevertheless (Volgograd and Penza). Suffice it to say that not only in the referendum in 1993 but also in the elections in 1991, all of these regions (except Kursk where the so-called 'Rutskoi factor' had a strong influence) voted against Yeltsin – only Tver' had a small majority in favour of Yeltsin on the first question in April 1993. Vladimir gave a 66% vote of confidence in Yeltsin and 58% to his economic policy, which is 5-7% higher than the average results throughout the whole of Russia. 35% voted for his re-election, which is 3% higher than the average figure. People's tolerance ran short after the 'last hope voting'. Similar things happened in Kirov where they had the same average rate of 58% and 52% on the first two questions, and the same 35% on the third question – a relative majority for the presidential election. In the non-black-earth zone, Yaroslavl' was the region affording the most support to *Russia's Choice*, with Gaidar (who played the role of the 'local Yavlinskii' during the period of his dismissal) running on a par with the *LDPR* – Kashpirovskii didn't manage to get to the *duma*, running only a few percent behind a local woman-candidate connected with the democrats.

As far as the rest of the non-black-earth zone is concerned, the local administration authorities were elected, although in practically every region an opposition representative was elected into either the Upper or the Lower Chambers – an agrarian deputy, a centrist connected with the Civic Union, a heavy industry manager. Conversely, in the black-earth zone very few democrats were elected (Voronezh –*Russia's Choice*, Penza – *Yabloko*); the authorities (with other political orientations) were elected there without problems. In each case there is a concrete situation behind this homogeneous picture, but there is not always enough information to understand it. As expected, the Baltic coast remained loyal to *Russia's Choice*, including the party-lists, except for the true Russian Königsberg region, which elected Shumeiko and the leader of the local administration to the Upper Chamber, as well as a military lawyer from the *RDDR* to the *duma*, but when voting by party-lists it voted for the *LDPR*: this area is home to many military men, including those in retirement, and people are uncertain of the future as far as keeping the zone as an enclave of Russia is concerned.

The South voted quite specifically: the success of the *LDPR* 'through television alone' (there were no other candidates at all except one in the Kuban) moved the *CPRF-APR* to the second/third place and with the exception of Volgograd where a *Yabloko* deputy was elected and two people in Rostov, the democrats were politically out of action. In the Don region four out of six elected Lower Chamber deputies belonged to the opposition (two from the *CPRF*, one from the *SPT*, one from the *APR*) which can be attributed to the local influence of the black-earth passions against Moscow. In the Kuban and Stavropol' regions almost no candidates belonged to any party (except one from the *APR* in each region); this was true for three candidates out of four in Volgograd. This situation is also characteristic of the middle Volga (four out of five in Samara, both in Ulyanovsk, all six in Nizhnii Novgorod). Except for Saratov (where three heads of the administration gave the population an opportunity to elect any of them not only to the Upper Chamber but also to the Lower Chamber), a non-Party candidate did not get enough votes: one from *Russia's Choice*, one from the *CPRF*, one from the *LDPR*. To the south of

Moscow the constitution passed in Samara and Tula with 57% and 58%, while in Kaluga, Rostov, Ryazan, Saratov and Ulyanovsk it was hardly adopted at 50-51% (all these regions have powerful authorities).

The results of the local elections introduced changes in the situation. In December in Nizhnii Novgorod, the local elite which had looked consolidated split into regional and municipal factions in the local elections. When B. Nemtsov understood that the ex-head of the regional Soviet E. Krestyaninov, a deputy in both the old and new Federation Council, was losing to the ex-city head D. Bednyakov, Krestyaninov withdrew and the elections were cancelled. Bednyakov was dismissed by presidential decree and I. Sklyarov, first deputy head of the regional administration, was appointed mayor. A real 'mini-Vladivostok', but with no direct violence and with legal sanction from Moscow. Similar conflicts (the governor vs. the head of the province) took place in Vladimir, Omsk, and Novgorod, ending in all cases with the 'top dog' winning. The situation in Saratov ended with the death of Y. Kitov, the former mayor who had lost the election to the Upper Chamber and had been dismissed. It is still unclear whether his death was suicide or murder.

In all these cases, the cowardly and cynical step of dismissing the mayor greatly damaged the reputation of each of the victorious governors. In the 'Nemtsov case' the cancellation of the election of the city head led to low attendance, although both the regional and the city *duma*s were elected (in the latter A. Maltsev from the *SPT* and ex-secretary of the CPSU-91 city committee became first deputy head, although he could have become the actual head if he had so desired). In any case, a sharp decrease of the reputation of the new local authorities and their influence over the way things are done in Nizhnii Novgorod on the whole became a reality: the idea of the fast creation of capitalism failed to succeed. Although the greater part of the electorate voted for Khakamada, the local democrats and businessmen have a feeling of complete 'nomenclature revenge'. Nemtsov plays the role of a local 'Boris', having the habit of granting people an audience and hearing them out, yet not really hearing anything and doing only what he wants.

In Tambov as well as in the Kuzbass, the Soviets took office again with the same leader. In Tumen (8 out of 17) and Ivanovo (10 out of 23) the factory directors triumphed. Vladimir *oblast'* turned out to be highly politicized, much to the chagrin and ill-fortune of administrators: representatives of four communist parties were nominated to the legislative council. Two out of four candidates from the *CPRF* were elected: the deputy manager of a factory and the headmaster of a village school. An unemployed man from the *VKP(b)* was also elected; candidates from the

CWPR [Communist Workers' Party of Russia] and the *RCP* [Russian Communist Party] failed; and two more directors were elected with the support of the communists.

There were five representatives from *Demrossia* (a head of department in the *Murommashzavod* enterprise was elected). The *LDPR* had three candidates but none were elected, and the head of the Kovrov Construction Works representing Zatulin's *Union of Entrepreneurs for a New Russia* was elected instead. The two solitary candidates from the *APR* and S*DPR* were unsuccessful.

In terms of social composition it should be noted that the directors dominate (7 out of 20, the elections not being held in one province only), along with six representatives of the administration (including the first vice-head and deputy head of the regional administration – out of 20 nominated in almost every district!). The rest of those elected are teachers and school headmasters (five in all) who now intend 'show the people how to live', as well as two unemployed persons. The former second secretary of the *oblast'* committee N. Vinogradov became head of the regional council; Along with A. Tuleev, Vinogradov defiantly refused to sign the Treaty of Social Accord. Another example of the success of the 'pure' *Communist Party* (i.e., without allies) is Astrakhan, where it secured 4 out of 17 seats.

In the case of the Volga area it is reasonable to look at the results of the election in Saratov on the 29th of May where there was a voting list of the parties (which is a very rare thing) according to which a dozen seats out of 35 were available. This allows us to compare the results of the elections in May and December. With an attendance of 38% (606,000 voters of a total number of eligible voters of over two million) the elections were held in 24 election areas out of 25 and all proved be valid, which is certainly not typical.

The norm for the registration of the list was reasonable – 20 thousand signatures (1% of the electorate) was needed to register. *Democratic Choice* and the *CPRF* got only one deputy elected, and other parties didn't manage to achieve even this result. Only one entrepreneur from the 'new' businessmen succeeded, as well as many administrators in rural constituencies and the former head of the regional Soviet. Consequently, a representative of the *Agrarian Party* was elected head of the local *duma*, with a communist as deputy head (they received 30 votes, with four against).

Below are listed the results of the vote by party-lists. The number of votes in thousands is in brackets; the second column shows the results of the voting on 12 December 1993.

	May	December
Za narodovlastie (*CPRF* + *Women of Russia*)	3 seats: 27,9% (169,3)	15,3% (159,7)
CPRF		9,9% (103)
'W.R.' *APR*	3 seats: 22,2% (134,6)	7,6% (79,9)
DPR (extreme nationalists, almost like the *LDPR*)	1 seat: 10,35% (62,8)	6,45% (67,5)
Union of Retired Officers (strict discipline with no clear ideology)	1 seat 10,23% (62,1)	
Democratic Choice (in December – *Russia's Choice*)	1 seat: 10,2% (62)	12,3% (128,6)
Yavlinskii's Bloc (here it is a moderate Democratic Russia)	1 seat: 7,9% (48)	8,6% (89,7)
3 more parties failed to pass the 5% barrier:		
Labour (alliance of the FNSR and city administration)	4,77% (28,9)	
Saratov zemskii soyuz (local 'white patriots', close to *ROS*.)	3,98% (24,2)	
PRES	2,44% (14,8)	5,7% (59,4)

After winning the party-list in the Saratov region with 375,300 or 22%, the *LDPR* didn't nominate anybody to the regional council either according to the list or by nominating candidates, proving once again that local elections are not its priority interest. The rest of the results are quite interesting. The *CPRF* retained its electorate, securing another ten thousand votes at the expense of its alliance with *Women of Russia*. With a much lower rate of attendance the percentage doubled. The agrarians, supported in town by the S*DPR*, trebled the percentage by doubling their electorate. The *DPR* received an increase in votes, proving the hypothesis that if the *LDPR* does not participate, dissatisfied people will vote for *DPR* and the agrarians. About 90,000 supported two other lists of the 'white opposition' – the officers (who got another candidate through in the majority election district) and representatives of the '*zemskii soyuz*'. *PRES* suffered an unprecedented defeat, showing that this was 'the phenomenon of 12th December' in Saratov: the electorate of *Russia's Choice* and *Yabloko* had decreased by half (110,000 for both) and even with the *PRES* this constituted less than one-fifth of the votes.

Voronezh *oblast'* is interesting as the biggest centre of the black-earth zone of European Russia. No-one was elected in eight districts in Voronezh (in the autumn bi-elections in the five districts where the election was finally held, the communists and their supporters were elected). The local united democratic bloc did not get anyone through (the same thing happened in Rostov, though deputies were actually elected there). Among the 36 elected, 15 are head chairmen of the local administration and six represent the executive branch. The bloc created by the *Communist Party* had 11 candidates elected (six members of the *CPRF* and five heads of collective farms and of an enterprise in one small town). The 'new business' bloc known as 'Peter the Great' had one entrepreneur elected, and two administrators were elected with its help. Apart from this, no one. On the Don the situation was very similar with a slight difference in numbers. The ex-chairman of the regional Soviet, I. Shabanov, became head of the Voronezh *duma* (he did not get elected into the Upper Chamber because a democrat was elected: there was a split of the electorate with the 'red director' G. Kostikov). Therefore it is not everywhere that the administration alone gets elected, although such regions do exist – 21 out of 45 deputies in Kaluga *oblast'*, 8 out of 12 in Ryazan *oblast'*, 12 out of 34 in Novosibirsk were administration workers, but almost nowhere were the democrats elected.

In the Kuban area, unlike all other areas where the deputies were finally elected in November 1994, the voters were going to the booths for the first time, almost a year after 12th December. In terms of the size of the electorate, the region has the fourth largest population in Russia – more than 3.5 million, just behind St.Petersburg (3.8 million, and where by this time the by-election was finished) and Moscow and Moscow *oblast'*. In December 1993 the Kuban area constituted a variation of the 'southern-opposition profile of voting', as M. Malyutin and O. Grigor'ev called the situation in those elections when (a) the *LDPR* receives over 30% by the party-list, (b) the *Communist Party* comes second and the agrarians third, (c) all of them get more votes than the average, and (d) attendance is higher than the average Russian figure. In this sense, the Kuban area was not the extreme example of opposition: the *LDPR* got only 25.5% – just a little more than the average indices (with 38.5% in the neighbouring Stavropol' and more than 30% on the Don), the *CPRF* got 16,8% (5% over the average, just as on the Don), the agrarians shared the third to fifth places with *Russia's Choice* and *Yabloko*: all three attained from 9.5% up to 12%.

Very peculiar regional deviations are concealed in these average rates and figures: for example, in Krasnodar *Yabloko* got first place (17.4%), coming ahead of the *LDPR* (17.3%). In the majority districts only the opposition representatives were elected to the *duma* (for example, a journalist and 'exposer of corruption' nominated by the *DPR* in the Sochi district outpolled K. Zatulin, who was nominated by *PRES*). The opposition was connected with the *ROS* headed by S. Baburin and concentrated in *Rossiiskii Put'*, although there was also a communist and an agrarian. N. Kondratenko, former first secretary of the CPSU regional committee and current Cossack chieftain, was the first elected into the Upper Chamber, having outpolled all other candidates. The second was the then-head of the regional administration and the current head of the State Committee for Nationalities N. Yegorov, but this was not easy for him. He was accused by other groups of the 'Party of power' and by the local democrats of falsifying the election.

What then was revealed with the unsealing the ballot-boxes in November? The attendance, as should have been expected, was less than in previous year, yet nevertheless was quite decent – around 50%, which was incidentally as much as in spring 1994 during the local elections all over southern European Russia. As a rule attendance is highest in the countryside polls. The Kuban *kraiduma* has been elected in full, all 50 seats, while approximately one quarter of the deputies have still to be by-elected to the municipal *duma* of Krasnodar, yet the result is 'on hand'. The elections to the *krai-duma* have been won by N. Kondratenko's *Otechestvo* [Fatherland] – 16 seats, or approximately one third of the total. This organization is a local version of *ROS* (or, according to the State *duma* – of *Rossiiskii Put'* – that is, the bloc of 'red-white opposition to the occupation regime'), which is tactically close to the former *FNS-93* [People's Salvation Front]. Furthermore, two *CPRF* deputies took their seats, three mandates went to Cossack chieftains of various oppositional trends, while the *Veteran Union* and the *Slavic Union* shared two seats; altogether, they nearly attained an absolute majority. One mandate was given to the *Kuban Revival Union* but that 'one' was indeed worth many, since it was assigned to the former chief (1991-1993) of the *krai* administration, Mr. V. Dyakonov, notorious for his tricks and scams (subsequently dubbed 'Vaska the toilet pan' by his opponents) and who was later eaten up by the 'Party of power'. During the 12th December elections he attempted to exact his revenge and to break through to the Upper Chamber, riding on the back of the local *Russia's Choice* adherents (which incidentally explains their considerable poll results attained as per party-list, and despite being 5% less than the national average, an elementary analysis has revealed that these two figures almost correspond.)

Today Mr. Dyakonov is again in opposition – now as an autonomist. The second and the third places with nine mandates each (one-fifth of the *duma*) are shared by the present 'Party of power', the locally named *Kuban* and the *LDPR*. In actual fact, the *Kuban* received more mandates due to the fact that most out of the eight representatives of the voters' groups were still oriented towards the *Kuban*- approximately the same one-third as the 'pure' *Otechestvo* possessed. In the country-side, the *APR* gave support to *Kuban*, as did the majority of the district authorities; in Krasnodar proper, an old conflict lingered on, which was only resolved on the eve of the elections by President Yeltsin's decree (with its extremely vague wording) to remove the municipal administration chief Mr. V. Samoilenko from office. The opponents referred to him as the 'godfather connected to the Adygeian mafia clan'; he himself considers this to be nothing but intrigues on behalf of the 'post-Egorov' *krai* administration. He has not yet managed to get elected to either the *krai* or the municipal *duma*, but nevertheless he intends to keep struggling.

Despite being nominated in about half of the total constituencies, not a single democrat from either *Yabloko* or *Russia's Choice* has been elected, yet since this is true of the situation everywhere in the Kuban, it is of little interest for discussion.

For its part, the *LDPR* phenomenon merits a detailed description. A quarter of all votes as per party-list had been collected by 12th December, mainly in the smaller towns (which corresponds to the general electoral model of this party, as outlined by O. Grigoriev and M. Malyutin). Today, this party has clearly won the electorate of the principal city – 10 mandates to the municipal *duma* of 27 seats – more than *Otechestvo* (four) and the 'Party of power' (five) put together. Out of its nine seats in the *krai-duma*, six were provided by Krasnodar. All this happens in a context when the 'führer' traditionally neglects local elections, regarding them as unworthy for a candidate for the presidency. Judging from the low attendance rate, the former *Yabloko* electorate – which had constituted 17% in Krasnodar – simply failed to show up on the day at the local elections and the *Russia's Choice* electorate voted instead for Mr. Dyakonov. As one apt remark by I. Klyamkin would have it, just as in times of old the formula that 'the cobble-stone is a weapon of the proletariat' had been true, now the ballot paper is the weapon of protest). Accordingly, the plebeian electorate, for whom both *Otechestvo* and *Kuban* are just varieties of local authority, used its modern day cobble-stone to batter them both, and Moscow to boot.

Naturally, all this electioneering has as yet little direct relation to the question of power. President Yeltsin cancelled the chief administrators' elections for the third time in 1994 (the first time having been in autumn 1991), but there were always some 'hard nuts to crack'. Y. Nozhikov in Irkutsk and V. Mukha in Novosibirsk still managed to hold gubernatorial elections in 1994, while Mr. Kondratenko had scared his opponents half to death. Long before that he had promised to put all of the present 'Party of power' in jail as criminals; his range of ideological curses is certainly rich and it is barely possible to find a plot (by the masons, Armenians, Chechens and so on) against which he has not pitted his might. Hence, the demand to elect the *krai*'s chief administrator becomes an ideal battering-ram in the hands of the new *duma.* Theoretically, we were able to clearly predict such a situation as far as the Ural and Primorskaya Republics were concerned, but E. Rossel and E. Nazdratenko – the indisputable leaders of the local establishment – abstained from appealing to the masses. For the same reason even A. Tuleev preferred not to 'rock the boat' despite his inveterate enmity towards E. Kislyuk, and never seriously tried to play this card in the Kuznetsk Basin. 'Father Kondratenko', much respected by a part of the 'old school' bureaucracy and at the same time the populist leader of a stratum of moderate anti-system opposition, is a unique figure – 'a new cultural specimen of the struggle for regional democracy'. Perhaps not merely regional. At one time Yeltsin and Lukashenko also seemed like entirely provincial 'scare-crows'. In general, the Kuban is a region of agrarian boom and internal market development; and judging by purely economic criteria in 1994, it gave no impression of decay. On the contrary, according to economic parameters it was predicted as a growth point, unlike in politics.

In November, the 'cobble-stone' poll could be observed in its clearest form in Voronezh. Compared to the opposition model in the Kuban south of 12th December, which was a little vague (the *LDPR* lacked almost 5% to overcome the 30% limit, and the agrarians barely reached the 10% level), the actual capital city of the central black-earth region proved classical for such a polling pattern, although not extremely opposed. In spring no candidates were elected from Voronezh to the regional *duma* because the voters failed to show. Somehow, the municipal *duma* was formed. Nine constituencies' representatives balloted to both *duma*s, and only five of them made it into each one. The results were similar: in the first case four communists and the head of *Trudovoi Voronezh*, and in the second, four communists and the head of the 'land tenure committee', put forward by the military. The latter collected exactly as many votes as a 'regular' communist, but so as to avoid having to organize by-elections, he was approved as a deputy although he had been unregistered earlier – a precedent no worse than any other! *Yabloko* had fielded four candidates, and there were a few more formally independent democrats, whose best achievement was 1300 votes, with a qualifying level of 3000.

This does not necessarily mean that in the south it is the opposition that always triumphs, while the authorities and liberals stampede in panic. In this respect, Rostov provides a vivid counter example in either autumn or spring. Three seats in the regional *duma* were taken by the *Yabloko* candidate, the chief administrator of the region and in the case of the third seat, as if specially trying to make life easier for Russian political science, the administration's protege came first, followed by the *Yabloko* candidate. In the municipal *duma Yabloko* placed two candidates out of four seats, and the elections to the two remaining seats failed to take place once again. The Don region is a very peculiar place in Russia (the proportion of the urban to rural population here is three to one compared to 50/50 in the Kuban). The local countryside still votes for the 'democratic alternative', and there are administrators who in principle are capable of winning the local campaign, taken in the context of the typically southern background of a two-thirds opposed electorate in the party-list ballot, and four out of six deputies stuck to the opposition in the majority constituencies in the *duma*, and so on. The Don region is the sixth largest Russian constituency (the fifth largest after the Kuban is Sverdlovsk *oblast'*) and the last in the 'over three million' group, followed by Nizhnii Novgorod. In Omsk the situation with the by-elections is similar to that in Voronezh (five mandates for the *oblast'* and six for the city). In spring, no one from 'Gubernsk' was elected to the regional *duma*, and the municipal *duma* was hardly formed.

In Murmansk the actual by-elections cannot be as clearly interpreted as the southern ones. The last time, the dismal turn-out made it impossible to elect the quorum at all. In Omsk everybody was by-elected one by one: a communist, a director, a 'new Russian' to both *duma*s, a social-democratic journalist to the regional one, a trade-union enthusiast – to the municipal *duma*, while the remainder were 'ordinary' people, not engaged in politics and without the burden of authority. Generally, the initial celebrity of a candidate is of minor importance. The voters assign him to either an ideological-political orientation or a particular position. From here on, everything depends upon the candidate's activity and money. In Murmansk the elections to the regional *duma* were arranged according to the 'Sakhalin pattern' – four three-mandate constituencies, and the number of those succeeding was seven – exactly enough for a quorum. As for the political 'colourings' of the elected organ, the first in the constituencies were: the regional trade-union chairman ('half-red' in the local democrats' opinion), a district administrator, a director of an enterprise, and a sailors' union leader. The second were: two women (from the women's union and trade union, with *Women of Russia* on the whole achieving their best national results in this region), an ardent communist and former USSR Congress deputy Mr. Zolotkov, and a 'green'; the third (i.e., the losers) consisted of a trawling-fleet captain, a geological research institute worker from the town of Apatites (RSDPP), a kick-boxing champion and a militia man, evidently to neutralise the kick-boxer. Party participation was displayed by the *CPRF* and *Yabloko* only (within the framework of the northern voting pattern, with its low attendance, the latter is not favoured).

Finally, we have the preliminary results of the laborious and sad story of how the Sobchak-St.Petersburg democracy had a relative and solely local triumph after three futile attempts to win. At the second round of the second stage all attendance restrictions were removed. (To put it simply, if three drunkards accidentally stumbled into a polling-station, one of them could be elected by a majority of two votes). The average attendance overall amounted to 13%! In such a situation even the most experienced professionals find it hard to discuss the comparison between the autumn and spring results. According to the first round of the autumn 'marathon', the situation was much akin to the 'cobble-stone' ballot, with one third (8 out of 24) balloting during the second round on behalf of *Communists of Leningrad.* The local 'Boldyrev model' of *Yabloko* named *Lyubimyi Gorod*' [Favourite City] fielded six candidates. In fact, in the end their chances balanced out and they received three mandates each (in spring *Yabloko* added five more mandates and took first place), as many as *Democratic Unity* did. In all three cases its nominees were disguised as if proposed by 'voters' groups'. In the end *Democratic Unity* shared the second place with ambitious businessmen/directors representing *All Petersburg*, but the latter failed to push through more than one of its members in the autumn. In all, there were seven mandates for each list. Three seats were taken by the communists as a whole and three by the movements *Petr Velikii* [Peter the Great] from Moscow. It is not very clear what distinguishes it from *All Petersburg* and *People's Consolidation* which has a leftist, self-administrative orientation – and both added two more seats to these three in the autumn.

Two seats were taken by *Democratic Choice*, in last place as per party-lists, and differing from *Democratic Unity* in nothing more than the leaders' personal ambitions and source of financial support. Extreme miscellany and terrible reciprocal altercations between all ideological orientations characterized the 1994 local elections in St.Petersburg, along with minimum electorate participation (the highest attendance of 25% was in the first round held in the autumn). It was not by accident that St.Petersburg was way ahead of any other region in Russia in the number of electioneering blocs (both proposed and registered).

In Sverdlovsk *oblast'* the segmentation was less insane. The grotesque capital-city ambitions multiplied by the provincial mentality have brought about the split-up of both the 'party of power' (into Maier's faction – with four loyal deputies deployed in spring and one in autumn – and the representatives' faction, genetically linked to the summit of the former municipal Soviet *Democratic Unity*) and others: businessmen, directors, opposition democrats and social democrats. In spring, the most ridiculous and mismatched alliances were mushrooming merely in order to collect the qualifying number of votes and to attain the right of nomination from the list, which was easier than from the voters' groups. Somehow, the communists' parties were the only ones to abstain from this orgy.

7 A Typology of Regional Voting Patterns

The typology of regional voting patterns can be seen as the political reflection of conditions of economic reforms. Using this approach, we can distinguish the following polling patterns, manifested at the referendum of 25th April 1993 and their further development:

1. The *northern 'export-based' pattern*, featuring relatively low attendance and a great degree of support for the president and his socio-economic policies, fading away as we move from East to West and from North to South. The party-list poll here favours the *LDPR*, *Russia's Choice*, *Women of Russia* and *Yabloko* (in descending order). Directors and administrators are elected to both parliamentary chambers. The local elections are scarcely attended and lack politicized deputies. In its pure form this pattern stretched from Murmansk to Vladivostok, although the total electorate of less than ten million is insufficient for parliamentary elections, especially per party-list and is therefore negligible. The steep reduction in attendance and the weakened impact of the democrats caused the 'capital city 1993' pattern to rapidly evolve here in 1994. Due to the scattered and feeble opposition the local authorities did not sense any serious menace in low election attendance. However, when it comes to permitting nation-wide gubernatorial elections – which have already been banned three times by President Yeltsin since 1991 – the excessive politicization will inevitably explode in an unpredictable direction and seize all electoral zones of one million voters and over.
2. The *Baikal region 'depressive' pattern*: low attendance and little confidence in the president and his policies. The *LDPR* prevails as per party-list, the *Communist Party* outpolls *Russia's Choice*, few politicized candidates make it to the *duma*

and the Federal Assembly, mostly representing the opposition. The data on local elections in this scarcely populated zone are not yet available and do not allow one to draw up a complete assessment, but what is obvious, however, is the domination of the administration and members of the economic leadership. There is an impression that growing public discontent regarding Moscow causes the smaller non-black-earth regions of European Russia to evolve in the same 'hopelessly depressive' direction, when the people have run out of stamina to even 'wield their cobble-stones' on a wide scale in elections. Chita in the Baikal zone is probably a logical extreme limit of such disintegration, when the opposition party-lists' results have nothing at all in common with the outcome of the elections in the constituencies.

3. The *southern Siberian pattern* is characterized by average attendance and a moderate pro-president attitude. Voting may vary from the approval of his policies to the wish to hold presidential reelections at the proportion 50/50. The *LDPR* won the party-lists with its average national results (even exceeding the 30% mark in Krasnoyarsk) in all regions except in the case of the Tomsk *oblast's* 'democratic anomaly', followed by the agrarians in some regions and by *Russia's Choice* in the other. *Women of Russia* performed admirably, as did *Yabloko* in some constituencies. It was primarily the opposition which ascended to the Federal Assembly as well as to the *duma*, although formally one-third of the Lower Chamber is composed of Sibirians who have no clear political position. Only in the Kuzbas were the local elections won by the opposition – generally it ranks second to the regional 'party of power'. The above polling pattern is typical for those large regions of European Russia where the communists are weak. The danger of an imminent detonation of conflict in 1994 along centre vs. Siberia lines has now abated.
4. The *Urals pattern* displays high attendance in densely populated regions in support of Yeltsin and his policies, regardless of its apparent incompatibility with the local economic structure. In the Urals proper, through an inertia of the 'last hope voting' as employed in December 1993, *Russia's Choice* marginally outpolled the *LDPR* as per party-lists and obtained approximately one-third of the total mandates in 'majority' districts. About one quarter of deputies represented a diverse opposition, but at that time those candidates concerned with local problems prevailed. Here, election to the Federal Assembly can hardly be adequately interpreted in broad ideological and political terms due to deputies' preoccupation with regional matters. The same situation could be observed in an

even more acute form in the local elections. Some parts of European Russia, such as Tula, display a similar pattern.

5. The *central-black-earth zone pattern*: high attendance and little confidence in the president and especially in his policies, prevailing eagerness to hold presidential rather than parliamentary reelections. This 'mass-opposition' regional type is concentrated in a geographical zone to the south of Moscow which is capable of providing itself with food, and where the influence of Yeltsin was minimal even as early as the presidential elections in 1991. Now this opposition stereotype has been ultimately fixed, its configuration having been slightly reshaped by the *LDPR*. The transitional pattern from this one to the 'hopelessly depressive' Baikal pattern is to be found in the 'new border' regions of Pskov and Smolensk, having low density of population and low attendance along with an undoubtedly pro-opposition bias. It is here that oppositional communist-agrarian-patriotic-Soviet political blocs were emerging in 1994 and often taking second place (but rarely first) in the number of attained mandates. In all regions but a few, the *LDPR* refrained from participating in local elections, and in those few (except the Kuban) – failed. The *APR* is not yet a political party but a territorial-professional corporation undergoing the first stage of its formation. Due to internal intrigues and lack of financial support the *CPRF* completely neglected the local elections and failed to organize the all-out nation-wide campaign. Nevertheless, in some regions both performed solidly.

   The myth about the Cossacks' predomination in the Don and Kuban regions proved to be strongly exaggerated – very few of their chieftains secured seats in the Federal Assembly, and in early 1994 the Cossacks' unions were far from triumphant at the local election, which is wholly understandable as this is not their line of preoccupation. With certain aberrations, this zone can be generally classed as following the 'central-black-earth region' polling pattern, which can be also called the 'south Russian' type.

6. There is, of course, an exclusively *'capital-city' regional polling pattern* in Moscow and St.Petersburg. These should be specifically distinguished for the mere reason that in Moscow and Moscow *oblast'* the number of voters amounts to 12 million – as many as in the whole non-black-earth-region, and in Moscow alone the electorate is greater than in either the eastern or western part of Siberia.

In terms of the referendum results the regions fell into similar groups in terms of preferred directions and prospects for their reconstruction, with clearly manifested transitional patterns. The northern polling pattern is primarily characteristic of the regions with a developed resource extracting industry, and some trade-industrial regions interested in liberal reforms and an open economy. Among such regions, however, there also exist those which support the notion of decentralised administration and independence in order to increase their share of the locally produced incomes.

The urban industrial regions, including those with a high percentage of the science-based military industrial complex, give active support to the president and his policies and are centre-oriented in the hope that they will not be neglected, counting on a reciprocation of support. At the same time, the deepening crisis and insufficiency of the much expected aid may lead in future to serious shifts in the public mood in such regions. Such a shift from the Urals to the Siberian pattern of voting had already occurred in late 1993 and in the local elections of 1994, especially in non-black-earth European Russia; in some places (Vladimir, Krasnoyarsk) it occurred rather in leaps and bounds, from 'last hope voting' to the fierce opposition of the electorate, although not of the 'south Russian' type. In Vladimir a kind of 'Baikal-hopelessness' emerged, while Krasnoyarsk is catching up with the Kuzbas – the current anti-Yeltsin steam engine of Siberia.

In those regions where the balance between industry and agriculture is properly established and which are oriented towards the local market, the prevailing type is either the black-earth regional one, which manifests stiff dissatisfaction with the president's policies as well as striving to slow down the reforms; or the southern Siberian pattern – more moderate, but with strong opposition. In the last classification we have specifically distinguished the Moscow and St.Petersburg subtype, although remarking its similarity to the Urals polling type. Today it is obvious that compared to the situation of 25th April and even 12th December, a qualitatively different electoral disposition is evident here (as well as in Nizhnii Novgorod and possibly in Samara), judging by local elections which took place in 1994. However, it is as yet difficult to know the precise consequences of such mutation. A sudden attendance drop (which caused the Moscow City *duma* by-election failure in December 1994) and weakening of *Russia's Choice* (here 'the last hope' voting took place on 12th December) cannot be denied, and the conduct of approximately one-third of the local electorate, which formerly attended regularly and polled in favour of moderate democrats, at the would-be nation-wide elections is vaguely predictable. Today the electorate has fallen into a stupor.

Regions falling into these groups are by far the most populated in Russia.

8 The Specific Character of the Past and Future Elections

It is not feasible to conduct a serious comparison of the results mentioned above without placing them within a definite framework.

The political sociologist I. Yakovenko (now a representative of *Yabloko* in the *duma*), has carried out the following research which has clarified the general vector of the process of change. A certain amount depends on the real presence and political skill of propagandists, but the mentality shift per se was objective. To help the reader visualize the essence of the lines of the shift, it is necessary to compare the key answers to the questions of the 25 April 1993 referendum with the situation in the middle of November 1993.

	November			April	
support of the government's economic policy	yes:	23.4	(-10)	yes:	33.8
	no:	51.7	(+21)	no:	30.3
support of Yeltsin's policies	yes:	31.2	(-7)	yes:	38.5
	no:	44.9	(+19)	no:	26
Support of Yeltsin's decision to call off the elections	yes:	22.1	(-8)		
	no:	46.5	(+14.5)		
(April - wish to have pre-term elections)				yes:	30
				no:	32

With respect to the qualitative analysis of public moods, to simplify it we may state that the alignment of forces at the referendum was turned upside-down in the autumn of 1993. Summing up Yakovenko's table one can draw a conclusion: the immediate result of crushing the unpopular Parliament, the breaking up the regional Soviets, pressure put on the autonomous republics' administrations, etc., turned out to be a 'Pyrrhic victory', although it was easily foreseen after April by serious researchers. After both the government and president had publicly accepted all the responsibility for the events that were taking place and the situation still had not improved (the government did not even attempt to create an illusion of effort – there was merely an internal squabble for power), while the political and social situation was slowly worsening regardless of all political sensations, the 'pendulum of unpopularity' inevitably started to swing in the other direction. In simple terms, those who had not yet adopted a firm position in April voted for the president and determined his victory by 7-10% in the first and second questions; we then termed this 'the last hope vote'. However, in April a relative majority, although a very slight one (by 2 million out of a total of over 30 million), wanted to have pre-term reelections of Yeltsin. In December, the 'indecisive one' swung back and the only question was, who will ride the wave?

The 1993 elections demonstrated, as if in a slow motion, the great mutation of the Russian mass mentality – in that sense the local elections of 1994 served only to reinforce and correct it. Secondly, there should be no doubt that if the next general elections are held in 1995 or 1996 – regardless of whether the parliamentary and presidential elections will be held simultaneously – the campaign will surely be very similar, with a minimum variety of characters.

Without understanding the 'small town phenomenon', the regional concept did not apply to Russia – or lacked the necessary foundation. So, the virtual defeat of *PRES*'s claims to be 'the party of regions' (not, of course, based on the understanding of the regions as a club of certain provincial officials), set against the overwhelming success of the super-centralist Zhirinovskii (for whom the very idea of 'lands' is purely minor) is a phenomenon of the same nature. Besides, the problem lay not in a weakness of the scientists' intellectual abilities or the politicians' incapacity to act; rather, the subject itself stayed passive for a while, so that any attempts to persuade it about its own interests were doomed to fail, which was frequently the case.

The last and most tragicomical example in this direction for the whole post-perestroika period are the endeavours of the majority of local officials to restrain all and absolutely all the participants of the September-October 1993 crisis. This they tried to do with most of the industrial and enterprise unions and directorate, although with a greater constitutional right, but their failure reaffirmed that there was no real organization behind the popular local leaders. Even the attempts of V. Volkov and N. Medvedev (who were responsible for the 'October course' in the Presidential Administration), to not just break up the Soviets, but also to create some kind of a unitary model also failed completely. The fact remains clear: in 1993 the regional leaders did not show the necessary qualities of organization and force, nor the minimum level of solidarity and psychological readiness to undergo a long struggle for their rights. This demonstrated that behind their claims lay nothing but a desire to exploit the break-up and of weakening of central authorities.

However, since the 'October regime', still not united, did not venture to use repressions (just as in August), the local authorities quickly recovered from their fright, and the triumphant success of V. Mukha, A. Tuleev, Yu. Nozhikov and other 'personal opponents' of Yeltsin in the 1994 local elections was quite natural. Yet if one looks below the surface of 'the personal struggle', the results of the 12th December elections not only confirmed the status of a small town as an independent phenomenon but also made it for the first time a significant political factor on a state scale. Like it or not, from now on this will always have to be considered. The results of the past elections allow us to sketch a tentative model of a small town's political behaviour, although it certainly needs a more exact background.

Millions of people have suddenly realized that their hopes will never come true, either now, or in the distant future, and with this occurred the collapse of all-Russian (and global) motivations and values. After the tremendous sociocultural provocation of Gaidar, not only were savings devalued but also all ideas of the prospects and course in life of the majority of the Russian population, which felt that it did not belong to this new 'carnival of life' enjoyed by the nouveau riche. However, in accordance with the centuries-old tradition of passivity and helplessness before the central government and its whims, for a long time they could not articulate the protest.

In the present conditions a small town has two fates. In those regions where agriculture is more or less developed, where it can keep up production, where the density of rural population is still high, a small town can change its orientation and become a normal well-functioning technical, cultural, social and commercial centre in its area. In those regions where agriculture is decaying, where the rural population is low and where there is a process of naturalization of farm production, small towns turn into centres of depression analogous to those in the Appalachians, Manchester and the Ruhr. Two ways, two models of political behaviour. The centres of agricultural areas become their political avant-garde.

Whereas the rural areas vote for agrarians, small towns vote for communists, as this is the way in which the political fundamentalism and traditionalism of rural population and its hate for the central regime are expressed today. Yet even more often small towns (and not only in the economically depressed zones) vote for Zhirinovskii. This thesis seems to be contradicted by the *LDPR*'s failure in all local elections – except in the Kuban region – but from the point of view of that part of the electorate, the farce is of no importance and there is no point in bothering about it. Considering the present helplessness of local dumas, it is not too surprising that voters do not attend the elections of other such political bodies. What is amazing is that they come to this farce at all. However, when a head of administration is elected by direct voting, voters always come. Mayors and governors were elected wherever the local authorities opted for this method, and not in all cases was the result known in advance. All of this makes it clear what the mouthpieces of the present order are so very afraid of, and why they postpone the presidential elections from 1994 to 1996 or even later. The citizen is now disillusioned with the notion of an independent role of local government bodies, since for a number of years the mass media have been showing him an enlargement of his own 'ugly mug', and what were all the Soviets but a company of sovoks?

Nevertheless, the democracy of appointment by election (judging from the estimates of the sociologist Igor Klyamkin) should not be doubted, provided we elect a person able to act, and not a bunch of irresponsible demagogues. This is the manner in which everyone in Russia – from Yeltsin to a drunkard in the street – perceives democracy, and that is the reality, whether you like it or not.

Yet, one cannot talk of a complete passivity of Russians in the local elections. It is true that the elections in St. Petersburg were a failure and that there are areas in Russia with a ridiculous average election attendance and invalid elections, which are by an odd coincidence those very places that during the referendum voted for the constitution by over 60-70%: namely Kamchatka, Magadan, Murmansk, Khanty-Mansiisk and Yamal-Nenetsk autonomous regions. In Sakhalin they even created such an election process (four four-mandate constituencies), whereby with an average attendance of 26% the elections are considered valid, whereas in Murmansk three mandates were not enough. However, in the case of the majority of the Russian Federation's subjects, valuable government bodies were elected even with such a procedure. Furthermore, the attendance does not depend directly upon geography (in Kostroma *oblast'*, which is far from being a southern one, it is 38%, in Novgorod *oblast'* it is 36%, in Kirov *oblast'* it is 35%), although the best attendance was observed in the Kursk *oblast'* (47.5%), while at the same time the elections fell through completely in eight districts. The local election attendance in the central and southern part of European Russia is relatively stable: 43% in Tambov *oblast'*, 42% in Kaluga *oblast'*, 39% in Voronezh *oblast'*, 36% in Bryansk *oblast'* and in Stavropol' *krai* (in the latter the elections were held in all districts), 35% in the Don area.

In Siberia, the highest attendance is in Kurgan *oblast'* (at 44%, with deputies being elected in all districts), and in Irkutsk *oblast'* (42.5%, but here three deputies in Irkutsk and two deputies in Bratsk and Ust-Ilimsk were not elected), around 40% in the Altai mountains (but an absolute failure in Barnaul), 37% in Omsk and Orenburg (also with a failure in the principal towns, or Gubernsks).

Even in this kind of situation, when the 'elections' had no particular outcome, one-third to a half of the citizens outside of the borders of the 'northern voting area' used their right to vote (with the prevalence of rural areas over small urban ones, and the latter over Gubernsks), demonstrating in this manner that it was the 'authorities' who had lost faith in 'democracy', realising that they would never again be legitimately elected, no matter how much they lie, threaten and cheat. However, the toy of voting has not ceased to amuse the most illiterate and patriarchal – rather they have only just discovered it.

9 Conclusion

1. The economic status of Russia's regions is determined by the nature of their restructuring. Today the impulses of reconstruction are generated from the centre, and as far as the regions are concerned, they merely react to a different extent to such impulses. One can ascertain that in the regions, both at the level of the administration and public opinion, people are well aware of how much the course of reform promoted by the centre correlates to regional development inclinations. However, by themselves and even as part of associations the regions are not in a position to independently work out and implement their own course. A few attempts of this kind, undertaken within the framework of the *Siberian Accord* and the Association of Central Russian *Oblasts* (initiated by A. Dolgolaptev, currently the deputy chairman of the Federal Assembly) did not meet with much success. The experience does, however, illustrate that by means of lobbying, the regions dispose of particular opportunities to affect the changes in the federal economic policy and to reorient it to their advantage. The presence of such opportunities (they gradually began to increase as of winter 1993) cushioned in great measure the contradictions between the Centre and the regions, and reduced the number and acuteness of separatist demonstrations. At the same time it deprived the activities of the federal government of predictability and consistency, and gave rise to complaints that there was no government economic policy at all. We should also take into consideration that the demands of the regions are becoming more and more complicated and diverse.
2. In 1991-1994 the factors determining the reconstruction process were changing constantly. Regional authorities were faced with the necessity of altering the priorities of the regional economic policy, which induced local political crises, linked to the discrepancy between the updated doctrines and the old governing

teams. In particular, today's crisis connected with transportation problems may endanger the position of the teams which based their calculations on raw resource export. Federal bodies have lately experienced serious pressure put upon them by the regions and aimed to exert strict control over the transportation tariffs and introduction of state subsidies. Pressure is also exerted in order to increase the dollar inflation rate. In case this does not work, an aggravation of the local political crises should be expected in the regions which are export oriented.

3. The process of restructuring in Russia is far from over. The situation in some regions is, thus, unstable. The factors which most of all determine the future of the reforms are the following:
   - the tariffs for transportation and energy resources;
   - the national currency rate; and
   - the policy of tariffs.

It is precisely these issues which are at the heart of a rapidly approaching struggle between the regions and the Centre. In this context, even the debates over the budget have now receded.

The near future is also expected to produce controversies based on disproportions in the banking and finance development. In particular, the regions welcome the idea of admitting foreign banks into the domestic market, regarding them as a means to create an efficient infrastructure of non-state investments.

In the political environment, the steadily increasing public discontent with both central and local authorities has not yet crystallized. All elections carried out in 1993-1994 were by their nature nothing but a public opinion poll (large-scale or regional), for no executive power leaders were elected on any level – except for a few governors opposed to Yeltsin – and to this day the representative organs are nothing more than an impotent decoration. Clearly understanding the context in which regional and central authorities undergo political and economic self-determination, the people have no means to directly affect it.

The parliamentary elections, the gubernatorial elections and the presidential elections (in ascending order of importance) should, by the very fact of their announcement, regardless of the degree of their legality or independence, create a totally new political reality – as should their renunciation by either central or local power in the near future. One way or another this problem should be solved in 1995 and new impulses will determine and transform federal policies along with regional political conduct.

10 Regional Economic Reproduction Typology

1. Financially Solvent
   - *Export oriented*: (under development): Komi-Perm', Khanty-Mansiisk, Evenk, Chukot, Yamal-Nenets autonomous okrugs, Sakha, Sakhalin
   - *Inhabited, partially self-sufficient*: Primorskii and Khabarovsk *krai*s, Komi Republic, Karelia
   - *Trade and finance-oriented*
     - Port-cities: *Arkhangel'sk, Astrakhan', Murmansk, Kaliningrad*
     - Capital-cities: *Moscow, St. Petersburg, Nizhnii Novgorod*
2. Self-Reproductive
   - *Southern Russian*: Krasnodar and Stavropol' *krai*s; republics of Mariy El, Mordovia and Chuvashia; Belgorod, Bryansk, Volgograd, Voronezh, Kursk, Lipetsk, Orel, Penza, Ryazan', Saratov, Tambov and Ulyanovsk regions, Rostov and Samara *oblasts*
   - *Siberian*: Tomsk, Irkutsk, Altai *krai*; Krasnoyarsk, Kuzbas, Omsk, Novosibirsk, Tyumen', Buryatia, Kurgan, Orenburg
3. Depressed
   - *With prospects for development*
     - *Traditional military industrial complex*: Vladimir, Kirov, Tula, Udmurtia
     - *Traditional heavy industry*: Ekaterinburg, Perm', Chelyabinsk, Yaroslavl'
   - *'Hopeless'*
     - *Science-based military industrial complex*: Moscow and Leningrad *oblasts*
     - *Light industry*: Kostroma, Ivanovo
     - *Non-vector* (having neither industry, nor agriculture, nor resources): The Jewish Autonomous o*blast'*, Amur, Vologda, Kaluga, Kamchatka, Magadan, Pskov, Smolensk, Tver', Chita *oblasts*, Koryak, Nenets, Taimyr Territories
   - *Ethnically dominated* regional orientation
     - *carrying out their own reforms*: Bashkortostan, Kalmykia, Tatarstan;
     - *hopeless without external support*: Adygeya, Dagestan, Kabardino-Balkaria, Karachai-Cherkesia, Ingushetia, North Ossetia, Tuva, Chechnya.

5

Risk Assessment of Russia's Regional Disintegration

N.V. Petrov and A.I. Treivish

1 Strengths and Limits of Quantitative Evaluations

Usually the possibility that Russia will disintegrate under the pressure of regional separatism is analysed only in a qualitative, verbal manner. Kommersant newspaper has published investment risk assessments of thirty ethnic regions of the Russian Federation, where the risk of their separation from Russia was considered to be of primary importance. However, separatism is not restricted to 'autonomous regions'. Moreover, it is unlikely that everything can be reduced to a single risk. The following questions seem to be reasonable in approaching the question of risk assessment. First, who is taking the risk? Second, what is the source of the risk?

The present study addresses three types of risks:

- The *primary risk of a region seeking independence*, i.e., the probability of its secession from the Russian Federation.
- The *secondary risk for the Russian Federation*: the consequences of the secession of a given region.
- The *secondary risk for the region*: the consequences of having to 'make it on your own'.

Finally, comparing the risks, we may determine who takes the greater risk. At the same time we must impose some restrictions on these calculations:

1. We do not attempt to foresee scenarios like coupling, repulsion or internal splitting of regions. To be more exact, 86 regions out of the 89 that make up the Russian Federation are involved in this study. Moscow and St.Petersburg are incorporated into their *oblasts* (regions) for greater comparability. The republics of Chechnya and Ingushetia are also represented in their former united form because there is a shortage of data on both of these republics.

2. Neither the Russian situation as a whole, nor the events which may become catalysts of a disintegration chain reaction, are discussed. In other words, general

political factors of disintegration are not being investigated, but solely regional factors.

Under general political factors of disintegration we understand the risk of such changes in the general structure of the state which (due to internal political or external influence) bring an end to Russia as a geographical entity and as a state. This outcome seems to be unlikely. Rather, it is much more likely that individual regions will break away from the 'rest of Russia'.

Economic policy leading to the severance of economic ties, destruction of the common transportation infrastructure, cultural and linguistic unity may be treated as factors of general political risk. All this may be the subject of a separate analysis, which goes beyond the scope of this paper.

3. Basic indicators utilised here reflect the objective situation in the region, rather than its political behaviour or degree of 'mobilisation', which may be compared later. Various indicators influence each risk group. Thirty indicators were chosen from the available statistical, historical, and cartographic data (see Appendix).

4. A basic, seven point scale, ranging from 0 to 6, was chosen for obtaining comparable rankings for each indicator.

2 Primary Risk of the Region Seeking Independence

The risk that Russia may lose a region through secession consists of three aspects: *geopolitical*, *ethnic-demographic* and *economic*.

2.1 Parameters of Geopolitical Risk

1. The *historical experience* of the region as a part of the centralised Moscow state, the Russian empire, or the USSR-RSFSR was calculated on average for those regions that had joined the Russian state at different times. The duration and frequency of 'independent periods' were taken into account if they existed. Map 1 shows the historical nucleus of the 500-year-old Moscow state. For the most part, other regions of Russia joined the empire 250-450 years ago. Some border regions such as those of the Northern Caucasus, Siberia and the Far East were incorporated later, and Tuva and Kaliningrad *oblast'* joined less than half a century ago. While translating the risk of separation from Russia into figures, we assumed that, all things being equal, the less time the region spent under Russian rule, the higher point score it will receive. The highest risk (6 points) was estimated for Tuva and Kaliningrad regions, whereas the areas of historical nucleus received the lowest

Map 1
Risk assessment of regional sovereignisation:
Historical stage of the region's affiliation with Russia

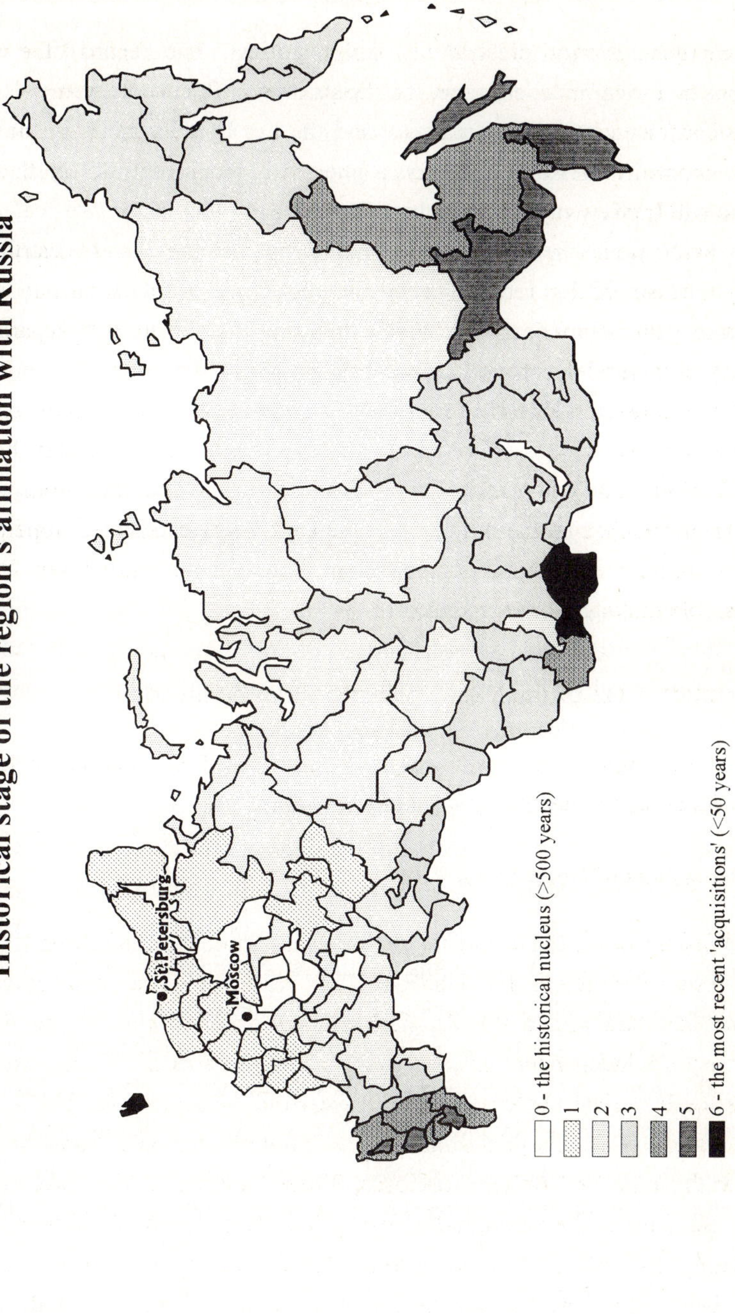

grade. Hereinafter this degree of risk will be noted when it is higher than the average, for the rest of Russia.

2. *Regional status*: present day and historical. The record of each region's previous historical independence, if it exists, may influence its status – for example, the independence of Tuva, Tatarstan, and the Far East Republic in the 1920's, the Soviet republic of Karelia, *oblasts*, *gubernii* [provinces] or other autonomous formations. In view of the difficulty of formalising this factor, we scaled it through expert evaluation. The highest risk ranking was assigned to the republic of Tuva alone because of its recent formal independence (protectorate of Russia and Mongolia). High rankings were given to Kalmykia and most Caucasian republics adjacent to it, as well as Karelia, Tatarstan, Bashkortostan, Buryatia, and Yakutia.

3. The character of *external contiguity* is determined by the length of the region's borders with old and new foreign countries, subjects of the Russian Federation of various ranks, and on marine boundaries, taking into account transportation and general importance of the basin. The greater the extent of contiguous borders of a region, the greater the risk of separatism. The regions in the south and west of Russia – from Dagestan to Sakhalin as well as the exclave of the Kaliningrad *oblast'* – are subject to this kind of risk, and accordingly, receive higher rankings. Some north-western regions have received higher than average rankings. Minimal rankings were received by the central regions and Yakutia.

4. The measure of *proximity to Russian and foreign centres* is considered to be the ratio of external urbanisation potential of countries bordering Russia to the Russian urbanisation standard. The potential of the population field is a well-known measure taken from physics, which indicates the position of a given location relative to that of external centres. The closer it is located to powerful centres – the higher the potential. The ratio of potentials in this study helps to evaluate the potential 'gravitational pull' of the regions to Russian external centres as well as the risk of separation connected with the influence of non-Russian external centres (Map 2). External potential taken alone is the highest in the west of Russian Federation. This location is also close to the main Russian centres. Only in Kaliningrad and Belgorod does this imbalance significantly benefit external centres. The potential influence of powerful Asian centres in the Far East diminishes because of the distance; nonetheless, the Asian influence is four times as great as the cumulative influence of Russian centres. The dominance of the external potential is also characteristic of Eastern Siberia.

Map 2
Evaluation of regions' gravitation towards Russian or foreign centres

Total geopolitical risk, represented in Map 3, is obtained as a simple sum of four equal factors. The risk is higher in the frontier Siberian regions, extending from Altai to Chukotka. The risk increases southwards and eastwards, with the maximal risk regions being Tuva, Primor'e, and Sakhalin.

The second risk zone stretches from the Caucasus to Astrakhan Astrakhan' oblast, where the risk is also higher in the south-east. In the European north and north-east, risk regions include Komi, Karelia, Pskov *oblast'* and especially Kaliningrad oblast. The block of the Volga and Urals autonomous regions (excluding Udmurtia but including Orenburg oblast) also belongs to the group of regions of higher risk.

2.2 Ethnic-Demographic Block

1. The *percentage of Russians in the population* ranges from 80% to 98% in the *krais* and *oblasts* and from 9% to 23% in some republics, especially in the Caucasus. It is understandable that the higher the percentage of Russians in the region, the lower the risk of separation.

2. The *percentage of native population* is important as a risk factor for 'autonomous regions', though sometimes the native population does not even exceed one-tenth of the overall population (e.g., in many of the northern okrugs, in the Jewish Autonomous okrug, etc.). According to this scale, all 'Russian' regions except those inhabited by large sub-ethnic groups have conditionally been assigned a ranking of zero. Those with large sub-ethnic groups – such as the Pomors in the Arkhangel'sk oblast, the Cossacks in the northern Caucasus and the Orenburg *oblast'* – received a ranking of 1.

3. *The concentration of non-Russians in the region* is also minimal for *krais* and *oblasts*, even if they are densely populated. The maximum percentage is in some national regions, up to 96 % in Tuva and in Yakutia, where additional risks arise for ethnic separatism.

4. A *majority of people of any nationality that were born in that region* strengthens their links with the motherland as well as their separatist moods. The percentage ranges from less than 1% in the north of Tyumen to 90% in Dagestan. The regions of higher risk form a wide band in the middle of European Russia, running from the western agrarian regions to national Povolzh'e: outside this band, Vologda oblast, Altai *krai* and Tuva may be mentioned. All data originate from the census of 1989.

2.3 Map 3 *Total geopolitical risk*

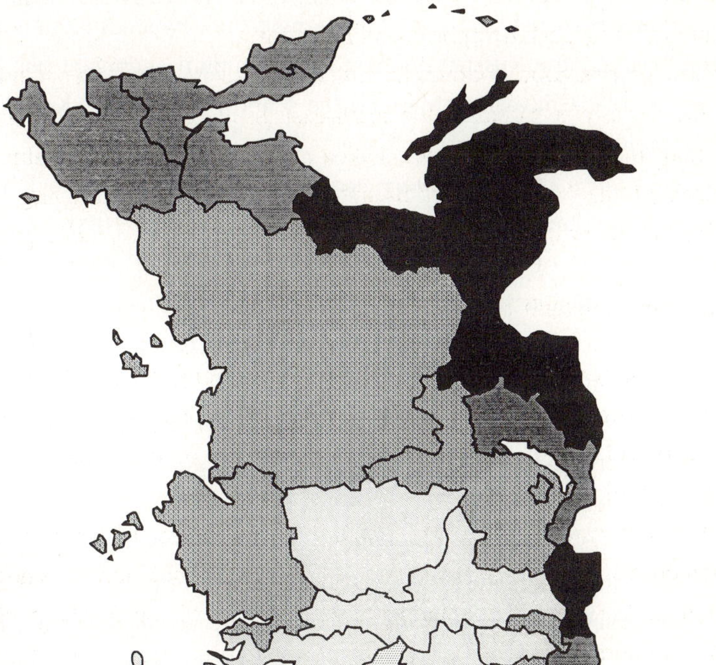

Map 3
Overall geopolitical risk

2.4 Total Ethno-Demographic Risk

In Map 4, some but not all autonomous regions stand out. For instance, the three Nenets, Khanty-Mansiisk and Evenk *okrugs*and the Jewish Autonomous *okrug* are represented as genuine Russian *oblasts*. The maximum aggregate risk was founded in Tuva, Yakutia, Chuvashia, Mari-El, the Komi-Perm okrug, Kalmykia, and the Caucasian republics.

Statistical values for the *primary economic risk* are represented by figures on gross national income and gross domestic product in 1989-1990. More recent data reflect the character of the transition and crisis period, but old and stable data still influence the regions' self-perception. The parameters are as follows:

1. *Per capita production:* the higher the per capita production, the higher the risk of separatism from other potentially poor regions. Tyumen' region, with its rich oil deposits, stands high in this chart. A higher risk also exists in the 'northern' regions ranging from Komi to Kamchatka, in the industrial regions of the Volga, in the Urals and 'capital regions'.

2-3. *Total per capita consumption and the gap between consumption and production* are used to capture the level of discontent of people in regions with low consumption levels, especially in the regions where production may, in theory, be increased. This risk factor is higher in Kursk and Orenburg *oblasts*, as well as in the Caucasus. It is slightly higher in the industrial regions of European Russia and in those regions of Siberia which are rich in oil and gas. Risk is minimal in regions with high production and consumption: Moscow, Murmansk, Magadan, and poor regions which are 'fed' such as Dagestan and Kalmykia.

4. The old industrial regions of the Centre (Leningrad, Perm, Orenburg and Udmurtia) had put significant investment into the *centralised distribution fund*. By the 1990's, when the flow of investments could no longer be maintained, the oil-rich region of northern Tyumen' joined the donor group. The recipients were many northern and eastern regions and 'national' frontiers of European Russia.

The *overall picture with respect to economic risk* (see Map 5) reveals three zones of higher risk. The first risk zone includes the Tyumen' okrugs, which are major suppliers of 'oil dollars' into the treasury, and the resource regions of Krasnoyarsk *krai* west of Tyumen'. However, the risk of their separation is much lower. The second zone encompasses the Middle Volga and lower Urals regions (especially Orenburg region). The third zone includes the less compact and risky

Map 4
Aggregate ethno-demographic risk

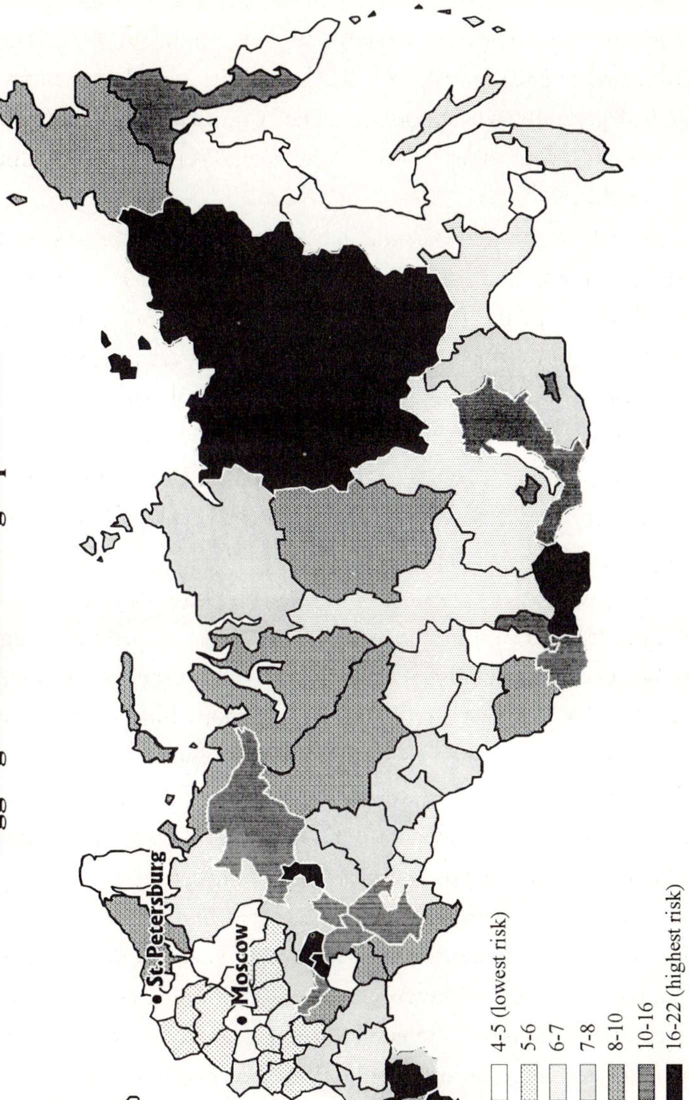

Map 5
Aggregate economic risk

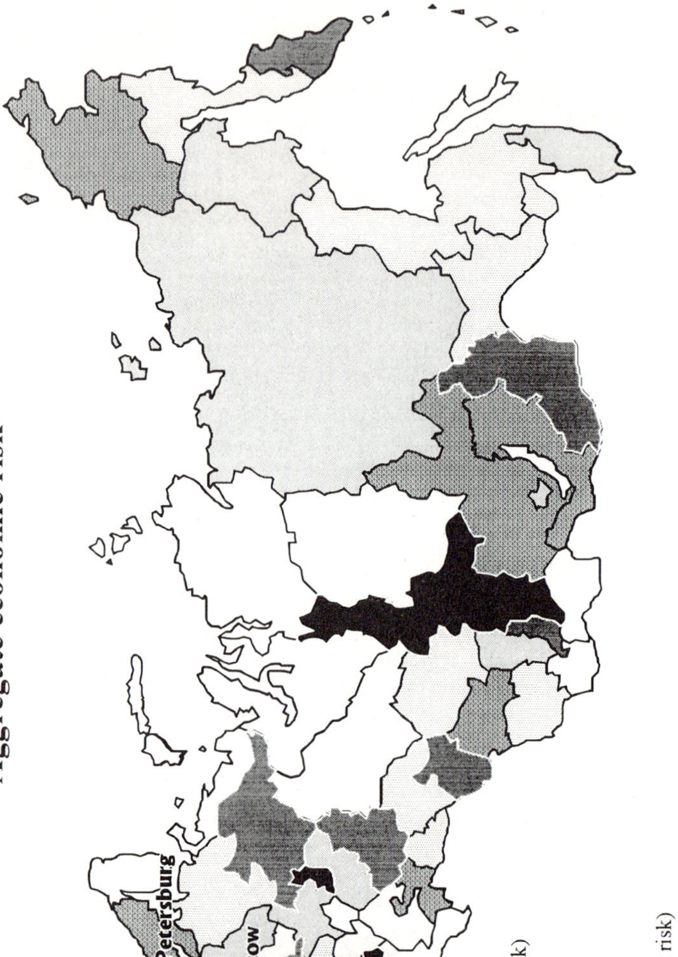

Map 6
Overall probability of sovereignisation

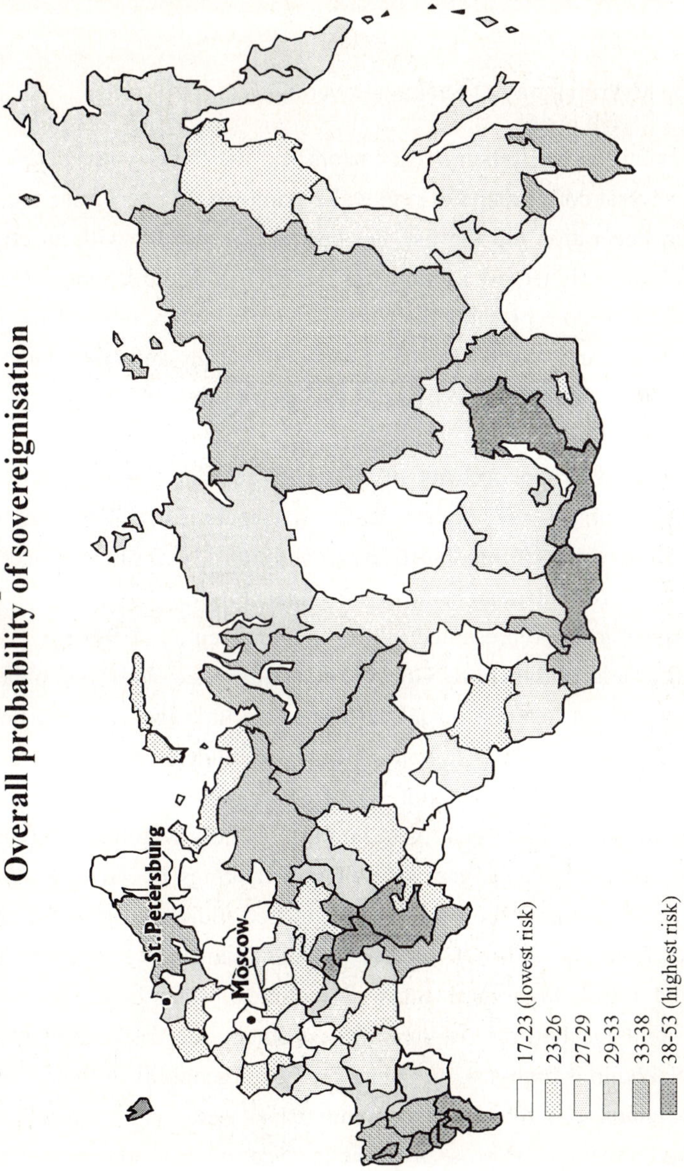

group of western and central regions. Regions to the east of Moscow require special attention.

2.5 Aggregate Probability of Seeking Sovereignty

The total of all twelve primary risk factors and the three types of risk allow us to single out several core groups of regional separatism. In every case the republics of the Russian Federation top the list, but one or two regions with an ethnic Russian population have a higher risk ranking, just below that of the republics (Map 6).

- The first group represents the Caucasus region, with the nucleus in Chechnya, Ingushetia, and North Ossetia. The neighbouring republics have higher risk evaluations. Slightly lower risk is assigned to the adjacent northern Caucasus region and Kalmykia.
- The second group consists of most of the Volga and Ural republics and Orenburg oblast. No explicit leader of separatism can be singled out here according to any of the objective preconditions. Nevertheless, according to the points scored, Tatarstan is the *de facto* leader.
- The third group, represented by the southern region of Siberia, is led by Tuva and Buryatia, and includes Gornyi Altai, Khakassia, and Chita oblast.

An extensive but less risky zone is formed by the regions of the north, ranging from the Komi Republic to Chukotka. These are holders of the main hard currency resources of oil, gold and diamonds. The frontier regions in the west and in the east have a significantly higher risk of separation, namely Karelia, Kaliningrad *oblast'* and Primorskii *krai*. The higher overall risk rankings of Tuva, Komi, Tatarstan, Buryatia, and Yakutia is the result of heightened individual risk factors. Although Komi and Buryatia did not receive high rankings on separate factors, they accumulated rather high total sums. Sometimes, when high rankings for some indicators are cancelled by low rankings on others, the final ranking is lower. For example, Sakhalin is high-risk only with respect to geopolitical factors, while central regions are characterised by high economic risk as well.

Naturally, this is only a hypothesis; reality is more complex. Regions contaminated by the virus of separatism are just as likely to be viewed as negative examples by their neighbours as they are to be imitated. This is particularly the case if the first experience of the 'leader' was unsuccessful, fraught with anarchy and a threat to the stability of normal life in the whole region (e.g., the case of Chechnya). On the other hand, the privileges that were successfully won from the centre by these regions (e.g., exemption from federal taxes) give birth to a certain kind of jealousy and create a desire to follow the 'leader' (e.g., Tatarstan).

3 Secondary Risk for Russia: Consequences of Losing the Regions

This class of risk is analysed without considering general disintegration scenarios. We single out each region and evaluate consequences of its secession for the rest of Russia. Six parameters have been selected:

1. *Length of the borders of the region that form external borders* of the Russian Federation – that is, the risk of the extension of unprotected external frontiers. The split-up of the USSR proved that this problem does exist in reality and that it increases secondary risks. However, the length of the border itself is a formal indicator correlating with the area of the region (except those that have long coast lines and borders with other countries). In this case, higher risk is expected in the vast trans-Urals regions. It is worth mentioning that risk of losing a part of the region is also high. However, frontier regions in the west and in the east create fewer problems with borders.

2. The *risk of 'interception' of Russian transport arteries* was evaluated using various transportation maps (except air traffic maps) and maps of communication passages, compiled earlier by the authors. The role of the region as a transit territory and the number and capacity of the inter-regional main roads controlled by it were taken into account. In the western part of Russia, where communication networks are better developed, the risk is usually not too high. Exceptions are two 'capital' transportation centres and Chelyabinsk oblast, through which two of the three main 'roads' to the east run. The threat to the system of transportation is higher in the northern Caucasus, where transportation arteries were constructed between the mountains and the sea, and where sea-ports of primary importance for the Russian Federation are located. Higher risk is associated with the southern Siberian zone, especially the trans-Baikal region. This zone controls the routes that allow Russia to be the Eurasian transit corridor. In the meantime, this zone as well as the Caucasus republics and the pre-Urals region are potential sources of separatism.

3. The *risk of loss of export resources*, especially natural resources, was also evaluated. Because the manufacturing and service sectors of the economy are largely inactive at present, their potential is difficult to assess. In 1991, when the Russian Federation saw the highest volumes of consumption of imported goods, the north of Tyumen', rich in oil and gas, had an outstanding export volume. In 1992 Samara

oblast, with its many branches of industry, left Tyumen' region behind, although the 'resource regions' remained the biggest net exporters and earners of hard currency. Such resource-rich regions, located in the north and the east, are marked with a higher degree or risk, with only a few rare exceptions.

Loss of the Kuzbass, most of the regions in the Urals and along the Volga, or the western regions of the Caucasus could cause a certain amount of damage to Russia; the contact zone from the Volga to the Enisei yields approximately two-thirds of all Russian exports.

4. *Regional monopoly* in the industries of the Russian Federation was calculated on the basis of a list of enterprises that control over 35% of national production of individual items. Monopolistic enterprises are unevenly distributed in all sectors of industry because of the structural differences of the industries. Many monopolies are found in metallurgy. Therefore, we have also considered the degree of concentration of industries in the regions, especially mining industries. Greater chances for monopolies to influence consumers were found in the leading regions, such as the two 'capital regions' of Moscow and St. Petersburg, Nizhnii Novgorod and Samara *oblasts*, the *oblasts* of the Urals as well as the mining and metallurgical Kuzbass and Rostbass regions. A marked discrepancy can be observed with primary risks: the threat to the Russian Federation is highest in those regions where the risk of secession is lower; the overall risk is subsequently more conditional.

5. *Tax losses* that would be experienced by the Russian Federation as a result of individual regions' secession are evaluated on the basis of the volume of taxes collected in each territory in 1992. Partial return of the federal taxes to the regions in the form of federal aid has been also taken into account. The behaviour of actual tax defaulters has influenced the data obtained. Among tax defaulters were the regions of Chechnya, Tatarstan, to some extent Bashkortostan, Yakutia, Tuva etc. Therefore the data have been adjusted, especially for Tatarstan, by the average level of tax receipts from defaulters. The central industrial zones and the band ranging from the Urals to the north of Tyumen stand out as high risk in this respect, just as in the case of the previous risk factors. Together with Krasnoyarsk and Krasnodar *krais*, these regions have contributed half of the total receipts to the Russian Federation treasury. Their loss, therefore, could mean the complete collapse of the Russian Federation.

6. *Loss of Russian-speakers*: The share of Russian speakers in the population is the only ethnic and demographic risk factor here. Its significance is clear: i.e., the same problems as with the disintegration of the USSR. Densely populated and advanced regions such as the two 'capital regions', Nizhnii Novgorod, Samara, two

Map 7
Overall evaluation of secondary risk factors

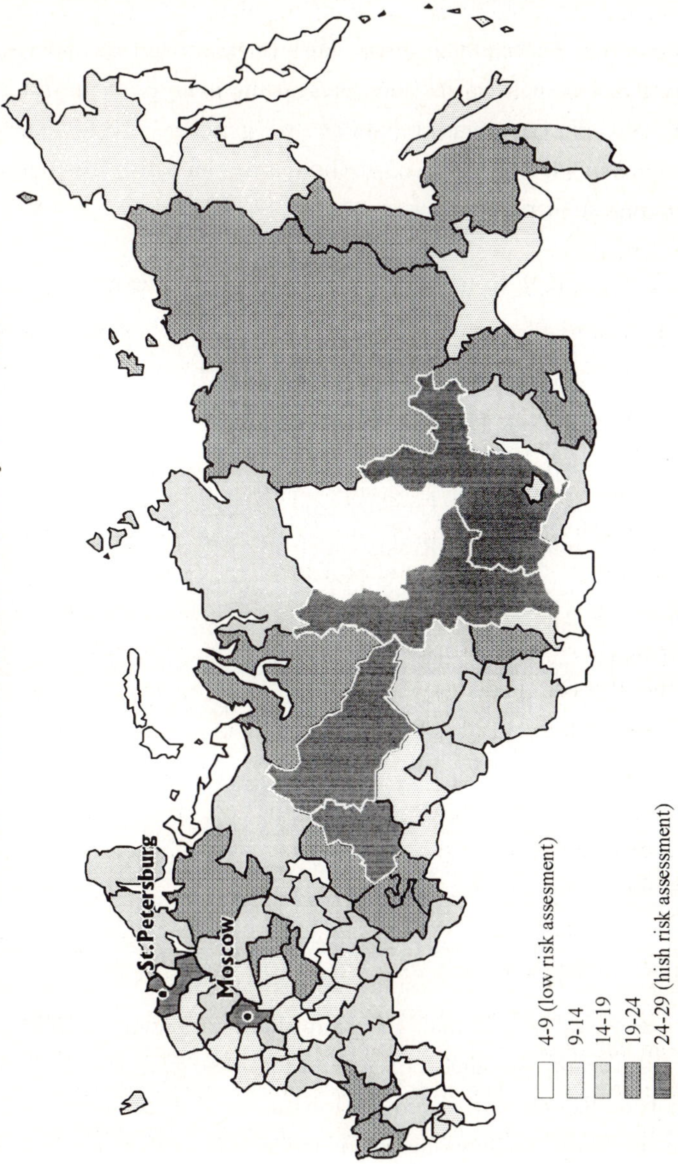

regions in the Urals and two Caucasian regions stand out here. They contain more than one-third of the total Russian-speaking population. The concentration parameter here is lower than the economic parameter. Tatarstan and Bashkortostan, home to 3.5 million Russian-speakers in 1989, present the main problem in terms of ethnic separatism. In all Caucasian republics the number of the Russian-speaking population is estimated at about 1.5 million, while in Tuva, it is only 160,000 and declining in recent years.

3.1 Total Evaluation of Secondary Risks for the Russian Federation (Map 7)

The greatest risk is in the 'capital regions' and in the vast Urals and Siberian band, which includes five regions: Chelyabinsk, Ekaterinburg and Irkutsk *oblasts*, Krasnoyarsk *krai* and the Khanty-Mansiisk okrug. Potential damage to the Russian Federation may also stem from the western part of the Caucasus inhabited by Russians and Cossacks, from Tatarstan and Bashkortostan and from a number of northern and eastern regions of Russia which are rich in natural resources.

To identify those regions that could cause the biggest problems for the federal government, we can simply multiply regions' rankings with respect to risk of secession by their rankings with respect to the consequences of secession for the Russian Federation. Thus, five regions may be singled out: Krasnodar *krai*, Bashkortostan and Tatarstan, the oil-rich Khanty-Mansiisk *okrug* and the Krasnoyarsk okrug. The risks of their secession, while not maximal, are still significant and, together with the secondary risks, they threaten the Russian Federation. The same may be said of those regions in the second-highest risk group, which includes Leningrad *oblast'* – the RF's 'second capital' (Map 8).

Regions in which the degree of primary risk exceeds secondary risk are viewed with 'fatal indifference'. It would be easy to lose them, and the negative consequences would be minimal. The Komi-Perm autonomous *okrug* occupies first place in this regard, far ahead of its 'rivals'. The correlation of risks in three republics of the Russian bloc is not very indicative. These republics are Mordovia, Chuvashia and Mari-El. Chuvashia, being the least Russified among them, stands out with its 'fatal' ratio of risks. Other minor risks can be found in small peripheral republics and districts on the border of Russia such as the Kaliningrad and Kamchatka *oblasts*. It is possible that the strategic damage to Russia through the loss of these maritime regions has been underestimated. However, the indicators for these regions are only slightly higher than the Russian average (Map 9).

Map 8
Combination of high loss potential and dire consequences of such a loss to Russia

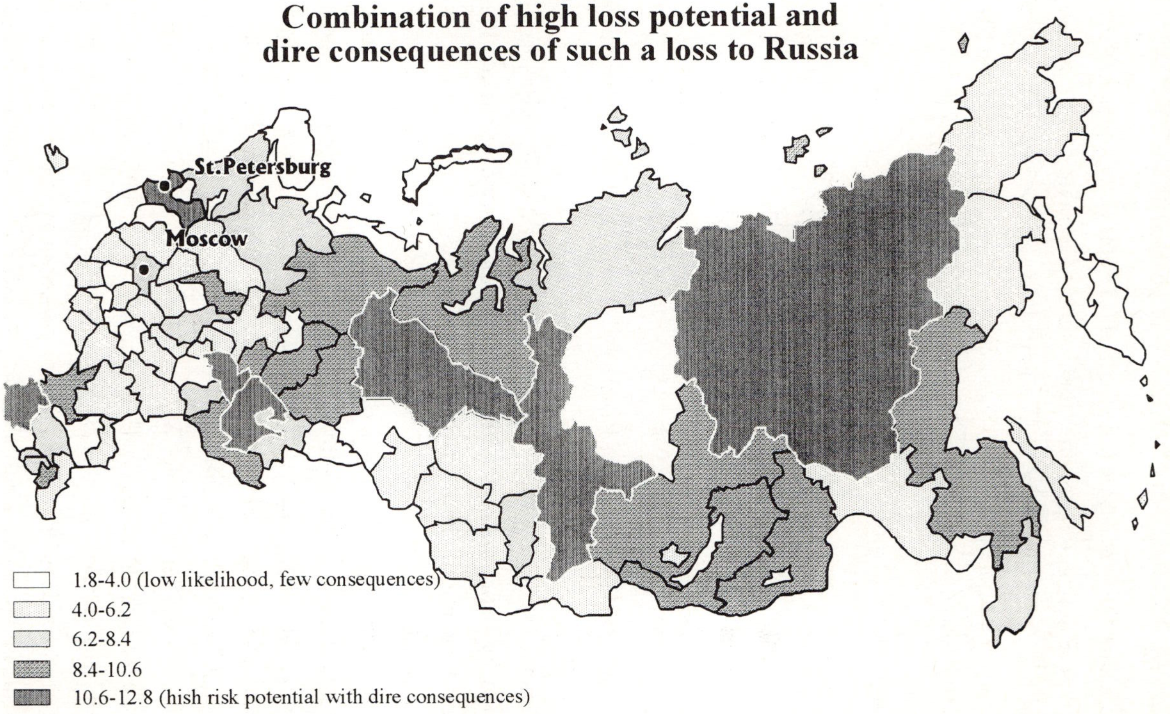

Map 9
Relationship between primary and secondary risk

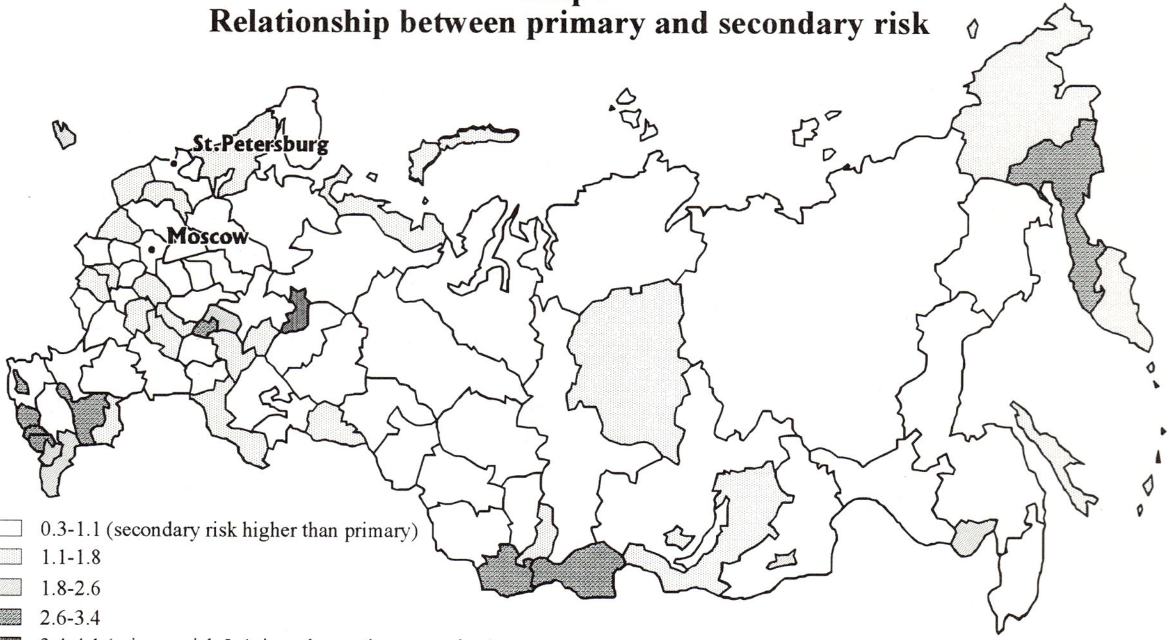

- 0.3-1.1 (secondary risk higher than primary)
- 1.1-1.8
- 1.8-2.6
- 2.6-3.4
- 3.4-4.1 (primary risk 3-4 times larger than secondary)

4 The Secondary Risk for the Regions

The danger of secession from Russia presents many consequences for the regions themselves. It is again worthwhile to study the issue by blocks of factors.

4.1 Geopolitical Block

The geopolitical block consists of four factors:

1. *Claims on the territory of a region*: Our information here is based on the data base of territorial and ethnic claims and conflicts at the Institute of Geography of the Russian Academy of Sciences. The degree of severity of conflict, up to the level of armed violence, is the basis for risk assessments. There are not sufficient data to take into account all risks connected with disputes between Russian regions and internal separatisms that threaten their integrity. Therefore, the frontier regions of the Russian Federation stand out. In the east is Sakhalin, which contains the Kurile Isles claimed by Japan. There are calls to re-unite three Buryatian territories at the expense of parts of the Irkutsk and Chita, the claim of Yakutia to the territory of Magadan region, etc. The second area is the north-west of the Russian Federation, where parts of the Pskov *oblast'* are officially claimed by Estonia and Latvia; Kaliningrad *oblast'* is claimed by Lithuanian and German nationalists. Although the claims were not supported by the respective governments, the nationalists continue to claim the entire region. The third area is the Caucasus, with an entire band stretching from Ossetia to Dagestan subjected to maximal risk. Conflicts along Russia's longest border – with Kazakhstan – are not so important as the counter-claims by the Volga regions.

The significance of this factor would increase sharply if secession of a region from Russia takes place. There may be no advantages of secession if the state is threatened by invasion of neighbours or by an internal split-up. Therefore this factor – claims upon territory – is the only risk factory to which we assigned a weight equal to double the usual weight.

2. The *extent to which a region is non-compact* was defined as the ratio of the real border perimeter to the circle perimeter of the same area. The higher the ratio, the less compact its form and the higher the risk of developing various 'bridges', 'divisions' and 'break-aways'. The Internal and external threat to the integrity of the region increases indirectly. Sakhalin represents an extreme with regard to this risk; since it consists of many islands. The risk is also high in the northern and eastern

regions. The band of substantial level of risk has the shape of a horizontally-placed question mark, embracing all the main resource regions of Russia.

3. *Risk of diplomatic non-recognition* threatens all of the regions. Those who have gone too far in their aspirations to be fully independent (like Chechnya) have already been convinced that this is a real risk. In the future much will depend upon precedent, that is, on whether the region had statehood in the past and whether it has it at the moment. Therefore, the general rule was omitted and two above-mentioned factors were taken into account. These factors include the period of time when the region was under Russian rule and its administrative and political status. Together they make up one indicator. It is clear that the small regions of central Russia which were absorbed by Moscow long ago and were deprived of any autonomy, have the highest risk of not being recognised. The risk is lower in the republics and some frontier regions that were incorporated later (such as Tuva).

4. *Remoteness from non-Russian centres* was evaluated by the method used for primary risks: in particular, the volume of the urban potential of the Russian Federation's neighbours. This potential has been used here by itself without correlation with domestic potential, although in practice it is closely related to the latter. Regions outside the sphere of interests of both external and internal centres are noteworthy in this regard. This applies to the underdeveloped north-eastern parts of Russia and, more widely, to most of the northern and eastern regions, except for the southern Urals and the southern regions of the Far East. The spatial distribution of rankings is of a regular zonal character.

Total geopolitical risks of the regions (Map 10) are defined basically by the first and second indicators of the risk block. The first indicator was multiplied by two (it was double-weighted). However, there are some deviations from the general pattern achieved in this manner. Chechnya and Dagestan in the Caucasus were excluded from the highest scale, but Krasnodar *krai* was included; both indicators were rather high. Krasnodar *krai* is claimed by the Adygeya enclave region that seeks to gain access to the Black Sea and to the republics of the Caucasus. The risk for Adygeya itself is very high because of its position as an enclave and its lack of compactness. In the north-west, Leningrad region faces higher risk, although the risk is lower in Karelia and Kaliningrad. The eastern part of the Russian Federation, however, is rather noteworthy in terms of differences pertaining to the second indicator – the same 'S'-shaped band appears, various parts of which are influenced by the remaining risk factors. One should remember that the northern Caucasus, the Volga and the autonomies in the Urals are potential and real leaders of separatist

Map 10
Overall geopolitical risk of the regions

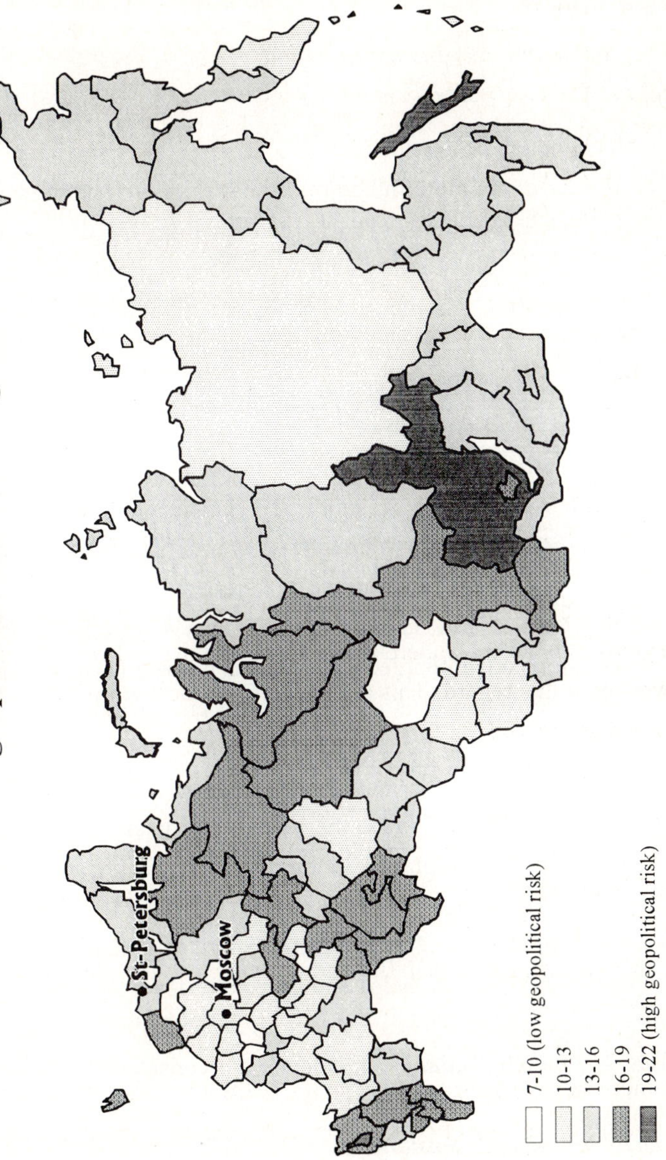

movements which may significantly damage Russia's interests. However, they are themselves vulnerable.

4.2 Ethnic Bloc

The ethnic block includes three factors:

1. *Ethnic structure*: the more mixed the ethnic structure, the higher the secondary risk. We took the composition of the population from the data of the last (1989) census. The following autonomies with a significant proportion of Russians are important: Bashkortostan, Tatarstan, to an extent Yakutia, and other northern and southern Siberian regions. However, in regions with a small proportion of indigenous peoples such as Karelia, Udmurtia, Khakassia, and the Jewish autonomous okrug, the risk is lower. The third group is formed by the Russian regions with a significant share of various minorities, such as in the Astrakhan, Ulyanovsk, Orenburg, Chelyabinsk, southern Tyumen, and Magadan *oblasts*.

2. *Extreme configurations of ethnic settlement* (visible zones of compact minority settlements, clearly defined frontiers, etc.), were analysed by expert evaluation on the basis of ethnic maps. Revisions of these estimates were made according to the potential support for native people of the region by people of the same nationality who live outside the region (this essentially concerns autonomies). Examples are: Tatarstan, supported by the Tatars dispersed across the former USSR; Adygeya supported by the Turkish Adygeians; Karelia, supported by the Finnish Karelians and Finns, etc. In the final analysis, the risk for Tatarstan, taking into account its complex ethnic nature of settlement, is lower than for neighbouring Bashkortostan. The risk for Chechnya is also lower because of the Chechen diaspora. The risk is higher for Kabardino-Balkaria, North Ossetia (South Ossetians themselves need help so they are unlikely to provide help) and especially for Dagestan, where the ethnic composition is very dense. Most of the northern and Siberian regions, which are characterised by 'blotchy' ethnic settlements, are considered to have a higher risk factor.

3. *De facto inter-ethnic tensions* are reflected in the reports of the Ministry of Internal Affairs on meetings, demonstrations and clashes with police classed as 'ethnic'. Data collected for 1990-92 takes into account developments in the regions. There are various problems associated with these data, including variation in the reliability with which such events were recorded. Regardless of the difficulties in reporting these events, the general picture is comprehensible. The whole of the northern Caucasus stands out vividly. Higher risks are observed in the southern

Map 11
Overall ethnic risk

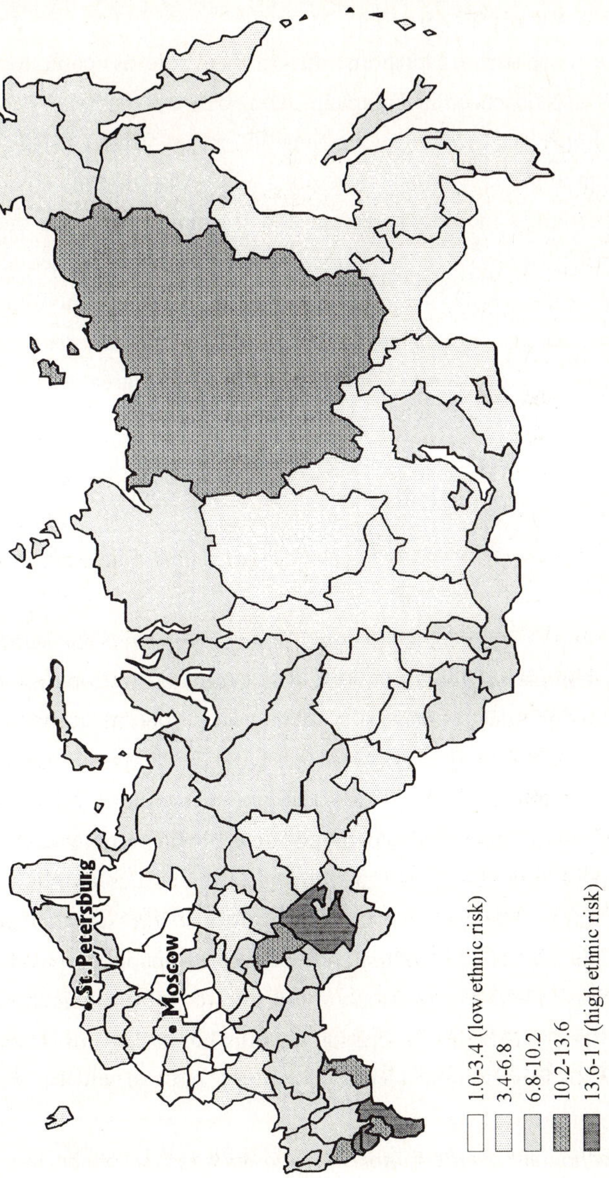

regions of the Volga, especially in Astrakhan *oblast'* ('peace' in Kalmykia may be regarded as a statistical artefact). Moscow region and to an extent Leningrad region both have more serious tensions, due to their role as 'capital cities'. Higher ethnic tension is also observed in Tatarstan, Altai *krai* and Tuva.

Total ethnic risk rankings (see Map 11) range from 1 to 17. The lowest rankings were assigned to purely Russian regions, while autonomies received higher rankings. The latter mainly include Tatarstan and Bashkortostan, and the risk factor of their neighbouring republics and *oblasts* was higher as a consequence. A second area incorporates the whole of the northern Caucasus where mountainous republics have very high rankings, except for Chechnya. The third vast area includes the north and the north-east (Yakutia and Chukotka). The fourth area consists of the republics of southern Siberia where, as usual, Tuva stands out in particular. In this block, the coincidence of increased secondary risks with primary ones is more evident. This means that potential separatists are likely to suffer first.

4.3 Economic Block

1. *Isolation due to underdeveloped transportation links*, which in turn makes it difficult to maintain economic ties, was evaluated by looking at means of external communication such as sea ports, main roads running through the territory of the region, or navigable rivers, compared with the length of frontiers. The degree of isolation is significant in the less developed northern and eastern regions, and is similar to the last factor of the geopolitical block: remoteness from foreign external centres. However, 'proximity to transportation routes' varies greatly. The external urban potential in the Chukotka region is four times lower than in the west of the Russian Federation and the distance between transport 'entrances' into the regions varies from 23 km in the Moscow *oblast'* to 1500 km in the Evenk and Koryak okrugs, with the Russian Federation average being 237 km. The average level of risk in relation to this is small (only 2.3 points), but the north-eastern area of maximal values is extremely large.

2. *Dependence on the import of foodstuffs* is one of the few indicators available through the statistics of inter-regional economic exchange. The data concerning consumption of non-food products depend greatly on fluctuation, demand, prices, etc. in the current atmosphere of instability. Once again, the north stands out, although on both sides of it (including regions with developed fishery industries) the risk decreases. Industrial and urban regions of the European centre, especially

Map 12
Overall economic risk of the regions

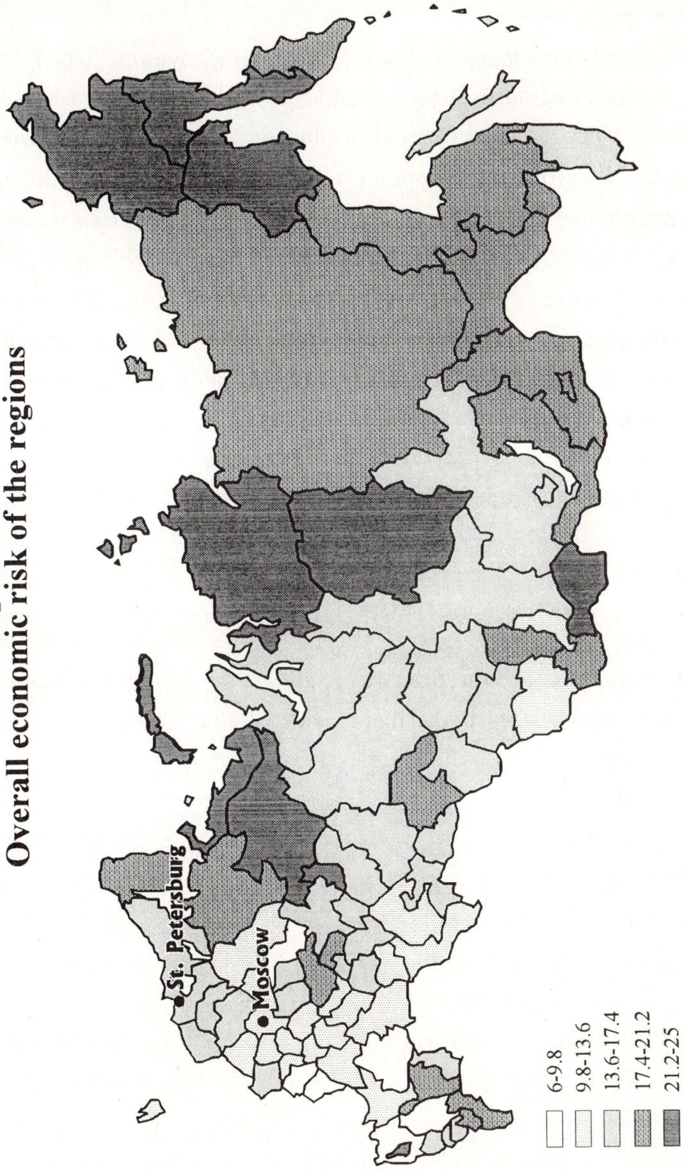

Moscow, and those of the Urals and southern Siberia may be considered as vulnerable in this regard.

3. The *level of diversification of economic structure* was evaluated on the basis of employment shares of agriculture and industry with the help of several statistical measures (variation, indices of branch localisation, etc.). Taken separately they are not sufficient; therefore, the overall evaluation is close to the one provided by experts. A number of regions have 'mono-economies'. The riskiest zones are in the North, ranging from Murmansk to Kamchatka, due to the dominant position of one or two branches of industry in their economy.

4. *Weak export potential* (per capita volume, taking into account the average trade balance outside the Russian Federation in 1991-92) is an important factor of secondary risk, leading to financial and hard currency 'poverty'. It is important to note that we evaluate export potential as a secondary risk factor for Russia on the basis of per capita volume in the region, not absolute values. In this case, the representatives of internal and external 'peripheries' are subject to the highest risk. This group includes the Volga-Vyatka republics and Kalmykia and the band of autonomies of southern Siberia. This risk is not characteristic for the main natural resource regions (except for Magadan).

5. *Budget losses of the regions* caused by the withdrawal of federal aid, just like the budget losses of the Russian Federation, were evaluated according to 1992 data. The return flow of taxes into the centre of the Russian Federation was considered as well. Once again, it was not the sum total of taxes which was considered (the sum which is important for the federal budget) but rather the sum relative to the population of the region. The 'winners' turned out to be not the small, densely-populated Caucasus autonomies (the risk of ending up without federal aid is still high in Dagestan and adjacent Kalmykia) but rather the northern republic of Komi and the Yamalo-Nenets okrug, the eastern Siberian regions as well as the adjacent Kuzbass, the trans-Baikal regions and north-eastern regions (where the Koryak region is leading).

Tatarstan, which did not pay taxes but instead received substantial material aid, even taking into consideration its large population, may be regarded as a very special case.

Total economic risk for regions (Map 12) is especially centred in the north-east of Russia. The present-day crisis is indeed particularly hard in the northern and eastern parts of the country. In the European part of Russia the risk is substantially lower and influences only the frontiers of the Caucasus and Volga-Vyatka separatist

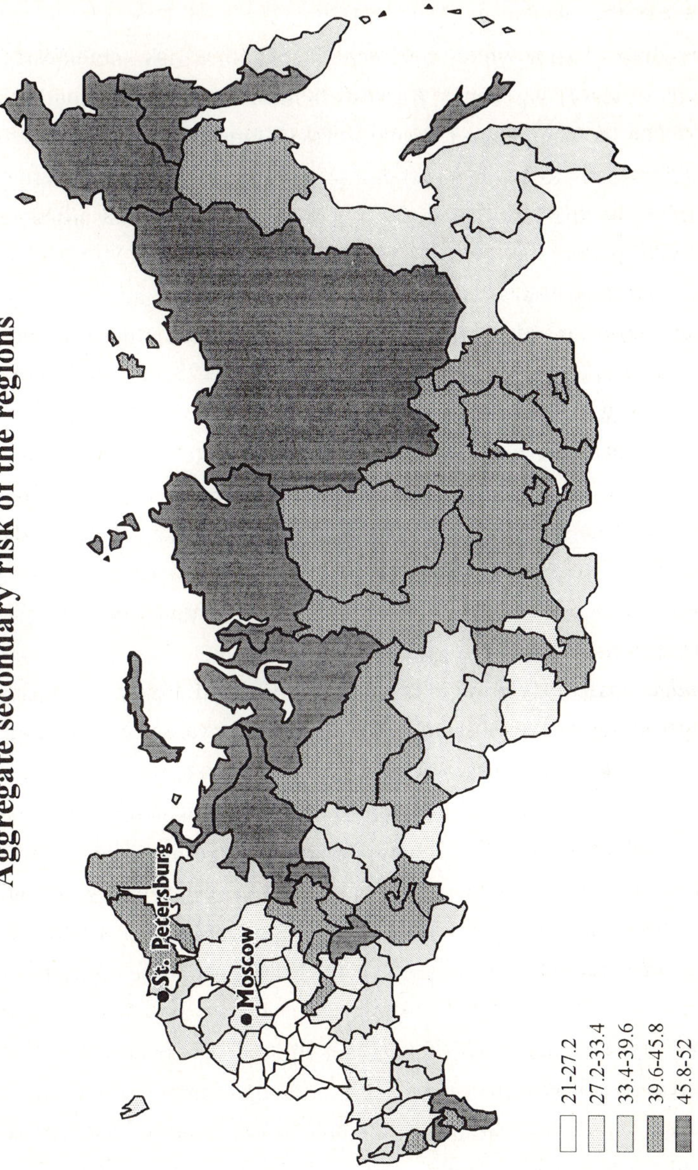

Map 13
Aggregate secondary risk of the regions

centres. Essentially it is the 'weak' regions which run the risk, such as the Komi-Perm, Yamalo-Nenets, Evenk, Chukotka and Koryak regions, as well as Magadan oblast. Meanwhile, heightened economic risk (sometimes significantly higher) is observed in some Russian *oblasts* which are usually considered as 'strong', such as Chelyabinsk, Novosibirsk, Kemerovo and the south of Tyumen'. The latter happens to be in a difficult situation without its northern part, which is demonstrated by the fact that in 1992 it received substantial aid from the Russian Federation.

Total secondary risk for the regions, estimated as the sum of these 12 factors is different from other risk factors. Indicators cancel each other out, and contrasts are eroded. The rankings within each block varied from 3.5 to 17 times, but the range in the overall ranking was considerably smaller – less than 2.5 times (21-25 points). This is close to a normal distribution, but skewed to the right: About 40% of all regions have 30-40 points (Map 13). Among them are many vast eastern regions. Therefore, even when we raise the level of the lower risk zone boundary (35 points, compared to an average of 30 for other indicators), we get the impression that this zone dominates in the Russian Federation. However, there are 35 regions that do not fall into this zone: all eastern and central regions including Moscow and Leningrad, Sverdlovsk, Omsk and Tomsk *oblasts* and Primorskii *krai*. In this risk zone, two Caucasian republics received maximum rankings (Ossetia and Dagestan) as well as two northern autonomies (Komi republic and Chukotka okrug); the zone extends between these two autonomies. Tatarstan and Bashkortostan also belong to this group. It is little wonder that, encompassing a large area, the secondary risk zone almost completely covers the regions with high primary risk of separatism. It is easier to point out exceptions such as Kaliningrad and Rostov *oblasts*, Khakassia and Primor'e, although the risk of their loss for Russia is not the highest.

Finally, the secondary risks for Russia and the regions have to be compared. We use the averages over each set of risks, since the number of parameters in each set varies. The Russian Federation as a whole has average risk of losses which is slightly lower than the regional average; the ratio is about 0.9. One can argue that the part is always more vulnerable than the whole, so that the ratio should be lower than 1. However, we are more interested in the regional deviation from the norm in order to find out which regions are most at risk. The difficulty lies in deciding how to scale the results. It may be either dichotomous – comprehensive either/or scale – or may

Map 14
Relationship between secondary risks to Russia and secondary risks to the regions

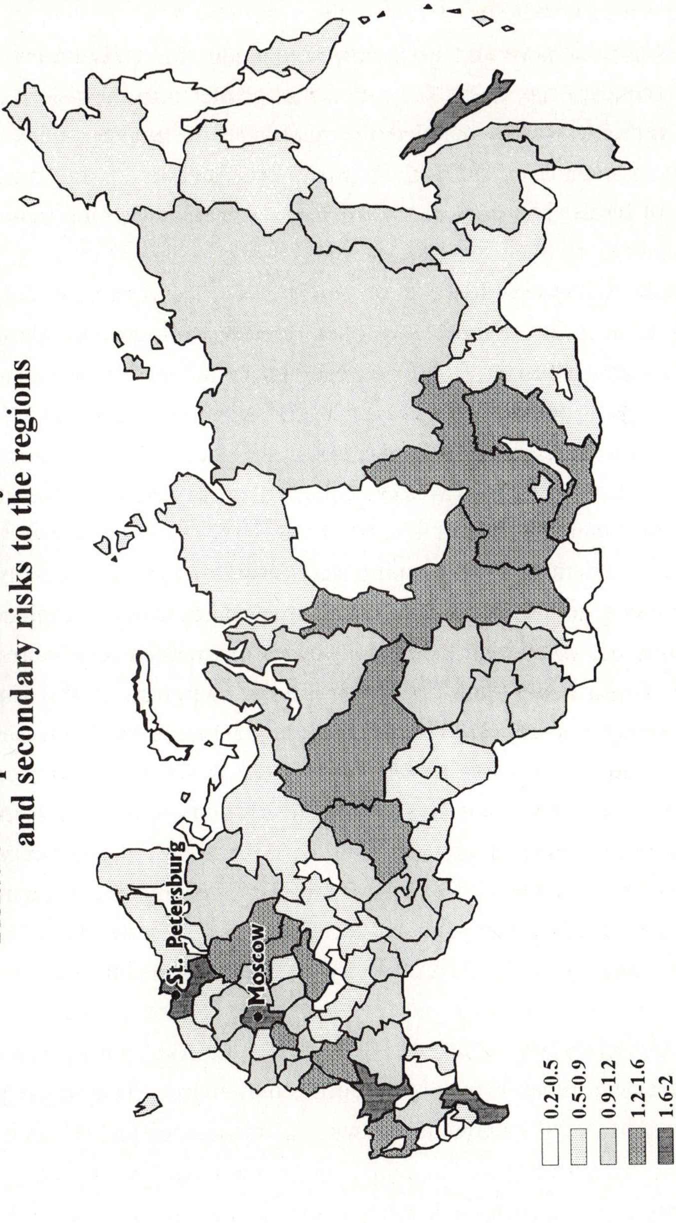

include a neutral group with approximately equal risks for Russia and the region. Both variants are given below.

In the first variant, we take a 1:1 risk ratio as the dividing line between groups. Thus, the secondary risk to the federation was greater than the risk to the region in 37 (48%) regions, which included the majority of European *krais* and *oblasts*, including both 'capital regions', the industrial Urals and half of the 'Russian regions' to the east of Urals. The only autonomy whose secession is more damaging to the Russian Federation than to itself is the oil-rich Khanty-Mansiisk region. The situation in the major separatist regions can be described as follows. All republics of the Northern Caucasus are more at risk than Russia, while *oblasts* and *krais* are less at risk. The same situation is to be observed in the Volga, Urals and southern Siberian regions. Moreover, the zone of local risk predominance includes a number of regions in the heart of central Russia and in the north-west, including Karelia and Kaliningrad oblast, as well as western Siberia. However, the degree of this higher risk is insignificant (Map 14).

The second variant of data grouping singles out a group of relatively equal risks (the ratio ranges from 0.8 to 1.2). This method yields an even greater number of those regions (31) for whom the consequences of secession are more severe than those they would impose upon the rest of Russia. There are only 17 regions whose loss would be more significant for the Russian Federation. In most cases, especially in those regions where the balance of risk is 1.5-2 times higher, these are small 'insignificant' territories. The Russian risk itself dominates (being up to 5 times greater) in both 'capital regions', as well as in the main industrial regions such as Rostov, Samara, Ekaterinburg and Krasnoyarsk. Even moderate attempts to raise their status of independence, such as declaring the 'Urals Republic', are painfully received by the centre. The probability of their secession is low, except for Chechnya, Tatarstan and Tuva; but they (especially Tuva) stand to lose more from seceding than Russia would lose. It is known that rational motives seldom stop the gears of 'self-determination' when the local elites succeed in imposing this slogan upon the masses of the population. However, this is a different topic. For, as the saying goes, 'measure seven times before you cut' [i.e., 'look before you leap' – editor's note].

5 Appendix: List of Initial Risk Indicators

1. PRIMARY RISK OF THE REGION'S INDEPENDENCE (loss of the region).
   A. GEOPOLITICAL BLOCK:
      1. Historical experience of the region being a part of Russia;
      2. Political and administrative status in the present day and in the past.
      3. Character of neighbouring countries and borders;
      4. Proximity to Russian and foreign urban centres.
   B. ETHNIC AND DEMOGRAPHIC BLOCK:
      1. Share of ethnic Russians in the population of the region;
      2. Share of indigenous people in the population;
      3. Concentration of native population in the region;
      4. Share of persons born in the region.
   C. ECONOMIC BLOCK:
      1. Per capita national income production and GDP;
      2. and 3. Per capita consumption and the difference between levels of consumption and production;
      4. Regional distribution of the income produced;
2. SECONDARY RISK FOR RUSSIA: CONSEQUENCES OF LOSING REGIONS
   A. Length of region's borders within the Russian Federation: the risk of growth of external unprotected frontiers;
   B. Control over national transportation arteries;
   C. Risk of loss of export resources;
   D. Monopolistic position of the region in Russian industry;
   E. Potential tax losses for the federal budget;
   F. Russian-speaking population in the region: risk of an increase in the number of Russians living abroad;
3. SECONDARY RISK FOR THE REGIONS: DANGERS OF SECESSION FROM RUSSIA
   A. GEOPOLITICAL BLOCK:
      1. Foreign claims upon the territory of the region;
      2. Lack of compactness of the region;
      3. Risk of diplomatic non-recognition of the region as an independent state;
      4. Remoteness from foreign (outside Russia) urban centres;

B. ETHNIC BLOCK:

1. Ethnic diversity;
2. Extreme configurations of ethnic settlement (with potential support of the native population by external diaspora);
3. Ethnic clashes, nationalistic demonstrations;

C. ECONOMIC BLOCK:

1. Transportation isolation of the region;
2. Dependence on the import of foodstuffs;
3. Lack of diversification (mono-structure) of the regional economy;
4. Weak export potential;
5. Significant budget losses of the region (without aid provided by the Russian Federation).

6

A Survey of Russia's Regional Economies

Il'ya Shkabara

1 The Analytical Procedure

The economies of Russian regions can be analysed on the basis of the following three factors: political, macro-economic, and micro-economic.

Political factors exert an indirect influence on regions' economies. They form the conditions within which the economy functions and they determine priorities and directions in the development of industry, agriculture, non-productive spheres, etc.

Macro-economic factors exert a direct influence on the economy. They determine the cost-effectiveness of production (profit and bank credit rates, etc.) and greatly influence consumption in the regions (incomes of the population, consumer expenditures, etc.).

Micro-economic factors shape the structure of production in regions, the volume of industrial output, the financial state of enterprises, etc.

In view of the above, the analysis was carried out in three blocks along the following lines:

- *Political factors*: a) local economic legislation, b) industrial policy;
- *Macro-economic factors*: a) profit rates in industry and commerce, b) banking activities in regions, c) unemployment;
- *Micro-economic factors*: a) industrial output, b) capital investments, c) changes in the structure of production, and d) financial position of enterprises.
- Comparison in monetary terms was made in constant prices (i.e., taking the rate of inflation into account).
- A comprehensive analysis of the above factors made it possible to distinguish between four types of regions:
- *Depressed regions*, where the most critical situation has developed in the economy (a drastic decline in industrial output accompanied by a reduction in capital investments and a high unemployment rate). The present situation in

these regions' economies and our analysis of prospects for their development lead us to conclude that economic recovery is very unlikely there in the near future.

- *Stagnating regions*, in which the critical economic situation is temporary and determined by the necessity of restructuring the national economy. The present state of the economy in these regions reflects the complexities of the transition period, but in the long run these regions may become 'points of growth' in Russia's economy.
- *'Sluggish' regions*, where the economic crisis is not so profound as in stagnating or depressed regions, but where this relative 'well-being' is achieved through procrastination with the restructuring of economy and industry. Therefore, the present stability may develop into a very complicated situation in these regions in the near future.
- *Stable regions*, in which the economic situation is the most favourable for business. These regions are the 'prime-movers' of Russian reforms.

2 Depressed Regions

The following can be considered depressed regions:

- Pskov *oblast'*
- Bryansk *oblast'*
- Vladimir *oblast'*
- Ivanovo *oblast'*
- Kostroma *oblast'*
- Yaroslavl' *oblast'*
- the Republic of Mari-El
- the Republic of Mordovia
- the Republic of Chuvashia
- Kirov *oblast'*
- the Republic of Kalmykia (Khal'mg-Tangch)
- Penza *oblast'*
- the Republic of Adygheya
- the Republic of Dagestan
- the Republic of Kabardino-Balkaria
- the Republic of North Ossetia
- the Republic of Ingushetia

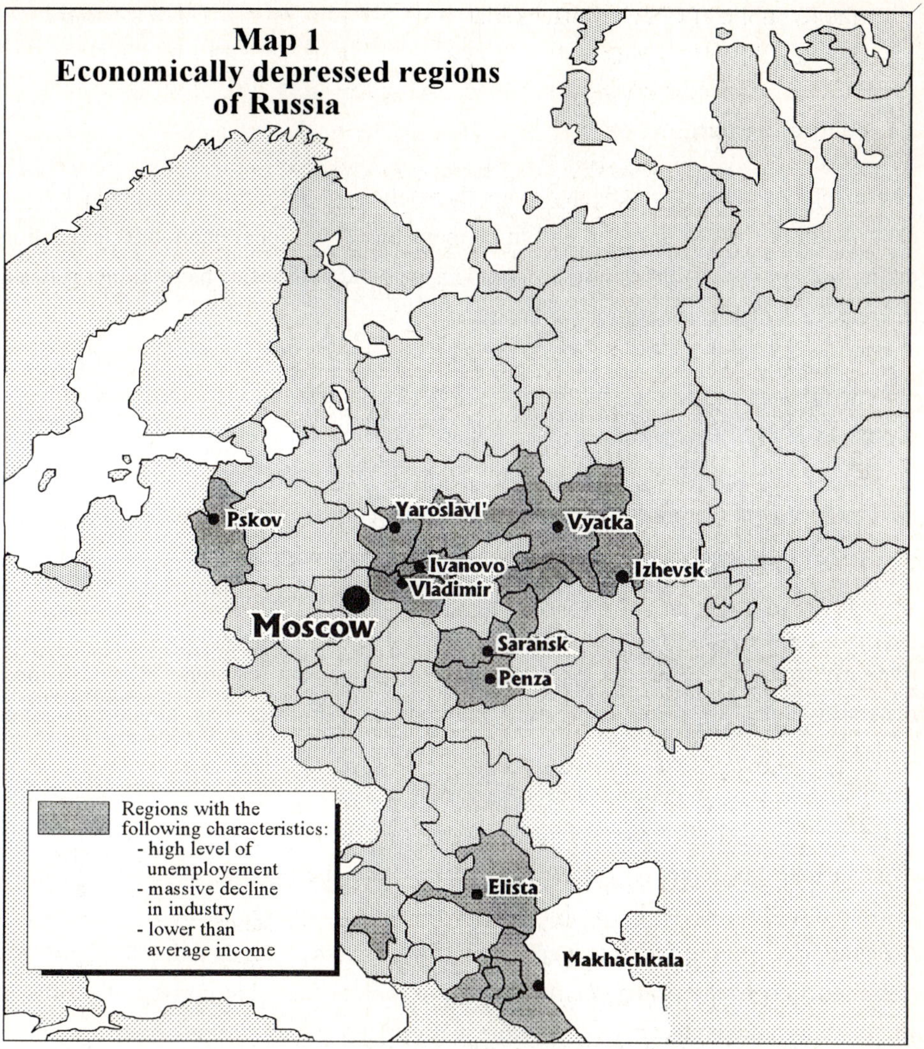
Map 1
Economically depressed regions of Russia
Pskov
Yaroslavl'
Vyatka
Ivanovo
Vladimir
Izhevsk
Moscow
Saransk
Penza
Elista
Makhachkala
Regions with the following characteristics:
- high level of unemployement
- massive decline in industry
- lower than average income

- the Republic of Chechnya (Ichkeria)
- the Republic of Udmurtia

2.1 Political Factors

These regions do not practically avail themselves of opportunities (given by the central authorities) to draw up and implement their own local economic legislation taking regional specificities into account. These local authorities have in fact refused to create acceptable conditions for business.

The presidential decree No 2207 of 27 December 1993 allows for variation in income tax rate in the regions from 13-25% (for banks and insurance companies – from 13-30%). Opportunities for lower taxation for regional industries and agriculture are not taken advantage of. None of these regions (except Kalmykia) have reduced the income tax rate, although this could support those sectors of the economy in the regions which are still capable of generating profit.

Admittedly, TV advertisements have been recently shown urging entrepreneurs to register their enterprises in Ingushetia, promising reduced taxation for them. It is still too early to comment on the results of this campaign, but the trend of establishing off-shore zones in some depressed autonomous republics has already become noticeable.

Budget deficits in depressed regions varied in 1993 from 12-30%. This situation developed for various reasons. Firstly, a great proportion of local budgets is derived from income tax funds and a third of industries in the regions are unprofitable or operate at a loss. Secondly, major budget expenditures (over 50%) go to subsidies for enterprises on the verge of bankruptcy. This system of funds redistribution leads to a reduction of the profit rate in production (since a sizeable portion of profits is absorbed into the budget), to all possible ways of concealing profits (especially those earmarked for capital flight from the regions) and to a greater number of unprofitable cost-ineffective enterprises dependent on funds from local budgets.

In depressed regions it is standard practice to finance and subsidise industries and agriculture. In Yaroslavl' *oblast'* over 30% of the 1993 budget expenditures went into subsidies and preferential credits for unprofitable agriculture. In such conditions, producers do not take opportunities of obtaining credits on the financial market and this results in a sluggish development of the market infrastructure (none of the 100 leading Russian banks are located in depressed regions).

Map 2
Budgets of the subjects of the Russian Federation in 1993

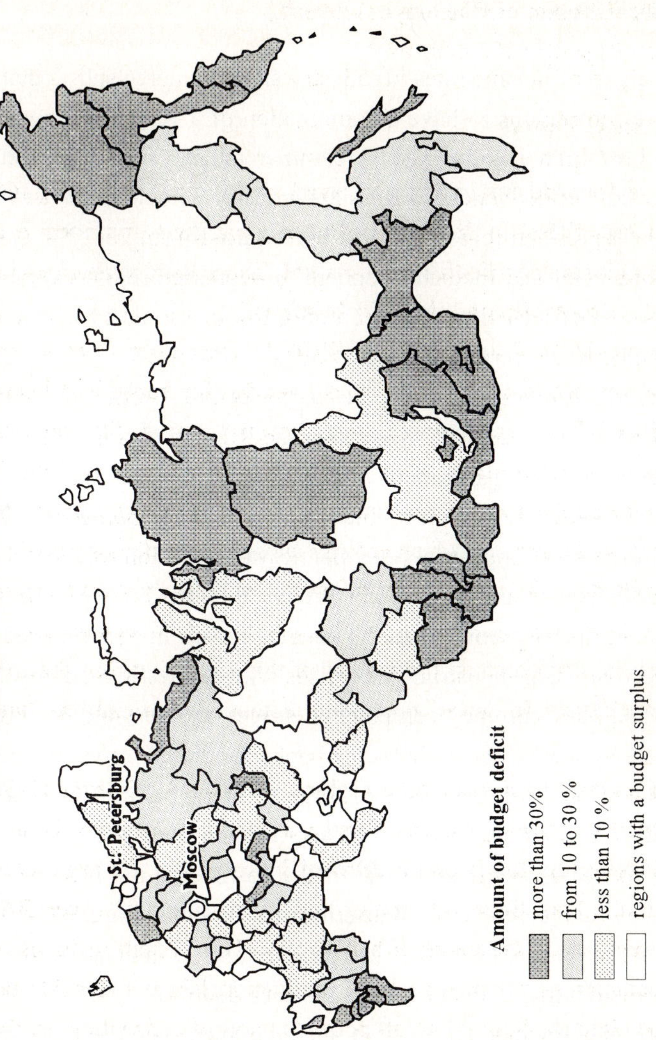

2.2 Macro-Economic Factors

Our analysis of income rates in industry and commerce shows that it is characteristic of depressed regions to have a combination of a very low income rate in industries and a very high income rate in commercial and mediatory activities. While the average cost-effectiveness in Russia's industry was about 40% in the first quarter of 1994, in depression regions' industries it varied from 26-37%. Cost-effectiveness in the commercial and mediatory sphere in depressed regions cannot be estimated on the basis of official data, but according to our estimates it amounts to 100-120%, with the Russian average being only 60%.

Banks in depressed regions are very inactive. Credit allocation growth rates in depressed regions are 40% lower than the Russian average. Moreover, indebtedness of enterprises and organisations to banks is much greater there (in Ivanovo *oblast'* in 1993 it exceeded 72 billion roubles while in Kaluga *oblast'*, which is similar to the former in terms of industrial potential, it was 25 billion roubles). Bank credit rates in depressed regions are 10-15 points higher than the rates for the same credits in St. Petersburg and Moscow. Banking operations are in fact reduced to settlement and cash services. Big industrial enterprises with stable financial positions make use of credit and hard currency settlement services and services for posting payments to suppliers, rendered by big Moscow banks. To take but one example, the *Dyagterev Plant* joint stock company, the biggest enterprise in Vladimir *oblast'*, uses the services of *Inkombank* (Moscow) for its foreign trade and payment posting, a branch of the *Moscow Industrial Bank* in the town of Kovrov for settlement and cash operations, and a number of Western banks for obtaining credits. Thus, the market of banking services in depressed regions is extremely idle and narrow and its expansion and intensification in the near future is very doubtful.

Depressed regions have a high unemployment rate (twice as high as the Russian average), and it is growing faster than in Russia as a whole. In many regions the unemployment rate is 5% of the able-bodied population, which, by world standards, is a critical threshold, beyond which unemployment adversely affects the amount of the gross national product of a territory. Among these regions are Ivanovo, Kostroma, Pskov and Yaroslavl' *oblasts* and the republics of Dagestan, Kalmykia, Mordovia and Chuvashia. Verging on the 5% rate are Arkhangel'sk and Kirov *oblasts* and the republics of Adygheya, Ingushetia, North Ossetia, Udmurtia and Chechnya.

Map 3
Unemployment and strike movement in the Russian Federation

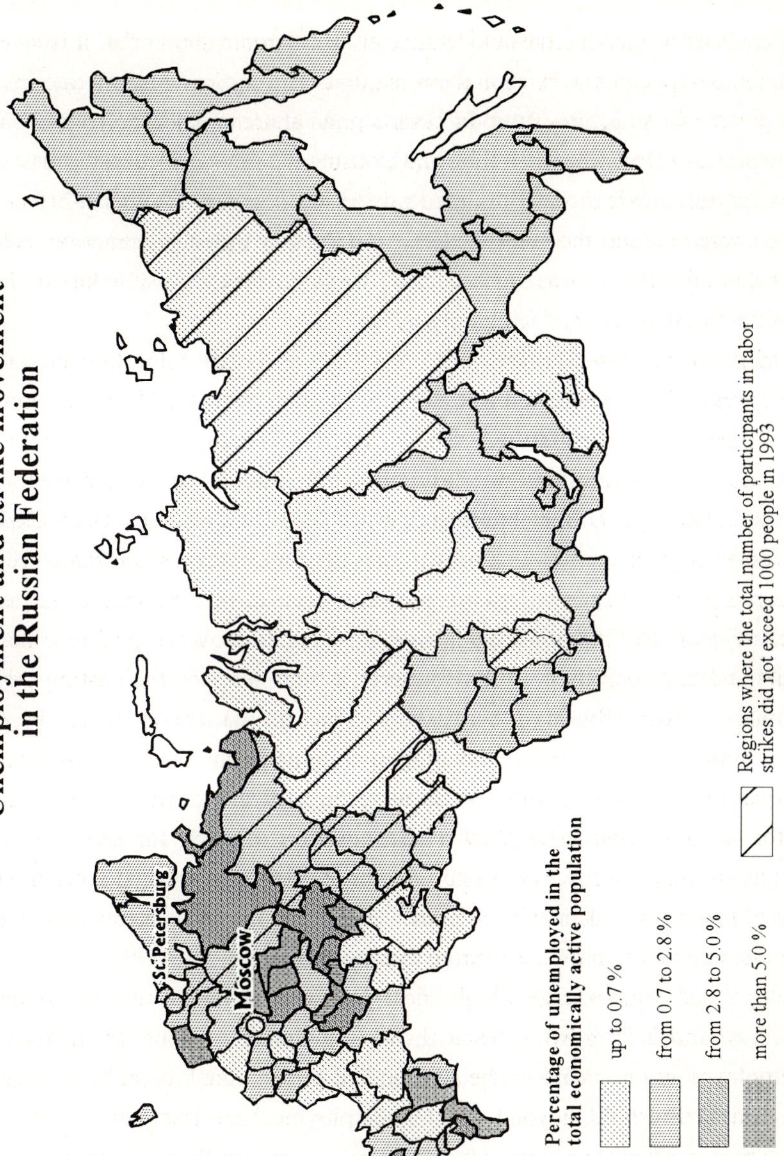

2.3 Micro-Economic Factors

In depressed regions there is a characteristic combination of a drastic decline in production, a decrease in capital investments (in comparable prices), insignificant changes in the structure of production, a great share of cost-ineffective enterprises, abnormal high unemployment rate and low income rates in industry and commerce.

Industrial output in 1993 dropped by 35% as compared with 1992. Practically in all the regions industrial output decreased by two times as compared with that in 1991, with the 1993 drop reaching 35% (Russia's average was 25%). So, the scale of the slump in production continues to grow.

The drop in industrial output in 1992-1993 was largely caused by the severance of economic ties between enterprises and the so-called 'mutual indebtedness and non-payment crisis'. The production structure in depressed regions is characterised by a very large proportion of enterprises of the manufacturing industry (machine-building, electronics, light industry, etc.) and the military-industrial complex. It is precisely these enterprises that mostly account for the drop in output. To exemplify, a shorter list of defence orders was the main reason for industrial output decrease in Udmurtia, where 25% of all the labour force are employed in the defence sector. A similar situation is observed in Mordovia, Chuvashia, Vladimir, Pskov, Kirov and Yaroslavl' *oblasts*. Ivanovo, Yaroslavl' and Kostroma *oblasts* experienced a large-scale drop (by more than four times) in light industry output. The non-payment crisis primarily gripped enterprises producing technological equipment (tools, machinery, automated and rotor lines, etc.) The proportion of such enterprises in depressed regions is also very high: up to 20% of those employed work at such enterprises in Kirov, Penza, and Vladimir *oblasts*. Thus, the suboptimal industrial profile of depressive regions caused, to a large extent, the scale of the 1991-1992 slump.

In 1993, the main reason for the drop in industrial output was a crisis of demand and an inadequate growth of working assets, which could not catch up with inflation. The demand for products designated for industries shrank much more than that for consumer goods. As a result, the industries in Yaroslavl', Kirov and Vladimir *oblasts* as well as the republics of the North Caucasus suffered great losses. A shortage of working assets turned out to be a logical consequence of the non-payment crisis, and in order to overcome it, sizeable funds were allocated from the federal and local budgets, with the major portion of them going to depressed regions. To take an example, in 1993 Udmurtia's enterprises received no less than 6.3 billion roubles in preferential credits for building up working assets; 4.7 billion roubles were appropriated from the federal budget. Structural changes in the stagnant industries of depressed regions are very sluggish.

The industrial crisis led to reduced capital investments. In Ivanovo *oblast'*, capital investments were reduced in 1993 to half in comparison with 1992 and in Kirov *oblast'* – by 40%, with the depressed regions' average being 28%, the Russian average being 15%

A decrease in capital investments into depressed regions' economies lead to a slow-down in rotation of fixed production assets. A decrease in commissioned fixed production assets, especially their active part – machinery and equipment – lead to a growth in capital consumption. In 1988-1991 commissioned production assets in depressed regions amounted to 6-8% of the total production capital value, while in 1992-1994 – only 3-3.5%.

The financial state of enterprises in depressed regions remains extremely pitiful. The cost-ineffective enterprises exceeds 25%. The debtor indebtedness of enterprises in Vladimir *oblast'* was, as of 1 January 1994, 230 billion roubles; while creditor indebtedness was 209 billion roubles, which is three times higher than the *oblast's* economic expenditures in 1993. A similar situation can be observed in all other depressed regions.

Economic recovery of the regions requires considerable funds for industrial restructuring. Since the federal budget is not in a position to finance the process, and local budgets are deficient, only commercial structures, including foreign investors, can become the sole source of financing. However, the economic and industrial policies pursued by the regions fail to facilitate the creation of acceptable conditions for large-scale investment programmes. Evidently, the economic situation in depressed regions will continue to deteriorate in the future. Adverse factors will compound one another and their multiple impact cannot be countered by the regions on their own.

3 Stagnating Regions

The following can be considered stagnating regions:

- the Republic of Karelia
- Vologda *oblast'*
- Novgorod *oblast'*
- Kaluga *oblast'*
- Ryazan *oblast'*

- Smolensk *oblast'*
- Tula *oblast'*
- Astrakhan *oblast'*
- Volgograd *oblast'*
- Rostov *oblast'*
- Perm *oblast'*
- Komi-Permyatsk autonomous *okrug*
- Sverdlovsk (Ekaterinburg) *oblast'*
- Chelyabinsk *oblast'*
- Altai *krai*
- Novosibirsk *oblast'*
- Omsk *oblast'*
- Primorskii *krai*
- Khabarovsk *krai*
- Sakhalin *oblast'*
- Kaliningrad *oblast'*

3.1 Political Factors

Local economic legislation in stagnating regions do not practically differ from the federal legislation. In their normative and legislative acts, local authorities do not, by and large, contradict the laws of the Russian Federation; their own decrees deal, in fact, only with regional industrial policy. Such inertness in creating a specific legislative basis (paying due attention to the regions' strategic objectives) for local industries and businesses complicates their functioning.

In 1993, the deficit of local budgets varied from 7-20%. There were several reasons for this. Firstly, local industries undergoing restructuring sharply decreased their outputs and, as a result, income and value-added tax funds in budget revenues also dropped. Secondly, drops in industrial outputs led to redundancies and forced unpaid leave, which, in turn, resulted in a decline in the average wage and lower tax revenues from physical persons reaching the budget. Thirdly, in stagnating regions' economic expenditures are very high and the restructuring of their economies requires considerable capital investments. About 40% of budget expenditures are allocated for these purposes. Finally, personnel redundancies mean a higher unemployment rate, and, hence, higher social expenditures.

Map 4
Drop in Industrial Production

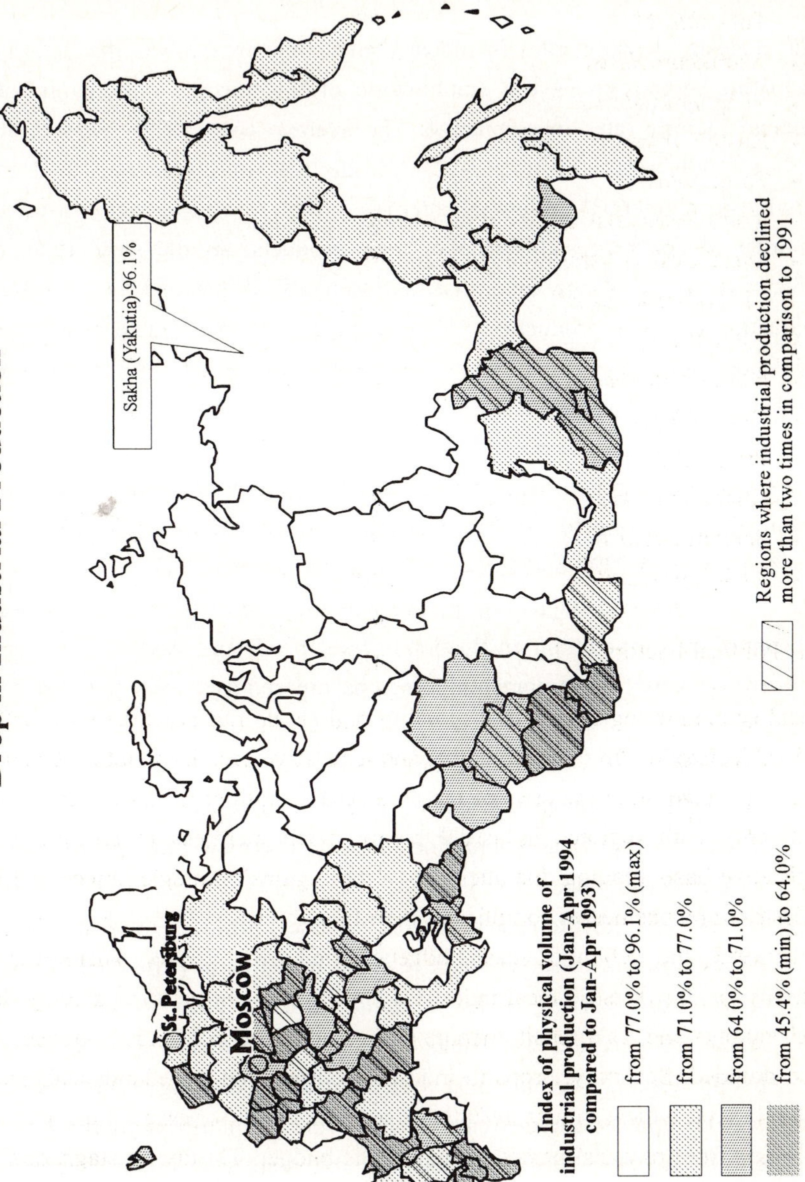

3.2 Macro-Economic Factors

Our analysis of profit rates in industry and commerce shows that it is typical of stagnating regions to have a combination of low income rates in industries and medium income rates in commerce. The average cost-effectiveness in stagnating regions' industries is from 17-32%, while that in commercial and mediatory activities is about 60%. Industrial enterprises often resort to lower cost-effectiveness in order to ensure a stable sale of their products. At the same time, the cost-effectiveness rate of new enterprises is essentially influenced by the system of re-evaluation of basic production assets adopted in Russia. Since re-evaluations are conducted once every two years with the increase rate of 15-20 times, total production capital value increases unevenly in conditions of rising inflation, and, more importantly, lags behind the inflation rate.

As a result, the cost-effectiveness rate of new enterprises turns out to be below the actual rate. Allowing for the fact that the major quantity of production assets was commissioned in 1992 and early 1993, one can surmise that the cost-effectiveness rate of enterprises in stagnating regions will increase in 1995 by 15-20% solely on account of the forthcoming revaluation of fixed production assets.

Banking activities in stagnating regions are reduced to a few main kinds of operations:

- Settlement and cash services for enterprises and organisations;
- Federal and regional investment credit servicing for industrial restructuring, mainly for the machine-building industry, chemical industry and the military-industrial complex;
- Extending credits to replenish working assets. In order to receive such credits, big enterprises co-found small regional banks or buy the controlling block of shares from existing banks. A similar practice leads to the development of small and medium-size banks in stagnating regions, with big banks being totally absent. The emerging system of amalgamating banks and enterprises may be a precondition of establishing financial-industrial groups.

The fact that banks become subjected to the interests of big enterprises adversely affects the state of the banking sphere: the crediting of small and medium enterprises shrinks, bank investment business is practically absent, and the banking sphere is incapable of implementing large-scale projects.

Unemployment in these regions is somewhat higher than the Russian average rate (by 15-37%). While the level of redundancies ix extremely high (in the defence sector, more than 50% of the personnel were made redundant in stagnating regions in 1992-1993), vacancies opening in other sectors of the economy can accommodate practically all people made redundant. Middle aged and pre-pension age people become mainly unemployed, while the proportion of unemployed youth (under 22 years old) is relatively small (less than 20%). Thus, unemployment in stagnating regions has a frictional character and is connected with structural changes in the economy.

3.3 Micro-Economic Factors

During 1993 the commercial production output in stagnating regions dropped by 25-30% but at the end of the year the rate of the slump in output somewhat decreased, which may be indicative of a possible stabilisation of industrial output in 1994 at the level of 80-90% as compared with 1993.

It is characteristic of stagnating regions to experience a sharp decline in the volume of production while capital investments are made on a grand scale and a great amount of new production assets are commissioned. To exemplify, in Karelia the share of new production assets in total production capital value of the machine-building industry amounted to 18% in 1993, which is four times as high as the industry's average.

In stagnating regions, changes in the structure of industry take place on account of the reduction of the share of capital goods production (machines, tools and technological equipment), military production and the growth of the proportion of consumer goods production. In practically all stagnating regions there is a large proportion of the defence sector industries (employing 5-12% of the able-bodied urban population). Up to the end of 1993 enterprises of the military-industrial complex had an opportunity to receive preferable credits for conversion purposes but at present, under the conditions of the government's austere crediting policy, the rate of defence conversion has dropped sharply. This situation entails three characteristic consequences. Firstly, the number of unaccomplished construction projects is growing in these regions. Secondly, the proportion of enterprises operating at full stretch is decreasing (in some sectors, i.e., electronics, radio-engineering, etc. it amounts to less than 40%). Thirdly, enterprises are increasing their demands for investment crediting for the completion of projects under construction, which influences positively the development of the market infrastructure (banks, financial intermediaries, etc.).

The financial state of enterprises in stagnating regions remains rather complicated. Because of considerable production restructuring costs and capital investments which can be recouped only in 2-3 years (and in the machine-building industry, in 5-6 years), many enterprises are suffering significant long-term bank credit indebtedness (in Karelia it is 35%, in Sverdlovsk *oblast'* – 26.9%, in Omsk *oblast'* – 26.8%, the national average being 15.5%). Many enterprises are liable for overdue repayment of debtor indebtedness, the share of which in the cumulative arrears of enterprises exceeds the Russian average by 20-70%. The share of cost-ineffective enterprises is close to the national average.

The situation in stagnating regions demands special attention on the part of local authorities which should pursue a purposeful policy in the field of industrial restructuring and market transformations. Greater interest is being displayed now in these regions by foreign investors and the preparation of foreign capital attraction projects is underway in all the regions (these projects envisage the participation of foreign consulting firms). Stagnating regions are potential points of growth in Russia's economic recovery and in the near future (within 2-4 years) they will witness an intensive production growth on the basis of a renovated industrial structure.

4 'Sluggish' Regions

The following can be considered 'sluggish' regions:

- the Republic of Komi
- Nenetsk autonomous *okrug*
- Arkhangel'sk *oblast'*
- Murmansk *oblast'*
- Orlov *oblast'*
- Belgorod *oblast'*
- Kursk *oblast'*
- Lipetsk *oblast'*
- Tambov *oblast'*
- Ulyanovsk *oblast'*
- the Republic of Karachai-Cherkessia
- Krasnodar *krai*
- Stavropol *krai*
- the Republic of Gornyi Altai
- Kemerovo *oblast'*
- Tomsk *oblast'*

- Tyumen' *oblast'*
- the Republic of Buryatia
- the Republic of Tuva
- the Republic of Khakassia
- the Krasnoyarsk *krai*
- *Evensk* autonomous *okrug*
- Taimyr (Dolgano-Nenetsk) autonomous *okrug*
- Irkutsk *oblast'*
- Oust-Ordynsk *Buryatskii* autonomous *okrug*
- Chita *oblast'*
- Aghinsk-Buryatsk autonomous *okrug*
- the Republic of Yakutia (Sakha)
- Jewish Autonomous *oblast'*
- Amur *oblast'*
- Kamchatka *oblast'*
- Magadan *oblast'*
- Chukotsk autonomous *okrug*.

4.1 Political Factors

Sluggish regions counteract, passively or actively, the reform process initiated by the government. Implementation of certain presidential decrees or legislative acts is impeded in these regions, which, given the absence of any coherent regional conception of economic development and the corresponding normative-legislative basis, creates preconditions for arbitrariness in regions' administration. Sluggish regions are sure to pay for their present stable situation when difficulties set in the future.

The category of sluggish regions includes primarily agricultural regions and the central black-earth belt, the Krasnodar and Stavropol' *krais*, etc. and mono-sectoral regions with a great share of extracting industries (the Far North, Siberia and the Far East). Characteristic of these regions is the fact that local authorities are composed largely of the former and present directors and managers of large enterprises.

The regions of the Far North, Siberia and the Far East have always been planned to operate at a loss and have always been dependent on the federal budget. An analysis of the regions' budgets (without federal subventions added) will show that practically all the regions, except for Irkutsk and Tyumen' *oblasts*, Krasnoyarsk *krai* and the republic of Sakha, have a budget deficit of over 30%. Under circumstances of reduced federal aid (which is envisaged in 1994) by 2.3 trillion roubles as per 1993 prices, the regions will need additional support in order to increase budget returns. However, since there are powerful industrial lobbies in regional bodies of power which will oppose any additional taxation of major regional industries, the budgets will be pruned in their social spending. So, hotbeds of social tension may arise and are indeed now arising in sluggish regions. To take one example, in January 1994 workers of the *Lukoil* extracting company, who were not paid their wages in full boycotted the election to the State Duma. Sluggish regions are the main breeding ground of the strike movement in Russia (they accounted for 70% of strikes in 1993).

Agricultural regions run a budget deficit of less than 15% and this is achieved solely due to the slashing of social spending. As a result, the population's incomes are lower there than the Russian average (the average wage did not exceed 130,000 roubles in March 1994 in these regions, compared to the national average of 164,000 roubles). Up to 20% of incomes are derived from personal plots of lands.

Industrial policy in sluggish regions is oriented towards supporting primary regional industries, to the detriment of other industries. Therefore, the regions' economies depend heavily on the situation in particular industrial sectors. Up to early 1994 the situation in the fuel and energy sector produced healthy profit margins (the reduced commercial rate of the rouble exchange, tax reliefs, etc.), the budget of Tyumen' *oblast'* had stable revenues from enterprise income tax funds but after a decrease in profitability of oil and gas extraction revenues sharply dropped. Large enterprises do not pay taxes to local budgets explaining this through lack of earnings from goods supplied to customers, while barter is actively used for settling payments for supplies. Regrettably, local authorities cannot take any actions to penalise enterprises, since stoppage of an enterprise in the primary industry can lead to various complications in the economic and social situation in the regions. Thus, industrial policy in sluggish regions is subject to the sectoral diktat.

4.2 Macro-Economic Factors

Our analysis shows that the profit rate in sluggish regions is abnormally higher than the national average. This is largely determined by the mining industry's export orientation and the monopolism of many enterprises which, in fact, dictate prices proceeding from their total production costs rather than the market situation. This

Map 5
Regions in which the share of loss-making enterprises exceeds 30%

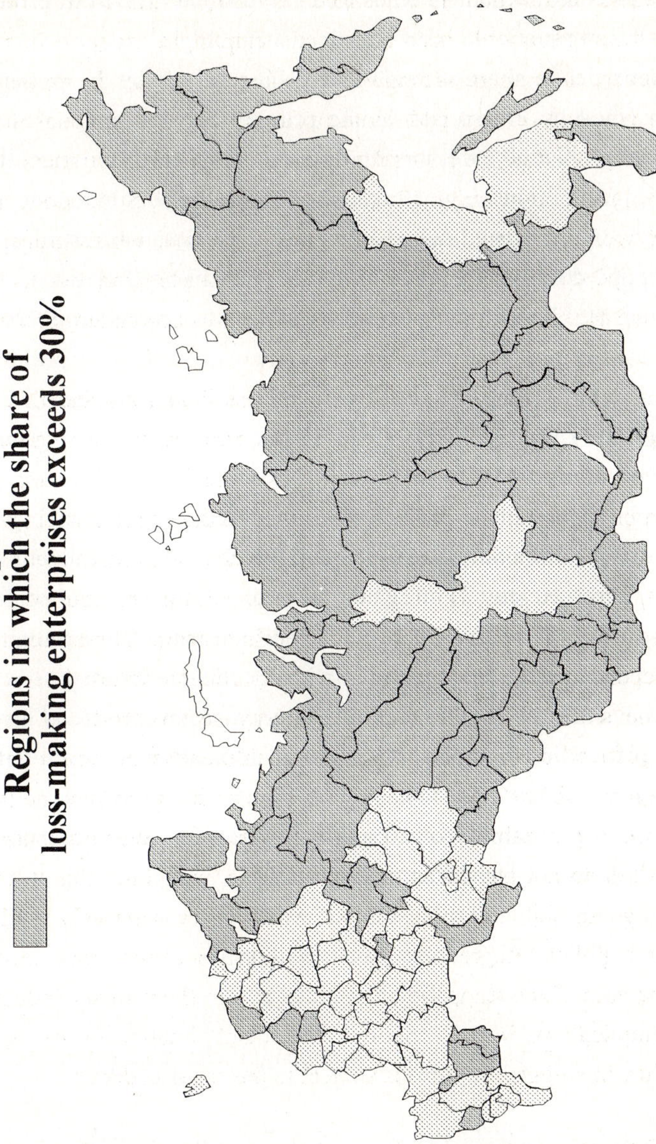

marginal cost pricing mechanism leads to an unjustified growth of production costs and restricts the introduction of new advanced technologies.

Banking activities in sluggish regions are characterised by the presence of a few large banks owned by enterprises of the primary regional industries (the former specialised banks). A high level monopolisation is typical of the market of banking services in sluggish regions, e.g., all operations with the population's deposits in the town of *Noyabr'sk* are carried out by one bank. This situation restrains competition on the market and does not facilitate introduction of market relations. Bank deposit attraction rates are 20-50 points lower than in Moscow. Large enterprises are extended the lowest interest credits, while small enterprises are imposed abnormally high interest credits. Thus, the peculiarity of the banking sphere stimulates the crediting of primary regional sectors of industry and impedes the growth of other sectors of the economy.

The unemployment rate is 1.5-2 times higher than the national average. This situation has arisen, first of all, due to the fact that the scope and level of production in the regions decreased least of all. At the same time, in the regions of the Far North there are practically no permanent residents and the redundant personnel leave for the regions of their permanent residence without being registered as jobless in the Far North. In agricultural regions the official unemployment rate is lower than the actual one because the members of the rural population who are only partially employed are not registered as jobless by social security bodies. On account of this, official statistics on unemployment are not reliable, indicating the unemployment rate to be 1.5-2 times less than is actually the case.

4.3 Micro-Economic Factors

It is typical of sluggish regions to have a combination of a small drop in output, a medium volume of capital investments and insignificant changes in the structure of industry.

Decline in output is different in various branches of industry. For primary regional sectors it is very small: in 1993 it did not exceed 20%, for other sectors – from 15-30%. Accordingly, the share of primary sectors in total industrial output has increased in sluggish regions. A narrow specialisation in production leads to a practically complete dependence of the whole region's economy on the situation in primary regional industries.

Since extracting sectors (oil, gas, etc.) are primary regional industries, the decline in industrial output in sluggish regions did not exceed 30% of the 1989 level.

Beginning in mid-1993, the demand for products of primary regional industries in sluggish regions has shrunk on account of a decrease in the efficiency of the export of all kinds of raw materials and an introduction of a system of specially assigned exporters (i.e., enterprises which have an exclusive right to export strategic products – various non-ferrous metals and the corresponding hardware). A drop in consumption of mineral raw materials within the country and the CIS resulted in a large-scale crisis of demand for mining industry products. Oil-extracting enterprises faced the crisis of demand for their products in spring 1994, when the agro-industrial complex was not extended a credit for purchasing fuel and lubricants. As a result of this, only the *Lukoil* joint-stock company, for example, had to temporarily close down over 50 oil wells and lower the daily yield by 20%. Further export efficiency loss and curtailment of production may occur if the purchasing power of the rouble with respect to the US dollar increases (at present, this policy is unswervingly pursued by the Central Bank of Russia).

Capital investments in sluggish regions in 1993 decreased by more than 25% (with Russia's average being 15%). The agro-industrial complex experienced the greatest reduction. In Voronezh *oblast'*, for example, the APK utilised half the amount of capital investments as in 1992.

Rotation of basic production assets in sluggish regions is very sluggish: newly commissioned production assets do not exceed 5% of the total production capital value. Capital consumption is on the increase: a half of all equipment has a wear and tear level of over 50%. The period required to write off debts for equipment is increasing (in the fuel and power resources complex it increased by 30-40%, in the machine-building industry – by 70-100%), which leads to the fact that primary regional industries become less receptive to innovations and the level of acquisition of sophisticated hi-tech products is falling.

In sluggish regions, there is a growth of the proportion of primary regional industries but on account of curtailment in production of other industries rather than expansion of production in the former. One-industry regions are becoming increasingly so, which adversely influences the development of market relations and a new market infrastructure in these regions.

The financial position of enterprises remains very complicated. As of January 1994, the proportion of cost-ineffective enterprises was more than 30% (in Chukotsk autonomous *okrug* it was 57%). Credit indebtedness is mainly short-term, accounting for 80-98% of all credit indebtedness. This indicates that enterprises do not have large investment programmes. Therefore, the regional policy in the sphere of financing enterprises boils down to 'eating up ' short-term credits. This is testified by the fact that less than 30% of short-term credits obtained are used to replenish working assets.

At present, the situation in sluggish regions is rather favourable in comparison with stagnating and depressed regions, but in the near future these regions' economies may experience substantial changes as a result of changes in the country's macro-economic situation. There are some fears about the future development of present-day trends which depends heavily on the existing structure of the economic complex. Dependence on the situation in primary regional industries and further growth of their share in regions' economies are leading to the emergence of one-industry regions in Russia. As the world's practice shows, such regions (e.g. the Ruhr, the Appalachian basin) are not capable of adapting quickly to changes and demand special attention from federal bodies of power (for drawing up development and social security programmes for periods of over 5 years).

5 Stable Regions

The following are considered to be stable regions:

- St. Petersburg
- Leningrad *oblast'*
- Moscow
- Moscow *oblast'*
- Tver *oblast'*
- Nizhnii Novgorod *oblast'*
- the Republic of Tatarstan
- Samara *oblast'*
- Saratov *oblast'*
- Kurgan *oblast'*
- Orenburg *oblast'*
- *Khanty-Mansiisk* autonomous *okrug*
- *Yamalo-Nenetsk* autonomous *okrug*.

5.1 Political Factors

Stable regions are actively forming their own normative-legislative bases taking into account regional peculiarities. Local authorities of stable regions pursue a flexible taxation policy. Taxation systems in these regions are improved by way of collecting full existing taxes from all enterprises and adjusting and simplifying the normative-legislative basis rather than introducing new taxes (though this right is granted to all regions by the presidential decrees No.'s 2268 and 2270 of 22 December 1993). Specifically, Tatarstan has rescinded inefficient taxes and levies (which did not pay back because of very high costs of their collection) – fees from dog owners, taxes and fees from racecourses, fees from use of local symbols. By trying to smooth over the normative-legal basis, local authorities very often run counter to the present Russian legislation in force but, at the same time, they create favourable conditions for the development of local businesses and industries.

Deficits of local budgets in stable regions do not exceed 10%. This can be accounted for, on the one hand, by the fact that tax funds can be easily calculated and prognosticated in a relatively stable economic situation, when there is a well-defined and clear-cut legislative basis, and, on the other hand, by the fact that practically all local authorities in these regions employ highly skilled specialists and groups of experts as economic consultants. In Nizhnii Novgorod *oblast'*, which, under rather favourable conditions, could have found itself among depressed regions (because of a very high share of industries badly hit as a result of industrial restructuring, specifically, in the machine-building and metal fabricating industries, and the military-industrial complex), they managed, due to the efforts of Boris Nemtsov, the *oblast's* governor, and the assistance of the think-tank *EPI-Tsentr*, headed by Grigorii Yavlinskii, to elaborate and implement a very efficient programme for the *oblasts* economic recovery. Given that the share of expenditures for the economic complex in the budgets and gross domestic products of these regions are roughly equivalent to the national average, the efficiency rate of such investments is much higher, first of all on account of the comprehensive nature of industrial restructuring programmes, targeted use of funds and the monitoring of their implementation by local authorities.

5.2 Macro-Economic Factors

Profit rates in industry and commerce in stable regions are somewhat lower (by 15-25%) than the national average rate. This is explained by the saturation of consumer market and rising competition.

Banking activities in stable regions are characterised by a number of peculiarities. Firstly, all leading banks provide the basic range of services in stable regions. Secondly, the process of bank stabilisation is underway, which creates conditions for a 'peaceful coexistence' of big banks specialised in extending inter-bank credits and servicing extended correspondent networks for postal payments; medium banks rendering settlement and cash services and managing the current and credit accounts of enterprises and small banks rendering banking services for population – deposits, currency exchange, etc. The development of banking networks, the diversification of banking services and the growing competition are leading to the formation of favourable conditions in these regions for the operations of both resident and non-resident producers. Many enterprises from other regions make use of the infrastructure of stable regions for their own operations. Bank credit rates in stable regions are 7-10 points lower than the Russian average.

It is typical of stable regions to have a low unemployment rate (half the national average). With an insignificant number of redundancies, practically all people made redundant find jobs within a year. There is a greater number of vacancies in stable regions related to low paid jobs and hard physical labour. Since unemployment here has a frictional character, vacancies are filled by casual workers from other regions and countries. The practice of inviting seasonal construction teams from Belarus and Ukraine and retail dealers from the North Caucasus and Transcaucasian republics is widespread.

5.3 Micro-Economic Factors

It is characteristic of these regions to have a combination of an insignificant (relative to the scope of the crisis) drop in output (in 1993, not more than 25%), an insignificant decrease in capital investments (in 1993, by 10-12%) and a small share of cost-ineffective enterprises.

Decline in industrial output was less than 25%; practically in all the regions industrial output decreased by less than two times, compared with 1991. The drop in industrial output was largely caused by a large-scale slump in manufacturing industries, with a great number of idle enterprises converted for other purposes during 1992-1993. Large diversified enterprises with a small proportion of military and related products in commercial output are prevalent in the MIC of the regions. Among them there are many technology-intensive enterprises which proved to be receptive to innovative processes, e.g., at Zelenograd *Kvant* plant (Moscow) the production of IBM computers was launched. Some defence-related enterprises started to produce or assemble medical equipment, audio- and video-recorders, etc.

The problem of replenishing working assets for enterprises was solved by means of special credits extended from the federal and local budgets and by commercial banks. The creation of prototypes of financial and industrial groups and an active participation of powerful banks in solving the problem of posting settlement entries, which was very acute until the end of 1993, made it possible for the regions' economies to remain stable over the recent period.

The decrease in capital investments into these regions' economies did not exceed 10-12% in 1992-1993. The reduction largely affected new construction projects, with the share of capital investments for converting and modernising existing capacities increased. Thus, the commissioning of new basic production assets amounted to 5-7% in 1992-1994 in stable regions (for the active part, it was 8-9%).

The financial positions of enterprises in stable regions are very different and dependent on the kind of industry and specific conditions. Among enterprises of the electronic industry, one of the most badly hit by the slump, there are enterprises which not only managed to keep up their commercial output but even succeeded in building it up by 20-25%. Therefore, the relative stability is obtained due to a great regional diversity.

Economic recovery has already begun in stable regions: according to preliminary statistics for the second quarter of 1994, the decline in output has stopped in Moscow and Nizhnii Novgorod *oblasts*, the republic of Tatarstan and in Moscow city. Since local authorities pursue a purposeful policy of creating normal conditions in these regions for the functioning of industry and market infrastructure and carry out a number of measures on realising the available potential, in the near future one can expect a normalisation of the situation and economic recovery in all stable regions.

7

Ethnic and Regional Conflicts in the Post-Soviet Space

Emil Pain and Arkadii Popov

1 Types of Ethnic Conflicts and Conflict Zones in the Former Soviet Union

In the period since 1987, when the first wide-scale ethno-political conflict (Nagorno-Karabakh) began, the former USSR territory has endured:

- 6 regional wars – long-lasting (at least for several months) hostilities involving regular troops and heavy arms (the so-called Karabakh, Tadzhik, South-Ossetian, Transdnestrian, Abkhazian and Chechen conflicts);
- about 20 short-term armed conflicts, lasting up to several days, causing casualties among civil population (Ferghana, Osh, Ossetian-Ingush conflicts, Baku and Sumgait pogroms and other);
- more than 100 non-armed collisions manifesting acute confrontation of states, ethnic groups, clans and confessions of faith (the majority of them being concentrated in Central Asia, Transcaucasus and the Russian North Caucasus).

Furthermore, there are vast territories in Russia and the former Soviet states (primarily Povolzh'e, South Siberia, Kazakhstan, Ukraine and the Baltic States) where the jeopardy of inter-community relations growing into various conflicts is quite likely (potential conflict zones). Some zones where to date no collisions have been reported remain seats of smouldering menace, because in most cases the reasons that have caused or are likely to cause confrontation have not been eliminated.

Once unleashed, the conflicts tend to expand and involve broader and broader population strata. More than 10 million people including several hundred thousand Russian-speaking members of the population live in the armed conflict zones (i.e., in the very regions affected by combat, bloody outbreaks and ethnic pogroms), and many of them have been compelled to abandon their homes.

According to the character and scale of existing and potential confrontation, all former Soviet states or republics can be divided into five zone types:

Armed ethnic and regional conflict zones. In this type combat operations are being conducted at present or there may be an unstable armistice, with random armed violence outbreaks and hostilities. This type lists:

- Chechen Republic territory,
- Nagorno-Karabakh and adjoining districts of West Azerbaidzhan, occupied by the Karabakh troops;
- Abkhazia;
- South and Central Tadzhikistan regions.

Acute ethnic and political confrontation zones. Those regions where armed force is either being used or highly likely to be used and where the reconciliation of the conflict achieved by separating the contending parties did not resolve the initial political and ethno-psychological problems which sparked the conflict. These regions are:

- Transdnestria;
- South Ossetia;
- the Prigorodnyi district in South Ossetia;
- part of the Chechen and Ingush Republics.

Ethno-political tension zones. This category includes the territories where the present context reveals ethno-psychological, ideological and/or political opposition between various communities and regions in the form of confrontation of leaders, parties, national organisations or authorities. Among such territories are:

- the Crimea;
- a few North Caucasian republics (Dagestan, Kabardino-Balkaria, Karachaevo-Cherkessia;
- the Lezgin-populated districts of North Azerbaidzhan;
- the Eastern and South-western parts of the Fergana valley.

Potential ethno-political confrontation zones. No direct ideological or political conflicts between ethnic communities or regional population groups have been waged so far, yet due to different reasons (primarily demographic conditions) there are real preconditions for ethnic tension to emerge and under some circumstances to develop into severe ethno-political conflicts. Such examples are:

- Tatarstan;
- Bashkortostan;

- Tuva;
- the regions of North and East Kazakhstan with a predominantly Russian-speaking population;
- the southern districts of the Krasnodar and the Stavropol *krais*, as well as the northern parts of the Caucasian republics situated along a band where these republics' titular nationalities and the Russian-Cossack and Nogai populations meet;
- some border territories in the Ukraine, inhabited mostly by the non-Ukrainian population (the Donbass, the Carpathians);
- the North-east districts of Estonia and the capital metropolis in Latvia where the proportion of the Russian population is high;
- the Talysh-inhabited South Azerbaidzhan districts;
- the northern district and around the Issyk-Kul' district in Kirghizia;
- the northern Turkmenistan districts adjoining the Khoresm oasis.

Ethno-political stability zones, where at present there are no manifest preconditions for any serious opposition or conflicts on ethnic grounds (the remainder of the FSU territories).

2 Ethnic Conflicts in the Russian Federation

2.1 General Factors in the Emergence of Conflict Situations in Russia

Four major types of ethno-political contradictions have been revealed on the territory of Russia, although not in the same acute form as in the other new independent states:

- conflicts between the federal government and the republics within the federation on account of the sovereignty of the former national autonomies;
- conflicts between the federation members (republics, *krais*, *oblasts*) over territorial claims (e.g., the contention between Ingushetia and Ossetia over the disputed Prigorodnyi district);
- inter-community contradictions within the republics, *krais* and *oblasts* (the most severe examples being between the numerous nationalities of Dagestan, and between the main ethnic communities of Kabardino-Balkaria and some other republics);
- conflicts between ethnic groups (i.e., between the ethnic majority and dispersed minorities), connected essentially with ethnic competition on the

labour market in the cities, land disputes in the countryside and a general escalation of various brands of ethnic phobia: in Central Russia the most manifested one is the anti-Caucasian prejudice; there also exist local-scale anti-Gypsy moods; and there is the threat of a resumption of anti-Semitic outbreaks, and in some republics – Russophobia.

After October 1993 throughout the greater part of Russia's territory (excluding the North Caucasus) the crisis in relations between the central power and the subjects of the federation was mostly overcome. Stabilisation of the political situation, reconstruction of the power structures and normalisation of relations with most autonomies (above all with Tatarstan – the leader of the struggle for sovereignty) considerably reduced the degree of overall ethno-political tension in Russia and lessened the likelihood of a number of potential conflicts to be exploding.

Nowadays it is reckoned that ethno-political or social-ethnic confrontation in the national minorities populated regions of the Russian North, Povolzh'e, the Urals and Siberia is unlikely. Although the possibility of ethnic tension arising due to social reasons cannot be completely eliminated, especially in the depressed regions of the Russian Federation (in particular in the Far North and Far East, Tuva, Kalmykia etc.), the major open and potential conflicts within Russia are concentrated primarily in the North Caucasus.

Today in seven North Caucasian republics (Adygeya, Kabardino-Balkaria, Karachaevo-Cherkessia, Chechnya, Ingushetia, North Ossetia, Dagestan) and two *krais* (Krasnodar and Stavropol') the number of nationalities amounts to over thirty with total population of 17.5 million people (in 1994). The multinational composition of the region's population and its proximity to neighbouring ethnic communities, which often have a controversial historical background, have proved to be a rich soil for the breeding of numerous rampant ethnic and political crises. In the case of the Ossetian-Ingush confrontation such tension led in autumn 1992 to a bloody armed conflict; in the case of Chechnya such tension indirectly caused the acute constitutional crisis which in late 1994 developed into a bloody war between federal troops and Chechen armed units, fighting to defend the President Dudaev's self-proclaimed regime (this conflict is addressed in the 'Policies of Russia in the Conflict Zones').

The following general factors heightening the ethno-political tension in the North Caucasus can be enumerated:

- presence of unsolved territorial and status-related disputes between different ethnic communities and national and territorial formations, derived from the colonial history of the pre-Soviet and Soviet periods when the borders had been arbitrarily altered and entire nationalities were deported etc.;
- the striving of the new national elite, formed in the *perestroika* era, to come to power by revolutionary means by riding the wave of self-initiated national determination movements and regarded as the endeavour of national autonomies and ethnic communities to acquire state independence;
- the destabilising effect of ethnic conflicts and hard fighting for power in the bordering Transcaucasian states, mainly in Georgia;
- the high concentration of vast numbers of refugees and migrants from the conflict zones in the Transcaucasus and Central Asia, which become another catalyst of ethnic tension in such regions;
- the high concentration of various weapons and the presence of numerous illegal and uncontrolled armed units operating in the region and formed according to ethnic or clan principle, often closely related to criminal structures;
- the weakness of the central power and local authorities, their incapability to establish effective control over the political and criminal situation in the region and to implement wise and consequent policies concerning inter-ethnic relations.

The Cossack movement has also become a significant political factor in the region, which is demonstrated by the self-proclamation of the 'Cossack republics'. The law on rehabilitation of the Cossacks created the legal basis for the restoration of Cossack self-administration on the territories originally settled by the Cossacks. However, this process is actually aimed at revival of the militant Cossack strata opposing the highlands' peoples. A specific political force is being formed which may possibly become another aggravating factor in the region.

2.2 The Ossetian-Ingush Conflict

The origin of this conflict lies in the dispute between North Ossetia and Ingushetia with regard to the Prigorodnyi district, which is claimed by the Ingush, but which since 1945, following the deportation of Chechen and the Ingush people and the abolition of the Chechen-Ingush autonomy, was transferred to North Ossetia and remained part of it after the reinstatement of the Chechen-Ingush Autonomous Soviet Socialist Republic. The dispute over this district, inhabited by about 40,000

Ingush people in autumn 1992 (according to Ingush estimations – up to 60,000), ignited the bloody Ossetian-Ingush clashes, claiming more than 600 lives.

The armed attacks of the Ingush guerrillas against Ossetian villages and Vladikavkaz were suppressed by Russian troops within a few days of the conflict's eruption, thus raising Moscow's authority among Ossetian society, but provoking extreme discontent among the Ingush population, which accused the Russian military of disregarding Ossetian law and of unwarranted brutality towards the civil Ingush population. Subsequently, the attempts of Moscow to convince the North Ossetian authorities to repatriate the Ingush to Prigorodnyi district were protested by the Ossetians and caused their rather guarded stance towards the Russian government. The negotiations conducted by the government with the two republics' leaders required much effort and only in June 1994 under firm pressure from the federal authorities was a principal agreement reached by both parties with regard to concrete steps to repatriate the Ingush refugees to the first four settlements in Prigorodnyi district.

Nevertheless, the implementation of this agreement and of the corresponding resolutions by the president and the government of Russian Federation dissatisfied both parties. During the next months the tension in the conflict zone was not alleviated due to incessant armed criminal incidents of a clearly ethnically motivated nature (arson, ethnic murders, seizure of hostages, etc.). Thus, from time to time the parties continue to exchange claims and accusations.

After the president of the Russian Federation had declared a state of emergency in the region, regional administrators took a number of measures to restore law and order, to search for the hostages and to disarm the militant, unlawful detachments. This enabled a certain 'freezing' of the conflict and averted further clashes, although it was not possible to ensure total stabilisation. This problem can only be resolved in the course of political dialogue, as long as the major controversies concerning the status of the district and the problems of the Ingush refugees remain unsolved.

The Ossetian side regards the very raising of the status question as provocative and unacceptable, referring to provisions of the Russian Constitution on the republics – Members of the Federation. The Ingush side insists on the re-transfer of the district under dispute, referring to the *Law on Rehabilitation of the Peoples Subject to Repression* passed in April 1991 by the Supreme Soviet, some articles of which actually stipulate the restoration of the former border-lines of the national-territorial formations of repressed peoples. As the preliminary condition for further negotiations, the Ossetian leadership demands the full renunciation by the Ingush authorities of any claims on Prigorodnyi district, while the latter agree to renounce their claims only on Vladikavkaz (a part of which also belonged to Chechen-Ingushetia before 1944) and as a compromise they propose to introduce direct federal administration, an idea which is entirely rejected by the North Ossetian leaders and public.

As far as the refugees problem is concerned, the Ingush insist that all Ingush people who had previously lived in Prigorodnyi district should have the right to return there as well as to have personal security guarantees; the Ossetian authorities do not formally object to this, but insist on step-by-step repatriation, alleging that 'the Ossetian population is not prepared to live jointly with the Ingush'. The Ossetians demand that Moscow give an official account of the 1992 events, and that Nazran admit that the conflict was unleashed by the Ingush.

Another significant problem in the continuing tension in North Ossetia's territory is the high concentration of enormous amounts of unregistered weapons, some of which are supplied from the other RF republics and from South Ossetia, while others were seized by the militants in the course of attacking federal troop units. Furthermore, during the conflict in the Prigorodnyi district, illegal national guards units of North Ossetia were formed, consisting of local and South-Ossetian guerrillas, which, following the introduction of the emergency state and the demand to lay down arms, were legalised by a decree of the Supreme Soviet of North Ossetia. These units also became the prototype of a republic's armed forces, being in many respects beyond the control of the central authorities.

The indefinite status of the Prigorodnyi district and the future of many thousands of Ingush refugees, the continuing high level of tension in the conflict zone and the lack of considered legislative and executive policies aimed at resolving the national disputes may lead to further clashes. The situation is aggravated by difficult socio-economic conditions in both republics. North Ossetia hosts more than 50,000 Ossetian refugees from Georgia, which makes economic hardships worse and induces social controversies. Besides the additional strain placed on the budget and social infrastructure, plans (partially implemented) to settle the refugees in former Ingush settlements in the Prigorodnyi district will have a destabilising effect.

One additional source of tension in the conflict zone is the ambiguous political status and the socio-economic conditions in Ingushetia. The republic of Ingushetia was founded by a decree of the Russian Federation's Supreme Soviet in 1992, yet its borders and territory have not been determined even today. The actual authority of the Ingush leaders is spread over three administrative districts of the former

Chechen-Ingush ASSR – Nazran, Malgobek and Sunzhen districts, although Chechnya's authorities have refused to acknowledge the Sunzhen district's transfer to Ingushetia. Prior to the separation of Chechen-Ingushetia (where Ingushetia was a indeed a far-flung province) into two republics, the Ingush share of productive capacity was less than 10% of the total, the majority of its enterprises having outdated and depreciated equipment. There is no developed social or production infrastructure, transport or communication networks or skilled administrative and industrial workers. The war in Chechnya has furthermore caused another wave of refugees to Ingushetia (50,000 according to official statistics), and has deeply worsened social-economic conditions, while the actual occupation of the republic by Russian military forces has raised ethnic tension in the region.

2.3 The Conflict Centres in Dagestan

Dagestan is potentially one of the most dangerous regions in terms of being prone to conflicts, especially due to its unique multinational population. Over 30 nationalities and ethnic groups living here consider Dagestan their historically native land, among them the most numerous being the Nakh-Dagestan language group (the so-called 'highland' people), the Avar (496,000 or 27%), the Dargin (280,000 or 15%), the Lezgin (204,000 or 11%), the Lakh (92,000 or 5%) and others. There are also a number of Turkic speaking peoples – the Kumyk (231,000 or 13%) and the Nogai (28,000 or 1.5%). The fraction of Russian speaking population including Cossacks is 9.1% (166,000).

The most menacing ethnic problem in Dagestan likely to cause conflict is that of the Lezgins. The problem derives from the aspiration of the leaders of the Lezgin national movement 'Sadval', founded in 1991, to create a specific national and state formation – member of the Russian Federation – a 'Republic of Lezgistan' within the area originally inhabited by the Lezgin and spread over Southern Dagestan and Northern Azerbaidzhan. Realisation of their plan would mean the annexation of part of Azerbaidzhan's and Dagestan's territories, and the authorities in both Baku and Makhach-kala are extremely opposed to the idea.

The situation here was exacerbated after the events of March 1993 when Azerbaidzhan authorities dispersed the meeting of many thousands of people organised by 'Sadval' in the Azerbaidzhan town of Kusary at which occasion a number of people were killed. Following this and other accidents on both sides of the Azerbaidzhan-Dagestan border, the slogans of the Lezgin national-radicals called the Lezgin people to arms in order to fight 'for freedom and independence'. Growth in the pro-federal disposition among the Lezgins and therefore possible conflict with Azerbaidzhan will inevitably bring forth not only an Azerbaidzhan-Lezgin confrontation in the Southern Dagestan (where there are over 100,000 Azerbaidzhan natives) but will increase the overall tension between the highland and the Turkic nationalities in the central districts, in the localities shared by the Kumyk and the 'highlanders'.

Furthermore, attempts to implement similar demands on the part of the Nogai people could involve the republic into a conflict with the authorities and population of neighbouring Chechnya, Karachaevo-Cherkessia and other regions. The claims of the Nogai national movement *Birlyk* (having its branches in Dagestan, Karachaevo-Cherkessia, Stavropol' *krai* and Chechnya) are geared towards establishing a Nogai territorial autonomy in the perimeter inhabited by the Nogai within the above named regions.

The Nogai are supported by another Turkic nationality of Dagestan, namely the Kumyk, who are also aspiring to gain a territorial autonomy of their own, but within the borders of Dagestan. They regard this as the only guarantee in the defence of their interests, since the republic's power structures are dominated by the highland peoples, the Avar, Dargin and Lakh. The latent 'highlanders' vs. 'Turkic' rivalry is aggravated by the ancient struggle for land, caused by the historical process – the highlanders' expansion into the plane, originally populated by the Kumyk and Cossack peoples. One of the most acute conflicts of recent years was that between the Kumyk and the Lakh, when the republic's authorities attempted to settle a part of the Lakh community (which had temporarily occupied the territory of the deported Akkins-Chechens, but was forced to withdraw after the latter returned in 1991) on the Kumyk's native territory. In 1992 this conflict was accompanied by armed clashes and Kumyk mass meetings and strikes. It remains a dangerous source of confrontation in view of the fact that the highlanders' national movements opposing the Kumyks dispose of armed detachments and are highly politicised.

The practically totally armed population and the passivity of law-and-order bodies, which are often interconnected with criminal and ethnic armed units, are the main factors leading to the escalation of crime. In the recent years a sharp increase in the number of assassinations and armed robberies of prominent politicians and administrators was reported yet almost none of the cases have been solved. Any nationalities other than native ones are being actively ousted from the republic. In 1993 alone around 5,000 Russian families were compelled to leave Dagestan, many of them having to sell their houses and property at knock-down prices. This process also had a degrading impact on the republic's industry, which is in need of qualified labour.

Another particular case is the problem of the Tersk (Grebensk) descendants of the Cossacks living compactly at Nizhnii Terek (around 15,000), officially represented by the Kyzlar department of the Tersk Cossacks. The leaders and ideologists of Cossacks' revival in Dagestan also insist on territorial autonomy, which, in their opinion, would help to re-establish the traditional Cossacks' economy and farming, undermined by the Soviet system, such as viticulture and fishing as well as helping to reverse the active demographic and economic expansion by the Avars, Dargins and other highlanders into the Cossacks' districts.

However, the territory bordering Chechnya and populated by the Dagestan Chechens (Akkins) has become the most menacing centre of instability in the republic. In the event that combat operations shift to this area, a chain reaction of clashes and conflicts will be inevitable and will grow into a powerful all-Dagestan ethno-political explosion.

2.4 The Conflict Situations in Kabardino-Balkaria and Karachaevo-Cherkessia

In Kabardino-Balkaria (KB) the main reason for tension is both peoples' (the Kabardin and the Balkar) political elite, who are seeking territorial and national demarcation, and their inability to come to a compromise concerning a possible border between the two mono-ethnic republics that would replace one KB.

It was the leading Balkar political public organisation – the *National Council of the Balkar People* – that appealed for the creation of the Balkar republic within the RF as early as 1991. Then, in January 1992 the idea to split KB was approved of by the Congress of the Kabardin People, which proclaimed the founding of the Kabardin republic within the RF and instituted an official parallel body to carry out this idea – the *Congress of Kabardin People* (CKP). Its new leaders proceeded with the transformation of this body into a weapon of the new Kabardin national and political elite's struggle for power and domination in the region, regardless of the threat of confrontation with the neighbouring communities.

Due to the Georgian-Abkhazian war, where the Kabardin national organisations assisted their ethnic compatriots, the Abkhaz, the relations with adjacent Georgia deteriorated. The CKP is an active member of the extremely politicised and belligerent organisation, the *Confederation of Caucasian Peoples* (CCP), allegedly uniting 16 national movements of highland peoples of the North Caucasus, South Ossetia and Abkhazia. Declaring their fight for freedom against Georgian expansion, the CCP equipped and sent to Georgia several thousand volunteers from North Caucasian republics, including KB, to fight on the side of the Abkhazian separatists. The anti-Georgian disposition of the Kabardins is not at all shared by the Turkic-speaking Balkars, whose organisations reject participation in the CCP, regarding it a means of political domination of the Abkhaz-Adygeyan and the Nakh-Dagestan ethnic groups in the North Caucasus.

The ethno-political situation in this sector of the North Caucasus is complicated by the view-point of many Kabardin leaders, who proclaim that the Kabardin republic will only set out the political unification of all Adygeyan (Cherkessian) ethnic branches – Kabardin, Adygeyan (native population of the republic of Adygeya), Cherkessian, Abazin (a part of the native residents of Karachaevo-Cherkessia) and Shapsug (a small community in the Black Sea coastal districts in the Krasnodar *krai* – and the Adygeyan diaspora abroad into one national state formation.

The prospects of KB's division into two separate mono-ethnic republics will be fraught with collisions concerning the frontiers between the Kabardin and the Balkar communities, and with respect to the foundation of a common Adygeyan republic – also between the Adygeyan and the Russian, as well as the Adygeyan and the Turkic (Karachai-Balkar) population. At the present rate of arms per person, the region faces a serious threat of becoming a new armed conflict zone.

In Karachaevo-Cherkessia (KC) territorial demarcation also constitutes a very severe problem, with both parties laying mutual territorial claims. In November 1990 the Congress of the People's Deputies of Karachai announced its all-out support for the establishment of a sovereign Karachai republic. Later, the same claims were put forward by the leaders of all other national movements in KC. However, demands to split KC into five mono-ethnic republics, the territories of which often overlap, can not be implemented peacefully. Any such separation will be accompanied by territorial altercations fraught with armed conflicts.

The same threat is implicit in the KC's Adygeyan (Cherkessian) communities' intentions to 're-unite' with 'ethnic brothers' in Kabardino-Balkaria and Adygeya, and furthermore to enclave the districts inhabited by the Shapsug (big resort areas around Sochi and Tuapse) into this national-territorial formation. Any attempt to alter the border-lines will detonate a chain reaction of mutual claims likely to develop into mass armed conflicts throughout the North Caucasus.

The social and political life in KC is embittered by the declarations of the local Cossack organisations which stand for excluding the lands inhabited by the Cossacks from KC and either annexing them into Krasnodar *krai* or merging them into a separate Cossack republic within the RF. An opinion poll in two districts (Zelenchuk and Urup) mainly populated by the Cossacks revealed that two-thirds of those questioned support the idea of a Cossack national-administrative formation and insist on dropping out of KC. Naturally, the authorities of KC strongly object to the territorial division of the republic. At the referendum organised by them in spring 1992, the majority of KC's population voted for a single and indivisible Karachaevo-Cherkessia.

3 Russia's Policy in the Conflict Zones of the Former Soviet Union (1991-1994)

For the whole period of the Russian Federation's post-communist government, its policy with regard to conflict situations in different regions of the ex-USSR was characterised primarily by *inconsistency* and *discrepancy*, reflecting both the complications of the internal political struggle in Russia and the unstable political situation in the CIS, as well as the discord in the very political establishment in Russia, consisting of heterogeneous components – the liberal union and the former communist *nomenklatura*.

Naturally, Russia's attitude towards the ethnic conflicts within the country somehow differs from its policies in the CIS conflict zones. But since there were no armed conflicts in Russia itself before 1992, we should start our analysis from the external policy aspects of the problem under consideration.

3.1 Russia's Policy in the FSU conflict zones

It was indeed Russia's historical achievement to hinder political efforts to retain all ex-Soviet republics in the USSR by force, which helped prevent the 'Yugoslavian pattern' evolving in the Soviet Union, i.e., armed conflicts between republics and their development into a Yugoslavian-style war.

The events of 1989-1991 in Tbilisi, Baku and Vilnius illustrated the tendency of forced (involving the army) retention of the republics in the USSR, revealed by that time. In these cases the Russian government acted as a counterbalance to such a tendency, and expressed its support to Georgia and Azerbaidzhan when Soviet troops invaded the capitals of these republics in 1989-90. In January 1991 it also rejected the actions of Soviet power in Vilnius. The proclamation of Russia's sovereignty and the independence of Russian policy from Soviet policy deprived the latter of the very opportunity to use Russia as a base to preserve the Soviet Union.

It should be noted that any reproaches again the Russian government concerning the shattered superpower have no grounds. The process of the USSR's decomposition by that time (1990-1991) was irreversible, which can be proved by the following:

- the all-out rise of national movements, with the aim of seceding from the USSR; this rise was proved by the results of general elections held in several republics, where nationally conscious leaders and structures came to power;
- the vast international public and governmental support of the Soviet republics' efforts to gain independence; in this respect the unanimity of the UN and European Council's members was very illustrative with regard to acceptance of the new post-Soviet states in these international organisations;
- the absence of any tangible support from the Russian population for the August coup as an attempt to restore the unitary Soviet state; as well as the steep increase of the centrifugal tendencies outside the RF, enhanced by the *coup*.

In the wake of the Ukrainian referendum on 1 December 1991 it was the emergency steps taken by the Russian government to keep the chaotic process of the USSR's decomposition civilised, such as the initiative of the Belovezhskoe Agreement to create the CIS, which helped the former USSR to avoid the fate of Yugoslavia and Russia and Ukraine – the fate of Serbia and Croatia. Another merit of the Russian government was that despite all mistakes and complications Russian diplomacy did manage to play an active and decisive role in the resolution of several conflicts in the ex-Soviet countries. Through the direct mediation of the president and the Ministry for Foreign Affairs of Russia, agreements were reached to cease fire and lay down arms, to demarcate the contending parties and to deploy Russian peace-keeping troops in Moldova (the conflict over Transdnestria) and Georgia (the conflict in South Ossetia). Due to these efforts the slaughter was brought to an end and the crowds of refugees were stopped, some of them even returned to their homes, even though a political solution to the problem of some territories' disputed status has not yet been found and has been in fact been postponed for an indefinite period.

The peace-making activities of Russia were generally successful in the Karabakh and the Abkhazian conflicts as well, especially in 1994. The arbitration efforts of Russian diplomacy (and in the case of the Abkhazian conflict, Russian peace-keeping military forces as well) allowed a cessation of the bloodshed, which has not been resumed for over a year already, although an adequate settlement of the problem of refugees and the future political status of the 'self separated' territories has not yet been found.

Nevertheless, analysing Russia's state policy in the conflict zones one can clearly ascertain some negative aspects. Among them we should note the *lack of distinct goals and priorities in state policy.* Until today, the state bodies of the RF have worked out neither an integral concept of national interests nor a set of state policy objectives or priorities in the conflict zones in the FSU. Both society as a whole and high political circles lack a distinct and civilised sense of justice when considering such key notions as a 'great power', 'presence in the region', 'political stability', 'defending compatriots abroad', etc. Therefore, these notions are often misinterpreted and even abused, which brings about negative political outcomes. For example, when applied to Russia the notion of 'great power' is often understood as the right to dominate over the less powerful neighbour-countries and even to wilfully interfere in their domestic affairs using the armed forces, rather than as a sign of responsibility – being a nuclear power and permanent UN Security Council member – for the world's stability. As for Russia's 'presence in the region': instead of seeking what is natural for any other state in the domain of international relations, namely to establish and maintain above all good diplomatic and economic positions of the state in a certain region, some Russian politicians regard this presence in purely military terms, which cannot but induce Russophobia in the neighbouring countries (as was the case for example in relations with Georgia and Moldova before 1994 and still is in the relations with the Baltic states).

The development of political and economic democracy, which is the only means to ensure long-lasting – *strategic* – stability in the just-recovering post-Soviet states, is often sacrificed in favour of the interests of certain authoritarian leaders, who promptly declared their eagerness to 'be friends' with Russia. In most cases such 'friendship' can be reduced to little more than the money-flow from Russia keeping the socialist-planned economy of the countries in question afloat and to feed their enormous power structures (e.g., as is the case in Russian-Uzbek relations).

Neither have Russia's policy goals and objectives been formulated with regard to specific regions. To a great extent this explains the executive power structures' inability to defend Russia's long-term strategic interests in the Caucasus, in Central Asia and in other regions, as well as their failure to take adequate measures in the cases of sudden aggravation of the situation outside and inside Russia (in Georgia, in the Crimea, in Transdnestria etc.). However, just as many problems resulted from the struggle to gain influence over different state levels as from the weak structure of vertical power or even the absence thereof.

The rejection of the former highly centralised command-administrative system, accelerating decentralisation processes in social life and the structural changes in the administration inevitable in such times of transition affected the traditional power vertical and brought forth many significant autonomous 'power centres' at different levels. Formerly these were the Supreme Soviet and People's Deputies' Congress, while today they include (either in fact or in aspiration) many republican and regional power bodies, the highest military ranks, as well as various ethnic or regional (e.g. Cossacks) organisations, which are often influenced by different criminal groups.

The above listed 'centres' complicate administration even in the more or less stable RF; in conflict zones their unconstrained activities have very detrimental impact on Russia's national interests and induce increases in violence.

The struggle for power between such 'power centres', which often exploit external problems in order to achieve their political goals regardless of the possible consequences the state policy, makes the co-ordination between the state bodies difficult and an integral Russian state policy in the conflict zones impossible.

Thus, there is complete discrepancy between the opinions and actions of various Russian state representatives over the same issues (e.g. in summer 1992 President Yeltsin declared that Georgia should remain indivisible and that the South Ossetian and Abkhazian conflicts should be solved by peaceful means, while vice-president Rutskoi openly threatened one of the conflicting parties that Russia would use armed force, and the Chairman of the Supreme Soviet Ruslan Khasbulatov stated that the possibility of Russia annexing South Ossetia might be 'positively considered' in the Supreme Soviet. The decisions of Russia's president and its former Supreme Soviet with respect to the status of the Crimea and the city of Sevastopol' were not just different but fully opposed to one another.

The federal power also faced opposition from some national elites and public movements. The Confederation of Caucasus Peoples and various Cossack and Russian extreme nationalist organisations deployed their illegal armed units into the Abkhazian conflict zone, and certain leaders of the North Caucasian republics gave *de facto* sanction to outfit and engage such armed units while their official representatives in Moscow assured Tbilisi of their neutrality and adherence to the principle of territorial integrity of the newly independent states (a similar situation could be observed in the Transdnestria conflict).

In many cases the military and political activities of the commanders of the Russian troops in the ex-Soviet conflict zones were uncontrolled (e.g. General Lebed' in Transdnestria, General Kondrat'ev in South Ossetia, General Sorokin in Abkhazia, and General Ashurov in Tadzhikistan). Unlike the 'autonomous' General Lebed's generally well-intentioned and positive political activities, the half-illegal deeds of Russian officers and their corps in Abkhazia in 1992-1993 and their actual fighting in support of the Abkhazian separatists only worsened the conflict, prolonged combat operations, and led to the loss of thousands of lives and hundreds of thousands of refugees.

The integrity of Russia's external policy course in the conflict zones also came apart due to a number of inconsistent steps taken by the state concerning the same problems (e.g. several unfounded changes in the Russian government's position with regard to the withdrawal of Russian troops from Lithuania, the problem of the division of the Black Sea fleet).

One of the principal drawbacks of the RF's state policy in the conflict zones were a number of unprofessional decisions made without proper consideration of the complex reasons which lead to a particular conflict situation and influence its evolution, and without estimation of the chain of consequences of such decision-making. For example, the decision to deploy national contingents of the CIS coalition forces in different districts in Tadzhikistan, which was taken after the proposal of a group of United Armed-Forces generals in September 1993, failed to take into account the historical peculiarities of ethnic relations in those regions (i.e., Uzbek units were positioned in districts where the dominating Tadzhik regional and clan ethnic groups had traditionally tense relations with the Uzbek etc.). Furthermore, this decision failed to observe the strategic interests of the RF: the deployment of the Russian contingent of the coalition forces in the Pyandz district inflicted both heavy casualties on the contingent's servicemen and it also increased the number of the political forces in the region which now regard Russia as an adversary.

Since 1988, various political forces in the USSR and later in the CIS have frequently attempted to arrange negotiations between the representatives of different national movements and parties in conflict, but unfortunately, most of the time they were unsuccessful. We can point out a number of reasons for this.

Firstly, negotiations were often conducted spontaneously, without preliminary preparations, without any special plan, programme or time-limit. Secondly, efforts to remove one of the main obstacles during any negotiations, namely the parties' fixation on their 'sole right' of resolution, were insufficient and unprofessional. Thirdly, 'informational noise', i.e., situations where the negotiating parties referred to incorrect and sometimes deliberately distorted information concerning the conflict's main circumstances and possible solutions, were not eliminated. Finally, the political status of the participants of the negotiations did not always guarantee the strict implementation of the agreements reached, because it was often overlooked that some of the conflicting parties were autonomous and often acted counter to the decisions of their nominal political 'patrons'. This was precisely the case in the Karabakh conflict, where the Nagorno-Karabakh republic's authorities, which for a long time were not allowed to take part in the negotiations, have for a long time constituted an independent political force, sometimes ignoring the recommendations of Armenia's central, official authorities.

This circumstance highlights one important problem which needs to be taken into account when organising negotiations over ethnic conflicts, namely that of searching for the most prominent representatives of the parties in conflict and for influential negotiators able to adequately gauge the positions of all parties and to deter them from violating the achieved agreements.

The participation of a big political figure as a mediator in the negotiations *per se* does not ensure their success, unless there have been thorough preparations in advance (as happened in 1991 in Zheleznovodsk during the negotiations over Karabakh, in which the presidents of Russia and Kazakhstan took part). Failures typically testify to the shortage of sensitivity to the sphere of ethnic conflict resolution, while compiled international and domestic experience in this domain is, as a rule, ignored.

In any event, the main shortcoming of all attempts to control ethnic conflicts on Russia's part was the weak connection between these attempts and the overall tendencies of international relations development in the post-Soviet world, as well as the absence of an integral, proven strategy in the state's policy with regard to conflict situations both in the ex-USSR countries and in Russia itself.

3.2 Russia's Policy in the Conflict Zones within Russian Federation

3.2.1 General Factors and Conditions of Constitutional Conflicts in the Russian Federation

Of all ethnic conflicts, the most dangerous in terms of the state's political stability are definitely the contradictions between the central power and the republics of the federation. Such contradictions or constitutional crises are reported to have created the grounds for the most acute armed conflicts in the post-Soviet space – Karabakh, South Ossetia, Transdnestria, Abkhazia. Among the general preconditions for the emergence of such conflicts in Russia we should distinguish between problems that are common to all regions in their relations with the Centre (underdeveloped federal relations, indefinite authority of the federation's members, inefficient taxation system, etc.), and the peculiarities of a national republic's relations with Moscow.

Why is it that the republics are at the head of the struggle for greater regional authority? Firstly, even the USSR Constitution formally stipulated a larger set of administrative rights for the republics than for the *krais* and *oblasts,* and so the republics' 'starting point' was already higher. Secondly, in their demands towards Moscow the leaders of the republics had greater public support and consolidation; all ethnic groups and especially the majority nationalities supported them at the peak of the 'surge' of the national idea, hoping to receive significant material benefits. Intensifying irrational mass consciousness, the national idea can temporarily suppress natural human needs of comfort and well-being, sacrificing them in favour of ideas of national independence. Therefore, national elites in the republics of the federation play the ethnic card and manage to attract vast public support, mobilising it in their own political struggle.

The most active demands made of Moscow were from the republics when the struggle between the two branches of federal power (the president and the Parliament) was at its highest in the spring and autumn of 1993. Both parties in this conflict needed allies and were trying to attract regional authorities. The latter, having comprehended their significance, asked a higher and higher price for their loyalty, pushing the Centre to more and more concessions.

After the October revolt in Moscow was suppressed, the position of the Centre towards the republics changed. It was not just a question of the Kremlin feeling stronger and having the possibility to impose sanctions on the republics without fear of opposition. It was mainly due to the concept of political and ethnic agreement which originated in the presidential structures, one of the main provisions of which was the doctrine of agreed relations, aimed at consensually distributing the authority between the federal power and the administrations of the regions of the RF. We should note, that this doctrine could not have appeared without several years of efforts on the part of Tatarstan's government, which was the first to prepare such an agreement.

This agreement enhanced the confidence between Moscow and Tatarstan, and reflected an almost optimal combination of the republic's demands with the integrity of the federation in the present conditions. This agreement, together with agreements with Bashkortostan and Kabardino-Balkaria helped to improve the relations between the republics and Moscow, which at that time demonstrated its denial of the 'policy of force' in relations with the former Russia's autonomies.

8

Regional Peculiarities of Privatisation in Russia

Aleksandr Kovalevskii

1 Introduction

Why is it only voucher privatisation that is considered here?

The Russian legislation on privatisation envisages the following kinds of sale of property to be denationalised:

- according to types of enterprises on sale: 'big' privatisation, when enterprises are sold with their ensuing transformation into public joint-stock companies, and 'small' privatisation, when small municipal trading enterprises and public service establishments are sold to privately established joint-stock companies;
- according to the condition of objects on sale: privatisation of operating enterprises, uncompleted construction projects and bankrupt enterprises;
- according to kinds of sale: auction sale, commercial bidding and investment bidding, as well as open and closed subscription and purchase of leased property;
- according to form of payment: free (voucher) privatisation and paid (money) privatisation.

In this paper we shall consider only 'big' privatisation of operating enterprises by way of voucher auction sales.

'Free' (voucher) privatisation began in Russia in December 1992 and finished on 30 June 1994. Paid privatisation was to begin on completing voucher privatisation. On 22 July 1994 the president signed the Decree No. 1535 *On Main Principles of the State Programme of Privatising State-Owned and Municipal Enterprises after 1 July 1994*. The document laid down basic principles of the programme of 'after-voucher' (paid) privatisation, but by the time this paper was submitted (15 November 1994) the paid privatisation has not as yet begun.

The fact is that there are actually two kinds of paid privatisation auctions in Russia. The so-called 'old' paid privatisation auctions are held in order to cover expenses of voucher auction organisers. Up to 10% of stock sold at voucher auctions may be put up for the auctions. At 'new' paid privatisation auctions large share packages of enterprises to be privatised were to be sold. However, 'regulations' on 'new' paid privatisation auctions have not been approved up to now. Draft 'regulations' submitted by the State Property Committee to the Ministry of Justice in October 1994 have not been approved by the ministry.

It should be noted that at present State Property Funds in some regions still do hold paid privatisation auction sales of large packages of shares. These auction sales are held, however, according to the rules set for 'old' auctions.

No statistics on paid privatisation auction sales are registered. The paid privatisation auction sales already held are very unlikely to be included in any case into statistical accounts, even if there is to be a central compilation of statistics.

That is precisely why in this paper we are considering only voucher privatisation outcomes. Moreover, the process of voucher privatisation has much greater geographical peculiarities than that of paid privatisation. The point is that, under the Russian legislation, a paid privatisation auction is always held after a voucher auction. This means that the results of a paid privatisation auction will most likely depend on those of the voucher auction. To take an example, if several big investors emerge as a result of voucher auction, who are competing for control of the enterprise, then at the paid privatisation auction the bidding price naturally will be high. As for voucher privatisation, it will be shown below that results of voucher auctions are largely determined only by the investment climate in the given region, i.e., they are of a definitely regional nature.

Below we shall consider reasons for peculiar geographical patterns in voucher privatisation.

2 Geographical Peculiarities of Voucher Privatisation

The following reasons why voucher privatisation has a clear-cut geographical pattern can be offered. As is known, voucher privatisation pursued the purely ideological aim of a free distribution of property among all Russia's population. It is this nation-wide character of Russia's privatisation (i.e., distribution of privatisation vouchers among the Russian population, except for the population of Chechnya who refused to accept privatisation vouchers) that determined a peculiar territorial pattern of Russia's privatisation. The original territorial distribution of vouchers coincided (except for some deviations connected with the fact that not all citizens have received their vouchers) with the territorial distribution (density) of Russia's population. Meanwhile, the distribution of property to be privatised in Russia's regions (i.e., the cost of enterprises to be privatised in various regions), the purchasing of which must be paid in privatisation vouchers, does not coincide at all with Russia's population density pattern. This led to a transfer of privatisation vouchers from regions with a lower market value of property to be privatised to those with a higher value. In its turn, the market value of property is determined not so much by its nominal balance sheet cost on the date of its valuation as by its real attractiveness for investors.

Among the factors of investment attractiveness of an enterprise there are purely geographical ones related to the micro-situation of an enterprise (i.e., the value of the land plot on which it is located), its meso-situation (i.e., advantages of the economic-geographical situation of an enterprise), and, finally, its macro-situation which is determined to a large degree by political-geographic factors, namely political aspects of the investment climate in the region where it is situated.

It should be noted that all three factors have a rather clear-cut territorial differentiation, especially on the territory of Russia, which is connected with the conspicuous heterogeneity of its 'economic space'. This is especially noticeable in the period of severed economic ties and with Russian regions striving for sovereignty.

The analysis of territorial peculiarities of voucher privatisation in Russia is given below.

3 'Special Zones' of Voucher Privatisation

Before giving a detailed analysis of regional statistics on voucher privatisation, we shall consider in some detail those Russian regions where voucher privatisation took a peculiar course.

First of all, among such regions are Russia's autonomies or regions with an undefined status and whose relation to Russia is somewhat difficult to define. First and foremost, this concerns Tatarstan, Bashkortostan, Chechnya, and the Republic of Sakha-Yakutia. Henceforth these and similar regions will be referred to as 'sovereign territorial units'.

Chechnya, for example, refused to receive Russian privatisation vouchers, largely for political reasons, in order to emphasise its status as a sovereign state. Privatisation in this republic has not in fact begun. It should be noted that although other republics of the North Caucasian region did not refuse privatisation vouchers, privatisation in these regions has not (practically) begun either. This is primarily the case with Ingushetia as well as North Ossetia and Adygheya.

Bashkortostan, as well as some other regions, decided to protect its property from being bought up by 'foreign businessmen'. This was done in an exceptionally simple way – at voucher auctions in the republic (which were held exactly after Russia's pattern), only vouchers with stamps of the *Republican Savings Bank* (vouchers issued in a certain region have the stamp of the Savings Bank of that region) were allowed for payment. Curiously enough, there were no restrictions on buying these vouchers by investors from other regions. In that way, 'foreign businessmen' could well take part in Bashkortostan's voucher auctions – but only by buying vouchers from people or the republic's legal entities.

In addition, voucher auctions in Bashkortostan, unlike those in Russia, were allowed to be held until 1 January 1995, and for some reasons the par value of a voucher there was announced to equal 40,000 roubles, while otherwise the voucher was not different from the Russian one: its face had the inscription '10,000 roubles' although, in general, the face value of a voucher, as any other security granting the right of property, is a purely fictional one.

They went much further in Tatarstan and, alongside with the Russian voucher they introduced their own privatisation security document which was called a 'personal privatisation deposit' (PPD) of Tatarstan. This deposit was placed cashless on its owner's personal account in the Savings Bank. After its withdrawal, a PPD was automatically transformed into a personal privatisation voucher (PPV). These vouchers could not practically circulate (since they were personal ones) – the right to sell and buy these vouchers was granted only to some vouchers investment funds of Tatarstan close to the republic's government.

Auction sales in Tatarstan are held according to a procedure that is different from that in Russia. At these auctions, Russian vouchers and Tatarstan's personal privatisation vouchers (as well as money) are acceptable as a medium of payment. There are no special restrictions on taking part in the republic's voucher auctions for investors from other regions.

Finally, one should also mention the special method of conducting privatisation in the Republic of Sakha-Yakutia. In this region, privatisation of enterprises proceeded, to all appearances, in the same way as in Russia. Usual voucher auctions were held in the republic. However, the procedure for privatising the republic's enterprises (and, especially, oil-extracting ones) was essentially different from the one stipulated by the Russian legislation. Besides, voucher funds in the republic obtained shares of the republic's enterprises in trusteeship on some unknown basis (actually, only one voucher fund – the Sakha-Invest Fund – was given an opportunity to become independent and thriving). As for outside investors, they have practically been prevented from taking part in the republic's voucher auctions.

Meanwhile, one cannot argue conclusively that anti-privatisation moods reign supreme in all Russian autonomous republics. Most autonomies conduct privatisation in the interests of their own population, which accounts for the very low voucher auction rate in the regions because the inflow of outside capital is, as a rule, limited.

However, this is not to say that Russian autonomies are completely unattractive for investors. Political risks of investing into the regions are paid for by huge profitability of investment which risk-taking investors may achieve by buying up local enterprises at the prices agreed upon with local authorities.

Individual ways of conducting privatisation were very likely to be observed only in Russia's 'sovereign territorial units' However, in other regions too, some peculiarities were observed in the course and procedure of privatisation. This will be discussed in the next section.

4 The Analysis of Privatisation Statistics in Russia's Regions

4.1 The Procedure

In selecting indicators which could be considered as indices of the course and pace of privatisation, we faced the problem of their 'cleansing' from 'extra-privatisational' factors. The fact is that indices of the pace of privatisation in a region are usually dependent on two quite different, if, as will be shown below, interrelated, groups of factors. The first group of factors includes objective ones, which do not depend on the attitude of authorities and a region's population to privatisation. These factors refer to the structure of a region's industry and the cost of fixed capital (they directly influence such indices as the amount of charter funds sold at voucher auctions, the number of enterprises sold, etc.).

The second group of factors includes subjective factors, namely, the attitude of the population and local authorities to privatisation (i.e., the degree of their market orientation). To this group of factors belong the following ones: 1) how active the workers (employees) of enterprises in a region are in submitting applications for making their enterprises joint-stock companies and 2) how active local authorities are in trying to sell their enterprises. In addition, this group also includes such factors as the degree of advertising sales of the property to be privatised in a region, the attitude to the influx of outside capital (i.e., to the admission of outside investors from other regions to participate in voucher auctions), etc.. While the first group of factors can be classified as a purely economic-geographical one (i.e., reflecting the location and structure of industry in regions), the second group can be considered as a group of political-geographical factors. Respectively, the first group reflects the degree of economic attractiveness of a region, and the second group – the degree of political risks in making investments.

Obviously, the factors of the first group are better reflected by means of absolute indicators – such as the cost of fixed capital on the territory of a region, the amount of charter capital to be sold – while the factors of the second group are much better reflected by relative indicators, such as the average price of a voucher auction sale, the ratio of actually privatised enterprises and enterprises planned to be privatised, the ratio of accepted and issued vouchers in a region.

In this paper, we shall mainly consider the second group of factors, since they are the most dynamic in terms of time. The point is that the factors of the first group have remained practically unchanged since the time of the USSR.

It should be noted, however, that the two groups of factors are not independent of each other. Specifically, such a basic index as the average voucher auction rate in regions is dependent on both groups of factors. In most cases, a voucher auction rate is determined by factors from the second group, although in some regions factors from the first group play a dominant part (this will be mentioned in each separate case).

We have chosen the average rate of voucher auctions in regions as the basic index reflecting the pace and course of privatisation. By the rate of a voucher auction we understand the total par value of shares per one voucher (in thousand roubles). For example, if one voucher was sold for two shares with a face value of 1000 roubles per voucher, the rate of a voucher auction then was two. If one voucher was sold for seven shares of the face value of 100 roubles, the rate of a voucher auction was then 0.7. Respectively, the smaller the amount of the total par value per voucher, the higher is the rate of an auction (i.e., the auction rate of 0.7 is considered to be higher than that of 2.0) The average auction rate in various regions is determined by the economic attractiveness of enterprises situated in them (the first group of factors) and the level of privatisation approval by population and local authorities, i.e., the market transformation support level of a region (the second group of factors). Obviously, the higher the auction rate in a region (i.e., the smaller the value of the number of shares per one privatisation voucher), the more open this region was for investors.

One should not forget, however, that an auction rate also depended on the investment attractiveness of enterprises located on the territory of the region, on the average amount of authorised capital of an enterprise (usually, the bigger the authorised capital of an enterprise, the lower is the auction rate), as well as on the purely geographical accessibility of the region itself for investors.

Still, it is precisely the openness of a region for outside investors and, hence, its attitude to privatisation which is reflected by the standard auction rate.

We shall explain why it is just the openness of a region to outside investors that allows one to maintain that the pace and course of privatisation in the region is favourable. The point is that the openness of a region for investors means not only any absence of refusal to accept applications for participation in a voucher auction (in many regions, applications from outside investors were not allowed to be accepted, though this ran counter to the corresponding laws), but also the information openness of a region (namely, the widest possible notification of the population about enterprises on sale), the active policy of transforming enterprises into joint-stock companies, etc. On the whole, all these factors reflect, as has been already mentioned, the level of the market transformation support by local authorities and the population, which is a good indicator of favourable political-geographical aspects of investment climate.

Economic regions were under scrutiny as objects of study. Sometimes a region as a whole produces a very favourable impression, and in this case indicators of subjects of the Russian Federation belonging to this region were not analysed. However if within an economic region great fluctuations of indices of its parts were observed, then extreme values in the region's parts were considered separately. As for other relative indicators, they were not considered in greater detail for lack of the corresponding data. The data on accepted vouchers in the current registers of privatisation statistical agencies in Russia have been classified until the results of voucher privatisation have been summed up. The latest date for which we have information on the data is 15th April, which certainly cannot be considered a reliable indicator. In most regions real voucher privatisation did not begin until spring 1993, and the data on collected vouchers have changed manifold since then. However, when necessary, we shall refer to these data.

Map 1
Average package of shares

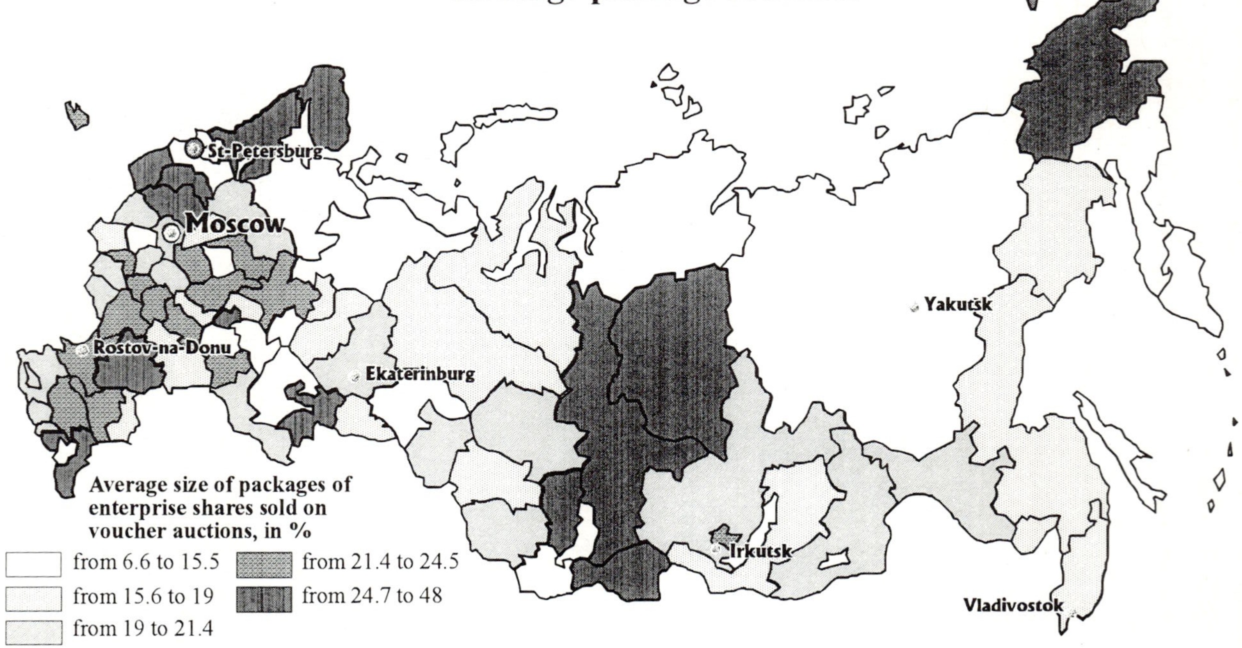

As far as the ratio of the number of enterprises transformed into joint-stock companies and enterprises to be transformed into joint-stock companies is concerned, the corresponding statistics are available, regrettably, only on the corresponding 20 best regions, which obviously cannot be a representative indicator. However, as in the case of the above-mentioned indicator, we shall refer to it from time to time.

4.2 The Analysis

Above, we have mentioned special 'sovereign territorial units' where privatisation either did not take place at all or was conducted in extremely peculiar forms. However, our analysis of statistical data clearly shows that other regions, too, differ from one another in various indices of the pace of privatisation.

To begin with, our analysis of standard auction rates reveals the following territorial peculiarities and regularities.

It should be noted, first of all, that auctions rates are rather well-differentiated according to economic regions. The highest auction rate was registered in the North-western region, especially in Leningrad *oblast'* and in St.Petersburg, due to the greater weight of which the region is the leader in the value of auction rates. Meanwhile, in two other *oblasts* of the region – Pskov and Novgorod – the auction rate was lower than Russia's average, the latter being 2.4.

A high auction rate was also observed in the Northern region, especially in the Republic of Komi, Murmansk *oblast'* and the Republic of Karelia. Although in Arkhangel'sk and Vologda *oblasts* the auction rate was a little lower than Russia's average, nevertheless, its value was also rather high. Incidentally, in one part of the Northern region – Nenetsk autonomous *okrug* – the auction rate was very low (8.1), which was determined largely by the low level of its industrial development, and, hence, the low attractiveness level of enterprises situated in this region's part, its difficulty of access, poor privatisation infrastructure (low number of offices for accepting privatisation vouchers, in particular) as well as low population density, etc. Henceforth such regions or parts of regions will be referred to as 'remote' ones.

The third part showing a high auction rate is the West Siberian region, within which especially prominent are Omsk and Tomsk *oblasts* and Yamal-Nenetsk autonomous *okrug*. Rather high was the auction rate in Khanty-Mansiisk autonomous *okrug,* too. In other parts of the region the auction rate was also, as a rule, rather high.

Map 2
Average voucher course at auctions

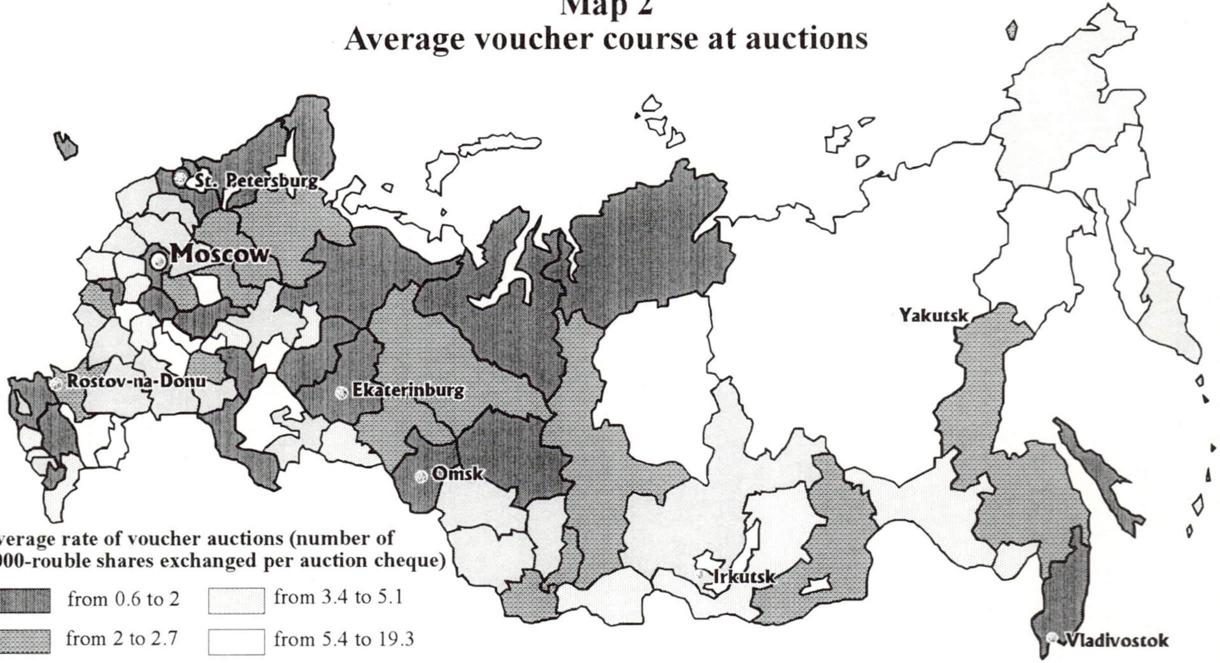

Average rate of voucher auctions (number of 1000-rouble shares exchanged per auction cheque)

- from 0.6 to 2
- from 2 to 2.7
- from 2.8 to 3.4
- from 3.4 to 5.1
- from 5.4 to 19.3

Comment: the smaller the number of 1000-rouble shares that is collected per voucher, the lower the voucher rate at that auction and the higher the 'auction rate'

A very high auction rate was also observed in the North Caucasian region. Here, however, was a typical case of two dominating parts – Krasnodar and Stavropol *krais*, and, to a lesser extent, Rostov *oblast'*. At the same time, in other parts of the region privatisation either has not begun at all (see the previous section of the paper), or has been very sluggish.

Finally, the last region, where voucher auction rate was higher than Russia's average, is the Baltic region represented by its only part – Kaliningrad *oblast'*.

Now we shall analyse reasons for these high auction rates in the above regions.

In practically all parts of the above regions, the number of accepted vouchers exceeded considerably the number of issued vouchers. In this respect, St.Petersburg became the 'record-holder': there the number of accepted vouchers exceeded that of distributed vouchers by two times. As has already been mentioned above, this means that the local privatisation agencies a) did not obstruct the influx of vouchers from outside investors, b) conducted a sufficiently efficient advertising campaign on sales of enterprises and c) that these regions were very active in putting up their enterprises for All-Russian voucher auctions – auctions where applications for participation were accepted in many regions and, hence, investors did not have to travel around to remote parts of the country in order to take part in auction sales. It goes without saying that these regions were rather active in transforming their enterprises into joint-stock companies. In practically all these parts, the number of enterprises sold was by far higher than that of enterprises to be privatised. This index was the highest one in Stavropol *krai* (859.9%).

Incidentally, the 'privatisation openness' of a region is not the only factor determining a high auction rate in it. Specifically, the North Caucasian region can hardly be called a region open for investors or a 'pro-privatisation' one; nevertheless, the auction rate in the region was above Russia's average. The reason for this is the following. In the North Caucasian autonomies, privatisation, as has already been noted above, did not practically begin, as a result of which the population of the autonomous republics (which, except for Chechnya, had received vouchers) had to invest their vouchers into enterprises of Krasnodar and Stavropol *krai*. Moreover, enterprises of Krasnodar and Stavropol *krai* (especially those of the former) had an additional appeal for investors – the point is that in Krasnodar *krai* a rather considerable quantity of ports and steamship lines were sold in the course of privatisation, which is of particular importance in the situation of developing Russian foreign trade ties with the Mediterranean countries and, at the same time, severed ties with Ukraine's ports. This is precisely why the few sea ports of

Map 3
Proportion of sold enterprises

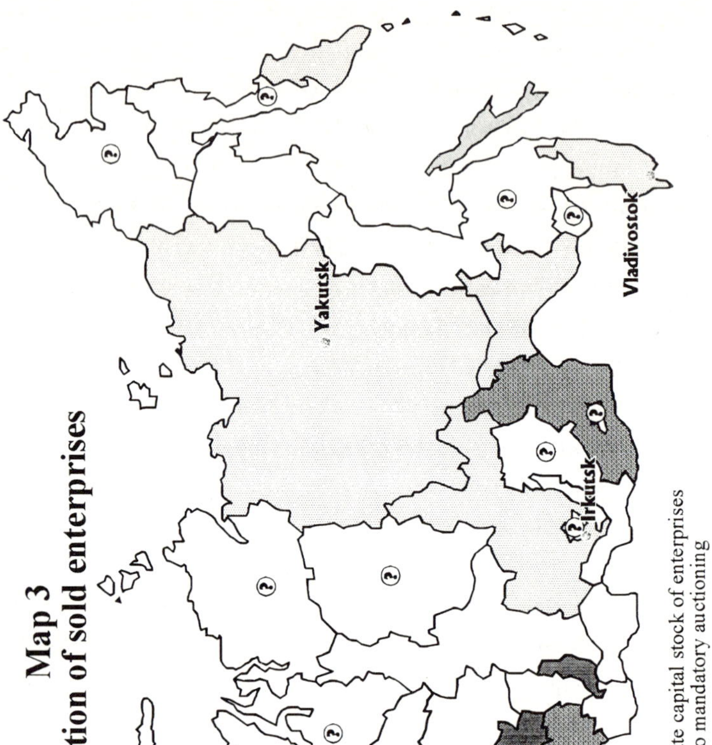

Krasnodar *krai* proved very attractive for investors, and this became the reason for the region's eventually highest auction rate in Russia.

More or less similar reasons account for high auction rates in the West-Siberian economic region. As the North Caucasian region, this region can hardly be called a 'pro-privatisation' one; nevertheless, the auction rate in it turned out to be rather high. Especially active in carrying out privatisation were Omsk and Tomsk *oblasts*. A high auction rate was also observed in two other parts of the region – in Khanty-Mansiisk and Yamal-Nenetsk autonomous *okrugs*. As is known, major Russian oil- and gas-extracting enterprises are located in these parts and they make up the basis of the region's industry. Since shares of these enterprises were very popular with foreign investors, the average auction rate in these parts proved to be rather high. Moreover, the privatisation of such a strategic industry as oil and gas extraction was political in nature – and that is just why practically all the enterprises were put up for All-Russian auction sales and these parts of the region could not 'protect' them from outside investors, though they wanted, undoubtedly, to do so.

Meanwhile, in other parts of the region the auction rate was somewhat lower than Russia's average, with the lowest rate observed in Novosibirsk *oblast'*, whose administration has always been known for its 'anti-privatisation' and anti-reformist frame of mind: some time ago they even tried to rescind privatisation or, at least, to prevent investors from other regions from taking part in the *oblast's* voucher auctions.

****

In other economic regions, the auction rate was below Russia's average. Somewhat lower than Russia's average was the auction rate in the Urals region, with Bashkortostan determining the region's average low rate (its index was 18.6, which was the second lowest rate after the Republic of Sakha-Yakutia on Russia's territory). Earlier, we have already mentioned peculiarities of privatisation in Bashkortostan. Also very prominent in the region is the low auction rate in the Republic of Udmurtia (7.9). This can largely be accounted for by the presence of a great number of defence enterprises in the republic, whose shares practically failed to evoke investors' interest. In addition, the regional authorities in the republic (as in most other autonomies) were reluctant to support privatisation.

Noteworthy in this respect is also Chelyabinsk *oblast'*. The point is that in spring 1993 the *oblast*'s minor Council came up with the initiative to rescind privatisation under the pretext that local industries would go over into the hands of 'alien' or outside businessmen. A little later this unlawful decision was cancelled but 'anti-privatisation' moods still remained there for a long time. This was displayed, specifically, by the fact that almost only shares of extremely unpromising enterprises were put up for voucher auctions, which resulted in a rather low auction rate for the *oblast*'s enterprises.

In other parts of the region, auction rates were close to Russia's average ones. Perm and Sverdlovsk *oblasts* are noticeable for their relatively high average auction rates. The administrations of these *oblasts* very much favoured privatisation. Withermore, securities markets have from the very beginning been rather actively developed in these highly industrialised areas.

Rather high auction rates were registered in the East Siberian region, with its index being, however, somewhat below Russia's average. A very dynamic privatisation policy was pursued in Khakassia (the only autonomous republic which may boast of this) and Irkutsk *oblast',* well-known for its 'skills' in forcing from the federal authorities the right to manage and administer the blocks of shares of Irkutsk enterprises proclaimed earlier to be part of the federal property. The pace of privatisation in Krasnoyarsk *krai* was also relatively brisk.

As well as noting parts of the region where the pace of privatisation was rather dynamic, one should also note some remote parts of the region, first of all the Aghinsk Buryat autonomous *okrug,* where privatisation has not begun at all, the Ust-Ordynsk Buryat autonomous *okrug* and the Evenk autonomous *okrug.* In any way, the weight of those parts was so negligible that it did not practically influence the value of the region's average index.

An extremely high average auction rate was registered in the Far Eastern region, with very high rates in three leading parts of the region – Khabarovsk *krai,* Sakhalin *oblast'* and Primorskii *krai* – being counterbalanced by other parts' low auction rates.

First of all, among the latter, one should mention the Republic of Sakha-Yakutia, where Russia's lowest average voucher auction rate was registered (19.3). Moreover, the region has the lowest ratio of authorised capital sold and of authorised capital put up for auction sales – it only amounts to mere a 6.6% (with Russia's average being 20%). 'Remote' regions (Koryak and Chukot autonomous *okrugs*), as usual, proved incapable of substantially influencing the average auction rate. The fact that the region's auction rate is not the highest was caused by the rather slack pace of privatisation in Amur, Magadan and Chita *oblasts* and in the Jewish autonomous *oblast'.*

In the Volga-Vyatsk region, the average auction rate turned out to be rather high, although in all its parts except Nizhnii Novgorod *oblast',* the average rate was very low. The lowest auction rate was registered in the Republic of Mordovia – for the same reasons as in Udmurtia. A low auction rate was also observed in Chuvashia and the Republic of Marii-El. However, due to Nizhnii Novgorod *oblast'* (whose governor Boris Nemtsov is well-known for his reformist frame of mind), the auction rate proved, on the whole, to be rather high. It is noteworthy that because of the *oblast*'s great industrial potential, the weight of the *oblast'* in the calculations of the index turned out to be greater than that of all other parts of the region taken together.

A low auction rate was registered in the Volga region. Despite a rather dynamic privatisation policy pursued in Samara and Saratov *oblasts*, the region as a whole manifested a rather low privatisation enthusiasm. This is also true of Kalmykia mentioned above, as well as Penza and Astrakhan' *oblasts.*

Finally, the lowest auction rate was registered, paradoxically, in the central and central black earth regions. As for the latter, here Lipetsk and Tambov *oblasts* are obviously trailing at the back. The reason for the slow pace of privatisation in the region may be the fact that a great segment of the rural population is considered to be conservative and is displeased with privatisation in general.

As far as the central region is concerned, the situation here is far from unambiguous. In practically all parts of the region the auction rate was rather low. But, as our data show, the lowest was the auction rate in Moscow.

Despite the fact that Moscow's mayor, Yurii Luzhkov, is known for his negative attitude to privatisation, privatisation in Moscow has nevertheless been completed. Certainly, Moscow is very much different from the former Russian capital – St.Petersburg. Most enterprises with good prospects have not been put up for Moscow's voucher auction sales. However, it should be emphasised once again that in the long run, privatisation in Moscow has been carried out.

Moreover, Moscow is a focus of financial capital concentration. The biggest voucher funds of the capital (one sixtieth of all the funds) have accumulated 15 million vouchers (one tenth of all the vouchers). Furthermore, the greatest number of voucher funds has been established in Moscow. Most big funds in the capital and practically all small ones invested their vouchers in Moscow. The largest voucher trading places were also located in Moscow. That is why voucher auction rates in the capital were, as a rule, very high. However, it is not clear at all what is behind the clearly unrealistic figure of 6.200 rouble share per one voucher.

One should bear in mind that Moscow is very attractive for investors not only because of the great attractiveness of its enterprises – another significant factor is, obviously, its status as Russia's capital and the corresponding advantages as well as the appealing feature of Moscow's enterprises as real estate.

It is precisely these reasons rather than any 'pro-privatisation' feelings in Moscow that account for a high rate of Moscow's voucher auction sales.

4.3 The Trends

The above analysis makes it possible to clearly define some regularities.

As to the analysis of 'pro-privatisation' policies of the regions as a whole, one can definitely see the following patterns.

On the territory of Russia's European part we can observe a trend of decreasing market orientation in the direction from the north-west to the south-east. The northern, north-western, and the Baltic regions are the most market-oriented ones.

Regions' market orientations also decrease as one moves southwards. This is especially noticeable in southern *oblasts* of the central and central black-earth regions, which, as has already been mentioned above, can be accounted for to some extent by the increasing share of the rural population, which is not especially well-disposed to privatisation.

Deeper down to the south, 'pro-privatisation' attitudes of regions considerably increase – in Rostov *oblast'* and, especially, in Krasnodar and Stavropol *krais*; however, this deceptive privatisation orientation is apparent and is actually explained by some other factors mentioned above. On the whole, the course of privatisation in the North Caucasian region cannot be considered successful.

A similar picture can be observed in the east of Russia's European part – the pace of privatisation slackens considerably as we go from the Volga-Vyatsk region to the Volga region.

As far as the Ural region is concerned, the situation there is approximately the same as in the previous case. Privatisation orientations decrease from the north (the Republic of Komi, Perm and Sverdlovsk *oblasts*) to the south.

The same is also the case with the West Siberian region. Moving from the north-west to the south-east, privatisation orientations are on the decrease. An especially quick pace of privatisation is observed in the north (Khanty-Mansiisk and Yamal-Nenetsk autonomous *okrugs*), while moving to the south-east, the rate of privatisation happens to be considerably lower in Altai *krai,* Novosibirsk and Kemerovo *oblasts*.

Map 4
Top-20 regions in working assets, sold through voucher auctions

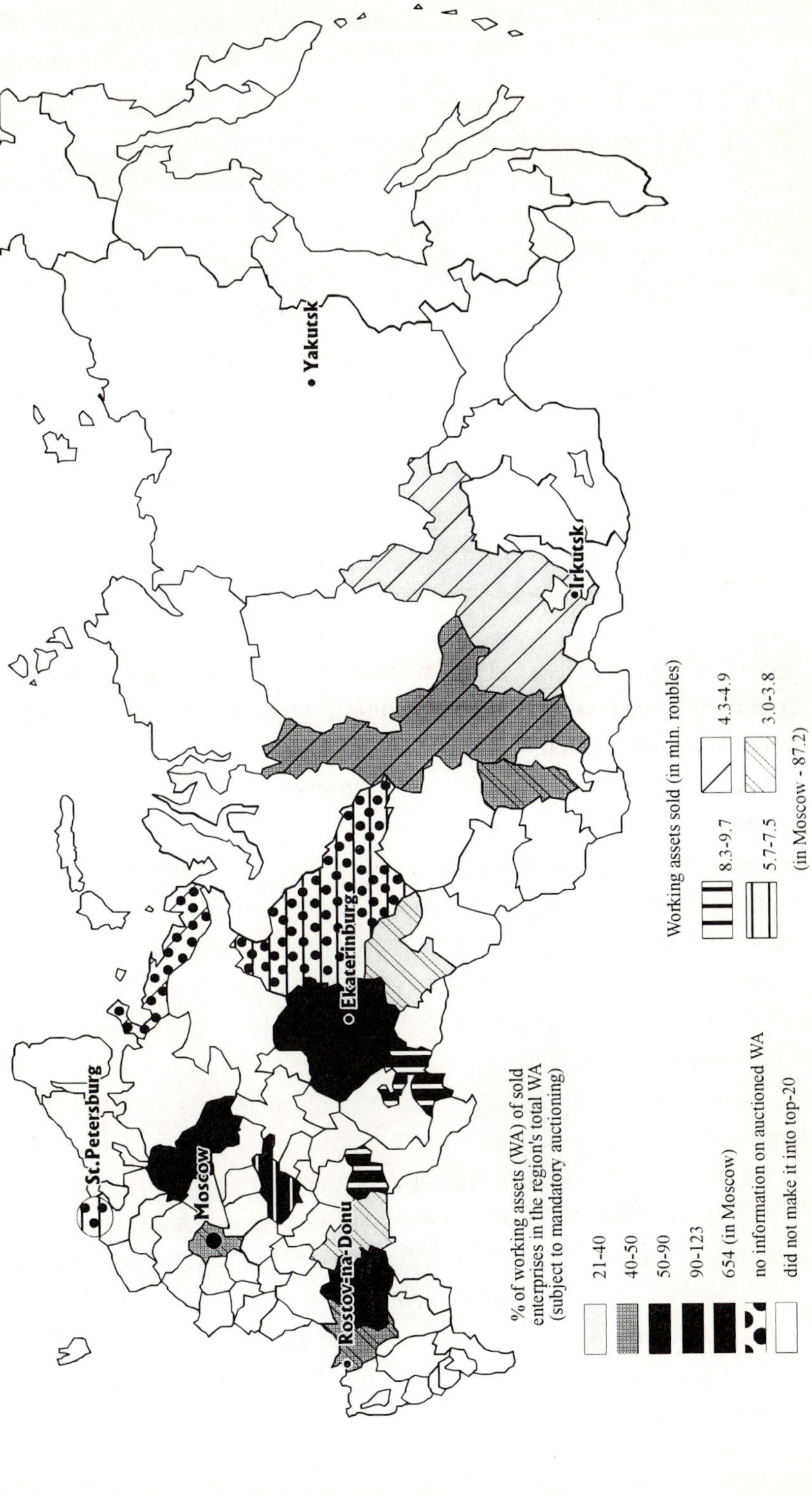

Map 5
Top-20 regions in number of enterprises, sold in voucher auctions

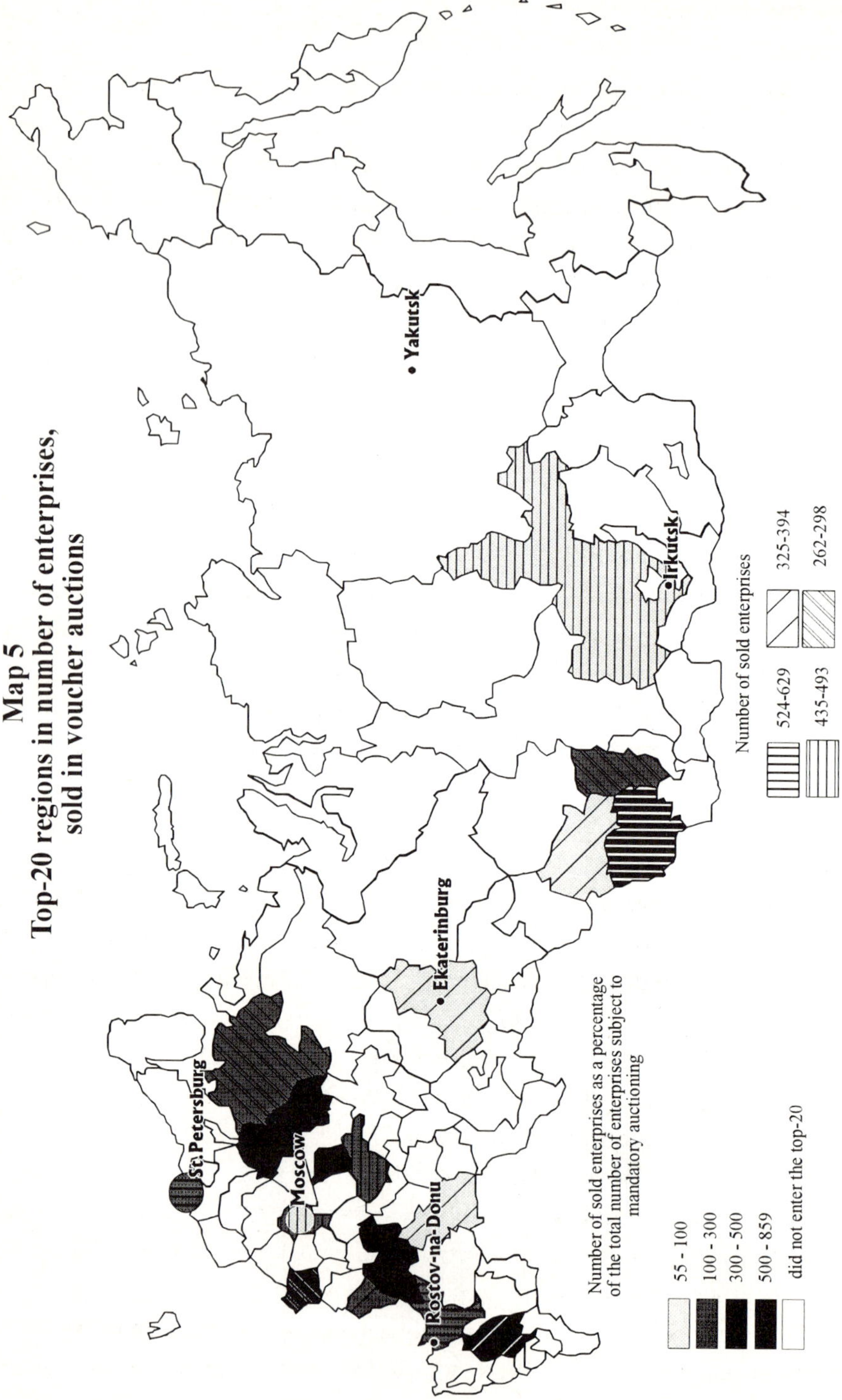

Privatisation activity of parts of the East Siberian and Far Eastern regions is somewhat different from the usual picture. The privatisation orientations of the East Siberian region's parts increase in the southward direction, because the remote parts (Taimyr and Evenk autonomous districts) are in the north of the region. Deeper down to the south, privatisation activity increases in industrial areas (Krasnoyarsk *krai,* Irkutsk *oblast'* and the Republic of Khakassia). Yet still farther to the south, the pace of privatisation slackens again in remote parts (Aghinsk and Ust-Ordynsk autonomous *okrugs* and the Republics of Tuva and Buryatia). As far as the Far Eastern region is concerned, in its north both 'sovereign territorial units' (e.g., the Republic of Sakha-Yakutia) and remote parts (Koryak and Chukot autonomous districts) are located. Privatisation dynamism is on the increase towards the south, reaching high rates in Khabarovsk and, especially, Primorskii *krais*, with substantially lower rates in Chita and Amur *oblasts* and the Jewish autonomous *oblasts*.

Thus, the analysis of territorial aspects of privatisation activities in regions makes it possible to discern the following prominent tendencies. On the whole, privatisation dynamism within a region noticeably decreases as one moves from the south to the north and/or from industrially developed parts to agricultural ones.

In some cases, however, the pattern is different; e.g., when remote parts are in the north of a region, then privatisation activity increases southward, where there are more industries.

Secondly, the factor of regional administration plays an important part. The pace of privatisation in a region depends on the political-administrative status of the region itself. The higher the status, the greater, as a rule, the region's independence in carrying out its privatisation policy. Correspondingly, the greater a region's independence, the higher the likelihood of its confrontation with the central authorities in Moscow. And since in the period of voucher privatisation the Centre's policy was definitely oriented towards privatisation, it is not difficult to suggest that the policies of regions having a high political-administrative status were either absolutely abstentionist or 'anti-privatisationist'.

We have already given some examples of this policy. One can, in fact, say that all Russia's autonomous republics, except for Khakassia, were rather ill-disposed towards privatisation, and reluctant to carry it out. In many of them, privatisation has not actually begun, while in others it was very sluggish.

Thirdly, within separate parts of some regions one can observe extreme values of privatisation activity indices, which do not conform to the region's regular pattern.

Map 6
Capital stock of privatised enterprises

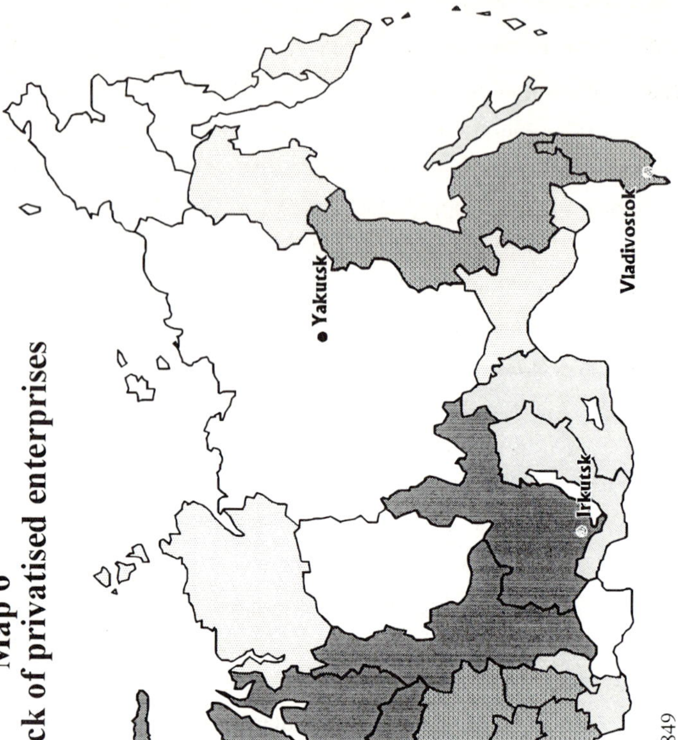

These are, as a rule, regions where local authorities are very strong, which makes it possible for them to pursue an independent policy of privatisation. In such cases privatisation dynamism can either considerably exceed average regional rates (e.g. St. Petersburg with its pro-reformist Anatolii Sobchak or Nizhnii Novgorod *oblast'* with its great reformer Boris Nemtsov) or go considerably lower, as is the case in Kemerovo *oblast'* with its opposition-minded Aman Tuleev, the head of the Legislative Assembly, or in Novosibirsk *oblast'*. In fact, this is also a manifestation of a purely political-geographic factor. These regions will be referred to as 'enclaves' (enclosed ones) (with their corresponding division into pro-market 'enclaves' and anti-market ones).

Fourthly, coastal border areas which have now become strategically important due to the growth of foreign trade are particularly noticeable for their privatisation activities. Krasnodar and Primorskii *krais* belong to such areas. In this connection it should be noted that despite a great demand for enterprises in the areas on the part of outside investors, foreign ones included, regional administrations are rather successfully competing with the former, buying up the property to be privatised through nominees or dummy companies. Primorskii *krai* represents a typical example of this: there managers and top administrators founded the Primorskii Association of Commercial Commodity Producers, which was busily buying up all property to be privatised at voucher auctions.

Finally, a number of regions were not quite so well-disposed towards privatisation; however, as a result of a not overly great influence of local administrations and rather energetic lobbying by investors (including foreign ones), their property was eventually put up for auction sales. Among such regions one should mention, first of all, Yamal-Nenetsk and Khanty-Mansiisk autonomous *okrugs* and the Republic of Komi, i.e., basic oil extracting regions of Russia. It is noteworthy, however, that other oil-extracting regions, e.g., Bashkortostan, managed quite successfully to preclude the influx of outside capital to its enterprises.

Thus, the analysis of territorial peculiarities of privatisation in Russia makes it possible to note the following regularities:

- Privatisation activity of regions decreases, as a rule, from the north to the south, and within an economic region – from the west to the east.
- Privatisation activity of a region depends on its political-administrative status. In all autonomous republics (the highest status), privatisation was, as a rule, considerably less dynamic than in other regions.

Map 7
Number of privatised enterprises

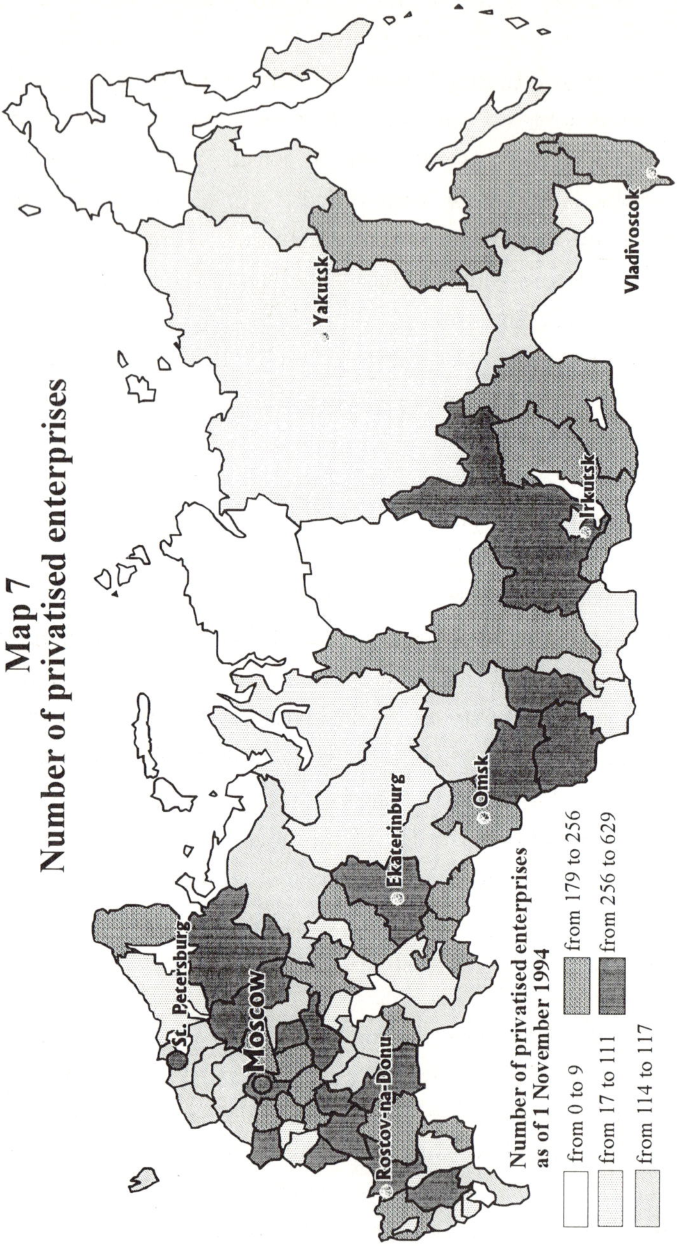

- On the whole, within one economic region all its parts have a more or less similar rate of privatisation activity, which is a manifestation of peculiarities of Russia's economic-territorial division coinciding, regrettably, with political-administrative division. In some regions there are, however, enclosed ('enclave') parts whose privatisation activity indices are essentially different from the region's average values. This is, as a rule, the case when the authorities in the regions wield strong influence and power.
- In addition, extreme values (as a rule, extremely low ones) of privatisation activity indices are observed in remote parts of regions. Such parts are, as a rule, situated in the Far North and, therefore, their privatisation activity rates are considerably lower than their region's average rate (which, it should be emphasised once again, is high in northern regions). However, because of the insignificant weight of such regions' parts, this does not influence substantially the regions' average privatisation activity indices.
- However, if a region includes autonomies, the latter substantially influence regional privatisation activity rates by downgrading them.
- There are special regions or regions' parts where reformist feelings and moods of local authorities are deceptive. These are, as a rule, regions or their parts with enterprises very attractive for investors, foreign ones included. Oil-extracting and 'coastal foreign trade' regions' parts (Krasnodar and Primorskii *krais* belong to such areas). Generally, these parts' administrations busily buy up the property to be privatised through dummy companies; that is why one can hardly consider such regions to be market-oriented.

5 Addendum: A Classification of Regions

The above account of privatisation peculiarities in various Russia's regions makes it possible for us to make a tentative classification of the latter. The below division of regions into groups can hardly be considered a classification in the proper sense of the term, for it lacks a single consistent classificatory principle. We classify regions into groups according to their market orientations and actual market reforms. So, the groups presented below give a general idea of the territorial distribution of investment climate parameters. The factors determining regions' attitudes to privatisation are entirely different in their origins and nature, that is why we are 'doomed' to arbitrariness in classification.

Map 8
Number of people employed in privatised enterprises

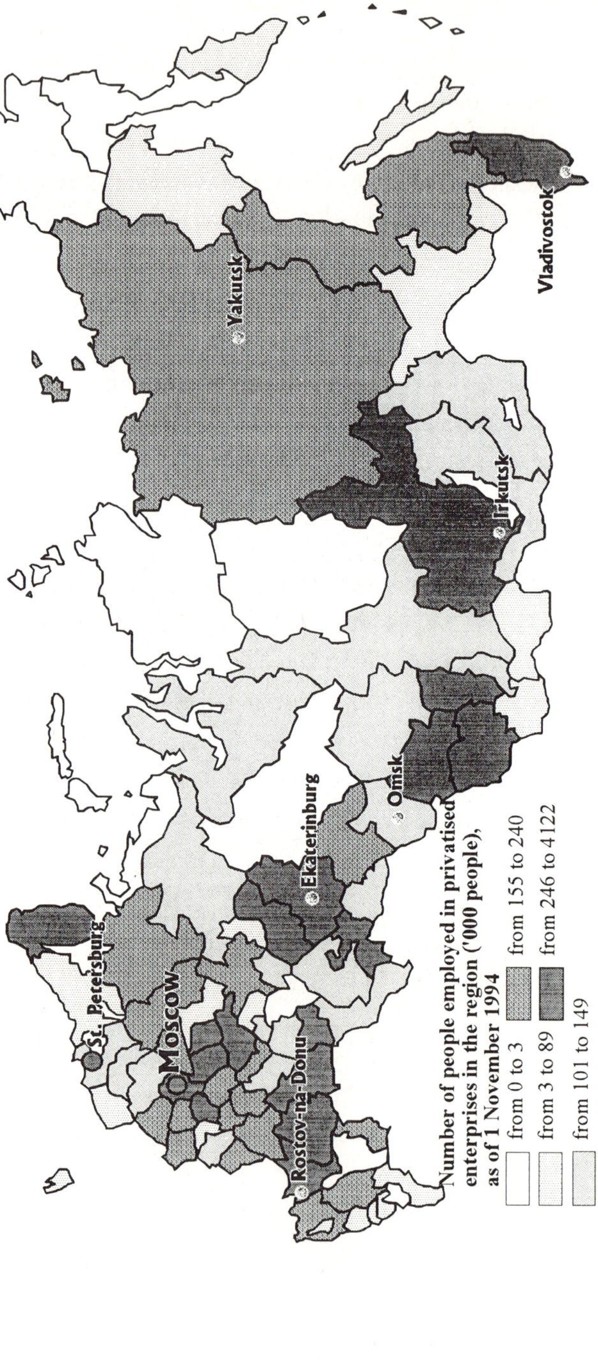

Map 9
Average capital stock of sold enterprises

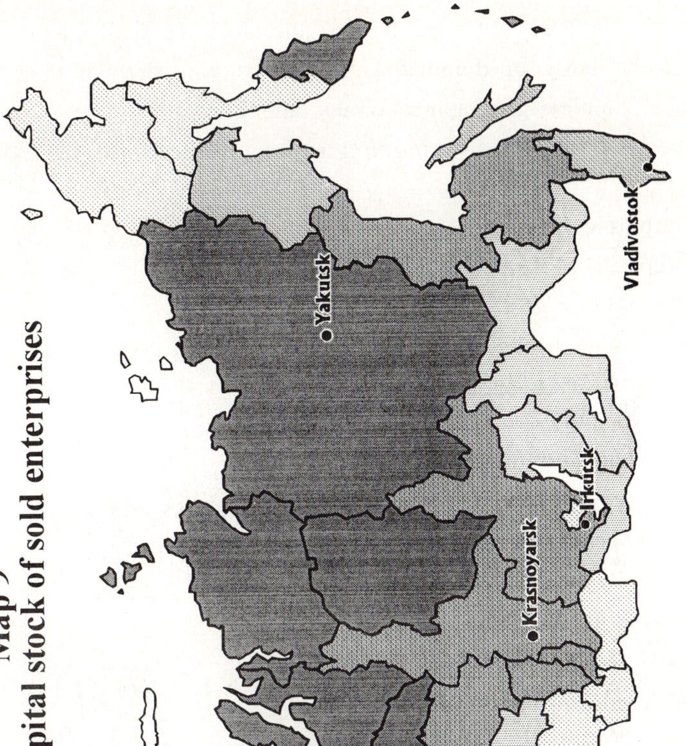

In each individual case, a region's actual market reforming index is a result of an interplay of completely different factors; therefore we shall classify regions into groups on the basis of dominating factors as we perceive them – economic-geographical, political-geographical or any other ones.

1. *Advanced (radical) market reforming* regions of the North, the North-West and the West:
   - the Republic of Karelia
   - the Republic of Komi
   - Arkhangel'sk *oblast'*
   - Vologda *oblast'*
   - Murmansk *oblast'*
   - Leningrad *oblast'*
   - St.Petersburg.
2. *Active market reforming regions* of the Urals and Siberia:
   - Perm *oblast'*
   - Sverdlovsk *oblast'*
   - Tomsk *oblast'*
   - Omsk *oblast'*
   - Tyumen *oblast'*
   - Krasnoyarsk *krai.*
3. *Market reforming regions* of the 'Golden Ring' (in the central European part of Russia):
   - Pskov *oblast'*
   - Novgorod *oblast'*
   - Vladimir *oblast'*
   - Kostroma *oblast'*
   - Yaroslavl *oblast'*
   - Tver *oblast'*
   - Smolensk *oblast'*.
4. *Moderate market reforming* regions of the Volga Basin:
   - Volgograd *oblast'*
   - Samara *oblast'*
   - Saratov *oblast'*
   - Ulyanovsk *oblast'*.
5. Coastal foreign trade regions:
   - Kamchatka *oblast'*

- Primorskii *krai*
- Krasnodar *krai*
- Kaliningrad *oblast'*.

6. Oil-extracting regions:
   - the Republic of Komi
   - Khanty-Mansiisk autonomous *okrug*
   - Yamal-Nenetsk autonomous *okrug*
   - Sakhalin *oblast'*.
7. Conservative regions of central Russia and the black-earth zone:
   - Ivanovo *oblast'*
   - Bryansk *oblast'*
   - Kaluga *oblast'*
   - Tula *oblast'*
   - Belgorod *oblast'*
   - Voronezh *oblast'*
   - Kursk *oblast'*
   - Lipetsk *oblast'*
   - Tambov *oblast'*.
8. 'Anti-market' southern regions:
   - Astrakhan *oblast'*
   - Penza *oblast'*
   - Chelyabinsk *oblast'*
   - Orenburg *oblast'*
   - Kurgan *oblast'*
   - Novosibirsk *oblast'*
   - Kemerovo *oblast'*
   - Amur *oblast'*
   - Jewish autonomous *oblast'*
   - Chita *oblast'*.
9. Remote regions:
   - Nenetsk autonomous *okrug*
   - Komi-Permyatsk autonomous *okrug*
   - Taimyr autonomous *okrug*
   - Evenk autonomous *okrug*
   - Ust-Ordynsk autonomous *okrug*
   - Aghinsk autonomous *okrug*

- Koryak autonomous okrug
- Chukot autonomous *okrug*
- Magadan *oblast'*.

10. 'Sovereign territorial units':

10 a. *Marginal ones* (Privatisation here either has not begun or is carried out in defiance of Russia's legislation)
- Chechnya
- Ingushetia
- Tatarstan
- Bashkortostan.

10 b. *Underdeveloped ones* (Privatisation is underway but at a very slow pace, largely because of the lack of enterprises attractive for investors and local authorities' ill disposition (negative attitude)):
- Kalmykia (Khalmg-Tangch)
- Kabardino-Balkaria
- Adygeya
- North Ossetia
- Daghestan
- Karachaevo-Cherkessia.

10 c. The ones *experiencing a structural crisis* (formally, privatisation is taking place here but the structure of industry, in combination with extremely high investment risks, is conducive to a practically total lack of demand for property to be privatised):
- the Republic of Mordovia
- the Republic of Marii-El
- the Republic of Chuvashia
- the Republic of Udmurtia
- the Republic of Buryatia
- the Republic of Tuva.

11. Enclosed regions ('enclaves') of advanced market reform:
- Moscow
- Moscow *oblast'*
- Ryazan *oblast'*
- Orel *oblast'*
- Nizhnii Novgorod
- Kirov *oblast'*

- Rostov *oblast'*,
- Stavropol *krai,*
- the Republic of Gornyi Altai,
- Irkutsk *oblast'*,
- Khakassia,
- Khabarovsk *krai*.

9

Russia's Transport Infrastructure: Problems and Prospects

Sergei Tarkhov

Transport and infrastructure play a pivotal role for Russia in light of the vast distances between cities and regions and because of the country's enormous circumference. Russia stretches from Kaliningrad to Vladivostok in latitude. This distance of 10,500 km can be covered within nine days by train and 14 hours by air (accounting for lay-overs). The meridian between Murmansk and Makhachkala stretches 4000 km which may be covered within four 4 days by train and six hours by air with a lay-over in Moscow. It is impossible for the economy to function properly or for the population to live on a day-to-day basis unless the transport system is reliable and well organised.

Official statistical reports are the main source of information for this research. While dealing with the data it should be kept in mind that road construction investments were dramatically reduced during the structural crisis of the 1990s. Therefore, the transport grid which took shape in pre-*perestroika* times has preserved its conservatism.

Following real economic reforms, the total volume of transportation has dropped by 25% in comparison with 1992 and has basically experienced a similar decline in 1994 as compared to 1993. Thus, by 1994, Russia's transport network showed a tendency towards reduction rather than towards growth. However, this does not necessarily mean that this trend is going to continue in the years to come.

Because of the enormous distances, each type of transportation in Russia developed its own spatial specialisation. The bulk of long- and medium-range haulage of cargoes is sent by rail, with the average transportation distance of one ton of freight being 1185 km. Motor transport takes care of the principal amount of short distance cargo haulage (the average distance for transportation is 138 km). River transport moves cargoes only in the summer-autumn time (on average 381 km) whereas sea transport provides long distance freight services between the basins and along the northern sea route with the average transportation distance for one ton being 4484 km. One ton of oil and one ton of natural gas are respectively relayed via pipelines over average distances of 2118 km and 2289 km respectively.

Cargo transportation has the following breakdown: 39% – motor transport (predominantly short distance haulage), 33% – railway, 10% – oil pipelines, 10% – conventional pipelines, 6% – river transport, less than 0.6% – sea transport and verging on 0% – airlines. A similar pattern is applicable for passenger transportation. Inter-city connections rely on coaches (68% of passengers), railway (24%), air transport (7% before the crisis) and river transport (1.5%), with sea transport shipments being close to 0%. The average distance covered by one passenger was longest by air (1632 km) and by rail (622 km), whereas in the case of river transport and coaches the figure was 170 km and 61 km respectively. These figures show that aeroplanes were mostly used for long distances, trains for medium distances and coaches for short runs.

The political disintegration of the Soviet Union and the subsequent economic crisis altered the transportation structure. These developments cut the volume of transportation by river, air and road, and also affected other types of transport – albeit to a lesser degree. For details, see Table 1.

Table 1 Changes in the volume of transportation for different types of transportation inside Russia

Type of transport	Freight transported (mln. ton)				Passengers carried in inter-city transportation (mln. passengers)			
	1991	1992	1993	1994	1991	1992	1993	1994
Railways	1956	1640	1348	1053	255	245	254	215
Motorway	2731	1923	1110*	1975*	790	520	420	390
Gas pipeline	546	523	511	483	-	-	-	-
Oil pipeline	497	421	362	318	-	-	-	-
Riverway	514	308	215	153	17	8	7	5.0
Sea	104	91	83	68	0,3	0.9	0.2	0.2
Air	2,2	1.3	0.9	0.4	82	59	37	34

* *Including the private sector*

The political demise of the Soviet Union and the emerging economic crisis were followed by the break-up of many economic ties between the former republics in terms of raw materials, semi-finished and finished products. Naturally, this reduced the transportation volume between the former constituent parts of the USSR and within Russia, which had been the key supplier and customer in these relations. The economic crisis, originally caused by political factors, took on a momentum of its own. A dramatic switch over to free market prices was the catalyst that precipitated the crisis and ultimately culminated in soaring prices for cargo and passenger transportation as well as for piped oil, conventional gas and petroleum products. The increase in these rates was the main reason for the decrease in the volume of both passenger and cargo transportation.

The economic space for duty-free circulation of cargoes and passengers became much narrower in the wake of the Soviet Union's disintegration. This was especially apparent in the western part of Russia which is the focal point for the country's economic connections with Eastern and Western Europe and, in particular, for the export of raw materials and semi-finished products, as well as for the import of European commodities. As a result of the political secession of the Baltic states and the strong isolationist stance displayed by Ukraine, the CIS experienced the emergence of customs, political and economic barriers between Russia and the rest of Europe. It is noteworthy that Belarus proved to be very loyal to Russia by granting the country privileged conditions for the transit of cargoes. The Baltics slipped away from the former Soviet Union which made Russia lose four large export/import ports. This loss made it much more difficult for Russia to maintain transportation links with its enclave in Kaliningrad *oblast'*. A proportion of cargo flows was diverted to neighbouring Russian ports on the Baltic and Black Sea and the Northern basin or was simply shipped over land through Belarus.

Customs transit duties for passage through Ukraine went up and, consequently, reduced the volume of Russian transit cargoes in Ukraine. The loss of the port of Odessa turned out to be a highly painful consequence for Russia. This port was used for large export/import transportation deals to south-east Europe and the Middle East. Today, the bulk of Russian cargoes goes abroad via Novorossiisk. By all accounts, Russia finds itself in a very precarious situation with oil and natural gas export pipelines which run through Ukraine *en route* from Russia to Eastern and Western Europe. In addition to the high transit duties set by Ukrainian authorities, fuel is also frequently siphoned off from the pipeline without permission. This inflicts serious economic damage on export operations and reduces the flow of hard currency earnings to the Russian budget. Thus, the main freight flows were redirected into the only available 'hatch way' (a favourable export/import corridor) – Belarus.

The transit conditions here are much more favourable than in Ukraine or the Baltic states, to say nothing of the transit distance, which is considerably shorter.

The Smolensk-Brest railway stretch is 680 km whereas the distance between Khutor-Mikhailovskii and Chop is 1100 km and from Valuek (Khar'kov-Belgorod region) to Chop 1 500 km. The establishment of a single economic and financial union of Belarus and Russia that was proposed in the spring of 1994 could make this corridor the chief, cheapest and safest way from Russia to Europe. The functions of the Baltic and Ukrainian ports that were lost by Russia will be taken over by neighbouring Russian ports which are likely to drastically improve their infrastructure facilities and terminals as well as increase cargo flows in the near future.

The European part of Russia 'looks out' mainly on Europe and partially on the Transcaucasus and the Middle East. Economic links with the Transcaucasian countries have recently deteriorated because of continuous military conflicts there. At the same time, the Urals and Western Siberia enjoy closer economic ties with Kazakhstan while Eastern Siberia and the Far East are on good economic terms with China, Korea, Japan and other Pacific countries.

A swift increase in transportation rates following 1992 led to a dramatic cut in transportation on the one hand, and to a growth of the share of transportation expenses in the prime cost on the other.

The haulage volume of certain commodities declined steadily: coal – by 11% in 1993 and 1994; iron ore – 7% and 5% respectively; raw materials – 25% and 26% respectively. However, it was typical for this period that against the background of a general drop in the volume of transit by rail, *export-oriented* transportation grew by 4% in 1994. This was primarily caused by the export of ferrous metals (which increased by 1.6 times), non-ferrous metals (1.3 times) and non-organic and mineral fertilisers (1.4 times). This means that the economic disintegration period of 1992-1993 when the transport network was losing its formerly integrated character is apparently drawing to an end. Exporters' interests make the transport infrastructure of Russia function in unison and with unprecedented efficiency. For instance, the total number of train carriages clustered at the border and port stations went down by 22% in 1994 despite the fact that these transit points handled an increased volume of goods. The average distance for transportation of cargoes was reduced by 13% over the same period of time.

Unfortunately, optimising changes in the structure of *domestic* transportation are lagging behind. A sharp upsurge of the share of transportation expenses in the price of some commodities can serve as an indication of structural reconstruction: e.g. for industrial coal that share went up to 54% of the price in 1994, for iron ore – 22% and for coking coal – 30% of the price. Regardless of the deep depression of the coal

Map 1
Railroad density
(km/1000 sq. km.)

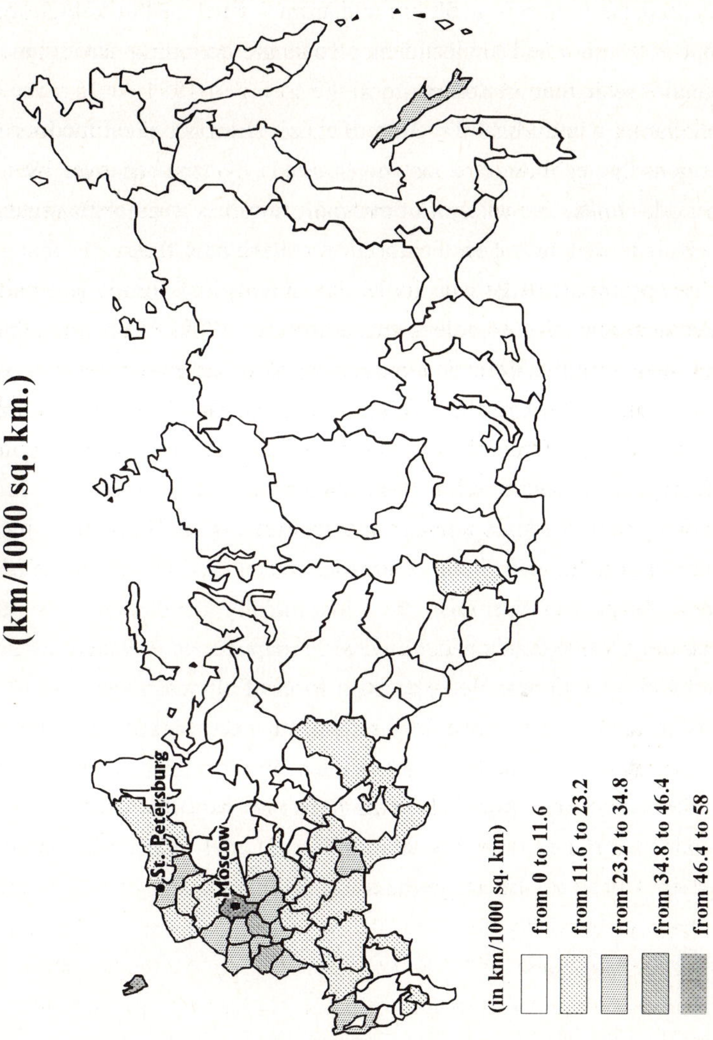

mining industry, coal exports increased by 2% in 1994. This testifies to the fact that the hauled coal is of prime quality and is competitive on the foreign market. At the same time, high-soot and low-efficiency coals are travelling across the country on a much smaller scale than in Soviet times.

By and large, a latitudinal direction of cargo flows is typical for Russia. However, in the densely economic zone constituted by the triangle St. Petersburg-Novorossiisk-Omsk, the network of transport lines has a radial character, converging on the city of Moscow. The territorial peculiarity of Russia is that its economic pattern is extremely heterogeneous. Only one-third of Russia's territory has been developed economically. However, this area houses 70% of the population. It should be mentioned here that four economic regions in its south-western sector alone – central industrial, central black-earth, North Caucasian and *Povolzh'e* regions – contain 50% of all residents. This is the area where the country's infrastructural skeleton is concentrated, with 95% of its economic centres. Throughout the remaining 70% of Russia's territory are scattered small isolated economic centres. The majority of them are mining centres for the extraction and export of mineral raw materials. Within the limits of the economically developed zone, the transport infrastructure is quite developed. However, untapped zones have poor and unreliable transport communications. Here the main form of all-season transport (and the most expensive one) is the aeroplane. In summertime a combination of river and sea boats can be used. Only oil and natural gas fields in Western Siberia and Komi have direct railway access and main pipelines to the European part of Russia.

Now let us move on to a description of the underlying problems in the development of certain aspects in the transport infrastructure.

1 Railway Transport

The total length of the Russian (general use) railway network is 87,000 km, including 38,000 km of electrified rail tracks. 58% of general use railways are single-tracked, which are mostly side branches and local lines, whereas almost all main lines are double-tracked. Basically all the railways have a broad gauge of 1524 mm, which is different from the European standard. The railways in South Sakhalin have the Japanese standard of 1067 mm. There is also a network of narrow gauge branches. Because of this gauge difference between Russian and all other post-Soviet rail tracks on the one hand and European ones on the other, it is necessary to change train carriages or reload containers and cargoes at the border stations. These operations are carried out at all major railway frontier facilities of the former Soviet Union. They are Chop, Mostiska, Khelm, Brest and Kuznitsa. Naturally this causes some delay to transportation and especially to cargoes. However this problem does not exist at the Russian-Finnish border or in the east where the Russian railways meet north-west China. These stretches have the same width gauge. Kaliningrad has a direct connection with the European railway network which also includes a rail track with standard width 1435 mm. Therefore there is no need to reload cargoes or change train carriages.

Changes in the geopolitical situation of the FSU brought some amendments to the railway network. Secession of the Baltic states and introduction of frontier checkpoints and customs regulations changed the itinerary for trains bound from St. Petersburg to the western border. The old route was replaced by a new one which made trains follow the direction Nevel'-Polotsk-Molodechno-Grodno in Russia and Belarus instead of Daugavpils-Vil'nius. Trains leaving Russia for the Czech Republic and South Poland now predominantly pass through Belarus instead of Ukraine as was formerly the case. The train itinerary for south-east Europe and Finland remained unchanged. The same goes for trains leaving for China, except for slight changes and the new Druzhba-Urumchi railway which was commissioned to open a direct route from Kazakhstan to China. However, this route is rarely is used by the Russian railway due to some worsening of Russian-Kazakhstan relations.

Railway communication between central Russia and the North Caucasus has experienced some difficulties. The main passenger line on this route runs through Khar'kov and the Donbass, whereas the freight line passes through Voronezh-Millerovo and at one point runs across Ukrainian territory. In the event of a further deterioration of political relations between Russia and Ukraine, the North Caucasus may be cut off from Russia's nucleus (the only remaining route would be via Volgograd or one which partially passes through Kazakhstan). Thus there is a necessity to build a back-up railway for the connection Michurinsk-Kalach-Morozovsk-Volgodonsk-Stavropol'.

The same problems may arise in Southern Siberia since a short stretch of the Trans-Siberian railway (Isil'-Kul'-Petropavlovsk-Mashukino, 205 km) passes through Kazakhstan. Should some complications set in it will be necessary to construct a by-pass stretch in Russia (Makushino-Nazyvaevsk) or a more expensive extension of the mid-Siberian railway over the marshland along the Ob' river.

Due to the uneven economic development of the Russian terrain the density of railway varies considerably (see Table 2). It is much higher in the western part of the country, reaching 26-27 km per 1000 square kilometres on average, but falls to 12-18 km/1000km^2 in the southern and eastern direction. The railway density is extremely low in Siberia, the Far East and the European North. The highest density at the *oblast'* level is observed in Moscow (58 km per 1000 sq. km), Kaliningrad (50 km), Tula (44 km) and Kursk (38 km). The density dwindles quickly as one moves away from Central Russia northward, eastward and south-eastward. This is connected with the falling population density and smaller growth of economic activities in to the east and north.

Table 2 *Density of the railroad network (km./1000 km²): 1 – density of the network of motorways with a hard surface (km./1000 km²); 2 – proportion of motorways with hard surface in the overall length of general-use motorways (in %); 3 – presence of light automobiles in the population (motorisation rate of the population – cars per 1000 people); 4 – index of all regions' data for 1992/1993*

	1	2		3	4	
	1992	1992	1993	1992	1992	1993
Arkhangel'sk	3	8	9	77	47	52
Vologda	5	69	71	92	45	50
Murmansk	6	16	16	93	69	92
Karelia	13	35	34	88	76	89
Komi	4	6	7	73	56	65
Leningradskaya	32	113	112	100	53	60
Novgorod	21	123	147	99	48	49
Pskov	21	125	151	99	64	71
Bryansk	31	128	129	98	34	35
Vladimir	33	150	157	100	54	56
Ivanovo	14	145	146	98	43	45
Kaluga	29	141	142	99	62	67
Kostroma	11	65	81	92	50	60
Moscow	58	260	300	98	69	81
Orlov	24	155	155	99	56	66
Ryazan'	26	123	145	96	55	58
Smolensk	25	106	107	99	61	67
Tver	21	111	120	99	53	61
Tula	43	189	191	98	58	65
Yaroslavl'	19	159	163	91	51	53
Nizhnii Novgorod	18	107	108	98	49	54
Kirov	9	62	63	85	51	53
Marii-El	9	104	107	96	41	44
Mordovia	21	133	138	88	44	58
Chuvashia	23	149	151	93	32	34
Belgorod	26	163	218	93	76	90
Voronezh	23	135	148	96	88	90
Kursk	37	167	167	93	36	37

	1	2		3	4	
	1992	1992	1993	1992	1992	1993
Lipetsk	33	153	153	98	61	60
Tambov	23	112	132	64	54	61
Astrakhan'	13	53	53	85	52	59
Volgograd	14	65	68	68	88	56
Samara	26	112	113	98	80	84
Penza	19	113	125	96	58	57
Saratov	23	88	89	94	81	85
Ul'yanovsk	19	118	120	95	60	63
Kalmykia	2	28	29	56	76	77
Tatarstan	13	146	149	97	48	54
Krasnodar	28	131	131	100	91	94
Stavropol	11	107	107	97	72	82
Rostov	19	99	100	92	86	90
Dagestan	9	127	127	97	35	39
Kabardino-Balkaria	11	186	187	100	79	87
North Ossetia	19	286	289	100	67	73
Chechnya-Ingushetia	19	152	160	98	54	-
Kurgansk	11	69	71	76	98	98
Orenburg	14	81	81	98	87	91
Perm	9	38	39	86	46	48
Sverdlovsk	18	43	46	74	64	67
Chelyabinsk	20	79	83	100	73	83
Bashortostan	11	101	111	92	64	71
Udmurtia	21	105	106	93	60	66
Altai *krai*	7	70	80	95	81	83
Kemerovo	18	45	49	100	71	75
Novosibirsk	9	41	46	72	70	73
Omsk	6	43	50	69	64	69
Tomsk	1	8	9	68	83	94
Tyumen'	2	3	3	58	73	86
Krasnoyarsk	1	4	4	96	76	82
Irkutsk	3	13	14	89	86	91
Chita	5	21	21	96	70	70
Buryatia	2	17	17	93	64	73
Tuva	-	16	16	88	52	52
Primorskii *krai*	10	43	42	96	82	96
Khabarovsk	3	4	4	76	56	72
Amur	6	16	17	99	73	85
Kamchatka	-	2	2	96	93	105
Magadan	-	2	6	89	70	86
Sakhalin	12	22	21	90	109	135
Yakutia-Sakha	0	2	2	44	73	79
Kaliningrad	50	306	306	100	79	106

The key latitudinal railway line for Russia is along the route Brest-Smolensk-Moscow-Urals-Omsk-Novosibirsk-Krasnoyarsk-Irkutsk-Khabarovsk-Vladivistok.

At the same time there are three double-track electrified railway lines which duplicate one another but bear an extremely intense level of traffic: Yaroslavl'-Nizhnii Novgorod-Perm', Murom-Kazan', Ryazan'-Samara-Ufa. The eastern length of this railway line, referred to as the *Transsib* (Chelyabinsk-Omsk-Vladivostok) is also partially duplicated by Barnaul-Novokuznetsk-Abakan-Taishet from the south and the BAM single track railway (Baikal and Amur Railway) from the north.

The main meridian line is that of Murmansk-St. Petersburg-Moscow-Tula-Belgorod; the line Arkhangel'sk-Moscow-Voronezh-Rostov-North Caucasus; the line Moscow-Tambov-Saratov-Astrakhan'-North Caucasus, and that running along the right-hand bank of the Volga river and the Transurals railway (Serov-Ekaterinburg-Chelyabinsk-Orsk).

The 'natural resources and raw material' railway routes Konosha-Vorkuta; Tyumen'-Surgut-Urengoi with branch lines, Tynda-Berkakit, etc. lead to newly developed regions.

Russia's largest railway junctions are Moscow, St. Petersburg, Samara, Ekaterinburg, Chelyabinsk, Novosibirsk and Rostov-on-Don.

Main cargo and passenger train lines go along latitudinal railways as well as radial railway lines from Moscow to St. Petersburg and the North Caucasus. Because of the heavy overload of these connections back in the 1980s, a design plan for a high-speed central-south railway through Khar'kov-Rostov was developed. However, it never became a reality because of the break-up of the Soviet Union. At present, construction of a high-speed railway (of the TGV type, with speeds up to 250 km/h) is under way. It is planned to connect Moscow and St. Petersburg and extend this a little further westward beyond the existing line. This railway is scheduled to be commissioned in 1997-98. Similar railway lines are also expected to be laid, creating the following connections; Moscow-Samara; Chelyabinsk-Ekaterinburg-Omsk-Novosibirsk-Kuzbass; Moscow-Smolensk-Minsk-Warsaw-Berlin. However, these are long-term plans indeed.

As far as regular railways are concerned there are some lines which are scheduled for construction. They are Berkakit-Aldan-Yakutsk (under construction already), Usinsk-Sea Coast (for exploration of the Shtokman field), a mid-Siberian railway and others. Many of them are not likely to be built because of lack of funds.

The basic problem facing the Russian railway transport system is the need for technical reconstruction of existing rail lines, replacement of train carriages and relief of overloaded railway conjunctions (Moscow, Samara, Chelyabinsk).

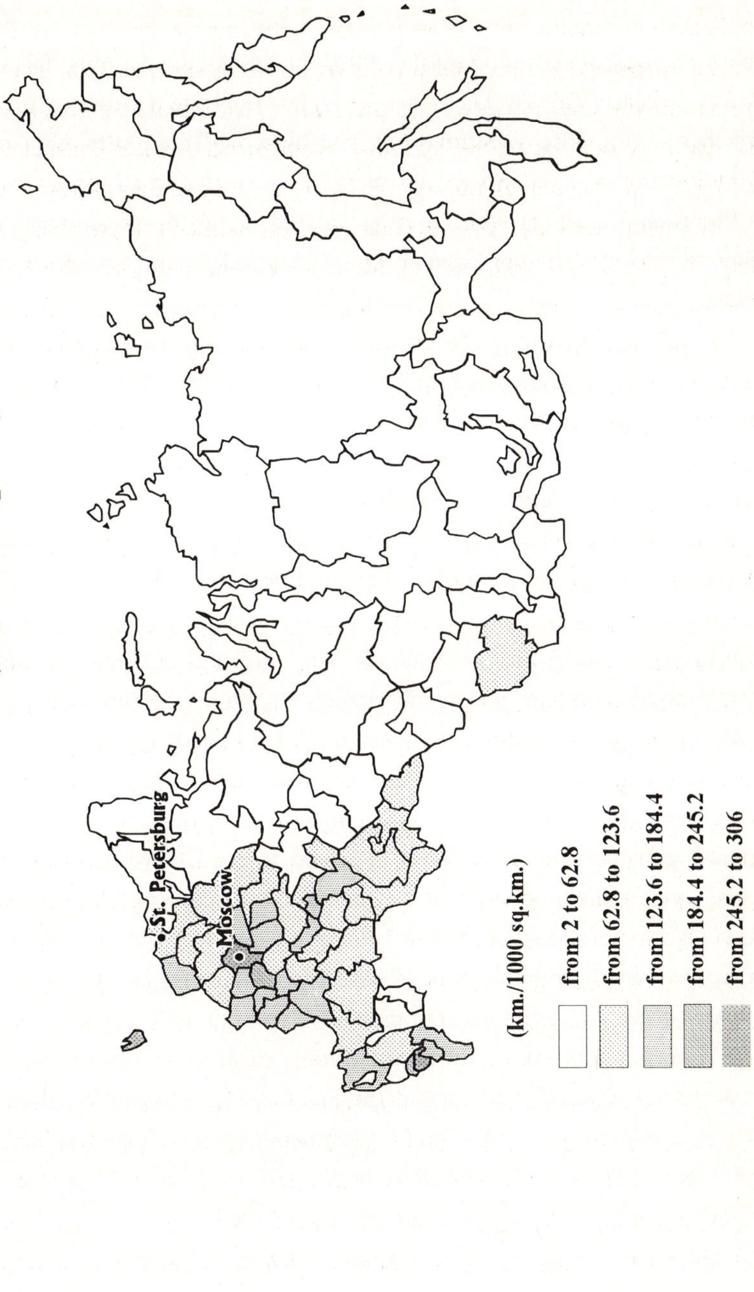

Map 2
Hard-surfaced motorway density
(km/1000 sq.km.)

2 Motor Transport

The total length of motorways is 902,000 km including 698,000 km which are surfaced (nearly 76%). There are very few top-rate roadways in Russia (short stretches of the Moscow-Simferopol' and Moscow-Riga routes and some others). In 1960-80 medium-class motorways were built connecting all large cities and regions in European Russia as well as cities located along the greater part of the Trans-Siberian railway. The only remaining missing link is one between Chita and Amur *oblasts*.

As with the railway network, the density of surfaced roadways (see Map 2) dramatically decreases as one moves north or east from the centre and the south of European Russia, with the highest density in the country being in Moscow *oblast'* and North Ossetia – 260 km per 1000 sq. km and 286 km per 1000 sq. km respectively. The density is much lower outside the fully developed economic triangle. Thus it is on average 15-16 km per 1 000 sq. km in Western Siberia and the Russian North whereas it ranges from 2 to 20 km per 1 000 sq. km in Eastern Siberia and the Far East. The core of the European part enjoys a higher density of surfaced roadways – 110-150 km per 1000 sq. km. As usual, Kaliningrad *oblast'*, being a more European place, is an exception with 306 km per 1000 sq. km.

Up to the 1970s Russia used to stand out for its lack of roads or, to be exact, for the poor quality of its roads (mostly dirt roads rather than macadamised ones). The proportion of surfaced roads has increased considerably in almost all regions because considerable funds were allocated to road construction over the last 20 years. Overall, the proportion of such roads in the total length of general-use roads in Russia has increased from 20% in 1960 up to 65% in 1980 and 90% in 1992. As far as the developed economic zone is concerned, the density is 94-100% (see Table 2), although there are some exceptions. Outside the zone the density decreases to 50-70%. The worst roads in European Russia are now in Kalmykiya – 56%; in the Asian part, the worst roads are in the Far East – Sakha and Khabarovsk *krai* with 44% and 76% respectively – and in Southern Siberia – Tyumen' *oblast'* with 58% and Tomsk *oblast'* with 68%. The best roads are located in the central industrial region, in the North Caucasus and Kaliningrad *oblast'*.

Unlike the railway system, Russia's network of motorways is predominantly radial. All of them actually lead to Moscow or St. Petersburg (although very few of them have multiple lanes). On the other hand, many neighbouring economic regions, especially in the Asian part, do not have surfaced good road links. The main radial

Map 3
Proportion of hard-surfaced motorways in overall motorway length (in %)

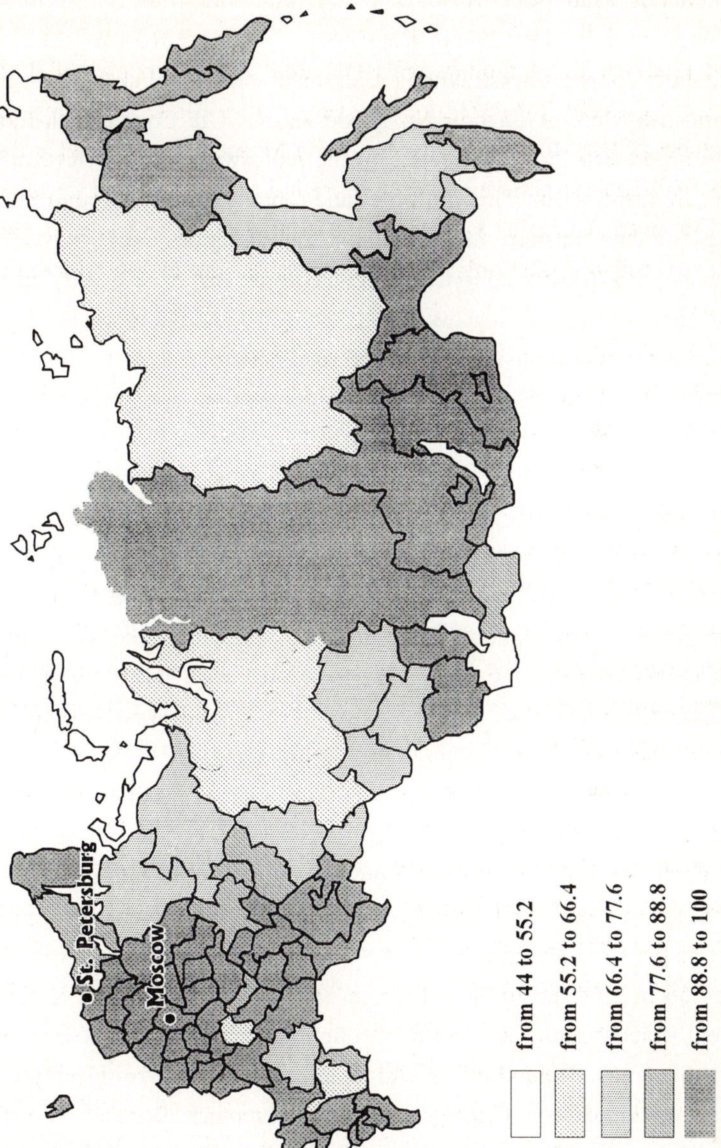

motorways lead from Moscow to the following cities: St. Petersburg-Murmansk, Velikie Luki; Orel-Kursk-Khar'kov; Voronezh-Rostov-Vladimir-Makhachkala; Tambov-Volgograd-Astrakhan'; Vologda-Arkhangel'sk. The motorway route Smolensk-Moscow-Nizhnii Novgorod-Kazan'-Ufa-Chelyabinsk-Ekaterinburg is the basic road line. It is duplicated by the motorway Moscow-Ryazan'-Penza-Samara-Ufa from the south. This multiple-lane route continues through the southern part of Western and Eastern Siberia along the direction Omsk-Novosibirsk-Kemerovo-Krasnoyarsk-Irkutsk up to Chita and has some very poor quality stretches. The North Caucasus as well as Moscow, Tula, Leningrad and Kaliningrad *oblasts* and the south of Primorskii *krai* have a fairly good road network.

Some road routes are the only communication link to the outside world for less developed regions because there are no railways. Here they are called 'tracts' – Biisk-Gorno Altaisk-Chinese border, Abakan-Kyzyl, Never-Aldan-Yakutsk-Magadan. In wintertime, so-called 'winter river roads' are arranged on some river stretches in North Siberia. Russia still has a low car per person rate. Its level of motorisation in 1992 was 69 cars per 1 000 residents. The highest rate is observed in the regions with higher living standards. These are the Far East (Sakhalin –109, Kamchatka *oblast'* – 95, Primorskii *krai* – 82, see Table 2) and the country's biggest centres (Moscow – 94, St. Petersburg – 76). The level is also high in steppe regions where the population enjoys higher living standards: Adygeya – 110, Khakassiya – 94, Kurgan – 98, Krasnodar *krai* – 91, Volgograd and Orenburg *oblast'* – 88 and 87, respectively, and Altai *krai* – 81).

Oddly enough, the motorisation rate in large cities did not increase dramatically until the economic crisis reached its pinnacle, with the emergence of different socio-economic strata. In Moscow and St. Petersburg the car per person rate rose from 71 and 56 in 1990 up to 94 and 76 in 1992, accordingly. Due to the emergence of a well-heeled stratum as well as through the activation of local foreign trade in the frontier areas, demand for second-hand cars imported from Europe, Japan and Korea went up immensely. Thus the growth in the motorisation rate from 1990 to 1992 was as follows: Kareliya – from 56 to 76, Kaliningrad *oblast'* – from 61 to 79; Far East: Sakhalin – from 74 to 109, Primorskii *krai* – from 62 to 82, Kamchatka *oblast'* – from 73 to 93 and Magadan *oblast'* – from 38 to 70. Unexpectedly the motorisation factor increased in the republic of Altai (from 56 to 78) which enjoys the closest access to China as well as Tomsk *oblast'* – from 63 to 83. In 1992, the most critical year of the crisis, the motorisation rate went up by 19 units in Sakhalin *oblast'* (from 90 to 109), Tomsk *oblast'* – from 67 to 83, Kaliningrad *oblast'* – from 63 to 79.

Map 4
Number of private automobiles in the population (motorisation rate - cars/1000 people)

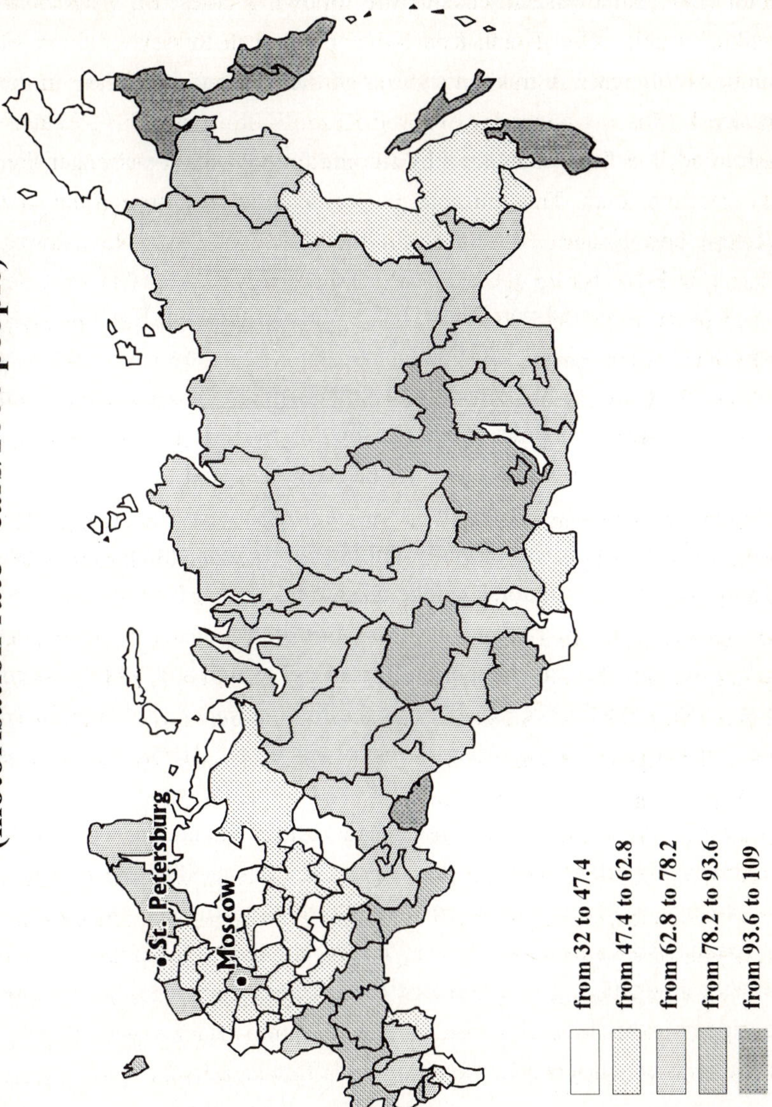

However, it increased by as many as 29 units in Magadan *oblast'* – from 41 to 70. Such a considerable growth in the motorisation factor serves as an indication of a significant increase in living standards of the population residing in these particular regions.

Inter-city and suburban coaches account for 68% of all passenger transport.

3 Sea Transport

The western export/import sector has suffered following Russia's loss of some sea ports in the Baltics and Ukraine. Therefore, cargo flows were diverted to Russian ports (Novorossiisk, St. Petersburg, Arkhangel'sk and Murmansk) and partially to land communication links. To make up for the lost ports, Russia is planning to commission new ports in Taganrog (the Azov Sea) and Ust'-Lug (the Finnish Gulf). It has also planned to expand the ports of Novorossiisk, Nakhodka and Vladivostok with new terminals. The partially military ports of Kaliningrad, Sovetskii Gavan', Murmansk and Severomorsk can be used to take some load off the above-mentioned ports. The port of Astrakhan' may also turn into a medium-size export/import port because of geopolitical changes and its access to Iran and Middle Eastern countries. Despite the reduction of export ports the foreign trade cargo turnover dropped only slightly. The main cargoes transported by sea are oil, petroleum products, timber and bituminous coal.

Ports in the southern Far East (Vladivostok, Nakhodka, Vanino, Kholmsk) are especially important for cargo haulage. They are used in the transit of cargoes to remote places in the Far North and North-east Russia – the ports of Magadan, Petropavlovsk-Kamchatskii, Pevek, Tiksi and Dikson. These routes are only used for summer navigation. The volume of cargo transportation to these regions has fallen considerably because of a rise in transportation charges over the last two years. Many ports are currently not functioning at full capacity.

4 River Transport

Russia's river transport system works on a seasonal basis. Navigation lasts from two to three up to seven to nine months a year, depending on the latitude. The total length of navigable rivers and shipping canals is 100000 km.

The volume of cargo transportation by river decreased by two times in 1992-1993 owing to a reduction of in the amount of construction goods. However, timber, oil and bituminous coal are still the main products carried by river transport. River vessels are obsolescent (new five year old ships account for just 3% of the cargo fleet). The volume of passenger river transportation has fallen by nearly two times, especially for inter-city and suburban communication, mainly because of increases in fuel and ticket rates.

The key navigable rivers are:

- *European Russia*: Volga (from Rzhev to Astrakhan'), Oka, Don, Kama and Belaya Vyatka; Sukhona, Vychegda, North Dvina, Mezen', Pechora (the Volga and Don basins as well as Lake Ladoga and Onega are linked by shipping canals);
- *Siberia*: The Ob' with tributaries Irtysh, Tobol, Ishim; Enisei; Lena with tributaries Vitim, Olekma, Vilyui, Aldan; navigable stretches of the rivers located in the Far North (Yana, Indigirka, Kolyma) and the Amur.

River transport only meets needs in domestic transportation. In the Far North a short navigation period is used for delivering supplies of prime necessity from the ports of the northern sea way to the main centres of the less developed zone. At the same time, raw materials are also funnelled to these ports to be picked up by railway transport. The Enisei and Lena rivers are used to pick up cargoes from the Trans-Siberian railway and its branches which are then shipped to the Far North and back. An increase in rates and fuel prices resulted in a drastic reduction of transportation volume.

5 Air Transport

This form of transport was at its peak just prior to the collapse of the Soviet Union. A network of 'A' and 'B' airports in partially and barely developed zones was almost complete by 1990. Here air transport is still the only regular all-season type of transport, the main function of which is to carry passengers, with a secondary function of hauling cargoes and mail. 1990 was the peak of the Russian air transport system. The aircraft of the civil aviation department carried 91 million passengers including 22 million from Moscow, 5 million from St. Petersburg, 2.7 million from Ekaterinburg, 2.3 million from Novosibirsk.

In 1991, Russia's 110 large and medium-size airports conveyed 86 million passengers while in 1992 this figure was 63 million. Such a drop in passenger volume was accounted for by an increase in prices for air fuel and, therefore, air tickets. The number of passengers flying Russian domestic routes declined immensely in 1992-1993 when the country was experiencing the worst stage of its crisis. Many passengers 'switched' to the railway. This affected the airlines operating from the heart of the country to the Far North, Siberia and the Far East to a lesser extent. Air transport is still a 'monopolist' in these areas. The number of passengers also decreased, although not so considerably as in regional centres of European Russia, i.e., there are several flights a day as opposed to 1-2 flights a week.

Prices of air tickets to CIS countries receiving oil products from Russia went up sharply following the disintegration of the Soviet Union and the rise in the cost of air fuel. Small and medium-size airports in Ukraine, Belarus and Moldova ceased to function because of the fuel shortage in 1992-1993. Flights from these towns to local capitals and even Moscow were cancelled. Now air tickets are more expensive than the railway fare and, therefore, airlines are not in a position to resume flights on these routes or to revitalise small and medium-size airports. This is only possible if there is a drastic reduction in the price of tickets. For instance, large airports in Ukraine run flights to large Russian airports (except for Moscow) once or twice a week. In 1993 medium-size airports in Kazakhstan, Uzbekistan, Kirgyzstan, Ukraine and Belarus cancelled some direct flights to Moscow. However, these developments did not apply to Transcaucasian airports which have run three flights to Moscow per day.

As the volume of transportation within Russia and to CIS countries decreases, the volume of international transportation to Europe, USA, Asia and the Pacific increases. Old traditional international connections to socialist countries (Berlin, Varna, Sofia, Belgrade and Havana) were replaced with new ones such as Tokyo, Seoul, Beijing, Shanghai, Singapore, Dubai, Turkish airports on the Mediterranean coast, the Canary Islands, Florida, California, London, Paris and New York). 3.5 million passengers were carried by *Aeroflot* planes on international routes in 1992. 90% flew from Moscow, 7% – St. Petersburg and the rest from Khabarovsk, Irkutsk, Petrozavodsk, Murmansk, etc. In Russia, *Aeroflot* split up in 65 local and regional air companies and enterprises.

Russia's largest air hubs are Moscow, St. Petersburg, Ekaterinburg, Novosibirsk as well as Sochi, Tyumen', Krasnoyarsk, Irkutsk and Khabarovsk.

6 Natural Gas Pipelines

In spite of Russia's sagging economy, the extraction of conventional gas remained at the pre-crisis level of 1990. In 1992 it was 641 billion cubic metres including 88 billion cubic metres for export to Europe and the rest for Russia and CIS countries, mainly, Ukraine, Belarus, the Baltic states and, partially, the Transcaucasus. Russia has the richest natural gas fields in the West Siberian plain (Berezovo, Igrim, Vyngapur, Urengoi, Medvezh'e, Yamburg, Bovanenkovo, Messoyakha), Komi and Nenetsk *okrug* (Shtokman), Middle Povolzh'e (Orenburg) and Sakhalin. 546 million tons in 1991 and 523 million tons in 1992 were transported through gas pipelines to customers in Russia, CIS and Western Europe.

The total length of gas pipelines was 140,000 km in late 1992. The main pipelines trail from Western Siberia and the republic of Komi to the industrialised core of European Russia and then branch out in three 'vectors':

- through Belarus to Poland;
- through Ukraine to West and South-east Europe;
- through the North Caucasus to the Transcaucasus.

The chief pipelines are the following:

- Yamburg-Urengoi-Surgut-Chelyabinsk-Tatarstan-Ukraine with an offshoot to the Caucasus;
- The 'northern lights': (Yamburg-Urengoi-Igrim-Ukhta-Centre-Belarus);
- *Soyuz* [Union]: (Orenburg-Ukraine-Western Europe).

In addition, Siberia also has small regional natural gas pipelines: Surgut-Kuzbass, Messoyakha-Noril'sk, Vilyuisk gas field-Yakutsk.

As has already been mentioned, natural gas in transit on Ukrainian soil was siphoned off without permission because of Ukraine's political isolation stance. This resulted in shortfalls of natural gas to Europe. At present there is an agreement on the construction of a direct gas pipeline from Russia to Germany through Belarus and Poland to correct the unfavourable situation. The quantity of natural gas transported will slightly decline because of new natural gas fields in Yamala and Shtokman.

7 Petroleum Pipeline Transport

The volume of oil extraction in Russia dramatically fell from 516 million tons in 1990 up to 399 million tons in 1992 and 295 million tons in 1994. These figures include 66 million tons of crude oil and 25 million tons of petroleum products exported in 1992. In 1994 the export volume made up 89.4 million tons of oil and 43 million tons of petroleum products. The largest oil fields are located in Western Siberia (Surgut, Shaim, Ust'-Balyk, Megion, Strezhevoi, Kholmogory) and the republic of Komi (Ukhta, Usinsk, Voivozh, Vozei). More exhausted oil fields are in the Middle Volga region and the Urals (Tatarstan, Bashkortostan, Perm' *oblast'*), the North Caucasus (Maikop, Malgobeck, Ozek-Suat) and Sakhalin (Okha).

Crude oil is pumped through main pipelines with a total length of 48,000 km. Refined oil products are transported through 15,000 km network of pipelines. 497 million tons of oil and petroleum products were sent through the pipes in 1991, whereas in 1992 this figure dropped to 421 million tons of oil and oil products including 381 million tons of oil and 41 million tons of products. The pipeline transport intensifies in terms of significance as the country is trying to rescue the economy at the expense of raw material export.

The main oil pipeline in Russia is that running from Western Siberia to the Volga region (where the refineries are located) on to the centre for secondary processing and then to consumers in Ukraine, Belarus, Slovak republic and Poland. The direction of this line is as follows: Usinsk-Ukhta-Yaroslavl'-Torzhok-Polotsk; Medvezh'e/Samotlor-Surgut-Perm'-Yaroslavl'-Moscow; Surgut-Chelyabinsk-Ufa-Samara-Mozyr'; Perm'-Almet'evsk-Samara-Petrovsk-Volgograd-Novorossiisk. Oil refineries are located in European Russia along the oil pipeline, most notably in Ryazan', Yaroslavl', Perm', Kirishi, Ukhta, Kostovo, Volgograd, Saratov, Novokyuibyshevsk-Groznyi, Tuapse, etc.

Siberia has the Trans-Siberian oil pipeline Almet'evsk/Tuimazy-Chelyabinsk-Omsk-Angarsk. There are oil refineries in Omsk, Achinsk and Angarsk which provide petroleum products for the whole of Siberia and the Far East.

As with natural gas pipelines there is a problem with transporting oil over the territory of Ukraine on the way to Europe. After the oil export port of Ventspils became part of the Baltics it became necessary to redirect the flow of oil and petroleum products to neighbouring countries.

The strategic importance of oil pipeline transport is increasing rapidly, since it serves as the infrastructural foundation for Russia's territorial integrity as well as for its integration into the Western European economy. The political role of oil pipelines is quite plain to see against the backdrop of the Chechnya crisis which has led to the idea of operating a new pipeline from the Caspian Sea to oil terminals of the Black Sea in order to side-step Chechnya. A draft agreement has been provisionally agreed between Russia, Kazakhstan and Oman (which is the main source of investments for the project) and was in fact ready to be signed by all parties by March 1995. However, this never happened because the representatives of Kazakhstan did not show up at the negotiation table. There is no doubt that construction of a new oil pipeline branch from the North Caspian area (Tengiz-Atyrau-Elista-Tikhoretsk-

Kropotkin-Black Sea) will be continued. For Russia this means the maintenance of geopolitical supremacy in the Central Asian region and the forcing of Turkey as well as of Western corporations like Chevron out of the region in question. Some Russian circles believe that some foreign companies have become too active on the former Soviet market.

The pipeline grid is also going to have an increasing importance for the CIS countries. Belarus has openly admitted that it is ready to reconstruct an economic union with Russia. As for other erstwhile republics of the FSU, Ukraine seems to be discreetly drifting in this direction, although more slowly and cautiously. Kazakhstan has been working on the conception of a Eurasian union and seems to understand that pipeline transport plays a pivotal role in the pattern of economic interaction with the world market and that this kind of transport is under Russia's control.

The near future and especially the prospects of a Russian-Kazakh Caspian consortium based on financial support from Oman will show how efficient pipeline transport can be in the post-Soviet era.

At the moment, the main problems of Russia's transport infrastructure are the high obsolescence of its material and technical basis and the low reliability of the system; the necessity of switching over to new and faster transport technologies; the heavy load of latitudinal lines; the absence of a network of highways in the developed part of European Russia; the narrowing of the export/import space in the western part of the country; the need for an all-out renewal of the rolling stock, ships and aircraft; the depletion of oil resources in the near future; and the excessively remote location of natural gas and oil fields from the areas of consumption.

10

Russia's Inter-Regional Associations

A New Form of State Life

Mariya Lyashevskaya

Introduction

The regional development of Russia is characterised by shifts between periods of tough centralisation and the autonomisation of regions. At the current stage (during the last three to five years), the process of dividing the whole territory into distinct areas has been proceeding stage by stage. This process seems to reflect the changing conditions of this division, which we have observed in previous periods of Russian history: from full autonomisation of regions to their economic interaction.

At the initial stage the territories were focusing their efforts on regulating trade (export, import, transit restrictions, etc.), fixing price and profit levels, regulating the circulation of money (including issuing money substitutes), basically manipulating purely administrative control levers. The logical completion of this situation was that the actions taken were legalised as decisions of local bodies of authority. The second step was to set up local security bodies (a kind of municipal militia), to enter into direct contacts with foreign partners, etc.

Further on, regional blocks were built, in the form of agreements promoting economic ties and mutual co-operation, while demands were also presented to the federal authorities. The climax of the development of those processes was in 1991, when regional associations started to be truly formed.

The final stages are linked with the legalisation of regional sovereignty. The confirmation of economic sovereignty comes with the declaration of munipalisation of federal property, the introduction or request of a one-channel tax mechanism, preparation for the release of local currency and the formation of gold reserves, institutional legalisation of sovereignty, (introduction of presidency, governorship, institution of legal representatives, etc.), transfer of internal affairs organs to

Russia's Regional Associations

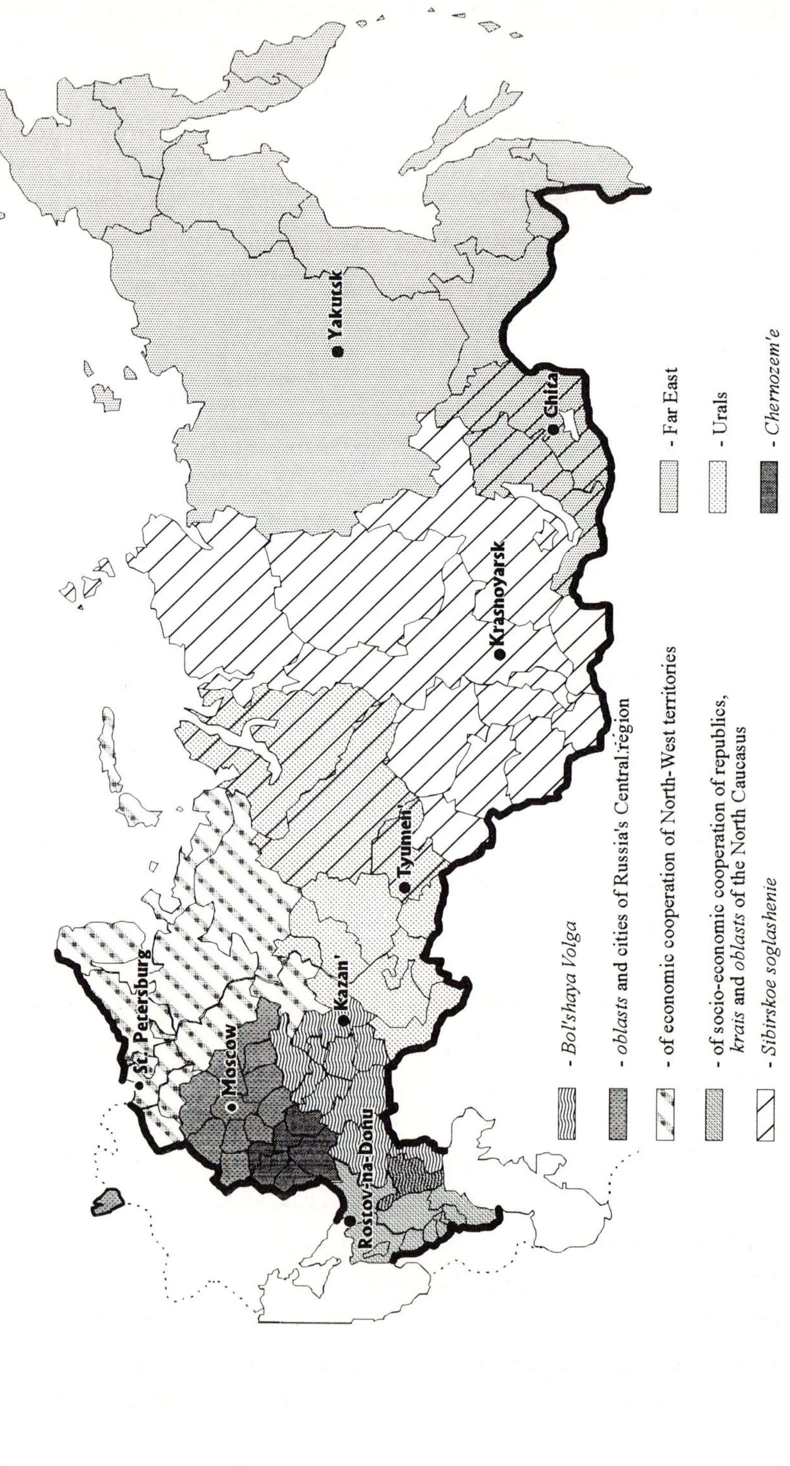

territorial jurisdiction. Nearly all of Russia's republics are now undergoing these stages.

2 Regional Associations: Economic, Political Or Elite Alliances?

The major goal established in the *Regulations of Associations* is to use the advantages of co-operation and co-ordination of republics' and smaller administrative units' efforts in order to stabilise their economies, to solve the regions' problems of social-economic development of regions and to reduce social tension.

In fact, the process of regional integration is far from being so homogeneous. The formally proclaimed goals do not entirely correspond to the essence of the presently formed regional alliances. At the current stage, a regional association may be considered from at least three points of view:

- as an economic alliance of territories;
- as a political alliance of territories;
- as a regional elite alliance.

The associations were being formed mainly in order to confront the Centre and to work out methods to protect regional interests at the federal level. The need for unity in light of the collapse of the Soviet state is evident, for it is hard to obtain any advantages, privileges, or benefits, when one acting as a single entity.

Displaying initiative and taking active measures greatly helped regional elites at the initial stages of forming associations. This may be accounted for by certain specific reasons.

Firstly, regional elites (heads of republican administrations and the administrations of smaller territorial units, representative bodies) are the founders of associations. It is the founders who assume the major responsibility for taking decisions at the regional level, as well as for working out and realising regional development concepts.

Secondly, regional elites are the specific link to be empowered in defending regional interests before the central authorities. They play the basic role in the application of the principle: 'achieving maximal accord with maximal consideration of peculiarities'.

Thirdly, the best way to control the situation is with the help of a local leader. Many of Moscow's solutions to regional problems seem oversimplified, and typically a number of complications have to be overcome which were not taken into consideration in the centre.

Finally, the reflex of solidarity is very important in the regional elites' defence against Moscow's regional policy.

The authorities in the regions are in immediate contact with the directorate which plays a quite important part in taking decisions at the local, and sometimes, federal level. The most weighty figures in the regions are the heads of monopoly enterprises, whose tax-revenues support the region. Many of the local leaders themselves used to head those enterprises.

The economic factor of territorial integration is the most fundamental one, although its importance is not always realised. By observing this factor it is possible to forecast the 'behaviour' of territories in the future.

The economic basis for integration of subjects of the Russian Federation is, as a rule, the heterogeneous economic structure of a whole region. This condition is not only linked with the initial natural pre-conditions, but also with a deliberate Soviet state policy which, in its drive to achieve overall economic efficiency, did not take local regional peculiarities into account. The priority of the principle of sectoral control during the recent decades led to the formation of what can be described as 'departmental' regions (i.e., Siberia is the major area for oil and gas extraction, the fuel and energy complex; the Urals – for the metallurgical complex, etc.).

The authorities of many Russian territories assume that the Centre prevents them from entirely availing themselves of the available economic advantages. These are, most frequently, skilled labour, developed agriculture, a powerful and diversified production potential, a monopoly on scarce export resources, large monopoly enterprises and a favourable geographical and geopolitical position.

The homogeneity of economic development brings about similar development strategies of macro-regional territories, similar problems, similar ways of protecting or forming an internal market, of entering the market environment, etc.

3 Regional Associations: Initiative from the Centre or the Regions?

One may encounter the opinion[1] that the formation of regional associations was initiated from the top (from the Centre), and that the elements of self-organisation were not the key-factor. In support of this assertion, one can adduce the extremely

1 E.g. in the work of the Centre for Political and Geografic Research, 1992. Compare also with Mikhail Rozhanskii's paper in these volumes.

concise periods of time taken for their organisation, the absence of substantial 'gaps' and 'bridges' in the network of associations and a close correspondence of the borders of associations to the borders of the economic areas of *Gosplan*.

Opinions such as this are controversial. It seems highly doubtful that the Centre would decide to form strong regional structures embracing the powerful potential of separation and possessing real economic levers. It was much more likely a forced reaction of the Moscow authorities during the 'sovereignty parade', when Tatarstan, Bashkortostan, Sakha, Tuva and Chechnya declared their independence, and many regions started to work out their own regulations. In this sense, it can be seen as some sort of an attempt to preserve the integrated expanse by creating apparent regional autonomy.

Whatever the case, the absence of a specific strategy of the Centre regarding relations with regions led to a situation where the processes of inter-regional integration are entirely controlled by local leaders. The basic discussions with the Centre are concentrated around the amount of power Moscow should grant to the regions.

One should also note that the associations with a higher level of economic development tend to make more demands from the federal authorities.

3.1 History of Regional Associations

If one considers regional associations as a combination of administrative and economic control, it is easy to find examples in the economic history of Russia of attempts to put these ideas into practice: administrative economic areas (1922-1930), *sovnarkhozes* (state economy councils, 1957-1965). Unlike their predecessors, contemporary regional associations have more opportunities to overcome the dictates of the Centre, and to move from sectoral control to territorial control.

Presently, eight associations of areas of the Russian Federation have been formed: the *North-West*, *Black-Earth*, and *Great Volga* associations, the *Siberian Accord*, the North *Caucasian*, *Far East*, and *Urals* associations, and the *Central Regions Association*.

In less than a year (by the beginning of 1992), the associations embraced all of the Russian territories, and their formation climaxed in the summer and autumn of 1991.

Siberia and the Far East were the first to declare the foundation of their associations. In December 1990, the Kemerovo, Novosibirsk, Tomsk, Tyumen' *oblasts* and Altai and Krasnoyarsk *krais* joined the *Siberian Accord*. At the beginning of 1991, the republics of Altai, Tuva and Buryatia, Irkutsk *oblast'* with the Ust'-Orda Buryat autonomous *okrug*, and Omsk *oblast'* joined them. The current *Siberian Accord*, embracing 19 administrative territorial units, was formalised in July 1992 by an agreement of the founders.

The formation stages of the *Siberian Accord* themselves show that the nucleus of the association is made up of Southern Siberian regions. Three of the above-mentioned members – the Tyumen' and Chita *oblasts*, the republic of Buryatia – declared their membership of two associations. Their 'dual membership' is easy to account for: Tyumen' *oblast'* wanted to get strong support from prospective partners; the trans-Baikal territories were attracted by an orientation towards the Asian Pacific countries instead of towards the economically weakening Russia.

The *Urals Regional Association* was preceded by the 'Association for the Economic Interaction of the Urals territories', formed on the basis of an agreement of the Soviet of People's Deputies of the Urals on 25-26 January 1991, when the Kurgan, Orenburg, Perm, Sverdlovsk, Chelyabinsk and Tyumen' *oblasts* joined the association. In the autumn of 1991, the republic of Udmurtia became a member of this association.

The *Central Regions Association* has experienced the most substantial compositional changes since it was founded. Before 1993 it was made up not only of *oblasts* but also of *oblast'* capitals. Initially, (in the spring of 1991, according to the Russian Federation Supreme Council's data), its members were the Vladimir, Ivanovo, Kaluga, Ryazan', Tula, Tver and Yaroslavl' *oblasts'*. In the summer of 1991 the number of its member territories was extended by the joining of Moscow, Kostroma, Bryansk *oblasts* and their capitals as well as the city of Obninsk (the Central Cities and Regions Association).

At a meeting of the council of associations in 1994, a question was raised about transferring the status of the administrations of *oblast'* capitals from founders to associate members, for, according to a presidential decree, only subjects of the Russian Federation can be given the rights of founders of an association.

1991 saw the formation of the *'North-West' Association*, which grew out of a co-ordinating committee for social economic development of the North-western regions, as well as the foundation of the *'Great Volga' Association* (June 1991) and the *'Black-Earth' Association (*October 1991). The only enclave region on Russia's territory, the Kaliningrad *oblast'*, joined both the *North-West Association* and *Central Regions Association.*

The last to make a regional alliance were the North Caucasian territories. In March 1992 the supreme executive and representative bodies of the republics of Adygeya, Dagestan, Kabardino-Balkaria, Karachayev-Cherkessia, North Ossetia, as well as Rostov *oblast'* and Krasnodar and Stavropol' *krais* became the founders of the *Association for Economic Co-operation of the North Caucasian Republics*.

In September 1993, the republic of Ingushetia was accepted as an independent member of the association. The interest for co-operation in the North Caucasian area is also increasing in the nearby areas. On 20 May 1994, representatives of the Volgograd *oblast'* participated in a session of the members of associations. As associate members, not only Abkhazia and South Ossetia, but also the Crimea, and as a permanent member – Volga Kalmykia joined in the North Caucasian association. The integration of regions of the 'near abroad' as associate members, according to the session report, purely signifies their will to integrate with the North Caucasian economy, and has no political basis.

The examples of regional integration simultaneously into several regional structures is, at present, the exception rather than the rule. The similar experience of Kaliningrad, Kalmykia, Tyumen', Chita and Buryatia deserves every possible means of support, for it facilitates the strengthening of inter-regional integration and the mutual interests of the regions.

3.2 Association And Economic Area: A New Structure Or Just Change Of Title?

The composition of the eight newly formed regions is highly reminiscent of the system of economic areas of the USSR. Regions in the former northern and north-western economic areas are covered by the *North-West association*, the ones of the former central area, except for the Orel *oblast'*, – by the *Central Regions Association*. The Orel *oblast'* and all the black-earth regions were covered by the *Black-Earth Association*; the Volga areas – by the *Great Volga Association*, the regions of Western and Eastern Siberia – by the *Siberian Accord*. The North Caucasus, Urals and Far East have completely inherited the composition of the respective economic areas.

However, the similarity in form conceals differences in content. An economic area is a product of a planned economy. Centralisation used to eliminate every opportunity for territorial integration. The development of the economic areas and the territories included in them was strictly subordinated to state interests – industrialisation of the national economy, increasing the defence potential; it was never intended to create appropriate living conditions, or take into account general territorial interests, ethnic peculiarities, etc.

In practice, the areas were neither subjects of economic activities, nor objects of any state control. The territorial aspect of the economic plans had a draft nature, with no specific direction. An economic area was not responsible for the realisation of forecast and plan- statements, for total planning would have required building an intermediate control link at the macro-regional level. In fact, economic areas always remained units for accounting, not for control.

Forming regional associations was and still is subject to absolutely different conditions. For the first time, regional authorities are faced with a variety of ownership forms and social, property-based and political division of society as well as with the growth of national self-consciousness and the problem of national separatism. This means that the leaders of associations are faced with the task of solving a series of real problems.

The second, more important condition is the current instability in the political, financial and economic spheres; significant changes among the high officials; continual corrections of the economic course and an absence of a specific strategy for implementing these corrections. The demand for security and stability implies a change of logic – instead of reforms from the top – self-development from the bottom.

Presently, the regional authorities first of all feel the link between the long-term political interests of the regions and their own economic interests, since politics is understood by them as a condition for economic stability on their territory. The higher the integration potential of a region, the more powerfully it exerts pressure on the Centre with regard to decision-making, the more weighty a political figure represents it. Strong regions seek to expand their rights in the sphere of law-making (the case of the Ural republic).

***Table 1** Conditions and factors of the formation of economic areas and regional associations and of economic interaction of* oblasts

Conditions and factors	Economic Regions	Regional Association
• Natural-historical • Resources (in the broad sense- nature, people, material valuables) • Economic specialisation and division of labour	consideration for the current natural-historical conditions and relevant peculiarities of the resources in the economic development of regions	
• Creation of a single economic space	single economic complex	single market space as a synthesis of regional internal markets
• The investment factor	absence of the free movement of capital and investments	creation of conditions for the region's maximal attractiveness to investment
• The financial market	absent	creation of new inter-regional financial structures as basis for a regional market infrastructure
• The foreign economic factor	territorially inequitable redistribution of income for foreign trade in favour of regions that are 'hard-currency-importers	'export potential' as the basis for future development and as a powerful basis for integration
• Social policy	residual funding of the social sphere	social well-being as the main and exclusive goal of the region's
• The political factor	absent	recognition of the region as a significant political actor
• The national factor	lifting up the territories to the level of developed regions	consideration of ethnic heterogeneity of the region
• The geopolitical factor	absent	orientation toward co-operation with other countries as a counterweight to an economically weakening centre

4 Activity Principles, Legal Status and the Organisational Structure of Regional Associations

The basic principles of formation and activity of the associations are the following:

- voluntary membership, mutually beneficial and responsible obligations of the members;
- freedom to be a member of any other inter-regional alliances;
- financial independence of the members, with partial transfer of the functions of forming funds of financial, currency and material resources.

- co-ordination of joint efforts and money to provide social guarantees for the residents of the territory of an association.

Before 1993, the regional associations of Russia existed as social organisations without legal status created to elaborate and realise programmes for the complex social economic development of regions. Heads of councils of people's deputies, as well as heads of regional administrations and administrations of big cities were their founders. The associations' joint activity was regulated by a founding agreement.

The associations were registered at the Ministry of Justice at the beginning of 1993. As independent juridical entities, they have statutes stipulating the functions of an association, their rights and duties, the types of membership (including the members' rights and duties), and the basic principles of the management and financing of their functioning.

The associations are given the following rights:

- to dispose of any income exceeding the fixed level of payments to be transferred to the federal budget by a single-channel system in accordance with the relevant legal provisions;
- during the functioning of the extra-budgetary federal economic stabilisation fund, all sums circulating on the territory of an association stand at the said association's disposal;
- to regulate on the territory of an association the order and size of transactions with natural resources, until the adoption of the relevant federal Russian legislation, as well as to regulate the size of fines and compensation for damage caused to the environment; to assign these sums primarily for environmental needs and development of the social sphere;
- to permit the members of an association to dispose of a stipulated part of the commodities manufactured by enterprises within the relevant territory and to trade these commodities both throughout the country and abroad;
- to set up, on the basis of equitable economic agreements with other areas and republics, direct ties concerning the supply of foodstuffs and agricultural goods;
- to regulate the independent level of the consumption funds of enterprises and organisations situated on the territory of an association, taking into account the balance between goods and the monetary mass on the territory;
- to allow barter relations, to license the export and import of goods (jobs and facilities) within and beyond the territories of an association by means of establishing quotas;

- to register enterprises and organisations as participants in external economic activity; to authorise the establishment of enterprises abroad, involving enterprises and organisations on the territory of an association;
- to allow enterprises on the territory of an association to dispose of a certain share of hard currency revenues, to sell the remainder to the currency funds of the Council of Ministers of the RF and the association.

Despite slight differences in their arrangement, all associations are based on a two-tiered principle. The supreme, representative body of an association is the association council (board of founders), consisting of the heads of the supreme executive and representative bodies of authority of the member *oblasts*, republics and *krais*. The board is authorised to resolve aspects of membership, as well as the most important problems of the region and the elaboration of strategies of regional development.

All day-to-day work is carried out by the executive body of an association – that of the general director (the general secretariat). This body ensures business contacts between the regions, relays operational information, puts the regulations adopted by the association council into practice. To promote a more reasonable and efficient functioning within the framework of an association, there also exist co-ordinate Boards (committees, commission, agencies, etc.), mobile structures to deal with a small range of problems or one problem at a high-skilled level. Such a body, as a rule, includes a representative of the Board of the Association, qualified experts, a working group.

In the *Siberian Accord*, there are co-ordinating boards dealing with external economic activity, the problems of resource extraction, transport, anti-crime measures, legislation, as well as environmental boards addressing the problems of the Baikal area and Eastern and Western Siberia.

The *Central Regions Association* includes agencies on transport, communication, technology and conversion, location of production potential, land utilisation, town construction and architecture, social and energy agencies, a commission on regional development problems, agreements on fiscal and financial matters.

The *Great Volga Association* includes 12 working groups (commissions) responsible for the major fields of economic activity, each of which is controlled by the head of the administration or government of an *oblast'* or republic.

5 Portraits of Regional Associations

Whoever wants to present a rough description of the regional differences of Russia, typically uses very stable geographic names: the Urals, the North Caucasus, the Volga territories, etc. Enumerating these, one would also be enumerating the names of the respective associations. Each of them, consequently, is very distinctive, having its own structure which links up all the territories of an association, rendering it unique and complete.

5.1 The Central Regions Association (CRA)

Established 1991

Composition: Bryansk, Vladimir, Ivanovo, Kaliningrad, Kaluga, Kostroma, Moscow, Ryazan', Smolensk, Tver', Tula and Yaroslavl' *oblasts* and the city of Moscow.

Headquarters: city of Moscow.

Administration: chairman – Anatolii Dolgolaptev (deputy chairman of the Federation Council). General director – Aleksandr Danusia.

Major advantages: highly qualified labour resources, has a monopoly in a number of branches of science and industry, capacious internal market.

Integration base: preservation of a unique innovative and social potential (the quality of labour resources), maintenance of the elite function of the central area.

The association may be regarded as one of the most powerful regional alliances. Covering less than 3% of the whole territory of the country, it accumulates one fifth of its population and one quarter of its industry.

The CRA's basic peculiarity, namely being concentrated around the capital, reveals itself not only in the close connection between the central regions and Moscow, but also in the distinctive leadership within the co-ordination board of the associations (headed by CRA chairman Dolgolaptev).

For the country as a whole, the CRA is not only vital as a giant of industry (primarily, in machine-building), and the biggest transport-distribution centre, but also as the major decision-making centre, innovator and distributor. A huge scientific potential, powerful staff training system and powerful military industrial complex chains are concentrated in this area. Central Russia has a well-developed internal market and high infrastructural concentration. One should emphasise the development of the market infrastructure, made up of a complicated network of banking, stock-exchanges and other financial structures.

The use of such a huge industrial potential requires a high proportion of highly skilled personnel among the population, although in fact the demographic situation in the area has become critical. The insignificant immigration cannot compensate for the low rates of natural growth and the rapid ageing of the population (the proportion of retired people is 23% with low birth rates).

The programme for bringing the territory out of economic crisis stipulates:

- forming centres of economic growth based on a stimulation of the development of small cities as priority areas of residence for settlers and as top class service centres for agricultural communities;
- reconstructing the agro-industrial complex, moving from immediate supply of agricultural produce to cities to a policy of local processing;
- as a possible variant of re-orienting the MIC, there is a suggestion to create financial industrial corporations, on condition of an increase of the amount of civil technologies financed through the sale of military assets ;
- to provide for the maximal profitability of the scientific complex, above all, by means of trading elaborations. By certain estimations, this measure could increase the scientific potential of the territory by almost two times.

5.2 The Black-Earth Association

Composition: the Belgorod, Voronezh, Kursk, Lipetsk, Orel and Tambov *oblasts*.

Headquarters: city of Voronezh

Administration: president – Alexandr Kovalev (head of the Voronezh region administration); general director – Grigorii Fedotov.

In its current form the association was formed in October 1991.

Major advantages: highly developed food and metallurgical base, has unique resources of iron ore.

Economic integration base: the development and modernisation of the agro-industrial complex.

This area is traditionally agricultural, lying between the industrial centre and the Donetsk coal field, and is one of the major food bases of the country.

The agro-industrial complex and full-cycle metallurgical industry based on the extraction of the unique ores of the Kursk Magnet Anomaly (more than a half of the whole Russian stockpile) form the basic economic nucleus of the area. The central black-earth regions produce over half of all granulated sugar in Russia, 20% of sunflower seed oil, 10% of meat and 12% of cheese. These regions produce over 40% of Russia's iron ore, cast iron production – 17%, rolled metal and fireproof material production – 13%. The area manufactures one-fifth of tractors, 17% of blacksmith equipment, 12% of computers, 19% of tyres and cement.

The area is notorious with respect to its intense demographic situation: negative natural increment, the highest amount of pensioners in Russia, resulting from the Soviet government's policy of encouraging young able-bodied people to move to the cities, to areas of development and industrial growth.

Nowadays, the population increment is mainly provided by immigration, with refugees from the Caucasian and Central Asian conflict areas showing a preference for the black-earth region. This territory is fairly homogeneous in terms of its internal structure, although the city of Voronezh clearly stands out as the regional leader. It is the only city in the area having a population of almost one million of people.

The basic trend of the activity of the association is the realisation of the 'Black-earth' programme worked out in 1991-1992, each of the parts of which is supervised by a particular region.

5.3 The Great Volga Association

Formed in June 1991

Composition: the republics of Kalmykia, Mary El, Mordovia, Tatarstan, Chuvashia and the Astrakhan', Volgograd, Nizhnii Novgorod, Penza, Samara, Saratov, Ul'yanovsk *oblasts*.

Headquarters: city of Samara.

Administration: president and co-chairman – Aleksandr Morozov.

Major advantages: located between the Urals and European Russia, powerful diversified industrial potential, big monopoly enterprises.

Economic integration base: solving the Volga basin's problems, maintaining a single infrastructural and energy complex.

The association covers *oblasts* whose economies are directly linked with the biggest European river. The Volga, with big cities and main transport routes concentrated around it, forms an infrastructural corridor, the axis of economic activity.

It is in the territories of the Middle and Lower Volga that the borders of the Muscovite state began to expand in the mid 16th century. At every stage of its history the economic situation of the area was favourable. Before the beginning of the 19th century, the Volga shipping route served as the main connection between the northern and southern territories of the country. Since the middle of the 19th century, cultivation of the right-bank areas and the development of agriculture turned the Volga territories into the leaders of bread production. In the 20th century, the elaboration of oil and gas deposits and the utilisation of the hydro-energy potential of the Volga became the base for developing a wide range of chemical and machine-building industries.

Covering 4% of Russia's territory, the Great Volga Association concentrates one-seventh of the whole industry and population and a quarter of grain production. The association has a monopoly in the aviation and car construction industries.

The association is famous for its multi-ethnic population structure. It embraces five republics of the Russian Federation. Even in Astrakhan' and Penza *oblasts*, the non-Russian population makes up 25%.

Considering the Great Volga Association, one can see the unnatural structure of the existing inter-regional economic ties. The structure of the regional and republican economies did not lead to a mutual supplementation within its framework but rather duplication.

The most homogeneous in terms of industry are the Nizhnii Novgorod, Samara, Ul'yanovsk and Saratov *oblasts* and Tatarstan, having developed the oil processing, oil chemistry and aviation and car industries, as well as machine-building for the defence sector. Strangely enough, however, this heavily agricultural area produces no agricultural machinery.

The economic interests of the association's republics and *oblasts* of require closer co-operation with timber industry regions, such as the Kirov and Kostroma *oblasts* and the establishment of close contacts with the Western Kazakhstan regions, especially in the exploitation of the Tengiz oil deposit which represents an alternative to the supplies from Tyumen' *oblast'*.

We are accustomed to mentioning the joint efforts of the Volga *oblasts* with regard to environmental problems. Despite the Great Volga members' economic heterogeneity, they have a common interest in maintaining and modernising the transport network of the area and in a single energy system.

The Volga territory is distinctive in that is has no distinctive leader city or region. The association numbers five cities with a population of one million plus (including the agglomeration of Saratov) and eleven cities with the population of over 500,000 people.

5.4 The Association for Economic Interaction of the North-West Territories

Formed in 1991

Composition: the republics of Karelia, Komi, the Nenets autonomous *okrug*, Volgograd, Kaliningrad, Kirov, Leningrad, Arkhangel'sk, Murmansk, Novgorod and Pskov *oblasts*, and the city of St. Petersburg.

Headquarters: St. Petersburg.

Administration: president – Aleksei Titov; general director – Lev Kolkolainen.

Major advantages: favourable position at the border with the North-western European countries, overlooking the Baltic and White Seas, immense export resources, the second largest city of the country is included into the association. The *North-West Association* seems to resemble a 'mini-USSR': excessive development of the centre, immense resource potential and developed industries are the major base for inter-regional integration.

After the collapse of the USSR, the European North-West became the representative of Russia's interests in Western Europe and the Baltic Basin. The Kaliningrad *oblast'* and the city of St.Petersburg were declared free enterprise zones. The expanding St.Petersburg harbour must now become an alternative to the Black Sea harbours that now belong to Ukraine.

The *oblasts* of the North and North-western economic territories are covered by the association. The members of the association vary in their geographical position, demographic, resource and economic potential. Thus, the association includes St.Petersburg, one of the biggest scientific, industrial and business centres, and at the same time also the Kirov *oblast'*, lying far off the beaten track and having low economic activity, stagnation in its timber industry and a low living standard among its population. The association has a diverse composition ranging from the highly populated Baltic *oblasts* (St.Petersburg, Kaliningrad) to the sparsely populated regions of the North (in the north of the Komi republic population density is less than one person per square km); from territories with a highly developed processing industry to those that have only primary raw materials processing. The whole area features a contrasting agriculture (flax growing areas in the south and timbering in the north) and has rich natural resources (forests, ores, coal), but it also suffers from a labour shortage, having an extremely scarce rural population (especially the Pskov, Novgorod and Kirov *oblasts*.)

During the two last decades, all the members were connected through a state programme for the complex development of the non-black-earth territories. The

Relative importance of Russia's regional associations

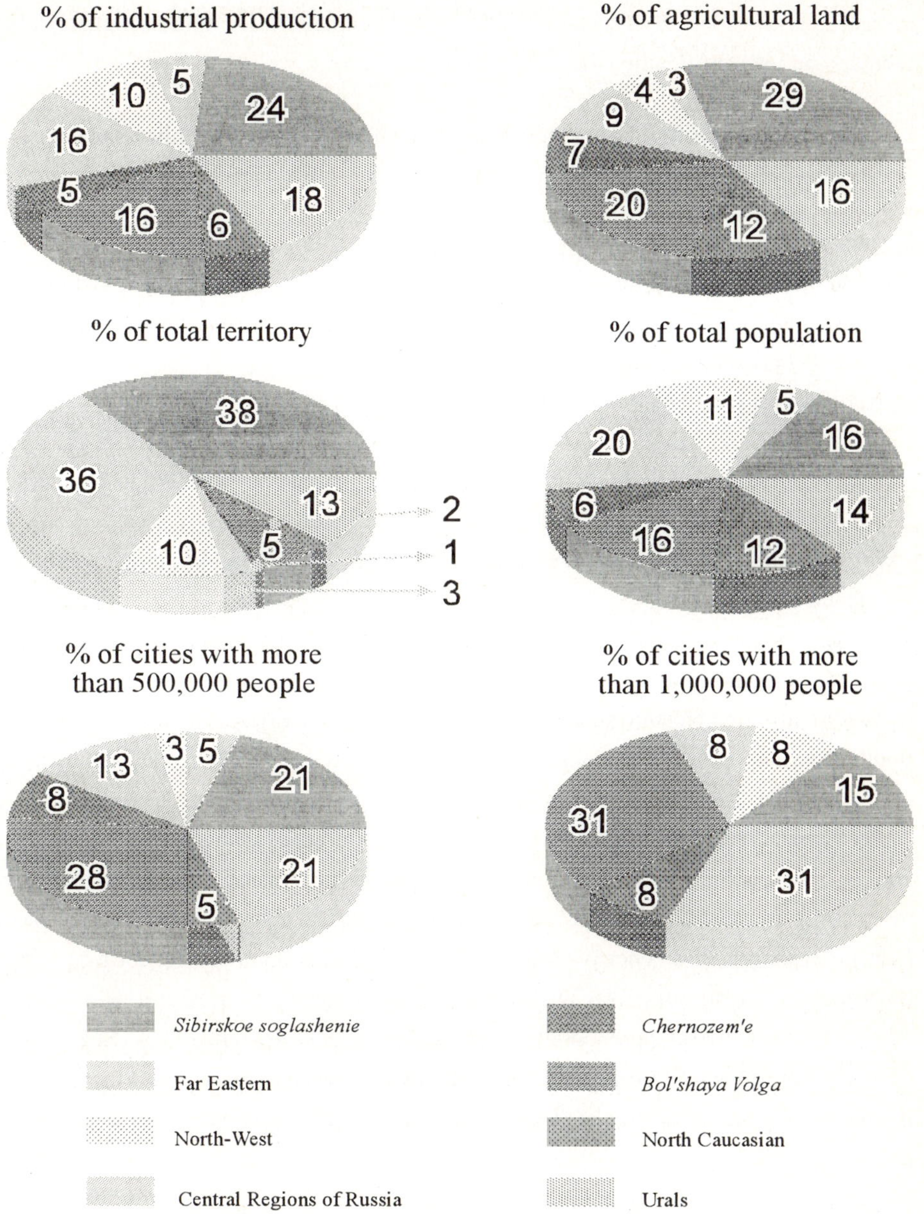

Numbers may add up to more than 100% because some regions belong to more than 1 association programme aimed at the complex resolution of the area's social and economic problems, above all the development of its agriculture and industry , as well as its social infrastructure.

Presently, priority funding is given to programmes for developing the infrastructural (especially transport) and energy complexes. The tourist industry also seems to be very promising (the 'Blue Ring' project).

5.5 The Association for Socio-Economic Co-operation of the Republics and Regions of the North Caucasus

Formed in 1991

Composition: the republics of Adygeya, Dagestan, Ingushetia, Kabardino-Balkaria, Kalmykia, Karachayev-Cherkessia, North Ossetia, Krasnodar and Stavropol' *krais* and Rostov *oblast'*.

Headquarters: city of Rostov-on-Don.

Administration: general director – Nikolai Pivovarov.

Major advantages: main food base in Russia, mediator in Russian-Caucasian relations.

Integration base: solving problems of the agro-industrial complex, reducing social and national tension.

Nowadays, the association is showing minimal initiative. In order to promote closer ties the territories of the association have to overcome national conflicts.

Historically, the North Caucasus is represented by two big sub-areas: the 'lowland South Russian' area, comprising the Stavropol' and Krasnodar *krais* and Rostov *oblast'* and the 'highland' area comprising the national autonomies.

For Russia, the North Caucasus is the biggest food base (grain, beets, sunflowers) and also has a high concentration of agricultural processing industries and is a monopolist in several types of agricultural production (the Rostov *Rostsel'mash* plant), transport and energy machine-building, manufacture of tungsten and molybdenum (North Ossetia). The area is unique because of its natural peculiarities (the Kuban lowland), recreational potential (the Black Sea and Azov Sea coast), transport significance (the biggest oil port in Novorossiisk), and it also serves as a mediator in relations with the Transcaucasian states. The North Caucasus covers about 2% of Russia's territory, produces a quarter of its grain harvest and 7% of industrial products. Its population represents 11.6% of the entire population of Russia.

The North Caucasus has a strong reputation as a centre of international tension. This can be explained by the problems in North Ossetia, Chechnya, Ingushetia, as well as the southern Russian *oblasts* (the issue of the Cossacks and the separatist moods in the Don Army *oblast'*). The territory of the association is both a 'supplier' and a 'receiver 'of numerous refugees.

At a meeting of association members held in the spring of 1994, priority was given to the problems of developing the North Caucasian transport system, co-ordinating the fight against organised crime and terrorism, regulating migration on the territory of the association and developing national culture.

5.6 The Inter-regional Association Siberian Accord

Formed in 1991 (in its current composition)

Composition: the republics of Altai, Buryatia, Tuva, Khakasia, Altai and Krasnoyarsk *krais*, the Ust'-Orda Buryat autonomous *okrug*, the Irkutsk, Chita, Kemerovo, Novosibirsk, Omsk, Tomsk and Tyumen' *oblasts*, the Khanty-Mansiisk and Yamal-Nenets, Taimyr(Dolgan-Nenets), Evenk and Aginsk Buryat autonomous *okrugs*.

Headquarters: city of Novosibirsk.

Administration: board chairman – Vitalii Mukha

Major advantages: immense resources that are appropriate for export.

Economic integration base: single foreign economic policy, re-orientation towards increasing the proportion of processing industries, development of the social infrastructure.

The '*Siberian Accord*' is the biggest association in terms of the size of its territory. It covers over one-third (38.5%) of Russia's territory, dividing it into three almost equal parts: European, Siberian and Far Eastern.

The enormous size of the territory, its severe climate, the sharp contrast between its North and South and its unique resources (in terms of both quantity and quality) are the main peculiarities of the area.

Siberia's proportion in Russian oil extraction reached 75%, gas extraction – 90%, coal extraction – 65%, electric power production – 25%, timbering – 25%, aluminium, copper and nickel production – more than 50% (the data refer to the early 1990s)

The priority given to raw material industries brought about immense structural imbalances in the economy, as the principle of 'super profitability' – the prevalence of dinosaur extracting and processing enterprises -, and the formation of the country's 'defence shield' necessitated the creation of huge defence plants (Krasnoyarsk *krai*).

The transfer of industry to the East was followed by the migration of labour. Besides enthusiasm, it was also caused by material incentives (salary adjustments for the conditions of working in the North), which have nowadays become meaningless. The fact that the development of Siberia was aimed at industrial growth, and not at social well-being, brought about mass migrant circulation. This form of temporary residence prompted the population to use a special kind of cash-money circulation. Today, the problem of retaining labour resources is acute. On the other hand, former camp-prisoners who mostly stayed in Siberia as permanent residents greatly contributed to local labour resources. They are considered to be the cause of a substantial crime increase on the territory (twice as much as in 1990).

5.7 The Far Eastern Association

Formed in 1991.

Composition: the republics of Buryatia, Sakha (Yakutia), the Primorskii and Khabarovsk *krais*, the Jewish autonomous *oblast'*, the Amur and Kamchatka *oblasts*, the Koryak autonomous *okrug*, the Magadan, Sakhalin, Chita *oblasts*, the Aginsk Buryat autonomous *okrug*, the Chukotka autonomous *okrug*.

Headquarters: city of Khabarovsk

Administration: general director – Anatolii Aksenov; executive director – Alexandr Panchenko.

Major advantages: favourable geopolitical position (neighbouring the Pacific-Asian countries), unique and little-exploited natural resources.

Economic integration base: enforcing the export potential of the territories and solving the problem of export quotas, preventing a mass emigration of the population, creating favourable investment conditions.

The major peculiarity of the Far East is its outlying position in the East of Russia. The great distance from the centre, broken links with the other areas of the country under conditions of a decentralised authority and economies coerce the Far Eastern regions to make contact with the Pacific-Asian countries. The first step towards achieving this was the creation of free economic zones in Nakhodka and the Jewish autonomous *oblast'*. Relations with China are being developed. Thus, in Amur *oblast'*, over half of the foreign trade operations are frontier trade operations.

Foreign investors are primarily attracted by the opportunity to utilise the region's unique natural resources and cheap labour.

The Far East shares many common features with the Siberian regions. Thus, it is considered to be a raw material area rich in ore, coal, timber and hydro-resources.

The Far East is a classical example of an outlying pioneer-developed area. In its economic structure, the proportion of branches of the extracting industry and primary processing of raw materials is even more immense than in Siberia. The region is clearly dependent on supplies of foodstuffs, machinery, equipment and mass consumption commodities.

It should also be noted that the Far East is important as a powerful navy base.

The territory of the Far East, as well as that of Siberia, started developing from the South, following first the newly constructed Siberian highway and then the Trans-Siberian and the Baikal-Amur railways. Consequently, the rather well-developed territories around the Amur and Pacific Coast contrast with the deserted areas of the North. The main cities of the Far East are Khabarovsk and Vladivostok.

5.8 The Urals Regional Association

Founded in 1991

Composition: the republics of Bashkortostan, Udmurtia, the Kurgan, Orenburg and Perm' *oblasts*, Komi-Perm' autonomous *okrug*, the Ekaterinburg, Tyumen' *oblasts*, the Khanty-Mansiisk autonomous *okrug*, the Yamal-Nenets autonomous *okrug*, the Chelyabinsk *oblast'*.

Headquarters: city of Ekaterinburg.

Administration: president – Eduard Rossel (head of Administration of the Ekaterinburg *oblast'*); chairman of the committee for regional economic development programs – Sergei Vozdvizhenskii.

Major advantages: key transport position at the junction of the western and eastern parts of the country, substantial industrial base with industries highly concentrated at separate enterprises, modern defence technology.

Economic integration base: overcoming the stagnation in industries, renewing the whole industry, dealing with environmental problems.

The Urals area has one of the most favourable positions among the macro-areas of the country, being a link between the European and Asian parts of Russia. From West to East, it is crossed by four main railway routes, and a great number of oil pipelines (from the Surgut, Samotlor and Volga areas) and gas pipelines (from Urengoi and Orenburg).

The picture of the association greatly depends on whether one includes or excludes Tyumen' *oblast'*. When one includes the Tyumen' *oblast'*, the association's territory covers 13% of Russia instead of 5%, the amount of national income it produces is 19% instead of 14%, and the volume of industries is 25% instead of 18%, whereas the population would increase only by 2%.

Having a prolonged development as the biggest metallurgical base in the country, the Urals area preserves the priority of this industry in its economy. Over 40% of cast iron, steel, rolled metal and 52% of metal pipes are manufactured there. The area is the leader in heavy machine-building (manufacturing a quarter of machine tools and over 60% of railway cars). Orenburg *oblast'*, Bashkortostan and Udmurtia specialise in oil extraction and processing. One of the area's characteristic features is the high concentration of industries at giant enterprises (the *Uralmash* machine-building plant, the Chelyabinsk metallurgical plant), having strong monopolies.

Taking into consideration strategic interests, a great number of military industrial complex enterprises were located in the Urals. The problem of conversion and the concomitant social consequences had a great impact on Udmurtia

In terms of its potential, the Urals (without Tyumen') are comparable to the Volga territories: the region covers 4.8% of Russia's territory; has 14% of the whole population; 15% of industry. Three-quarters of the population of the area live in cities (conforming to the degree of 'industrialisation' of the *oblast'*, the share of city population swings from 87% in the Sverdlovsk *oblast'*, to 29% in the Komi Perm' autonomous *okrug*).

Ekaterinburg is the traditional centre of the area. However, there are a number of other sizeable regional centres – Perm, Ufa, Chelyabinsk, numbering over one million citizens.

6 Major Results of the Activity of Regional Associations

The associations' three year existence is clearly insufficient to draw any substantial conclusions about their work. Each association, with varying degrees of enthusiasm and activity, has chosen its own course of development.

The areas of Russia beyond the Urals – Siberia and the Far East – look the most independent. The Far Eastern Association seems to be in danger of becoming defunct, with inter-regional integration frequently being replaced by direct contacts with Asian and Pacific countries (especially China and Japan).

The '*Siberian Accord*' is the most remarkable regional alliance. The so-called 'Siberian span' embraces everything from large-scale decisions (e.g. the programme for the 'rescue of Siberia') to the presentation of a lavishly packed image (constant presence of VIPs from Moscow at board sessions, frequent reports in the central press). The association is the most bureaucratised of all the associations. Its administrative style in fact tends to lead to the replacement of attempts to find internal growth reserves with ever increasing demands for additional state funding.

Presently, the interests of the centre and of the *Siberian Accord* are contradictory with regard to price regulation, especially for fuel and electric power. Siberia is ready to suggest its own concept for such regulation, which meets with resistance from the state.

The Urals regional association has not played a very visible role. Its commonly recognised leader, the Ekaterinburg *oblast'*, was more preoccupied with its own struggle to secure additional powers and to legalise the constitution of the Urals Republic. Perhaps the October 1994 session of the heads of the Ural *oblasts* and republics in Orenburg can be viewed as the start of genuine co-operation.

The most successful examples of regional integration seem to be the associations of the Central and Black-Earth regions. A session in January 1994, where 17 heads of *oblasts* of the territory met to discuss the programme for the 'revival of Central Russia', stressed the need to develop agriculture as well to resolve the problems of the indigenous rural population, which represents a majority in the area.

The 'Black-earth' programme is being developed step by step. This is an example of a highly flexible regional programme, where each part can expand through the integration of new sub-programmes meeting the current needs of the association. The most successful is the development of sub-programmes for manufacturing sugar, metal, chemicals and other products. Sub-programmes entitled *Spiritual Revival*, *Environment*, *Health Care*, *Resources* and *Energy* are currently being elaborated.

Unlike the previously widespread regional programmes of the 1970s and early 1980s, the programmes of the associations have one clear advantage: there are specific structures which are responsible for all decisions taken.

The political activity of the associations is probably the most successful aspect of their activities. Although only a year has passed since they were formally recognised, they have secured the following considerable advantages:

- an independent legal status;
- the signing and ratification of a 'Co-operation Agreement' between all the associations and Parliament (14 July 1994). In particular, the agreement contains the following elements:

- draft laws regulating the life of the regions may only be considered by the Federal Assembly after they have been reviewed by the associations.
- the associations have the right to supervise fulfilment of the Federal Treaty.
- the associations have the right to participate in elaborating the development strategies of the economy's major sectors; the creation of a two-way link is envisaged, whereby federal programmes would be integrated into inter-regional ones, and vice-versa

- The problem of separating the powers of Moscow and the regions regarding the budget, taxes and financial spheres constantly arises. There was a preliminary agreement whereby discussion of the budget draft for 1995 would proceed from initial approval by the associations. In the near future, the formation of a permanent session on budgetary and taxation policy involving representatives of the State Duma, Federation Council and regional associations is planned.

Territorial leaders are becoming more and more confident of their own abilities. Here are two examples of association leaders' views stated at different times:

- A. Kovalev in January 1993: 'The commonwealth of regions is still a rather fragile formation, and still regions barely trust each other'[2];
- A. Dolgolaptev in May 1994: 'Regional associations are the only body to co-ordinate and carry out all the decisions taken'[3].

Similar statements were heard at the July 1994 session in the Kremlin.

Nevertheless, the growing pressure from the regions towards the centre is still mainly limited to statements. Vladimir Shumeiko is sure that the associations will never manage to replace the current federal authority, and that the centre will be able to reform the regional system of Russia by using the structures of the associations.

A further strengthening of the regions' influence on decision-making processes in the centre may be facilitated by the rapid promotion of some regional leaders in the political sphere, e.g., the appointment of A. Dolgolaptev, the chairman of the Central Regions Association, as deputy chairman of the Federation Council. On the other hand, the merging of central and regional elites can only occur if the latter use the associations purely as a means of political promotion.

---

2 *Izvestiya* 14 January 1993.
3 *Segodnya* 17 May 1994.

7 Perspectives of Regional Associations: Possible Scenarios

The destiny of regional associations can be presented in the form of four possible variants deriving from different political scenarios.

1. The associations become a *mediator* between the Centre and the subjects of the federation. This variant is logically based on the current situation.

   In this variant, the situation is politically contoured as follows: weak central authority, decentralisation of state regional policy, transfer of responsibility for the reform to regions. This signifies that regional associations are assuming the role of lobbyist structures, a means to protect regional interests, self-arrangement of regions. In this event, the role of Moscow is restricted, but not denied. The major discussions with the Centre will be with regard to separating powers. This scenario does not foresee preserving key-positions within the Centre.

   The main danger for the state coming from the associations is the danger of separatism, the risk of turning into a puppet controlled by the territories. One can state that presently the Centre is maintaining its levers of control over the territories. These levers are not sufficient to conduct the Centre's policy, but suffice to be involved in the situation. At present the territories do not have completely formed influential political forces; there are contradictions among regional elites (between authorities and entrepreneurs) and the population does not seem to be united or to possess features of a common regional culture.

2. A change in the political course may lead to the *strict subordination* of regional alliances to the Centre: the priority of vertical ties over horizontal ones, reinforcement of Moscow's exclusive right to take decisions. A policy of tough centralisation does not allow for a controlling intermediate link between the federal and regional level. In this kind of situation, regional associations either fade away, or are actively destroyed through a policy to this end.
3. Within a climate of increasing social chaos, the associations may acquire *full independence*. In such a situation, regional alliances would try to apply the potential of separation. It is likely that the territories of Siberia, the Far East and the Urals would be the most independent. An extreme variant of such sovereignty is the transformation of the associations into independent states. This scenario does not seem to be probable, for even in case of a total collapse, the territories would inherit a considerable degree of dependence on each other

and would not possess enough financial resources to overcome this dependence.

4. A *mitigated variant* in which regional associations would temporarily assume the functions of a higher authority in order to rebuild a Russian state based on new principles. This variant does not seem particularly probable either, although this variant enjoys some popularity, being close to Solzhenitsyn's 'zemskoi' variant. It would require that the territories act in the political sphere as subjects of a new federation, capable of assuming responsibility for implementing state economic and national policies. The state strategy itself would have to be substantially transformed in order to combine in its regional structure both efficient local self-control and state integrity.

8 Can Regional Associations Be Objects of a Regional Policy?

The problem here is how a new state strategy concerning the regions can be worked out without relapsing in the Soviet variant of territorial planning. The declared principles of territorial justice and of making the development level of regions equal could not be put into practice. In fact, the results turned out to be the reverse: the expansion of total planning, the levelling off of regional differences at the expense of efficiency of regional development, etc.

If one is to assume that the associations are to become the basic object of a regional policy, then one would expect a move away from the manipulation of statistic or 'accounting' units, i.e., economic areas, into the direction of territories of voluntary integration, i.e., regional associations.

Unlike economic areas, the associations already have structures of control and co-ordination. Each of them already fulfils the function of supporting internal and inter-regional ties. They have the right to choose a course of regional policies by either accepting or refusing suggestions of the Centre or by putting their own initiatives into practice. The latter may include such steps as the formation of regional non-state funds whose financial resources may be used to carry out regional programmes and for rendering assistance to separate territories (cities, regions, etc.).

Opinions are frequently voiced that not macro-territories should become objects of a regional policy, and not subjects of the federation such as republics, *krais* and *oblasts* but rather certain 'average' territories[4]. Different authors select about 20-30

---

4 See e.g. Lifshitz, A., A. Novikov, and L. Smirnyagin. *Regional'naya strategiya Rossii* [Russia's Regional Strategy]. Moscow, 1993; and Podkolzin, V. and V. Kiryanchuk. *Krupnyi* different territories such as the Pacific area, the Kama river area, etc. These suggestions are based on valid factors which are not to be disputed. There is one main hindrance to the implementation of these suggestions – the territories are not legally formalised.

Regional associations are legalised formations; nowadays they are practically the only ones, except for the most active republics, *krais* and *oblasts*, which may serve as objects of regional policies without some sort of considerable organisational or financial expenditures on the part of state bodies. It is important to realise that the associations can fulfil this function temporarily, during the so-called transition period.

Choosing regional associations as an object of regional policies would have to be seen as the optimal solution by all territories at all levels, from the lowest – the *oblast'*, over the medium level – the macro-territory, to the highest level, i.e., the country as a whole.

In the first case, the interest is based on the cross-cutting of 'rich' and 'poor' regions' interests on an inter-regional market.

In the second case, the association allows a territory:

- to achieve a minimal level of self-sufficiency and/or to create sufficient export or trade potential;
- to solve similar problems of its component parts through joint efforts;
- to protect (or to create) the internal market of a territory;
- to elaborate regional programmes taking into account the particular features of a territory and to support their implementation;
- to send representatives to state bodies of authority in order to push for protectionist policies with regard to decisions of federal authorities.

The basic role of the associations at the state level:

- the opportunity to build a state regional strategy, relying on formed regional alliances with their administrative co-ordination bodies;
- the opportunity to co-ordinate the separation of powers between the Centre and regions.
- the opportunity to bring the process of regionalisation under control.

In case the current quasi-balance of the political situation in the country is maintained, i.e., a situation where the division of power in Moscow has reduced its overall ability to influence territories, one may expect further growth of the activity

---

ekonomicheskii raion kak sub"ekt Rossiskoi Federatsii [Major Economic Areas as Subjects of the Russian Federation]. Moscow, 1992.

of inter-regional associations and/or individual big territories. It is possible that they will occupy the 'vacancy' of a controlling intermediate link between the capital and the subjects of the federation. However, in this event, one should not expect that the activities of each of the eight associations will be equally efficient or successful.

11

Policy Subjects and Factors in Povolzh'e[1] (Volga Region)

Ol'ga Senatova, Aleksandr Kassimov, Vladimir Gel'man and Sergei Ryzhenkov

1 General Outlines

1.1 Definitions

Throughout this paper, the notion of 'area' will be used in the meaning of 'region as a whole', the notion of 'region' in the meaning of 'subject of the Federation'. Under policy subjects we understand both politically shaped and unshaped groups that exist *de facto*, have some joint interest and participate in local policy formation making use of influence mechanisms. Under policy factors we understand objective factors that influence the situation in the regions directly or indirectly. The policy factors are, as a rule, the least subjective aspects of the specific regional character.

1.2 Specific Features of the Volga Region

Unlike the other economic regions, the Volga region is not geographically compact. This is one of the main reasons for the relative weakness of the horizontal links, those of an economic, social and political character. One of the consequences of this is the predominantly formal character of the 'Great Volga Association' founded in 1990. In contrast to the others similar organisations ('The Great Urals', 'Siberian Accord') it is presently inactive, and the Marii-El republic even withdrew from it. The regions are looking for some other forms of interaction such as the signing of bilateral agreements, Tatarstan in May 1994 joined the association of the oil extracting regions, etc. One should mention here that the very concept of economic areas under the contemporary Russian conditions is a quite abstract one[2]. Weak

---

1 This article was written in Saratov and Moscow in June 1994. The authors used materials from the programme *Political monitoring* of the Institute of Humanitarian and Political Studies.

2 In Soviet geography Povolzh'e formed a so-called 'economic region', including Ul'yanovsk *oblast'*, Kuyibyshev *oblast'*, Penza *oblast'*, Samara *oblast'*, Saratov *oblast'*, horizontal links are their main distinctive feature; the only *bona fide* areas seem to be just the North-West and the Urals (and even in these cases, with reservations). The Volga region itself is the best example of the break-up of the economic social and political space of the country.

Another fundamental peculiarity of the Volga region is the determinant *role of the individual.* If we look into the reasons for the present economic and political situation in the Volga region, we can state that the personal qualities of the former and present leadership (naturally, along with objective economic reasons) are the major ones. One can say that the political situation in the Volga region is defined, in the first place, by the region's leadership. Economically, the situation is highly complicated, but even in this area the personal features of the regional leaders are of great importance (with the exception of economically doomed regions like Mordovia or the Marii-El republic).

A sovereignty trend can be clearly seen in most of the regions of Povolzh'e. Tatarstan and Bashkortostan are the leaders of the sovereignisation processes there, but clear deliberate aspirations toward more independence are found in many regions (Samara *oblast'*, Nizhnii Novgorod *oblast'*). The Volga region also differs through the *ideological diversity* of the political views of the regional authorities. The whole possible spectrum is represented: from 'support of reforms' to 'rejection of reforms'[3]: on the one hand Nizhnii Novgorod *oblast'* ('the stronghold of the reformers'), on the other Ulyanovsk *oblast'* and Bashkiria (in opposition to Gaidar's reform ideology); from Marii-El republic obediently fulfilling the Centre's orders, to

---

Volgograd *oblast'*, Astrakhan *oblast'* as well as the Tatar, Bashkir and Kalmyk Autonomous Soviet Socialist Republics. The Volgo-Vyatskii economic region included Yaroslavl *oblast'*, Kostroma *oblast'*, Kirov *oblast'*, Gorki *oblast'* and the Mari, Mordov and Chuvash Autonomous Soviet Socialist Republics. Generally seen, Povolzh'e consists of the regions along the Volga from Nizhnii Novgorod to Astrakhan. In this article the republics of Bashkiria and Kalmykia are also considered to be a part of that region.

All *oblast's* and republics in Russia were part of 'economic regions' according to the principle of self-sufficiency. However, due to natural or historical reasons regions' links with the Centre were much closer than economic ties to neighbouring terrirories. Neither the Volgo-Vyatskii nor the Povolzh'e 'economic region' had self-sufficiency in the true sense of the word.

A good example for the relative randomness of the 'economic regions' are Bashkiria and Kalmykia, who do not belong to any region. On the map Bashkiria first belonged to the Ural region, then to Povolzh'e region (the most powerful in economic terms). Kalmykia first belonged to Povolzh'e, then to the North Caucasus. The same was the case with Udmurtia, whose inhabitants neither identifed themselves with the Ural nor with the Povolzh'e economic region.

3 The word 'reform' is not used here in the true sense of the word, rather it is meant as an ideological concept implying the forced transformation of economic mechanisms which was imposed by a 'team of reformers' (with Yegor Gaidar as one of its most prominent members).

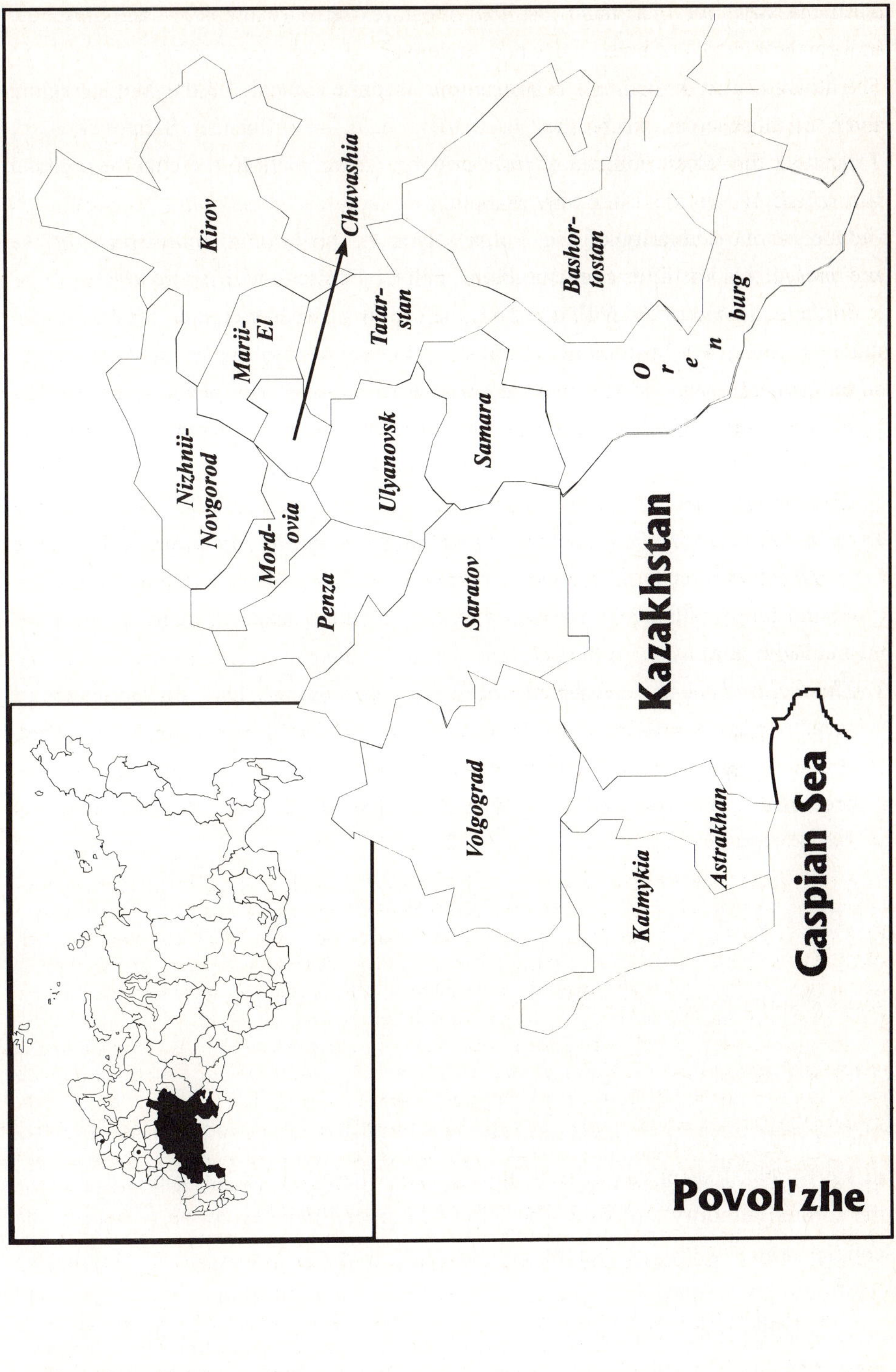
Kirov
Chuvashia
Marii-
El
Tatar-
stan
Bashor-
tostan
O r e n burg
Nizhnii-
Novgorod
Mord-
ovia
Ulyanovsk
Samara
Penza
Saratov
Kazakhstan
Volgograd
Kalmykia
Astrakhan
Caspian Sea
Povol'zhe

Bashkortostan (or Tatarstan as the most extreme example) defending the independent choice of both tactics and strategy.

The *weakness of political organisations* is quite typical for the Volga region. Even in those areas where they used to to have an influence (Saratov *oblast'*, Tatarstan), the 'clean politicians' have now been forced out to the edge of political life. Volgograd *oblast'* is the only exception.

One more peculiarity of the Volga region is the *relative significance of the national factor*, viz. inter-ethnic problems in the republics and diaspora issues.

In the *economy* of the Volga region, the following characteristics can be singled out:

- the general *predominance of industry over agricultural production*. Samara *oblast'* is the most striking example, where the overall share of agricultural production is 5%. One exception is Kalmykia and to a certain extent Astrakhan *oblast'*.
- *the predominance of the military-industrial complex (MIC) in industry*. The share of industries directly or indirectly connected with the MIC reaches 90% in Marii-El and rarely falls below the 50% mark (exceptions again are Astrakhan *oblast'* and Kalmykia).
- *The fuel and energy complex and oil and gas processing*. These industries are of great importance for Nizhnii Novgorod (oil processing), Saratov, Volgograd, Astrakhan *oblast'* and, prospectively for Kalmykia. Oil extracting and oil processing are determining elements in the economies of Tatarstan and Bashkortostan.

2 Policy Subjects

2.1 Executive Power Structures

2.1.1 Republics

The current presidential model of the republics' state formation took shape gradually in 1991-1994. Executive power is almost everywhere headed by representatives of the former authority structures (but only Mintimer Shaimiev formerly headed the corresponding CPSU committee.) Another variant are regional politicians [*vykhodtsy*] who made their career in Moscow (Kirsan Ilyumzhinov in Kalmykia and Nikolai Fodorov in Chuvashia). The exception was Vassilii Guslyannikov who was elected as the President of Mordovia. Being a marginal figure in *Democratic Russia*

[*DemRossiya*] and having neither administrative abilities nor connections within the elite, he was torn away by the republic's political community and thrown out of his presidential post, along with its abolition. As a result, Mordovia is the only republic in the region where there is no presidency.

As a rule, the number-one figure of a republic's executive branch has complete control over the situation in the regions. The extent of such an influence does, however, differ: M. Shaimiev both *de jure* and *de facto* determines the economic and political situation of the republic; K. Ilyumzhinov liquidated the political system in the absence of the significant opposition from the other policy subjects. In Bashkortostan, Murtaza Rakhimov plays an absolutely dominant role. Here we can speak about a constantly toughening authoritarian power without the disappearance of the outer attributes of the division of power. In other republics, the leaders' influence is less pronounced.

It is necessary to mention that all the heads of the executive branch of the republics have passed through elections and by the autumn of 1993 also had to reckon with their own Supreme Soviets (K. Ilyumzhinov is an exception here). As a rule, the republics' political leaders do not strive to encroach upon the power of the representative branch as it is their backing and support. Legitimisation and juridical legality are the primary factors behind this: to oppose the Centre's authority (which once in a while spreads the threat of liquidation of the republics' political system and reducing their economic rights down to the region level) is only possible with their support.

2.1.2 Regions

In 1991-92 heads of administration were appointed in the regions. Among them are both old administrators (Ivan Shabunin in Volgograd *oblast'*, Anatolii Guzhvin in Astrakhan *oblast'*, Yurii Goryachev in Ulyanov *oblast'*) and some new people from the ranks of Yeltsin's political supporters (Boris Nemtsov in Nizhnii Novgorod *oblast'*, Konstantin Titov in Samara *oblast'*). The appointment of new administrators did not bring any obvious 'disasters', with the exception of Aleksandr Kondratev (Penza *oblast'*).

The system of executive power that emerged in the *oblasts* after October 1993 is simple: the head of administration is subordinate to the president and responsible before him only. The election of the heads is not envisaged in the 'transitional period'. All new executive branch appointments in the regions were made from candidates that had been nominated by the governor.

Part of the head of the administration's authority extends down to districts and towns which causes conflicts of vertical subordination within the region. By now, this has already led to a phenomenon described by Anatolii Sliva, (chairman of the Committee on Local Self-Rule of the State *Duma* of the Russian Federation) as a 'pestilence of mayors' [*mor merov*]. The heads of administrations did not allow any limitation of their absolute rule, which lead to numerous conflicts bursting out into scandals.

The trend towards the formation of a 'mini-authoritarian' model is dominating in the regions. The leaders in this respect are Ulyanovsk, Nizhnii Novgorod and Samara *oblasts*, the governors of which are *de facto* the sole masters. At the same time, Nizhnii Novgorod and its governorship are referred to as a shining example of democracy; Konstantin Titov, the governor of Samara *oblast'*, has been elected as deputy chairman of the political board of the party *Demokraticheskii Vybor Rossii* [*Russia's Democratic Choice*].

2.2 Regional Soviets, *duma*s and Assemblies

Supreme Soviets elected in 1990 are still functioning in Tatarstan and Bashkortostan. By our estimation their qualitative structure and political and ideological orientation will barely change after the coming elections – we only expect a cutback in the number of federal representatives in Tatarstan. In April 1993 K. Ilyumzhinov transformed the Supreme Soviet of Kalmykia into his own 'personal' parliament; the State Soviet in Marii-El is turning into an ever more independent political power; during the elections in March 1994 the State Soviet in Chuvashia was not elected and we cannot expect the formation of a sound representative institution in the near future. Finally, the Supreme Soviet of Mordovia under the leadership of the former first secretary of the regional CPSU committee N. Biryukov cannot be regarded as a stabilising factor (the general political situation there has no positive prospects).

Regional *duma*s and Assemblies (organised during winter 1993-spring 1994 under the direction of the heads of administrations) personally as well as institutionally do not play an independent role with regard to their administrations. Perhaps this is the reason why the level of the voters' enthusiasm was very low. In order not to have to conduct repeated elections some regions came up with their own schemes for declaring the first round valid: Nizhnii Novgorod *oblast'* changed the ballot calculation rules *post factum*, in Astrakhan *oblast'* the winners were those candidates who received the majority in the electorates where less than 25% of voters took part in the elections, in Samara and Saratov *oblast'* polling was carried out over a period of three days and concurrently with the election campaign.

The number of executive branch officials in the regional representative organs can reach up to 50% (Penza *oblast'*). A very influential group is formed by managers of enterprises (mostly agricultural); from other social groups only medical workers are represented (Penza *oblast'*, Marii-El). As for the elected heads of regional representative organs, there we primarily find people that were 'created' by the administrations (Penza *oblast'*, Volgograd *oblast'*, Nizhnii Novgorod *oblast'*). We should point out that in Saratov *oblast'* the majority of deputies in the local *duma* were representatives of commercial structures and financial capital, both close to administration and independent (a unique case, not only in the Volga region but in Russia as a whole).

In the other regional representative organs, the 'new Russians' are not so well represented, and the same can also be said about 'democratic' politicians – in some regions they did not get into the *duma*s, while in the rest they managed to receive only two or three mandates. But more or less major fractions (e.g., Communist party, Agrarian party) are represented everywhere. We can evaluate the work of the new representative organs by looking at the situation in the Volgograd *oblast' duma* (elected in December 1993). The head of their district administration (a former KGB agent) took charge of it. Only six full-time deputies work in the *duma* and four commissions have been formed: budget control and law-making work remains a dead letter. Proposals are made by the administration, the deputies can only correct a few things. There are no people in the *duma* to deal with these problems, and deputies' interests coincide first of all with the interests of the regional administration.

2.3 Directorate of Enterprises and Pressure Groups

2.3.1 Military Industrial Complex (MIC)

Up to 1991 MIC enterprises have formed the basis of the social infrastructure and economy in regional centres and factory-towns. They received money and resources from their branch ministries. People used houses and cultural and community facilities built by enterprises, and therefore the role of the MIC directorate in the political elite was very considerable. In Tatarstan, the MIC directors and democratic-federalists united against the republican administration and their policy of 'distanciation' from Moscow. Now there is neither money nor orders for the MIC.

As a result there are no salaries, no work, 'strangers' have to pay huge sums of money for the use of kindergartens etc., and some buildings were sold to commercial structures. At the same time, salaries of managers (being under neither state nor public control) come to millions of roubles (this is essentially a topic for special investigation).[4] That is why the MIC directors failed both at the federal (*Civic Union*) and the local level. Everywhere, the MIC directorate left local politics; and we feel they will not return to it any time in the near future, but will instead concentrate their efforts on the federal level.

2.3.2 Agro-Industrial Complex (AIC)

During the 1994 elections AIC leaders retained their positions in the local representative bodies and continue to form a very powerful group both at the local and the federal level. They were successful in almost all regions and they were able to form fractions in legislative organs. The main reason for this was the importance of self-reliance with respect to food – the key factor of independence from the Centre. Pressure from the President's team also helped to consolidate the position of AIC leaders through the idea of 'recollectivisation' and 'forced farmerisation'. The struggle against such policies and then against an increase of custom taxes on imported food united the AIC leaders and initiated the formation of the *Agrarian Party of Russia* (APR). Both at the local and the regional level, the APR is a purely lobbyist structure, and not a part in the classical sense of the word. Of course, this did not prevent them from succesfully competing in the elections by party lists. The general AIC and APR perspectives in the Volga region look very promising.

2.3.3 Fuel and Energy Complex (FEC)

Up to 1991 FEC leaders were oriented toward the Union Centre since oil production was centralised. Right from the beginning of 1991 republics and regions began to take charge of the extraction of their territories' energy resources, which acquired priority in both barter and export operations. For example, Tatarstan's policy of 'entering the market gently' was based on 'oil-dollars'; in Kalmykia, Kirsan Ilyumzhinov aims to make his republic self-profitable by organising oil-production.

---

4 In May 1994 the president of Bashkortostan gave the example during a public meeting of a director of a plant in distress, where workers for several months had not received their salaries, who put his signature in his schedule of wages at the rate of 110 mln roubles.

Thus, the previously highly discernible influence of oil- and gas people has sharply increased.

2.3.4 Others

Car factories play an important role in the regional economy of Povolzh'e: in Gorkii – *GAZ*, in Tolyatti – *VAZ*, in Ulyanovsk – *UAZ*. While the economy (and with it the car industry) is going through a general crisis, car production remains a considerable source of profit. In Ulyanovsk, the car factory is controlled by the administration (personally by Yurii Goryachev) and supplies the regional 'barter fund'. The situation with *GAZ* and *VAZ* is quite different. Being the main factory in Tolyatti, *VAZ* co-ordinated not only the town's economy but also the entire *oblast'* economy. In 1991 its leaders initiated an attempt to move towards direct federal subordination ('in order not to have to sustain the *oblast'*'). Later the conflict calmed down but Tolyatti remained another *oblast'* 'capital' with a nearly independent political system. In June 1994 the second *duma* and mayoral elections took place there, and the factory's hegemony became obvious: nearly all deputies have links to *VAZ*, the head of administration of the car-factory district became mayor.

A real 'public fight' took place between the governor of Nizhnii Novgorod Boris Nemtsov and *GAZ* director B. Vidyaev. Vidyaev was accused of violations of the law during the *GAZ* privatisation. The fight ended in a draw, even though the Russian Prime-Minister Viktor Chernomyrdin also took part in it. Vidyaev was put 'under the control of the administration' (Nemtsov initiated the proposal of electing N. Pugin, former Minister of the USSR car industry, as the president of the joint-stock company *GAZ*), but in fact – and taking into account Nemtsov's role in the *oblast*'s political and economic life – he was the winner in the fight with the administration.

2.4 Business

We can subdivide businessmen who try to take part in the political life of the country into two groups: those who are close to the administration and those who are independent. The first group can use the administration in their own interests by investing in its projects, and can also be the heads of structures formed by the administration and for the administration. There is a trading firm in Nizhnii Novgorod called *Nizhegorodskaya Yarmarka* that enjoys the administration's support. Their manager ran the elections and became a deputy.

In Samara *oblast'* such businessmen as mentioned above established an *Association for the Support of Economic Reforms* (ASER) or *Titov's Party* (Titov is the regional governor). As a result of this 'connection' ASER managed to form a powerful fraction in the *duma* that was ready to fight for the interests of both administration and financial capital. Cases like that are more characteristic of *oblasts* rather of republics, where the position of commercial capital is weaker.

Businessmen who are in conflict with the administration attempt to penetrate the local authorities through political activity in order to champion their own interests and for the sake of prestige. These people are well-known, financing various publications, political organisations, often giving interviews in the press and on TV (e.g., in Kazan', S. Shashurin – an ex-criminal; R. Kadyrev, who failed during the presidential elections in Bashkortostan). The only positive example of a businessman and a political leader at the present moment is Kirsan Ilyumzhinov – President of Kalmykia. One can find respectable people among those businessmen who are ready to be political leaders, people who are dissatisfied because their status does not correspond to the power of their enterprises. For example, A. Skorynin, president of the concern *Povolzh'e-S*, began as an economist and made his way up in the *post-Komsomol* business world. He took part in both local and federal elections, in which he successively headed the local chapter of the *Party for Economic Freedom* and of *PRES*. Both attempts failed, but he is sure to find other ways to achieve his goals.

A *Ilyumzhinov syndrome*, as one of the authors has already mentioned, did not take root during the elections. Only those businessmen who had very strong administration ties won. Some famous businessmen who expanded beyond the borders of their own regions (e.g., the founders of *Khoper-Invest* and *Russkii Dom Selenga*) did not take part in the elections at all, seeing no economic necessity. Evidently, they knew more rational ways to spend their money.

2.5 Politicians from the Region in Moscow

The Volga region has never acted as a supplier of administration staff for top-level organs (the South of Russia is quite the contrary). Only a few exceptions (V. Gusev, chairman of the Council of Ministers of the USSR, former secretary of the Saratov CPSU regional committee and at the moment, president of the State *Duma*'s Committee on Industry) confirm the rule. At the same time, many politicians from the Volga region maintain contacts with their particular region of provenance and play a certain role in its life (e.g., A. Makashov, a leader of the *anti-Yeltsin* opposition and former commander of Povolzh'e military district; or I. Rybkin, the chairman of the State *Duma*). Indicative is also the 'castling' of the leadership in Chuvashia in 1993/94: V. Viktorov, former chairman of the Republican Council of Ministers, became vice-chairman of the Soviet of the Russian Federation; and V. Fedorov, former Minister of Justice of Russia – became President of Chuvashia.

Amongst the politicians of federal stature, who play an important role in the political life of the region, we want to single out one of the leaders of the CPRF Alevtin Aparin (the most popular politician in Volgograd). On the whole, however, the regional political elite is independent from Moscow and has an impact on all-federal processes primarily from a positional point of view, by using status and resource endowments (e.g., we do not have to talk about the importance of Mintimer Shaimiev and Mustaza Rakhimov as independent factors of all-Russian policy).

2.6 Federal Structures in the Region

2.6.1 Power Structures[5]

Regional departments of the power ministries – security, internal affairs, public prosecutor's office, defence – were always directly subordinate to Moscow. However their apparat was deeply integrated into the local surroundings, so we can not call them fully independent from the local authorities. Under the current circumstances, this integration is increasing significantly. Let us take, for instance, the fact that during the crisis in 1993 the heads of all republics and of some regions announced they were assuming control over of all the power structures on their territories. The leaders of these structures either supported this move, or remained silent.

According to the authors' sources of information, the intelligence services are the most integrated into the regional elite and independent from Moscow. In some republics it is possible to speak of their direct subordination to the local executive authorities. Indirectly, this can be confirmed by the absence of any hints about possible dissatisfaction with the activity of the intelligence services, while at the same time ideas about their subordination to the Ministry of the Interior or about the creation of similar regional structures surface regularly.

As for the armed forces, they only take a minimal part in the life of the regions. Traditionally, military garrison commanders were members of the *oblast'* Soviets

---

5 The successful struggle of Tatarstan's leaders for the right to coordinate the appointment of the heads local of power structures will not examined in this article.

(according to certain accounts, this prevented the last *oblast'* Soviets from being dispersed with the use of force during the autumn of 1993). But nowadays, barring a couple of exceptions, active-service military personnel were not elected to local bodies of power, nor did they show much interest in the elections. Being deprived of executive rights and serious financial resources, these bodies of power cannot solve the problems of the conscripts, and the expenses involved in participating in an election campaign by far exceed the financial possibilities of a normal soldier.

2.6.2 Presidential Representatives

This rudimentary political institution was established in August 1991 as a counterbalance to the local Soviets. After the creation in the autumn of that same year of an executive 'vertical' oriented towards the president, representatives lost their primary meaning. As they had to act within the limited powers that had been delegated to them, writing reports about the situation in their region became their main and unique (and fully futile) function. Only some of them managed to become powerful persons, with the help of old contacts (e.g., V. Golovatchev, in Saratov *oblast'*, a very important 'shadow' person; the local administration failed many times to retire him), but most of the representatives were marginal-democrats who had contacts neither in the Centre nor in the region.

After the elections in December 1993 the heads of administrations who became members of the Federal Council put forward the demand to the president to liquidate this institution. The government agreed but the institution does still exist, mainly because one can always find politicians in the Centre who want to use this network for their own interests.

The president's representatives in the republics are a special case. Up to October 1993 they existed in Russia only in Kabardino-Balkaria and Chuvashia. Nikolai Zaitsev in Chuvashia meant nothing as a political leader (his assistant Valentin Alekseev, for instance, gained far more political power). In October 1993 the president publicly announced the appointment of his representatives to all republics, in order „to prevent giving all power to the Soviets“ (in fact, the situation in Mordovia was behind this statement). A representative was appointed for Mordovia, but the Centre left its measures at that. Attempts to appoint presidential representatives to powerful republics could cause a political crisis in Russia as a whole.

2.6.3 Governmental Representatives in Regions

Representatives of different ministries and departments do not exert any influence on the local policy. Shakhrai's point of view that they have to represent the *executive vertical* in the region (while the executive organs of the subjects of the federation should be elected by citizens and be responsible only before them) is only of academic interest as one of the possible concepts of Russian federalism in the future. In fact, these representatives have neither resources (these come from Moscow, by-passing them) nor influence in the region, where the administration resolves all important problems.

The only exception on this score are the branches of *Goskomimushchestvo* (*GKI*) [the State Property Committee], which were also given competence over bankruptcy proceedings. These structures have a strong base for participating in political life, namely the right to dispose of federal property. There are cases when the administration uses them as a staff reserve (in Mordovia, V. Konakov, head of the regional *GKI*, was appointed as a presidential representative). In autumn 1991 the local departments were headed by democrats, but then these people either left their posts, or were integrated into the local establishment. As a result, the *GKI* has stopped working in the Centre's interests, having become *de facto* a local organ. Therefore it is quite clear that it will carry out bankruptcy proceedings in the interests of administrations and local elites.

2.7 Parties

The latest election campaigns showed the real influence of political parties of the 'democratic spectrum' which had been strong in 1990-1992. The representatives did not manage to gain a majority in the election to the State *Duma* or in the local administration (there were instances where candidates hid the name of the party they belonged to). People rejected both their ideas, which were no longer so popular, and the candidates themselves.

Only respresentatives of the Agrarian Party (which, as was already pointed out, is not a party properly speaking) and the Communists were successful. They managed to form some functioning structures at the regional level, thereby mimimising the amount of resources spent on the electoral campaign. The communist can be said to have succeeded in creating a stable *ecological niche* for them in the administrations of many regions: their representatives have already become chairmen in commissions on social questions in practically all regions, and in some regions (e.g.,

Astrakhan *oblast'*) they also headed the representative organs of power. It is interesting that communists are suffering greater difficulties in Tatarstan than they have ever had, mainly because the stable political system is pushing out all *informals*.

On the LDPR, is has to be pointed out that its success at the federal level was due exclusively to the qualities of its leader. In local elections *not a single member of the LDPR was elected in a single subject of the Federation*, and there are also no organisations as such.

2.8 National Movements and Organisations

What was just said about parties, also applies to national movements: neither *Marii Ush* in Marii-El Republic, nor *ChAP* in Chuvashia, nor a great number of other national organisations in Tatarstan and Bashkortostan had any real influence on decision-making or on the outcome of the elections. Their leaders lost and once again failed to get elected into the organs of power (e.g., *ChAP* leader Anter Khuzangai nearly became president in 1991 but failed in 1993). The decreasing influence of national organisations as well as their small increase in 1990-1991 does not reflect the role and the importance of national problems in the political life of the subjects of the Federation. They primarily reflect certain elite struggles that transcend the scope of this paper. Let us just point out that the 'nationals' did not manage to establish either a 'political Islam', political' paganism (Marii-El) or protestantism (Mordovia). This clearly indicated that the level of their leaders' influence on their own national population is very low.

The hypothesis about a re-emergence of Russian nationalism in the regions did also not receive confirmation, as its representatives did not meet with any great success. *Overall, the elections showed people's negative attitude towards parties, policy and politicians.*

2.9 Political Prospects of Policy Subjects

We believe that this list of subjects of local policy is exhaustive at the present time and for the near future (trade unions and social organisations as well as mass media play no independent role). For the further future, tt is doubtful that any serious 'role change' will occur.

Almost in all regions of Povolzh'e the position of the *executive power leaders* is very stable (except in Saratov region). Most probably, all political actions against them will have no chances. However, in the medium term, a deterioration of the economical and political situation could cause great problems for the present leaders of Bashkortostan, Chuvashia, Marii-El and Nizhnii Novgorod *oblast'* (especially if personal alternatives were to enter the arena). The problems are quite different in Mordovia, where the appearance of a new prospective leader is unlikely. At the same time M. Shaimiev, Y. Goryatchev and A. Guzhvin will dominate in their regions for a long time.

It should be noticed that in reality not a single regional leader can be displaced from the 'top' (as foreseen in the constitution). This is practically impossible, since the position of the regional elite is too strong and that of Centre is too weak, because of the absence of levers of control over the local executive power.

It is difficult to foresee any changes in the position and role of *the representative organs* in relatively stable republics, but in the *oblasts* a expect gradual or sudden increase of their influence is possible. The adoption of Regional Charters is a privilege of *duma*s and Assemblies. It is highly likely that they will use this opportunity to try to usurp executive and control functions. If they manage to do that in one region, the process will instantaneously spread throughout the whole of Russia. The near future will show the ability of the *oblasts*' political system to regenerate itself.

Politicians who originated from regions will naturally maintain their interests in their 'small motherlands' (if only to retain a place to which they can return). It is typical that regional leaders who are members of the Federal Assembly do not regard elections as a step forward in their career and a chance to move to Moscow (today staying in the region is far more profitable for them). Directors come back to their plants after working in different ministries, and they frequently enjoy the backing of the heads of administration, which strengthens the unity of the local elite.

According to the results of the local elections *MIC directors* left local politics, but they have no other place to go and the consequences of their failure can influence the social climate of regions and republics. The *agro-industrial lobby*, which structured and consolidated itself into a political party, is quite the opposite, being on the rise and set to increase even further in the future. Before 1993 *oil-production and oil export* were a 'gold mine', and therefore administrations aspired to develop deposits on their territories (the plan of oil-producing in Volgograd and Saratov *oblast'*s drawn up by the French firm *Elf-Aquitaine* gained support from administrations but was blocked by the Soviets). With the reduction in profitability of oil export, however, it is certainly possible to expect a slackening of the tendency to stress oil production which will be good news for the environment. After the formation of *Gasprom*, uniting FEC leaders that had previously been dispersed across Russia's regions, the political role of *gas production and processing*, as well as of the structures that are related to it, is increasing, The existing enterprises that produce, process and transport energy carriers will keep their place in the industrial 'infrastructure', and the political influence of their directors will rise on the power bodies at all levels.

The role of *federal institutions* is decreasing with the exception of *Goskomimushchestvo*, but since this structure is linked to administrations it is difficult to speak about its possible independent political role, although that might still come (in 1993 there were efforts to form a party on the base of the *GKI*).

The elections showed that *political parties and organisations* (including national ones), with the exception of the Communists[6], lost all confidence of their voters. Their leaders thus lost a unique chance to join the *oblast'* and republican elite. After August 1991, these leaders ended up in the administrations of many oblasts, but today they no longer hold any serious positions. A united and well-structured regional elite shut off 'additional' patterns of renewal – now career advancement is possible only using the old Soviet way – from the 'bottom' up or by being a member of the 'necessary' family. Changes in this pattern can only occur if the prestige of elections and the respect towards politicians were to increase, but that will be probably a task for a new non-marginal generation of politicians.

Representatives of business without links to the administration lost the elections with only a very few exceptions, since people did not trust them. They will protect their interests in the corridors of power by other means, e.g. by using bribing (buying) deputies.

3 Policy Factors

3.1 State Regional Policy

In the Soviet Union, *Gosplan, Gossnab*, and the CPSU Central Committee apparat were in charge of all regions. Big enterprises were to a large extent ex-territorial and turned to the branch ministries with their questions. There are no such structures any more and regions were left to solve their industrial giants' problems themselves.

---

6 The activity of the Communists can not be viewed in the regions alone, but should be analysed in combination with its structural and organisational principles of party-formation.

Rights that belong to the joint competence of the Centre and regions according to the Federatal Treaty, required a mechanism of implementation. The Centre dragged out this work and it has not been finished up to this day – the definitive division of the joint competence spheres turned out to be unprofitable for many leading structures in the Centre. As a result, the Centre deliberately ignored the Federal Treaty after 21 September 1993. As it turned out, the Centre still has nothing to offer to the regions: their refusal to support *Russia's Choice* and the unanimous election of regional executive branch leaders to the Federal Assembly showed the total incompetence of such a policy.

The result of this was the signing of an agreement on the division of powers with Tatarstan, which was held up as a model for co-operation (we have to point out that it was precisely the referendum on sovereignty in Tatarstan that accelerated the signing of the Federal Treaty in 1992, after which this republic became the generally acknowledged locomotive of souvereignisation).

Republican politicians that are oriented towards Moscow do not receive any support from Moscow, so they either integrated into the local political landscape or became fully marginalised and lost their influence and popularity (as in Tatarstan).

3.2 Economy

3.2.1 Central Economic Policy and Regions

In 1992 the regions of Povolzh'e were split between *those who adhered to and those who resisted the Centre's credit-financial policy.* Rejection of reforms 'a la Gaidar' prompted them to look for other ways – regional economic programmes appeared, more or less successfully:

- in Tatarstan the policy of 'entering the market gently' is suffering great difficulties because of a decrease in the efficacy of energy-carriers export, but the prices are still lower there because of the preservation of certain traits of a Soviet-style economy;

  in 1993 in Ulyanovsk *oblast'* production fell by 2 % (compared with 1992);

  in summer 1992 *oblast'* loan bonds of the regional loan were issued to compensate the shortage of cash in the Nizhnii Novgorod[7].

---

7 At the same time, economic 'creativity' in unregulated circumstances often has peculiar results: in April 1994 the head of the Samara administration, K. Titov, put forward a proposal to invest 50% of the salaries of the *budzhetniki* (received from Moscow) into local industry with 'subsequent compensation'.

The development of those regions that implement their own methods of economic transformation can generally be said to be much more successful (Ulyanovsk *oblast'*, Tatarstan etc.) than of those following Moscow's guidelines (Penza *oblast'* under Kondrat'ev, Mordovia under Guslyannikov).

If the Centre's non-interference is good in the case of strong regions, weak regions cannot survive independently. In Marii-El, Mordovia and Chuvashia, where the economic situation is disastrous, effective economic assistance was not given. The Centre does not prevent the 'incapable' from sinking in the 'market sea'. Had the right of reselection of heads of administration been preserved, incompetent leaders would have been replaced (as was the case in Penza *oblast'* and Chuvashia), but in the face of the conservation of the power pyramid the regional populations become hostage to their leaders who are appointed from above.

3.2.2 The Social and Economic Situation

The basic problems of the social and economic sphere in Povolzh'e are common for the whole federation: industrial recession causing unemployment; the failure to finance science, education, and health care resulting in an increase in mortality rates and shorter life expectancy; criminalisation of the economy; the influence of criminal elements both in entrepreneurship, industry and the existing business atmosphere in general; shortage of ecological restrictions in the activities of enterprises. The unregulated nature of privatisation and the lack of assiatance from the State exacerbate the effect of these negative elements. Even in the relatively successful Astrakhan *oblast'* all industrial branches, except the FEC, are suffering a slump of some 20-30 %. The fall in industrial production in Tatarstan during the first quarter of 1994 reached 28.4 %, in March 35.1 %. This decrease depends neither on the regional strategies (ranging form 'socialistically coloured' in Tatarstan, Astrakhan and Ulyanovsk *oblast'* to the 'statistically average reform' projects of Volgograd and Samara *oblast'*) nor on the state status and experience of leaders. *The general reasons are connected with the economic policy of the Centre.*

Among the particular reasons are the 'non-payment crisis', the shortage of material resources, the overstocking of production and lack of money resources for salaries. There is also a shortage of a qualified staff together with an unwillingness and/or impossibility of the state or the people (shareholders) to take action against incompetent or corrupt administrators. The tax system precludes any significant profit margin, and so we cannot speak about production development and expansion.

Finally, inflation depreciates all long-term projects and does not permit the reconstruction of the industry.

The social aspect of the economic crisis is clearly negative – unemployed groups (such as pensioners, disabled workers, students, children) in particular have no prospects. A lot of formally employed people are on compulsory unpaid leave or are engaged on a part-time basis. On a psychological level, this has already led to the appearance of certain type of 'post-Soviet' man: a combination of total exasperation, dissatisfaction with the existing state of affairs and a general indifference towards political activity.

The traditional character of the population in various regions can explain the uneven spread of mass declarations on the part of different groups in defence of their economic rights: while numerous demonstrations take place in Volgograd, so far these have only been dark pre-strike rumblings from trade unions in Saratov, but in spite of good co-ordination these actions have no real power.

3.2.3 The Criminal Economy

The criminal economy in Povolzh'e (as throughout the whole of Russia) is diverse and fundamentally implanted. It is characterised not only by external demonstrations (racket, skirmishes between different groups), but also by the foundation of small factories, companies and trade houses which operate on the premises of state enterprises and which speculate with state resources and state production in their dealings at ridiculous low prices; by privatisation at ridiculously low prices and auctioning under the control of criminal groups; 'administrative business' e.g. conducting trade in different licenses and rights; and finally, universal tax evasion (using cash clearings) and utilisation of deposits by on-the-budget enterprises at the expense of holding back workers' salaries.

The participation of the administration of financial, industrial and business groups in these activities is becoming common practice. There is indirect evidence that top-level administrative workers have very close ties with criminal leaders but it is obvious that such information cannot be verified. The inability or unwillingness of our organs (e.g. militia) to at least partially take control of the situation complete the picture of a unique collective guarantee in which the criminal element has captured the economy and the polity.

For the foreseeable future, the economic development is likely to continue in the same direction, with may lead to unforeseeable consequences. The most likely variant for Povolzh'e is not a confrontation between criminal and 'honest' business but between local capital and that from Moscow, the Caucasus and above all from abroad in the near future.

3.2.4 Non-Economic Crime Aspects

The social background of public and private life over the last 2 years is characterised by an increase of crime, including organised crime, structural changes in crime, leanings towards economic and serious 'big time' crimes, crimes perpetrated with cruelty and of dubious motivation (causing the response 'it's too dangerous to go out into the street').

The criminal factor is one of the reasons for the people's political apathy. Politicians use it as a means of manipulating the public consciousness, twisting the issue to their advantage (e.g. from appraising the criminal factor as inevitable and temporary to declaring an uncompromising struggle against it).

3.3 National Problems

3.3.1 Indigenous Povolzh'e Inhabitants; Activity of the Tatar Diaspora

Living both in separate and in compact settlements, the Mordvans, Mari, Chuvash, Bashkirs and Udmurtians as a rule exert no influence on local policy as national minorities, nor do they put forward any demands. The Tatar diaspora is quite different. Tatar national and cultural organisations operate throughout almost the entire territory with their demands for national and cultural autonomy. They also initiated the inter-regional religious co-ordination of Moslems in the Saratov, Volgograd and Penza *oblasts*[8]. A sociological survey on the level of potential

---

8 The split among the Moslem clergy caused the formation of several organizations oppositional to the Clergy Administration of Moslems of the European part of the Community of Independent States and Siberia-Ufa (CAMEUS). The organisations co-existing with the CAMEUS are the Clergy Administration of Moslems of Bashkortostan; The Clergy Administration of Moslems of Tatarstan; the inter-regional Administration of Moslems in Saratov, Volgograd and Penza *oblast'*. The split among the Moslem clergy is due to an elite-based conflict between young ambitious Imams on one, and Talgat Tadzhuddin, the head of CAMEUS who dominated the sphere of international contacts, on the other side. In Bashkortostan it was vice versa: the local Moslem organization was established by a small group that opposed the republic's domination of Moslem life by Tatars.

conflict among different nationalities in Povolzh'e revealed the following surprising picture[9]:

1 – *oblast'* experts;

2 – republican experts;

3 – consultants on the national problems to the heads of administrations;

4 – independent experts (scientists, journalists).

	1	2	3	4
Caucasians	20%	8.3%	46%	60%
Tatars	8.5%	8.3%	15.5%	-
Azerbaidzhani, Turkmens	2.5%	-	7.7%	-
Gypsies	2.5%	-	7.7%	-
Vietnamese	2.5%	-	7.7%	20%
other nationalities	5%	8.3%	23%	-
Jews	2.5%	-	-	20%

We can see that while the' Caucasian factor' was largely a product of the mass media, Tatars cause *oblast'* and republican leaders to become agitated. Although during the local elections there was no confirmation of the importance of the national factor, we are inclined to think that it will arise only there where the urgent problems of life are being solved (it is mainly non-elected organs that deal with them). If the influence of elected organs increases we will see representatives of the Tatar diaspora ascend to their ranks.[10]

3.3.2 German and Cossack Problems

Two national groups in Povolzh'e want to create their own state formation in Russia: Germans and Cossacks. The German interests in Povolzh'e are mainly found throughout a large part of the Saratov and Volgograd *oblasts*, and those of the Cossacks through a part of the Volgograd *oblast'* (plus a part of the Rostov *oblast'*).

---

9 The survey was done by N. Malikova in February 1993 during a meeting of Povolzh'e representatives dedicated to national problems. (Malikova is a member of Russia State Committee for the problems of national and regional politics).

10 As an illustration, we can refer to D. Ayatskov – Saratov's vice-mayor and a deputy of the Federal Council. He played an important role in a scandal with Saratov's ex-Mayor U. Kitov who committed suicide in the aftermath of that scandal. Ayatskov is characterized as a politician closely linked to a powerful Tatar group in Saratov doing business in industry and trading (more generally called 'the Tatar mafia') and to other criminal groups. At the moment he is working out laws against crime. For some experts, Ayatskov's next political goal is to become head of the regional administration.

While the Cossack movement is increasing and the ideology of the formation of a Cossack republic or *oblast'* is flourishing, the Germans, following the failure of their policy to recreate a German state entity, are busy building settlements (also somewhat unsuccessfully), developing the national okrugs and regions in Siberia and Povolzh'e, as well as addressing the problems of moving back to their historical motherland. However, the German and Cossack problems differ very much indeed and as such constitute a topic for a more detailed discussion.

3.4 Ecology

3.4.1 Chemical Weapons

The problem of chemical weapons is related not just to their existence in various depots, but also to the necessity of their disassembly and destruction. Chemical weapons are kept in military depots in Udmurtia, Marii-El, Tatarstan, Saratov and Nizhnii Novgorod *oblast'* (as a rule in relatively inaccessible wooded regions). Their very transport to places for destruction is fraught with danger and their storage is becoming an increasing headache for regions. As the storage period comes to its end, the leakage of poisonous substances can start, the consequences of which cannot be predicted.

The Centre planned to locate the equipment for the destruction of the weapons at two plants which had produced such weapons – *Khimprom* in Novocheboksary (on a bank of the Volga, 20 km from Cheboksary) and the military settlements Shikhany and Gornyi in Saratov *oblast'*. The former administration of Chuvashia tried to make the Supreme Soviet agree but invariably met with hostility (the new president of Chuvashia N. Fedorov is against such a move). The administration of Saratov *oblast'* also tried many times to start annihilation on their territory which is not surprising since the Centre promised considerable investments, but this became possible only after the dispersal of the regional soviet. Now these works are carried out without any publicity and control. We have to expect the new *duma* to examine this question (together with that of an atomic power station in Balakov, the construction of which has been 'frozen' by the same *oblast'* Soviet). A new round of conflicts is inevitable.

3.4.2 Cheboksary Hydro-Electric Power Station

During its construction in the early 1980s vast territories of Marii-El were flooded (there is a shortage of land suitable for agriculture in the republic). The same situation affects Nizhnii Novgorod *oblast'*. The station is situated on the territory of Chuvashia, which disposes of all energy produced here, while Marii-El (which has no hydro-electric installation of its own) has to buy it.

The parties involved (above all Marii-El and Chuvashia) send mutual claims to each other: Ioshkar-Ola demands its share of the produced energy, as well as a part of the Volga territories that belong to Chuvashia; Cheboksary maintains that Marii-El has already received huge compensation from the federal budget but did not know how to use it. The problem seems to defy resolution and it can become aggravated if the general economic situation in Russia changes for the worse.

3.5 The Influence of Different Factors on Regional Policy in Povolzh'e in the Near Future

The main factors determining local politics are related to the economic development of the country in general, a forecast of which is not a goal of this study. It is evident that the collapse of the MIC will be painful for the social situation in the subjects of federation in the area and will increase levels of tension, leading to the activation of non-parliamentary forms of life. It is also possible that people's apathy will increase, especially if the criminal state is confirmed in the Centre (a secanrio for which all the pre-conditions are present).

Regional policy (or rather the lack of such a policy) enables the elite (in spite of their goals) to consolidate in 'strong' regions (above all in republics), and to form horizontal regional unions. *Rossiiskaya Gazeta*[11] announced the intent of 23 territorial governors to ask the president to transfer the power of the local federal organs to the heads of administrations. We shall not present a list of all those leaders but we would point out that it includes the names of the heads of the Povolzh'e *oblasts*.

In case the Centre were to move towards real federalism (e.g., would give them rights and responsibilities to take charge of the corresponding part of the budget, and would revert to the election of the heads of the executive branch of power), the political climate would improve and the prestige of the local policy would increase.

---

11 22 June 1994.

Yet we do not expect any changes in the Centre's policy along these lines. They are not profitable for those heads of local administration who are members of the Federal Council, especially those who are incapable of carrying out their own economic policy. Most probably the existing policy of periodically widening/narrowing regions' rights according to the state of affairs will remain. Ultimately such a policy will lead to a total break-down of the federal Centre and the economic collapse of the weaker subjects of the Russian Federation.

National conflicts in the republics of Povolzh'e, contrary to the wide-spread opinion which is disseminated in the mass media, cannot be regarded as defining factors; at this stage they exist in a latent form and can become aggravated only if the economic situation changes for the worse in *comparison with Russia as a whole*. However, for many reasons such a situation is unlikely.

The external factors (i.e. those coming from the Centre) are still very important for *oblasts* but they become less important for republican policy. Republics are becoming more and more independent and are establishing horizontal relations in a very active way. The authors of the study believe that in their lifetime, the region will also rid itself of the dominating role of the Centre.

12

Russia's Palermo in the Far East: Politics and Economics in Primorskii *Krai*

Peter Kirkow[1]

The regional thrust of democratic institution-building and economic reform in Russia includes the depoliticisation of the economy and institutional restructuring, which are to be implemented by provincial politicians.[2] However, there is a profound conflict between the current national policy agenda and regional leaders' interests. Hanson[3] first formulated this conflict between the macroeconomic stabilisation effort by the national leadership, with its intention to provide a stable currency as a national public good, and the lack of interest among regional authorities in pursuing financial discipline. Local and regional politicians favour naturally their electorate, since they are now faced with the threat of being voted out of office. This caused serious tensions in centre-periphery relations, ultimately challenging the viability of the contemporary Russian federal system.

---

1 The research programme and three consecutive trips to Vladivostok between August 1992 and September 1994, on which this article is based, were funded by the School of Social Science of the University of Birmingham. The author wants to thank Philip Hanson who read an earlier draft and gave useful comments. The help and inspiring discussions with Jeremy Bristow, the producer of the BBC film 'Lord of the East', who generously provided records of interviews and shared information with this author while his TV-team was filming in Vladivostok in September 1994, are gratefully acknowledged.

2 'Region' or 'province' refer to the first sub-national, administrative unit of *kraya, oblasti*, autonomous *okruga* and republics, while 'local' is associated with the next lower city and *raion* level. Earlier ideas on this topic were expressed in Kirkow, P. „Regionale Politik und wirtschaftliche Ausdifferenzierung. Eine Fallstudie über Rußlands fernöstlichen Primorskij Kraj." *Osteuropa* 1993, no. 8: 754-770; Kirkow, P. „Regional Warlordism in Russia The Case of Primorskii Krai." *Europe-Asia Studies* 47 (1995), no. 6 (forthcoming); and Kirkow, P. & P. Hanson. „The Potential for Autonomous Regional Development in Russia: The Case of Primorskiy Kray." *Post-Soviet Geography* 35, no. 2, 1994: 63-88. The analysis of this article covers the events until early summer 1995.

3 Hanson, P. „The Center versus the Periphery in Russian Economic Policy." *RFE/RL Research Report* 3, no. 17, 29 April 1994: 24.

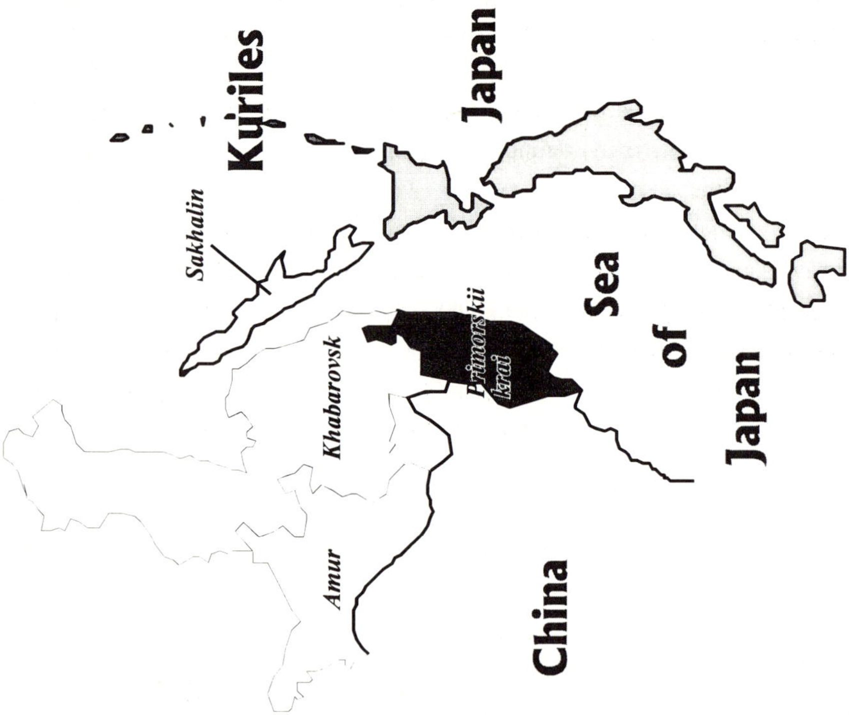

Primorskii krai

A conspicuous example of these tensions was presented by the Russian Far Eastern region of Primorskii *krai*. What made it differ from other regions, though only in its extreme appearance, was the assertive style and intransigence exhibited by regional leaders in demanding preferential treatment from Moscow (subsidies, soft credits), their continuous search for a special economic regime, the ruthless suppression of all oppositional forces, who were perceived as a threat to the current administration, and the emergence of an absolutist leader as governor. It will be argued that the centre was not only too weak to resist these developments, but that certain national leaders had a particular interest to keep, in the periphery, such an authoritarian governor in power.

The investigation of Primorskii *krai* evidenced that there was, alongside an incipient functional differentiation between politics and economics, also a revitalisation of power exerted by former *nomenklatura* members and an activation of previous social networks. However, in contrast to the opposite gateway province of St.Petersburg, Primorskii *krai* did not experience, at the early stage of political liberalisation in 1989-90, 'horizontal networks of reciprocity and civic engagement' (Putnam)[4] and a democratic self-organisation of new institutions and the press. Vladivostok was a closed city over many decades subjected to military rule and hierarchically-structured power. Compliance and patronage poured in all capillaries of social life. This provided the ground for a criminalisation of all social spheres following the physical and moral decay of the Russian army, which has many parallels with Southern Italy, making even the authoritarian governor to a hostage of the war between criminal gangs.

After briefly outlining the geostrategic importance of Primorskii *krai* for Russia, both political actors and institutions in place will be examined. The second main part looks at particular policy issues including the open showdown with Moscow, economic policy and issues of nationalities and environmental pollution. It will pay a particular attention to shifting alliances of interest groups, techniques of rent seeking and new institutional arrangements. This insight story of a peripheral Russian region should shed some light on more complex issues concerning the struggle for the control over territorial resources, the distribution of wealth, political power and, ultimately, the viability and future of the Russian Federation.

---

4 Putnam, R.D. et al. *Making Democracy Work. Civic Traditions in Modern Italy*. Princeton: Princeton University Press, 1993. The authors found predominantly horizontal networks of reciprocity and civic engagement in Northern Italy compared with elitist policy and vertical patron-client relations in Southern Italy. This, it was argued, is the main reason for the difference in performance of regional institutions between North and South Italy.

1 Strategic Location and Economic Importance

Located in the Southern tip of the Russian Far East, the Primorskii *krai* is a gateway for Russia to leading Asian financial and trade markets such as Japan, South Korea and the growing giant of China. Within the geographical triangular between Russia, China and North Korea, the Russian side is faced with an increasing competition for providing the infrastructure to bridge economic cooperation between these markets and the resource-rich mainland. Primorskii *krai's* territory of 165,000 square km makes it three-fourths the size of Britain, but it has a population of only 2.3 mn[5], one million of whom live in the industrial agglomeration of Vladivostok-Nakhodka in the South.

Access to well-equipped port facilities and a developed transport system became key issues after both Russia and China opened their economies. Officials in China favoured a free economic zone (FEZ) along the Tumangan border river[6], which would mean, in fact, giving the Chinese an extension of their Eastern Chinese Railtrack and freeing access to the Sea of Japan for the transshipment of predominantly agricultural products to Japan.[7] This would cause serious competition for the Transsiberian Railtrack on Russian territory.[8] It naturally clashed with Russian geostrategic interests and Moscow's desire to become a new key economic player in Pacific Asia. Russian regional authorities elaborated their own 'Greater Vladivostok' FEZ programme,[9] which applied only to Russian territory, but which, in conditions of economic crisis, political turmoil and a lack of substantial state support, never materialised.

---

5 Goskomstat RSFSR. *Narodnoe khozyaistvo RSFSR v 1990g* [The National Economy of the RSFSR in 1990]. Moscow, 1991.

6 Korkunov, I. „O proekte svobodnoi ekonomicheskoi zony 'Tumen'tsyan' na territorii Rossii, Kitaya i KNDR [On the Project of the Free Ecnomic Zone 'Tumentsyan' on Russian, Chinese and Korean Territory]." *Problemy Dal'nego Vostoka* 3 (1994): 17.

7 Since the last few miles before the Tumangan river enters the Sea of Japan are along Russian-Korean border, the Chinese proposed to build a canal through the territory of either of the sides. Their plans also envisaged the set up of a major port at the site where the river reaches the sea (*Vladivostok* 7 December 1994: 11).

8 *Utro Rossii* 15 November 1994: 1.

9 This initiative was supported by a 'pre-investment study' of the UN Organisation for Industrial Development in 1991. Troyakova & Christofferson (Troyakova, T. & G. Christofferson. „The Greater Vladivostok Project: The Russian Far East's Opportunity for Integration with the Asia-Pacific Region?" In *Gumanitarnye problemy stran aziatsko-tikhookeanskogo regiona (ATR)* 1 (1993), no. 3: 73) assert that it was, in fact, the Japanese government that had requested UNIDO to do this study in order to create an alternative to the Tumangan project, which would heavily depend on Japanese investment.

This failed attempt also indicated the problems of transforming a formerly closed military district and one of the most militarised areas in the world into a gateway of active economic integration into Pacific Asia.[10] The Pacific Fleet, the former pride of the Soviet army, and, in particular, its 10th squadron which was present at the Persian Gulf war, is now in a state of unprecedented physical and moral decay. Its fighting capacity is under question and naval ships and submarines are scrapped or simply 'disappear' (sold abroad). A lot of navy servicemen were made redundant[11] and developed their private business in arms trade. While naval missiles are being dismantled to sell precious metals, nobody knows what to do with the huge stockpiles of ammunition, which are often simply thrown into the sea.[12] People in this former military fortress are now sitting on top of a volcano, frequently suffering from explosions of ammunition due to poor maintenance.[13] Nuclear weapons are stockpiled at an estimated two million t in this region alone.[14]

Moreover, the land border of 1,162 km with China has again become a very sensitive issue.[15] About 74 mn people live in the two Chinese provinces adjoining

---

10 Governor Evgenii Nazdratenko expressed during a BBC interview on 1 October 1994 his unease with the government that he still does not know how much of the region's territory remains for eventual military mobilisation. This clearly clashed with the regional authorities' interest to start new businesses and to issue concessions for foreign investors to extract natural resources.

11 The Vladivostok-based Pacific Fleet had about 100,000 navy servicemen in 1993 compared with a total military personnel of 500,000 in the whole Russian Far East at that time (Terskii, M. *Konkretnye predlozheniya po formirovaniyu Severo-Vostochnogo ekonomicheskogo soobshchestva* Concrete Proposals for the Creation of a North-East Economic Community]. Vladivostok, 1993 (mimeo): 2).

12 Interview with the military correspondent of the Pacific Fleet, G. Pas'ko, on 17 September 1994. Former highest officials of the Ministry of Defence in Moscow were reportedly involved in the sale of the two aircraft carriers *Minsk* and *Novorossiisk* to the Koreans to be dismantled (*Segodnya* 22 November 1994: 13). It was expected that this deal would bring a profit of US-$ 8-9 mn (*Izvestiya* 7 December 1994: 4), which was partly to be used to build housing for military personnel (*Kommersant-Daily* 28 March 1995: 9). From a total of 498 Soviet ships sunk into the sea by the end of the Soviet era, 232 belonged reportedly to the military (*Segodnya* 22 November 1994: 13).

13 Primorskii *krai* became not only a stockpile base for ammunition from the Baltics (*Izvestiya* 21 June 1994: 7), but also a transshipment hub for arms deals (conversation with Mikhail Terskii from the Far Eastern Technological Institute on 22 September 1994). On 14 May 1994, 1,500 t of ammunition exploded at an airbase in Novonezhino, causing devastation within a radius of 6-8 km (*Utro Rossii* 19 May 1994: 1). In the spring of 1995, a fire started at an artillery depot in a distance of only a few miles from the settlement of Pogranichnyi close to the Chinese border (*Izvestiya* 1 April 1995: 2).

14 *Izvestiya* 1 April 1995: 2.

15 There are still open territorial questions. About 21 km have yet to be redrawn in Primorskii *krai*, in particular, in the centre of river channels (Kireev, G. „Granitsa s Kitayem:

Primorskii *krai*, and these mountainous areas have a relatively high rate of unemployment. This caused, after the Russian government introduced visa-free entry following President Yeltsin's visit to China in December 1992, a mass influx of Chinese people. Up to 200,000 Chinese citizens were estimated to have crossed one of the five checkpoints in the region alone in 1993 and many of them remained there after the expiry date on their stay in Russia.[16] A special commission, which was set up in Moscow in May 1994 to combat the perceived problem of emerging Chinatowns in Russia, claimed, reportedly, that there were 150,000 Chinese citizens resident in Primorskii *krai* at that time.[17] This has to be compared with an annual average of 10,000 Chinese people who were officially under labour contract in construction and logging businesses in the region since the end of the 1980s.[18]

While some national politicians clearly fuelled these resentments against the Chinese,[19] regional authorities had already taken the law into their own hands. They restricted visa-free entry for citizens of neighbouring countries in September 1993,[20] a decision which violated the prerogative of the Russian government in international relations. A special police operation called 'Foreigner' was launched in early summer 1994, but only 1,000 illegal residents were identified during the first months.[21] With such actions Primorskii *krai* authorities are trying to switch from the traditional role of a military spearhead to that of a defender of Russian national interests in the periphery, while setting more and more the political agenda by themselves and becoming independent of Moscow's supervision.[22]

---

emotsii i real'nost [The Border with China: Emotions and Reality]." *Utro Rossii* 29 July 1993: 1-2). It is doubtful, in view of the long-standing nature of this dispute, that an early resolution is in sight. For border demarcation with China, see also *Segodnya* 22 December 1994: 2 and *Segodnya* 17 February 1995: 3. Governor Nazdratenko tried to delay further proceedings by denouncing the 1991 Russo-Chinese treaty on border demarcation, effectively taking a strong nationalist stance and declaring, in early 1995, the 1,500 ha of land, which Russia would have to hand over to the Chinese according to the treaty, as strategically important territory (*Segodnya* 14 February 1995: 2).

16 *Utro Rossii* 16 November 1993: 1.

17 *Kommersant-Daily* 26 May 1994: 3.

18 Interview with the deputy head of the committee of foreign economic and regional relations of the Primorskii *krai* administration, V.Tikhomirov, on 14 September 1994.

19 Shakhrai, S. „Neobkhodima strategiya otnosheniya s Kitaem [We Need a Strategy in our Relations with China]. " *Izvestiya* 20 May 1994: 4.

20 Interview with Tikhomirov on 15 September 1993.

21 *Izvestiya* 14 July 1994: 2.

22 Governor Nazdratenko considered the redrawing of borders as the real problem. 'One should stop with it... We strengthened Russian statehood in the Far East by closing the border. I did a good job for our country.' (BBC interview on 1 October 1994).

Fishing was traditionally the most important sector of industry in Primorskii *krai*, which accounted for 32.8% of the gross value of industrial output in 1990, while machinebuilding (military hardware) was ranking second with 23.7% at that time.[23] The region produced traditionally 80% of all fluoride concentrates and 90% of boron in the former USSR.[24] It also has substantial deposits of ferrous and precious metals (tin, lead and silver); timber, copper and furs were exported; and the territory delivered 9% of the rice and 15% of the soybean production in the Russian Federation.[25]

Finally, because of its geographical location, Primorskii *krai* plays an important role as a transport junction, not only for the supply of goods to regions in the Russian Far North (Chukotka, Magadan), but also for East-West trade. Civil and military ships are now mainly hired to cope with the increasing demand of Russian export products abroad, which consist mainly of fish, lumber and wood products, precious metals and mineral fertilizers. In Russian perception, Vladivostok now ranks highest, along with St.Petersburg, as a Russian-controlled gateway region, after access to the Baltic Sea and the Black Sea was reduced with the end of the Soviet Union.[26]

2 Policy Actors and Institutions

This section examines the configuration of political power in the province by focusing on both the provincial and federal institutional setting and key political players. Two opposing political camps can be personified in the present governor, Evgenii Nazdratenko, who is backed by the industrial management, the military and other federal structures, on the one side, and the former mayor of Vladivostok city, Viktor Cherepkov, who receives support from various democratic groupings and the local media, on the other. The former camp has he main influence on regional policy-making today and they are responsible for market reform and institutional restructuring, while the role of trade unions and parties in this process remains

---

23 Goskomstat RSFSR. *Narodnoe khozyaistvo Primorskogo kraya v 1990 godu.* [The Economy of the Primorskii *krai* in 1990]. Vladivostok, 1991: 131.

24 Osipov, B. (ed.) *Ekonomicheskii potentsial i problemy razvitiya Primorskogo kraya* [The Economic Potential and Problems of Development of Primorskii *krai*]. Vladivostok, 1992: 13.

25 Savalei, V. „Primor'e: poisk ekonomicheskoi nishi [The Maritime Area in Search of an Economic Niche]." *Problemy Dal'nego Vostoka* 1991, no. 5: 73.

26 Leksin, V. & E. Andreeva. „Territorial'naya dezintegratsiya Rossii [The Territorial Disintegration of Russia]." *Rossiiskii ekonomicheskii zhurnal* 1992, no. 8: 32-41.

marginal.[27] However, this constellation became more complex after members of the new private business and the criminal underworld entered the political scene, while the alliance of Nazdratenko's camp was splitting up following a growing diversification of interests.

2.1 Key political players

The ruling establishment in Primorskii *krai* consists of members of the second echelon of the former party and management *nomenklatura*, who came to power at the wave of public disillusionment with rapid systemic reforms, while being able to rely on considerable private capital.[28] The first governor of the region, Vladimir Kuznetsov, was for this alliance a newcomer and intellectual troublemaker. He was devotedly reform-minded and embarked on different economic experiments in 1991-92, the most prominent of which was the above discussed 'Greater Vladivostok' project. His liberal market approach and his liking for extended travel abroad caused strong resentments among traditionalists in the old regional soviet and industrial management.

After Kuznetsov suspended the regional communist newspaper *Krasnoe znamya* in the aftermath of the August 1991 coup, its editor-in-chief, V.Shkrabov, started a campaign against him with the aim of promoting a new governor, who would be closer to the regional elite's thinking.[29] He joined traditionalists in the regional soviet to launch a coup against Kuznetsov in April 1993, after the Russian parliament had withdrawn its support of Yeltsin's power to appoint provincial governors (one of the temporary, special powers granted him in late 1991). The regional soviet suggested to the President the new candidature of Evgenii Nazdratenko, assuring him in advance of the support of the majority of the soviet.[30] Shkrabov revealed later [31]that they had chosen Nazdratenko because of his 'practical experience' and his allegedly close connections to Yeltsin.

---

27 For an examination of the role of trade unions and parties in privatisation in Primorskii *krai* see: Vacroux, A. „Privatization in the Regions: Primorsky Krai." In *Russia: Creating Private Enterprises and Efficient Markets*. Washington, D.C.: The World Bank, The Private Sector Development Department, 1994: 39.

28 Savvateeva, I. „Evgenii Nazdratenko kak zerkalo rossiiskikh reform [Evgenii Nazdratenko as a Mirror of Russian Reforms]." *Izvestiya* 1 December 1994: 5.

29 BBC interview with V.Shkrabov on 28 September 1994.

30 *Utro Rossii* 19 May 1993: 1.

31 BBC interview on 28 September 1994.

The new governor was originally described as having a 'progressive conservatism'.[32] In 1983, he finished a degree at the Far Eastern Technological Institute and became in 1990 the director of the mining company *Vostok* in Dal'negorsk, as well as a deputy of the Russian parliament.[33] Nazdratenko provides an excellent example of how industrial management was pouring into power in Russian regions, seeking advantage in the combination of public office with private business. In a special interview, he referred explicitly to his friends, who are directors of enterprises of the defence industry and local entrepreneurs, which he called a 'legal union of industrialists'.[34]

Over a period of four months, Nazdratenko managed to appoint a new team in his administration[35] in which a number of deputies (A.Pavlov, I.Lebedinets, V.Shkrabov) were, at the same time, leading executive members of the joint-stock company PAKT.[36] This was devised as a 'model to rule the Primorskii *krai* independently of Moscow'[37]and the responsibility for large-scale privatisation gave the additional opportunity to control the regional economy.[38] It allowed the combination of tax-evasion, embezzlement of public money and control of political power (including the issue of export licences and distribution of regional quota), which became famous as 'Primorskii Watergate'.[39] Pavlov, the former head of the regional trade administration during the late Soviet period, who is today the director of the company *Kommersant*, originally held the reins as the general director of PAKT.[40] In 1992, the year when PAKT was set up, he seemed to be the real key player of the whole business, while Nazdratenko may have been at first only a political puppet.[41] Pavlov alone was accused of tax-evasion in *Kommersant* of R 2.5

---

32 Gainutdinov, D. „Pobedili li Primortsy? [Did the Primorians Win?]" *Utro Rossii* 12 June 1993: 2.

33 *Utro Rossii* 20 May 1993: 1.

34 *Utro Rossii* 2 June 1993: 2.

35 Nazdratenko claimed in an open letter to *Rossiiskaya gazeta* (20 October 1994: 3) that he had to change the personnel of his predecessor completely because of corruption. He frequently tried to justify his authoritarian rule because of the necessity to fight crime.

36 This stands for 'Primorskii Shareholding Company of Commodity Producers'.

37 BBC interview with Shkrabov on 28 September 1994.

38 Vacroux, A. „Privatization in the Regions: Primorsky Krai." In *Russia: Creating Private Enterprises and Efficient Markets*. Washington, D.C.: The World Bank, The Private Sector Development Department, 1994: 43.

39 *Izvestiya* 1 December 1993: 5.

40 *Utro Rossii* 4 November 1993: 1.

41 This was confirmed by Shkrabov during his BBC interview: 'Nazdratenko did not conquer power, he was promoted to power'.

bn in 1992.[42] While Pavlov was trying to control the newly emerging commercial sector, Nazdratenko attempted to control the military-industrial complex. He takes a strong nationalist stance and wants Russia to restore and maintain its leading position in global arms sales alongside the United States: 'I support, by nature, a strong military-industrial complex ... Without the help of this complex, I would never be able to run the economy of the region'.[43]

Another important member of PAKT is the former deputy head of the provincial tax inspection, Igor Lebedinets, who became later Nazdratenko's chief of staff, and is today not only the chairman of the new regional Duma, but also the deputy director of the Vladivostok-based trawling and refrigerator ship fleet.[44] Finally, the fourth decisive player of PAKT was originally Shkrabov, a former member of the Primorskii CPSU committee and, as mentioned above, the editor-in-chief of the regional newspaper *Krasnoe znamya* (the former party organ), who was appointed as the head of the committee for mass-media in the regional administration, becoming, in fact, his own boss.[45] He described himself as the 'ideologist' of PAKT.[46] The administration acted as the co-founder of this newspaper in an attempt to get its own media-mouthpiece. This fusion of politics and business in the activities of the highest ranking regional leaders marked a decisive step towards absolutist power in the second half of 1993.

On the other side of the barricade was the first democratically elected mayor of Vladivostok, Cherepkov, a former prosecutor in the Pacific Fleet, who took over his new office in summer 1993 and became the spokesman for democratic groupings. However, systematic measures were undertaken by leading officials of the provincial administration to undermine his authority, including the switching-off of water and electric power, a cut in the city's share of the consolidated regional budget from 16.8% to 8.4%, the sudden off-loading of one third of the total housing stock of Vladivostok from former sectoral ministries onto the municipal authorities and acts of sabotage on heating systems.[47] Cherepkov embarked on a number of measures that were unpopular with the huge administrative apparatus in the city. His main proposal for administrative reform was to dissolve city districts, which would reduce

42 *Utro Rossii* 19 October 1993: 2.

43 BBC interview with Nazdratenko on 1 October 1994.

44 *Izvestiya* 1 December 1993: 5.

45 Ibidem.

46 BBC interview on 28 September 1994.

47 Smirnova, T. „Syuzhet dlya dramy [Topic for a Drama].“ *Utro Rossii* 23 November 1993: 2.

the number of state employees from 6,500 to 1,000.[48] In reply, the regional administration issued a statement that city district councils should not comply with Cherepkov's commands.[49] The mayor, for his part, sought popular support by providing free public transport and trying to break the bread and fish monopolies through opening new bakeries and fish markets.[50]

The campaign against Cherepkov was re-inforced at the end of 1993. On 30 December 1993, Lebedinets sent an emergency call to Moscow, reporting the alleged break-down of the heating system, paralysed public transport and medical aid not working in Vladivostok, for which he blamed Cherepkov.[51] On 11 February 1994, an apparent plot was started against the mayor, when the city procurator and a number of armed policemen investigated his office for alleged acceptence of bribes. During the inspection, R 1.2 mn (approximately US-$ 600) were reported to have been placed in his safe and another R 1 mn to have been left in one of his coats, during an investigation of his flat.[52] Cherepkov was kept in custody for a day or so and his son was also arrested, being accused of theft of a computer in his school a year earlier, for which he was later sentenced to prison to seven years.[53] At this time, Vladivostok's mayor had to be released after public protest; he was later evicted from his office on 17 March 1994 by armed police under orders from Nazdratenko.[54] He was also beaten up by criminal gangs on 2 August 1994.[55]

In late 1994, Cherepkov was cleared of all charges of accepting bribes by the Russian attorney general A.Il'yushenko.[56] However, only a few days later Yeltsin sacked Cherepkov for 'violating the legislation of the Russian Federation and for not fulfilling his public duties for a long period of time'.[57] For Cherepkov, who was kept in custody and not allowed to get into his office for more than four months, this could not have been a more ridiculous statement, and it is questionable whether Yeltsin really knew what he was signing. In spring 1995, three former police officer,

---

48 *Utro Rossii* 8 October 1993: 2.

49 *Utro Rossii* 11 March 1994: 1.

50 Smirnova, T. „Syuzhet dlya dramy [Topic for a Drama]." *Utro Rossii* 23 November 1993: 2.

51 *Utro Rossii* 6 January 1994: 1.

52 *Utro Rossii* 15 February 1994: 1.

53 *Financial Times* 27 October 1994: 3.

54 *Utro Rossii* 18 March 1994: 1.

55 *Kommersant-Daily* 4 August 1994: 14.

56 *Segodnya* 6 December 1994: 2. It is interesting that this official statement was made by Il'yushenko, who is one of Nazdratenko's closest allies in the centre (see below).

57 *Izvestiya* 27 December 1994: 4.

who took part in Cherepkov's eviction from his office, were made to scapegoats and arrested, while no charges were made against Nazdratenko by the time of writing.[58] One of the 'famous representatives of the local criminal underworld',[59] and a close ally of Nazdratenko, K.Tolstoshein, who received less than one per cent of the votes during the election of the new mayor of Vladivostok in June 1993,[60] was appointed by the governor as Cherepkov's successor. He sought popular support among former military officers and soldiers who had served in Afghanistan and war veterans.[61]

2.2 Institutions

The strong stress on personalities in the analysis of the configuration of political power in Primorskii *krai* is not only due to the blurred regional institutional structures, but also the weak coherence of national parties with their representation in the province. Institutional restructuring in Primorskii *krai* did not proceed toward a division of power as envisaged by national leaders and established in the new Russian constitution, but toward a subordination of regional legislature and judiciary under the executive power and, in particular, the concentration of authoritarian power in the hands of governor Nazdratenko.

2.3 Executive branch

Nazdratenko's predecessor, Kuznetsov, had already taken over a huge bureaucratic apparatus and he did not change the structure of the former executive committee and retained almost all of the old personnel. In September 1993, the Primorskii *krai* administration employed 718 people and consisted of 16 committees and 28 departments.[62] In late 1994, Nazdratenko announced a cut of members of staff down to 300 people altogether, including the cut of deputies from thirteen to only five, and also structural changes between committees and departments.[63] This was hardly an attempt to save public expenditure, but to get a close entourage of state employees,

---

58 *Kommersant-Daily* 25 May 1995: 14.

59 Interview with Cherepkov's former adviser, I.Sanachev, on 19 September 1994.

60 *Utro Rossii* 16 June 1993: 1.

61 *Rossiiskie vesti* 11 May 1994: 3.

62 Interview with the deputy head of the committee for economy and planning of the Primorskii *krai* administration, G. Sorokin, on 17 September 1993.

63 *Utro Rossii* 5 November 1994: 1. *Segodnya* (10 November 1994: 3) reported a cut from 920 people employed in the Primorskii *krai* administration to only 90, which could be exaggerated bearing in mind the number of committees and departments.

which would be more easily controllable, particularly the kind of information leaking out from the administration.

The distinctive approach of Nazdratenko's team was to take over the role of former central branch ministries and to converge, within the structures of PAKT, to an all-encompassing conglomerate aiming to control the main spheres of the regional economy. Administrative measures were taken to stop large-scale privatisation in 'crucial and socially significant' enterprises in August 1993. This category encompassed 64 regional and 108 federal enterprises.[64] In its organisational goals, PAKT claimed the leading role in structural reorganisation of the regional economy, the setting up of a financial system and a 'socially stable and economically protected structure for voucher investment'.[65] This would not only mean a replacement of old sectoral monopolies that dominated the regional economy until then, but also a new institutional entanglement of politics and economics at the regional level and a fierce resistance towards outside competition. In a letter to the President, signed by Egor Gaidar and other members of the democratic fractions in the State Duma, it was claimed that PAKT controlled more than 200 of the total of 360 large enterprises in the province in September 1994.[66]

The system of regional quotas and export licences left also a strong lever of control over foreign trade for the authorities of the executive branch. The administrative distribution of fishing quotas for export in the region, for example, implied price agreements and financial help for the former regional monopolist (in terms of sale of fish on foreign markets) *Dal'moreprodukt*, which led naturally to new cartels and conglomerates.[67] Moreover, in order to pursue its populist price policy for fuel and energy, the regional administration initiated in May 1994 the creation of a new conglomerate, *Energiya Vostoka*, in which the regional energy company *Dal'energo* and the mining company *Primorskugol'* were incorporated.[68] The executive branch backed reportedly Central Bank credits by passing on subsidies from the federal budget,[69] which is a clear example how regional authorities contribute to the federal budget deficit.

---

64 Vacroux, A. „Privatization in the Regions: Primorsky Krai.“ In *Russia: Creating Private Enterprises and Efficient Markets*. Washington, D.C.: The World Bank, The Private Sector Development Department, 1994: 41.

65 Ibidem: 40.

66 *Segodnya* 29 September 1994: 2.

67 *Utro Rossii* 28 January 1994: 2.

68 *Utro Rossii* 6 May 1994: 2.

69 *Segodnya* 20 October 1994: 11.

Finally, the Primorskii *krai* administration did not only try to control former sectoral monopolies of the regional economy, but also interfered into newly emerging market structures. In late August 1994, Nazdratenko set up a new commission for securities under his administration which was supposed to control the issue and turnover of securities in the region.[70] It gave members of the commission the right to check on participants of Vladivostok's stock exchange and to give obligatory instructions.

The head of the regional property fund, V.Lutsenko, issued a decree in September 1994 to stop the free sale of shares of privatised enterprises at the city's stock exchange.[71] This was part of a new attempt at manipulating large-scale privatisation by the use of closed, non-public auctions to which leading executives of PAKT had access. *Rossiiskaya gazeta*[72] reported that officials in Lutsenko's property fund allowed applications by serious competitors and independent entrepreneurs to 'disappear', making sure that PAKT members could cheaply acquire the best enterprises in the region. At a press conference in October 1994, Nazdratenko made the following statement after being accused of mixing public office with private business: 'One cannot separate me from industry ... I am not against privatisation, but I am against the methods being used. For that reason, I tried to keep a large package of shares in the hands of the administration to talk with the commercial structures in a civilised way'.[73]

2.4 Legislative branch

The traditionalist majority in the regional soviet rejected Yeltsin's edict 'On the Stage-by-Stage Constitutional Reform in the Russian Federation' of 21 September 1993[74] and Nazdratenko declared on 22 September: 'There is only one solution to this mess: the whole Far East has to split up'.[75] However, after Yeltsin forcibly disbanded the Russian parliament in early October 1993, Nazdratenko made a complete U-turn, pledging allegiance to the President and ordering strong subordination of the local executive power under his command.[76]. Moreover, he

---

70 *Kommersant-Daily* 27 August 1994: 7.
71 *Kommersant-Daily* 3 September 1994: 6.
72 *Rossiiskaya Gazeta* 28 September 1994: 7.
73 *Segodnya* 26 October 1994: 2.
74 *Utro Rossii* 28 September 1993: 1.
75 *Rossiiskie vesti* 1 October 1994: 2.
76 *Utro Rossii* 6 October 1993: 1.

decided to disband the regional soviet on 28 October 1993[77]: a move which affected most of those deputies, who originally proposed his appointment.

This gave Nazdratenko the opportunity to rule without being faced with a legislative counterbalance for more than a year, since he postponed in March 1994 the elections to the regional parliament, which were originally scheduled for that month by presidential decree, until 23 October. Whether he did not feel safe enough remains an open question, but he claimed that there was not enough money to pay for them.[78] Moreover, there was a rising apathy among voters, being disillusioned with local politics. A public survey conducted in the run-up to the elections of the new regional Duma in October 1994 still indicated that one third of the eligible voters were willing to participate at the elections.[79] But the results of the elections had to be declared invalid because of low turnout. In only 19 of the 39 voting districts the necessary quorum of 25% was achieved.[80] Nevertheless, the analysis of candidates and elected deputies by workplace background[81] gives a clear indication of the revitalisation of power by former *nomenklatura* members as is shown in table 1.

Table 1 *Candidates and elected deputies to the Primorskii krai Parliament by workplace background, 23 October 1994*

	Candidates	% of	Elected	% of total
Total	149	100.0	19	100.0
Executive power	41	27.5	8	42.1
Khozyaistvenniki	55	36.6	8	42.1
Military	9	6.0	1	5.3
Intelligentsia	22	14.8	1	5.3
Social organisations	8	5.4	-	-
Other	14	9.4	1	5.3

Note: *Percentage figures in the last column do not add to 100.0% because of rounding. 'Executive power' includes heads and deputy heads of regional and local administrations. Khozyaistvenniki refers to directors, managing directors and chief engineers of joint-stock companies, state enterprises, banks, kolkhozy and sovkhozy. Intelligentsia includes academics, teachers, doctors and engineers. 'Social organisations' apply to members of independent trade unions, consumer associations,*

77 *Utro Rossii* 29 October 1993: 1.

78 *RFE/RL Daily Report* 22 March 1994.

79 *Utro Rossii* 11 October 1994: 2.

80 *Utro Rossii* 3 November 1994: 1.

81 For some of them, both workplace background and party affiliation were indicated at the candidate list. However, the latter played during the pre-election campaign only a minor role and most of them were proposed by 'voters' groups' (*Utro Rossii* 12 March 1994: 2).

*etc. 37 of the candidates (24.8%) were former deputies of the regional soviet (*Utro Rossii *15 March 1994: 1).*

Source: *Compiled from* Utro Rossii *12 March 1994: 2 and 3 November 1994: 1.*

Even if the regional Duma had convened at that time, it is clear that it would have been dominated by representatives of the executive power and industrial management. Both members of the intelligentsia and social organisations lost considerably in this tentative estimate of the configuration of power.

Like in other Russian provinces,[82] there was a particularly low turnout in urban areas such as Vladivostok, Artem and Nakhodka.[83] Unpleasant candidates like Pavlov, who departed from the PAKT alliance only a few weeks before, were reportedly denied of their proper number of votes.[84] Moreover, new procedures for the re-elections scheduled for 15 January 1995 were adopted which clearly violated the President's decree on voting regulations: (1) the candidate had now to collect signatures from only one per cent of all eligible voters instead of three per cent; (2) the candidate could be proposed by only one supporter instead of a group of at least 30 supporters before; and (3) better conditions were provided for members of the executive branch including the possibility to be relieved from public duty for the time of the pre-election campaign.[85] It is intriguing that no further information on the new deputies elected in January 1995 was released in the local press.

The first information came in the national press, reporting on the attempt of some of the new deputies to declare the primacy of the legislative over the executive branch in the new provincial statute, but its new chairman and close ally of Nazdratenko, Lebedinets, quickly distanced himself from this clause)[86]. Two committees of a total of five are headed by two former deputies of the regional soviet, while the head of the federal treasury, N.Sadomskii, is, at the same time, the head of the budget committee of the regional Duma,[87] resulting in overlapping administrative competences between federal and provincial institutions. Moreover, the leadership of the new regional parliament pursued a provocative policy against the centre right from the beginning, trying to functionalise various trade unions during the miners strike in the province in spring 1995 by declaring, allegedly in

---

82 For an excellent analysis of this urban-rural cleavage and the 'ruralisation' of Russian politics, see: Petrov, N. „Regional'nye vybory-94: itogi i uroki [1994 Regional Elections: Results and Lessons]." *Rossiya regionov* 1994, no. 2 (November 1994): 8-12.

83 *Utro Rossii* 25 October 1994: 1.

84 *Utro Rossii* 3 November 1994: 1.

85 *Utro Rossii* 17 December 1994: 1.

86 *Segodnya* 22 February 1995.

87 *Utro Rossii* 24 February 1995: 1.

their name, to block ports and the Transsiberian Railtrack if the centre would not deliver further subsidies and soft credits for defence-related enterprises[88] and the coal industry.[89] This was widely considered as a deliberate attempt by highest provincial officials at using industrial action to destabilise the political situation in the region.[90] Lebedinets announced also his support for the election movement *Gosduma-96*, according to whom the centre of its activity should be in the Primorskii *krai* in order to get more industrialists in the new federal parliament.[91]

2.5 Industrial management

The strongest impact on economic decision-making in the region is made by the above mentioned industrial conglomerate PAKT, whose members are closely linked with the provincial administration. The 213 founders (people, not enterprises) of PAKT represented 36 leading industrial enterprises, including 6 defence plants (among others, *Varyag* and *Radiopribor*), 4 fishing and fish-processing companies, producers of chemicals and electronic circuits.[92] The member enterprises of PAKT employed 90,000 people or 9% of the total regional workforce in August 1993.[93] PAKT became a vehicle for its founders' interests. It acquired 236,000 shares of privatised enterprises for half the market price through manipulated, non-public auctions.[94] This was justified under the pretext that the local economy has to be protected against the capital pouring into the region from outside.[95] Credits were taken at *Promstroibank* and afterwards PAKT executives distributed loans among themselves to buy a majority of shares of privatised enterprises. Lebedinets, for

---

88 *Nezavisimaya gazeta* 30 March 1995: 2.

89 *Nezavisimaya gazeta* 7 April 1995: 1.

90 *Segodnya* 11 April 1995: 2.

91 *Utro Rossii* 15 April 1995: 1.

92 *Russian Far East Update*, March 1994: 11.

93 Vacroux, A. „Privatization in the Regions: Primorsky Krai.“ In *Russia: Creating Private Enterprises and Efficient Markets*. Washington, D.C.: The World Bank, The Private Sector Development Department, 1994: 41.

94 *Rossiiskie vesti* 28 September 1994: 7.

95 Vacroux, A. „Privatization in the Regions: Primorsky Krai.“ In *Russia: Creating Private Enterprises and Efficient Markets*. Washington, D.C.: The World Bank, The Private Sector Development Department, 1994: 41. Prokop's interpretation (Prokop, J.E. „Industrial Conglomerates, Risk Spreading and the Transition in Russia.“ *Communist Economies & Economic Transformation* 7 (1995), no. 1: 47) of PAKT representing 'a rational attempt by industrial managers to spread economic risks while pursuing restructuring' seems to be a complete misperception.

example, acquired more than 28,000 shares through this kind of procedure.[96] PAKT founders received also interest-free loans from the regional budget, which totalled R 500 mn in 1993.[97] The former representative of the President in Primorskii *krai*, V.Butov, claimed that PAKT embezzled money from the consolidated regional budget to the extent of R 25 bn in 1993 alone,[98] compared with a total budgetary income of R 753.7 bn in that year.[99]

Nazdratenko tried to justify the set up of such a financial-industrial group by drawing parallels to Japanese conglomerates, arguing that they would be better suited to absorb economic shocks.[100] PAKT executives have reportedly a particular interest in the fuel and energy complex (TEK), ports, oil pipelines and sites of resource extraction, while all programmes of geological investigation in the region are under personal control of Nazdratenko.[101] According to Savvateeva,[102] PAKT did never engage in any new production activity; it did only redistribute money and industrial assets. Finally, in late 1994, the Moscow-based *ONEKSIM* bank was chosen by the regional administration to operate as its financial agent in foreign economic activities, to settle payment arrears between provincial enterprises for which bank officials hoped to get treasury bills from the Ministry of Finance, and to engage in new investment projects in the region.[103] The regional administration's attempt to halt privatisation and to set up new conglomerates impeded proper institutional restructuring, resulting in a net drain for both the federal and the regional budgets. In return, industrial managers' response was to lobby for new subsidies and soft credits, while not undertaking thorough-going structural changes at the enterprise level. The mining company *Primorskugol'*, for example, which had

---

96 *Rossiiskie vesti* 20 October 1994: 3.

97 *Rossiiskie vesti* 28 September 1994: 7.

98 *Utro Rossii* 12 January 1994: 1.

99 Interview with the deputy head of the budget office of the Primorskii *krai* administration, V. Rybakova, on 7 September 1994.

100 *Utro Rossii* 27 August 1994: 2.

101 *Novoe vremya* 1994, no. 40: 14.

102 Savvateeva, I. „Evgenii Nazdratenko kak zerkalo rossiiskikh reform [Evgenii Nazdratenko as a Mirror of Russian Reforms]." *Izvestiya* 1 December 1994: 5.

103 *Kommersant-Daily* 16 December 1994: 5. Executives of commercial banks in Primorskii *krai* sensed the potential threat of large Moscow-based banks operating in their region under the shield of the provincial administration. After *ONEKSIM* bank acquired the controlling package of shares of the local bank *Primor'e* in March 1995, leading officials of the Far Eastern Banking Association declared their intention to fuse all 24 member banks into two or three large banks to be able to compete with the Moscow-based banks (*Kommersant-Daily* 3 March 1995: 6).

to be subsidised almost completely by the state as a result of regional authorities' price policy for fuel and electricity, started with privatisation only in autumn 1994, employing reportedly, at that time, more people for management and subsidiary jobs than miners.[104] The only solution is to close a number of unprofitable mines, but no programmes for retraining were started until the miners' strike broke out in spring 1995.[105] Moreover, the provincial administration still claims the right to dispose over federal subsidies handed down for this company, from which R 17 bn were reportedly embezzled and passed on to commercial structures.[106]

The institutional entanglement of politics and economics in the Primorskii *krai* resulted in growing cartels along the regional boundary, the institutionalisation of inflationary behaviour and rent seeking, which was politically supported by the executive branch. Monopolies in timber-processing industries were exempted from local taxes,[107] while the set up of a new transport conglomerate sponsored by regional and Moscow-based banks was reported.[108] The management of the fishing company, *Primorrybprom*, acquired 55% of all shares after having received money from the regional budget for 23% of the shares alone.[109] Finally, former structures of the agro-industrial complex (APK) were lobbying for the set up of a regional grain fund to guarantee the sale and get additional subsidies.[110]

2.6 Private business

It is certainly hard to set up a new business in Primorskii *krai* without being subjected to administrative control by the executive branch or blackmail by criminal gangs. There is an insider scheme for the issue of export licences and the distribution of regional quotas, which was extensively used by those new private companies which were in close connection with the regional administration like Pavlov's *Kommersant* to export natural resources.[111] The Vladivostok stock exchange, which is trading shares of Siberian and Far Eastern enterprises, can only run its business with the blessing of governor Nazdratenko.[112] In the meantime, Western

104 *Utro Rossii* 29 September 1994: 1.
105 *Izvestiya* 26 April 1995: 1.
106 *Izvestiya* 7 April 1995: 1.
107 *Utro Rossii* 19 April 1995: 2.
108 *Utro Rossii* 1 April 1995: 1.
109 *Utro Rossii* 20 April 1995: 2.
110 *Utro Rossii* 8 April 1995: 1.
111 *Izvestiya* 1 December 1994: 5.
112 *Utro Rossii* 30 August 1994: 2.

businessmen are trying to turn a blind eye on human rights' abuses in the province, while not operating in cash to avoid racketing.[113] One of the few successful private companies is *AKFES*, which was set up by young engineers of defence-related enterprises,[114] running a wide range of activities including fishing, freight transshipment, tourism and car service. Its construction business seems to be particularly profitable due to the provision of alternative systems for the supply of water and electricity.[115]

2.7 Federal institutions

Nazdratenko tried also to get the structures of federal power in the region under control. With the first representative of the President in Primorskii *krai*, Butov, he was at loggerheads. Butov was a former soldier in Afghanistan and later the deputy military procurator of the Pacific Fleet)[116], who started, in the second half of 1993, to report more frequently on abuse of power by the administration and to reveal publicly cases of corruption by leading executives of PAKT. Nazdratenko started a campaign against Butov and pressed the centre to replace him. On 4 January 1994, Yeltsin acceded to the demands of the regional administration and sacked his representative. In a later interview, Butov referred to the personal friendship between Nazdratenko and the head of the President's bureau, V. Ilyushin, who not only suggested to the President the candidature of Nazdratenko as the new governor in May 1993, but also the sacking of Butov.[117] Whether Yeltsin knew what was going on in the region while signing this document remains an open question. The new representative, Vladimir Ignatenko, is clearly Nazdratenko's man, a former head of a local administration in the province. He condemned democratic groupings and the mass media supporting Cherepkov as scandalous and provocative[118] and openly resisted the reinstatement of the sacked mayor in his former office.[119]

Two attempts were made by the governor to suggest in Moscow the former head of the Dal'negorsk police office (where Nazdratenko's company *Vostok* is based),

---

113 *Financial Times* 27 October 1994: 3.

114 *Utro Rossii* 4 October 1994: 2.

115 Interview with the former director of the economics institute of the Far Eastern Branch of the Russian Academy of Science, V. Savalei, on 14 September 1994.

116 *Utro Rossii* 26 November 93.

117 *Utro Rossii* 12 January 1994: 1.

118 *Utro Rossii* 13 August 1994: 2.

119 *Izvestiya* 27 December 1994: 4.

Lieutenant-Colonel Shul'g, as the new head of the regional tax police.[120] The appointment of the new head of the regional police department, V.Ipatov, was largely promoted by Nazdratenko's team,[121] who, in return, then showed his gratefulness by delaying the legal investigation into the case of PAKT's tax-evasions and embezzlement of public money by special commissions from Moscow.[122] One year later, Nazdratenko promoted Ipatov to the rank of a general.[123] Moreover, the commanders of the regional office of the secret service, the border guards and the Pacific Fleet are, reportedly, in 'close relations' with the governor.[124]

This applies also to newly set up federal committees and federal funds. The head of the tax police in the province, Bondarenko, is one of Nazdratenko's close allies.[125] The head of the pension fund, P.Nazarov, gave Nazdratenko's administration R 25 bn in July 1994, because the governor decided to increase pensions by 1.5 times, which was a populist action in Nazdratenko's campaign to be elected as governor in October 1994.[126] Whether the newly created treasury office, which is supposed to bundle the flow of federal finances,[127] will stay independent from the regional administration's intrusion remains doubtful, all the more so as its head, Sadomskii, had already become a member of the commission for securities of the administration as well as the head of the budget committee of the new regional Duma as was discussed above. Finally, the regional parliament claims now also the right to confirm the appointment of heads of various federal institutions in the region,[128] which is only another way to legitimise the governor's authoritarian power.

2.8 Political parties

Political parties and social movements had no real impact on regional policy-making due to a lack of institutional coherence between the national headquarter and the representation in the province, while viable political programmes were absent.

---

120 *Utro Rossii* 26 November 93: 1.

121 *Utro Rossii* 16 November 93: 1.

122 *Utro Rossii* 26 November 93: 1. The close relation between the regional judiciary and Ipatov was confirmed by the deputy head of the provincial court, V. Razhev (*Utro Rossii* 15 September 1994: 2).

123 *Utro Rossii* 6 January 1995: 2.

124 *Segodnya* 29 September 1994: 2.

125 *Novoe vremya* 1994, no. 40: 14.

126 Interview with P.Nazarov on 20 September 1994.

127 Interview with the head of the treasury office of Primorskii *krai*, N.Sadomskii, on 21 September 1994.

128 *Utro Rossii* 23 February 1995: 2.

Voters' preferences and political sympathies are scattered, as shown in the analysis of the results of the elections to the new Russian parliament in December 1993 in the following table (table 2).

Table 2 *Results of the federation-wide election to the State Duma in the Primorskii krai by party consideration compared With Russia as a whole and Nizhnii Novgorod oblast', 12 December 1993 (in % of the total vote)*

Party	Russia	Primorskii *krai*	Nizhnii Novgorod *oblast'*
Liberal Democratic Party	22.8	21.9	19.2
Russia's Choice	15.4	13.2	13.4
Communist Party of RF	12.3	8.1	11.8
Woman of Russia	8.1	14.3	9.3
Agrarian Party	7.9	2.3	8.7
Yavlinskii-Boldyrev-Lukin	7.8	7.9	11.6
Party of Russian Unity & Accord	6.8	7.5	5.3
Democratic Party of Russia	5.5	6.8	6.8
Russian Movement for Dem.Reform	4.0	5.2	n.a.
Other	9.4	12.8	13.9

Source: *Compiled from* Kuranty, *28 December 1993: 1;* Utro Rossii, *16 December 1993: 1 and Cline, M. „Nizhnii Novgorod: A Regional View of the Russian Elections."* RFE/RL Research Report *3, no. 4 (28 January 1994): 51.*

One of the striking features was that the Communist Party and the Agrarian Party received a considerably smaller share of the vote in Primorskii *krai* than they did in both Russia as a whole and Nizhnii Novgorod *oblast'*, which was widely perceived as a region with a strong reputation for reform.[129] While Women of Russia got substantially stronger support in the Far Eastern region due to the prominence of its regional leader and former Yeltsin aide, Svetlana Goryacheva, the same importance of personalities applied to Nizhnii Novgorod for the Yavlinskii-Boldyrev-Lukin bloc, since Yavlinskii had chosen this region for his market reform experiment.[130]

There was not only a lower turnout in the 1993 elections compared with those before, but also a lot of confusion about different policies pursued by national parties in the regions. For example, while Zhirinovskii's party is widely perceived in the West as an ultra-nationalist party, the local office of this party joined the 'Club of Democrats' in Vladivostok and supported the former mayor Cherepkov.[131]

---

129 Hanson, P. „The Center versus the Periphery in Russian Economic Policy." *RFE/RL Research Report* 3, no. 17 (29 April 1994): 28.

130 For first results of this experiment see: Yavlinskii, G. (ed.). *Nizhegorodskii prolog. Ekonomika i politika v Rossii* [The Nizhnii Novgorod Prologue. Economics and Politics in Russia]. Nizhnii Novgorod/Moscow, 1992.

131 Interview with I. Sanachev.

Moreover, the activities of national political parties in Primorskii *krai* is also characterised by low membership and generally weak support as indicated in table 3.

Table 3 *Estimated membership and potential voters for leading national parties in Primorskii krai, September 1994 (in absolute figures)*

Party	Members	Potential Voters
Communist Party	150	20-30,000
Party of Russian Unity & Accord	100	n.a.
Social-Democratic Party	40	300-400
Russia's Choice	20-30	500
Democratic Party of Russia	15-20 200	
Party of Economic Freedom	15	150-200
Liberal-Democratic Party	5	n.a.

Note: *'Communist Parties' refers to both the Russian Comunist Workers Party and the Communist Party of the Russian Federation.*

Source: *Compiled from interviews with lecturers of the department of political science of the Far Eastern State University in Vladivostok, I. Sanachev and G. Kulikov, on 15 and 19 September 1994*

Although the estimates in table 3 are only tentative, they appear to support the notion of a revival of Communist Party structures, as has already been found in other Russian regions.[132] Members of the provincial Communist parties tried to integrate the Social-Democratic Party and the Democratic Party of Russia in a patriotic movement 'Accord in the Name of Russia',[133] but it remains open what real impact this could make on regional policy-making. The representation of political parties in the new regional Duma was only marginal, as was shown in table 1 above, and they could not organise strong opposition to the rise of authoritarian power in the province. In contrast, Nazdratenko became the Far Eastern coordinator of Chernomyrdin's centrist political bloc 'Our House-Russia' in spring 1995,[134] which gives him additional institutional backing for his power.

2.9 Mass media

Central and local mass media could be considered as one of the few forces of resistance against autocratic rule in the province. Critical journalists were denied of

---

132 For a strong influence of Communist parties in local politics in Altaiskii *krai*, for example, see: Kirkow (Kirkow, P. „Regional Politics and Market Reform in Russia: The Case of the Altai.“ *Europe-Asia Studies* 46 (1994), no. 7: 1182-1183). The Communist Party of the Russian Federation claimed in this region an active membership of 12,000 people in April 1994.

133 *Utro Rossii* 10 September 1994: 1.

134 *Segodnya* 13 May 1995: 2.

technical facilities to carry on with their reporting and their lifes were under permanent threat. The commercial TV channel 'PKTV' was prevented from running its programmes, after compromising Nazdratenko's reputation by showing him publicly embracing putsch leader, Alexander Rutskoi, and an assassination attempt was made on the author of this programme, M.Voznesenskii, on 15 November 1993.[135] Under the command of Lebedinets, fierce attacks were launched against the oppositional newspapers *Bolshoi Vladivostok* and *Utro Rossii*. Both were suspended on 21 March 1994, when it was claimed that there was a shortage of paper, while electricity and heating in their offices were switched off.[136]

Critical journalists were regularly beaten up by hired criminal gangs.[137] When the former deputy governor and member of PAKT, Shkrabov, started to express a different opinion to that of Nazdratenko's team, there was an attempt to sack him as editor-in-chief and to suspend his newspaper *Krasnoe znamya*.[138] The regional publisher's monopoly, *Dal'press*, was under Nazdratenko's control and could deny newspapers of paper, office space and other technical facilities.[139] For example, the sale of those central newspapers, which kept critically reporting on the events in Primorskii *krai*, was restricted under the pretext that there was no sufficient paper.[140]

2.10 Criminal underworld

The involvement of criminal gangs in local politics, privatisation and foreign economic activities is evident, but it is hard to estimate their real impact on policy-making in the province. This is not surprising for a region, which used to be a closed military district for many decades, subjecting.people under military rule and patron-client relations, and where now many military servicemen are made redundant. Criminal activities are not only pouring in all capillaries of social life, but they produced a special public atmosphere of compliance and patronage.

---

135 *Izvestiya* 1 December 1993: 5. Nazdratenko reportedly threatened Voznesenskii's wife: 'You know that I could liquidate you physically, but I wouldn't do it.' (*Novoe vremya* 1990, no. 40: 13). He also started his populist daily programmes 'The Governor's Hour' on local television to brainwash the population. One has to bear in mind that TV became the main source of information for ordinary Russian people in recent years, while the sale of newspapers dropped rapidly.

136 *Izvestiya* 6 April 1994: 2.

137 *Kommersant-Daily* 22 July 1994: 14.

138 *Utro Rossii* 17 September 1994: 2.

139 *Kommersant-Daily* 14 December 1994: 3.

140 *Izvestiya* 17 November 1994: 1.

Criminal gangs established close relations with the executive branch. They were reported to have offered their services to the regional administration.[141] Foreign visitors were frequently attacked and robbed, while information on their place of residency was reportedly released by local administrations.[142] One clear example of their methods and political influence was provided by the criminal gang *Sistema*, which hired highest ranking security officers from the Pacific Fleet and copied, with their help, the structure of the fleet's espionage system to carry out racketing and blackmail of new commercial structures.[143] A sophisticated scheme was set up to acquire the control package of shares in the privatisation of *Vostokrybkholodflota*.[144] Each district in Vladivostok has its own criminal hierarchy with a *Polozhenets* on top, who sorts out troubles between the groupings and disposes over money. This structure not only parallels official state power, but former procurators and police officers are now working for the criminal underworld.

2.11 Trade unions

Trade unions in the region are still dominated by former structures and officials, which makes them more susceptible to be functionalised by the new political authorities. Industrial action gets then easily linked with political demands. This was the case in a joint statement by trade unions of mining companies, the VPK and fishing industries issued to the Russian government in protest of high inflation, rising unemployment and falling standards of living.[145] Economic and political demands were reinforced by the new regional Duma, announcing industrial action if the demands would not be met.[146] About 4,000 miners employed in 24 different pits striked reportedly in the first quarter of 1995 alone.[147] The rising political importance of trade unions could not be ignored by governor Nazdratenko, who sought their political support in his conflict with central authorities.[148]

---

141 *Novoe vremya* 1994, no. 40: 14.
142 *Segodnya* 5 November 1994: 3.
143 *Utro Rossii* 12 May 95: 2-3.
144 *Utro Rossii* 13 May 1995: 2.
145 *Delovoi mir* 28 October 1994: 1.
146 *Utro Rossii* 30 March 1995: 1.
147 *Utro Rossii* 27 April 1995: 2.
148 *Utro Rossii* 5 November 1994: 1.

3 Main Regional Policy Issues

While the first section focused on main policy actors and institutions in terms of their impact on regional policy-making, this one examines more complex issues of centre-periphery relations, economic reform, nationality policy and environmental problems.

3.1 The Open Showdown with Moscow

At a press conference on 20 March 1994, just a few days after Cherepkov was evicted from his office by armed police, Nazdratenko announced not only the delay of elections to the new regional parliament until October 1994, but also his renewed demand for a special economic status for the province as well as the administrative subordination of the Kurile islands to the jurisdiction of Primorskii *krai*.[149] These two demands remained among the most important regional policy issues challenging the centre for most of 1994.[150]

In summer 1994, Nazdratenko announced still more assertively his proposal to the President to subordinate the Kurile islands to his (Nazdratenko's) control, claiming to have a stronger position than Sakhalin *oblast'* officials to help the islands' economic problems. This came at the time when his own campaign to become the elected governor started. It was then considered as an additional attempt to get votes from fishermen as a potentially supportive electorate.[151] Using the fact of a difficult demographic situation with a high rate of out-migration in 1993 (261 from a total population of about 5,000 in the Northern Kurile islands),[152] Nazdratenko accused the Sakhalin authorities of not supporting these territories and promised large investments by Primorskii *krai* fishing and mining companies, if these islands would be put under his rule.[153] As with fighting the mass influx of Chinese people into Russian territory, he tried to present himself again as the defender of Russian national interests, since all four islands are still under territorial dispute with Japan.

---

149 *Izvestiya* 22 March 1994: 1.

150 The third important issue was that of Nazdratenko's attempt at scheduling the election of the governor of Primorskii *krai* for 7 October 1994, a devise to get a democratic mandate to concentrate more authoritarian power in his hands, since the success of his manipulated re-election was without any doubt. This challenge of the centre will be discussed below.

151 *Kommersant-Daily* 3 August 1994: 3.

152 The Southern Kurile islands suffered an out-migration of 931 people in 1993, but no figures for their total population were given in this report (*Segodnya* 6 September 1994: 3).

153 *Segodnya* 6 September 1994: 3.

Yeltsin passed Nazdratenko's proposal on to governmental authorities for 'further investigation',[154] but more important was that Nazdratenko could rely on strong encouragement by top officials in Moscow, notably the head of the Russian secret service, S.Stepashin, who mentioned the possibility of an administrative fusion of Sakhalin *oblast'* and the Kurile islands with Primorskii *krai* at a meeting with businessmen in Nakhodka in June 1994.[155]

Nazdratenko also reiterated in summer 1994 his intention to get a special economic status granted to the province. He announced that a development programme for his region had been elaborated which included a 'preferential tax and investment policy regime for two to three years'.[156] However, this press release could be a big understatement of the scale of the special regime plans. In March 1994, he had already given a hint of a long term 'Hong Kong solution' during an interview for the American business journal *GQ*. The internal version of his economic programme, which was made available to this author in September 1994, contained demands adding up to a total of R 175.3 trn (in August 1994 prices) to be paid by federal institutions in the period up to 2010.[157]

These demands included among others: (1) higher revenues for regional authorities from state-controlled transit cargoes and freight transport which are crossing provincial territory; (2) federal subsidies for fuel and energy; (3) additional payments for regional enterprises in form of a special federal programme; (4) the consignment of all federal taxes to the region for a period of 10 years; (5) the consignment of all state customs duties to the region for a period of four years; and (6) restricted entering to the province for non-residents for a period of 10 years. Nazdratenko justified these requirements later on the grounds that the region faced high transport charges for shipments from the rest of Russia, and that customs duties, export quotas and most taxes were controlled by central authorities.[158]

The third and politically most serious challenge to the centre was Nazdratenko's announcement of the election of the governor of Primorskii *krai*, which was to take place on 7 October 1994 in the form of an 'experiment'.[159] After the October 1993 events, Yeltsin had reasserted his right to appoint heads of regional administrations

---

154 *Kommersant-Daily* 18 August 1994: 3.

155 *Rossiiskie vesti* 1 October 1994: 2.

156 *Rossiiskie vesti* 19 July 1994: 2.

157 *Rezhim khozyaistvovaniya dlya ekonomicheskoi stabilizatsii i razvitiya Primorskogo kraya*. Kraevaya administratsiya Primorskogo kraya Vladivostok, 1994: 12 (mimeo).

158 BBC interview with Nazdratenko on 1 October 1994.

159 *Kommersant-Daily* 30 July 1994: 3.

(a special power which he was granted in late 1991 and later deprived of by the old Supreme Soviet), but the new Russian constitution, adopted in December 1993, left open whether governors are to be elected or appointed by the President.[160] The date when there would be elections of governors was a matter of dispute, but, in the case of Primorskii *krai*, it was peculiar that this election was scheduled before the elections of the new regional parliament on 23 October 1994, which alone would have the legislative power to call for elections of the head of the executive body.[161]

Five local democratic parties united to fight Nazdratenko in this election and announced Igor Ustinov, the former head of the Nakhodka FEZ administration and current deputy of the State Duma, as their candidate.[162] However, Nazdratenko took unilaterally the decision that 32,000 signatures would be necessary to be registered as a candidate (the Russian legislature requires merely 10,000) in an attempt to make sure that he would not face any serious competition.[163] Ustinov could collect only 25,000 signatures,[164] which left merely two 'puppet opponents', who were promoted by Nazdratenko to give the whole campaign a democratic appearance.

This scheduled election had strong political implications. It was widely believed that this was a new attempt at separating the region from the Russian Federation. A new constitution of the province was already in preparation,[165] as the President requested from all provinces, and the day after the election a referendum could have been called for setting up an independent republic.[166] Only when the leaders of the democratic fractions in the State Duma, Egor Gaidar, Boris Fedorov and Grigorii Yavlinskii, published a report in late September following their independent investigation of human rights' abuses, corruption and authoritarian power in the region,[167] was the attention of the Russian public attracted. At this point, President

---

160 Wishnevsky, J. „Problems of Russian Regional Leadership." *RFE/RL Research Report* 3, no. 19, 13 May 1994: 9.

161 *Kommersant-Daily* 12 August 1994: 3.

162 *Kommersant-Daily* 19 August 1994: 3. is worth noting that Ustinov's economic programme, which was summarised in *Kommersant-Daily* (19 August 1994: 3), did not differ substantially from Nazdratenko's project. He also demanded a special economic status and relied on the support of the traditional industrial lobby.

163 *Segodnya* 29 September 1994: 2.

164 This author was told that Ustinov received 10,000 signatures from Cherepkov to enhance Ustinov's chances (Interview with I. Sanachev).

165 *Vladivostok* 20 September 1994: 4.

166 *Rossiiskie vesti* 1 October 1994: 2.

167 *Segodnya* 29 September 1994: 2.

Yeltsin issued a new decree to strengthen his power in appointing governors until 1996.[168]

3.2 Moscow's position

In Moscow, opposition to Nazdratenko's autocratic power is of a somewhat ambiguous nature. Although the State Duma had a hearing on human rights' abuses in the Primorskii *krai* on 5 October 1994 [169]and several governmental commissions had already been sent to the region to investigate, Nazdratenko is still, at the time of writing, firmly in power. The only explanation for this seems to be that certain top officials in the centre have a particular interest in keeping such an authoritarian governor in power in Russia's periphery.

In his attempt to schedule the election of the governor of Primorskii *krai* for October 1994, Nazdratenko got the backing from influential national leaders. The head of the President's administration, Sergei Filatov, tried to delay Yeltsin's new decree, which would reassert the delay of elections of provincial governors until the next Presidential elections in 1996, until the last minute.[170] The chairman of the Federation Council, Vladimir Shumeiko, supported publicly the election of the governor in Primorskii *krai*.[171] Apart from Nazdratenko's allies Stepashin and Ilyushin, who were already mentioned above, he could also use his contacts with the attorney general, Alexei Ilyushenko, to delay all investigations against him when he was accused of violating human rights.[172] Direct access to the office of Vice-Prime Minister, Oleg Soskovets, was used while lobbying for preferential treatment.[173] Soskovets was Nazdratenko's boss as the former Minister for Metallurgy in the USSR,[174] when the latter still worked as the director of the mining company *Vostok* in 1991. The Russian Vice-Prime Minister also headed several governmental meetings to solve financial problems in Primorskii *krai*.[175]

The positions of President Yeltsin and Prime Minister Chernomyrdin are ambivalent. Nazdratenko accompanied them frequently when they went on state

---

168 *Rossiiskie vesti* 7 October 1994: 1.
169 *Segodnya* 4 October 1994: 2.
170 *Segodnya* 29 September 1994: 2.
171 *Segodnya* 5 October 1994: 2.
172 *Utro Rossii* 18 March 1994: 1.
173 Interview with I. Sanachev.
174 *Izvestiya* 19 January 1995: 5.
175 *Utro Rossii* 29 October 1994: 1.

visits to Asian countries. Yeltsin rewarded Nazdratenko with the medal 'For Personal Bravery' after the rather mysterious explosion at an ammunition store in Novonezhino in May 1994.[176] Nazdratenko reportedly used to spent his weekends in the President's dacha. In late 1994, Nazdratenko was invited to join the President's Club, an infomal group of advisers consisting of 30 members.[177]

Chernomyrdin reportedly supported Nazdratenko's election as governor scheduled for October 1994.[178] The Russian Prime Minister was also a strong supporter of subsidies for the region to keep prices for electricity at a level of R 40 per kWh. For this purpose, R 134 bn were received in the first quarter of 1994.[179] However, the centre seems to have used these subsidies also as a strong political lever, since they were not given after the beginning of August 1994, when Nazdratenko announced the election of the governor, while payments were resumed after he backed down.[180]

This suggests an ambiguous and dangerous policy on the part of national leaders. They were apparently not prepared to challenge authoritarian rule by politicians like Nazdratenko even at the price of human rights' abuses, corruption and crime; at the same time, they seem to have resisted an attempt on his part to acquire democratic legitimacy. The latter element in Yeltsin's and Chernomyrdin's handling of Nazdratenko - regardless of whether the elections would have been rigged (they probably would have been) - suggests a fear of leaders in the regions who could claim a popular mandate more recent than the President's.

3.3 Economic policy

Since regional authorities in Russia had to implement economic reform and institutional restructuring, this section also examines their impact on economic change in Primorskii *krai*. Quantitative data are provided in comparison to the Russian average to draw some preliminary conclusions on their attitude towards market reform, focusing on privatisation, regional price policy, fiscal arrangements, capital investment and foreign trade in subsequent sections.[181]

---

176 *Kommersant-Daily* 12 August 1994: 3.

177 *Utro Rossii* 19 November 1994: 1.

178 *Utro Rossii* 13 October 1994: 2.

179 *Kommersant-Daily* 30 July 1994: 3.

180 *Kommersant-Daily* 14 October 1994: 11.

181 However, available quantitative data should be treated with considerable caution. Reported results on privatisation differed substantially between various provincial institutions, while budget figures were permanently corrected and non-registered retail trade and non-

3.3.1 Privatisation

Provincial officials played an important role in determining in which way and at what speed privatisation would be carried out as well as who the potential beneficiaries would be. Table 4 indicates results of privatisation of medium and large-sized enterprises by industrial sector relying on data provided from the regional committee of property administration.

Table 4 *Privatised medium and large-sized enterprises in Primorskii krai by some sectors of industry, 1 September 1994 (in absolute figures and % of applications)*

Sector of Industry	Applied	Privatised	%
Light industry	23	73	0.4
Food industry	107	181	6.8
Construction industry	172	462	6.7
Construction materials	73	152	0.5
Agricultural industry	323	2.0	100
Transport industry	73	4	5.5
Wholesale trade	622	33	7.1

Source: Osnovnye pokazateli khoda privatizatsii na territorii Primorskogo kraya po sostoyaniyu na 1 sentyabrya 1994. *Vladivostok: Komitet po upravleniyu gosudarstvennym imushchestvom Primorskogo kraya, 1994 (mimeo).*

Although figures for privatisation by industrial sector for Russia as a whole were not available, Primorskii *krai* probably lagged far behind the national average as a result of Nazdratenko's stop of privatisation in 'vital spheres of the economy' in August 1993, subjecting a large amount of enterprises under the control of the regional conglomerate PAKT. According to regional *Goskomstat* information, a total of 1,195 enterprises were privatised in Primorskii *krai* in the first quarter of 1995,[182] but this gives no indication of the number of all enterprises (including those not released for privatisation) in the region. One intriguing fact is that in the statistical report used in table 4 none of the defence-related sectors (machinebuilding and metalworking) nor those structures under state control (fuel and energy production) were included.

There was a somewhat greater availability of data for privatisation in the spheres of retail trade, public catering and services, as evidenced in table 5, but a great deal

---

licenced foreign trade remained unreported. Information on statistical data received from regional administrations and *Goskomstat* provincial offices will be preferred in this discussion, while adding some qualitative analysis for background information.

182 *Utro Rossii* 27 April 1995: 2.

of caution for interpretation is necessary here as well. In Vladivostok city, 250 outlets were reportedly privatised by the end of 1993, which amounted to 75.7% of the total according to official statistics.[183] However, the comparison with 1990, when Vladivostok had more than 1,000 shops, catering and service outlets, reveals that at least two-thirds of the original premises were restructured, closed or passed on to other commercial structures, without the city authorities getting control of them, which gives reason to doubt any favourable interpretation of the official statistics.

Table 5 *Results of small-scale privatisation in Primorskii krai compared with Russia as a whole, September-November 1994 (in absolute figures and % of applications)*

Sphere	Primorskii *krai* (1 Sept 1994)			Russia (Nov 1994)		
	Applied	Privatised	%	Applied	Privatised	%
Retail trade	811	680	83.8	84,857	57,703	68.0
Public catering	133	114	85.7	21,056	14,739	70.0
Services	361	288	79.8	38,451	29,992	78.0

Source: *Compiled from table 4 and* Russian Economic Trends *3 (1994), no.4: 97.*

By comparing tables 4 and 5, a certain pattern of privatisation policy becomes clear. While the region was fairly slow in medium and large-scale privatisation, its authorities adopted a high-speed small-scale privatisation with reported results far exceeding those of the Russian total even two months earlier.[184] But this resulted reportedly in the breakdown of retail trade and public catering in many rural areas in the province.[185] Moreover, the change in ownership rights did not necessarily lead to an improvement in the quality of provided services, with many new owners just closing down or trading with their premises,[186] while the region was, at the same time, 'flooded over' with cheap import products, particularly from neighbouring China.

---

183 *Utro Rossii* 11 December 1993: 2.

184 Slider (Slider, D. „Privatization in Russia's Regions." *Post-Soviet Affairs* 10 (1994), no. 4: 380) provided figures from the central privatisation committee (GKI) for medium and large-scale privatisation according to which Primorskii *krai* ranked among the regions with the highest results of privatised enterprises, but this was before voucher privatisation was stopped by Nazdratenko. His data for small-scale privatisation in the province by October 1993 (ibid.: 384) could rather be an understatement, since Primorskii *krai* was indicated among those provinces with the lowest results. This shows the difficulties with using central data, while not taking local reports and qualitative analyses into account at the same time.

185 *Utro Rossii* 21 April 1995: 2.

186 Competitive tenders and selling-off of leased premises, which were the most frequently used forms of small-scale privatisation in Russia, included special clauses prescribing a particular time period for maintaining the profile and workforce, but this was often ignored.

Regional authorities' attitude towards institutional restructuring is also reflected in results of private farming as shown in table 6.

Table 6 *Private farming in Primorskii krai compared with Russia as a whole, 1994-early 1995*

Indicators	Russia (1994)	Primorskii *krai* (first quarter 1995)	% of Russia
Number of private farms	279200	4022	1.4
Used arable land ('000 ha)	12005	673.3	0.6
Average size of land per private farm (ha and % of Russian average)	43.0	18.2	2.3
Average percentage of the total arable land in the examined territory	5.2	10.0	-

Source: *Compiled from* Russian Economic Trends *3 (1994), no.4: 69-70 and* Utro Rossii *27 April 1995: 3.*

Although 10% of the total arable land in Primorskii *krai* is privately owned (which is twice the amount of the Russian average), the average size of land per private farm amounts merely to less than half of the national average, which indicates a lower proportional total of arable land in this province.[187] However, one should not read too much out of these figures. In 1994, 20,000 ha of land were reportedly given to Cossacks for farming,[188] but it is not clear whether they really engaged in private farming, since they were used by regional authorities as an additional force to protect the Russian border against Chinese illegal migration.[189]

---

187 These results indicate that a critical mass of the number of private farms and privately used arable land seems to be achieved under current circumstances in early 1995, since the percentage figures are almost identical with those for the beginning of 1994 (Kirkow, P. „The Siberian and Far Eastern Challenge for New Centre-Periphery Relations in Russia: A Comparison between Altaiskii and Primorskii Kraya." In Gibson, J. & P. Hanson (eds.). *Transformation from Below. Local Power and the Political Economy of Post-Communist Transitions*. Cheltenham: Edward Elgar, 1995 (forthcoming), table 8). Although there were still high fluctuations with 1,780 private farms going bankrupt in the province in 1994 (*Utro Rossii*, 27 April 1995: 3), the 10% share of arable land privately used was maintained over the last two years.

188 *Utro Rossii* 25 October 1994: 3.

189 It was also reported that regional officials intend to give Cossacks in the region another 15.5 mn ha of state reserve land (*Utro Rossii* 25 October 1994: 3), which would make the above indicated figure of 73,300 ha of privately used land look fairly small. However, it is ironical that many private farmers in the province have to employ a few dozens of Chinese people if they want their business to survive (*Utro Rossii* 2 August 1994: 1 and 13 April 1995: 1).

Moreover, the committee for land reform of the regional administration had a distinguished anti-reform stance, calling for 'regulation of the state agro-industrial complex' and 'new cooperation'.[190]

3.3.2 Regional price policy

Regional authorities in most of the Russian regions had a considerable leverage over price liberalisation, developing a populist 'consumption bias', through which they tried to increase their votes at the ballot box by lowering transformation costs.[191] This applied also to the investigated region, where price controls impeded structural reforms and provincial officials had to pay an increasing bill for industrial and consumer price subsidies.

As outlined before, industrial prices for coal and electricity were heavily controlled by the Primorskii *krai* administration. For example, industrial enterprises in the region were charged for electricity with R 40 per kWh in mid-1994, while those in Sakhalin *oblast'* had to pay R 218 at the same time,[192] which amounted to a price difference of more than 1:5. As a consequence, payment arrears accumulated between coal mines, energy producers and industrial enterprises. Debts of *Primorskugol'* customers were reported to total R 70 bn by the end of 1994.[193] This became a vicious circle, since coal producers could not pay for used electricity either, and the only solution was considered in pressing for new subsidies and soft credits from the centre.

Table 7 compares the increase of the industrial price index (IPI) and consumer price index (CPI) in Primorskii *krai* with that in Russia as a whole and relates this to the increase in money supply.

190 *Utro Rossii* 13 April 1995: 2.

191 Berkowitz, 1994: 193.

192 Goskomstat Rossii (Primorskii Krai Office). *Nekotorye pokazateli, kharakterizuyushchie khod ekonomicheskikh reform, po Primorskomu krayu v sravnenii s drugimi regionami Sibiri i Dal'nego Vostoka na 1 iyulya 1994.* Vladivostok, 1994: 23.

193 *Utro Rossii* 24 December 1994: 1.

Table 7 *Comparison of increased IPI and CPI in Primorskii krai with Russia as a whole and rise of money supply, 1993-early 1995 (multiples to previous time period)*

Indicator	Russia			Primorskii *krai*			
	1993	1994	Q1'95	1993	Q3'94	Q1'95	
IPI	10.0	3.4	1.1	1	1.6	3.3	4.3
CPI	9.4	3.0	1.1	1	1.63	6	2.9
Money supply	n.a.	n.a.	1.1	1	3.8	5.7	1.2

Source: *Compiled from* Russian Economic Trends *3 (1994), no.4: 38;* Finansovye Izvestiya *18 May 1995: II;* Segodnya *25 May 1995: 2;* Utro Rossii *3 February 1994: 2;* Utro Rossii *29 October 1994: 2 and* Utro Rossii *27 April 95: 2.*

Increases of IPI and CPI in Primorskii *krai* exceeded the national average considerably in 1993 and early 1995, while the money supply in this region was above the increase of both IPI and CPI. This is probably due to two main reasons. First, its gateway location is linked with a large amount of 'shuttle trade', which increases the inflow of hard currency and the demand for rubles. The trade of Japanese second-hand cars in the province results in an additional inflow of Russian domestic currency from other parts of the country.

Second, there is also a large inflow of cash into the province due to the trade of shares of enterprises from Siberia and the Russian Far East at the Vladivostok stock exchange.[194] The total of its financial transactions amounted to R 7.37 bn in September 1994 alone [195]or US-$ 2.95 mn at that time. It paid reportedly R 3.5 bn in taxes into the regional budget in the first half of 1994.[196] The inflow of cash into Primorskii *krai* increased even further after the sale of 3.7% of *Gazprom* shares, the Russian leading gas company, at the Vladivostok stock exchange was announced in November 1994, which was apparently personally agreed between Nazdratenko and Prime Minister Chernomyrdin.[197] One per cent of *Gazprom* shares was estimated to be worth US-$ 2 bn,[198] which immediately unleashed financial speculations in which traders acquired options to buy shares in order to resell them afterwards.[199]

However, the considerably higher increase of IPI and CPI in Primorskii *krai* compared with the national average in the first quarter of 1995 is clearly a result of previous price controls in the region, which were not longer tenable by the end of

194 *Utro Rossii* 30 August 1994: 2.

195 *Utro Rossii* 4 October 1994: 1.

196 *Utro Rossii* 30 August 1994: 2.

197 *Segodnya* 5 November 1994: 2.

198 *Utro Rossii* 6 December 1994: 2.

199 *Kommersant-Daily* 9 November 1994: 5.

1994. Despite first signs of stabilisation in Russia as a whole in the first quarter of 1995, the substantial increase in money supply is still worrisome.[200]

3.3.3 Fiscal arrangements

The current federal system in Russia has no transparent, fair and consensus-based intra-governmental financial framework, but consists of a series of bilaterally bargained, ad hoc deals and has no clear equalisation formula, despite some modifications in 1994-95. With traditionally only a small percentage of Primorskii *krai* enterprises under local jurisdiction, as in the former Soviet Union generally, regional authorities possessed a quite meagre independent income base and depended almost entirely on union and republic subsidies and allocations handed down as a percentage of locally-collected but centrally-determined turnover taxes and personal income taxes. This high budgetary dependence on the centre did not change with the fiscal reform and introduction of new taxes (VAT, profit tax) in 1992.Table 8 indicates a tendency of an increasing guaranteed income in the province.

Table 8 *Main income sources of the consolidated budget of Primorskii krai, 1992 - mid-1994 (in mn R and % of total)*

Income Source	1992	%	1993	%	mid-1994	%
Total	35,829	100.0	751,905	100.0	820,074	100.0
Profit tax	9,894	27.6	212,041	28.2	217,965	26.6
VAT	3,235	9.0	93,701	12.5	87,707	10.7
Personal income tax	7,819	21.8	97,088	12.9	142,161	17.3
Excise duties	1,411	3.9	15,516	2.0	12,048	1.5
Other	4,654	13.0	181,698	24.2	154,149	18.8
Total guaranteed income	27,013	75.4	600,044	79.8	614,030	74.9
Subsidies	-	-	72,923	9.7	195,944	23.9
Federal budget	7,286	20.3	73,792	9.8	-	-
Federal loans	1,526	4.3	5,146	0.7	10,100	1.2

Note: *Because of rounded absolute figures, percentage figures do not always add to 100.0%.*

Source: *Compiled from interviews with the deputy heads of the budget office of the Primorskii* krai *administration, L.Popova, on 13 and 20 September 1993, and V.Rybakova on 7 September 1994.*

200 The former adviser to Prime Minister, Chernomyrdin, and current director of the Moscow-based Institute of Economic Analysis, Andrei Illarionov, estimated the increase of money supply at 10% for the first quarter of 1995 and another 20% in April 1995 alone (*Segodnya* 25 May 1995: 2).

Although mid-1994 figures do not reflect the real picture due to end of year transfers from the federal and local budgets, table 8 shows that regional authorities depended to one-fourth of the budgetary income from federal transfers, loans and subsidies for the examined period. There seem also to be problems with the tax collection system, particularly with personal income tax, the share of which decreased substantially between 1992 and 1993, probably because of hidden, unreported income or a real decline in personal income.

There were some minor modifications of the Russian fiscal system in 1994-95, including the set up of a federal fund for the financial support of regions as a first attempt at equalising budgetary income between Russian provinces, from which Primorskii *krai* got a 2.8% share allotted in 1995 or, in absolute terms, R 416 bn.[201] However, bearing in mind the continuing inflation in 1995, this will probably not change substantially the financial situation in the region. In contrast, revenue from the 15 local taxes in the province provided reportedly less than 10% of the regional budget income in 1994, while some of the local taxes (auctions and lotteries, ownership of dogs) could be considered as nuisance taxes.[202]

The two main spheres of expenditure in the region in 1992-94 were the regional economy and the social and cultural sphere as indicated in table 9.

---

201 *Rossiiskie vesti* 7 April 1995: 4.
202 *Utro Rossii* 20 April 1995: 3.

Table 9 *Main spheres of expenditure of the consolidated budget of Primorskii krai, 1992-mid-1994 (in mn R and as % of total)*

Sphere of Expenditure	1992	%	1993	%	mid-1994	%
Total	31,893	100.0	513,541	100.0	795,936	100.0
Regional economy	13,242	41.5	245,659	47.8	375,287	47.1
of which:						
Agriculture	573	1.8	33,076	6.4	n.a.	-
Transport	1,446	4.5	19,122	3.7	n.a.	-
Housing	1,030	3.2	163,800	31.9	n.a.	-
Other	10,193	32.0	29,661	5.8	n.a.	-
Social and cultural sphere	14,779	46.4	199,489	38.8	306,967	38.6
of which:						
Education	6,928	21.7	99,482	19.4	164,452	20.7
Culture	596	1.9	6,984	1.3	13,462	1.7
Health and sports	6,499	20.4	85,912	16.7	118,465	14.9
Social services	756	2.4	7,111	1.4	10,588	1.3
Administration	919	2.9	13,902	2.7	22,847	2.9
Other	2,953	9.2	54,491	10.6	90,835	11.4

Note: *Because of rounded absolute figures, percentage figures do not always add to 100.0%. It also appears that the figure for 'housing' in 1992 is not quite accurate, bearing in mind the traditional high subsidies for housing and its high proportional percentage in 1993.*

Source: *See table 8*

The regional economy experienced increasing total expenditure in 1993, while the social and cultural sphere had a corresponding decline of almost the same percentage share, most conspicuously, in the health service. Percentage shares for different spheres of expenditure were remarkably stable in 1993 and mid-1994. Moreover, what becomes clear by comparing the data in tables 8 and 9 is that the province did not have a budget deficit during the examined period, which was virtually impossible because Russian regional authorities couldn't increase the money supply by printing new money and the issue of municipal bonds was only in its infancy.

However, official budgetary figures do not reflect the whole picture, since various other flows of public money are not included in them. Table 10 gives a rough estimate of actual regional public-sector income and expenditure in the region in 1993-94, incorporating extra-budgetary resources.

Table 10 *Aggregated budgetary and extra-budgetary income and expenditure in Primorskii krai, 1993 - mid-1994 (in bn R)*

Source	Income		Expenditure	
	1993	mid-94	1993	mid-94
Total regional budget	751.9	820.1	513.5	795.9
Central Bank soft credit	45.4	n.a.	45.4	n.a.
Memorandum items	58.0	377.4	58.0	377.4
Total	855.3	1,197.5	616.9	1,173.3

Note: *'Memorandum items' contain 'off-budget funds', finances from state programmes and subsidies.*

Source: *Compiled from several issues of UR and interviews with officials in the region in 1994.*

Table 10 included federal extra-budgetary resources, or 'off-budget funds', which are channelled through federal institutions at the regional and local level (pension fund, social insurance fund, employment fund, etc.), regional extra-budgetary funds, state programmes, and certain subsidies and soft credits. These resources provide much more scope for autonomous regional development than official statistics would reveal, and help to account for the bargaining power different regions have in reality. These resources were frequently used to meet increasing budgetary expenditures.[203]

3.3.4 Capital investment

One important issue of economic transformation is to find new forms of resource allocation by which the traditional state dominance in investment policy has to be reduced, while private entrepreneurs and foreign investors are expected to play a much more important role. Table 11 shows that enterprises' own funds became a major source of capital investment in recent years, while state investment went mainly in the fuel and energy sector, agriculture, and the defence and coal industries.

---

203 The provincial pension fund provided R25 bn in July 1994 for Nazdratenko's populist measures in his pre-election campaign (interview with the head of the Primorskii *krai* pension fund, P. Nazarov, on 20 September 1994).

Table 11 *Capital Investment by Sources of Financing in Primorskii krai Compared with Russia as a Whole, 1994 (in % of total)*

Source of Investment	Russia (1994)	Primorskii *krai* (mid-1994)
Total	100.0	100.0
State investment	24.1	27.0
from federal budget	(13.6)	(14.1)
from sub-national budgets	(10.5)	(12.9)
Preferential state credits	1.4	1.4
Centralised off-budget investment fund	5.9	7.8
Enterprises' funds (own and borrowed)	64.5	63.0
Joint ventures and foreign firms	4.1	0.8

Source: *Compiled from* Russian Economic Trends *3 (1994), no.4: 68 and* Utro Rossii *28 July 94: 3.*

Percentage shares of investment sources are remarkably similar between Russia as a whole and the investigated region. However, the 0.8% share of foreign investment in Primorskii *krai* is somewhat surprising for such a gateway region, but probably due to the frightening criminal situation in the province as discussed before. The cities of Vladivostok and Nakhodka have certainly a higher share of foreign investment, which amounted for the latter, for example, to 18.4% in the first quarter of 1995.[204] Moreover, the use of mid-1994 figures could also deviate the results.

3.3.5 Foreign trade

Liberalisation of the regional economies is one of the main cornerstones of economic change in Russian provinces. In terms of revenues generated from foreign trade, Primorskii *krai* should be naturally in a more advantageous position than other Russian regions due to its close geographical location to Asian-Pacific markets and its disposition of resources that are tradable on the world market, mainly fish and precious metals.

---

204 *Utro Rossii* 27 April 1995: 3.

Table 12 *Foreign trade activities of Primorskii krai compared with Russia as a whole, 1993-94 (in mn US-$ and % of Russia)*

Indicator	Russia		Primorskii *krai*			
	1993	1994	1993	%	Q3'94	%
Exports	112,000	83,000	442.3	0.4	279.9	-
Imports	75,100	66,600	253.0	0.3	118.4	-
Freight transport (in mn t)	3,600	n.a.	45.0	1.2	26.7	-

Note: *RF exports include gold, but exclude gold swaps. RF imports include non-registered 'shuttle trade'. Primorskii* krai *data include only trade with non-CIS countries. Freight transport includes export and import cargos.*

Source: *Compiled from* Russian Economic Trends *3 (1994), no.4: 73-81;* Ekonomika i zhizn', *no.6 (February 1994): 7;* Utro Rossii, *3 February 1994: 2 and* Utro Rossii, *29 October 1994: 2.*

For a region with 1.5% of the Russian population, Primorskii *krai's* percentage share in exports and imports was far below the national average and confirms earlier findings, that foreign investors were extremely cautious to get involved in official trade activities under conditions of autocratic political rule. If one would include unreported 'shuttle trade', the share of the region's foreign economic activity would probably increase significantly, but it is hard to estimate what real difference it would make. In contrast, the incorporation of figures for trade with CIS countries in this statistical analysis would probably not make much difference.[205] However, figures for freight transport also indicate that capacity was underutilised. The volume of trade loadings had reportedly decreased to 78% in the province in the third quarter of 1994.[206] This is mainly due to relatively high domestic tariffs for transport over long distances from and to European Russia.

As in most of the other Russian regions, the export structure of this province was dominated by natural resources as shown in table 13, while consumer goods, machinery and equipment were mostly imported. While Russia as a whole had a clear domination of fuel, minerals and metals in its export structure, exporters from Primorskii *krai* were mainly selling fish products and lumber and wood products on the foreign market. In 1994, 70% of the total catch of the region's fishing fleet was reportedly exported to Asian-Pacific countries.[207] The export of predominantly

---

205 The region's exports to non-CIS countries amounted to US-$ 99.4 mn in the first quarter of 1995 compared with only $ 0.7 mn with CIS-countries (*Utro Rossii* 27 April 1995: 3), which makes trade with the latter category statistically almost negligible.

206 *Utro Rossii* 29 October 1994: 2.

207 *Utro Rossii* 22 April 1995: 1.

primary products is a clear indication that diversification has not taken place during recent economic reform.

Table 13 *Export Structure of Primorskii* krai *Compared with Russia as a Whole, 1993-94 (non-CIS, in % of total in US-$ prices)*

Export products	Russia		Primorskii *krai*
	1993	1994	1993
Total	100.0	100.0	100.0
Machinery and equipment	6.5	5.3	n.a.
Fuel, minerals and metals	63.7	66.7	n.a.
Food products (fish)	2.7	2.8	75.8
Lumber and wood products	3.7	3.8	15.1
Chemicals (fertilizers)	3.0	4.2	1.9
Other	20.4	17.2	-

Source: *Compiled from* Russian Economic Trends *3 (1994), no.4: 76-78 and Komitet po vneshne-ekonomicheskim i regional'nym svyazyam administratsii Primorskogo kraya.* Vneshne-ekonomicheskie svyazi Primorskogo kraya: sostoyanie, problemy, perspektivy. *Vladivostok, 1994: 9 (mimeo).*

Finally, in contrast to comparatively low officially registered exports, there was an above national average import of consumer goods in Primorskii *krai*, which is certainly due to the region's geographical proximity to the Asian-Pacific market.

3.4 Nationality policy

According to the 1989 census, the population of the investigated region consisted mainly of Russian nationality (85.9%), while Ukrainians amounted to 8.1% and Belorussians to 0.9%.[208] Although there are no figures available for out-migration by nationality, one can probably assume that the percentage share of Ukrainians is currently much lower, but the dominance of Russian nationality is still evident. This was reinforced by the nationalist stance of the regional leadership and its xenophobic paranoia against all non-Russian nationalities.

This applied particularly to people from neighbouring China. In the border town of Ussuriisk, local officials declared Chinese traders as criminal elements, intimidated them with armed police and stopped all foreigners from trading at the local market.[209] According to witnesses, Chinese people were regularly robbed and beaten up by the police, while a special repatriation camp for Chinese citizen was set up in one of the suburbs of Vladivostok during the police operation 'Foreigner',

208 Goskomstat RSFSR, *Natsional'nyi sostav naseleniya SSSR. Po dannym Vsesoyuznoi perepisi naseleniya 1989 goda*. Moscow, 1990.

209 *Utro Rossii* 25 October 1994: 2.

from which arrested people could only get free after paying US-$ 300 to the police.[210] This was encouraged by the Russian central press, which reported about mass in-migration of Chinese people, the robbery of Russian resources and the set up of Chinatowns on Russian territory, which could lead, according to Russian commentators, to renewed territorial claims.[211] One of the few realistic reports in the Russian central press was published in *Izvestiya*,[212] in which the author dismissed the Russian hysteria about a 'silent colonisation' by the Chinese, after he carried out close investigations in the Russian bordering regions and conducted interviews with their governors.

However, this xenophobic atmosphere was used by Nazdratenko to present himself as the defender of Russian nationalist interests in the periphery and to denounce the 1991 Russo-Chinese treaty on border demarcation in early 1995, declaring the 1,500 ha of territory under question as 'strategically important'.[213] This was reiterated by the new regional Duma,[214] effectively embarrassing foreign minister Kozyrev before he left for his official visit to China.[215] This was in striking contradiction to the region's destiny as one of Russia's gateways for active integration into the world economy. But the below national average data on foreign investment and foreign trade provided above are a logical consequence of this nationalist attitude by its leadership. However, ordinary people in the region do, in their majority, not share these positions. A public survey conducted in several Far Eastern provinces showed that only 20% of the respondants think that Russian interests are threatened by the 1991 Russo-Chinese treaty.[216]

Nevertheless, Nazdratenko pressed ahead with his policy of local protectionism, which clearly favoured business interests of the PAKT conglomerate. He gave reportedly the local secret service full freedom to investigate and prosecute foreign

---

210 *Segodnya* 3 March 1995: 6.

211 Figures on Chinese illegal migration into Russia published by Russian sources are highly contradictive. *Kommersant-Daily* (5 November 1994: 4) claimed that 5 mn Chinese people lived in Eastern Siberia and the Russian Far East in late 1994, while *Segodnya* (3 March 1995: 6) reported 2 mn for Russia as a whole. *Delovoi mir* 6-12 March 1995: 42.

212 *Izvestiya* 16 March 1995: 3.

213 *Segodnya* 14 February 1995: 2. is interesting to note that Nazdratenko voted, as a former deputy of the Russian Supreme Soviet, for the ratification of this treaty in 1991 (*Rossiiskie Vesti* 16 March 1995: 2).

214 *Segodnya* 23 February 1995: 2.

215 *Izvestiya* 3 March 1995: 3.

216 *Segodnya* 4 March 1995: 3. This was confirmed by another survey, concluding that entrepreneurs of small and medium-scale businesses and the majority of ordinary people in this province have a rather positive attitude towards Chinese citizen (*Segodnya* 25 March 1995: 2).

businessmen, independently of their nationality.[217] The war in Chechnya was used to legitimise attacks against Chechen people, who allegedly controlled the car import business and several banks in Nakhodka.[218] All attempts at setting up autonomous territories by indigenous people in the North of the province were rigorously opposed.[219] This indicated not only a fear of outside control of provincial enterprises by non-residents, but also of local self-government by residents. While authorities in Primorskii *krai* tried to regulate the influx of Chinese citizen through employing 15,000 Chinese people under official contract,[220] first voices were raised, after Russian regional officials stopped visa-free entry for Chinese citizen in late 1993, that new shortages of consumer goods appeared on Russian territory.[221]

3.5 Environmental issues

The natural environment in Primorskii *krai*, particularly unique biotopes in the northern part, is under severe threat through the ruthless extraction of natural resources (fishing, logging, precious metals), poaching of rare animals (Siberian tiger) and the scrap of military hardware. Primorskii *krai* became a major junction of Russian arms deals, where stockpiles of ammunition are frequently exploding due to poor maintenance. Moreover, 1,700 t of radioactive material are reportedly stored in the province,[222] with a large amount of nuclear waste simply being dumped to the sea.[223] After Japanese officials raised their concern and offered help to process nuclear waste, Nazdratenko sensed a new business opportunity and wanted to prevent Moscow's officials to get involved.[224] His concern about outside control became clear after 70 kg of non-registered plutonium were reportedly discovered while radioactive material was recycled by the Japanese, which would be sufficient to produce eight nuclear warheads.[225]

---

217 *Segodnya* 29 November 1994: 3.

218 *Segodnya* 21 December 1994: 2.

219 *Utro Rossii* 20 April 1995: 2.

220 *Delovoi mir* 26 December 1994-1 January 1995: 44.

221 *Izvestiya* 16 March 1995: 3.

222 *Izvestiya* 3 November 1994: 4.

223 For spots of the Russian Pacific Fleet dumping radioactive material to the Sea of Japan, see BBC-film 'Lord of the East'.

224 *Izvestiya* 2 December 1994: 3.

225 *Izvestiya* 29 December 1994: 5.

4 Conclusions and Outlook

Although Nazdratenko's apparently omnipotent power has been cut short in October 1994, at the time of writing, he is still firmly in control of his public office and private business.[226] While some of the leading executives of PAKT defected (Pavlov, Shkrabov), Nazdratenko's power base, which is represented by the regional management *nomenklatura*, is still intact. The regional Duma, which started its legislative work after the re-elections in mid-January 1995, is mainly composed of local heads of administration (who were appointed by Nazdratenko before), managers and the military, headed by Nazdratenko's close ally and former chief of staff, Igor Lebedinets. Thus, there is a complete subordination of the legislative branch under the executive administration.

Moreover, the judiciary at the law courts provide no guarantee of due process and proper legal order in the region. Oppositional political forces can be brutally intimidated and suppressed with the help of criminal gangs. The local media can be muzzled. Finally, national leaders in Moscow seem not only to have no real leverage over Nazdratenko (which is a remarkable feature of current centre-periphery relations in Russia, considering that Nazdratenko was supposed to be a Yeltsin appointee), but they also appear to have a strong interest in keeping such an autocratic politician in power in a peripheral province, which is perceived to be vital for Russian national interests. Thus, there seems to be a real danger for regional warlordism and little constraint on authoritarian power.

This applies particularly to institutional arrangements. Nazdratenko controls not only the appointment of officials of both the regional executive and legislative branches, but also of authorities of the federal structures in his province (army, police, tax inspection). He could simply capitalise on the fact that institutional arrangements in Russian centre-periphery relations remained blurred, administrative competences were not clearly defined and that Moscow did not draw a clear line between central and provincial/local property and taxes which left the struggle for control over economic resources open-ended. Most importantly, there were a number of contentious constitutional issues in which shared functions between the centre and standard provinces (ownership of territorial resources, foreign trade) were

---

226 A the time of writing, it is still not clear whether Nazdratenko has any ambitions for higher political office in Moscow. He was apparently offered the job of the head of the federal committee for precious metals, which would be the rank of a minister, but he refused (*Kommersant-Daily* 29 October 1994: 3).

not clearly defined. The sheer mountain of contradictory central decrees and regulations made regional authorities to interpret law to their own advantage.

This also strengthened existing elitist policies and vertical networks of patron-client relations in Russian regions. Not functional separation of politics and economics at the provincial level, but institutional entanglement and local corporatism appear to drive the dynamics of Russian regional development. This could confine economic activity to particular clusters of regions and strengthen regional monopolies. Instead of powerful central branch ministries, Russia might end up with all-embracing financial-industrial groups growing along regional lines. One might speculate whether an organisation like PAKT can succeed in monopolising the regional economy in the long term, in particular if operating in geographic proximity to leading financial and trade centres like Japan and South Korea, but it can clearly slow down the development of an open and competitive regional economy in the short term.

For the last few years, Vladivostok became one of the main centres of drug trafficking, arms deals and money laundering in Russia. Its autocratic leadership, pursuing a policy of insider control and administrative protectionism of the economy, strong nationalism and political suppression of all oppositional forces, could be on the best way to marginalise the city's potential to take on a role for Russia what is Palermo for Italy. Hopes for a successful transformation from a formerly closed military fortress to a gateway for active integration of the Russian economy into the world market, even in Nazdratenko's vision of an authoritarian Hong Kong solution, could then be buried soon.

13

A Search for Place and Time: Siberia between Russia and Moscow

Mikhail Rozhanskii

Libraries in Irkutsk get newspapers and any other informational or analytical materials from the neighbouring *krais*, *oblasts* and republics only from time to time. The editorial rooms of Irkutsk newspapers do not have these materials and newspapers (not even all 'regional' newspapers to be found there) and the same applies the library of the local administration or that of the legislative assembly. The 'Siberian Accord' does nothing to fill this gap – a gap which is just not acknowledged. The *oblast'* administration structure does not cover the situation in the neighbouring regions. Only the periodic editions of Novosibirsk are satisfactorily represented in the libraries of Irkutsk. These publications help to understand the situation in Novosibirsk and try to give a true picture of the situation in Siberia as a whole. Yet despite the efforts by the Novosibirsk periodicals to acquire an all-Siberian status, from the point of view of their contents and readership they nevertheless remain Novosibirsk newspapers. Their view of Siberia is nearly as 'central' as that of the Moscow newspapers, although it is closer and more detailed. As for a more natural source of information on Siberia, namely personal impressions, conversations and interviews, they are inevitably geographically limited. Siberia is not only immense, but also extremely diverse, and that diversity raises the further question as to what can be considered Siberia. Physical geography subdivides Siberia into three zones – the Western Siberian plain (stretching from the eastern slopes of the Urals to the Enisei river), the Central Siberian Plateau and Southern Siberia. But it is history that has given the same name to the three geographical regions. Economic geography contradicts physical geography, when it excludes from Siberia the huge territory of three million sqare kilometres occupied by Yakutia, a substantial part of the Central Siberian Plateau.

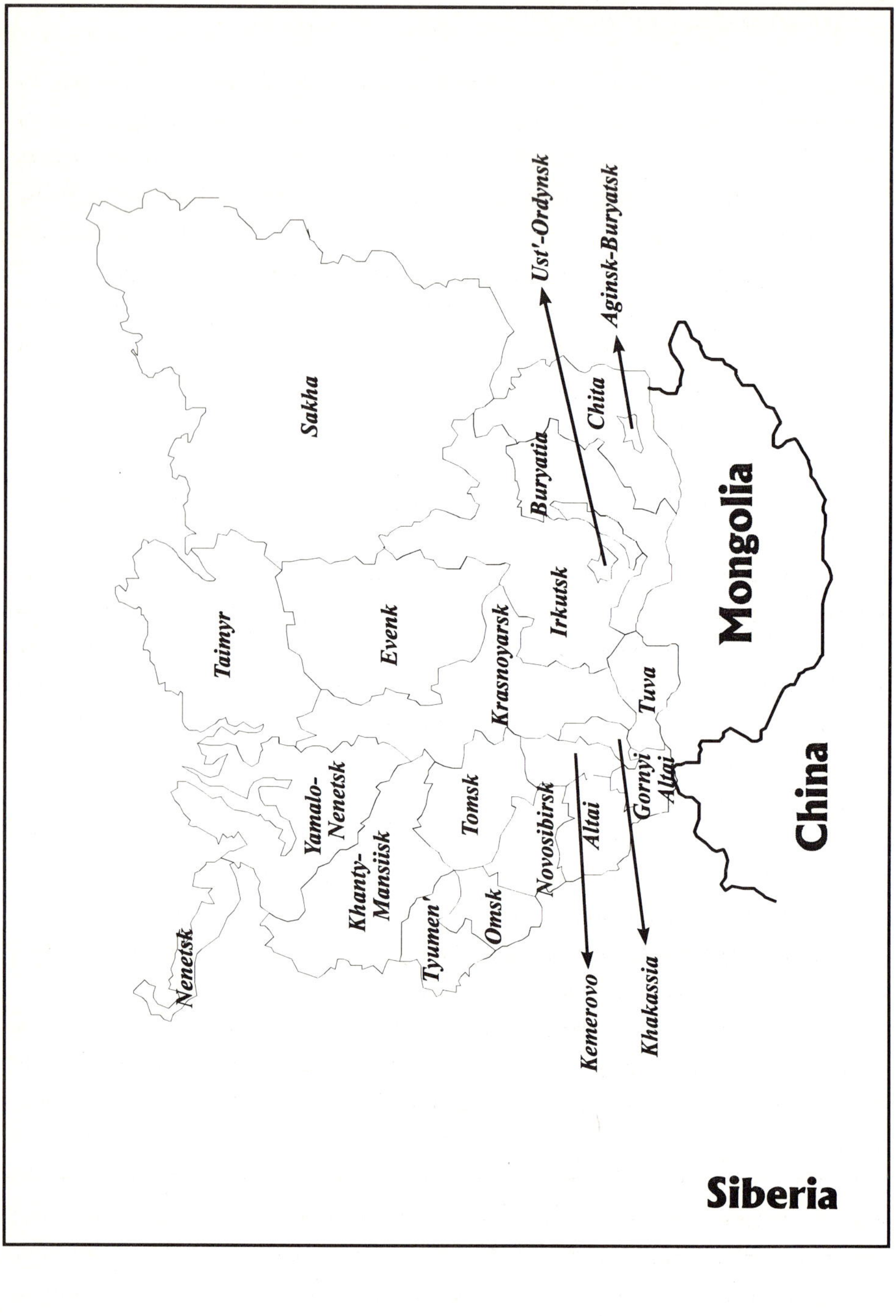
Siberia
Sakha
Ust'-Ordynsk
Aginsk-Buryatsk
Chita
Buryatia
Irkutsk
Mongolia
China
Taimyr
Evenk
Krasnoyarsk
Tuva
Gornyi Altai
Yamalo-Nenetsk
Khanty-Mansiisk
Tomsk
Novosibirsk
Altai
Tyumen'
Omsk
Nenetsk
Kemerovo
Khakassia

1 With Yakutia and without It

In the pre-*perestroika* years an unexpected definition of Siberia was given by prominent Novosibirsk economist A. Aganbegyan: Siberia is the aggregate of territories where the subdivisions of the Siberian branch of the Academy of Sciences work. This definition is not only a witty attempt to give a definition defining nothing, it also contains a heuristic insight: the changing borders of Siberia are drawn on the basis of the inner-Siberian developments and interests, approved, of course, but not totally inspired by Moscow. It combines two contradicting understandings of Siberia. One of them has existed since the times when the name of one captured settlement on the other side of the Urals spread across the whole territory, together with those serving Moscovia (Moscovia is a historical name for the Moscovite Russian state) who their hunted sable and built frame houses. The other understanding belongs to those whose ancestors were driven beyond the Urals either by the authorities, their love of life or through various other circumstances, and whose personal destiny cannot be separated from Siberia because it is so deeply rooted in its soil. This is the problem of the descendants of the settlers. The concept of 'a Siberian' is of no interest and of no consequence to a person belonging to those peoples that already lived in Siberia before the 16th and 17th centuries, if this man is not related by birth to the descendants of the settlers (and more often than not, he is related to them). Moreover, if we take into account the fact that a considerable number of people living in Siberia represent only the second if not the first generation of the Siberians, then this issue acquires also a humanitarian aspect. However, the humanitarian aspect can seriously affect economics and politics if an opportunity for an unexpected and unauthorised turn in developments or even a ghost of such opportunity presents itself.

The Siberian 'cellar' as well as the 'window into Europe' allowed Russia in the 18th century to postpone the issues of domestic development and creation of economic ties. This 'geopolitical' outlook upon Siberia resulted in the immunity of the central government to the idea that the unique potential of Siberia could be used in other ways. The word 'geopolitical' is taken into the quotation marks because well-considered geopolitics would have surely taken into account not only the resource potential of North-eastern Asia but also advantages due to its geopolitical position. Such a broader approach to Siberia, regarding it not only as the 'cellar' but as the 'window' if not the 'door' into Asia emerged only twice. Peter I's dream to turn the Third Rome (i.e., Moscow) into a new Jerusalem was interwoven with a thoroughly imperial intention to become Europe's ambassador in Asia, converting all the 'pagans' on the way, starting with the Chinese emperor, to Orthodox Christianity. However, the Siberian non-Russians upset all calculations and China even more so. On the other hand, the people chosen by the resolute monarch to carry out that mission turned out to be more resistent and more viable than that dream and the barbaric methods that it involved. Ignoring the inert Moscow patriarcy enfeebled by the docile serf parish, Peter I sent priests from western Russia bordering on Catholic Europe to Siberia to enforce moral order and to convert local peoples. The first foundations of the culture of Siberian cities, which, like European culture is cosmopolitan in nature and open toward other cultures thanks to its frontier character and its orientation to the values of christianity, were laid at that particular historical moment.[1] Siberia entered the European world and for this reason *Rus'* began to become Russia.

The second geopolitical programme envolved S. Yu. Vitte's plans of a large-scale Russian economic expansion into Asia through Siberia and with the active participation of the latter. The trans-Siberian railway is the monument to that programme and it is the most impressive heritage of the 19th century. The energy and resources of Siberia concentrated at the places where the railway crossed the great Siberian rivers and these pin-points on the map have swollen in the course of the 20th century to the size of large cities, though they are not collosal by European standards. These cities along with the innumerable small towns turned Siberia into an area of quasi-civilized urbanization. The key role was played by the trans-Siberian railway which acted not only as a gigantic magnet attracting resources[2] but also as an instrument in the hands of the Centre, used to develop the virgin lands, first at the turn of the century when Stolypin was the Russian prime-minister and then it contributed to industrialization under Stalin. The prospects for the creation of a Siberian processing industry adjusted to the natural conditions and economic situation of Siberia were reduced practically to zero and in the first decades of the 20th century hopes of opening Siberian industry and trade onto the Asian market faded. The interests of the Centre, behind which stood the interests of entrepreneurs from in and around the capital, prevented any idea of Siberia as an equal part of Russia and led to a renewal of the uni-directional geopolitical outlook of medieval Moscovy.

---

1 For details see Rozhanskii, M.Y. „Prishestvie v Sibir'[Coming to Siberia]." *Svoi Golos*, no. 2 (1992).

2 See Lamin: 30.

Lenin's intention to turn Russia into the leader of the great revolution of the peoples of Asia could have advanced Siberia geopolitically. That intention had as its consequences the national-territorial divisions that imitated autonomy and the encouragement of the multi-national diversity of Asian Russia. Encouragement of absolute and indisputable power resulted in the radical and, for the majority of the indigenous population, irreversible corruption of their ethical norms and mode of life. This was aggravated by the accompanying didactic arrogance of the 'enlighteners' and the typical chauvinism (if not racism) of the middle level bureaucrats. Moreover, formal autonomy cemented the idea of the national-territorial divisions, which proved to be an impasse for the multi-national region. This might be fatal not only for the Siberian peoples but also for the sovereignty of Russia, which does not take proper notice of its Eurasian potential, excited by the scanty rewards of cultural and political levelling.

Russian 'geopolitics' is nothing but ambitions nourished by the complex of its European inferiority, and by the huge Siberian expanses and resources, and by its military muscles (which also consume Siberian energy). Real geopolitics, that is the geopolitics that would pursue vital interests and would be based on the advantage of the geographical position could provide Russia with the status of a Eurasian power which would be a welcome and an equal partner both to the European and the Asian countries.

It would be correct to say that Russia does not yet have the geopolitical awareness that it should have, and it still acts in the world arena like Muscovite Russia, regarding the two-thirds of its territory beyond the Urals merely as a mineral resources appendage. Siberian infrastructure has not become a source of interest or concern, as the creation of an infrastructure has never been among the priorities for the Russian authorities anyway. But, in the case of Siberia, the insufficiently developed infrastructure does not only reflect bad management on the part of the authorities, but it is also indicative of the approach of the central authorities towards Siberia: when it became necessary to suck dry the next resource reservoir, far from the trans-Siberian railway, a whole process of organizing a system of expensive air-transport was put in motion to carry workers, materials and the extracted resources. Transport over water remained a secondary matter, and the urgency of its development, not requiring so much effort and money compared with the costly projects of new railroads and 'air bridges', was simply overlooked. In fact, it was just not noticed under the planned economy, which essentially favoured large-scale projects, otherwise the Siberian rivers would have remained free from the hydroelectric stations that tightly blocked them.

It would be very hard nowadays to find good reasons for considering Yakutia as a Far East region. It has always been so, except for the brief period of the Sovnarkhoz reform between 1963-1966, which was the most favourable and natural for the different regions of the USSR, a period which is still remembered with nostalgia by veteran managers . Here, it would be very much to the point to recall an analogous situation with the division of Moscow into districts, carried out according to the principle that every district should have an equal number of Communist Party organizations. The same was done in Siberia. The Far Eastern region and the East-Siberian regions were cut with the intention of equalizing their respective populations and, accordingly, the number of the Party organizations. Yet one never knows with such grandiose decisions, when they are made exclusively in the dark corridors of power in the capital. One can never tell whose personal preference or dislike affected the cooking of this or that decision. However, the fact that such decisions were repeatedly made and that possible alternatives were not even regarded is of interest to us not from the point of view of the history of Soviet bureaucracy, but from the point of view of its connection with the history of Russia and, especially, its impact on the future of the country, because even today Siberia is still perceived along the horizontal line of Moscovia's expansion, in other words, along the 'West-East' axis instead of the South-North meridian line.

The principal results of that policy are the separation of the 'North' from the 'South', or more precisely – the fact that the industrial production that spreads from the south of Siberia to the north, is fully unadjusted to the extremely fragile natural environment, and the fatal lack of experience of coexistence between an industrialised culture with the cultures of local nations dependent on the ecological balance of the environment.

The South and the North are metaphors, but no more than the West and the East. The peoples of Southern Siberia depend on the ecology as much as those living in the north of Siberia, but the ecology in the north is particularly vulnerable and the northern nations are especially defenceless against mass intrusion because of their isolation from the rest of the world. Siberian history reproduces the stories of the Mongols' invasion of Russia and Muscovite Russia's invasion of the northern Russia of olden times. 'Iron' flows of people directed by a centralized and absolute power swept over the people who were predetermined by nature itself to be independent. Moreover, despite the fact that the history of Siberia was begun by fugitives from

Moscovia with its system of servitude, there were people among them who could find a common language with the indigenous population of Siberia and who had become masters and builders of their own life. They needed the protection of the law but no supervisors. Those people could be justly defined as marginal. Their marginality helped them adjust themselves to a different natural and cultural environment. However, it must also be taken into account that in the course of Muscovite Russia's expansion, many cultures with their own traditions turned out to be in marginal relation to that state. They had their own internal stability and perfectly fitted the broader context of Russian nature. So, the fact that the descendents of those smaller communities that were swallowed by the expanding Moscovia managed to secure a place for themselves in Siberia shows the contribution made by those cultures and communities to the formation of an integrated Russia. Primarily we mean northern Russia, the people of which were the first to come to Siberia, not as wandering hunters and gold-prospectors but as permanent settlers. It is they who started the process of Siberia's contribution to the renewal of Russia's cultural potential so that Russia became something very much different from feudal *Rus'*.

It is northern Siberia and its economic potential that relieved Russia's economic disintegration and helped Russia to gain time, live through the crisis and eventually join the rest of the world. Now the north itself is being torn apart by a severe crisis. In the 1980s migration into the northern regions and the regions of 'northern status' was about 235 000 people per year (up to 1988), but over the period 1990 to 1992 a reverse movement stripped the north of 470,000 people, over half of whom left in 1992.[3]

The reasons for this are the reduction of high incomes, the abolishment of a wide range of privileges, the discontinuance of many large programmes, the drop in construction activity and the rapid growth of unemployment. According to the estimates by the Centre of Demography, by the end of the 1990s the northern territories will lose around 1.3 to 1.4 million people.[4]

It is primarily people of reproductive age who are leaving. Birth rates are dropping and the proportion of pensioners is growing accordingly. The reduction in the population might have been of benefit to the north if it was not for the fact that it

---

3 Rybakovskii, L.L. and N.V. Tarasova. *Vnutrirossiiskaya migratsiya naseleniya: nyneshnyaya situatsiya i prognoz* [Migration of Population in Russia: Current Situation and Prognosis]. *SI*, no. 1 (1994): 31.

4 Ibidem: 34

is not just the short-term residents who are leaving but also those who have grown up in Siberia – adaptation to Siberia requires more than one generation. If the Irkutsk administration realizes its plan to evacuate the Mamsk-Chuisk district then, when the economic weather changes for the better again, it will require enormous expenses to attract a temporary work-force to work gold or any other deposits (in the event that such a necessity presents itself), and even more money to attract prospectively permanent settlers. Now we witness that programmes of development of the north are being changed spontaneously and solely for considerations of momentary advantages. The governor of Irkutsk, Nozhikov, despite the populism that is so characteristic now of the heads of administrations, suggests (although not too frequently in public) that the 'northern bonuses' are pernicious: the north can accommodate only those who are needed there, and not one man more! The governor of the Yamal peninsular has reached an agreement with the president of Ukraine, according to which Ukrainian citizens who are entitled to the 'northern pension' after many years of work in Yamal and who left for their homeland but retained their registration as Yamal inhabitants, will lose that registration and the 'northern bonuses' to their pensions as well. The City Duma of Salekhard has submitted to the State Duma a draft that would restrict entry into the *okrug*.[5] In the north of Russia live more than four-fifths of the northern population of the globe, and yet only a small percent of all them, for instance, in Tyumen' *oblast'* are oil workers, the rest provide services for those few.[6]

The breakdown of the heating system in Deputatskoe (a district centre in the north of Yakutia) required an immediate evacuation of its population right at the height of winter. The population of that district (Ust-Yansk *ulus*) decreased in 1989 from 43 000 to 26 000 people. It was planned to reduce the number of those living in Deputatskoe by autumn 1994 from 10 000 to 6 000 people, only one in ten of whom worked in the industrial complex, for the sake of which the town had been built. The head of the district gave an interview which was given the following heading in the central newspaper: 'The exodus will be beneficial to all'[7]. In that district they extract tin and gold. As for the Kularsk district, where the joint-stock company 'Gold of Yakutia' operates, even more reductions are needed.

---

5 Dudnikov, N. „Servernyi shlagbaum [Northern Barrier].“ *Rossiiskaya Gazeta* 21 December 1994.

6 Tarasov, A. „Krainii Sever doshel do kraya [The Extreme North Is in Dire Straits].“ *Izvestiya* 12 January 1994.

7 „The Exodus Will Be Beneficial for All.“ *Respublika Sakha* 18 February 94 (interview with G. Polushkin, head of the Ust-Yan *ulus* administration).

The bulky and awkward infrastructure created by the supercentralized command economy that was orientated towards large-scale and 'blitzkrieg' projects proved fatal to the north. But whether the north is going to survive has become a question of vital importance to Russia. The Centre can either help or impede the resolution of that question but it is up to Siberia itself to answer it, since it is the question of the integration of Siberian economy into one viable whole that would be able, if it succeeded, to combine the industrial mode of life and exploitation of Siberian resources with the preservation of the environment. This combination would be the realization of the old principle of a balanced coexistence with the world of nature that had been so natural to the indigenous population of northern Asia before the arrival of the Russians. This principle also helped the native peoples to find forms of coexistence with 'Russian Siberia', that is, with civilization at the turn of this century.[8] How far these processes could have gone had they been given a chance no one knows now. Today the two traditions – industrial civilization on the one hand, and the ecologically balanced life of the native peoples on the other – seem to be totally incompatible. The mildest version of this incompatibility is represented by Tuva[9], which was not spared large-scale exploitation of its resources but which, nevertheless, survived on the roadside of industrial development of Siberia, and those people became an equal object of the Soviet nationalities policy only 50 years ago. The situation with Yakutia is more characteristic and not for purely scientific reasons did we dwell on the question of whether it is included in Siberia. Whether it will it ever cease being a cluster of territories around main transport lines connecting it with the European Russia is a question to be answered not by the Centre but by Siberia and, at the same time, without Russia and the Centre, it will remain unanswered for the foreseeable future.

The situation in Yakutia highlights the dependence of Siberia on the possibilities opened to it by industrial civilization, and the Siberian peoples, at least the largest of them, constitute no exception here. It is also true that the industrial invasion of Siberia retains its alien character with regard to Siberian nature and to the different Siberian cultures that constitute an organic part of that nature, and to a traditional Siberian economy, including its agriculture which is now on the verge of extinction.

---

8 See for example M. Filippovich.

9 See for example Balakina, G.F. „Sovremennaya Tuva: sotsiokul'turnyi aspekt razvitiya [Modern Tuva: The Socio-Cultural Aspects of Development]." *Sotsiologichesky issledovania*, no. 10 (1994): 159-161.

2 Yakutian Diamonds

We use here the word 'Yakutian' not only because they are extracted on the territory of the Republic of Sakha, but because economic issues prompted by the times are becoming increasingly affected by nationalist overtones. This issue is an economic one, and its national colouring comes not from the history of Russian-Yakutian relations but is a result of the principle of national-territorial division and of the fact that the Yakutian mining industry employs migrants from other regions of Russia. Nevertheless, this mining industry is the backbone of the Yakutian economy and without it the future of Yakutia seems uncertain, if not dismal.

Development of the mining industry has proved to be disastrous for Yakutia because it introduced into management and mass consciousness the 'left over principle' i.e., resources are directed towards production or some other priority area and the social sector gets only that what remains after this disproportionate distribution of resources. Yakutia, the least populated territory in the world, today holds the 72nd position in Russia according to housing criteria (among a total of 78 regions). We are referring, of course, to the city and village population. Traditional occupations of the native peoples – hunting and deer-breeding – have been almost completely abandoned. Absurd economic policies that for decades pressed for an increase of the number of cattle fed by the hay delivered from Amur *krai* and by the mixed feed from Kazakhstan, forced the introduction of the sedentary way of life, forced collectivization and the merging of villages in order to turn them into a bigger settlement. All these and other economic absurdities resulted in the marginalization of the people, which was especially detrimental to the native peoples. There are only 380 ethnic Yakutians among the 40,000 employees working at the industrial complex in Mirnyi.[10] A person who has neither the skill nor the inclination to be a deer-breeder is left without any alternative. Having been uprooted from the soil of tradition, he has no ambitions except, perhaps, a wish to live in a town. The new agricultural mode of production has proved to be a still-born baby. Orientation on the high-efficiency lifestock stock-raising was an economic absurdity because Yakutia could not provide feeding stuffs of its own.

When Yakutia, having announced itself as the Republic of Sakha, declared its sovereign right to its mineral resources, the Moscow newspaper *'Kommersant'* printed on its front page the following ironic headline: 'Yakutia has become the

---

10 Dyakanov, Kh. „Bezrabotitsa – real'nost' [Unemployment Is a Reality]." *Respublika Sakha* 12 January 1994.

richest country in the world.' In 1993 Yakutia sold diamonds for one billion dollars and in 1994 it plans to sell 1.2 billion dollars worth of diamonds.

The newly introduced budget clause 'rent for unrestorable natural resources', accounted in 1993 for one-fifth of republican income, and together with other payments for the use of natural resources of the republic this clause brought Yakutia about 40% of its total income.[11]

As a result, Yakutia could afford a very generous system of social security envied by all its neighbours. Furthermore, when academic structures were being ravaged by the crisis in Russia, Yakutia managed to set up its own Academy of Science. But gold and diamond mining cannot be the basis for self-determination and economic independence without preserving the temporary workforce made up by the people from all republics of the former USSR. As far as gold mining is concerned, it is becoming a loss-making sector due to a sharp rise of prices for equipment and fuel and because of high transport costs. Given all this, Yakutian leaders turn out to be staunch supporters of a more just and a more market-like, though Moscow-centred, administrative command system. For the time being, however, the Yakutian authorities, have to resort to their own form of state regulation: chairmen of the joint-stock companies which only yesterday were state enterprises, are appointed by the president of the republic. The government issued a special degree on 'attraction and consolidation of the labour force' to the diamond mining enterprises and ordered the *'ulus'* (district) administration to send teams of workers to extractive enterprises as well as to take on new full-time workers and to conduct a professional orientation campaign among the countryside schoolchildren. The government also compells radio, television and newspapers to inform the public on that subject. Will this political line have any far-reaching effects? It is a forced reaction to the pressure of

---

11 See *Yakutskie novosti*, no. 3 (1994). The quota of Yakutia-Sakha is bought by *De Beers* by agreement with Russia (nearly 200 mln $ per year). The recent scandal, initiated by the diamonds monopolists *De Beers* company and their demand to toughen the agreement with Russia is justified by the leakage of diamonds. It can result in a sharp fall of prices on the world market for diamonds. The reason for the leakage is the termination of the state monopoly in Russia that took place after the agreement with *De Beers*. It is quite natural to suspect Yakutia and the *Almazy Rossiya-Sakha* [Russian-Sakha diamonds] company. Furthermore, *De Beers* strongly relies on its powerful lobby in the Russian state machine and on the fact that Russia will hardly ever want to destabilize the diamonds market in the present situation. So, either Yakutia joins the agreement between Russia and *De Beers* preserving the status quo but becoming dependent on Russian foreign economic functionaries, or it acts as a third side or even makes a separate agreement with *De Beers* without having sufficient experience and being still dependent on Moscow, because it cannot support diamonds production itself. See Guseinov, Eldar and Aleksandr Skalnev. „Skhvatka almaznykh korolei [The fight of the Diamond Kings]." *Izvestiya* 15 December 1994: 2.

circumstances, and if it does come to fruition, it will not be soon. But the need to keep diamond extraction going and to make it the preserve of Yakutia is still urgent. The current propaganda campaign is certain to focus on the national interests of the people of Sakha. The power structures of the republic will recruit new, ethnically Yakutian people. The attraction of the rural population (that is of the Yakutians), especially school-leavers, to the enterprises of Mirnyi by means of high salaries, guaranteed housing and privileged status in admission to the University of Mirnyi (soon to be opened), will entail conflicts between different ethnical groups and an outflow of people from the republic. This problem could be solved in other ways, less costly to the people and the republic, and this solution is possible only under the condition that Russian authorities will adopt a protectionist political line towards Yakutia. Theoretically, investments could be foreign, but that is virtually impossible in the case of the workforce. The native population is mostly rural and it is not just a question of acquiring a qualification and of adapting to a specific job, it is also a conflict of different lifestyles and the intensity of this conflict depends on the degree of marginalization of these contradicting lifestyles. On the one hand, there are rural people who have practically forsaken their traditional occupations and on the other hand there are people who consider their job in the north as a temporary one or if they have no other place to go to, which is often the case, as forced employment.[12]

Problems of this kind are resolved over several generations. However, problems of ethnic and political self-determination and international relations are very often solved on the spur of the moment and in pursuit of a momentary advantage. This knot has become so tight in the 20th century, having been drawn during the two or even three previous centuries. Having considered the possibility of reversing the marginalization of the Siberian nations which is a key issue for Siberia, we come now to another question which, if answered, should determine not only the future of Siberia but also the future development of Russia. This question reads as such: Is a market economy compatible with the inevitable state protectionism towards the resource and industrial sector and towards the military-industrial complex?

This question will be answered in the coming years.

---

12 On the more general problem, see *Arkticheskaya politika: chelovecheskoe izmerenie* [Arktic Policy: The Human Dimension]. Tyumen', 1990; Vinokurova, U.A. *Value Orientation of Yakuts in Urbanisation surroundings*. Novosibirsk: Nanka, 1992; *Problems of the Historical and Cultural Environment of the Arctic* (*Proceedings of an International Symposium Held in Syktyvkar on 'Etnics of the North'*). Tomsk, 1991. 2 volumes.

3 The Siberian Boomerang

The collapse of the Soviet economy is usually explained by the fact that Tyumen' oil stopped bringing in enough profit to maintain the ever-growing expenses of the military-industrial complex. However, the new course of Russia's integration into the world economy has not changed the status of Siberia as a natural resources supplier. The Siberian energy-consuming military-industrial complex (MIC), which is more of a burden now, has been pushed into the shade but it remains very important as another unique resource. Thanks to the MIC and the natural riches of Siberia, Siberia is now much better represented in the power structures of Russia, but unfortunately, it is so to the detriment both of Russia and Siberia. It is not because of their exceptional business talents that former industrial 'generals' and party functionaries jumped into Moscow offices from the Urals or from beyond the Urals. These 'tough guys' were brought forth by the political and economic situation in the country which is now very similar to the constant 'emergency ' atmosphere on Siberian building sites. These tough guys managed almost single-handedly to finish industrial monsters and 'projects of the century' within the allitted time, sacrificing the living conditions of workers as well as the environment in the process. They are used to bending the rules, this being a synonym of courage and manhood in their eyes. To their mind, victory covers up all losses and success in life is obtained to enter by a reliable team and by nurturing one's own 'faithful men'. They are perfectly aware of two main ways of treating those whose life depends on them: the first is foul language and bullying and the other is the born' benevolence. They often act as benefactors sponsoring art and sport in order to make up for their lack of internal culture. These are the features of a personality which can be easily recognised in a Moscow office by any Siberian who happened to witness the 'golden age'of BAM, Bratskgesstroi, Samotlor. The popular label of 'technocrat' does not objustice to those people. The only respects in which they fit this description are their business-like approach to things and a kind of an ideological pragmatism.

They believe neither in a special role of science nor of technology. They place their stake on 'toughness' and on their ability to act decisively. Siberia is not the only place that produced such characters personifying the command economy, but Siberia offered them many more possibilities to prove themselves and, finally, it returned them to Moscow as if thanking them for its fast development and revenging the consequences of this development. It is not likely that the command economy will be given another chance, but thanks to this Siberian or – more precisely – Ural-Siberian boomerang, attempts to bring it back to life will continue for a long time.

The collapse of the state and the economy has created conditions favourable for that generation of leaders. It is another matter how and to what extent their character determined actual events, the general atmosphere, and the prevalence of harsh tones. Tone has proved to be an important factor in the recent political history of Russia because too much was decided by the ease with which that human type set the tone of the anti-Party meetings, adding to the general chorus of ideological cynicism and helping them to become anti-Communist. The presence of Siberia in the Centre is manifested not only through its representatives, though, of course, it is hard to underestimate the role of that lobby. Siberia has no rivals in the other, material sense: both the array of political forces and distribution of posts and offices depend more on the scramble for western Siberian oil, eastern Siberian aluminium, for the gold of Bodaibo, Norilsk tin, Yakutian diamonds and Transbaikal copper, than on the results of elections in different *oblasts* and *krais*. So what is the harm? It comes from the fact that the tight knot of Centre-province relations is not being loosened, neither by the Centre turning its attention to Siberia, nor by the Siberian lobby in Moscow. On the contrary, they have all tightened it even more.

For the first time, the dependence not only of the economic but also the political development of Russia on the state of affairs in Siberia was revealed during the Gorbachev-Yeltsin conflict when Yeltsin added the strike activity of Siberian miners to his half of the scales. During the early 1990s many Siberian cards were played in the political game, regardless of whether they had been important enough to occupy the newspaper headlines or not. By the end of 1994, the same happened with the publication of a scandalous message written by Korzhakov to 'TEK' Chernomyrdin, with the promotion of 'aluminium' Soskovets and in the wrangling about the industrial giants turned into joint-stock companies. These cunning tricks were not invented yesterday and will not fall into disuse tomorrow. Their essence, however, was tersely formulated by an *'Izvestiya'* journalist, A.Tarasov, who said while analysing the situation around the Krasnoyarsk aluminium factory: 'The State has lost its monopoly on the pillaging of Siberia!' [13]

4 East-Siberian Aluminium

The joint-stock aluminium giants only survived because of a *tolling* arrangement. Their chief partner and their largest share-holder is an off-shore company Trans-CIS

---

13 Tarasov, A. „A Battle for Aluminium with Criminal Implications." *Izvestiya* 21 December 1994: 5.

Commodities Ltd. Under conditions of the tolling, Trans-CIS supplies alumina and is the owner of the aluminium smelted from it. The company is exempt from duties, which considerably reduces production prices.

The origin of Trans-CIS's enormous financial resources is still subject to pure guess-work. Neither is it clear why the (well-versed in business) general managers of KRAZ, BRAZ and others agreed to such unfavourable conditions. What was the personal interest of the industrial bosses, what role did Trans-CIS play in lobbying the idea of the tolling in Moscow – all these questions are still open. We know only that the benefit to the territories is, so far, dubious. The budgets of Krasnoyarsk *krai* and Irkutsk oblast profited from the taxes on currency earnings and demand on electric power is again resurgent. But the aluminium giants themselves remain under external control and local suppliers of alumina that are firmly tied to the giants have lost their sales. Having survived and recovered, the aluminium bosses started thinking about alternative partners and now dream about independence. They now wish to turn their attention back totheir own region which, it proves, cannot be wholly neglected after all. KRAZ is now engaged in a new struggle for the redistribution of power.[14] BRAZ, judging by the articles in the local press (apparently paid for by BRAZ itself), is trying to lessen its dependence and to combine the interests of its partner with the interests of the region.[15] However, the Centre also has its own interests and may object to local solutions to the problem. The Centre wants foreign investment into production development and wants to retain its control so that the functionaries of the Centre can use this control at their discretion. The new chairman of the State Committee on Property pronounced in December his intention to deprivatize the aluminium industry, although the same idea had been categorically refuted by his predecessor. Needless to say his statement caused an enormous uproar. Vladimir Polivanov (the temporary chairman) promised in his interview given on that subject to Russian television that the mistakes made in the course of a hasty privatization would be gradually corrected (through repurchasing) and admitted that 'they had lost control of the aluminium industry' and that the government had no money yet to repurchase it. The government suspended the sale of the aluminium factories shares, but where the money for the buyout was going to come from and how swift the buyout would occur, the official did not tell the interviewer. He kept silent about a fact known to everybody and not

---

14 Ibidem.

15 Gofova, Natalya. „BRAZ – reference-point for industrial giants.“ *Vostochno-Sibirskaya Pravda* 14 December 1994.

voiced aloud by anybody, namely that the government has its own means of insisting on the variant that it prefers. Moreover, although Victor Chernomyrdin said that Polivanov's accession to the post of chairman of the SCP was also a great mistake, it is clear that Trans-CIS company would be taking a great risk by simply waiting for some Moscow official to change the rules of the game, and likewise by short-sightedly launching long-term projects for production development. Instead, it should get what it can from the situation as it stands at this very moment. Powerful western partners will interfere, of course, to prevent Trans-CIS from strengthening its position and will demand guarantees for a long-term participation on mutually beneficial terms. It is also clear that the aluminium industry can no longer make do with lobby efforts in the Centre. In addition it needs political power in the region and real freedom to do business with foreign companies. As for the 'industrial bosses', apart from the interest of the industries that they represent, they start to have their own personal or group interests (of the same nature but on a much more ambitious scale) and acquire new skills corresponding to these expanded interests: while just yesterday, lying on their death-bed they trusted themselves to their partner in tolling without any second thoughts and with the sole intention of freeing themselves from brain-racking strategic worries, now they are themselves trying their hand at political games (including the argument about state security), are using politics to achieve economic goals and vice versa. KRAZ has excluded Trans-CIS from the list of its shareholders. One can suppose that that was done to make shares fall in order to corner them afterwards. Now it is estimated that 25 to 30% of the shares are controlled by the same hands as a result of this operation. The governor of Krasnoyarsk stated to the public that the situation had been artificially created for political purposes.

5 Tyumen' Oil[16]

Unlike the aluminium industry, the oil-extraction branch is almost 100% Russian. The biggest block of shares belonging to a foreign shareholder amounts to 10% (the *'Noyabrskneftegas'* company), but the issue of foreign participation is being raised because of the crisis that the oil industry is now suffering. The fuel-energy complex (FEC) contributed to the 1993 budget of Russia 38% of its credit and only 7% of its debit.

The FEC accounts for 70% of all currency earnings of Russia. These are oil, oil products and natural gas. The share of Siberian oil in Russian oil export is 88%, of Siberian gas – 99% and oil products – 12%. Western Siberia became a centre of oil extraction in the mid-1970s. Then, it was unreasonable to increase the volume of oil extraction, but the USSR command economy needed currency, oil prices kept rising and by the end of the 1970s oil extraction increased faster than new oil deposits could be prospected. By 1988, extraction of Tyumen' oil doubled and accounted for 70% of the total Russian oil extraction. After that oil production began to drop because of exhaustion of oil deposits. In 1993 oil extraction in Russia dropped by 50 million tons. In 1994 every seventh oil well in Russia was not being exploited, in Tyumen' every forth. To overcome the crisis, the oil industry needs large investments in oil prospecting and urgent investments in exploitation of oil deposits that are situated in places where the environment is even more vulnerable than in the

---

16 Frenkel, A.A and V.I. Galitskii. „Prognosis on the Branches of Industrial Production. Survey 'Economy of Russia in January-October, 1993'." *EKO*, no. 1 (1994); Kovaleva, G.D. and E.G. Koklyagin. „Export and Import in the Mirror of Customs Statistics." *EKO*, no. 2 (1994): 3-24; Medvedev, Zh. „Oil of Russia." *EKO*, no. 5 (1994); Savvateeva, I. „Neftyannye lobbisty stavyat Rossii na gran' finansovoy katastrofy. [The Oil Lobbyists Are Putting Russia on the Edge of a Financial Catastrophe]." *Izvestiya* 8 December 1994; Vyzhutovich, V. „Iskusstvo trebovat' zhertv. TEK, VPK, APK: tri istochnika i tri sostavnykh chastei rossiiskogo lobbizma [The Art to Request Sacrifices. FEC, MIC, AIC: Three Sources and Three Units of Russian Lobbyism]." *Izvestiya* 6 December 1994; Roketskii, L. „Tyumen' Oil Is Necessary for All Russia and Tyumen' Problems Are Only for Its Inhabitants." *Russkaya Aziya*, no. 39 (1994): 2; Trifonov, A. „Priobskiy sled." *Novaya Sibirskaya gazeta*, no. 2 (15 October 1994); Kryukov V. „Oil Policy of the State: As Much as Possible and Right Away if Possible." *Russkaya Aziya*, no. 43 (1994); Roketskii, L. „Speech at a Meeting of Representatives of the Federal Authorities, the Subjects of the Federation, and the Inter-Regional Associations of the Urals, Siberia, the Far East on the Draft Budget (2 December 1994)." *Novaya Sibirskaya gazeta* 10 December 1994; Gol'dberg, R. „Komu i pochem dostanetsya tyumenskaya neft' [To Whom anf for How Much Is Tyumen' Oil Delivered]." *Sibirskaya gazeta*, no. 25 (1993); Shafrannik, Yu. „My sozdadim neftyannoe lobbi [We Will Build an Oil Lobby]."; and Muravlenko, S. „Ya prizvan obespechit' zhizn' lyudei [I Am Required to Guarantee People's Lifes]." *Sibirskaya gazeta*, no. 2 (1994).

areas where oil extraction has been underway for a long time already. After 50 years of exploitation, 'Ob' region oil deposits still contain, according to the estimates of experts, about 700 million tons of oil. However if technologies employed today by the Russian oil industry were used there the ecological balance of the whole northern hemisphere would be irrepairably upset. The other important consideration is the fact that Tyumen' oil is the most expensive in the world now and, considering that transportation costs cannot be reduced to zero anyway, really modern technologies have to be used. There is a western company that has won the contest for an ecologically acceptable and therefore costly project, and the credits are already agreed upon, but it is not yet clear whether political opponents to the idea of western participation in the strategic branch will give their consent. There are also Russian industrialists and investors who are very interested in short-term partial oil extraction that promises hyperprofits for a certain period of time. Really up-to-date technologies are also needed for further exploitation of the already worked deposits, especially if these technologies will help to maintain low prices on Siberian oil. The West is very eager to get closer to the oil and gas of Tyumen' but the arrival of western technologies will be a catastrophy for unqualified workers. The Siberian north is now flooded by refugees from the former USSR countries, and those Siberians who hoped to live there temporarily in order to make some money have nowhere to go to and no money to do so.

The oil and gas industry plays the key role in Russia's budget and will remain the key industry in the exploitation of Siberia for the foreseeable future. The future of the Russian market economy will be heavily conditioned by the outcome of collisions of interests over Tyumen' oil. For the last three years of reforms the smell of oil hangs in the offices of Moscow officials who take responsible decisions. It is no coincidence that the oil issue emerged on the surface of Kremlin intrigues in 1994.

This issue became a background to the struggle for a change of the political course. It also emerged in 1994 in the State Duma where the 'oil' lobby took shape as a faction headed by V. Medvedev who is the chairman of the oil industrialists' union. Oil and gas trade-unions threatened to go on strike if the president and the prime minister did not sign drafts prepared by the oil bosses.[17] Trade-union leaders refered to the hard living conditions of the north, three to four month delays in payment of salaries, yet their ultimatum was merely channelled around through the

---

17 *Sibirskaya gazeta*, no. 6 (1994).

corridors of power, used as an instrument in big politics rather than helping to uphold the social rights of the workers. The governor of Tyumen' remarked that 'oil is now extracted in Moscow'. The Russian capital now is the arena of clashes of different interests over a wide range of issues: 'the concept of the regulation of the oil industry of Russia', export quotas, export licenses, 'balancing of internal supplies with exports', foreign investments and, of course, taxes, transport tariffs, export duties. These interests group around two poles, the first being *government monopoly* under which the oil industry would become part of the state-owned financial-industrial monsters (for example, through 'two-tier management of oil industry'). The second is *external trade freedom* supported by state protectionism. These are two poles of attraction which means that the interests related to them do not always contradict each other. These interests and their agents form a very complex fabric of relations. One thing, however, is clear – a branch of the ailing Russian economy is trying to overcome crisis by means of hypermonopolization and combination of market and directive methods.

What are the interests of the Tyumen' region? What can it expect? The 'oil lobby' is connected with the region in a very indirect way. The 'oil lobby' promotes the interests of the 'oil general' and the interests of oil industry giants headed by them, and above all, the interests of *'the seven sisters'* – regional monopolies and their respective ministries. All the seven sisters are either Siberian or connected with Siberia by their origin, but all are registered in Moscow except *'Surgutneftegas'*. This company, which has become the biggest in the world after its merger with *'Noyabrskneftegas'* in 1994 has its headquarters in St. Petersburg. The 'oil lobby' is primarily pre-occupied with the issues of independent setting of prices on power resources, state regulation of transport tariffs, revision of the tax system, and, last on the list of their concerns, both the local and national budgets. Of course, battling out reasonable concessions over taxes and transport tariffs contributes to local budgets, just as the importance of the oil industry secures for its workers the highest salaries in the Tyumen' region, but are even such scraps from the industry's table as these sufficient to solve all the problems that it creates for the region? How is the industry's development linked with the development of the region? In order to establish this relationship it is necessary to acknowledge that firstly, this relationship differs between Tyumen' region where the oil is extracted and the regions where this oil is processed. Secondly, this difference places obstacles in the way of the projects inspiring Moscow reformers whilst simultaneously stimulating the Centre's command functions and ambitions (as well as the ambitions of those very same reformers).

Formerly, development of the Tyumen' oil extraction region was determined by its intensive exploitation. This fact accounts for its fast growth as well as for the abnormal character of this growth and the 'left-over principle' in the financing of the social sphere. Today the place of this principle is taken by the usual delays of payments from the federal budget, by enormous wages recieved by the oil workers which triggers inflation, and by a tax policy that makes renovation of infrastructure impossible. Modern reform principles and the inflationary situation put oil processing industries in a much more favourable position as compared with oil extraction industries and regions. Tyumen' *oblast'* does not yet have a gas supply system, whereas in Irkutsk oblast, the four cities of which (including the oil processing city of Angarsk) are the CIS leaders in terms of atmospheric pollution because their heating plants are coal powered, a plan has already been launched to convert heating plants to gas. This is an initiative of to the Angarsk integrated industrial complex. Despite the fact that it is working at one-third of its capacity, its exports (23% of its output) provide enough currency both for development and for fifting up financial gaps in the *oblast'* budget. Omsk *oblast'*, which has a large oil processing plant, draws far greater profits from Tyumenian oil than the Tyumenians themselves. Ten years ago Tyumen' *oblast* resisted ecologically lethal plans to build five oil processing plants on its territory. Now, however, as the governor of Tyumen' *oblast'* Leonid Roketsku states, they dream of having even just one, although they are fully aware of the disadvantages of constructing such plants there (more expensive labour and remoteness from the sales markets). Of course, there is an alternative dream – the creation of a Tyumen' oil and gas company. Akin to this dream are plans to create a Yamal gas conglomerate and an export-oriented energy-production on its basis, as well as other analogous plans for an accelerated creation of an East-Siberian oil and gas conglomerate. All of this, however, needs investments, and in order to obtain them financial flows must be reversed in order to build the economy starting from the base line and working upwards. This in turn requires concordance of interests of all Siberian regions in order to change the current situation into a more favourable one for Siberia. However, it is precisely this situation and the very development of reform processes which strengthen a new version of the old economic monocentrism and promote the 'divide and rule' principle, rendering the possibility of a common Siberian economic policy rather doubtful. Too many interests and too many careers depend on the oil industry which is trying desperately to keep itself afloat, to make 'Moscow oil workers' relinquish their control over it. Now Siberian regions face an untoward choice between ecological and social catastrophy and feel the inexorable approach of both while the fierce scramble for oil continues.

6 Gold of Bodaibo[18]

Gold in the Bodaibo district (north-east of Irkutsk oblast) is extracted by the *'Lenzoloto'* company and by individual teams of gold-prospectors. In 1995 *'Lenzoloto'* plans to extract seven tons of gold and teams of prospectors will extract 3.5 tons. In 1992 *'Lenzoloto'* was turned from a production association into a closed corporation (its founders are the State Committee on Property and the Australian company *'Star'*). The scandal surrounding this company broke out not just because of the economic injustice (gold goes to the country, profits go to Moscow, to gold bosses and the mysterious Australians, whereas all worries about the infrastructure fall on the shoulders of the district and Irkutsk oblast). The main cause of the flare-up was the fact that the 'underground' transformation of *'Lenzoloto'* was connected with a practical move to start exploitation of Sukhoi Log, a deposit capable of

---

18 See Berezin, Vl. „Narodu est', chto teryat' [People Have Something to Loose]." *Sovetskaya Molodezh'* 28 August 1993; Pyanov, A. „Ne spasayut vlasti ot lichoi napasti [Power Does Not Save from Troubles]." *Sovetskaya Molodezh'* 28 April 1993; Volkov, N. „Kto lishnii v zolotom al'yanse [Who is Not Wanted in the Gold Alliance?]" *Vostochno-Sibirskaya Pravda* 2 February 1993; Ignatenko, V. „Zayavlenie dlya sredstv massovoi informatsij [Declaration for the Mass Media]." *Vostochno-Sibirskaya Pravda* 17 February 1993; Udodenko, U. „Ikh plany byli tak gromadnye [Their Plans Were Enormous]." *Sovetskaya Molodezh'* 28 April 1993; Udodenko, U. „Sest'-to on sest', da kto emu dast [Sitting, Sitting, Nobody Gives Him]." Ibidem; Udodenko, U. „Bodaibinskomu Paionu s Irkutskoi oblast'yu ne po puti." *Sovetskaya Molodezh'* 9 September 1994; Alekseev, G. „Zoloto Suchovo Loga: boroda echche ne podrosla [Gold Sukhoi Lug: Its Beard Hasn't Grown Yet]." *Sovetskaya Molodezh'* 5 November 1994; Semkin, A. „Sukhoy Log: rabota plyus khleb [Sukhoy Log: Work Plus Bread]." *Sovetskaya Molodezh'* 5 November 1994; Semkin, A. „Na zolotom krylze sideli [We Were Seated on a Golden Roof]." *Sovetskaya Molodezh'* 24 November 1994; Freedman, V. „Bitva za Sibirskoe Zoloto [Fight for Siberian Gold]." *Moskovskie Novosti* (1994); Antonenko, A. „Zoloto vernoe: vernoye zoloto [Gold Is Real: Real Is Gold]." *Vostochno-Sibirskaya Pravda* 7 December 1994; Antonenko, A. „Zoloto vernoye - vernoye zoloto [Gold is real – Real Is Gold]." *Vostochno-Sibirskaya Pravda* 8 December 1994; Kirilov, S. „Moskovskie pirogi [Moscow Pies]." *Zemlya*, no. 19 (1994); „Meir Bodaibo vstupaet v borbu [Mayor of Bodaybo Joins the Struggles]." *Zemlya*, no. 20, 1994; „Udokanskaya Med' [Copper of Udokan]." *Delovoi Sibir'*, no. 37 (1994): 13. See also Pavlov, D. „Ob'yavilsya khosyain 'mednoi gory' [The Master of the Copper Mountain Appeared]." *Sovetskaya Molodezh* 6 April 1993; Karpov, A. „Zabaikal'e bedy i radosti [Zabaikal'e: Joys and Misfortunes]." *Delovoi Sibir'*, no. 41 (1994); Matapova, E. „Chto obechtchayut zvezdy [What Do the Stars Lighten]?" *Sovetskaya Molodezh'* 27 December 1994.

yielding 20 tons of gold per year and which contains considerable reserves of platinum. This project was regarded as one that could save the economy of Russia as it will not only contribute to the growth of Russia's gold reserve but can also change the situation on the world gold market. Formerly, if that project had been launched, it would have been carried out under an absolute state monopoly, budget financing, compressed terms, and the *oblast* and the district would have simply complied to the commands from Moscow and served the production. Now the ambitions of *'Lenzoloto'* were regarded as a challenge: prospector teams as well as other enterprises of the district did not want to be pushed aside and the Bodaibo authorities clung to the project because it would have provided high incomes and normal living conditions both for the *'Lenzoloto'* employees and the rest of the district population. It would have also changed the infrastructure of the district. As for the oblast authorities, they were counting on the project saving the *oblast'* budget. Other foreign companies appeared who were willing to join the project, offering modern technologies and skilled labour (*'Star'* participated in the project only financially and its share of profits is apparently bigger that its contribution). The *oblast'* administration tried to revoke the transformation of *'Lenzoloto'* into a joint-stock company and to revise it with the aim of adding the 'territory' and the inhabitants of the district to its shareholders. A license to start working the Sukhoy Log deposit was also a matter to be decided by the *oblast'* authorities. Sukhoy Log is now being prepared for exploitation. The government has passed a resolution to start work on the deposit and the contract for the construction of an industrial complex at the site is at the tender stage. It is planned that this complex will start working in 1998. The whole issue seems to be nearing the stage of completion.

The *oblast'* contented itself with 10% of the shares and the question of listing the inhabitants of Bodaibo district among the shareholders is also being considered. The participation of *'Star'* has also been agreed, provided that guarantees of its business reliability will be given. *'Star'* proved not so much its reliability as its entrepreneurial talents, having issued shares that proceeded to rise very quickly. The *oblast'* administration showed that it can conduct both consistent and flexible politics. *'Minatom'* is doing everything it can to take the financing of the project into its hands. The *'Lenzoloto'* managers proved themselves incapable of displaying business flexibility and the power of compromise. Being omnipotent in Bodaybo, they rudely attacked their opponents in the district and threatened the *oblast'* with the secession of their district. This situation is quite usual after many years of absolute power enjoyed by the industrial bosses on the territories that had became hostages to industrial monopolies. These last two years witnessed many things, including blackmail, ultimatums, radical changes of position by authorities of all levels, and by the Moscow and Irkutsk press. The tone of the recent publications suggests that investors still have some hope. The stand taken by the Duma committee on state security (that the West must not be involved, that Irkutsk *oblast'* must not be given any shares) is a clear indication of the fact that the ambitions of state monopolies have not yet been abandoned.

The most important lesson, however, is that without a compromise between the federal government and the regional authorities any large-scale exploitation of resources is virtually impossible. But there is another aspect of the problem that may become crucial in this aspect, namely that foreign participation can turn the conflict of different economic interests into political battles fought to the music of patriotic rhetoric. This rhetoric rages through the region on the pages of the local press and in speeches made by certain jingoists in the local legislative assembly that barely affect actual decision-making, if this rhetoric were to be exported to Moscow this could dramatically delay the realization of any project, hovewer important it might be.

7 Udokan Copper[19]

The former Soviet Union failed to open up athe well-known copper deposit in the Transbaikal region which according to the estimates of experts is capable of yielding 20 million tons of copper every year. Attempts at this had been made every five years since 1956, but the difficult terrain, permafrost and frequent earthquakes (in 1925 a force-eleven earthquake was registered there) upset all plans.

The importance of Udokan copper for Russia increased with the break-off of other ex-Soviet republics although, of course, the importance of copper for Russia is less than that of Tyumen' oil. However, for Chita *oblast* Udocan copper is the only means of entering the world markets. All Russian uranium is extracted on the territory of Chita oblast, but, of course, there is absolutely no hope of pushing that state monopoly aside. Therefore, Udokan is the only hope, all the more so since BAM makes exports possible. The initiators of Udokan plans are the Chita authorities. They quickly tendered for mining of the deposit and gave a license to a

---

19 „Udokanskaya Med' [Copper of Udokan]" *Delovoi Sibir'*, no. 37 (1994): 13. See also Pavlov, D. „Ob'yavilsya khozyain 'mednoi gory' [The Master of the Copper Mountain Appeared]." *Sovetskaya Molodezh* 6 April 1993; Snegur, A. „Zabaikalskie robotniki [The Workers of the Zabaykal'e] 11 December 1993; Karpov, A. „Zabaikal'e: bedy i radosti [Zabaykalye: Joys and Misfortunes]." *Delovaya Sibir'*, no. 41 (1994).

promptly created Udokan Mining company (UMC), which is a joint Russian-American enterprise. This was done in violation of the law regulating exploitation of Russian mineral resources, according to which the question of the initial mining of the deposit must be decided through a contest and the tender must be only for exploitation. Chita authorities argued that only minor formalities had been violated and that this mistake could be easily corrected. They also emphasized that Udokan copper was discovered in 1949 and that it would have remained unused but for their efforts. The project requires 1.3 billion dollars. Russian founders headed by '*Uralmash*' provide 55% of the capital and foreign investors (Udokan Mining Company's partners) furnish the other 45%. Moscow's argument is that Chita oblast has no right to grant a license on Udokan copper and that this issue falls under federal jurisdiction. Apart from the issue of the tender, Soskovets and the State Committee on Industrial Policy objected to UMC's plan to send half of the all to China for smelting. In 1993, on Shumeiko's orders the State Committee on Industry, Ministry of Metallurgy (i.e., Soskovets) and the Finance Ministry organized an expert commission consisting of 25 members, 13 of which were representatives of the above-mentioned departments and some of the others be were claimed by the Chita authorities obviously biased. After six months of work the commission pronounced its verdict to cancel the Udokan project on the garants Chita *oblast'* cannot manage it alone. This, however, was not the end of the story. UMC is building up its activity and its chief rival, the Australian BHP company hopes that the whole issue will be revised in its favour. Soskovets threatens to invalidate the results of the tender and that creates many difficulties for UMC in its relations with investors as well as opening up possibilities for 'replaying the game', refering to the legal incapacity of UMC.[20] Chita's reaction is negative, of course. Chita *oblast'*, which is the farthest of all Siberian regions from Moscow, has not yet become part of the Far East but it is very much willing to connect its future with the Asian-Pacific region. It is being badly hit by transport tariffs as well as by both the attention and inattention of the Centre. Anti-Moscow feelings are very strong there. In the course of the 1993 referendum every tenth voter was asked his opinion on the issue of transforming Chita *oblàst'* into a republic of the Russian Federation. The result of that poll was negative, but the 'againsts' only slightly outnumbered the 'fors'. This is not separatism but a decision for a higher status and more opportunities for the region. Nevertheless, the hope for radical measures is rather

---

20 Matapova, E. „Chto obeshchayut zvezdy [What the Stars Promise]." *Sovetskaya Molodezh'* 27 December 1994.

characteristic, as reflected success in December 1993 Zhirinovski's, who looked there to be a collective challenge to Moscow. The LDPR leader gaining 30% of the vote in the *oblast'* and the majority in the 'uranium' settlement Krasnokamensk. Neither is it coincidence that the political leader of local associations of businessmen, Nikolai Postrigan is making advances to the Liberal Democratic Party of Russia (LDPR). Even if it 'behaves well' Chita is treated like an outcast by Moscow, not because of any explicit dislike but simply because Chita can be much more safely ignored than Irkutsk or Krasnoyarsk, to say nothing of the republics. Moreover, the logic of economic and administrative relations of Moscow with the regions is just the same, with Moscow paying attention to their interests only if it is forced to. It would be a gross simplification if these events were considered as an opposition of the Centre and the regions, though on the surface they indeed look like a chain of local conflicts.

At the same time as the Bodaibo affair, Irkutsk was wrestling with Moscow over its hydroelectric power stations. Turning power stations into joint-stock enterprises, the Centre left thermoelectric power stations under control of the regions but retained control over hydroelectric power stations under the pretext of the threat of monopolism in East Siberia which has redundant energy resources. The Irkutsk authorities hurled themselves into the fight together with Krasnoyarsk and finally succeeded after they appealed to the Constitutional Court. Today, the *oblast'* pins many hopes on the *'Irkutskenergo'* joint-stock company. Its shares are quoted at very high prices. However, the region has won only the juridicial stage of the fight, leaving the final outcome yet to be decided. When the Chita *oblast'* construction industry was on the verge of bankruptcy because of the exorbitant energy tariffs imposed by the Russian Energy and Electrification Association (REEA) and divided to buy Irkutsk energy at considerable lower and mutually beneficial tariffs, REEA threatened to raise the tariffs still higher in order to compensate for the losses that it suffered because of its Irkutsk rivals. This story, the Bodaibo, Udocan, oil, diamond and aluminium 'sagas', as well as the problems that are faced today by the timber and wood processing industries illustrate a complex system of clashing centrifugal and centripetal forces in the Russian economiy set in the present distabilized situation where 'the state has lost its monopoly on the pillaging of Russia'. A new equalization, if it will ever be found, is a very remote prospect, because all these interests and the logic of their agents are determined by a centralized economy that reacts irrationally to the challenges of life and imposes its *modus vivendi* upon the economy and the people.

Far more serious than just the Moscow-Siberia confrontation is the fact that today Siberia plays a key role in the process of making the Russian economy face up to the real world, since Siberian regions are so vitally important for the Russian economy and suffered from so many large-scale projects. Thus, the present moment can be a turning-point in the economic history of Russia.

Today, Siberian managers and politicans ascertain that the reforms of the early 1990s caused the spiralling of economic hypercentralization. Transport and energy tariffs as well as taxes stifle production and disrupt internal economic ties. By the time products from the Angarsk oil processing plant get to Vladivostok they become 300% more expensive. In 1990 costs of transportation were 2% of the cost of products, and now their share reaches 50% /1/. The state monopoly on foreign trade is replaced by the monopoly of Moscow companies specializing in foreign trade ('foreign trade associations'). In 1993 they controlled 50% and for some Siberian regions – 90%. Proceeds that are to be returned to the regions take a very long time to get back there via financial channels, and on their way back this money enriches those who control these channels. Inflation and currency exchange rates, artificially raised, increase the profitability of exports but undermine development of local industry. Capital is turned over through speculation on the currency market and through trading cheap low-quality mass goods, which orientates people towards consuming and forms vulgarized consumer preferences, 'Africanizing' the country, as an Irkutsk political scientist, Gennady Novikov puts it. In fact, it is rather the case that Siberia is falling under China's influence as Chinese consumer goods flood its markets. Moscow, compared with Siberia, seems to be an island of European life, providing ample evidence that the gap between the living standards of the capital and the provinces has widened even more. In 1994 the average Muscovite could buy twice as much as an average Irkutsk inhabitant with his salary. Of special importance is the fact that financial rivers flow to Moscow which is now a place where the interests of industrial as well as trade and financial elites are concentrated. Moscow possesses 10% of Russian industry and 80% of its financial capital. One can conclude that efforts to change the current situation are not in vain – regional export and import structures are already taking shape, an unjust system of taxation is about to be compensated by the creation of financial centres in the regions which will handle tax money that is supposed to return to regional budgets. At the same time, it is hard not to notice that the hypercentralization, so much feared by Siberian elite, has begun and will continue to embrace those managers and regional authorities that promote their interests using power levers in Moscow. In the event that Siberian enterprises and regions succeed in obtaining a degree of independence that would correspond to their economic importance, their contribution to the development and strengthening of the Centre would be quite proportional to this importance. Being highly pragmatic people they cannot fail to realise this. After giving an interview lavishly stuffed with complaints and protests against the Centre's interference in the local affairs of the regions, regional leaders return to their everyday concerns, which include trying to establish good relations with Moscow financiers as well as to lobby presidential edicts by influencing his administration and other officials surrounding him. The more they rely on Moscow power structure levers while promoting their personal plans, the more they solidify these structures.

8 Phantoms of Pan-Siberism[21]

The virus of separatism only slightly affected Siberian regions, almost without any outward symptoms. The idea of Siberia's independence has not gathered many supporters under its colours, though being much liked by the press it contributed considerably to the noise that in the spring of 1992 preceded the All-Siberian Congress in Krasnoyarsk. The All-Siberian emergency conference convened in Novosibirsk in September of 1993 is a separate episode. The participants of this conference, representing those who cared more about federal interests and declarations rather than Siberian ones, threatened to stop the operation of the trans-Siberian main line and to declare the Siberian Republic. They did so to influence events in Moscow. If that is to be regarded as an example of separatism, this separatism has an ethnocratic character and people who support it have an imperial mentality, considering Siberia to be a special zone of preservation of Russian national potential. Just like the ethnocratic separatism in some of the republics of Siberia, this kind of separatism does not exert much influence on the situation in Siberia, though it has to be scrutinized in detail when considering problems of Siberia and the future of Siberian self-determination. Here we shall just state that Siberian separatism as a special case of pan-Siberism is the other side of hypercentralism. The development of more loyal pan-Siberian aspirations, articulated as a general redrawing of borders along more rational lines and a radical change of Siberia's position in Russia, prove that this is a common feature of all types of pan-Siberism that regard Siberia as an integrated whole and fail to notice

---

21 The term pansiberism was introduced during the joined work on an article by a lawyer from Irkusk S. Shishkin.

the details without which the subject is an empty abstraction. For this reason projects, good for this abstract whole, collapse immediately when they run into the concrete facts of reality. The evolution of the 'Siberian Accord' can serve as a vivid illustration of the modern political history of Siberia.

The 'Siberian Accord' was the first interregional association to emerge in Russia. It was one of the most active and conspicuous, too. Now, however, it seems to be the least influential of all interregional associations. The 'Siberian Accord' was founded in 1990, its main goal being to work out a coherent and a uniform Siberian economic policy as well as to obtain the right to set real prices on Siberian raw-materials and goods. Now, excecutive directors and experts of the interregional association 'Siberian Accord' (IASA) talk about the necessity of protectionism.

In June 1993 IASA had the well-formulated goal of uniting not only the industries but the territories as well, that is to become an association of *krais* and *oblasts* that would have equal status and a new mechanism of financing as well as a common legislature regulating this union. At this time the IASA was at its height, but in October and November 1993 leaders of regional administrations grew cold towards it. Together with A. Tuleev, who founded the association in October of 1990, it lost the core of its political intentions. Vladimir Ivankov, the highest ranking IASA's official, said in an interview given to the press in March 1994: 'We co-operate with any authority'.[22] The emphasis was obviously placed on the word 'any'. In the same interview he attributed IASA's flights and falls to the 'heavy tread' of the president and Parliament in their actions since 1992. This dependency of IASA is due to its advocacy of protectionism which it openly admitted to be the principal aim of its activity. Focusing on co-operation with the government, IASA now shuns the idea of a Siberian Republic. V. Ivankov threatened to sue the journalists at a press-conference to the tune of 100 million roubles if any of them associated the 'Siberian Accord' with this idea.[23]

In 1994 the association held its sessions in Moscow simultaneously with those of the Federal Council. That gave high officials of the Centre a chance to visit IASA's sessions, which would have been difficult if they had taken place in Siberia. The 'Siberian Accord' is gradually trying to adopt a new role as the Centre's chief counsellor and agent of state regulation in Siberia, although Moscow, which it acknowledges as its director, might not necessarily approve its suggestions.

---

22 *Sovetskaya Sibir'* 30 January 1994.

23 *Sovetskaya Sibir'* 19 January 1994.

This is vividly illustrated in the only document of some consequence issued by IASA, a published draft of a law 'on state economic policy in Siberia'.[24] Its authors and the association are concerned with the attention of the state towards Siberia, and Siberia is defined in the draft as an 'object of state regulation'. As Aganbegyan remarked, the only thouroughly worked-out part of the draft is that dealing with the mechanism of forming the revenues of the budget of the 'Siberian Accord'.[25]

IASA sells itself as a mediator in the protectionist policy, claiming the role of the advocate of the interests of Siberia, but being at the same time unable to formulate them. But do they exist, these Siberian interests? Every individual region of Siberia has its specific interests, they may even coincide or contradict each other, but is it possible to embrace all of them by one consistent programme? These are inevitable questions and they are inevitable for the same reason that it is impossible in Irkutsk to find newspapers from neighbouring regions, or that protectionism cannot be avoided and that an attempt to co-ordinate relations between Siberian regions is doomed to turn into the state regulation of the Siberian 'subjects of the Federation'. And that should preferably be purely economic regulation, and not bare-faced politics, because politics would mean inevitable skirmishes between the regions and suspicions of the Centre. This is of little use to anybody. It is far better for every region to develop its relations with the Centre independently, joining forces with a specific neighbour if need be, as was the case of Irkutsk and Krasnoyarsk in their court battle with Moscow over their hydroelectric power stations.

The idea of a centralized regulation of Siberian economics is mostly supported by Novosibirsk, which is just another indication of the principal source of pan-Siberism – the material as well as psychological and anthropological heritage of the command economy. Novosibirsk owes its existence to the trans-Siberian railway and the military-industrial complex, as well as to corporate state-supported science. Now, having been 'abandoned' (as the Novosibirsk press likes to say) it suffers from its dependence on the good graces of the central authorities. It rushed headlong into

---

24 *Russkaya Aziya*, no. 2 (1994).

25 *Russkaya Aziya*, no. 3 (1994). See also Kisilev, L. „Sibir' ustavshaya [Siberia Is Tired]." *Krasnoyarskij rabochii* 11 April 1992; Sobolevskii, A. „Sibir': belo-zelenij variant [Siberia: A White and Green Variant]." *Sibirskaya gazeta* 5 February 1992; Sobolevskii, A. „Sibirskii Put': pokushenie na prognoz. Stsenarii na vozmozhnovo otdeleniya Sibiri ot Rossii v 1995 godu [The Siberian Way: Scenarios of a Possible Disintegration of Siberia from Russia in 1995]." *Sibirskaya gazeta*, no. 23-24 (1992); *„Sotsiologicheskie issledovaniya ili sotsialnyi zakaz. S kem vy, gospoda deputaty sibirskovo s"esda?* [Sociological Research or Social Necessity: Whose Side Are You on, Deputies of the Siberian Congress]?" *Sibirskaya gazeta*, no. 14 (1992); „Sibir' prosypaetsja [Siberia Is Awakening]." *Sibirskaya gazeta*, no. 14 (1992).

the fight for the independence of Siberia. The intelligentsia of Novosibirsk as well as businessmen and even politicians sincerely believe that the interests of Novosibirsk fully coincide with those of Siberia. They consider Novosibirsk and Novosibirsk *oblast* to be the lever that, if properly used, could radically change the situation in the Siberian economy and even that of Russia, raising it from ruins to prosperity. They indend to introduce in Siberia power-consuming industries and high technologies instead of plundering its resources. Yet this obvious and well-argumented idea also smacks of optical distortion and centralist ambitions. Otherwise, they would not have put forward an idea of making Novosibirsk the Siberian capital and would not have proposed to make its airport the only international airport of Siberia (under the pretext of saving money). The evolution of the *'Siberian Accord'* would have been more successful if leaders of other Siberian regions had not feared Novosibirsk's rapacious ambitions. Shifts in the IASA's administration when L. Polezhaev became its chairmen in 1994, succeeded by V. Zubov in this office, most naturally coincided with the revision of goals and ambitions of the association. Having lost its central core, however, the association also lost its drive.

The knot has indeed been drawn tighter, but after many years of chaotic reform, the way to undo it has finally been found in the combination of independence with state regulation. It would be absurd to ask Moscow to decolonize Siberia, as that would be ruinous for the Russian economy. However, the Centre is far from being a homogeneous institution capable of strategic planning and of consistent realization of its plans. The above-mentioned combination is possible only if the federal structures and mechanisms will provide the necessary balance between the Centre and the local authorities. That is well understood by all pragmatic politicians, but it is still uncertain whether this will ever take place and whether the principles declared by the constitution will ever reflect the real situation in the Russian Federation.

One must be ideologically blinkered to consider the late Gosplan (State Planning Committee of the USSR) responsible for the current difficulties of Siberia and to hope for an 'invisible hand of the market' to lead blind Siberians to the fairyland where they will feel that they live in a 'second Kuwait', that they will learn to sell Baikal water and will restore happy farm oases. The plight of Siberia goes back in history to the very origins of Russia, and the heritage of the Soviet period has just intensified contradictions on which Russia had been built for centuries. It has always moved in a see-saw motion from tyranny to rebellion, both of which are becoming more fierce with every cycle. The contradiction between the hypertrophied centre and the rest of the country which was turned into one large province with no chance of self-determination is the drama of the country, of a Russia which cannot handle its space and time, or more precisely, it cannot reconcile the time in which it would like to live with the space that it must seemingly control.

Diversity of the natural environment and economic traditions as well as numerous modes of life and cultural traditions throughout the immense expanse of Eurasia presupposed that in order to control this huge territory and the nations populating it the state had to fill the vacuum of the as yet unborn societal links by excessive control and interference. Society needed some time to mature, whereas governors could be appointed or replaced at one stroke of a pen. The state made up for that. Political cultivation of new territories was achieved through state initiatives, everyday life was likewise subjected to state regulation, and immature morals were compensated for by exemplary punishment and the state character of the Orthordox Church. As law-awareness had not become either an attribute of power or a part of public consciousness, its absence was replaced by the arbitrary rule of the state bureaucracy. Temptation to strengthen the power through its build-up and penetration into every sphere of life was always very strong in Russia. An accompanying facet of this tendency was formed by the periodic crises of authority: the country was so tightly bound by governmental control that it could not live and develop through public aspirations and initiatives, but if control weakened, anarchy sprang up immediately. Anarchy or a threat of anarchy caused a further concentration of the power in the Centre, and the two ends of the vicious circles met again. This peculiarity of Russian history and maybe of its future is especially characteristic of Siberia. It was Siberia that gave the empire the possibility of postponing its internal development for centuries, and as a melting-pot of nations and traditions it is Siberia that has become the place of their final unification and that has preserved Russian diversity as a hope for an alternative, as a potential means of breaking the vicious circle.

In the example of Siberia it is possible to identify the central contradiction of Russia, namely the fact that it cannot be reduced to *Rus'* (the early Russian state, more or less ethnically homogeneous). Now Russia stages a drama of historical existence of nations that are unhistorical by their nature, not because they are insignifant or make no contribution to history but because their nature does not accept history as a mode of existence. Along with the advancement of *Rus'* into Siberia, Russia was being born, a country of European culture and European values oriented at transformation and at finding a proper place in the world community, but which does not properly care about its internal development and is often unaware of its real interests.

The advancement took place as an invasion into the natural environment and into the conservative and fragile world of the peoples who live in close contact with nature. This contradiction between history and the world, which has a different face in the Middle East, Latin America and Middle Asia, was presented in Russia as Siberian problems, Siberian alternatives. For this reason, levels of industrialization are especially obvious in Siberia – we can already see the ecological consequences, and the experience of ecophilic peoples is real and not just living in our memories.

At the same time, the results of the industrial development in Siberia cannot be removed – we can only find its proper measure and its forms that could co-exist with nature. That is why we talk about Siberia as something indivisible. Unlike the Far East, Siberian regions have this common contradiction as a basic feature. The Far East has a separate development, determined by the access of Russia to the Amur and to the Pacific Ocean, and it will seek its self-determination in within the Asian-Pacific region. This region is not situated very far from Siberia, and Siberian regions have their interests there, but it has totally different priorities. The illusion of universalism is not popular here, whereas it is common within the Sadovoe Koltso (central part of Moscow) and is to an extent practical in the off-shore zones of the Far East, that is to say, the illusion that Russia can become a part of the 'civilized world' without mastering its experience, but rather, by adopting certain universal recipes.

For this reason, if we turn to politics and ideological and political sets and models that mould Moscow's political life after the European image, we can see that they are especially unconvincing in Siberia. That is why Siberian affairs and Russia's future are so closely interconnected. That is why Eurasianism in Siberia is rather an applied orientation than an ideological conception.

9 Federation and Democracy

Eurasianism exists as a yearning for empire and as a perception of the diversity of cultural experience. The fact that these concepts are different but bear a common name is far more serious for Russian history than the everlasting struggle between westernism and russophilia. Indeed, it is this contradiction that makes us use the term Siberia, a word from the history of the Russian Empire, in order to define this land as an anthropological and cultural phenomenon, as a historical space but not as an administrative territory. In this sense, today's attempts have inherited the regionalist tendencies of the turn of the century to the same extent that federalist declarations are the manifestation of the state feelings of the Eurasians, who understood that an integrated Russian State is impossible without true federalism. However, there is something that allows us to hope for a dialogue between the 'cultural' and state forms of Eurasianism and for a solution to this coincident contradiction. We talk about an applied Eurasianism, in other words, about the Eurasian character of the problems that have to be solved by regional politicans, about the Eurasian character (pre-determined marginality) of their decisions and Eurasian nature of the society under formation on which they could lean and to which they more and more noticeably appeal.

Today's politicians of Siberia, whose activities have gone beyond the limits of economic management, are putting into practice or have to put into practice this applied character of Eurasianism, whether they know about this conception or not (as a rule, they do). The governor of Omsk, Leonid Polizhaev, runs into the Eurasian problems in his own way, because he is planning his policy in terms of the development of his region, bordering Eurasian Kazakhstan. In Buryatia this problem arises as a question of concordance of a Central-Asian cultural heritage with the region's existence as a part of Russia (the majority of the population in the republic is Russian). Yakutia is trying to enter the world community independently, claiming the leading position in the resolution of the problems of the northern peoples. Tuva, the only Siberian republic where international conflict has taken a long-lasting criminal form, places the accent on creating its own manufacturing industry, which presupposes further dependence on Russia and the influx of non-Tuvan population. There is the problem of the survival of the ethnic Khakass population, constituting 11% of the population of the republic of Khakassia. Its leaders decisively broke away from Krasnoyarsk *krai* for economic reasons, but in no way because of the problems of the indigenous nationality, trying to claim special rights for the sake of survival. The programme of creating an economical-ecological zone is being put into practice in the Altai Republic. More than a half of the territories of Tyumen' *oblast'* and Krasnoyarsk *krai* is occupied by national *okrugs*, the economy of which cannot be imagined without the mineral resources found in those territories. Industrial managers are still the masters of those regions, but local self-government and governing bodies of okrugs have already started the painful redistribution of power, often partly hidden. Irkutsk leaders will have to deal with large neighbouring ethnoses, first of all Buryats (the Buryatia and Ust-Ordinsk *okrug*) and with Chinese and Mongols, even if they will be able to significantly delay making decisions on the future of small nations and the problems of the north. Furthermore, a clumsy, almost panic-ridden policy towards the 'yellow peril', which resembles antisemitic hysteria at the beginning of the century, proves more effectively and better than any debates that the meeting of East and West in Siberia has not take place. An inner meeting takes place here, so we write about it. This meeting, Eurasian in its essence, is only just forming and without dwelling on its features in each of the Siberian regions (these features have their own significance in each of them and thus we can unite the situations in only the most general sense) we can simply say that today's stage of this meeting is focused on the problems of concordance of economical regional interests with federalist and democratic values and with the rights of small nations.

These problems spilled into the political arena during the discussion of the problems of federative organization, where Siberian 'subjects' were the most active and persistent participants of the discussions on equalization of the rights of the 'subjects of federation'. The fact that Yakutia and Irkutsk *oblast'*, which actively defended contradictory arguments, could independently agree on a search for possible means of compromise gives us hope. The potential of the meeting under discussion is created by Siberian history, but the most difficult questions are not solved. The constitution does not satisfy anybody and it is generally accepted that a federation does not yet exist.

Why is Siberia the most disquieted region in this respect? Because here the federation is not only an economic, political and national question. It is more accurate to say that the acute nature of the economic, political and ethnic problems of federalism can be explained by the fact that we do not simply talk about the urgent problems of the exploited territories, but also about the urgency of the historical and cultural self-determination of the region, which itself represents industrial society implanted in an environment alien to the changes. The question of the official state legislative structuring of the diversity of Russia is not only a question of the way out of the economic crisis for Siberian regions (although politicians and industrial managers emphasise this, it is naturally not the only problem), but is a necessary condition for overcoming the ecocultural crisis. This is true for all the national republics of Siberia as well as *krais* and *oblasts* (with the possible exclusion of Novosibirsk which was not by coincidence the leader of pan-Sibirism tendencies). Everybody proceeds from the statement that a federation is a chance to include the state in the solution of Siberian problems, using the potential of Siberian initiatives, and practically nobody tries to solve the ecocultural crisis by escaping from Russia.

Historians have noted that *'oblastniks'* (regionalists – defenders of oblasts separatism and independence), gathering their ideas in the student groups of St.Petersburg, Moscow and Kazan where people passionately discussed the problems of the Siberian colony and the inevitable departure of the colony from the Centre, stopped being separatists without renouncing their ideas when they returned to Siberia. Persuasive alternative conceptions could hardly be the reason for this (we cannot name them even today) and, of course, it is also not a question of sudden Russian patriotic inspiration. A man with a democratic outlook (and intelligentsia oblastniks groups consisted of such people, unlike, the pan-Siberian groups of the merchant class) should become even more convinced of his outlook on everyday experience of contacts with the virtually absolute power of local authorities, as demonstrated by the high and the lower officials. These people, usually intelligent and educated, became accustomed to the idea that the Tsar was 'sitting high' and that they were out of the reach of the law. In this sense, the fresh example of Vladivostok clearly illustrates the things that are usually covered in Siberia, and Siberian 'tough guys' in Moscow's chambers demonstrate that the habits of unlimited power are deeper than the populists' democracy. That is why it is not amazing that Grigory Potanin proved the vital necessity of *oblast'* federalism by Kant's categorical imperative.[26] Persistent reference on the part of the present Irkutsk governor Nozhikov to the list of philosophers who spoke about a man as an end in his own right is quite surprising. This sincere philosophical rhetoric in interviews and speeches goes beyond the framework of populistic liberalism and the superficial erudition of his speech-writers. These words help to explain the steps of Yurii Nozhikov towards civil society, though these steps are dictated not by a liberal sense of justice but by everyday experience, just like the liberals' fears concerning the unlimited power of the new elite. The everyday experience of the Irkutsk governor forced him to overcome the Kremlin's resistance and to insist on the direct elections for the post of governor, thus becoming the first directly elected governor of Russia. The same experience additionally prompted him to introduce simultaneous direct elections of the mayors of the *oblast's* towns and districts and to doggedly establish a procedure for impeachment for each of these positions through the Legislative Assembly of the *oblast'*. Of course, this self-limitation of power is

26 Potanin, G. „Guarding Oblast' Interests and the Dictatorship of Proletariat." *Sibirskaya gazeta*, no. 6 (1991); see also Svatikov, S. G. *Russia and Siberia*. Prague, 1924.

limited. When an opportunity presented itself to dismiss the *oblast'* Soviet and to become the source of legislative power for several important pre-election months, Nozhikov grasped it immediately. Self-limitation of the executive power which the Irkutsk governor obtained was the necessary condition for its strengthening. The regional leader could not afford to preserve full dependence of his position on Moscow because interests of regional origin conflict with the Moscow policy too often. Special foresight is not necessary here, though Nozhikov has the experience that taught him to be far-sighted after the widely-known history of spring 1993.

On this occasion, Yeltsin, announcing the forthcoming referendum, dismissed Yurii Nozhikov and the head of Novosibirsk *oblast'* Vitalii Mukha from their positions. Very soon the president had to go back on his word: the Siberian leaders, who could not agree with the Centre's manner of behaviour, whereby orders concerning positions of regional leaders were issued over the radio, united in lending their support to Mukha. In the case of Nozhikov's dismissal, the Irkutsk reaction demonstrated that the president could lose the referendum in this *oblast'* as a result of his actions. The central authorities either had to publish evidence of clear violation of the law and present facts pertaining to corruption in the Irkutsk administration, or to restore the rights and position of Yurii Nozhikov and silently admit that this dismissal was an exemplary attempt to punish a leader who defended the interests of the region too persistent. On his way from the Western hemisphere to Moscow Yeltsin made a stop in Bratsk where a scene of public reconciliation took place, or more exactly, it was demonstrated that nothing had really happened between these two leaders and they even had something to talk and to think about at the round table. But referendums and elections do not take place often enough to consider this precedent a guarantee for a relatively independent position. In this endeavour Yurii Nozhikov visibly demonstrates the process of forming the regional administrative elite of Siberia. The first wave of these leaders in 1989-1990 produced a flow of populists with experience of participation in political parties. This flow could have swept away the former Party governors, who in order to save their positions had to learn to please everybody with their speeches or their silent thoughtfulness that was to reflect a certain Siberian firmness and to underline independence of character. More often than not the flow did eventually sweep away these people appointed by Moscow since they were not used to pleasing the local population because career progress depended rather on their skills in pleasing the people who nominated them to the position. Generally speaking, however, owing to their large-scale industrial activity and 'major communist projects' that demanded spontaneous democracy, the Siberian regions were not only able to supply Moscow with leaders who combined populism with administrative experience, but they left some for local needs as well. The sincerity of this populism could be doubted but it had to be demonstrated as proof that a man can adapt to the situation or adapt the situation to himself. That proof was sufficient for those who counted on this man as well as for the voters who could distinguish right away between pragmatic populism and glib rhetoric. In any case, the 'Siberian Accord' was founded in 1990 by inveterate officials and the first secretaries of the Communist Party retained their positions because they were not aliens in these places, but it was always local people who made their careers there.

First secretaries became presidents, populists started putting accents on economic expediency and in general, a considerable number of the leaders of the first wave and even more people from their surroundings managed to materialize power through financial and industrial corporations and secure positions among the elite. Nevertheless, this does not mean that they are operating direct power levers. The fact is that the first wave inevitably uplifted those who were sufficiently prepared to ride it, or to put it more precisely, those who were supported and promoted by the groups ready to act at the first convenient moment. They took advantage of the moment, introduced 'their own' people into the financial sphere and empowered them with a right to make decisions. The definition 'mafia' which is in general use in Siberian regions merely reflects the clan character of the political power of economic groups. The processes that were stimulated by the preparations for the second wave show that this clan character will be rejected or at least considerably corrected. Already during 1994 the regional leaders stepped out from the ranks into the centre of political life of Siberian districts and became the only influencial political force. They act through unions of businessmen and industrialists which unite production bosses and provide a possibility to search for common interests and to work out common positions. One can say that the industrial party is the only party in the regions and territories for the foreseeable futur. This party flatly rejects the centralism characteristic of the parties established from Moscow. It tries to understand and defend the interests of the region where its enterprises are situated.

The industrial party selects and pushes into positions of power either professional politicians with economic experience (and thus hoping to find in these politicians the party's executive directors), or promotes one of the industrial bosses who does not wish to pursue a political career in the capital or quietly finish his career in the region and who simultaneously showed abilities in curbing clan traditions in his own surroundings as well as creating and heading the union of the top men of the region.

Today their only rivals are financial-industrial clans which have had a taste of power. Political parties cannot be considered as rivals. Siberian political life proved to have no party spirit, or perhaps even an anti-party spirit.

The necessity of constant conflict with Moscow over the questions that we have defined as contradictions of centralism requires people with a juridical background as its leading actors. Yet if they are people with natural senses of law and order, then the region's 'tough guys' who make their living selling raw materials or at the expense of the industrial giants, will not let them behave independently, giving them second positions or using them as highly controlled Federation Council Deputies. The tough guys do not care for law and order; the law must serve the necessity. The story of Viktor Ignatenko, speaker of the Irkutsk region Council of People's Deputies is quite didactic: scrupulousness in matters of law which proved to be useful in conflicts with Moscow turned out to be an annoying obstacle for industrial-clan decisions. Mutual dissatisfaction accumulated, resulting in an open struggle during the elections i.e., at the time least suitable for the clarification of juridical rightness, at the time when images are of paramount importance. Voters preferred to see Pavel Golishev in the Federation Council; he is not a man of high education but he owns a large building company. His main interests are focused on his own profit. Rhetorical phrases about support and care of the region were backed by the image of a tough and serious leader. Having a slight majority of votes in Irkutsk, Ignatenko dramatically lost to Golishev in the northern towns and districts of the region, where the people's past is inseparable from the command economy and the present is inseparable from large enterprises/monopolists. Contitutionalists, upholders of the law, can be suitable enough in the elite of national republics with an evident majority of Russian population – Yakutia and Buryatia – and in some national autonomous areas, especially if the constitution is incomplete or is at least considered to be incompleted in the Republics. But even regional and district authorities will have to deal with constitutional issues when legalizing a certain degree of economic autonomy and when securing the right to speak and act in the name of the region.

Several years ago one could puzzle oneself with the question of whether Russia exists as a single indivisible economic and political entity. Its infrastructure is so immature and possibilities of independent relations with the rest of the world are so tempting that a really vigorous effort would lead either to a breakaway of important regions or to the hopeless and destructive attempt at a forced return of the regions back into the state. Neither of these dangers have receded, but their possible scale no longer seems to be global.

Centripetal tendencies were considerably more powerful even in the period of state and economic desintegration. Firstly, the national and cultural unity of the state, so sorely missed by Russia's patriots, is deeply rooted in the psychology of the people and in their political behavior. Secondly, it is precisely the soberly realized fear of the *process* and not of the *fact* of desintegration that plays a key role. Theoretically, regions could fare better separately but only without any quarrels and severance of necessary links. However, everybody sees that things will not go this way, and through clashes, conflicts, grumbling, occasional blackmail and threats of a decentralized union the Centre grows stronger. On the other hand, the centre is obliged to conduct decentralization, knowing that it is necessary, but it does so in fits and starts which only aggravates the situation.

When trying to convinc Yurii Nozhikov to cancel the elections for the post of governor, the head of the department for relations with regions explained that these elections violated the executive vertical line. During the struggle between the branches of the power that permeated political life during the last few years, certain problems were pushed aside which, if not resolved, will leave democracy with a purely symbolic status and will legalize hypercentralization of the state. Gorbachev's Congress of People's Deputies is still the main step on the road to the settling of Centre-province contradictions. The decision to found the Congress was made in view of the necessity to undo the knot of differences. The last General Secretary understood its importance clearly ('It is impossible to develop at Moscow's bidding').

To resolve these difference, the establishment in the capital was guaranteed a number of places at the Congress in a completely undemocratic way, that is by depriving the provinces of the right to vote for Moscow candidates. In response the provinces, (especially Russian provinces and above all Siberian) actively promoted the politicians rushing to join the new political elite, which was enough for this elite to start forming. In this sense, today's Federal Assembly of Russia is a step backwards because the new elite narrows the access to the positions of power and prevents undesirable situations by strengthening the executive vertical line. One half of the members of the Duma was elected from the parties' electoral lists and scores of people in these lists had Moscow registration. As a result of this, only 11 people representing six political parties from Siberian regions were elected in the Duma, and their connection with these regions is extremely tenuous. Loginov from

Zhirinovskii's party, who occupied an important position in Parliament and was active during the events that preceded the war in the Caucasus, had been practically defeated in the *okrug* elections in Novosibirsk and nowadays attends lectures at Moscow Military Academy. Nazarchuk – member of the Agrarian Party from Altai is already making a career in Moscow, Alekseev, member of *Russia's Choice* from Irkutsk works in Russia in presidential circles. Furthermore, the right of those elected from the party lists to represent the interests of the regions is generally under considerable suspicion because of almost absolute failure of parties' candidates in okrugs. If you take the party that named itself as the party of Russian provinces *(PRES),* 16 of 18 candidates who passed through the elections represent Moscow and on the list of the ecological movement *'Kedr'* ('Cedar') which did not qualify, there was only one candidate from Siberia. Paying attention to Siberia became just a political manoeuvre for the parties. Though this manoeuvre is necessary, it does not deceive anybody.

Given the hypercentralized nature of the country, parties could only form as Moscow parties and party life did not become a catalyst for forming civil society in the provinces, and thus throughout the whole country.

The fact that 46% of deputies in the Duma are Muscovites i.e., people elected 'over the TV set' gives grounds for new critical collisions around the law on elections. Even Vladimir Shumeiko shows discontent with the Muscovite nature of Parliament, but as a rule he makes these declarations in the provinces. The speaker of the Upper Chamber of the Parliament makes it clear that it is in fact his chamber that has the right to represent and co-ordinate the interests of the country sincee it represents all the subjects of the Russian Federation. The idea of creating the Federation Council was introduced and worked out by the presidential team in 1993. The idea was to establish a controllable body which could speak in the name of Russia. The first session of the Federation Council was planned to be held on 18 September but was postponed with the bombardment of the seat of the Russian Parliament, the White House, which put an end to dual power as well as to fears of a new diarchy. These fears are quite natural, and the requests and needs of the regions as well as the necessity to declare them openly and to co-ordinate them with national interests is the most acute factor that demands separation of powers. According to the constitution, the next composition of the Federation Council must be formed from the heads of the 'subjects of the Federation' and from the top lawmakers.

The executive vertical line will make the top of the legislative vertical line controllable. Voters do not feel that the situation in the region depends on their representatives in Parliament or those in the local legislative bodies. Lack of a real division of powers comes from the limited power of Parliament as well as from the absence of a 'horizontal' division of power. Yeltsin's attack on soviets of all levels immediately after the October events was certainly linked, as was declared, with the fear of a formation of a 'vertical' line of legislative bodies and with the fact that administrations of the regions are controlled quite easily.

A dread of surprises from the province typifies the character of the new Russian political elite. Judging by the section of it that has passed through the presidential circles or constitutes them, we can refer to the following two reasons for the 'dread of the regions'. In the first place, the team of reformers does not see the essence of the conflict between the Centre and the provinces. They content themselves with political stock-taking and their own familiar terminology in order to understand the processes that are taking place in the country. Otherwise, true analysis would not be replaced by deep remarks about the reactionaries and provincial conservatives, or by hysteria on the subjects of a Urals republic and of Siberian separatism. State subsidies and the centralized financial system are used for political control of the regions.

This produces very short-term results that do not solve the problem: one will not find any Siberian region where the administration and the mass media do not complain about the injustice of financial charity from Moscow and do not think that their neighbour is more obedient and, therefore, more fortunate. It is evident that this situation is characteristic both of that part of the political spectrum that has the power and of the Moscow party elite. Even if they were offering to change the system, they would still regard Russia's integrity in terms of its 'controlability'. The second reason is also characteristic of the whole of the political elite but it became apparent in the political and legal moves of Yeltsin's team: it consists in using the regions according to the political conjuncture and no more. We also see it most distinctly in relation to Siberia. Siberia as did not serve a means of support for Yeltsin in his conflict with Gorbachev and later with the Supreme Soviet, but as a means of blackmail. The Supreme Soviet leaders used Siberia in the same way. When the next onset of dread shook the provincial Vende'e or when Siberian regions tried to act as an independent force, Moscow tried to put Siberia its place. Having barely recovered from the events in Moscow that took place in the beginning of October 1993, Yeltsin 'opened fire on the territories' in his address of 6 October by ordering the dismissal of the Soviets and by directly accusing the regional authorities of their alleged readiness to support the putsch. One could distinctly hear notes of revenge in this address. Revenge for the feelings that the President experienced in the last days of September and on 1 October, on Friday, 'the day before', when regionalists at a meeting in St.Petersburg showed their ability to become the only real mediator whose initiative could not be ignored by both sides. This could have meant not only a peaceful resolution of the crisis but also a vigourous step towards the drastic redistribution of political power in favour of some federative body and a forced refusal on the part of the presidential team to implement the presidential edict No. 1 400, that bore the idea of obtaining personal control of the key factors of constitutional reorganization. These notes of revenge are the most powerful arguments proving that the tragic acceleration of events on Saturday/Sunday was in keeping with the interests of the presidential team because it deprived the peacemakers of their initiative. The fire on 'Soviet power' in Siberia was supported at different levels by the heads of regions' administrations even if there was no conflict with their local lawmakers.

They were proposed the most convenient option – to obtain a completely free hand for several months and the opportunity to shape the future scheme of power interrelations on their own. The situation in Irkutsk was typical for Siberia, though in some cases (Novosibirsk, Yakutia) removal of lawmakers from the office looked more civilized: the succession between the old and the new bodies was marked, the leaders of the old bodies took part in the elaboration of the basic documents but the leaders of the executive power had the only real authority and they did not allow any attempt to limit it. The fact that this 'gift' was gladly accepted does not mean that the leaders of regions reconciled themselves with their removal from participation in the constitutional establishment of the state. Nevertheless, a gift from the president is not a precedent which permit a one to count on the support and 'presents' from the Centre as a basis for efficient policy in the regions. There will be more and more of these presents, no matter who will occupy the throne Moscow. In this sense, political relations between the Centre and the province will change but they will not become political because of that. Currently, we can define these relations as a possibility to reign and rule on the base of mutual support. Relations between nearly every head of Siberian administration and the Centre illustrate this formula. Of course, this is necessary for the embryonic regional elite, but it is not enough. Whilst leaning on the region for support and defending its interests, the regional elite is now interested in those political relations that help to avoid quarrels with the Centre, and in the same time help to preserve some autonomy.

The only thing that can compensate for the hypercentralization of financial levers is the possibility of co-operation in lawmaking i.e., the foundation of real federalism. The Moscow elite that personifies the Centre is interested in protecting itself and the country from disturbances, from an 'anti-Moscow' conspiracy of regional leaders and simply from their unpredictable political behaviour. So, taking into consideration the contradictory nature of different interests and projects, the Centre proves to be strategically interested in the construction of a civil society or, in other words, in stimulating the creation of political public institutions in the regions. It is impossible to provide this kind of support by ad-hoc intervention in everyday troubles; it can be provided only constitutionally. There are no other remedies to prevent troubled times from becoming real rebellion.

The foundation of actual federalism seems to be more and more doubtful because of the political heritage and orientation of political elites towards gaining momentary advantages, the ensuing hypertrophy of the Centre and the predominantly Muscovite nature of legislative power. If the Federation Council becomes a directly elected body, it will nevertheless have to constantly choose between federalism and retention of the status quo of the central powers (their conflict is a catastrophe for the country and every step towards federalism provokes conflict because it limits executive power while tempting legislative power). The power distribution system will continue to form for a long time and with considerable difficulty, because there are no formulas that can satisfy all the parties concerned 'right here and right now'. If it is at least theoretically possible to find such a formula, specific political demands and requests in each of the regions and in Moscow will lead to criticism as well as to lobbying and to slowing down of the introduction of this formula. The knot is being drawn more and more tightly and prompts us to consider it ever more intently. Political opposition will reveal itself during the adjustment of the electoral system, the formalization of political autonomy and the struggle between the interests of different groups of regional elites. It will put the problems of the hypercentralized country in the foreground of the struggle in the course of the local and All-Russian elections and push aside ideological and political phrases. The results of the presen.t confusion will be somewhere between the following two models. According to the first, after taking independent decisions on the issue of their unification and consolidation, regions will renounce their right to quit the union in favour of a federative agreement that will be one of the two main parts of the constitution. The other mainpart will deal with human rights, the protection of which will be the most important argument for the self-preservation of the Centre. The leaders of the regions will be elected to their position and the Federation Council will be at the head of the legislative branch of power, which itself will be genuinely independent from the central executive power.

The second model will be characterized by highly developed local self-government, from the *'zemstvo'* (elective district council in pre-revolutionary Russia) up to the *oblast'* level, but the governor will be appointed by the president after consultations with the representative body of the region. Governors will act under surveillance of the prefect sent from the Centre. Neither model is optimal for Siberia nor for Russia, both of them being practically impossible in their ideal aspect but, modified by reality, they are the only possible ones. Forces strongly interested in rebuilding the state's power system, provided that they have a possibility to obtain it, will save themselves and the whole system only by finding a compromise between federalism and unitarism. Where will this compromise be and what shape will the conflict between these forces take? This depends on them and, of course, not on the external conditions of Russia's existance. However, it is also possible that one of these forces will decide to change the external conditions and thus resolutely win in the competition for internal organization.

A further exploration of the basic themes of our research would require more intent attention regarding the specific peculiarities of each of the Siberian 'subjects' of the federation. Owing to the peculiarities that cannot be explained solely by the processes taking place inside Siberia, each of these subjects will find its own way in the complicated rivalry of regional and ethnocratic (including imperialist) tendencies, and will solve their own national problems. It will be impossible to overcome the ecocultural crisis without solving these problems. Thus, their self-determination will develop in the general Siberian context of geopolitical self-determinition (within the frames of Russia and the whole world) and on the basis of federalism.

14

North Caucasus

Ol'ga Vasil'eva

1 Principal Characteristics of the North Caucasian Region

The North Caucasian economic region includes Rostov *oblast'*, Stavropol' and Krasnodar *krais*, the autonomous republics of Adygheya, Karachaevo-Cherkessia, Kabardino-Balkaria, Northern Ossetia, Chechnya, Ingushetia and Dagestan.[1] The region's territory is 355.1 thousand sq. kms (or 2.1% of the Russian Federation's territory), its population in 1989 was 16.75 million people (11% of the Russian Federation's overall population). Since 1959 the region's population has increased by 4.4% (in Russia as a whole – by 25.4%).

The economy of the North Caucasus specialises in agriculture (Table 1): it accounts for 22% of Russia's agricultural output compared with only 7.6% of industrial output. The region accounts for 22% of the Russian grain production, 45.4% of Russia's sugar, 37.9% of Russia's preserves and canned food, 22.5% of vegetables, 16.2% of meat, 50% of vegetable oil, 34% of wool. Especially noteworthy are Krasnodar *krai* and Rostov *oblast'*, the country's two greatest agricultural producers of staple agricultural produce. Favourable natural and climatic conditions determine the leading role of the North Caucasus in the production of rice (Krasnodar *krais* produces 60%), tea, and industrial vine-growing and wine-making.

---

1 In some recent works the region is referred to as the 'South of Russia' and is considered to include also Volgograd and Astrakhan oblasts and Kalmykia (see, e.g., *Mezhdunarodnaya Zhizn'* March-April 1992), although it is not clear from the journal what administrative units of the Russian Federation precisely are included into the 'South of Russia'.

Table 1 *Agricultural Produce Output:*
1 - Total grain yield, average per year, 1986-1990
2 -Total beet-root yield, average per year, 1986-1990
3 - Granulated sugar output in 1990
4 - Total yield of sunflower seeds, average per year, 1986-1990
5 - Total yield of vegetables, average per year, 1986-1990
6 - Preserved/ canned foods output in 1990
7 - Meat output in 1990
8 - Wool output, average per year 1986-1990.

	1	2	3	4	5	6	7	8
Russian Federation	100	100	100	100	100	100	100	100
North Caucasus	22.0	22.7	45.4	53.1	22.5	37.9	16.2	34.2
Adygheya	0.46	0.5	2.4	1.0	0.7	2.9	0.4	0.14
Daghestan	0.45	-	-	0.3	2.1	5.2	0.6	6.27
Kabardino-Balkaria	0.54	-	-	1.2	0.8	2.2	0.4	0.61
Karachaevo-Cherkessia	0.19	1.0	1.3	0.1	0.5	0.2	0.3	1.28
Northern Ossetia	0.35	-	-	0.3	0.6	2.4	0.3	0.19
Chechnya-Ingushetia	0.41	0.5	0.3	0.4	1.4	2.8	0.1	1.71
Krasnodar *krai*	7.9	18.	39.1	19.3	8.5	14.2	6.1	1.76
Stavropol *krai*	4.7	2.5	2.3	8.4	2.7	3.0	2.8	14.63
Rostov *oblast'*	7.	-	-	22.1	5.2	5.0	5.0	7.61

Source: The Russian Federation in 1992: Statistical Yearbook. *Moscow: Goskomstat Rossii, 1993 (in Russian).*

However, since 1992 the output of agricultural products has been decreasing, which is connected with a reduction in sowing areas, a decrease in supplies of mineral fertilisers and fuel, a shortage of water resources and a curtailment of land improvement work in the region. Prospects for the development of agriculture will depend on how successful the commitment of additional sources of water-supply for irrigation will be, especially in Stavropol' *krai*, Rostov *oblast'*, and Northern Dagestan, which is unlikely in the near future.

Shortages of fuel in Rostov *oblast'*, Krasnodar and Stavropol' *krais*, amounting to 7 or 8 million tons (according to the estimates of the Ministry of Economy), are caused by the general economic crisis in the Russian Federation and the aftermath of the political crisis and the civil war in Chechnya, where major oil refineries are located. At present fuel supplies come from the Volga region. However, these supplies are of low cost-efficiency. In October 1994 the Ministry for Fuel and Power Resources passed a decision to build oil pipelines bypassing Chechnya, which will make it possible to refine oil extracted in Dagestan and Stavropol *krais* at other

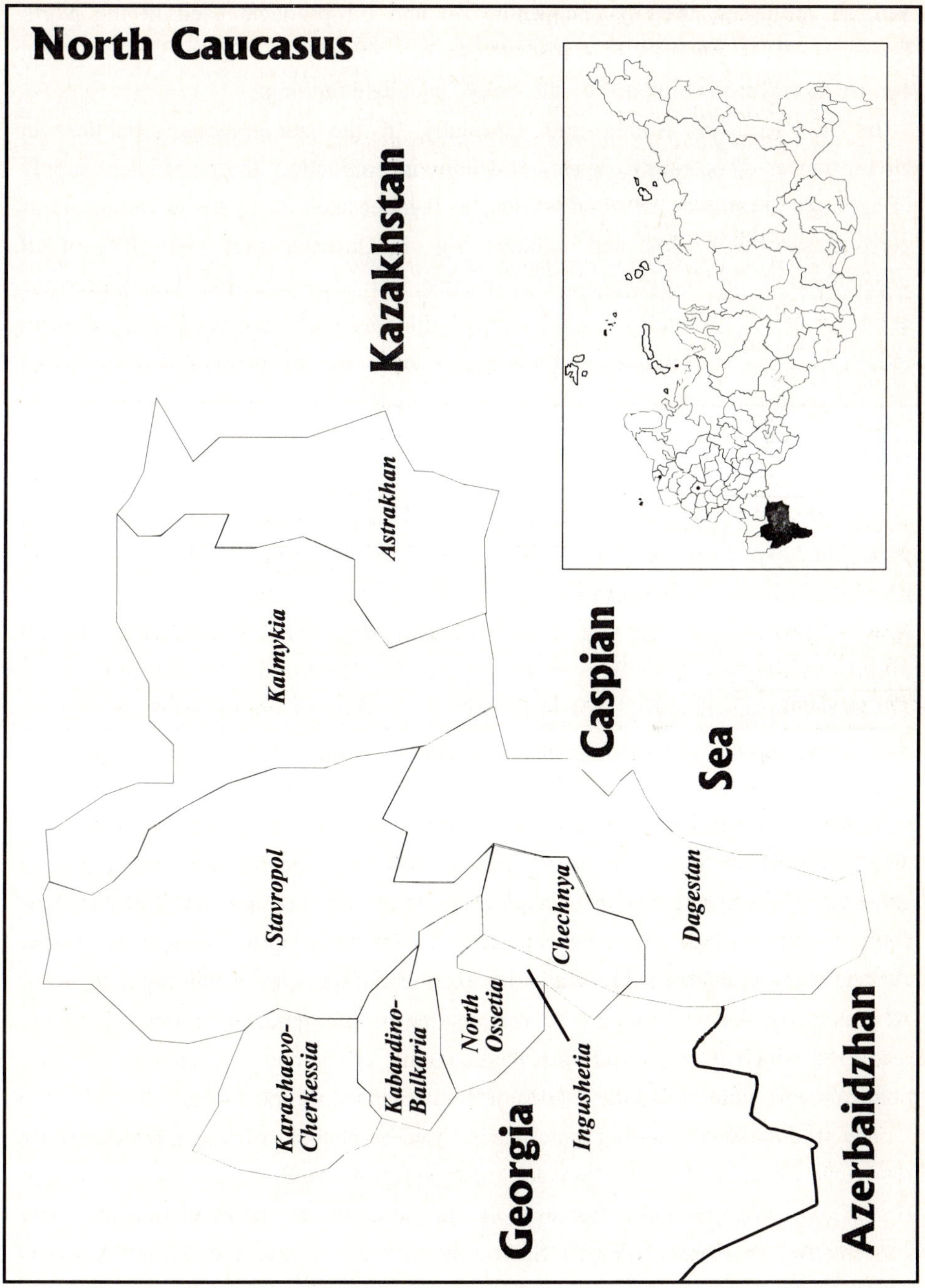
North Caucasus
Kazakhstan
Astrakhan
Kalmykia
Caspian
Sea
Stavropol
Dagestan
Chechnya
North Ossetia
Ingushetia
Kabardino-Balkaria
Karachaevo-Cherkessia
Georgia
Azerbaidzhan

Russian refineries, thereby cheapening oil and oil products used in the North Caucasus. It is planned to construct an oil refinery in Krasnodar *krais* but construction work is impeded by the lack of adequate funding.

In the 'Russian' South, and especially in the autonomous republics, in circumstances of economic crisis and decline in production, the insufficient supply of agricultural produce and food products is compensated for by the development of personal subsidiary plots and holdings: e.g., in Dagestan they yield 70% of all vegetables, 50% of potatoes and 45% of meat. The economic crisis has spurred the exodus of ethnic Russians from the national republics who were mainly employed in industry and had no relatives in the countryside, as well as the exodus of the urban population to rural areas. This factor has, however, some negative consequences as well, since it will lead to the further growth of inter-ethnic tensions because of scarce land resources.

The *mineral and raw material resources* of the North Caucasus are not great. All in all, they extract here about 7 million tons of oil (Dagestan, Stavropol' *krai*, and Chechnya – half of the overall output), 5 billion cubic metres of natural gas (the Krasnodar *krai*, Dagestan and Chechnya), and 30 million tons of coal (Rostov *oblast'*, ranking second in the coal industry output in the Russian Federation).

The region accounts for 3.5% of non-ferrous metallurgy output: here they extract tungsten and molybdenum (Kabardino-Balkaria), lead and zinc (North Ossetia) and other components of polymetallic ores. However, deposits have been largely exhausted as a result of long and continuous mining. For example, while in 1971 about 17.9 million tons of oil and 4 768 million cubic metres of natural gas were extracted in Chechnya, in 1991 the output was 3.5 million tons and 1 460 million cubic metres respectively. The capacity of Tyrnauz tungsten and molybdenum concentrating mill (Kabardino-Balkaria) exceeds the capacity of the mines by 30%. At present we are witnessing a general decline in the amount of mineral products recovered which is connected with the economic crisis, and in Chechnya – to the political confrontation and the exodus of Russian-speaking specialists.

The production of building materials is based on deposits of schist, plaste, quartz sand, marl, etc., which are of local and regional significance.

The *industrial potential* (Table 2) of the North Caucasian economic region is concentrated in Rostov *oblast'*, Stavropol' and Krasnodar *krais* (the 'Russian' South) which account for 77.5% of the industrial output of the North Caucasus (5.9% of Russia's gross industrial output).

Table 2 *Shares of Industries in the General Output Volume (in percentage)*
1 - all the industries
2 - electric power engineering
3 - fuel sector
4 - ferrous metallurgy
5 - non-ferrous metallurgy
6 - chemical industry
7 - machine-building sector
8 - forestry/timber industry
9 - construction materials-producing industry
10 - light industry
11 - food industry.

	1	2	3	4	5	6	7	8	9	10	11
Russian Federation	100	100	100	100	100	100	100	100	100	100	100
North Caucasus	7.6										
Adygheya	0.2	-	-	-	-	-	0.1	0.5	0.2	0.1	0.6
Daghestan	0.4	0.3	0.1	0	-	0.2	0.4	0.1	0.5	0.3	0.6
Kabardino-Balkaria	0.3	0	-	0	1.0	0	0.4	0.1	0.3	0.3	0.5
Karachaevo-Cherkessia	0.2	-	0	-	0.1	0.8	0.2	0.1	0.5	0.1	0.2
Northern Ossetia	0.3	0	-	0	1.2	0.2	0.3	0.3	0.3	0.2	0.4
Chechnya-Ingushetia	0.4	0.5	2.3	0	-	0.2	0.2	0.1	0.6	0.1	0.4
Krasnodar *krai*	2.2	0.5	0.7	0	-	0.7	1.1	2.2	2.8	2.1	5.7
Stavropol *krai*	1.3	2.0	0.1	0	-	1.5	0.9	0.4	1.1	2.9	1.6
Rostov *oblast'*	2.3	1.3	1.2	2.0	1.2	2.7	2.9	1.2	2.1	1.9	3.0

Sectoral Structure of Industrial Products Output (in percentage)

	1	2	3	4	5	6	7	8	9	10	11
Russian Federation	100	3.0	6.9	4.7	5.9	6.8	23.9	5.6	3.6	16.6	17.8
North Caucasus	100	1.9	4.0	1.3	2.7	5.7	20.6	3.8	4.1	18.1	31.0
Adygheya	100	0.3	0.7	-	-	-	10.9	15.3	4.1	11.2	51.6
Daghestan	100	2.4	1.5	0.1	-	4.0	23.9	1.9	4.6	15.5	32.8
Kabardino-Balkaria	100	0.1	-	0.1	19.2	0.5	27.7	1.9	3.6	15.0	26.4
Karachaevo-Cherkessia	100	-	0.1	-	1.7	27.6	22.9	4.4	10.4	9.0	19.8
Northern Ossetia	100	0.3	-	0.2	22.5	4.7	24.1	5.6	3.5	12.1	21.5
Chechnya-Ingushetia	100	4.2	40.9	0	-	4.0	12.9	2.1	5.7	6.2	18.5
Krasnodar *krai*	100	0.7	2.2	0.1	-	2.2	12.2	5.7	4.7	16.0	47.4
Stavropol *krai*	100	4.6	0.7	0.1	-	7.6	16.2	1.7	3.1	36.9	22.2
Rostov *oblast'*	100	1.7	3.5	4.1	3.0	8.0	30.3	3.0	3.3	14.1	23.5

Source: Indices of Economic Development of the Republics, Territories and Oblasts in the Russian Federation. *Moscow: Goskomstat Rossii, 1992.*

In many sectors of machine-building the Russian South is the monopolist in the Russian Federation and the CIS. Examples of this are combine harvester factories in Rostov and Taganrog, which produce 80% of combine harvesters in the Russian Federation, the cultivator factory in Rostov accounts for 50% of the cultivators produced in the CIS, while a third of steam-boilers and most nuclear power units in the Russian Federation are produced in Taganrog and Volgodonsk, two-thirds of main line diesel locomotives used in the CIS are turned out in Novocherkassk and Rostov plants supply 60% of welded tubes in the Russian Federation. Krasnodar *krai* specialises in producing equipment for the chemical, oil and food industries, while Stavropol' *krai* specialises in producing mineral fertilisers.

Unlike the 'Russian' South, the industries of the autonomous republics (making up 1.7% of the industrial potential of the Russian Federation) are characterised by narrow specialisation and a low level of production complexity. Additionally, up to 70% of the industrial potential of the autonomous republics is concentrated in their capitals. A drop in production can sharply aggravate social problems in the republics and make Russian-speaking specialists flee from them. Among the North Caucasian republics only Chechnya-Ingushetia had a developed industrial potential, featuring oil-refineries with a total output of 14 million tons (for the treatment of Chechen, Azerbaidzhani, Dagestani and Stavropol oil), plants producing oil-refining and oil-extracting equipment and the Oil Research Institute, the largest in the Russian Federation. However, at present the republic's petrochemical complex is practically disabled, the specialised equipment has been plundered and vandalised, and the drop in production in Chechnya was as great as 30% in 1992 (Russia's average drop was 18%).

The North Caucasus imports ferrous metals, timber, cement, oil products, gas etc. from other regions of the country. Electric power import ranges from 60.4% for Krasnodar *krai* to 95% for Kabardino-Balkaria, although all the autonomous republics have considerable electric power resources. Only Dagestan exports electric energy (in 1991 export was 27%), but, as in other regions, strict economy operation procedures are introduced in winter. The development of hydroelectric power production is constrained by land shortage and shrinking lands for agriculture, which may lead to inter-ethnic tension.

The North Caucasus has an *advantageous geo-economic* position characterised by its access to the Azov, Caspian and Black Seas: there is the Volga–Volga-Don canal–Don water transport system that ensures the region's connection with the CIS countries, other Russian regions and the Black Sea countries, as well as European nations. The region has important motor and rail routes: Rostov-Baku and Novorossiisk-Sochi-Tibilisi, linking Russia with the Transcaucasus. At present, however, the importance of roads for Russia's trade with the Transcaucasus has been practically reduced to nought. The 1989-1992 war in South Ossetia caused the blockade of the Georgian military road, linking the Russian Federation and Georgia.

After the beginning of the Karabakh crisis it became the road of 'survival' for the blockaded Armenia which had earlier been connected to Russia via Azerbaidzhan. The resistance movement of supporters of Georgian ex-President Zviad Gamsakhurdia in Megrelia and the Georgian-Abkhazian war brought about the paralysis of the railroad and the Novorossiisk-Tbilisi road link, and after the beginning of military actions in Chechnya in August 1994 the Transcaucasus found itself completely cut off from the Russian Federation because of the paralysis of the Rostov-Baku motor road.

Under the above circumstances, an ever greater importance for cargo and passenger transportation in the region is assumed by sea and river transport, but a drastic increase in transport tariffs resulted in the conservation of the basic funds, e.g., 42% of the Kuban' river steamship line fleet were tied up in 1994, and freight charges for ships at the Novorossiisk port render transportation of cargoes cost-ineffective. Nevertheless, the transport significance of the North Caucasus, especially Krasnodar *krai* and Rostov *oblast'*, is likely to increase. After the disintegration of the USSR, Krasnodar *krai*, where passenger port of Sochi and the largest naval and trade port of Novorossiisk are located, has turned out to be the only access route to the Black Sea in the Russian Federation. Azov and Taganrog (Rostov *oblast'*) may also become important ports, but the Taganrog port reconstruction project will require US $ 4 billion.

After the collapse of the USSR, the North Caucasian economic region, due to its unique natural, climatic and weather conditions, became the most important *recreation area* in the Russian Federation. It includes the Black Sea coastal area of Krasnodar *krai*, more than 100 sanatoria of the Caucasian mineral spas area and rehabilitation centres based on mineral springs in the autonomous republics. In the past about 10 million people used to spend their annual holidays at health resorts in the Caucasus. But at present the number of holiday-makers and those who receive treatment at health resorts has dropped sharply, especially in the autonomous republics, on account of interethnic and social instability and exorbitant charges for vouchers and passes to sanatoria which makes holiday-makers spend their holidays outside the Russian Federation. A further development of the network of health resorts and sanatoria will require not only the stabilization of the socio-economic, political and crime-fighting situation in recreation areas, but also the development of communications, the reconstruction of health resorts and sanatoria, as well as improved public catering and other services.

All parts of the North Caucasus except for Rostov *oblast'*, are subsidized from the federal budget. In 1993 the North Caucasus was allotted 22% of all state subsidies in the Russian Federation.

Table 3 *Intensity of Population Migration (Balance of Migration per 1 thousand persons, on average per year) and Natural Population Growth*
1 - in the average per 1981-1985
2 - in the average per 1985-1990
3 - in 1991
4 - the natural population growth per 1000 in 1991

	1	2	3	4
Russian Federation	1.2	1.4	0.3	0.7
North Caucasus	-0.0	1.3	8.7	4.0
Adygheya	2.1	2.9	10.5	-0.3
Daghestan	-11.0	-9.8	1.1	19.2
Kabardino-Balkaria	-2.3	-0.1	-1.8	10.3
Karachaevo-Cherkessia	0.2	4.0	0.0	8.2
Northern Ossetia	-3.3	-1.6	72.7	6.3
Chechnya-Ingushetia	-5.6	-5.0	-14.7	15.5
Krasnodar *krai*	2.2	3.6	13.6	-1.2
Stavropol *krai*	5.2	7.5	12.4	2.1
Rostov *oblast'*	1.4	2.0	4.3	-0.9

Source: *Indices of Economic Development of the Republics, Territories and Oblasts in the Russian Federation. Moscow: Goskomstat Rossii, 1992.*

The different parts of the North Caucasus enter various classification clusters depending on their level of *socio-economic development* and the *quality of life*. Rostov *oblast'*, the most developed part, belongs to the third economic development group (of a total of six groups) and to the second of six life quality groups, Krasnodar *krai* (including Adygeya) and Stavropol' *krai* (with Karachaevo-Cherkessia included) – to the fifth and second groups respectively; Kabardino-Balkaria – to the fifth group, while Dagestan and Chechnya-Ingushetia – to the sixth group on the both counts.[2] It should be noted that living standards in the North Caucasus are determined not only and not so much by high wages in the agricultural sector (Table 3) as by the presence of health resorts in the region and personal subsidiary plots of land (i.e., by the production of agricultural produce exempt from taxation). After economic decline had begun, it was precisely this factor that proved to play the role of 'social discontent absorber'. The lower living standards in the autonomous republics can be accounted for by the land shortage and unemployment among the rural population resulting from the development of the single priority sector in industry and the drawing of the work force from other regions.

2 Peculiarities of the North Caucasian Region

The disintegration of the USSR, the economic and political crisis in the Russian Federation as well as the crisis of the national-state structure were compounded with the internal problems of the region. This brought about a sharp aggravation of the region's interethnic, political and socio-economic problems.

The high factor of conflict in the North Caucasus is determined by a number of factors which are characteristic of this region only.

'Natural' causes of conflicts are related, first and foremost, to the ethnic variety of the region which is due to an extensive migration of various ethnic groups in the region over the course of several centuries and the preservation of ethnic communities and cultures because of the mountainous relief of the region. At present, more than 50 autochtnonous ethnic groups, belonging to several language groups, live in the region: the Abkhaz-Adyg group (Abkhazians, Adyghians, Abazians, Cherkessians, Kabardinians, Ubykhs); the Turkish group (Balkarians, Karachays, Kumyks, Nogais, Azerbaijanians); the Nakh group (Chechens, Ingush); the Dagestanian group including several subgroups – the Avar-Ando-Tsez subgroup (Avarians, Karatinians, Andians, etc., the Dargin, Lack and Lezgin subgroups (Lezginians, Tabasaranians, Agulians, Rutulians, etc.); the Iranian group (Ossetians), etc.

Believers of several denominations of the world's religions live in the region: Orthodox Christianity, Sunnite Islam (which came here via two routes from Iran to North Ossetia via Dagestan and from the Crimean Khanate to Ossetia via Adygeya),

---

2 Dmitrieva, O.G. *Regional'naya ekonomicheskaya diagnostika* [Regional Economic Diagnosis]. St.Petersburg: Izdatel'stvo Sankt-Peterburgskogo universiteta ekonomiki i finansov, 1990. See also Tables 6 and 7.

Monophysite Christianity (Armenians), Shiite Islam (Azerbaijanians), with the areas of their settlement, which changed in the past centuries because of natural reasons, wars and Russia's policy of resettling people in the region, now being compact.

The region is characterized by a high population density which is 47.1 people per sq.km (for Russia, this index is 8.6) with the share of the rural population varying from 29% in Rostov *oblast'* to 59% in Chechnya-Ingushetia.

The problem of land and water shortage is very acute in the national mountainous republics of the North Caucasus, where the population density varies from 29.6 people per sq. km in Karachaevi-Cherkessia to 79.2 people per sq. km in North Ossetia.

The situation is compounded by a high population growth rate, especially in the polyethnic and overpopulated eastern Caucasus; e.g., from 1979 till 1989 the number of Ingush increased by 27%, Chechens by 27% and Avarians – by 24% (for Russia, this index was 7.2%). A high birth rate in the region is determined by the considerable number of the rural population and a low level of education, traditionalism of the North Caucasian peoples and fear of being assimilated by larger ethnic groups.

A high population growth rate, an inadequate volume of capital investments and their structure (creation of large enterprises) led to a high hiden unemployment rate. Typical of practically all the indigenous peoples of the Caucasus is the practice of seasonal work, mainly, on construction sites in rural areas. At the same time, in the republics themselves a process of enlisting industrial specialists from other regions was taking place; e.g. in Dagestan, where every fifth adult is only temporarily employed, there were 7 000 vacancies at industrial enterprises in 1991. In Chechnya, the priority development of the petrochemical industry and the recruitment of specialists from Central Russia led to a high unemployment rate among Chechens and Ingush which was instrumental in forming the social basis of the 1991 Chechen revolution.

Another set of factors responsible for high level of conflict in the region is linked to the history of Russian conquest of the Caucasus, to the national, ethnic and state structural transformations in the North Caucasus under the Soviet power.

Russia's colonial policy – the extermination of the mountain peoples and the construction of Cossack fortification lines during the Russian-Caucasian was (1816-1864); the subsequent forced emigration of Moslem mountain people (according to various estimates, from 0.5 to 1.5 million people, mainly Adygs and Vainakhs were deported) to Turkey; the resettlement of mountain people onto the plains and the settling of Slavs in the Caucasus in the late 19th century and early in the 20th century – all these factors have to a considerable extent changed the socio-demographic situation in the Caucasus.

The *resettlement policy in the Caucasus* was continued under Soviet power. Especially great changes in the ethnic map of the Caucasus were brought about by the deportation of Karachais, Balkarians, Ingush and Chechens who had been accused of collaborating with the Nazis during World War II and deported from the Caucasus to Central Asia in 1943-1944; the ensuing resettlement of other ethnic Caucasian groups to the territories of the repressed peoples, the ousting of mountain peoples onto the plains in the 1950s and in the 1970s, the accelerated industrialization of the North Caucasian region in the 1930s trough to the 1960s, and, as a result, the migration of Soviet European ethnic groups to the region. That policy led to the fact that ethnic Russians have become the major ethnic group in the Caucasus (67.5% of the population), although they are largely settled in the western Caucasus and the capitals of the autonomous republics.

Changes in the areas of settlement of ethnic groups in the Caucasus have become another consequence of that policy. They may be conducive to a chain reaction of territorial claims in in the event of various conflict erupting in the region, or should there be an attempt to implement the Law on the Rehabilitation in the region or of the Repressed Peoples passed in April 1991 and providing for their 'territorial rehabilitation'. To take an example, the Chechen-Lak and the Chechen-Avar conflicts caused by the reinstitution of the Aukhovskii district in Dagestan led to the aggravation of relations between Laks and Kumyks after the beginning of Laks' resettling to the plains where Kumyks have traditionally lived.

One of the objectives of that resettlement policy was the assimilation of the mountain peoples but its practical results are rather contradictory: alongside the growth of integration of ethnic groups (e.g., an increase in the number of mixed marriages), a growth of ethnic self-awareness and self-identification was observed.

The forming of autonomous republics in the region alleviated the process of the mountain peoples' assimilation to some extent, but at the same time brought about the forming of a hierarchy of ethnic groups in the Caucasus, their division into the 'titular' ones, which gave their names to the corresponding autonomous republics, and the 'non-titular' ones, which do not have a state of their own. This caused increasing tensions between representatives of various ethnic groups in polyethnic republics of the North Caucasus, since in traditional societies of the Caucasus (the colonial policy of Russia failed to disrupt traditionalist structures – clans, councils of elders etc.), tribalism led to the domination in bodies of power and administration of certain territorial clans of the dominating ethnic group. The struggle of national elites and/or various clans of a particular ethnic group for power became one of the major factors of instability and, in the case of an autonomous republic's breaking away from Russia, will become a determinant process, as has been the case in Chechnya.

The *creation of national autonomies* did in fact constitute the 'historical right' of the 'titular' ethnos (or the dominant ethnic group) to the territory of the national state formation and the preferential representation in bodies of power (the so-called 'process of indigenization of cadres', i.e., appointing natives of a region to key administrative positions), which has especially become a standard practice over the recent few years and a significant factor of the rise in ethnic tension under the conditions of property redistribution, increase in unemployment rate and decline in production.

In addition, national bureaucracies of the North Caucasian republics which have retained their positions since the time of Communist rule[3] are making use of this factor in order to split the national-democratic opposition and to strengthen their positions. The political confrontation (in 1990 and especially after the *coup* in August 1991) between new democratic and national movements on the one hand and the Communist Party and managerial elite on the other, changed into a confrontation of political organizations along ethnic lines: between various nationalist movements in Dagestan on the question of making the republic a federative state and reinstating 'historical' territories of ethnic groups, between Kabardinian and Balkarian parties in Kabardino-Balkaria on the partitioning of the republic and forming new borders, the Karachai and Cherkess movements in Karachaevo-Cherkessia.

One of the most conflict-ridden issues in the Caucasus is the *formation and repeated changes of administrative and national state borders.* Before the 1917 revolution, the North Caucasian territory was successively part of the Don military *oblast'*, Stavropol' province, abd Kuban' Dagestan and Tersk *oblasts*. During the civil war, various Cossack and mountain peoples' republics were established there: the 'South-eastern Union of the Cossack Forces, the Mountain Peoples of the Caucasus and the Free peoples of the Steppes' (established on 20 November 1917

---

3 In nearly all the regions of the Northern Caucasus the managerial and Communist Party elites have managed to remain in the leadership: Northern Ossetia's President Akhsarbek Galazov, Kabardino-Balkaria's President Valerii Kokov, Adygheya's President Aslan Dzharimov once were the first secretaries of regional committees [*obkomy*] of the CPSU.

but liquidated very soon); the 'Union of Towns of the Tersk-Dagestan Territory' (December 1917; existed for 1.5 months); the 'Tersk People's Republic' March 1918 - February 1919), the 'Kuban' – Black Sea Republic' and other quasi-state formations. In January 1921 the All-Union Central Executive Committee (the Soviet government) established by Decree the Autonomous Soviet Socialist Republic of Dagestan and the Autonomous Soviet Socialist Mountain republic which consisted of six administrative provinces (Kabardinian, Balkarian, Ossetian, Karachayi, Ingush and Chechen). In July 1924, the Mountain republic was liquidated and the Kabardino-Balkarian, Karachaevo-Cherkessian, Chechen, North Ossetian, and Ingush autonomous *oblasts* were set up as part of the North Caucasian *krai*, which in 1934 was divided into the Azov-Black Sea *krai* (with the centre in Rostov-on-the-Don) and the North Caucasian *krai* (with the centre in Pyatigorsk). In December 1936 Kabardino-Balkaria, North Ossetia, Chechnya-Ingushetia were granted the status of autonomous republics but their borders were changed many times.

The administrative borders of the North Caucasus were changed just as often. To take an example, the present territory of Rostov *oblast'* was part of Don *oblast'* in 1920-1924, in 1924-1934 they were part of the North Caucasian *krai*, and in 1934-1937 tey were a part of the Azov-Black Sea *krai*. It was established as a separate unit, in September 1937 and in 1957 it was divided into Rostov and Kamenetsk *oblasts*. In 1957 two districts of the Rostov *oblast* (the 'western'and Stepanov ones) were incorporated into the Kalmyk autonomous *oblast'*. In 1958 Kamenetsk *oblast'* was included into Rostov *oblast'*. Equally complicated is the history of the formatiom amd alteration of the administrative borders of Stavropol' and Krasnodar *krais*.

Alongside the process of changing the national-state structure of the North Caucasus, administrative borders of districts were also changed. The process was especially active in the 1920s after the notorious circular of the Central Committee of the Russian Communist Party concerning a ban on the Cossacks (1919), after the deportation of the Ingushes, Chechens, Balkarians and Karachais in 1944.

Moreover, the demarcation of borders did not take into account established patterns in the settlement of ethnic groups and, as a result, the Nogai found themselves divided between Stavropol' *krai*, Dagestan and Chechnya-Ingushetia; the Lezgin – between Dagestan and Azerbaijan, the Osetins – between Russia and Georgia, etc. There were also established the 'two-subject' republics of Kabardino-Balkaria and Karachaevo-Cherkessia, without due consideration of the ethnic proximity of Karachais and Balkarians, Cherkessians and Kabardinians.

In the present situation, any attempt to 'restore historical borders' will bring about a chain reaction of similar claims throughout the Caucasus, because each ethnic group and leaders of national movements prefer to choose a reference point on the historical plane of their own liking, with the borders most advantageous to them. Very indicative in this respect is the creation of the Ingush republic. The Law of the Russian Federation on the Creation of Ingushetia (June 1992) does not specify the republic's borders. Incidentally, Ingush national movements, supported by the whole population at the December 1991 poll on the issue, spoke for the creation of the republic on the basis of Prigorodnyi district (North Ossetia) and Nazran district (Chechnya-Ingushetia), which had been part of Ingushetia before 1944, and the Maglobek and Sunzha districts whose territories were not part of the autonomous *oblast'*. However, at present these districts are largely occupied by Ingush, after a natural 'shift' of the areas settled by Chechens and Ingush to the north-east (after a number of districts of Stavropol' *krai* were made part of Chechnya-Ingushetia in 1957).

The next knot of contradictions increasing the chances of conflict is connected with changes in the geopolitical position of the Caucasus, which following the USSR's collapse became a border area.

Conflicts in the Transcaucasus directly influence the stability of the North Caucasus, with population migration being on the increase, and the arms smuggling and drug trafficking routes are being formed. Moreover, a segment of the North Caucasian population is being drawn into the Transcaucasian conflicts, which has led to the formation of paramilitary units in all regions of the North Caucasus. This situation is primarily brought about by the close ethnic relation between Abkhazians in Georgia and Adygs in Russia, the divided territories of settlement of Osetins and Lezgins in two different states (Russia and Georgia, Russia and Azerbaijan respectively). Moreover, conflicts in the Transcaucasus resulted in formation of paramilitary groups even in the 'Russian South', e.g., Cossack units in Stavropol' and Krasnodar *krais* which actually function as customs and borderguard outposts.

The closure of the border between Russia and the states of the Transcaucasus, which is demanded by the Russian-speaking population in the south of Russia, is capable of significantly destabilizing the situation in the North Caucasus. The demarcating and and establisment of border lines will be considered as an 'imperialist' action aimed at assimilating the mountain peoples. This might alienate the national mountain movements from Moscow and strengthen separatist aspirations in the Caucasus.

Finally, we should mention reasons related to the full-scale crisis in the post-Soviet space. The crisis is largely determined by the simultaneity of several processes – the transformation of the national state structure of the ex-USSR, the transition from the command administration and management system to a market-oriented economy, and the quests for a new development ideology in Russia. The crisis of the state is also manifest in the weakening of control over and within the structures of law enforcement and the armed forces, which has led to arms trading and thriving black markets, illegal arms manufacturing, the forming of armed militant groups with a semi-legal status, i.e., whose existence was endorsed by some legislative acts but runs counter to other acts. For example, the National Guard of North Ossetia[4] was established on the basis of acts of the republic of Nortn Ossetia which contradict federal legislation. The Russian leadership is also involved in the formation of illegal armed units, financing (and, perhaps directly supplying with arms) the opposition in Chechnya during its 1994 civil war.

The character of the modernization of the nation-state relationships which began in 1990 with the Declaration of Sovereignty and changes in the status of former autonomous republics and *oblasts* was determined by the struggle between the Russian and Union Centres and, later, between the legislative and executive branches of power in Russia. It was precisely the confrontation and the practices of granting privileges to regions (on the part of both branches of power) in exchange for their leaders' loyalty that determined the spontaneous chaotic nature of the process of national and state transformation in Russia and the codification of inequality among the federation subjects in the Federal Treaty (March 1992) and the Constitition of the Russian Federation (December 1993).

Rather significant factors inviting conflict are the renunciation of Communist ideology and the lack of a federal ideology of development, which brought about the forming of the 'titular' ethnos nationalism as the new ideology of the former Russian autonomies. The conducting of the process of modernization of Russia's national and state structure on the initiative and under the control of local national 'titular' bureaucracies led to the realization of ethnocratic models of statehood (the process of bringing indigenous cadres into the administrative apparatuses of autonomies), which is destabilizing the situation in polyethnic republics, especially at the stage of property redistribution.

---

4 After the Ossetian-Ingushetian clashes, it was reorganized into a militarized security service for national economy objects.

The crisis of the national and state structure of the Russian Federation also manifested itself in the formation of structures speaking on behalf of the people or whole ethnic groups: Peoples' Congresses (with their undefined ways of electing delegates), Congresses of People's Deputies of All Levels. The powers of these structures were not defined in the legislation in force[5], and they could be considered as public organizations. But the referendum on the creating of the Ingush republic, held on the initiation of the Congress of the Ingush people, became the basis for passing the Bill of the Russian Federation on the Creation of the Ingush republic. This decision of the Russian leadership was explained by a desire to reduce the territory controlled by the Dudaev's government which in October 1991 proclaimed Chechnya's independence.

The overall economic crisis of the post-Soviet 'space' in the North Caucasus is aggravated by the structure of federal investments used for setting up large production complexes and attracting qualified labour force from other regions of Russia. This has led to the realization of the 'Asian pattern in employment' (the indigenous population is employed in agriculture, while migrants are employed in industry) and has been the source of interethnic tensions between natives and migrants over the past few decades. In conditions of declining production and high dependence of personal living standards on one's own personal subsidiary plot of land, the appointment of indigenous cadres to high posts is fraught with transforming social conflict into interethnic conflict.

Shortage of land will also call into question the forthcoming land reform in the region, since the realization of reforms may result in aggravation of not only interethnic but also clan contradictions in the republics of the North Caucasus.[6]

All these factors have triggered several interethnic conflicts over the past five years on the territory of the North Caucasus: in Dagestan – the Avar-Komyk, Chechen-Lak, Chechen-Avar and Lak-Komyk conflicts (and have put the question of Lezgin and Nogai autonomies on the agenda); in Chechnya-Ingushetia – the Chechnya-Ingush confrontation, the Osetin-Ingush war, the confrontation between various ethnic groups in Kabardino-Balkaria and Karachaevo-Cherkessia, between Cosacks and the mountain peoples both in the autonomous republics and in

---

5 In Kabardino-Balkaria, after the Congress of the Balkarian people and the Congress of the Kabardinian people convened in 1991, in May 1992 a Bill on the Peoples' Congresses was introduced for consideration at the plenary session of the Supreme Council of the Kabardino-Balkarian Republic.

6 After the issue of private ownership of land had been put on the agenda, they began to shoot and kill herdsmen whose herds trespassed the lands of another, alien, taip.

administrative units of the 'Russian' South. The conflicts took various forms; ranging from rallies and pickets, main line blocks, derangements of work of municipal councils and strikes to armed clashes, etc.

Up to now no conflict has been settled and a further intensification of confrontation is to be expected. A certain stabilization of the situation in the autonomous republics has been achieved due to an overall abatement of the population's political activity in the Caucasus in 1993. Small ethnic groups have, however, a great mobilization ability, and a rise of Russian nationalism (to a large extent, as a tardy response to the rise of nationalism of the mountain peoples) is capable of encouraging and spurring on nationalist movements in the republics. Tis is all the more so since Russian policy in the region has been conducive, to a large measure, to the destabilization of the situation.

3 Russian Policy in the North Caucasus

Over the past few years, Russian policy in the North Caucasus has been characterized by lack of a ceonception and strategy of regional policy and lack of co-ordinated actions on the part of federal structures; by decision-making solely determined by momentary advantages (changes in the status of autonomies, administrative borders in the Russian Federation, the adoption of the Law on the Peoples Subjected to Repressions, the Law on the Establishment of the Ingush republic, etc).

All this led to the fact that various functionaries and politicians act in accordance with their own particular understanding of Russia's future state structure. With regard to the North Caucasus, there are two major approaches to realizing Russia's policy. The military experience of conquering the Caucasus in the 19th century underlies the so-called 'historical' approach. On this approach, the peoples of the North Caucasus are divided into traditionally loyal (Osetins), hostile (the peoples of the eastern Caucasus – Chechnya, Ingushetia, Dagestan) and 'undecided' (the western Caucasus – the peoples of Abkhazia, Adygeya, Karachaevo-Cherkessia and Kabardino-Balkraria), who have different attitudes towards Russia in various historical periods. The major goal of this policy is to retain the Caucasus as part of the Russian Federation at any coste, withthe main principle being 'divide and rule'.

The other approach (a 'democratic' one) is based on the principles of equal partnership with all the peoples in the region, the forming of approaches and institutions for settling interethnic conflicts, and a wider use of negotiating practices at all levels – from the federal level to that of national movements, and others.

The two approaches are often realized simultaneously, and this complicates an objectively ambiguous perception of the federal policy by the various peoples in the Caucasus. Nevertheless, one can discern several stages of Russian policy in the North Caucasus.

The first stage: a latent period (1989-1990) characterized by a confrontation of the Union's Centre and the Russian leadership, the forming of national political movements which supported the Russian democratic movement in the presidential election (due to the emphasis placedon the concept of making all national-territorial units of the USSR equal in their rights). However, neither the Russian nor Union authorities pursued an active policy in the region.

The second stage: a stochastic period (1991-1992), characterized by the attempts of the Russian and Union Centres to use the regional elites and national movements in their confrontation with each other. That is precisely why the actions of the Russian Centre undertaken to stabilize the situation in the Caucasus were rather inconsistent and dependent on the situation.

Measures taken by the federal leadership to settle conflicts very often brought the opposite result and resulted in increased tensions. To take an example, the Law on the Rehabilitation of the Repressed Peoples of the Russian Soviet Federative Socialist Republic passed in April 1991 without any provisions for a mechanism of realizing such territorial rehabilitation became a cause of increased tensions throughout the North Caucasus because it was impossible to implement the law on account of the high population density, the 'chain character' of territorial claims, etc.

The third stage: attempts to stablilize the situation (1993). Early in 1993 the Russian leadership made an attempt to work out a single policy with respect to the North Caucasus, based on a 'democratic' approach. The actions succeeded in dampening down the conflicts in the North Caucasus, but this stage was short-lived and ended in September-October 1993 when the crisis of authority broke out in Moscow.

The fourth stage: Intensification of Russian policy in the Caucasus began to manifest itself in spring 1994 during the crisis of relationships between the Centre and Chechnya (which had proclaimed its independence in autumn 1991). However, the new policy of the Kremlin turned out to be nothing more than a realization of the 'historical' approach: Moscow politicians staked on one of the groupings in opposition to President Dudaev and began financing and supplying it with arms in order to change the authorities in recalcitrant Chechnya.

Such practices are extremely debatable not only from a pragmatic point of view (even if Dudaev is removed from power, Moscow's control over the situation in Chehny will remain extremely problematic), but also from a juridical point of view. In fact, Russian politicians responsible for the situation in the North Caucasus (e.g. head of the Presidential Administration Sergei Filatov, vice-premier Sergei Shakhrai, and others) facilitate the organization of an illegal armed formation on the territory of Russia. In addition, such tactics on Moscow's part with respect to Chechnya may speed up disintegrative processes in the federation, since formal leaders of Russia's regions may draw their own conclusions, seeing how one of the opposition groupings is financed with a view to installing a regime more loyal to Moscow. The second conclusion of regional leaders will concern their relationships with their opposition: it is quite evident that authoritarian trends are being strengthened and pressure on the opposition is mounting at the regional level.

The incoherent, inconsistent Russian policy in the polyethnic North Caucasian region torn apart by internal contradictions made it impossible to finally settle the crises in the whole of the North Caucasus. The Russian leadership does not just have any means, ways and finances for a military solution of conflicts, while a political solution, which requires time and harmonization of interests, will be problematic in the circumstances of continuing economic decline, the absence of a modernization philosophy for Russia's national-state structure, and the unco-ordinated efforts and actions of politicians and functionaries. Under the present conditions, the Russian leadership can only 'freeze' the present contradictions (by political or military methods). At first it may try to stabilize the socio-economic situation in Russia.

4 Prospects for the Region's Transformation

In the North Caucasus, as in the whole post-Soviet 'space', there are two simultaneous processes under way – a disintegrative and an integrative one.

4.1 Integrative Processes in the Caucasus

At present, the political situation in the North Caucasus is largely determined by the evolution of the idea of North Caucasian integrationism, which is part of the general process of regionalisation of the post-Soviet space. The integrationist movement in the Caucasus has many levels.

The first level of integrationism is connected with *political alliances of the region's new national elites*. To these belong the *Konfederatsiya narodov Kavkaza* [Confederation of Caucasus Peoples], incorporating 16 national movements in the region; the *Soyuz Kazakov yuga Rossii* [League of Cossacks of the South of Russia]; *Severokavkazskii demokraticheskii kongress* [the North Caucasian Democratic Congress] formed on the initiative of the Federal authorities and, hence, enjoying no support among most popular national movements of the North Caucasus.

The most numerous, although they too are undergoing an organisational crisis, are the *League of the Cossacks of the South of Russia* and the *Konfederatsiya gorskikh narodov Kavkaza* [Confederation of Mountain Peoples of the Caucasus (CMPC)]. The major objective of the CMPC, created in August 1989, is the co-ordination of the actions of national movements for solving the problems of the 'small' Caucasian peoples:

- inter-ethnic problems (settling border disputes in the Caucasus by initiating and holding talks between the confronting sides);
- political problems (solving problems of the repressed peoples, enhancing the prestige of national movements at the regional and federal levels, struggling for upgrading the status of the 'autonomous nationalities');
- problems of cultural integration of the peoples of the North Caucasus;
- economic problems (e.g., after the natural calamities in the vicinity of Tuapse in summer 1991, national movements of the CMPC allotted money for the reconstruction of destroyed bridges and motorways in 'Shapsughia'.

The covert struggle of blocs of indigenous peoples for leadership (e.g., between Adygheans and Vainakhians), the creation of alternative organisations of ethnically cognate peoples[7], border problems, and the personal ambitions of mountain leaders circumscribed the range of major programme guidelines of the association. The Confederation is in fact used by its members for defending the interests of their ethnic groups, e.g., by Ossetians for winning over support in the conflict with Georgia and repelling Ingush territorial claims; by Ingush, on the contrary, for their quickest possible territorial rehabilitation; by Chechens as a means of exerting pressure on Russia and a way of consolidating the Chechen influence in the neighbouring republics and in the region as a whole, etc.

---

7 For example, the World Cherkessian Association which includes Cherkessians, Kabardinians, Adygheyans, Shapsughians and related Abkhazians and Abazians, advocated the creation of a confederation of Adygheyan-Abkhazian states. In summer 1992 the idea was discussed at the state level as well, and bilateral agreements were signed between the Adygheyan states.

The Federal policy in the Caucasus to a large extent encourages the radicalisation of this integrationist movement. Wavering of the Russian leadership on the issue of a future federative structure and Moscow's harsh and inconsistent response to the events in Chechnya in October 1991 provoked the adoption of a course of action that lead to the gradual formation of a Mountain Republic outside the Russian Federation (November 1991). However, for most leaders of national movements of the North Caucasian peoples the orientation toward a union with Russia remains predominant.

The *League of Cossacks of the South of Russia* includes the Tersk Cossack Host, the All-Kuban' Cossack Host, the League of the Cossacks of the Don Host Region, the League of the Cossacks of Stavropol. Despite some contradictions between the Cossack leagues (having to do primarily with political ambitions of the Cossack atamans and with attempts of official authorities – both regional and Federal ones – at initiating 'dehorned' tame Cossack movements), the *League of Cossacks of the South of Russia* put forward a number of common co-ordinated demands:

- to recognize the Cossacks as a people that were repressed by the Soviet power;
- to be granted the right to organize national-territorial formations[8] in any area inhabited by Cossacks and to re-establish the traditional territorial administration (the Ataman rule);
- the revival of the historical tradition of Cossack representation at all levels of state power;
- a ban on selling land to migrants (in the 'Russian South');
- the forming of Cossack units to guard the state borders of Russia.

The growth of the Cossacks' popularity is facilitated by, first of all, the national self-determination of the Caucasian peoples. Thus, claims to establish national districts in Krasnodar *krai* led to a growing activity of Cossackdom not in their traditional places of settlement in the North but also in the South of the Kuban'. Secondly, the aggravation of inter-ethnic contradictions fuelled demands to reinstate Cossack administrative-territorial units and even to allow some districts to secede from the autonomous republics. Such demands were put forward by the Kislyar section in Daghestan, the Mozdok and Sunzha sections in Northern Ossetia and

---

8 In the South of Russia, the following Cossack groupings stood up for creating Cossack Republics: the Tersk Cossacks (a reinstitution of the Sunzha District within the 1928 borders of 11 *stanitsas* [large Cossack villages] of Northern Ossetia and Ingushetia); the League of the Cossacks of the Region of the Don Host; the Kuban' Cossacks (a creation of the Zelenchuk-Urupsk and Batalpasha Cossack Republics in Karachaevo-Cherkessia). It should be noted that one is to expect a new intensified wave of similar demands during the privatisation in the region.

Ingushetia, the Nauri section in Chechnya (the Tersk Cossack Host); the Upper Kuban' section of the All-Kuban' Cossack Host in Karachaevo-Cherkessia.

It should be noted that while the aims of the League of Cossacks and the CMPC are very different, they still have quite a few things in common: an internal amorphism coupled with rigid outward hierarchy; militarised formations; and similar stereotypes in thinking. But the principal similarity is their resorting to traditionalism which ensures wide popular support of the movements in the region. What is more, traditionalism (i.e., use of traditional methods in conflict resolution between peoples in the Caucasus; references to common history and roots; use of traditions in forming organisational structures) may be seen as a peculiar analogue of nationalism at the regional level. This phenomenon does indeed share the main features of nationalism: heedfulness of a common past, hopes for the future, a specific role for the poly-ethnic Caucasus as a bridge between two civilisations – the Moslem and Christian ones, between the East and the West. It was precisely this traditionalism that helped to smooth down the confrontation between Cossacks and 'Caucasians'[9] and to hold 'round tables' with the leaders of both integrationist structures in 1993-1994. But, at the same time, it was also traditionalism that brought about, at least in part, the crisis in the two organisations: prospects for their development have not been elaborated and an outside factor of assistance or counteraction is required in order to consolidate these organisations.

The second level of Caucasian integrationism is the *North Caucasian Economic Association of Local Councils and Executive Bodies of the Regions of the North Caucasian Economic Area* which was founded in summer 1991. The activities of the Association have so far been rather limited: in practice, it does not conduct any serious work on developing general economic, ecological or electric power engineering programmes. This situation is partly determined by the structure of economic ties of regions in the former USSR. Krasnodar *krai*, for instance, largely had ties with industrial areas in Siberia and the Urals rather than with its neighbours. The present economic crisis, lack of financial resources and a drift toward isolationism also influence the elaboration and realisation of joint programmes.

The third integrationist factor is at the *inter-state* level. The idea of a 'Common Caucasian home' was put forward in 1989 by the Movement of Georgian Greens and the CMPC, independently of each other. The CMPC regarded the 'Caucasian home' as a way of solving inter-ethnic and regional tasks in the North Caucasus

---

9 Both leaders of national movements and Cossack atamans are of the opinion that the Cossacks and the mountain peoples are 'the two indigenous peoples of the Northern Caucasus'.

(admittedly, this aspect was not elaborated by the new political leaders of the Caucasus), while the Greens of Georgia saw it as a mechanism to establishing a single eco-system in the region. Georgia's ex-President Gamsakhurdia, having taking over the slogan in 1990, added some political colouring to it: to break away from Moscow in order to solve regional problems (whereby the role of the new integrating centre in such a 'Home' was assigned to Georgia). After the 'Chechen revolution', Chechnya's President Dzhokhar Dudaev supported Gamsakhurdia on this point.

At present, this idea is not popular enough to become a serious threat to the Russian leadership's dominant influence. Beside the socio-economic crisis that has gripped all parts of the region, national-territorial contradictions and armed conflicts reduce to a large extent the chances of having the Caucasian republics unite into a single 'Home': the Ossetian-Ingushetian conflict showed the unfeasibility of such a union in the North Caucasus, to say nothing about the inter-ethnic conflict in Transcaucasia. However, in the future this initiative may have some prospects (although the number of members and composition of such a union still remains undefined) on account of the volatile political situation in Transcaucasia, the inconsistent policy of the Russian leadership in the region, and the lack of funds in the Federal Budget for regional programmes in the North Caucasus. All this can become an impulse for regions to try to break away from Moscow and to intensify the 'horizontal ties' between various regions. It is indicative that in June 1994 Kalmykia, the Crimea and Abkhazia joined the Economic Association.

4.2 The Pace of Transformation

Nevertheless, at present intra-regional *disintegrative processes* are the determinant factor in the situation in the Caucasus. In the first place, they are connected with prospects for economic transformation of the region: the pace and the direction of getting out of the economic crisis and modernising the economy are different for different parts of the region. In the first approximation, one can distinguish between two blocs - the 'Russian' South of Russia with good chances of getting quickly out from the economic crisis and the autonomous republics of the Caucasus where a change in the negative trends in the economy and politics can hardly be expected in the near future.

The 'Russian' South belongs to regions of relative stability. Its economic potential is considerably higher than that of the national republics. The former has, first of all, a solid industrial and agricultural basis: it accounts for 77.5% of the industrial output and 90% of sowing areas of the North Caucasus. It should also be noted that the all-Russian agricultural register mentions this region as the zone with the 'least hazardous farming'.

After the disintegration of the USSR, this region remained the only access way of the Russian Federation to the Black Sea, which is important in light of the fact that 25% of Russia's foreign trade passes through the Bosporus and Dardanelles.[10] The use of Black Sea ports (Novorossiisk, Sochi, Tuapse) and ports on the Azov Sea (Taganrog, Azov) for international trade is limited at present because of very high freight rates and the need to reconstruct ports. The export potential of the 'Russian South' is small and makes up only 1.3% of Russia's export potential. However, practically all regions of the Russian Federation that produce power sources, raw materials and semi-finished products are interested in projects of sea transport development, and in the nearest future one should expect a bustling investment activity of these regions in the 'South of Russia'. Speeding up the transport potential renovation in the South of Russia is possible within the framework of the Treaty on Black Sea Economic Co-operation (BSEC), the declaration for which was signed on 25 July 1992. The BSEC is important to Russia for several reasons[11]:

- first of all, the member-countries of the BSEC account for 10% of Russia's foreign trade with the 'far abroad', and the importance of the BSEC countries for Russia 's export (especially, for the machine-building sector) will grow even more;
- secondly, as the social-economic situation in the Russian Federation becomes more stable, the importance of the recreation potential of the BSEC member-countries will grow ever more as well;
- and finally, Russia is interested in importing a number of goods produced in the BSEC: Greek bauxites, Bulgarian soda, and Turkish chromites.

The 'Russian South's' industrial structure differs from that of the national republics by its complexity and the availability of 'local' labour resources (75% of those employed in the North Caucasian industry). The 'Russian South' is a region of relative stability: the drop in production in 1992 is close to Russia's average (18.8%), the share of unprofitable cost-inefficient enterprises in 1992 was 11% (Russia's average was 17%), which makes it possible to expect a more peaceful economic recovery than in the autonomous republics.

---

10 *Vneshnaya Torgovlya*, nos. 7-8 (1994).

11 Vardomskii, L. „Ekonomicheskiye Interesy Rossii i Chernomorskoye Sotrudnichestvo [Russia's Economic Interests and Black Sea Co-operation]." *Vneshnaya Torgovlya*, nos. 7-8 (1994).

Characteristic of the latter are economic[12] and political instability, inter-ethnic confrontation, which lead to the flight of Russian specialists from the republics, while the lack of 'national' (native) cadres in industries makes any modernisation of industries in the national republics rather doubtful within the next few years. Moreover, the whole of the republics' industrial potential, in contrast to the regions of the 'Russian South', is actually concentrated in the capitals, which considerably compounds social and inter-ethnic problems in the period of economic recession, presents an extra stimulus for Russian-speaking specialists to flee from the republics, and becomes the reason for the fact that most funds allocated from the Federal Budget are spent for social security needs rather than modernisation.

The second aspect determining a practical disintegration of the North Caucasian economic region is connected with the rise of nationalism in the region. The growing nationalism of the mountain peoples became one of the causes of a rise of Russian nationalism in the South of Russia. Among 'external factors' for the rise of Russian nationalism one should also mention the national humiliation experienced by many Russians after the collapse of the USSR and Russia's loss of the role of a world leader. These feelings are constantly being nourished by the awareness of the position of Russians in the CIS countries and autonomous republics of the Russian Federation and the fate of Russian refugees in the South of Russia.

The differentiation between Russian and non-Russian national movements in the North Caucasus is also a consequence of the policy pursued by the Federal authorities. Thus, the confrontation between the mountain peoples and the Cossacks increased after the President of the Russian Federation had signed a number of decrees on the rehabilitation of the Cossacks as a military class (*soslovie*). A rise of Russian nationalism can, in its turn, bring about a new intensification of national movements in the North Caucasus even there where they have been on the decrease since early 1993.

The inter-ethnic tension in the national republics is greatly hindering economic modernisation. Apart from the above-mentioned problem of Russian specialists' flight from the republic, modernisation will be impeded by a set of socio-economic problems that are typical of the region: the use of finances for liquidating the aftermaths of inter-ethnic conflicts rather than for economic transformations. To exemplify, after the Ossetian-Ingushetian war in 1993, about 23 bln roubles were spent only on financing the provisional administration in the region, while 100 bln

---

12 In 1992, In Kabardino-Balkaria the drop in production was 32.5%, in Karachaevo-Cherkessia - 27.7%, in Northern Ossetia - 26.1%, and in Chechnya-Ingushetia - 30%.

roubles were spent on relief operations for refugees (to compare, the draft budget of Northern Ossetia for 1993 provided for general expenditures to the amount of 25.2 bln rouble, and in Ingushetia – 5.9 bln roubles).

The differences between the 'Russian South' and the autonomous republics are also connected with the actual paralysis of communications. Inter-ethnic tensions in the national republics would often result in the obstruction of the main transport lines. After the outbreak of the civil war in Chechnya in summer 1994, the eastern part of the North Caucasus found itself completely cut off.

It has to be emphasised that it would be overly premature to maintain that there is a unified bloc of autonomous republics. The Ossetian-Ingushetian conflict in autumn 1992 divided the North Caucasus geographically into two parts: the Eastern (Chechnya, Ingushetia, Daghestan) and the Western (Adyghea, Karachaevo-Cherkessia, Kabardino-Balkaria) ones. That conflict also paralysed the Confederation of the Mountain Peoples of the Caucasus which included both the Ingushetian and Ossetian national organisations. Notwithstanding the economic and political complications that are characteristic of all the republics of the North Caucasus, the Western Caucasus has a more favourable geographic and economic position, as compared with the Eastern Caucasus.

The former gravitates toward the 'Russian South' and its economic modernisation will directly depend on economic transformations in Rostov *oblast'*, Krasnodar and Stavropol *krais*. The index of the Western Caucasus' ethnic diversity is also considerably lower than that of the Eastern Caucasus, which leads to a far lower level of inter-ethnic confrontation.

The Eastern Caucasus has the most adverse conditions for economic and political transformation: here are intertwined complex economic, inter-ethnic and political problems. This is the region of the lowest living standards and the highest unemployment rate, underdeveloped communication lines and great industrial specialisation employing predominantly specialists from other regions, who are now inclined to leave the republics. This is the region with the highest ethnic diversity index in the Russian Federation, the highest population growth rate, and, at the same time, the greatest scarcity of land and water. Its administrative borders and areas of settlement of ethnic groups have changed repeatedly, and the process of property redistribution greatly sharpened the competition of national elites in their struggle for power. In the predictable future, the maintenance of stability in this region of the North Caucasus will become a weighty burden for the Russian budget and will require considerable political and, most likely, military activities on the part the Federal bodies of power.

4.3 The Unity of Russia

Finally, the differences between the 'Russian South' and the autonomous republics are also determined by their attitudes toward the idea of breaking away from the Russian Federation. In Rostov *oblast'*, and Stavropol and Krasnodar *krais*, there are no political groupings that support separatist ideas. This is primarily due to its developed economic ties with other regions of the Russian Federation. The attitude to Moscow as the political and economic centre of Russia is, however, not so unambiguous. Up to now, the most popular politician in the Kuban' has been Nikolai Kondratenko, the former first secretary of the territorial committee [*kraikom*] of the CPSU[13] who once put forward the slogan 'We will not let the Centre plunder the Kuban'!'. However, this local patriotism is most probably a reflection of the traditional confrontation between Moscow and the regions, which is characteristic of other Russia's regions as well.[14] This factor has lately become more important due to the uncertainty about the principles of Russia's regional policy and the lack of clear-cut and well-grounded differentiation of powers among the subjects of the Federation.

In the autonomous republics, attitudes toward Moscow and the integrity of the Russian Federation are varied. Local bureaucracy is well aware of the fact that economic development and living standards are largely determined by subsidies from the Federal Budget (see Table 5). Furthermore, official elites are interested in winning (financial and military) support on the part of the Federal Centre to retain and stabilise their positions. The confrontation between the Russian and Union Centres In 1990-1991, and the permanent confrontation at the Federal level in 1992-1993 created very favourable conditions for the republics to extract economic and political privileges and subventions in exchange for their loyalty to this or that branch of power. It was precisely in that period that the republics' Acts and

---

13 At present, a deputy to the Federation Council who won the greatest number of votes at the election.

14 Very indicative, for example, is the following fact. Under the 1994 Budget, Moscow – a financially well-to-to region – was allotted 3 bln roubles subventions which is equal to the amount planned to be spent on programmes of regional development and free housing all over Russia.

Constitutions, which ran counter the Federal legislation[15], made their appearance. In addition, possibilities for the Federal Centre to interfere in the internal affairs of the republics are very limited (with the only exception being in cases of violation of human rights): the local bureaucracies resort, as a rule, to arguments about an alleged sharp destabilisation of social situation, inter-ethnic conflicts and social upheavals, in case the status quo is offset. Such uncontrolled actions of the local bureaucracies may well be considered as a 'soft' variety of secession. Contradictions between the 'feudalisation' of power in the republics and violations of human rights and rights of various ethnic and social groups do exist, but their solution, as well as the stabilisation of the socio-economic and inter-ethnic situation are possible only after Russia's economy has recovered.

As far as the national movements of the region are concerned, the idea of seceding from the Russian Federation has supporters everywhere, except for in Northern Ossetia. The situation in this aspect is determined by the complex history of Russia's relations with the Caucasian peoples, and the inconsistent policy of the present Russian leadership in the region. One should also mention another important reason for the lowering of Moscow's profile in the North Caucasian region: the wavering of Russian foreign policy with respect to Transcaucasian conflicts. The Abkhazian-Georgian war, the Ossetian-Georgian war and Russian leadership's support of the idea of creating the unitary Georgian state[16] were met with disapproval by all the mountain national movements. The conflicts in Georgia and the inconsistent policy of the Russian Federation regarding Chechnya in 1991 became major reasons behind the proclamation by the Confederation of Mountain Peoples of the Caucasus of a course toward creating a Mountain Republic outside the Russian Federation. The motives for this decision were different for the national leaders of the CMPC: for the leaders of the 'Abkhazian-Adygheyan bloc', those harsh declarations were designed to attract the Russian leadership's attention to the Abkhazian-Georgian war, while the Chechen leaders considered this statement as a

---

15 According to Vladimir Lysenko, the Chair of the subcommittee on the development of Federative relations of the State Duma, the Constitutions of the national republics of the Northern Caucasus, adopted in 1994, all ran counter the Constitution of the Russian Federation. For example, Chechnya's Constitution is in complete contradiction to the Russian Constitution. The Constitution of Daghestan defines the republic as a subject of international law, and Daghestan's laws are superior to Federal laws. Adygheya's Constitution provides for ethnic quotas in Parliamentary elections.

16 This was proved by agreements on settling the conflicts in Southern Ossetia and Abkhazia in 1992.

regional (even if at the level of unofficial political elites) support for separatist aspirations.

Nevertheless, the very appearance of the slogan is quite symptomatic. The weakening of Russian influence in the Caucasus creates a precondition for a change in the regional balance of power. Now some Moslem countries are already sizing up their opportunities in the region. And although at present the Moslem-belt countries, despite the expectations of Moslems in the former USSR, are not pursuing any activist policies in the region (one can hardly consider insignificant activities of foreign businessmen or the participation of volunteers from Turkey in the Abkhazian-Georgian conflict as serious), but construction of mosques and programmes in the field of education may become factors of political influence, even in the absence of solid investments into the region's economy.

Internal contradictions in Russia and the inconsistent policy of the Russian leadership have led to a considerable lowering of Moscow's rating in the Caucasus and a search for new ‘centres of influence’, first of all on the part of the region's new political elites. At present we can discern the emergence of a whole number of centres of regional influence in the Caucasus, with each specific problem of an ethnic group determining its appealing to this or that ‘centre’ (Moscow, Groznyi, Ankara, etc.).

At the first stage (late 1991-the first half of 1992), Turkey became a new ‘centre of influence’ for leaders of the national mountain movements. This trend emerged, first of all, under the influence of economic (the Russian mass media were popularising of the ‘Turkish model’ – a peculiar ‘Oriental’ analogue of the slogan about ‘a bright capitalist future’), historical (Turkey's active role in the region during several centuries, and the presence of a sizeable Caucasian diaspora in Turkey after the Russian-Caucasian War) and political stereotypes in the minds of nationalist leaders in the North Caucasus. In the second half of 1992 the leaders of the ‘Abkhazian-Adygheyan block’ came to be disenchanted with the role of Turkey in the region (since the outbreak of the Abkhazian-Georgian conflict in August 1992, official Ankara had been giving humanitarian aid to Georgia). At that time, a rift emerged between Adygheyan nationalist movements, on the one hand, and Turkish – Balkarian, Karachai and Nogai – ones, on the other.

At present, the choice of ‘centres of influence’ by political elites depends on the situation and very often it may be rather contradictory. For members of the Balkar national movement, who had been constantly swearing allegiance to the idea of Russia's unity and integrity, Chechnya's President Dzhokhar Dudaev was, up to the outbreak of the civil war in Chechnya in 1994, the indisputable regional leader in the North Caucasus.

At the present stage, the idea of breaking away from Russia is not popular among national leaders of the North Caucasus. The main reason for this became the obvious three-years long 'independent' experience of Chechnya which is one of the most ethnically homogeneous republics of the region. It should also be pointed out that, unlike in other republics, the idea of breaking away from Russia was popular among most Chechens.

In the former USSR, Chechens were considered by Communist Party leaders as the most politically unreliable people: Chechnya-Ingushetia was one of a few Russia's autonomies where the *oblast'* committee of the CPSU was headed by a Party functionary appointed by Moscow. Only in July 1989, Doku Zavgaev, a native of the Nadterechnyi district which has traditionally been loyal to Moscow, became the first secretary of the *oblast'* committee of the CPSU. This was the first step in changing the previous balance of political elites. Natives of the Nadterechnyi district who had been well represented in administration bodies well before 1989, now came to dominate all levels of power. The 'Chechen Revolution' of September 1991 was undertaken under the slogan of expelling the Communist *nomenklatura* and was supported by many confronting clans (taips) and groupings. But the overthrow of Doku Zavgaev brought about a further split in political and taip-groups struggling for power and resources. The outbreak of the civil war was provoked by actions of the Russian leadership in the region. But the eruption of the military-political conflict was primarily connected with the internal conflict potential within the republic itself. It should be noted that a change in the balance of forces of the present ethno-political groupings in the autonomous republics, especially if it is done by violent methods, will lead to a drastic destabilization. And this is well understood in the North Caucasus.

Table 4 *Main Conflicts in the North Caucasus Region*

1 *Territory ('000 km²)*
2 *Population ('000 people)*
3 *Population density (people/km²)*
4 *Rural population (%)*
5 *Main ethnic groups*
6 *Number of people ('000)*
7 *% of total population*
8 *Main conflicts*

	1	2	3	4	5	6	7	8
Daghestan	50.3	1802.6	35.4	56.4	Avars	496.0	27.5	• Federalisation of Dagestan; demands of the national movements of the Kumyks, Cossacks and Nogai
					Dargins	280.4	15.6	
					Kumyks	231.8	12.9	• Recreation of the Aukhskii-district (Chechens)
					Lezgins	204.4	11.3	• Conflict between Chechens and Avars in Kazbegovskii district
					Russians	165.9	9.2	
					Lakhs	91.7	5.1	• Conflict between Chechens and Lakhs in Novolakskii-district
					Tabasarans	78.2	4.3	
					Azerbaizhani	75.5	4.2	• Conflict between Kumyks and Avars in the fight for power
					Chechens	57.8	3.2	• Creation of a Nogai autonomy
					Nogai	28.3	1.6	• Separation of the Kizlyarskii-district
					Rutulcians	15.0	0.8	• Conflict between Lakhs and Kumyks in Khasav-Yurta
Kabardino-Balkaria	12.5	759.6	60.8	38.8	Kabardins	363.5	48.2	• The recreation of the administrative borders of 1944 by the Balkars lead to the demand of a Balkar Republic (March 1991), while the Kabardins still recognise the borders of the 1863-treaty
					Balkars	70.8	9.4	
					Russians	240.8	32.0	
					Ukrainians	12.8	1.7	
					Ossetians	10.0	1.3	
Northern Ossetia	8.0	634.0	79.2	31.2	Ossetians	334.8	53.0	• Conflict between Ossetians and Ingush in the Prigorodnyj-district
					Russians	189.2	30.0	

					Ingushen	32.8	5.2	• Demands of unification of Mozdokskii-district with Stavropol′ *krai*
					Armenians	13.6	2.2	• Ossetian refugees from Georgia
					Georgians	12.3	1.9	
					Kumyks	9.5	1.5	
Chechnya-Ingushetia	19.3	1275.5	66.2	58.5	Chechens	734.5	57.8	• The inner political crisis in Chechnya (Nadterechnyj- and Urus-Martanovskii-districts)
					Ingushen	163.8	12.9	• Conflict between Chechens and Ingush about the Suzhenskii- and Malgobegskij-districts
					Russians	293.8	23.1	• Ingush refugees from Northern Ossetia
					Armenians	14.8	1.2	• Conflict between Ingush and Ossetians
					Kumyks	9.9	0.8	•
					Nogai	6.9	0.5	
					Avars	6.3	0.5	
Adygheya	7.6	432.6	56.9	47.9	Adygheyans	95.4	22.6	• feud between Cossacks and the authorities
					Russians	293.6	69.4	• feud between Russians and Adygheyans about the 'nationalisation' [*korenizatsiya*]of political authority
					Ukrainians	13.6	3.2	
					Armenians	10.5	2.5	
Karachaevo-Cherkessia	14.0	417.6	29.6	51.2	Karachaevs	129.5	31.2	• the partition of the Republic: the declaration of the Republic of Karachai (Oct. 1990 and April 1992), of the Cossack Republics of Batalpashinskaya and Zelenchuksko-Urpskaya (August 1991) and of the Republics of Abaza and Cherkessia (October 1991)
					Czechs	40.0	9.7	
					Russians	175.9	42.4	
					Abazins	27.5	6.6	
					Nogai	13.0	3.1	
Rostov *oblast'*	100.8	4308.6	42.7	28.7				• The problem of migration and refugees • Cossacks (their administration and armed groups) • the problem of the Armenians and other 'Caucasians'.
Stavropol *oblast'*	56.6	2439.6	35.4	46.4				
Krasnodar *krai*	76.0	4680.5	61.2	45.7				
Northern Caucasus	355.1	16750.6	47.1	43.0				
Russian Federation	17075.4	147400	8.6	26.4				

Source: *1989 Population Census*

Table 5 *Exports Structure in 1991 (in percentage):*
1 - machinery and transport vehicles
2 - fuel and mineral raw materials
3 - chemical produce, fertilizers, rubber
4 - raw materials and processed products
5 - raw materials for food products
6 - alimentary products
7 - consumer goods
8 - others
9 - share of exports in the 1991 industrial goods output (in percentage).

	1	2	3	4	5	6	7	8	9
Russian Federation	100	100	100	100	100	100	100	100	100
Northern Caucasus	15.1	53.3	9.6	8.4	0.3	5.8	6.9	0.6	2.9
Adygheya	5.4	0	0	0.6	11.6	53.3	29.1	0	0.9
Daghestan	8.4	0	67.6	4.7	1.7	5.9	10.1	1.6	1.0
Kabardino-Balkaria	18.4	0	0	17.8	4.9	57.8	1.0	0.1	0.3
Karachaevo-Cherkessia	10.0	0	3.3	26.7	0	3.3	0	56.7	0.1
Northern Ossetia	6.2	1.6	0	84.4	0	0	7.8	0	0.2
Chechnya-Ingushetia	1.2	90.0	8.8	0	0	0	0	0	1.9
Krasnodar *krai*	7,0	31.8	7.2	7.7	0.2	29.8	8.8	7.5	2.0
Stavropol *krai*	4.1	4.1	66.1	17.3	0	5.1	2.2	1.1	0.8
Rostov *oblast'*	55.5	4.9	30.2	5.3	0	0.9	0.7	2.5	3.9

Imports Structure in 1991 (in percentage)

	1	2	3	4	5	6	7	8
Russian Federation	100	100	100	100	100	100	100	100
Northern Caucasus	36.3	6.4	7.1	5.6	19.9	7.7	15.9	1.1
Adygheya	18.7	0	0	0	3.5	16.5	61.3	0
Daghestan	4.5	4.2	3.7	2.1	30.9	43.8	10.3	0.5
Kabardino-Balkaria	10.9	1.7	2.2	0	55.5	1.5	26.9	1.3
Karachaevo-Cherkessia	0.5	9.1	22.1	68.1	0	0.2	0	0
Northern Ossetia	12.7	8.0	10.7	3.3	44.7	20.3	0.3	0
Chechnya-Ingushetia	18.5	9.8	5.4	0.7	20.2	43.7	1.7	0
Krasnodar *krai*	16.5	0.5	2.7	13.7	51.4	8.7	6.4	0.1
Stavropol *krai*	21.3	3.6	10.6	14.5	42.1	1.1	5.7	1.1
Rostov *oblast'*	24.4	4.7	7.9	0.6	12.3	8.1	41.6	0.4

Source: Indices of Economic Development of the Republics, Territories and oblasts in the Russian Federation. *Moscow: Goskomstat Rossii, 1992.*

Table 6 *Budget Estimates for 1993:*
1 - Expenditures (mln Roubles)
2 - Federal Budget Subsidies (relative to expenditures in %)
3 - Federal Budget Subsidies (relative to overall amount of subsidies in %).

	1	2	3
Northern Caucasus	517,782.8	27.1%	21.9%
Adygheya	14,290.9	32.1%	0.7%
Daghestan	61,657.2	73.7%	6.9%
Kabardino-Balkaria	26,357.0	63.9%	2.6%
Karachaevo-Cherkessia	14,823.9	45.4%	1.0%
Northern Ossetia	25,189.6	41.8%	1.6%
Ingushetia	5,958.3	92.9%	0.8%
Chechnya	30,711.9	32.4%	1.5%
Krasnodar *krai*	134,716.6	11.1%	2.3%
Stavropol *krai*	83,906.2	37.3%	4.8%
Rostov *oblast'*	120,171.2	-	-

Source: The Budget Message of the President of the Russian Federation for 1993.

Table 7 *Indices of Social Development (relative to the national indices):*
1 - Number of hospital beds per 10,000 in 1991
2 - Number of doctors per 10,000 in 1991
3 - Dwelling space per one dweller (in sq. m)
4 - Selling space (in sq. m) per 1,000
5 - Number of seat in public catering facilities per 1,000
6 - Number of students of higher educational establishments per 10,000
7 - Number of students at specialized secondary educational establishments per 10,000)
8 - Volume of paid services per 10,000 rendered per 1 person.

	1	2	3	4	5	6	7	8
Russian Federation	100	100	100	100	100	100	100	100
Northern Caucasus	90.6	93.8	97.6	86.9	87.3	77.4	86.5	97.1
Adygheya	90.3	76.5	107.3	83.2	70.9	67.2	100.7	86.3
Daghestan	88.3	97.9	94.5	73.2	62.0	79.6	75	45.1
Kabardino-Balkaria	93.5	111.0	89.0	84.5	97.5	86.0	79.7	118.9
Karachaevo-Cherkessia	81.8	63.5	100.0	92.0	96.2	53.8	73.7	89.3
Northern Ossetia	88.9	138.6	101.2	81.2	91.1	138.2	112.8	87.5
Chechnya-Ingushetia	76.0	58.9	78.0	67.1	59.5	68.8	60.1	54.9
Krasnodar *krai*	94.1	98.2	99.4	90.6	93.7	52.7	77.7	129.0
Stavropol *krai*	87.5	112.6	96.3	99.5	92.4	62.9	69.6	22.5
Rostov *oblast'*	94.8	81.5	103.7	88.7	92.4	107.5	114.9	82.0

Table 8 *Consumer Goods Output per Capita in 1991 (relative to the national indices):*
1 - Consumer goods output per capita in 1991
2 - Food products output
3 - Non-food goods.

	1	2	3
Russian Federation	1	1	1
Northern Caucasus	0.83	1.16	0.61
Adygheya	1.2	1.66	0.48
Daghestan	0.37	0.44	0.33
Kabardino-Balkaria	0.72	0.86	0.63
Karachaevo-Cherkessia	0.84	0.89	0.92
Northern Ossetia	0.89	0.78	0.81
Chechnya-Ingushetia	0.39	0.49	0.27
Krasnodar *krai*	1.10	1.96	0.63
Stavropol *krai*	0.73	0.97	0.56
Rostov *oblast'*	0.90	1.01	0.79

Source: Indices of Economic Development of the Republics, Territories and Oblasts in the Russian Federation. *Moscow : Goskomstat Rossii, 1992.*

Table 9 *Money Incomes of the Population:*
1 - average monthly wages/salary of workers and employees in 1985
2 - average monthly wages/salary of workers and employees in 1991
3 - average monthly wages of collective/state farm workers in 1985
4 - average monthly wages of collective/state farm workers in 1991.

	1	2	3	4
Russian Federation	100%	100%	100%	100%
Northern Caucasus	84.9%	86.9%	98.8%	120.7%
Adygheya	76.7%	86.8%	91.6%	108.7%
Daghestan	72.6%	62.8%	56.0%	40.5%
Kabardino-Balkaria	84.1%	80.3%	87.4%	104%
Karachaevo-Cherkessia	83.8%	86.8%	103.0%	110.1%
Northern Ossetia	84.7%	78.3%	107.2%	101.4%
Chechnya-Ingushetia	79.3%	74.6%	82.5%	74.8%
Krasnodar *krai*	82.6%	92.1%	101.8%	140.5
Stavropol *krai*	86.1%	90.7%	112.1%	140.5
Rostov *oblast'*	91.0%	92.0%	103.0%	118.6%

Source: Indices of Economic Development of the Republics, Territories and Oblasts in the Russian Federation. *Moscow: Goskomstat Rossii, 1992.*

15

A Qualitative Analysis of the Situation in the Donbass

Grigorii Nemir'ya

The situation in the Donbass in considered in this paper from three angles: first, from the viewpoint of the specificity of Ukrainian regionalism; second, from the point of view of Donbass area specifics; third, with due attention to the dynamics of forming elites, both national and regional.

Present-day Ukraine is often viewed as a country with two 'poles': the Eastern one (with the centre in Donetsk) and the Western one (with the centre in Lviv). These two key regions differ from each other *ethno-linguistically* (a considerable presence of ethnic Russians and prevalence of the Russian language in the East and domination of Ukrainians and the Ukrainian language in the West), *religiously* (Russian Orthodox Church *vs.* Catholic Church), *socio-culturally* (traditions of collectivism and state paternalism *vs.* traditions of individualism) as well as *in the types of economic orientation* (state-owned property *vs.* private property), *in geopolitical preferences* (pro-Russian, Eurasian *vs.* pro-Western, European) and *in the perception of the past* (e.g., contradictory views on the significance of the Treaty of Pereyaslavl with Moscow of 1654 and some events of World War II).

The centre of this 'Western Ukraine – Eastern Ukraine' axis is Kiev, the capital and focal point of power, and, at the same time, an object of incessant attacks by the two competing regions trying to acquire resources and influence over the process of political decision-making. The bureaucratic centre, in this model, plays the role of a mediator in the conflict between the East and the West, making efforts to see to its own interests, to preserve stability in the country and to preclude its disintegration.

Clearly, this simplistic model reflects real facts, both modern and dating back to the remote and recent past (for example, the fact that various parts of Ukraine used to belong for a very long time, sometimes for centuries, to different states that were often hostile towards one another – to the Polish-Lithuanian, Ottoman, Austro-Hungarian and Russian empires, Romania and others). However, this model cannot be sufficient for a detailed analysis of Ukrainian regionalism.

On the Meaning of the Term 'Region'

Under the present administrative-territorial division, Ukraine consists of 24 *oblasts*, two cities subject to the central government (Kiev and Sevastopol) and the Crimean Autonomous Republic.

Despite the fact that the terms *oblast*' and 'region' are often used interchangeably, the term 'region' is widely used to denote a combination of several *oblasts*, with the areas of individual regions being interpreted both narrowly and broadly. For example, Western Ukraine is treated narrowly as consisting of three *oblasts*: those of Lviv, Ivano-Frankivsk and Ternopil, while in a broad sense, five *oblasts*, with Rivne and Volyn *oblasts* added. Eastern Ukraine is perceived in the narrow sense as comprising two *oblasts*: Donetsk and Lugansk one, in the wider sense – as consisting of five *oblasts*, with Zaporizhya, Dnipropetrovsk and Kharkiv *oblasts* being added to the above two. In popular literature one can come across identifications of Left-Bank Ukraine with Eastern Ukraine and Right-Bank Ukraine with Western Ukraine.

Designations with historical and geographical connotations are also very current: Galicia, Volyn, Transcarpathia, Bukovyna, Podillia, Transdniepria, Slobozhanshchina (*Free Peasants*' *Ukraine*), Novorossiya, the Donbass.

The most recent works of Ukrainian sociologists use a geopolitical division of Ukraine into 11 regions:

- Kiev
- The Northern Region (Zhytomyr, Chernihiv and Kiev *oblasts*)
- The Central Region (Vinnytsya, Kirovograd, Poltava, Cherkassy and Khmelnytsky *oblasts*)
- The North-Eastern region (Sumy and Kharkiv *oblasts*)
- The North-Western region (Volyn and Rivne *oblasts*)
- The Dnieper region (Dnipropetrovsk and Zaporizhya *oblasts*)
- The Western region (Ivano-Frankivsk, Lviv and Ternopil *oblasts*)
- The South-Western region (the Transcarpathian and Chernivtsi *oblasts*)
- The Southern region (Mykolaiv, Odessa and Kherson *oblasts*)
- The Crimea
- The Donetsk region (Donetsk and Lugansk *oblasts*)

Characteristically, practically all political forces in Ukraine do not consider the official administrative-territorial division of Ukraine as something unchangeable and fixed for ever. Though adopting different models of state structure (as a unitary, unitary-decentralised or federative state), they admit the possibility for administrative-territorial units to become larger in future.

Problems of the quest for an optimal administrative division of Ukraine have been posed several times before the nation's architects. In 1918 Mikhailo Hrushevsky, the President of the Ukrainian People's Republic suggested to divide Ukraine into 30 lands, three of which – the cities of Kiev, Kharkiv and Odessa, together with suburban areas – were to become separate districts. The issue of a future administrative-territorial reform as part of the nation-building agenda, even if remote, is today already influencing the behaviour and policies of some representatives of regional elites. The main statistical data on the regions' economies are indicative of the great territorial differentiation.

Table 1 *Levels of Economic Development of Ukraine's Regions (Regions'/Oblasts' Share of National GNP, in %, 1992)*

Region/*oblast'*	Region's share in production of GNP (in %)	Region's share in production of national income (in %)
1. Donetsk *oblast'*	16.40	13.95
2. Dnipropetrovsk *oblast'*	12.65	11.59
3. Lugansk *oblast'*	8.40	7.92
4. Kiev *oblast'*	7.12	7.63
5. Zaporizhya *oblast'*	5.54	5.10
6. Odessa *oblast'*	5.24	6.80
7. Kharkiv *oblast'*	4.74	4.45
8. Poltava *oblast'*	4.58	4.25
9. Lviv *oblast'*	3.94	3.90
10. The Crimea	3.17	3.59
11. Vinnytsya *oblast'*	2.82	3.19
12. Cherkassy *oblast'*	2.30	2.40
13. Sumy *oblast'*	2.25	2.19
14. Khmelnytsky *oblast'*	2.20	2.64
15. Kherson *oblast'*	2.19	2.25
16. Chernihiv *oblast'*	2.18	2.33
17. Zhytomyr *oblast'*	2.13	2.44
18. Mykolaiv *oblast'*	2.08	2.18
19. Ivano-Frankivsk *oblast'*	1.90	1.92
20. Kirovograd *oblast'*	1.68	1.76
21. Rivne *oblast'*	1.64	1.95
22. Ternopil *oblast'*	1.47	1.72
23. Volyn *oblast'*	1.33	1.58
24. Transcarpathian *oblast'*	1.19	1.19
25. Chernivtsi *oblast'*	1.00	1.08

In some regions of Ukraine the transformation crisis is especially acute, first of all because of specifics of regional economies. We will take the Donbass as an example where the economic potential is largely determined by industries. In Donetsk *oblast'* they account for about two-thirds of the produced national income and 82% of profits made. Approximately 45% of industrial and white collar workers are employed in these industries.

Four-fifths of industrial output fall to heavy industries. Products of non-ferrous metallurgy and fuel industries, which determine the *oblast*'s specificity, account for over 41% of general industrial output. In machine-building the share of heavy metallurgical, mining and transport machine building amounts to 54%. At the same time, less than 25% of industrial products are produced in the *oblast*' for the needs of consumer goods.

The level of capital consumption in the *oblast*' is as high as 55%. About 80% of coal mines have not been subject to reconstruction for more than 20 years. More than 90% of open-hearth furnaces, 35% of oxygen converters, 70% of bar mills and 85% of sheet mills are run beyond normative deadlines for operation and must be either replaced or radically reconstructed. For this reason, the region's industry bears essential economic losses related to increased labour consumption, unreasonable diversion of funds for capital repairs of plants and equipment facilities, while in the general volume of its production the share of products that are competitive on the world market is small.

An excessive concentration of heavy industrial plants in the region has resulted in the pollution of the *oblast*'s air, amounting to over 92 tons of pollutants per square kilometre, which is 6 times higher than Ukraine's average. The *oblast*'s territory is polluted with 3 billion tons of industrial waste. Given the high density of population in the *oblast*' – 202 persons per sq.km, the ecological situation here is critical. This is witnessed by a growth in the population's (especially children's) sick rate.

The situation is aggravated by an obvious heterogeneity of situation in various industrial conglomerations of the region. This differentiation is compounded with changes in the states of business and the market, depletion of mineral resources, dilapidation of production facilities, resulting in ever smaller volumes of production and the deteriorating environment. The region's urban agglomerations find themselves in a particularly difficult situation since they specialise in *only one* sector of production, mainly in coal mining.

Here, another peculiarity of industrialised regions must be noted – *the combination of productive and social spheres*. Typical of the *oblasts* in the Dnieper, North-Eastern and Donetsk regions is a great number of 'departmental' blocks of flats, hospitals, kindergartens and the so-called socio-cultural organisations owned and financed by large plants and mines.

To take an example, the municipal council in Donetsk owns 2,088 dwelling houses, various enterprises – 3,003. This means that structural changes in industries will unavoidably entail closures of some enterprises which would be detrimental to the whole of social sphere connected with the latter. Furthermore, all of this is taking place in a situation where today, by social norms in force, shortages of dwelling accommodations in the region already amount to 20% and in the case of hospitals – 35%.

An essential role in providing the *oblast'* with consumer goods and products has always been played by imports from other regions of Ukraine and from the states of the former USSR. With long-established economic ties severed and regions' economies separating from one another, the supply of food and goods to the population is getting worse. This still further complicates a highly vexing disproportion between money incomes of the region's populace (incidentally, the highest in the country) and its supply with goods (the last place in Ukraine as to sales of goods and services). Incomes of one category of workers (miners), greatly increased for the past several years and not covered by a corresponding amount of goods and products, have been pushing prices up and the other categories out beyond the poverty line. Naturally, this imbalance causes *the nation's highest rate of inflation* and increases social tensions in the region.

It must be emphasised that the processes described above could also be observed during the USSR's existence. We must recall that one of the causes of the miners' strike in the Donbass in 1989 was their conviction that Moscow had been 'plundering' the region, and the USSR Minister of Coal-Mining had been taking more care of the Kuznetsk basin in Russia rather than the Donetsk basin in Ukraine. In the perestroika years, hopes came to be pinned on 'regional self-accounting', and in the peculiar situation of the early 1990s hopes were pinned on 'national sovereignty', which was seen to be the only possible means of getting rid of the monopoly of the Moscow centre.

It was these considerations that inspired more than 83% of the Donbass electorate to vote for Ukraine's independence at the 1 December 1991 referendum.

Therefore, a short time later, some indications were evident that a new Centre would form (in Kiev) instead of the old one in Moscow – a spitting image of the previous Centre. This brought about, on the backdrop of a deepening economic crisis, a second centrifugal wave – this time within Ukraine. The idea of 'autonomous regions' received a second wind.

This seems to be inevitable. At the moment of gaining independence, Ukraine did not have a coherent system of state institutions (indeed, their formation has even now not yet been completed), and, quite naturally, much attention was paid to their establishment. Nevertheless, it would be wrong to overlook the emergent harsh struggle among regional elites for influence on political processes underway in Kiev.

Due to the heterogeneity of Ukraine's political space, the process of elites' reformation and regeneration, stimulated by the ban on the *Communist Party*, was gaining greater momentum in western Ukraine and in Kiev, which ensured their greater co-ordination and, for a short time, influence, despite the numerical minority of national democrats in Parliament.

However, the initiative was gradually being taken over by political forces and interest groups which derived their influence from eastern Ukraine's industrialised regions. During 1992-1993, Donetsk saw constitutory conferences and conventions of six parties: the *Labour Party*, the *Party of Slavonic Unity*, the *Communist Party*, the *Liberal* and *Socialist Parties*, and the *Civic Congress of Ukraine*. Local elites began to effectively play the card of 'defending the region's interests' in order to exert pressure on Kiev by resorting to the major mobilising mechanism – miners' movements and their structures (strike committees and the *Independent Trade Union of Miners*). By means of the June 1993 miners' strike in the Donbass, the fuel-energy lobby succeeded in blocking the cautious attempts of Leonid Kuchma's government to liberalise the economy. The 'red directors corps' found its ally in the form of the collective farmers agrarian lobby, interested in obtaining state credits and preserving the administrative and command system of management and administration.

The history of the first stage (December 1991 – March 1994) in the development of Ukraine's regionalism leads us to come to a conclusion about the *instrumental role of economy* in its conception. At this stage, regionalism was encouraged not only by temporarily matching group interests of industrialists and regional elites, but also by the inconsistency of Kiev's policies. Peculiar conditions in Eastern Ukraine and the Crimea made these regions 'epicentres' of regional politics.

The priority of economic preconditions in spurring regionalism does not imply that there are no other causal factors, for example, that of *ethnicity*. It is true that the new wave of regionalism is primarily a reaction to the national economic crisis. However, at the same time, it is also true that the most crisis-prone sectors of industry are located in the regions which are united by the following specifics:

- The proportion of the Russian-speaking population is significant in them;

- It is these regions that as a rule border with Russia;
- They are the most 'Soviet' of all Ukrainian regions;
- There are influential leftist forces which voice their desire for a strategic alliance (or union) and integration with Russia within the framework of the CIS.

Typical of discussions and debates on regionalism among many East Ukrainian politicians has become the abuse of two topics: the region's 'self-sustenance' and highlighting differences between the region, Kiev and western Ukraine. A telling illustration of this may be the following excerpt from the pre-election leaflet of Alexandr Bazilyuk, one of the leaders of the *Civic Congress of Ukraine*: „Nearly all Ukraine's industry is in the south-east. A major proportion of products is manufactured here, and here the biggest money is made. But all these are pumped into Western Ukraine. Money is expropriated by Kiev, while only 20% of it is returned to the region. There are, on average, three times less budgetary funds per capita in the Donbass than in Galicia (Western Ukraine)". The leaflet is crowned with the slogan: „With Russia – for ever! Yes to a Union with Russia! Yes to the Donbass' autonomy! No to Ukraine's independence!"

An ethnic element underlies this kind of thinking. Despite its obvious political character, the presence of an ethnic component is indicative of a real process of national identity being formed in ethnic groups inhabiting a multi-ethnic country. Of particular importance for Ukraine's nationhood is the 'Russian factor'. With which nation will 11 million Russians living in Ukraine identify themselves? How far are they ready to go in order to translate their cultural specificity into political demands?

It is evident that the choice will be different among Russians, for most of them are inclined toward a 'mixed national identity' in which, besides the ethnic factor, there are other components in various proportions.

A significant proportion of Russians lives in the eastern and southern regions of Ukraine. They have been living in these regions, together with Ukrainians, for a sufficient length of time to associate their identities first and foremost with the territory in question rather than with their 'historical native land'.

In the Donbass the forming of a special regional identity has been influenced by the experience of the region's development in the former Soviet Union. The land of heavy industry, the Donbass was a 'showcase' of socialism, a privileged region with its own type of mentality which entitled a native Donbass inhabitant to taking pride in his/her coming from the 'all-Union stoke-hold'. The feeling of uniqueness developed in the region's population was augmented by a continuous 'intermingling of cadres' with Moscow and Kiev, through which natives of the Donbass were in a position to defend the interests of Donbass people in the top echelons of power. A stereotype of being a special region, entrenched in the minds of many people in the Donbass, was actually strengthened by traditionally higher living standards as compared with the neighbouring Rostov *oblast*' in Russia.

We can advance the hypothesis that for the Donbass Russians the ethnic component is not a dominant one. More important for them are territorial and economic factors. Hopes for economic welfare in an independent Ukraine along with a strong, preserved feeling of living in a 'vital' region were major motives for voting in favour of Ukraine's independence at the December 1991 referendum. A great number of ethnic Russians in the east of Ukraine, together with an even greater number of the Russian-speaking population (according to data obtained by Valerii Khmelko of the Kiev-Mohyla Academy, 48% of the adult population are Russian-speaking Ukrainians, 30% are Russian-speaking Russians, 15% are Ukrainian-speaking Ukrainians) proved a significantly influential factor in the minds of the region's inhabitants to preclude any possible fears of an ethno-linguistic nature (a potential threat of being 'Ukrainianised').

An essential role is played by the positive fact that Ukraine, unlike other former republics of the former USSR, managed to avoid the influence of the ethnic criterion for redistributing of social wealth in the course of privatisation among ethnic groups and for allowing access to top posts. No law was passed in Ukraine which would interfere directly or indirectly with ethnic Russians taking part in privatisation and the filling-up of positions in the state apparatus. Top posts in the Ukrainian government are held by many people who are not ethnic Ukrainians. To give an example, ethnic Russians are chairmen of five standing commissions in Parliament: those on defence and national security, finances and banking, economic policy and national economy management, the Chernobyl disaster and youth, sports and tourism. A substantial mutual ethnic tolerance between ethnic Russians and Ukrainians is an important indication of the minimal role of the ethnic factor in the development of regionalism in Ukraine.

A typical example of how the 'regional identity' of North-Eastern Ukraine and the Donbass is being expressed can be found in a number of multilateral inter-regional agreements concluded between bordering *oblasts* of Russia (Belgorod, Kursk, Bryansk, Voronezh *oblasts* and Krasnodar *krai*) and Ukraine (Sumy, Kharkiv, Zaporizhya, Donetsk, Lugansk *oblasts*). There have already been four conferences held by the *oblasts*' ruling bodies (twice in Kharkiv, in Belgorod and

Donetsk), at which problems in co-ordinating border trade and establishing production and other links between Russian and Ukrainian regions were discussed. On 27 January 1995 an agreement on co-operation between bordering *oblasts* was signed in Kharkiv.

In assessing these new developments, one cannot agree with those analysts who are inclined to consider these facts as 'covert' or 'crawling' separatism. We would rather speak here about manifestations of common sense and pragmatism on the part of the regions, a natural response to the inefficient policies of the Ukrainian and Russian leadership. Nevertheless, one should not ignore here a peculiar regional economic 'egotism' when the region's borderline status is used as a pretext for securing special privileges and preferential treatment by the Centre. Therefore, it is no coincidence that the regions are trying to combine their efforts in this direction. At two conferences regional mayors and heads of local presidential administrations addressed joint appeals to the presidents of Ukraine and Russia.

It should be mentioned that there have been some warning signs about the treatment of the role of such cross-border co-operation. There have been attempts to link the 'international relations of regions' not only in conjunction with the general problem of the future of the CIS, but also with some very peculiar integration processes within the CIS. A special role in this is assigned to financial-industrial groups in which the leading role is played by Russian companies. Also peculiar is some Russian politicians' understanding of the 'economic basis for integration'. „Since many of the Russian Federation's debtors do not have the financial resources to settle their accounts with Russia for fuel and energy deliveries," says Russia's Vice-Premier Sergei Shakhrai, „we must pursue an unswerving and hard-line policy of acquiring debtors' assets and lands as a means of debt repayment, *i.e. to create the economic basic for integration*" (emphasis added)[1].

Occasionally the argument is adduced that, in a situation where various regions of the country are more loosely connected with one another than with other republics of the former USSR, the encouragement of external regional ties, especially in border areas, may increase disintegrative impulses. One can imagine a scenario whereby established channels of co-operation between border regions and the corresponding preferential juridical treatment can be utilised for influencing the situation from the outside, thereby making foreign policy more ethnocentric and providing plausible arguments for „supporting and defending fellow-countrymen abroad". However, it

1 *Nezavisimaya gazeta* 12 May 1994.

would appear that there is more theoretical thinking behind such conjecture than any realistic accounting of trends and dynamics of regional developments in present-day Ukraine.

Parliamentary, presidential and local elections, held in Ukraine in the spring-summer period of 1994, marked the end of the first stage of Ukrainian regionalism, the characteristic features of which were rather impromptu and chaotic bids by regional elites for places in the new conditions, and attempts at finding the most efficient ways of influencing the Centre's policies.

With respect to the prospects for consolidating Ukraine's nationhood, not so much the relative victory of the leftist political forces should be regarded as the most important outcome of the parliamentary elections, but rather the awakening of the deputies' and voters' awareness to the priority of active regional policy. Most of the deputies were elected to Parliament precisely due to their expression of this interest. The deputies from Eastern Ukraine gained a clear majority during the allocation of parliamentary posts. The deputies from the Donetsk, Dnieper and North-Eastern regions took the chairmanship of 12 out of 23 standing commissions of the *Verkhovna Rada* (Ukraine's Parliament). Among the chairmen of parliamentary commissions there is only one deputy from Western Ukraine who heads the commission on culture and spiritual values.

It is noteworthy that a highly important commission on budgetary affairs includes six deputies from Donetsk *oblast'* and is headed by Volodymyr Shcherban, also a Donetsk deputy, later also elected as the chairman of the Donetsk *oblast'*s council of People's Deputies. „Our commission", says V. Shcherban, „does not suffer from separatist feelings and does not intend to address only regional problems... The most essential point is to change the principles for determining the nation's budget. It is no good to do it the way it is now being done, whereby the regions relinquish their funds to the budget in Kiev and then the centre gives them back to the regions as subsidies and subventions. The regions will have to solve their problems on their own. All contradictions between them and the centre, between the East and the West of Ukraine will ultimately fade away when money resources come to be earned at the national level. To do so, it is necessary to set enterprises free economically, to give them economic freedom rather than to tie them up with administrative commands, quotas and other conventions"[2].

---

2 *Gorod* 16 June 1994.

The signing of agreements on co-operation between Mariupol and Lviv, Donetsk and Ivano-Frankivsk appears to indicate a new form of (constructive) regionalism. The two regions jointly (Western and Eastern Ukraine) drew up within a short period of time a program to attract investments from the West, in particular, from the World Bank. First Vice-Premier Viktor Pinzenik, a leader of the parliamentary group *Reforms*, gave a very apt definition of the essence of the new regionalism when he said: „If the centre is not in a position to unite the nation, this must be done by regions“[3].

Naturally, one should not overestimate the significance of emerging positive changes in the regional dynamics of Ukraine. The real challenge for Ukrainian politicians today to ensure, under new conditions, *the connection of regional development strategies and the general strategy of Ukraine's nation-making.*

An aggravation of social tensions caused by a greater radicalism of economic reform will inevitably stimulate tensions between regions (competing for scant state resources) and between the Centre and the regions. This latter factor was indeed one of the reasons for the lack of political will of Leonid Kravchuk, Ukraine's first President, who, not without some grounds, feared that the dynamics of reforms might tear Ukraine to pieces.

President Kuchma is taking a risk, but, judging by some indications, he has taken into account the pitiful experience of L. Kravchuk. For the first 100 days of Kuchma's presidency he:

- initiated the setting up of structures through which regions could be more actively associated with the mechanism of making decisions which are of concern to the regions;
- stimulated the process of constitutional division of powers both vertically and in the Centre;
- offered a program of radical economic reforms.

On 20 September 1994 the *Decree on the Institution of the Regions' Council* was signed. Under the Decree, the Regions' Council is instituted „in order to conduct consultations, to draw up draft decisions on the most important problems in economic and social spheres, on issues arising in relations between the government and local executive branch administrations and bodies of local self-rule“. The council consists of chairs of regional councils, Kiev and Sevastopol city councils and the head of the government of the Republic of Crimea. Besides the function of

---

3 *Zhizn'* 18 October 1994.

solving immediate tasks of „providing for a vertical harmonisation and co-ordination of measures on economic reform“[4], the new consultative body can be feasibly be viewed as a step toward a two-chamber parliament with a *Chamber of Lands* consisting of representatives from all regions. An important detail: before presenting his address on economic reforms to the plenary session of the *Verkhovna Rada*, President Kuchma discussed its main points at a Regions' Council meeting.

The sooner the agreed 'rules of the game' are adopted, i.e. the forms of state structure and government are decided upon, the greater the chances that economic reforms in Ukraine will proceed unswervingly.

Contradictions between the hierarchy of soviets as representative bodies and the system of state power vertical is one of the major components of the conflict between branches of state power in Ukraine, as, incidentally, in many other post-Soviet states, too. In Russia, in October 1993 similar contradictions resulted in an armed confrontation. To avoid even the slightest possibility of repeating a similar scenario in Ukraine, it is necessary to legislatively codify the relationships between the Centre and the regions with regard to basic mechanisms of forming individual tax bases and financial resources of the regions. At the same time, along with a *regional macro-policy*, we need special *regional micro-policies*, taking into account the peculiarities of the different Ukrainian regions, especially depressed and border ones. The Regions' Council could possibly become the main body responsible for elaborating such special regional programmes. Within its framework, the natural competition of regions and contradictions arising between them could be settled on a legitimate compromise basis.

A devolution of some powers from the Centre to the regions will be healthy in its core, since it will:

- urge local authorities to become more responsible for their decisions and accountable before their electorates, reducing to the minimum the tradition of blaming the central government for all shortcomings;
- facilitate a quickening of the pace of economic reform, especially privatisation, ridding the central government of many uncharacteristic functions and getting regional structures involved in the process;

---

4 *By Way of Radical Reforms: Ukraine's Presidential Address*. Kiev, October 1994: 29 (in Ukrainian).

- encourage regional elites to co-operate more actively and pragmatically on the horizontal (region-region) level, speeding up the emergence of new inter-regional links within Ukraine;
- assist in developing direct economic and cultural cross-border ties of Ukrainian regions with neighbouring countries, which is especially important, given the specific geopolitical position of Ukraine and the lack of general national consensus with regard to priorities in foreign economic and political co-operation;
- demonstrate (notably, in eastern Ukraine), the inevitable difficulties in self-government and stimulate more mature and responsible relations between Kiev and the regions, thereby removing some present symptoms of 'romantic autonomisation'.

To what extent are the regions, the Donbass and its political elite in particular, ready for such a policy from the Centre? The dynamics of forming regional elites in the Donbass can be described as an interaction of several processes characterised by different speed and intensity. The old (*Communist Party*-managerial) structure of the elite is being gradually eroded and substituted by a new (post-Soviet/post-totalitarian) one. We can discern three types of elites undergoing transformation:

- the most ideologically conservative part of the previous Communist Party elite, 'leaving the regional stage' and the group of directors and managers of coal-mining, metallurgical and petrochemical enterprises who still retain their positions;
- the younger, more flexible and pragmatic elite, adapting to the new conditions and representing, as a rule, the second and third echelons of the old Communist Party-managerial nomenklatura;
- the emerging nouveaux riches who formerly were not part of the traditional regional elite (this group is characterised by the greatest dynamism and consists largely of former 'shadow' economy entrepreneurs who have made money by mediatory and commercial operations, and people who came to politics in the roaring years of the 'perestroika democracy' and managed to transform their political capital into material wealth).

In the two *oblasts* of the Donbass (Donetsk and Lugansk) the above-mentioned groups have definite signs of different proportions and shares. If in Donetsk *oblast*' the first roles are being taken over by representatives of the third group (V. Shcherban, Donetsk's mayor; M. Pozhivanov, Mariupol's mayor and others) together with members of the second group; in Lugansk *oblast*' neither of the groups has won a stable majority, though the positions of managers-traditionalists of the first group are stronger. The fact that P. Kupin, the leader of Lugansk Communists is at the same time the chairman of the Regional Council of People's Deputies, supports this conclusion.

The political structuring of Ukrainian society is far from being completed. This is also the case with Donetsk oblast. No matter what formal ratings the activities of political parties' have in the region, an in-depth analysis testifies to the fact that the parties' structures are not mature and do not wield any great influence at the local and regional levels. This is also indicated by a poll of regional echelon functionaries and rank-and-file members of political parties acting in Donetsk *oblast'* (the poll was conducted by the *Centre for Political Studies* in April-May 1994).

Table 2 *Distribution of Responses to the Question „What is your assessment of political parties' influence on the following levels..." (in percentage)*
A. LOCAL LEVEL

	Very significant	Noticeable	Medium	Weak	Very weak
The *oblast'* echelon functionaries of the Party of Ukraine's Democratic Revival (PUDR)					100
The PUDR's rank-and-file members				40	60
The Popular Movement of Ukraine (Rukh), *oblast'* echelon		11	11	45	33
Rukh's rank-and-file members		12	22	44	22
The Ukrainian Republican Party (URP), *oblast'* echelon				66	34
The URP rank-and-file members			16	51	33
Congress of Ukrainian Nationalists (CUN), *oblast'* echelon		20		60	20
CUN's rank-and-file members			40	40	20
The Civic Congress (CC), *oblast'* level			68	16	16
The CC's rank-and-file members	16	34	34	16	
The Labour Party (PL) *oblast'* level	25	50	25		
The PL rank-and-file members	40	20		40	
The Liberal Party (LP), the *oblast'* level	30	40	10	10	10
The LP's rank-and-file members	30	60		10	

B. REGIONAL LEVEL

	Very significant	Noticeable	Medium	Weak	Very weak
The *oblast'* echelon functionaries of the Party of Ukraine's Democratic Revival (PUDR)					100
The PUDR's rank-and-file members			20	40	40
The Popular Movement of Ukraine (Rukh), *oblast'* echelon			10	80	10
Rukh's rank-and-file members			33	44	23
The Ukrainian Republican Party (URP), *oblast'* echelon				34	66
The URP rank-and-file members			16	51	33
Congress of Ukrainian Nationalists (CUN), *oblast'* echelon		20		60	20
CUN's rank-and-file members		20	20	20	40
The Civic Congress (CC), *oblast'* level		67	33		
The CC's rank-and-file members		16	68	16	
The Labour Party (PL), *oblast'* level		100			
The PL rank-and-file members	20	60		20	
The Liberal Party (LP), *oblast'* level	20	50	10	20	
The LP's rank-and-file members	20	50	20	10	

Noteworthy is a recent trend which indicates that representatives of the third group are definitely striving to go beyond the borders of their region and to incorporate into their ranks some of the most prominent leaders from Kiev and the Right-Bank Ukraine (to the west of the Dnieper river). There are many indications of this: the ambitious Oleg Soskin has been asked to 'rule over' the *Liberal Party*, which Volodymyr Lanovoi has joined; liberals are intending to form their own faction in Parliament; the *Liberal Party* has been strengthened by such politicians as Mikhail Pozhivanov (People's Deputy, mayor of Mariupol), People's Deputy and manager of the *Pravda* coal-mine of the production association *Donetskugol* Volodymyr Ampilogov, People's Deputy and *Aton* corporation president Evgeny Shcherban. In addition, the third group elite enjoys the protection of Volodymyr Shcherban, the Budget Commission Chair in the *Verkhovna Rada* and the Head of

Donetsk *oblast'* Council. All this is indicative of a serious regrouping of forces in the ranks of regional elites and the beginning of preparations for new election campaigns.

The top priority objective of Kiev reformers is to secure support and understanding for those reforms which are commencing in critically important regions (those of Donetsk, the Dnieper and the North East) not only on the part of local elites, but also on the part of the population. The latter task will be very difficult because the reforms will most of all hit workers in coal-mining and heavy industries concentrated in the regions. The presence of sufficiently organised structures there (the *Independent Miners Union*, standing striking committees, and others) which have a significant mobilising potential, forces the central authorities in Kiev to resort to an active 'preventive diplomacy' and to extend the practices of regional self-government (in some spheres to be agreed upon in advance) to the budgetary, juridical and other spheres of Kiev's relationships with the regions.

An active regional policy in conjunction with an immediate elimination of the indefinite status of powers, a realisation of a coherent program of economic reforms and the West's solidarity and assistance present a unique opportunity to consolidate a political and multi-ethnic society in Ukraine.

16

Regionalisation, Federalisation and Separatism in Ukraine: Historical Roots, New Realities and Prospects

Nikolai Shul'ga

The three notions in the article's heading belong to the same semantic series – they designate phenomena related to separation, differentiation or division of the whole into parts. These are concepts which reflect processes taking place in the spheres of social and state life. At the same time, each of them has its own specific features and denotes a separate quality. Their heuristic role dramatically increases in transitional periods in the life of society and the nation. It is in such periods that differences in the process of regionalisation, federalisation and separatism reveal themselves.

The development of these processes is in practice effected by their actual agents, subjects of social actions – individuals, political organisations, political movements, state bodies, etc. Each social subject frequently tries to orient these processes in a direction which is beneficial, first of all, to themselves but also which differs radically from the intentions of other subjects. Thus, each of the phenomena in question becomes an object of a harsh political struggle in society.

Ukrainian society is not, in this respect, an exception. Problems of administrative-territorial structure and restructuring, regionalisation and the status of territories sprang up just after the first steps had been taken in the process of democratisation and the policy of *glasnost'* in the USSR. This resulted in the Crimean referendum (early in 1991) on the restoration of the Crimean Autonomous Soviet Socialist Republic and the proclamation by Ukraine's *Verkhovna Rada* (Parliament) of the autonomy of the Crimea. This initial period was characterised by the facts that political parties were only just forming, that there were no significant theoretical studies on federalisation and regionalisation, and that differences in approaches of various political forces to the problem of administrative territorial structure were hardly noticeable. However, the problem in question very soon became extremely topical and politicised, and the positions of political parties and individual public figures in relation to it became quite clear. Today in Ukraine there are both ardent supporters and proponents of the idea of federalisation and a greater role of regions in the economic, social, cultural and even political life of society and the state, and active opponents of these notions. As far as separatism is concerned, one would rather avoid being called its proponent, since this has an inherently negative sense. For this reason, supporters of the idea of breaking several territories away from Ukraine prefer to speak about autonomy and self-determination rather than separatism.

1 Basic Initial Notions

1.1 Region, Regionalism, Regionalisation

In practically any state there is a at least one part of its territory which is notably different from other parts. These differences include natural-climatic conditions of life, history, ethnic composition of population, language, culture, religion and other natural and socio-historical factors. Interaction of these factors takes on an integrative, systemic character and results ultimately in a qualitative specificity of the given territory. So, regionalism as an objective phenomenon is intrinsic in practically all the nations of the world.

Regionalism is perceived by social subjects in the form of certain socio-economic, political and cultural ideas, as well as in the form of specific needs and interests of the territory in question. The needs and interests acknowledged by its subjects take the form of ideas, concepts and doctrines. Naturally, social and political subjects differ considerably in their views of regions' problems, not to mention means of resolving them.

Doctrines reflecting views of various socio-political subjects on regions' problems; a political process accompanied by confrontation of viewpoints and positions on these issues; an elaboration of political and legal points related to the issues by political parties and state bodies; a process of interaction between the Centre and the regions and among the regions themselves – all these are characteristics of the process which can be called regionalism.

Hence, regional differences as an objective phenomenon are an inalienable attribute of any nation. But regionalism as a complex socio-political phenomenon springs up only under certain conditions, namely in those periods when regional problems become more acute in society, when contradictions between the Centre and the regions, between certain regions, or simultaneously between the former and the latter become more intense and pressing.

As a rule, such exacerbations occur in periods of global social crises and revolutions. Then, revision and reassessment of ideas about the administrative-territorial structure of the state, forms of territorial administration and status of regions appear on the agenda. Similar frames of mind permeate the whole of society and all the regions. Furthermore, the situation may become aggravated in one or several regions. As a rule this is connected with the fact that, with time, radical changes of an economic, social, demographic, ethnic or any other nature take place on these territories, while forms and methods of governing regions remain the same.

The processes of socio-political life, linked with the realisation of the idea of regionalisation, of granting territories a special status and the establishment of the corresponding state bodies and bodies of local self-government can be defined as falling under the notion of regionalisation.

1.2 Federation, Federalism, Federalisation

Regional diversity is an objective precondition not only of regionalism and regionalisation but also of federalism and federalisation. A federation is a form of state system. A peculiarity of the classical federative state is that it is formed through unification, the union of lands, princedoms, counties, cantons and even states. Naturally, the unified states were in themselves integral social bodies and had their own identities and qualitative peculiarities. For this reason, once having formed a federation, the states constituting it continue to preserve their distinctive features. These are the characteristics of a federative state.

However, over the past decade federations have been formed not only by way of combining several unitary states into one state. Ideas of decentralisation and autonomisation have gained currency in many countries of the world. As a result, there has emerged a trend of forming federations not only by way of unifying unitary states but also by making some territories of a unitary state autonomous, with major criteria for autonomisation being essentially different in various countries. To exemplify, in Canada this is language (French Canadians), in Great Britain – religion (Catholics), in Spain and France – ethnicity (Basques, Corsicans). While in the above states aspirations for autonomisation and federative state structure exist as trends, in Belgium they were realised in political and legal norms fixed in the constitution.

Social and political processes resulting in federations, as well as theoretical and political conceptions of organising such states, are termed federalism.

The immediate process of laying the foundation and organisation of a federation, of making and passing legislative acts and instituting corresponding bodies of state power is called federalisation.

1.3 Separatism

In contrast to the notions of regionalism and federalism, which are first and foremost theoretical-cognitive, gnoseological notions designating certain phenomena of reality, the concept of separatism has, first of all, an evaluative character. (However, within the context of certain situations the former notions may also acquire an evaluative – either positive or negative – character). The latter notion designates a certain political position, a social subject's attitude toward the processes connected with autonomisation, with the secession of a part of a state. The notion 'separatism' typically evokes a negative connotation. But this same phenomenon can also have a positive meaning for certain subjects under evaluation, in which case other notions are employed to this end, for example, decentralisation, sovereignisation, struggle for independence etc.

Today, in Ukraine's socio-political life, trends of each of the three phenomena mentioned above are emerging: regionalism, federalism and separatism. Furthermore, all of them have already become issues of both theoretical and political consideration.

2 Conceptions of Ukraine's Administrative-Territorial Structure

The country's top leadership, political parties, their leaders and representatives of local elites are divided in their approaches to the problem of administrative-territorial and state structure of Ukraine.

Some believe that reform is a necessity while others maintain that the problem is not urgent. The former are rightist and centrist political parties – *Rukh* (Popular Movement of Ukraine), the Ukraïnian Republican Party, the Party of Democratic Revival and some others. The latter belong to the leftist parties – the Communist Party of Ukraine, the Socialist Party of Ukraine, the Agrarian Party.

Proponents of the idea of administrative-territorial restructuring put forward the following arguments to substantiate the need for reforms in the sphere of Ukraine's territorial structure:

- the existent territorial structure is a legacy of the former administrative-command system and, therefore, does not correspond to the stage of building a democratic state ruled by law and to the stage of forming a market-oriented economy;
- the present territorial units (*oblasts*) are not identical or even similar in their economic and demographic potentials. For example, the population of Donetsk *oblast'* is 5.3 million people, while that of Volynia *oblast'* – only one million;
- it is expedient to make the administrative-territorial units larger, which will make it possible to cut down excessively inflated administrative apparatuses in the regions;
- Ukraine's gaining independence has led to a situation where 11 *oblasts* are border regions, while earlier there were only 7 such regions;
- within the framework of the existing structure of the states' territory, there are regions 'infected' with separatist ideas and feelings. Reform will allow to single out these territories and to diminish the organising capability of the leaders of such groups.

Scholars and politicians offer a multitude of variants for the division of Ukraine's territory into new administrative units. Practically all proposals are connected with the enlargement of the present *oblasts*, with the suggestion that instead of the Autonomous Republic of the Crimea and 24 *oblasts*, some 12 to 15 new territorial units (lands, districts, etc.) should be formed. Supporters of the territorial restructuring are not unanimous, however, and do not have a common approach to the problem. Their positions can be summarised as follows.

As to the question of when the territorial restructuring should be undertaken, some hold that it should be done immediately, while others – only after nationhood has been consolidated and the country's economy stabilised. There is also a point of view that such reform should be implemented in stages within six to eight years. At the first stage, the federative principle of state structure should be codified in the constitution. At the second stage, it is necessary to work out a model of the state's administrative-territorial structure. At the third stage, corresponding decisions of legislative bodies will be taken. Finally, the fourth stage entails a practical restructuring of administrative-territorial bodies[1].

---

1 Savelev, V. "Pribichniki ta suprotivniki zemelno-administrativnogo ustroyu Ukraini u spektri ii suchasnogo politichnovo zhittya [Proponents and Opponents of Ukraine's Territorial-Administrative Structure and the Spectrum of Today's Political Life]." In *Administrativno-territorialny pereustri Ukrainy: shlyakhi i perspektivi* [Administrative-Territorial Restructuring of Ukraine: Problems and Prospects]. Kiev, 1994: 33.

Today, the first and most critical question concerns Ukraine's state-territorial structure. There is a wide range of opinions on the matter, but in political circles only three plausible alternatives to the state structure are being discussed: a unitary centralised republic, a unitary decentralised republic, and a federative republic.

In addition, there is also the point of view that Ukraine is not capable of building an independent state, and that the problem lies in entering into a new union (of the former USSR type) rather than in restructuring the territorial composition of Ukraine. This idea is most popular in the Crimea. It is supported by a number of Crimean political parties and has even been discussed by the Presidium of the Supreme Council of the Crimea. In particular, early in November 1994, the Presidium discussed the possibility of holding a referendum in the Crimea. The inclusion of one question in the ballot-paper was suggested, namely: „Are you for the Crimea's independence within a union with other states?" No decision has yet been taken on the referendum.

Nevertheless, the topic of Crimea's possible entry into a new union of states continues to be discussed, one indicator of this being the *Declaration on the Denouncement of the Belovezha Agreement* which was adopted by the Crimea's Supreme Council in the last week of 1994[2]. The trend in question must be considered within the context of processes and developments taking place in other states of the CIS. Specifically, one should not overlook the fact that the adoption of the above-mentioned declaration by the Crimean Parliament coincided with the convention of the Second Congress of the Peoples of the USSR in Moscow, at which the restoration of the Soviet Union was discussed.

However, notions of possible economic, political and military unions between Ukraine and other states differ not only across the various political parties but also to a considerable extent across the various regions.

Firstly, one of the territories speaks resolutely and consistently against a union with Russia, since it sees in this a threat to Ukraine's sovereignty. The territory in question is Galicia.

Secondly, a proportion of the population of Galicia and other regions of western Ukraine, and the local political elite in particular, may still reconcile itself with the idea of an inter-state economic and political union, but only with the neighbouring states to the west and north-west, and under no circumstances with Russia. In particular, the idea of a Baltic Sea-Black Sea alliance is quite well-known and is

---

2 Pritula, V. "U Krimy vidnovlyuyut Radyansky Soyuz." *Molod Ukraini* 27 December 1994.

supported by some political parties whose social basis is concentrated in western Ukraine.

Thirdly, people in the eastern, south-eastern and southern regions are supporters of firmer ties within the CIS and speak out insistently for Ukraine's accession to the CIS Economic Union and for closer all-round relations with Russia.

Fourth, a considerable part of the Crimean population voice their support for a military union with Russia, for a single Black Sea Fleet under joint Ukrainian and Russian command.

Concerning the positions of the state's leadership on the issue, they are clearly and unambiguously defined. The former president of Ukraine, Leonid Kravchuk, was a proponent of a unitary-decentralised state: „Proceeding from world experience as well as the conditions in which Ukraine's nationhood is being formed, it would seem that the optimal solution for Ukraine may be a unitary-decentralised type of territorial organisation“[3]. However, Kravchuk failed to specify in what forms decentralisation will occur, what shape territorial units will take and what their status may be.

Ukraine's ex-speaker of Parliament, Ivan Plyushch, takes a somewhat different stand. He suggests for Ukraine a type of decentralised state with broad administrative autonomy on the regional level. „I do not believe“ he says, „that such autonomy will shatter Ukraine's integrity. It will turn it into a federative republic like Germany or other democratic nations“[4].

Incumbent Chair of the *Verkhovna Rada* of Ukraine, Olexander Moroz, as the leader of the socialists, stated that his party's position „lies in Ukraine's unitary character with broad freedoms for territories, stipulated by the constitution. The issue of federalisation has, undoubtedly, some prospects but nothing can justify a discussion of autonomy for the *oblasts* at the present time. We may risk provoking the Transdnestria scenario in the borderlands...“.[5]

A quest for responses to the challenge by those regions that differ significantly in their political attitudes led to the idea of Ukraine's federative state structure. The popularity of similar ideas can be seen in the fact that they were proclaimed not only

---

3 Kravchuk, L.M. "Kontseptualnye osnovy regionalnoi politiki v Ukraini [Conceptual Bases of Ukraine's Regional Policy]." In *Aktualni problemi upravlinnya teritoriyami Ukraini* [Current Problems in Governing Ukraine's Territories]. Kiev, 1990: 6.

4 Plyushch, I. "Kontseptualni printsipu upravlinnya teritoriyami Ukraini v suchasnikh umovakh." In *Aktualni problemi upravlinnya teritoriyami v Ukraini*. Kiev, 1993: 24.

5 Moroz, O.O. "Pro deyaki politichni aspekti derzhavnogo upravlinnya." In *Aktualni problemi upravlinnya teritoriyami v Ukraini*. Kiev, 1993: 185.

by political parties, but were also taken up by many independent candidates running for parliament as well as by candidates for the presidency. During local elections the appealing character of federalisation manifested itself not only at the national level but also at the regional level. In the elections to the local councils, people voted for those candidates who staunchly supported a greater freedom for the regions.

Discussions on the issue of Ukraine's territorial structure are still continuing. Proponents of a federative structure for Ukraine put forward the following arguments. Firstly, the state will be strong only when historical, natural and regional specifics have been taken into account. Secondly, a regional policy cannot be shaped in the Centre. It can only be formed and developed naturally, organically and comprehensively in the regions themselves.

The fears of opponents to federalism that a federative structure in Ukraine could swiftly result in separatism, in dismemberment of the country and in annexation of some of its parts by other states are refuted by the following arguments. Firstly, territorial integrity and the indivisibility of the state will be codified in the constitution, and, secondly, the federative character of Ukraine will be based on territorial demarcation and on the endowment of the regions with a degree of state powers, rather than on a contractual unification of autonomous territories with their own constitutions.

The anti-federalists, however, lay down further doubts and adduce new arguments in favour of a unitary state. In particular, they maintain that to create federative units under the present conditions would, in the first place, be unnatural and even forced, would furthermore complicate the process of consolidating the Ukrainian nation, and thirdly, they argue that it is not necessary to carry out the decentralisation of power by way of territorial restructuring. Moreover, the Crimea's experience in pursuing an autonomous policy – the political confrontation between the president and the Supreme Soviet, the neglect of economic and social problems, the upsurge of organised crime – has led to the emergence of a certain type of negative example. This example leads one to conclude that a greater independence of a region and the granting of autonomous status cannot bring anything good and will have negative rather than positive consequences. It equips opponents of federalisation with numerous arguments for considering it inexpedient to renounce unitarianism in general and in the period of nation-building and general economic crisis in particular.

There is also no doubt that events in Chechnya will in their own way also become a warning to those who are trying to accelerate the process of state-territorial restructuring of Ukraine on a federative basis. For opponents of the idea of federalisation those events will become an additional argument proving that their position is correct.

Over the past several years, problems of regions' autonomisation have ceased to be discussed exclusively by a narrow circle of politicians, theoreticians, and managers. Practically the whole of the adult population of the regions is involved in discussions on this topic by means of various polls and referenda. Among these one can mention a referendum on the territorial self-government in Transcarpathia, a referendum on the status of the Crimea as a member of a future union of states, and regional polls in Donetsk and Lugansk *oblasts* on the status of the Russian language on their territories. Thus, millions of people are becoming involved in these processes which, as a result, have taken on the character of a fully-fledged political issue.

3 Preconditions of Regionalism and Federalism in Ukraine

Processes of regionalisation have as their basis deep-seated phenomena which have various causes: both modern and historical, economical and cultural, technological and linguistic, social and ethnic.

3.1 Historical Preconditions

Let us begin with the historical preconditions of regionalism in Ukraine. Under the influence of dramatic events in history, the Ukrainian ethnos formed on the territory of several states. The process of unification of the Ukrainian lands within modern borders came to an end only in 1954. During World War I, the October revolution and the Civil War autonomous formations emerged claiming to be independent states. Those were the West Ukrainian People's Republic, the Donetsk-Kryvorizk Republic and the Crimean Tatar People's Republic.

Galicia, Transcarpathia, Bukovyna and a part of Bessarabia had for a long time been separated from Ukraine and had been parts of other states. For this reason some regions have up to now considered themselves as regions with specific histories which are noticeably different from those of other parts of the country. A complete consolidation of Ukraine in socio-psychological terms has as yet not been achieved. A great number of people in these territories identify themselves first of all as Crimeans, Transcarpathians etc. and only then as citizens of Ukraine. Among such territories are Galicia, Transcarpathia, Bukovyna, Bessarabia and the Crimea. There are people in these territories who began to tread their life road in other states, without leaving their homeplaces.

3.2 Economic Preconditions

Obviously, the historical factor is one of the main reasons for the country's regionalisation, but it is not the foremost reason. This factor is always present but becomes prominent and effective only in certain periods.

The economic factor is certainly of primary importance. The economic crisis gripping Ukraine has, on the whole, its specific regional manifestations. It is compounded by the energy crisis. That is why it first of all became evident in regions with a great share of mining and metallurgical industries in their economies, and in the second place, in regions home to enterprises of the military-industrial complex which are undergoing military conversion and are experiencing a sharp drop in orders for military production.

However, regionalisation is activated by a broad array of factors specific to each region rather than individual factors. In each of them there are specific parts of the national economic complex. Let us consider some regions whose economic specifics are very prominent.

In the Crimea, this comprises a health recreation complex which was of all-Union importance, as well as enterprises of the modern military-industrial complex. To these one should also add naval bases of the Black Sea Fleet. Each of the components comprising the specific economic character of the Crimean area is in a state of profound crisis.

Over the past three to four years the recreation and resort industry has diminished rapidly. As a result of this, hundreds of thousands of people have lost their jobs as well as their additional earnings which they made by letting their apartments to those coming to the seaside resorts and by providing various services etc. The workers in Crimea's industrial complex have also lost out heavily since many modern defence plants and factories are concentrated in the region. These, as is well-known, have suffered most of all in the process of conversion and severance of economic ties. The unsolved problems of the Black Sea Fleet and the fate of Sevastopol are a serious negative factor which substantially aggravates the moral-political situation in the peninsula.

The matter of the return, settling, housing and adaptation of several hundred thousand Crimean Tatars and other unlawfully deported peoples is a separate political, social and economic problem. These problems seem to be knotted together tightly and the very impossibility of disentangling and resolving them quickly provokes separatist feelings.

The external factor cannot be disregarded either. Unlawful claims by some state bodies of the Russian Federation, such as the Declaration on Sevastopol adopted by the previous Russian Parliament, will sharpen the Crimea's problem and will therefore intensify separatist feelings.

The industries of the Donbass are characterised by technological backwardness, capital consumption, lack of investments for their renovation, technological dependence on enterprises of the former USSR states, especially Russian ones. A lot of social problems have amassed in the region: housing shortages, inadequate cultural, personal, medical and sanitary services. This territory suffers from a colossal anthropogenic pressure on the environment which is not properly protected. As a result of this, the ecological situation here is close to catastrophic.

Transcarpathia's specific regional problems are derived from labour force redundancy and scarcity of arable lands. To these are added the problems of the health resort and recreation complex, similar to those of the Crimea. There are also other difficulties resulting from the fact that Ukraine's major transport routes pass through the region and that the territory is a border region with an intensive cross-border traffic flow.

3.3 Ethno-cultural Preconditions

All three above-mentioned regions have one more common peculiarity in that all of them have a complicated, intricate ethnic structure. To take an example, the Republic of the Crimea is the only administrative unit in Ukraine where most of the population is not Ukrainian, 67% being Russian. The 'Russian card' is being actively played by politicians. It was extensively employed during elections to the Crimean Supreme Soviet as well as during the presidential elections in Ukraine and the Crimea. The matter also becomes very pressing as the problem of the Black Sea Fleet substantially intensifies. Powerful pro-Russian political formations are active there which speak for joining the Crimea to Russia. The problem of resettling Crimean Tatars, Bulgarians, Greeks, Germans and Armenians, unlawfully repressed in the years of World War II, remains a particularly painful matter for this region.

Over the past five years the Crimea has accepted more than 250 thousand Crimean Tatars, Armenians, Bulgarians, Greeks and Germans ousted and deported from this territory during World War II. One can only imagine what sort of a complex socio-political task is now being dealt with, given that the number of those resettled already amounts to 10 per cent of the Crimea's population. This one problem alone is capable of generating an extremely dangerous situation in the region since its solution may infringe upon the interests of hundreds of Crimeans, both those who settled there several decades ago and those who are just returning. Moreover, its solution is being sought in the conditions of a most acute economic crisis and against a background of spiralling inflation.

No other state of the CIS from which masses of population were deported on an ethnic basis has taken the risk of attempting to solve such a tremendous task. To exemplify, Georgia has flatly refused to tackle the problem of bringing Meskhetian Turks back to their homeland.

The 'Russian question' in the Donbass region (i.e. in Lugansk and Donetsk *oblasts*) is not less urgent than in the Crimea. Though the proportion of ethnic Russians is smaller (of 8.2 million people in the region, 3.8 million or 46.4% are Russian) there are 2.4 times as many of them as in the Crimea. In other words, every third Russian in Ukraine lives in the Donbass.

In addition to Ukrainians and Russians, about a hundred thousand Greeks live in the Donbass, in and around the town of Mariupol. In the past several years they have experienced an upsurge of ethnic self-identification and are trying to revive the Greek culture and language. Given the high level of urbanisation in the Donbass, one has to pay attention to the fact that many Belorussians, Tatars, Jews, Armenians, Gypsies and people of other ethnic groups live dispersed throughout the towns of the Donbass.

Despite the fact that the climate of inter-ethnic relations in the Donbass is quite agreeable, there remain many unsolved problems in this sphere. Up to the present day no one has thoroughly and comprehensively analysed the problem of ethnic Russians in Ukraine at the level of state bodies. There is no state programme for the development of education, book-publishing and mass media in Russian. An average ethnic Russian has only a vague idea of how his spiritual, cultural and educational needs will be met in the future. Until now, the mass media preferred to produce the impression that Russian culture was threatening Ukrainian culture. In so doing they were in fact deliberately confusing notions and terms – under Russian culture they meant not only the culture of Russia, but Russian culture in Ukraine. All this formed an implicit feeling of guilt in the minds of ethnic Russians, an inferiority complex, as if they were unloyal citizens of the Ukrainian state. The above attitude towards ethnic Russians was largely manifested by the national (central) mass media – the impulses came from Kiev. In the Donbass and southern Ukraine another social atmosphere was prevalent. Ethnic Russians and their language and culture did not experience any pressure from the local authorities and mass media. Furthermore, with regard to these regions we can say that the Russian culture and language prevailed and dominated there. At the same time, more attention should be paid and more support should be given to the Ukrainian culture and language there.

However, on experiencing pressure on the part of the Centre, the Donbass and the South manifest centrifugal trends in order to preserve the cultural and linguistic status quo. This is one of the causes of powerful propaganda-based support for the idea of regionalism rendered by the local Russian-speaking intellectuals, with the cultural-linguistic problem being that point which unites the local elites of every political tendency.

A no less complex ethnic picture is presented by Transcarpathia. Here, four ethnic groups, the largest in the region, are in close contact: Ukrainians (78.4%), Hungarians (12.5%), Russians (4.5%), and Romanians (4%). Moreover, Transcarpathia is inhabited by several thousand of Gypsies, Germans, Jews, and Belorussians.

The so-called 'Ruthenian issue' is a separate problem for the region, the crux of the matter being that a part of the area's population differentiates itself from Ukrainians and identifies itself ethnically as Ruthenians. Today, this issue has not so much an ethnocultural colouring as a political one. The 'Ruthenian card' is played in its strictly political form. Those who play it are concerned not so much with the development of the so-called Ruthenian language and culture as with establishing a differentiation and then secession of Transcarpathia (or, in their terms, Transcarpathian Rus') from Ukraine. This is clearly illustrated by attempts to create the *Government of Transcarpathian Rus'* which claims the role of a parallel body of power in the region.

The ethnic specificities of the regions discussed above do not necessarily coincide with their peculiar linguistic features. That is why it is necessary to consider the *linguistic factor* as a separate cause of growing regionalist aspirations in Ukraine. In the Donbass and the Crimea, a sizeable segment of non-Russian population holds that their native tongue is Russian. It is precisely in these regions that hundreds of thousands of Ukrainians state their mother tongue to be Russian (incidentally, all in all in Ukraine over 4.5 million people).

Therefore, a typical feature of these two regions is the fact that the overwhelming majority of people uses Russian in everyday life, in places of work and in public places. This condition should be taken into consideration in implementing the *Law on Languages*. Otherwise, attempts to introduce a wider use of the official, Ukrainian, language in everyday communication will be perceived by people as a threat to their native tongue, as a supplanting of the Russian language, as forced Ukrainisation, while the *Law on Languages* stipulates a wider development of Ukrainian-Russian bilingualism, a balanced use of the two languages, a greater culture in their use.

Especially unhealthy is the reaction to such moves on the part of the authorities such as the discontinuation of radio broadcasting in Russian, executed without any prior notice (as was the case with *Mayak* broadcasting), or when state television does not transmit in Russian, and, as a result, excludes some 17 million people from its sphere of influence (this many people from various ethnic groups, according to the 1989 census, mentioned Russian as their mother tongue).

The volume of negative responses to the language policy of the central authorities in these regions reached a critical point at the beginning of 1994. The population formed negative images and stereotypes both of politicians who are apologists of such a policy line of state bodies with respect to the Russian language, and of the mass media which ignore the linguistic needs of the Russian-speaking citizens of Ukraine. This is proved by opinion polls on Russian-Ukrainian bilingualism in Donetsk and Lugansk *oblasts*. Whatever one's attitude towards the legality of those polls, one cannot disregard their impressive outcomes without risking being politically incorrect. Bilingualism was, after all, supported by 82 to 90% of those polled on 27 March 1994, a fact which became a feature in Leonid Kuchma's election platform. Support for Russian is so great that the former President Leonid Kravchuk, Kuchma's rival, also had to include the point about granting Russian the status of official language. It is worth noting that the linguistic argument in the presidential race had opposite roles to play in the East and the West of Ukraine. While in the East the pledge to upgrade Russian to the status of the second official language found considerable support among the electorate and the population as a whole, the same point aroused an equally emotional but negative response in the West.

Thus, analysis shows that the accumulation of internal factors in each of three regions under discussion, which in their totality create a negative trend, determines, in the first place, the development of regional egotism, confrontation with the Centre and rise of separatist ideas. It is not only in the regions in question that the striving for autonomy and isolation can be noticed. It is gaining momentum in some other parts of Ukraine. In this respect we could mention Bukovyna as a potentially explosive region. In action here is a historical factor (the rather late joining of this area to the Ukrainian state), a multi-ethnic factor (hundreds of thousands of Moldovans and Romanians are a part of the indigenous population), and a foreign policy factor (the idea of creating a Greater Romania), all combining to invite an isolationist outcome.

Separatist aspirations are gaining strength to the same degree with local elites in western and south-western parts of Odessa *oblast'*. Here, the influence of historical and ethnic factors is considerable (several hundred thousand Bulgarians, Gagauzians and Moldovans live in close proximity to one another). The situation is influenced to a certain extent by the examples of separatism set by the Gagauz Republic and the Transnestrian Moldovan Republic which freed themselves from the rule of Kishinev.

However, possibly the greatest threat to the Ukrainian state is that of a division into Eastern and Western Ukraine, rather than local and regional separatism.

3.4 Political and Juridical Preconditions

The rise of regionalist aspirations is influenced by the fact that many social and political processes under way in society are incomplete and contradictory in nature. For example, the change in forms of property and the emergence of the strata of proprietors are occurring extremely slowly and haphazardly. A fierce political struggle is taking place with regard to the question of privatisation of state-owned property and the possibility for individuals to buy and sell plots of land, and these clashes are especially conspicuous in Parliament. The process of forming private farms has been practically stalled. As a result of these processes, the social structure is amorphous and unstable and since there are no definite social strata, no proper awareness of their interests and prospects, this, in turn, negatively influences the emergence and consolidation of political parties and the strengthening of their role in political life. Ukrainian society is not permeated with comprehensive political ties and relations. In the final analysis, this all combines to encourage regionalism.

These processes are occurring against a background of a growing polarisation of wealth in society, political tensions and confrontations, and people's confusion and loss of faith in the future. Because of an extreme politicisation of society, any problem in the sphere of interrelations between the Centre and the regions and among the regions themselves assumes political overtones. Politicians of various orientations, numerous political parties and social and public organisations are exploiting factually existent and objectively emerging problems to their own advantage by interpreting the problems in a profitable way.

In this situation of legal and political confusion about the status of territories, centrifugal trends are becoming ever more prominent. They can be observed in the political, economic, social, and cultural spheres. The 1994 election to the *Verkhovna Rada* and the presidential election very clearly showed regional differences in political preferences and foreign policy priorities. The East and South of the country voted for the left-wing forces to be represented in Parliament, whose platform denounced isolationism and severance of ties with the former Soviet Republics, and voted for a president who pledged to make Russia a top priority partner in Ukraine's foreign policy and to upgrade Russian to the status of the second official language. Conversely, the West of Ukraine voted against any rapprochement with Russia and against Ukraine's accession to the CIS, etc.

The problem looms even larger given that in Ukraine, which does not have deep-rooted traditions of nationhood of its own, any consolidating ideas that could unite the nation have practically disappeared. The attractive idea of independence, the realisation of which would bring to its supporters personal benefits and advantages of a 'rich Ukraine' being separated from its 'poor' neighbours, was very soon discredited and even transformed into its opposite – „Why should we have separated? Our neighbours live better!" The slogan of building an independent state has not been translated into a governmental programme which could be put into practice and would be acceptable to the majority of the population, and in which everybody could discern his/her own interest. That is why this slogan merely began to evoke annoyance in the long-term.

The all-round economic crisis is a factor aggravating the situation. The alignment of political forces in Ukraine is such that this makes it impossible to adopt a new constitution. Notwithstanding the fact that the Constitutional Commission was set up as far back as 1990 and that a draft constitution has been drawn up and publicly discussed in great detail, a Basic Law has not as yet been adopted. The draft constitution has not given an unequivocal answer to the question about the status of the regions. In one of its versions, a two-chamber parliament was envisaged. Its upper chamber was allotted the role of a forum for representatives from the regions, since election to it was not supposed to be direct but effected via the election of deputies to local councils of various levels. However, it is very unlikely that a clause concerning a two-chamber parliament will be preserved in the new constitution since Ukraine lacks traditions of such a parliament and its political parties are too numerous and weak. This would suggest that such a parliament would produce a confrontation between the chambers and, hence, would function very inefficiently.

Therefore, we can prognosticate that the future Ukrainian Parliament is very likely to have only one chamber.

Forms of state government have changed several times since 1991. After the presidential branch of power had been instituted and Ukraine's first president had been elected, a new hierarchy of state government and administration was introduced in 1991 – the so-called presidential representatives and their local (regional) administrations. Given the fact that a hierarchy of soviets (councils of People's Deputies) continued to exist, two parallel branches of power formed which began to compete and confront each other on every level. This resulted in their becoming practically disabled by the strife and in a weakening of state power in society as a whole. This stage finally came to an end in 1994 when the *Verkhovna Rada* of Ukraine passed a resolution on a new reorganisation of power structures. The hierarchy of presidential representatives was abolished and the role of soviets (councils of people's deputies) was increased.

Especially augmented were the positions of the councils' chairs at all levels, since they were to be elected by the whole electorate of a constituency. This generated a threat of having local leaders who might ignore the central authorities and the law, transformed into 'independent princes', as it were. However, in the opinion the chairman of the *Verkhovna Rada* Olexander Moroz, such a threat should not be overestimated since, in the first place, „heads of local authorities, especially in the regions, are themselves as apprehensive of separatist trends as the Centre. They are just the same patriots of Ukraine as we are. In any case, they perceive problems of their own regions as being part of the state's problems". Secondly, the speaker of Ukraine's Parliament believes „a mechanism, stipulated by the *Law on Local Soviets*, provides for some checks, for example that local authorities are subordinated to the top structures of power. Some revisions will be made later during the final reading of the bill but we are of the opinion that it gives grounds to believe that the unity and integrity of the state will be guaranteed"[6].

After the summer 1994 elections to local soviets, the chairs of these councils became heads of local executive bodies which were once again reorganised. However, that was not the end of transformations. The point is that the degree of imbalance and disharmony of functions and actions between various branches of power and between various levels assumed threatening proportions by the end of 1994. President Leonid Kuchma introduced into Parliament a *Bill on State Powers and Local Self-Government* which came to be known as the 'smaller constitution'. In his address to Parliament he had to admit the following: „Today Ukraine is not practically governed by any one. Everyone is trying to pull his/her own string, leaving aside the people's interests and practical matters of managing the economy. Moreover, the first indications of the state's disintegration are to be seen„.[7]

Heated political debates began to be waged about the bill. Hard line proponents of a unitary state structure saw in it a threat to Ukraine's territorial integrity. This threat lies, in their opinion, in the clause which provides for the election of heads of regional and district administrations by the whole electorate of the corresponding territory. „... by voting for the head of a state administration, the voters vest him or her with a mandate to exercise state power", maintains People's Deputy of Ukraine Stepan Khmara, the Republican Party leader. „The head of an administration, by realising this right, may run into a serious collision with Ukraine's sovereignty at best, or with its integrity at worst"[8]. At the time of the writing of this article the bill had been subjected to the first reading and its future has not been decided upon as yet, just as the future of the hierarchy of power in the state has not been defined either.

Considering it very important to keep the balance of interests between the Centre and the regions, in the first weeks of his presidency Leonid Kuchma suggested a new organisational form for co-operation. He decreed the institution of a *Council of Regions* to act as a consultative body under the president, which includes the chairs of all the *oblasts'* councils. He also relies in his work on another public body set up earlier – the *Association of Town Mayors*. Under circumstances whereby the model of governing the territories is not codified by law, the above bodies strive for a

6 Moroz, O.O. "Mi ne povinni grati rol prokhacha." *Holos Ukrainy* 22 July 1994.

7 President Leonid Kuchma's address to the plenary session of Ukraine's *Verkhovna Rada. Holos Ukraini* 24 December 1994.

settlement of contradictions which arise between various territories as well as between the Centre and territories. Public bodies can, naturally, play a positive role in co-ordinating the efforts of central and local authorities, but they are not in a position to solve all the problems which arise in this sphere. For this reason, many public figures and scholars suggest the establishment of a specialised ministry or department within Ukraine's Government which would tackle the problems of territories.

Thus, since the proclamation of Ukraine's independence, the executive branch of power has been in a state of permanent transformation. This naturally generates a peculiar mood among state officials and shapes a psychological atmosphere of insecurity and transitoriness in all echelons of the administrative hierarchy, great fluctuations in the ranks of civil servants and a loss of managerial skills and abilities. Furthermore, since the driving force behind each new wave of transformations is provided by the Centre, a subconscious defence of their interests by civil servants in the regions is quite understandable. They begin to entertain a hope that on gaining a higher autonomous status for their territories they will be able to make their positions more secure and avoid any destructive organisational influence from the outside.

In such a situation where common goals unifying the whole of society are disappearing, regional goals assume a greater importance. There come into circulation new myths of a well-to-do existence on a separate territory, in a self-contained region. Old arguments that this or that region is very rich but is plundered by the Centre are once again resorted to. Moreover, being left to face the local population, local administrative elites have to independently seek possible ways out of the crisis, given the collapse of major social and public structures, the onset of uncertainty in all spheres of life and the weakening of the central authorities. Such quests result, as a rule, in the drawing up of a regional project that is based on self-reliance, because nobody now believes that it is possible to expect assistance from the Centre. At the same time, local elites realise their own interests in such projects, paying heed, very often, to their own political ambitions.

Among regional elites, the idea of the territorial restructuring of the state is extremely popular. This can be accounted for by their dissatisfaction with the present state of relations between the territories and the Centre. They are displeased with their status in state structures and want to play a more active role in the development

---

8 Droshkevich, V. "President Ukraini rozrobiv model derzhavnoi vlady. Chy na koryst?" *Holos Ukraini* 27 December 1994.

of the economy, to have more rights, greater powers and a greater freedom to act in this sphere. Regions demand the right to pursue their own taxation policy and to have their own financial resources. In each region one or two regionalist ideas have taken shape and meet with considerable popularity amongst people in that region. Particularly in Transcarpathia, Bukovyna and Odessa a sizeable segment of the population supports the idea of establishing free economic zones. In 1990-1991 local referenda were held in those regions and their outcomes showed that the idea was extremely popular.

In Lugansk and Donetsk *oblasts* and in Kharkiv and Mykolaiv the question on linguistic autonomy has met with a wide response. Being a mouthpiece for these ideas, local elites are building a more attractive image of themselves. This is confirmed by a public opinion poll conducted in 1994 in the Crimea, the Donetsk and Lugansk *oblasts*, in Sevastopol and Kharkiv[9].

The fact that a constitutional court has not been formed is another political and legal precondition for the rise of regionalism. The state does not, in fact, have any legal method or mechanism for resolving contradictions arising between the Centre and the regions, between bodies of autonomous local self-government and central authorities. The case of the Autonomous Republic of the Crimea vividly shows how many problems may amass in this sphere in the absence of a constitutional court. Over the past three years of this republic's existence several dozen legislative acts were passed by the Crimea's Supreme Soviet which contradict the Ukrainian constitution. Ukraine's *Verkhovna Rada* had to declare 37 of them unlawful and having no legal force, and demanded that they be amended in accordance with Ukrainian legislation. However, the Supreme Soviet of the Crimea has so far failed to comply with the demand and it is not as yet clear how the Crimea's Supreme Soviet can be made to do so.

Neither should one disregard the phenomenon of inertia of social consciousness and action by power of suggestion as a reason for the popularity of the ideas of regionalism and autonomisation. This phenomenon has an imitative nature, a sort of an aftermath of the sovereignisation of the former USSR republics, which was 'en vogue' and widespread during Gorbachev's *perestroika* in 1987-1991. The model of gaining independence in breaking away from a Centre became a fad in the ex-USSR. It was tried at all levels: at the level of autonomous republics (breaking away from the Union Centre or from the Union Republic's Centre – suffice it to recall the

---

9 Melnichenko, V. "Chi zagrozhue Ukraini 'krimizatsiya'?" *Democratichna Ukraina* 8 August 1994.

sovereignisation of Chechnya, Tatarstan, Bashkortostan, Tuva, Yakutia-Sakha, Buryatia in Russia, the Crimea in Ukraine, Abkhazia and North Ossetia in Georgia, Transdnestria and Gagauzia in Moldova), then at the level of *oblasts* (the ideas of creating the Vologda, Urals and Far Eastern Republics on the basis of the respective *oblasts* in Russia or the Transcarpathian Republic in Ukraine). These and similar ideas and their bearers have not completely vanished.

4 Conclusion

An analysis of the positions of various political parties, statesmen, representatives of local (regional) elites and some scholars in relation to the problem of Ukraine's territorial structure shows that, firstly, this subject has been one of the central topics in the past three years in the state's social and political life. Secondly, over the past several years considerable insights into this area have been gained by scholars and politicians, the Centre and the regions. Mutual relations between the Centre and the territories have been extensively covered by the mass media and hence people have been educated and informed on this matter. Conditions have been formed for any citizen of the country to clearly ascertain his or her own point of view on such problems.

The third conclusion to be made is that there is no stable understanding in Ukraine about the problem of the state-territorial structure, nor about the question of principles and forms of pursuing regional policy. There is no consensus of opinion on the problem among political parties but, admittedly, the position of state institutions has not been elaborated either. To exemplify, in late 1992 Ukraine's then president, Leonid Kravchuk, set the task of drawing up a conception of territorial administration[10]. Two years passed, and late in 1994 Professor V. Grinyov, L. Kuchma's advisor on regional matters, had to admit that there was no national programme on regional policy in Ukraine [11].

In this connection, the adoption of a new constitution of Ukraine is of primary importance, by establishing the major principles of Ukraine's territorial structure, defining the status of the regions and the character of their interrelations with the Centre, and instituting a vertical system of power structures. To further procrastinate

---

10 Kravchuk, L.M. *Upravlinnya teritoriyami v umovakh rozbudovi demokratichnoi pravovoi v Ukraini.* Kiev, 1993: 4.

11 Grinyov, V. "Ya ne khochu obmanyvat lyudei. Budushchee za kapitalizmom [I Do Not Want to Cheat the People. The Future Lies with Capitalism]." *Kievskie Vedomosti* 16 November 1994.

in adopting a new constitution or at least passing the *Bill on State Powers and Local Self-Government in Ukraine* means the continuing weakening of the central authorities, the growth of separatist movements and the threat of the secession of some of Ukraine's regions.

17

List of Authors

Gel'man, Vladimir Yakovlevich (1965, Leningrad), graduate of the Leningrad Polytechnical Institute; political scientist, research fellow at the St.Petersburg branch of the Russian Academy of Sciences' Institute of Sociology; deputy director of the Moscow Institute for Humanitarian and Political Research (*IGPI*).

Grigor'ev, Oleg Vadimovich (1960, Moscow), economist and mathmatician; deputy chairman of the apparatus of the State Duma's Committee on Economic Politics.

Kaganskii, Vladimir Leopol'dovich (1954, Moscow), geographer; director of the research project at the Interdisciplinary Academic Center for Social Sciences.

Kassimov, Aleksandr Grigor'evich (1966, Nal'chik), journalist, consultant at the Moscow Institute for Humanitarian and Political Research (*IGPI*).

Kirkow, Peter (1966, Jena), M.A. in social sciences; research fellow at the Centre for Russian and East European Studies, Birmingham.

Kovalevskii, Aleksandr Romual'dovich (1972, Moscow), graduated from Moscow State University's faculty of geography, chair for economic geography of foreign countries; independent expert for foreign investment and as such observer with the magazine "Kommersant-Weekly", Moscow.

Lyashevskaya, Mariya Nikolaevna (1972, Moscow), graduated from Moscow State University's faculty of geography, chair for economic geography of Russia; independent expert for investment politics.

Malyutin, Mikhail (1955, Vladivostok), *kandidat* of philosophical sciences (Moscow State University); consultant with the Expert Institute of *RSPP*.

Medvedev, Sergei Aleksandrovich (1966, Moscow), graduated from Moscow School of International Journalism, studies at Prague, Columbia University; senior analyst at the Foreign Policy Association, Moscow; head of section at the Russian Academy of Sciences' Institute of Europe.

Nemiriya, Grigorii Mikhailovich (1960, Donetsk), historian; director of the Donetsk Center for Political Research.

Neshchadin, Andrei Afanas'evich (1950, Moscow), *kandidat* of social sciences; executive director of the Expert Institute of *RSPP*.

Pain, Emil' Abramovich (1948, Kiev), *kandidat* of historical sciences; member of the Presidential Council, deputy head of the analytical department of the President of the Russian Federation.

Pavlenko, Sergei Yur'evich (1958, Novosibirsk), economist, sociologist, *doktor* in economic sociology; director of the Russian governments' Working Center for Economic Reforms (*RTsER*), senior research fellow at the Institute for Russian Economy Studies.

Rozhanskii, Mikhail Yakovlevich (1954, Irkutsk), *kandidat* of philosophical sciences; senior researcher at the Center for International Studies of the Irkutsk University, head of laboratory at the Irkutsk Institute for the Training of People Working in Higher Education.

Ryzhenkov, Sergei Ivanovich (1959, Saratov), linguist and political scientist, assistant to member of the Russian State Duma Vyacheslav Igrunov; head of the Volga region research group at the Moscow Institute for Humanitarian and Political Research (*IGPI*).

Senatova, Ol'ga Olegovna (1964, Moscow), lecturer of history and the foundations of Soviet state and law; political scientist, senior researcher at the Moscow Institute for Humanitarian and Political Research (*IGPI*).

Shkabara, Il'ya Anatol'evich (1971, Ivano-Frankovsk in Ukraina), graduated from Moscow State University's faculty of geography; expert with the commercial bank "Olimpiiskii" in Moscow.

Shul'ga, Nikolai, minister for National Questions of the Ukrainian government.

Tarkhov, Sergei Anatol'evich (1953, Moscow), geographer; senior research fellow at the Laboratory for Economic and Social Geography of the Russian Academy of Sciences' Institute of Geography.

Treivish, Andrei Il'ich (1950, Moscow), geographer specialized in economic and social geography; fellow at the Russian Academy of Sciences' Institute of Geography, contributer to the department for regional research at the analytical center of the Russian public television ORT (*Obshchestvennoe Rossiiskoe televidenie*).

Vasil'eva, Ol'ga Valentinovna (1962, Cheboksary), from Moscow Physical-Technical Institute; expert for interethnic conflicts in the post-Soviet space with the Gorbachev Fond.

18

Index

A

B

C

D

E

F

G

H

I

J

K

L

M

N

O

P

R

S

T

U

V

W

Y

Z

19

Cumulative Table of Contents